PENGUIN BOOKS

AS I SAW IT

In his long and multifaceted career as soldier, teacher, foundation president, and diplomat, Dean Rusk has served at the vortex of history. Born on a small, red-clay farm in Cherokee County, Georgia, he worked his way through Davidson College and won a Rhodes Scholarship to Oxford University. In 1950, Rusk took what he calls "the best job in the world" as president of the Rockefeller Foundation. Then, beginning in 1960, Dean Rusk served as Secretary of State under Presidents Kennedy and Johnson. He is now a professor of international law at the University of Georgia. Richard Rusk is currently working on his second book and is driving a tractor trailer. He lives in Athens, Georgia. Daniel S. Papp, the editor of *As I Saw It*, is the director of the School of International Affairs at Georgia Institute of Technnology.

As I Saw It

by

DEAN RUSK

as told to

RICHARD RUSK

Edited by DANIEL S. PAPP

PENGUIN BOOKS

PENGUIN BOOKS
Published by the Penguin Group
Viking Penguin, a division of Penguin Books USA Inc.,
375 Hudson Street, New York, New York 10014, U.S.A.
Penguin Books Ltd, 27 Wrights Lane,
London W8 5TZ, England
Penguin Books Australia Ltd, Ringwood,
Victoria, Australia
Penguin Books Canada Ltd, 2801 John Street,
Markham, Ontario, Canada L3R 1B4
Penguin Books (N.Z.) Ltd, 182–190 Wairau Road,
Auckland 10, New Zealand

Penguin Books Ltd, Registered Offices:
Harmondsworth, Middlesex, England

First published in the United States of America by
W. W. Norton & Company, Inc., 1990
Published in Penguin Books 1991

1 3 5 7 9 10 8 6 4 2

THE LIBRARY OF CONGRESS HAS CATALOGUED THE HARDCOVER AS FOLLOWS:
Rusk, Dean, 1909–
As I saw it/Dean Rusk with Richard Rusk and Daniel S. Papp.—
1st ed.
p. cm.
ISBN 0 14 01.5391 8(pbk.)
Includes index.
1. Rusk, Dean, 1909– . 2. Statesmen—United States—Biography.
3. United States—Foreign relations—1945– I. Rusk, Richard.
II. Papp, Daniel S., 1947– . III. Title.
E748.R94A3 1990
973.92'092—dc20 89–34461

Printed in the United States of America

For Virginia Foisie Rusk

Contents

Dean Rusk's Preface

When I joined President Kennedy as his secretary of state in January 1961, I announced that I would never write a memoir. Several reasons lay behind this decision. Among them was my desire to let foreign leaders know that if they wished to talk with me in confidence, they could do so. I would not rush to write a book about our conversations. I was also influenced by a remark attributed to George Marshall: "If I were to write memoirs I would owe it to myself as a matter of integrity to tell the full truth. But were I to tell the full truth, I would injure a great many people including myself. So I will leave this to the historians." Also relevant is my view that documents generated in the course of public business belong to the government and not to those temporarily serving in government. When I left the Department of State, I took away only my appointment books—they are available to anyone in the Kennedy and Johnson presidential libraries—and copies of my income tax returns; all else I left in Washington.

In June 1984 our son Richard came home to Georgia after many years in Alaska, years spent, I now realize, attempting to understand and make peace with the events of his youth and of my public service.

He could not do this, could not reforge the broken chain, without me. Thus, together we have explored the memories and have written not a formal memoir or a book based on documents but a human story, father to son.

Our many dozens of taped interviews will be found in the University of Georgia Library. This is as much Rich's book as mine. I have shared with Rich my best recollection of what my colleagues and I had in mind about the many issues which arose in the 1960's. If my memory is faulty at times, the responsibility is mine. There are many anecdotes in these pages, and a few I did not myself eyewitness. Even these are a part of the Washington folklore of that period.

Any future historian must sift through the blizzard of paper work that has fallen upon the world in our century. During my eight years in Washington 2,100,000 cables went out of the Department of State over my signature. Of these I personally saw fewer than 1 percent. The extensive documentary record cannot tell the whole story. Documents are surrounded by much discussion among those handling policy, and these discussions are, of course, nowhere in the record. There may be some value in my attempt to reconstruct what was in our minds as we worked through the jungle of events.

A central theme helps sort out the extraordinary complexity of this postwar period. We have now put behind us forty-five years since a nuclear weapon was fired in anger—perhaps the most important single development of the postwar years. Our young people should be reminded of these forty-five years as a platform to build upon and a partial antidote to the Doomsday talk with which they are being battered. I recognize my generation's shortcomings. We left America an abundance of serious problems. Even so, I wish that those who follow can move into the future with a measure of hope and confidence. Optimism is vital to the workings of a democracy and an operational necessity in the nuclear age. I am profoundly confident about the prospects for avoiding nuclear war.

I am deeply moved by the attitudes and performance of the American people in this postwar period. The Kennedy and Johnson presidencies in particular were years of crisis; there was little of Camelot about them. There have been mistakes and disappointments in these four decades; we have learned some hard lessons. But in the longer view the American people have conducted themselves with responsibility, restraint, and even generosity. Never has so much sheer power been harnessed to the rather simple and decent purposes of the American people. There is nothing for which to be ashamed as we look to the future.

I deeply regret that limitations of space did not permit me to give adequate credit to the talented people with whom I served. This includes the leaders of a professional diplomatic service which is second to none in the world. I mention only a few: Ted Achilles, Tap Bennett, Charles Bohlen, Martin Hillenbrand, Foy Kohler, Alexis Johnson, Carol Laise, Thomas Mann, David Newsome, Joe Sisco, and Llewellyn Thompson.

Some were not members of the Foreign Service: George Ball, Lucius Battle, McGeorge Bundy, William Bundy, Ellsworth Bunker, David Bruce, Abe Chayes, Harlan Cleveland, Adrian Fisher, Arthur Goldberg, Jim Greenfield, Averell Harriman, Philip Jessup, Nick Katzenbach, Bill Macomber, Robert Manning, Bob McCloskey, John J. McCloy, George McGhee, Len Meeker, Ben Read, Eugene Rostow, Walt Rostow, Tony Solomon, Adlai Stevenson, Phillip Talbot, Barbara Watson, and many others. I was particularly blessed in having secretaries and personal assistants such as Phyllis Bernau Macomber, Jane Mossellem, Andy Steigman, Harry Shlaudeman, and Emory Swank in the State Department and Ann Dunn at the University of Georgia. Surely no secretary of state in this modern period has been surrounded by such talent. A full listing would fill many pages.

Together, Richard and I have worked hard to write about life as it really was. He decided what should be included or left out in a book of this size. I greatly hope readers will profit from reading it as much as he and I have enjoyed making it.

Finally, the Rusks of Cherokee County have found it difficult to talk about things they feel most deeply. I must, however, express my loving appreciation for that talented and gallant lady who has tolerated me for more than fifty years—Virginia Foisie Rusk. She has combined grace and commitment to the duties which have fallen upon her throughout our lives—especially as the wife of the secretary of state. She has been the same person in the presence of presidents, princes, and potentates as she has been with my country cousins in Georgia. Our three children, David, Richard, and Peggy, and their respective spouses and our six grandchildren have been blessed by her love and dedication.

Foreword

"What was it like to have an American secretary of state for a father?"
I've been asked that hundreds of times, and I always answered as
offhandedly as possible, with a glib "No big deal" or "It gave me a shot
at some girls I never had a chance at otherwise," knowing that people
might have had reasons of their own for asking and that a serious answer
might be germane to their own experiences. Well, it *was* a big deal, and
twenty years later it became time to answer that question.

Aware that he had special talents, not wanting to overwhelm or
influence us unfairly, my dad worked hard to keep his career separate
from the lives of his children. Fourteen years old at the time of his
appointment in 1960 and move to Washington, D.C., I joined Pop in that
effort, wanting as normal a life as possible, free from the pretense and
frenzy that drive the lives of high public officials. But despite our best
efforts, his working life and its influence upon me became pervasive. We
did fine up until the mid and late 1960's, and then our combined efforts
were just swept away.

This book is an attempt to reconstruct a life, my attempt to know my
aging father. I had grown up as his son, spent eighteen years in his home,
and, at age forty, really didn't know him. I also wanted to know as a
sixties-era Marine reservist and college student whose classmates were
called upon to serve in Vietnam. To some extent, the nation was entitled
as well to learn more about Dean Rusk, a man who hadn't yet told his
own story, a man who was an architect of a war that killed fifty-eight
thousand Americans and nearly a million Vietnamese. My private quest
had a public side to it.

"Rich, my life was more than the Vietnam War," my father would say
patiently, sometimes in a voice edged by exasperation. I knew that,
having read what little had been written about his career, yet I needed to
place my father's life and the war in a wider context. I needed a better
way to remember him. So in June 1984 I sold our home in Nome,
Alaska, and moved my wife and two children five thousand miles to
Athens, Georgia. I parked myself on his doorstep, said in a brave voice,
"We're going to write a book, Pop," and turned on the tape recorder.
We went back to his birth on a forty-acre farm in Cherokee County,
Georgia, and traveled his eighty years together.

As a retired professor Pop now had the time. To take one's aged father by the hand and go back to the earliest memories of his youth is a rich and fascinating experience. For long and wonderful hours in his office I listened to him talk about his life. He warmed to the project as we became involved with each other. I think he secretly welcomed our excursion into the past, touching once again the events of his career and the dreams of his youth. He even became excited about "this book of yours, Rich," realizing that much of what we talked about was very dear to him and that publishing this story was simply another way of spreading a message he had personally delivered all over the South.

But we were in for a checkered experience. "I've always had a sense of inner self that was impenetrable," he once told me. "That's been characteristic of me all my life. I try never to completely expose myself to anybody."

"I am amazed that Dean is allowing you to do this," said a former girl friend from Davidson College when I told her of my project. "Good luck!" said others who knew him.

With the tape recorder rolling, my dad talked easily and at length about policy, the job of the secretary of state and how government works, even about his boyhood, his career, and his life in a narrative sense. He talked less easily about himself. And he would say nothing at all about areas crucial to his story: a stiff and mystifying relationship with his father; personal disappointments; moments of failure; differences with his presidents; critical observations of the men he served with. Most disappointing of all, he remained somewhat tight-lipped on Vietnam, revealing little of his inner struggle, saying less about conflicts within the administration over policy.

My dad was reluctant to talk even about his wife for publication. In their letters, within our family, I had seen many evidences of my parents' love and heard the stories of their courtship at Mills College. Yet when I asked him for more comment about my mother, explaining that what we had was skimpy, he replied, "That's no one's business but ours."

For profound reasons of his own, he had never wanted to tell his own story. Doing so would have violated his sense of integrity and certainly invalidated his privacy. Only a son could have talked him into this project. I had reasons of my own, which he guessed were also profound.

"I'm not much on stream of consciousness," he confessed at one point, rather proudly. "Rich, you're far more introspective than I am," he said on another occasion, mildly disapproving of my questioning. "I never brooded about that," he replied when I pressed him for qualities about his presidents that he didn't like. He never said anything even slightly critical about either John Kennedy or Lyndon Johnson. Psychohistorians in particular drew his contempt. No one should try to penetrate a sacred preserve of the inner mind, and he suggested politely that I back off. "I am a much simpler man than you perceive me to be," he advised. "You may be my biographer, but you're not my father confessor," he gently reminded me when I questioned his religious beliefs.

My dad did talk willingly with me, but his inner censor was always screening. Examples are legion. My grandfather Robert Rusk had died in 1944 while Pop was in the China-Burma-India (CBI) theater. "I have always regretted not telling my father what I truly thought about him," my dad told me.

"What did you think of him?" I asked.

"Let's move on to something else." He begged off.

I pressed on, with my dad squirming in his chair.

"What *did* you think of him?" I repeated, grinning. Two days later, determined not to repeat my dad's mistake, I marched into his bedroom and, wearing that same grin, told my befuddled pop that I loved him.

"Aw, come on, Rich," he said, very uncomfortable.

"Well, what did he think of you?"

"I don't know," he said.

"Did he love you?" I asked.

"I suppose that he did," replied my father, "although I never heard him say that."

"Well, did you love him?" I asked.

"Knock it off, Rich! You know I don't talk about these things."

I kept after him.

"Of course, I loved my father!" He finally exploded, glaring at me.

My father's relentless inscrutability wasn't our only problem. The format we chose—a tape recorder book—was awkward for us both. Despite Pop's gift with language, oral communication does not translate directly into publishable text. Regrettably, I have changed words, added sentences and even occasional paragraphs. Although I read everything to him for his comment and suggestions, because of failing eyesight, he could never actually see the material. We worked around this as best we could, although losing his reading vision—in 1985—was a terrible loss for one so viscerally involved with the affairs of mankind. "For the first time I feel like I am in my declining years," he told me.

Let the reader beware. This son is not neutral. Of all possible author-editors about Dean Rusk, I am the only one who for forty years knew him as Pop and loved him unabashedly. In going back through the oral histories, his congressional testimony, press conferences, hundreds of speeches, many hours with him, and hundreds of thousands of words, cutting and pasting together and splicing and editing, I was always putting the best possible spin on his story. I never deliberately altered meaning. But there is enough of me here that my dad might say if pressed, as he laughingly threatened to do, "Did my son say that?" or, "Rich got that all wrong!"

Although in this book my father tells his story in his own words, a son's perspective might be helpful. I remember little of my father from early childhood, a clear sign that he was fully involved with career even then. Those early memories remain distant and clouded by forgetfulness. But as is true with many small children, my dad was larger than life to me, a giant I adored. In a child's world of fantasy, I remember wanting to be like him, without having the slightest idea what he did. At age four I asked for a suit so I could be "a businessman just like Pop," complete with dress shoes, tie, even a top hat. My indulgent parents quickly supplied the suit and as quickly realized their error; as soon as I appeared outside, the laughter of my playmates drove me off the sidewalks. And beyond age four, I have a flood of memories.

Generally, my father made the command decisions, but he modeled his family along democratic lines, with all the disorder and license—and anarchy—that accompany democracy. He treated his children like sovereign souls, in whose lives he would rarely intrude. Perhaps reacting to his own stern upbringing, he flopped to the extreme of permissiveness. He really thought that we would flower best in a climate of pure freedom. My brother and sister blossomed, but when I came up a weed, even then he refused to assert himself or modify his approach. When teachers complained about my behavior, he would tell his anguished wife, who preferred a firmer approach, "Let the boy alone. He'll turn out all right." When my grades plummeted in high school, he never inquired or even offered a word of reproach. But he was alarmed; in Georgia I found his correspondence with my high school counselor and his plaintive question, "Is Richard showing any signs of wanting to go to college?"

In their married life my mother and father fought rarely and never in the presence of children. But when they did—and both confirmed this years later—it was often about me. Late one night they began to quarrel in the living room. I moved to the top step and heard every verbal blow, shocked by the intensity of the debate. From early childhood I can remember wanting discipline, sometimes even aching to be spanked. In this midnight summit, from the shadows, I agreed with my mother. But it was the father I adored who would have to wield the paddle, and he never did.

My father, a gentle soul, would intervene only to protect us from bodily harm. After the stories of my shooting up the neighborhood got back to him (I was eleven), he made me give up BB guns, although he sweetened the deal by promising to buy me a .22 rifle when I turned fourteen. My playmates and I once dug a row of foxholes in a vacant field, then connected them with underground tunnels. Concerned about cave-ins, my dad made us seal them off. When, at age sixteen, I hitchhiked from California to Washington without first asking his permission, he was very unhappy. Later, when I called him from Cornell to ask his permission to go skydiving, summoning up that special courage of parents, he gave it—reluctantly. "He was nervous as hell," remembers his press secretary Jim Greenfield. But that was the level at which he involved himself.

In office, my father's patience was legendary; even with family, he never raised his voice or uttered a cross word, however deserved or whatever the provocation. He never tried to guide us in any explicit way. Not wanting to "threaten our integrity," he would suggest, he would reason with us, but he always allowed us to decide. He never sought to impose his will. From my earliest memories, I recall clearly that the standard was "Do your best." But he rarely said that; it had to be inferred. He preferred to lead by example. It didn't always work. Once while driving through Nevada, Pop decided to teach us kids about the futility of gambling. Spotting a one-armed bandit, he dropped in a silver dollar, pulled the lever . . . and hit the jackpot, in front of his astonished children. Still, fatherhood for him was a code of conduct from which he never deviated. Rather than talk about his beliefs, he lived them, for the witness of his children.

As a father, during the 1950's, Pop tried to be involved in his kids' activities. As president of the Rockefeller Foundation he had a normal job and regular schedule, and we saw him often. Riding the commuter train daily from our suburban home in Scarsdale, New York, to Rockefeller Center in Manhattan, he was home most nights and weekends. We always sat down to an evening meal.

In Scarsdale Pop was active in community affairs, serving on the education board and library committee. He also helped coach our baseball and football teams. As head coach he once guided my brother's sixth-grade baseball team to an 0 and 7 record. But he played every boy on the team, not always the rule in Scarsdale. At elections my mother worked as a poll watcher while Pop sat beside a polling booth, pulling the string to open and close the curtain as each person came to vote. "There was a tradition in Scarsdale that everyone should pitch in and help," remembers my dad. The tradition fitted him like a glove.

His civic-mindedness never included running for public office, despite his growing prominence in Westchester County. Local Democrats once asked him to run for the U.S. Congress.

"You must be kidding!" he told them. "You're asking me to resign my job at the Rockefeller Foundation, run for Congress, get twenty-five percent of the vote in a district overrun with Republicans, and then start looking for a job." Elective office never appealed to him. "I simply didn't want to open myself up to that kind of scrutiny," he explained.

In Scarsdale we were a functioning family unit, often traveling and vacationing as a family, including five long car trips from the East Coast to California and back. For hobbies Pop enjoyed an occasional game of golf, Double-Crostic puzzles, bridge, reading. He also enjoyed gardening. I groused mightily at the time but now recall with much love the fall leaves we raked together, cutting the grass, planting pachysandra by the thousands, breaking up bales of peat moss by hand and spreading it, installing a garden fence. I remember him best sitting on a lawn with a weed puller, his bald head shielded from the sun by a handkerchief knotted in the corners, pulling weeds by the hundreds, listening to ball games on the radio while our play swirled around him. Perhaps we wondered at the time, perhaps we didn't, why the president of the Rockefeller Foundation would pull weeds by hand when commercial weed killers were available with crews to administer them. "Those gardening chores were in part an expression of my affection for the family," he told me years later, "an affection I never put into words."

If there were flaws in Pop's "fathering," they've been forgiven. Having become a parent with two children, having learned for myself the challenges of raising children, I see my own imperfections; they sometimes mirror the mistakes of my father! But I do remember from childhood a sense of aloneness, a hunger that was constant and rarely satisfied. It seemed that as a child I could never retain more than a fraction of my father's attention. Even when he was home, it often seemed that he was away. He lived in a different world, and it was hard for him to enter into the play and fantasy of small children. He would never wrestle on the rug or play children's games. Later in Georgia I once found Pop on his knees in his Athens apartment, at age seventy-five not an easy trick, putting together a Lego creation with his three-year-old grandson asleep on the couch. Rather than build something with Andy, he would leave to Andy the mystery of where it came from.

Many fathers ask, "What am I going to do today with the kids after get home from work?" My dad was different; with his work at the foundation and later as secretary of state, he was concerned with the question, "What kind of world can we build for our children?" That is the level at which he lived his life. I will not fault him for this.

Still, during my childhood at times Pop seemed painfully distant. In the family lives of my Jewish friends in Scarsdale, I saw how love and anger were lived right on the surface, and I knew that we Rusks were different. As a child I hadn't yet heard the stories of his upbringing in rural Georgia or realized that he was doing only what his own father had done, buried love for family deep in his heart. I hadn't yet pondered the implications of what my dad's vow to President John Kennedy of "one term only" meant when he was named secretary of state: the need to provide for family. Even though short of money in the sixties, Pop somehow paid for my Ivy League education. Although he was never wealthy even after leaving Washington, every two or three years Pop sent tickets to the entire family—scattered in Alaska, New Mexico, Virginia, and Georgia—to bring us together for family reunions at Christmas. Rummaging through his files in Georgia, I found a letter he had written to a building materials supplier when I started building houses in Alaska, asking him to extend to his son Richard a sizable credit line for which he would be responsible, "but please don't tell my son." More serious was his reference letter to my insurance company, by implication pledging his personal assets to help me secure bonding for a new contracting business in the high-risk world of Alaska construction.

As a child I knew nothing of this impulse. Yet even as a child, despite some lonely moments, I appreciated his efforts at fathering. We were always at the heart of our parents' decision making, whether the issue be schools, where we lived, the vacations we took. They never flew together in the same airplane, out of concern for surviving children if that plane went down.

On occasions that were entirely too rare, my dad and I would do something together that was really special. We once drove up to Indian Lake in the Adirondacks, where he and I shared a wall tent at a camp run by Quakers and cooked our food over an open fire. Although he couldn't swim and was uncomfortable on such adventures, we paddled a canoe across the lake, and from the bow I cast for bass and crappie while he worked us along the shoreline. We fished well into the evenings, and I worked those little poppers among the lilly pads with his quiet encouragement behind me. These were magic moments; for four days that man belonged to me.

On another occasion, lying sick in bed with a stack of *Field and Stream* magazines, I decided that the Dean River in northern British Columbia had the best trout fishing in all of North America. I told my dad, who to my astonishment said, "Let's go up there and try it." He drove the entire family across country and rendezvoused in Seattle to pick up my grandfather. There we sailed up the Inside Passage by ferry to Bella Coola. We never made the Dean River but spent a week in virgin country and fished in rivers black with salmon. With the family flying back ahead, my dad and I drove the car across country to New York.

It was adventures like these—when a busy father, totally involved with his job, put everything aside and did his best to make up in a few days for long periods of absence—that sustained me. During those years when a son's relationship with his father overrides everything and when a blemish in that relationship is acutely felt, my mind would return to Bella Coola and those rivers black with fish or to my dad and me gliding across a lake in the Adirondacks or driving across country as we did many times, with me so young I couldn't even see over the dashboard as his "copilot." As the "navigator," my brother, Dave, had a functioning role; he would at least read the map and tell us where we were. But I was a proud member of the crew, driving through the prairie states and across the American West, with Pop always finding a motel in time for a late round of golf.

What was it like, having an American secretary of state for a father? In large part my experience was no different from any son's. Yes, during the sixties there were unique qualities to our family life, considering the pomp of official Washington, the excitement of the Kennedy-Johnson years, Pop's awesome responsibilities, and the somewhat unnerving experience of life as a "cabinet kid" in a goldfish bowl like Washington, D.C. But strangely, these special times with my father, the experiences of childhood, seem more important and more lasting than anything that occurred during his years as secretary of state. Such experiences are within the reach of all families, and as such, "life with father" was no different. Despite a busy, event-filled career of great achievement, Pop found time to be a father.

Looking back, I am impressed most by my father's utter lack of pretentiousness. A genuinely humble man, throughout his career he refused to take advantage of perks or use his status in any way we kids could recognize. Robert Lovett, Dean Acheson's undersecretary of state during the Truman years, remembered my father once coming to the office exhausted, almost green with fatigue. Shocked, Lovett asked him what was wrong. My dad replied that he had been up all night washing sheets for me, sick with my second bout of scarlet fever. Lovett was appalled. "My God, Dean!" he exclaimed. "We have people around the department for things like that." On another occasion when he was secretary of state, our washing machine went on the blink. Rather than call for help, Pop piled a load of dirty clothes in the family car, drove to the local Laundromat, lined up alongside the housewives, and fed quarters into the machines.

It may have been this modesty, or perhaps his lack of assertive leadership, or perhaps his reluctance to fight for his policy views that led some people to a serious misjudgment: that as secretary of state Dean Rusk was mainly a technician who acquiesced readily to superiors and had few principles of his own. Those who make such arguments have profoundly misread him. My dad felt passionately about foreign affairs and American democracy; his thinking was as fully developed, his views as strongly held as those of any of his peers. As I researched his story, the reasons became apparent. They derived from his experiences, his education, and a lifelong interest in foreign affairs, dating back to grade school, when he carried a sign supporting Woodrow Wilson's fight for the League of Nations. They came as well from his soul, where they had been deeply implanted by a series of formative experiences, the product of the CBI, Hitler's Germany, Oxford University, Western indifference and aggression unmet, the loss of friends and fifty million lives, a world war that vitally affected his generation and viscerally seared Dean Rusk. His views derived from Davidson College, with its emphasis on service and moral values; from his Atlanta boyhood and his attending the finest public schools the "New South" had to offer. They came also from parents who stressed morals and character and who gave the Rusk children a passion for education and from teachers who constantly urged him to "be somebody" and "do something with your life." They derived from southern Presbyterianism with its Calvinist overtones, the Christian Endeavor, reading aloud from the Bible as a boy, and earning "pearls" for passages memorized. They derived from life in the American South, with its respect for patriotic values and military service. "Love of God, love of country," said his brother Roger. "They were as natural to us as living and breathing."

They derived as well from poverty, scratching a living on a red clay farm, living in a house built by his father, with three rooms and unlined walls and cracks through which the wind blew. They came from wearing clothing made of flour sacks sewn by their mother; throwing rocks at passing trainmen in hopes they would throw coal back and then picking up the pieces with which to heat their house; eating a diet low in calcium and other nutrients that left him with bad teeth as an adult. When Robert Rusk butchered the pig—the only source of meat—"we ate everything but the squeal," said his sister Margaret.

His views on foreign affairs came from reading books about the Rover Boys and "rags-to-riches" stories on which he was weaned as a youth, which preached that in America, through education and hard work, even the poor can get ahead. He saw the American dream come true for him. And through FDR's New Deal, improved public education and public health, rural electrification, and increased agricultural productivity, he lived to see the Cherokee County of his youth transformed.

"I believe in democracy," my father will say unabashedly, having seen it work in his own life. "I believe in our constitutional system." With an innocence and enthusiasm that seem almost quaint by modern standards, he grew up believing in the words "freedom," "justice," "government by the consent of the governed," "the responsibilities of citizenship," "the rights of man." Such concepts have profound meaning for Dean Rusk. I have never heard him utter a cynical word about them. He really believes that democracy best fulfills the needs of people that a free society is most consistent with human nature, and that American democracy confers unique privileges—and responsibilities—upon its citizens.

Richard Rusk

Acknowledgments

It is not possible to list all those who helped make this book possible. But I must name a few:

· Buisfeuillet Jones and the Trebor Foundation for their generous financial assistance.

Peter and Julia White and the Southern Center for International Studies for assistance of all types and for capturing my father on film in a way the printed page could never do. The Southern Center's thirteen-hour television series with my father and Edwin Newman as interviewer beautifully supplements this volume.

Anne Cox Chambers and the Rockefeller Foundation for funding the gathering of Dean Rusk's papers and related materials.

The University of Georgia for housing the Dean Rusk Research Collection, with special thanks to archivist Sheryl Vogt and her crew.

Tom Schoenbaum, director of the Dean Rusk Center of International and Comparative Law, for office space and collaborating on research and interviewing.

Ann Dunn, "keeper of all the secrets," who shared a few about her boss.

Marty Ledford, Nelda Parker, and Ann Wills for transcribing hundreds of hours of interviews with Rusk and colleagues.

Savanna Jackson Mapelli for collecting and organizing research for this book and the Dean Rusk Collection.

Dean and Virginia Rusk's hundreds of friends, fellow professors, and former colleagues who helped jog my parents' memories and contributed stories of their own.

My mother, brother, David, and sister, Peggy for their own stories and encouragement, and thanks to the extended family as well, especially my uncle Parks Rusk, who collected hundreds of clippings on his brother's career beginning with the Truman years.

Ed Barber at W. W. Norton, for his patience and gentle touch.

Professor Dan Papp of the Georgia Institute of Technology for his many hours of editing and rescuing this project after I encountered unforeseen difficulties along the way.

My father, "victim" more than "instigator," who, despite having pledged for years never to tell his own story, finally agreed to this first-person account only because he recognized its importance to me.

And finally, my children, Andy, Sarah, and Ryan, and my wife, Fran, who started me on this journey with a letter during the spring of 1984, and in reality, far earlier than that—a cold, blustery day in an Eskimo village in Alaska. . . .

—R. R.

SECTION I

THE
EARLY
YEARS

Why Dean Rusk? Even years after he became secretary of state, the idea that my modest and gentle father had left Scarsdale, New York, to guide the nation's foreign policy remained totally incongruous to me. Pop himself never got over how a "freckle-faced boy from Cherokee County, Georgia," became an American secretary of state. Even at the age of eighty, looking back on a life of great achievement, he insisted that the "roll of the dice best explains what happened to me." With evident sincerity, he said repeatedly to friends, students, audiences of all types that "accident, chance, happenstance" are what moved him up the ladder. "In tracing my journey", he said, "one should not try to find rare talents and special qualities, because whatever ability I had was shared by millions of others."

Undoubtedly there is some truth to this, but beware of old men and their modesty. Dating back to childhood, the evidence suggests my father had unique talents and high abilities. He never admitted it; throughout the course of our father-son journey he took no credit for his own talents or for achievements—always crediting others—and he usually used the pronoun "we" rather than "I." It took the stories and recollections of friends, family, and classmates to flush him out. And even if they were biased, and even if they lived in the reflected and nostalgic glow of a man who rose from their midst to great heights, and even if we acknowledge that such people would rarely tell a son about the shadows in his father's past, their stories of his early years, indeed, of all stages of his life, are remarkably the same.

Judged by their tales, Pop had obvious potential even as a young man, dreaming big dreams, painting big scenes on the canvas, taking giant strides. The dreams were evident when he became the dean of faculty at Mills College. At age twenty-nine he taught a full schedule, maintained his Army Reserve commission, and studied law at Berkeley, between classes driving at breakneck speed across the Oakland hills between Mills and Cal to keep a schedule. Somehow he found time to court and marry Virginia, his wife of more than fifty years.

My father had also lived this pace at Oxford University, England, in the 1930's, first acquiring a Rhodes scholarship and then heading with an instinct for history in the making to the Nazi rallies in Germany, where he heard the roar of a million Germans and a madman who soon plunged Europe into world war. Nearly out of money, he locked himself in a Berlin hotel room for five days and wrote nonstop, producing a draft paper without a single footnote that won the Cecil Prize and funds to pay his way back to Georgia. "Dean was lionized at Oxford," said a classmate, David French. "The whole incident was so typical." His friends at Oxford were already betting that he'd be an American secretary of state.

I followed his trail to Davidson College to search the archives and talk with those who remembered him there. His teachers were gone, but his surviving classmates told me stories of the man they called Elijah: how he worked his way through the "Poor Man's Princeton," how he took top honors and won a Rhodes, and how they saw him dashing day after day across campus, from his classes to his job at a bank, then to basketball practice, and then to the Kappa Alpha fraternity house to wait on tables, his second job.

"Dean would come running in from the bank, or wherever, maybe fifteen or twenty minutes before class," said his former roommate James Caldwell, nicknamed Spec because one could place a thumb anywhere on his face and cover at least fifteen freckles. "He would lean up against a wall, open the book on which he was being tested, and flip through the pages like this," said Spec, turning a page every three to four seconds. "He was taking sight pictures, and he'd go through the whole book that way because he had no free time, his schedule was so tight. And then he'd ace the exam."

"How did he ever acquire a reputation for dullness?" I asked Spec.

"Schlesinger!" he spit, referring to Arthur Schlesinger's *A Thousand Days*, in which the Harvard professor suggested that Rusk wasn't smart enough for the job.

"Richard, I've been in this business forty years," added University of North Carolina Professor of American History Caldwell, "and Dean Rusk was the most brilliant man I've ever known. And his brilliance was matched by a character that made him a man transcendent. He was the most admired and respected man on campus, the only one I knew who literally worked his way through. He would run from one thing to the next. I don't know how he did it."

Pop's talents were evident even as a boy in Atlanta, where the Rusks moved after heavy rains had washed them off their farm in Cherokee County. At Boys High he was president of everything and won top honors in Atlanta's finest public high school. When his possible appointment as secretary of state was publicized, my dad's former high school classmates began to receive calls from the national press, wanting background information on a man virtually unknown to the American people, obviously looking for the shadows in his past.

"One reporter stopped me after I had mentioned 'exemplary moral character' and 'unquestionable integrity,' " said John Candler, class of 1925, "to let me know that he had already heard about the 'goody-goody stuff.' He said that dirt could be dug up against anyone, that he intended to find it on this man right here in Atlanta, and that he expected his schoolmates to know and to tell.

" 'This interview is concluded,' " Candler said he told the reporter. "I'm confident the negative-minded vulture went back to New York without the first tidbit for character assassination."

At age twelve Dean Rusk wrote a paper entitled "What I Want to Do with the Next Twelve Years of My Life," laying out with uncanny accuracy his career at Boys High, Davidson College, and Oxford as a Rhodes scholar. At age eleven he was driving all over the state of Georgia in his dad's Model T Ford, barely tall enough to see over the wheel, making inspirational speeches about the work of the Christian Endeavor, his church's youth group.

Earlier the six-year-old boy who one day became my father pulled a little red wagon through a black shantytown, delivering groceries for Mr. Leatherwood to help pay his family's bills. And even earlier, it really started with infant David Dean Rusk lying in a basket of freshly picked cotton, "making policy," insisted his brother Parks, while the rest of the family worked the forty-acre farm in Cherokee County, Georgia.

—R. R.

1

The Rusks
of Cherokee County

The Rusk family cemetery in Cherokee County, Georgia, thirty miles north of Atlanta, holds the graves of my great-grandmother Jane Rusk and of her husband, David Rusk. On Jane's tombstone is this inscription: "Born in Ireland, 1776. Died in 1854. She believes and sleeps in Jesus." For David: "Born in Ireland, 1773. Died in 1841. An honest man, the noblest work of God." In a very few words, their children said it all. For the Rusks, that little family cemetery in Cherokee, surrounded by loblolly pines and oaks and rolling pasture, is almost hallowed ground. I have returned to it many times. In walking among the nearly hundred stones that mark the graves of my ancestors, I have often reflected upon the fact that only four Rusk generations—and with my own children a fifth—have spanned the life of our nation. It means both that we Rusks grow very old and that our country is very young.

David Rusk sailed to America from Northern Ireland around 1790 with two brothers. He landed first in Charleston, South Carolina, then moved on to Cherokee County, mostly Indian country at that time. David staked out several hundred acres of piny, red clay farmland, on

territory that was still in dispute between the Cherokee Nation and the
state of Georgia, and there he raised his family. We Rusks have been
Georgians ever since.

David and Jane Rusk had seven children, the youngest of whom was
my grandfather James Edward Rusk, who kept the original homeplace
going after his father's death. That took some doing. That effort can be
measured by a picture my brother Roger has of the meat box in grandfather's smokehouse. That box, hewn out of a poplar log, measured
nearly three feet wide and deep and nine feet long. The reason for a
meat box of this size was simple: two parents, three old-maid sisters,
two slaves, and eleven children. Feeding eighteen people three meals a
day required a lot of salt bacon in Grandfather's meat box.

At the outbreak of the Civil War James Rusk rode off at the head
of a band of Cherokee County men to fight for the Confederacy. He was
not alone in this; eventually over eighteen hundred Cherokee County
men fought in the Civil War, one-eighth of the county's population. My
grandfather on my mother's side became a bugler, was wounded, and
carried a minié ball with him for the rest of his life. After my own
experience with Army buglers, I wondered if one of his own men put
that bullet into him.

Of the Cherokee County contingent, hundreds were killed or
maimed, but James Rusk was fortunate. After riding back to Cherokee
County at war's end, he resumed farming and became a justice of the
peace. Life and the settlement of disputes were simpler then. When
neighbors had problems, they simply met with my grandfather under
a tree and got them settled. Rarely did anything go as far as the county
courthouse.

The third youngest of James Rusk's eleven children was my father,
Robert Rusk. In 1890 he enrolled in Davidson, a Presbyterian liberal
arts college in North Carolina, hoping to become a Presbyterian minister. Had he graduated, he would have been a member of the class of
1894. At Davidson he played center on the football team and learned
the violin. During his senior year his father—my grandfather—died.
My dad came home to bury him and never returned to Davidson. As
with many American families, we can trace this country's progress in
the history of our own family. Of my grandfather's family, only Robert
went to college. Three of Father's five children went to college. All of
his grandchildren would go to college.

My father never won his degree, but Davidson provided a lifetime
of rewards. One of my father's classmates, Joe Clotfelter from Rockdale
County, Georgia, thirty miles from Cherokee, took my father home

during Christmas vacation to meet his sister Elizabeth. A schoolteacher who had gone to the normal school in Milledgeville, Georgia, "Fanny" Clotfelter was said to be the prettiest girl in Rockdale County. I can believe it; she was always a handsome woman. And she came from good stock. Her father had emigrated from the Black Forest region of Germany, and her mother came from Ireland. Everybody approved of the match, and in 1899 they married.

If a Davidson degree was not possible, one motivation remained strong: Father wanted to be a Presbyterian minister. So he attended Louisville Theological Seminary and was soon ordained, only to be thwarted again when he developed a throat ailment which made it difficult for him to speak out. He kept an atomizer at his bedside for nighttime spraying of his throat. Father was so soft-spoken we had to strain to hear him, and in those days that wouldn't do in a preacher. Ministers were expected to holler and shout, especially in the rural South. Not having the voice for it, Father left the ministry, taught school for a while, and in 1907 made his way back to Cherokee County.

My older brother Parks said that our father returned to Cherokee County at the specific request of his mother, that one day Grandmother told him, "Bobby, I'm getting old and the family is all scattered. How would you like to come up here, pick out a piece of land to farm, build a little house, and spend some time here in my final days?" And so it was. Father, Mother, my brothers Roger and Parks, and my sister Margaret moved back to the Rusk farm in 1907 and took up residence on forty acres.

Farming in Cherokee and working those red clay hills tended to make stern people of all the Rusks. Father was a gentle man, but when he spoke harshly, we knew that he meant it. His occaisonal burst of temper wasn't easy to get around. Farming life was gentler and more productive in the flatlands of Rockdale County, and that showed in the attitudes of the "valley people." Family relationships among the Clotfelters were more expressive and affectionate than among the Rusks. Indeed, whenever someone had a fit of temper, my mother would say, "That's the Rusk in him!"

Father may have been disheartened about returning to farm life in Cherokee after having been college-educated, but he never spoke of it. Choosing the second-highest spot on the farm—Grandmother's house was the highest—he first dug the well. No farm is worth the name without water. Using a pick and shovel—again according to Parks— Father dug for thirty days with a sharecropper for a helper. At twenty feet he hit rock. He drilled holes by hand, using a steel drill and a sledgehammer. These holes he filled with dynamite and blasted through the rock. After ten days of drilling and blasting, he had penetrated nine feet of rock. Now at twenty-nine feet, Father had to go down another twenty-six to find water, but that fifty-five-foot well provides excellent water to this day.

Father built our house himself, close to the well so that the water pump could be on the front porch. The brick chimney fireplace was central to the house, and around it were three rooms: a bedroom for my parents and any one of the children who needed a corner to throw down a pallet; a second bedroom perhaps ten feet by twelve feet for the children; and a kitchen-dining room with a wood stove in the corner. Built of pine, the house had weatherboard siding over rough studs, and the inside walls were uninsulated and unlined. Father eventually tacked paper over the walls in his bedroom. The ceilings were paper-thin—literally wallpapered. When we children went up to the attic, we had to take care not to step between the joists. The roofing was wood shakes. As my brother Roger says, "When the wind blew, we felt it!"

There was no central heating and, of course, no air conditioning, but shade trees around the house helped cool things down in summertime. Father put in window glass. Our house was one of the first in North Georgia to have glass windows. Our night-light came from kerosene lamps, and that meant the lamps' chimneys had to be washed every day. I must have washed several thousand of them as a boy. During the winter we read by the light of an open fire.

I was born in that house on February 9, 1909, the youngest of three sons and the second youngest of five children. Only my sister Helen came later, born three years after me. For a long time I thought I had been delivered by my uncle Roberts, a veterinarian who lived next door. But in fact, a doctor rode out eight miles from Woodstock on a dark, stormy night to assist in my birth.

We lived in Cherokee County until 1913, when I was four. I was too young to remember details of those farming years, but I often heard my parents and older brothers and sister reminisce about those difficult times. I learned about this life years later, when as a teenager I summered in Cherokee County, living with kin and helping with the work. But I do remember a few things: men playing a marbles game called Tennessee Nines in our yard and the quarter-mile walk from our house through the trees to Grandmother's down the road. It was scary to walk along there at night, when every stump became a lurking monster. I can remember riding atop a wagon to the mill with a load of sorghum cane to be ground up for syrup, and scampering on winter nights through the cold to our outdoor privy. I also recall the death of my grandmother and the way her sons sang together at her funeral. They sang her husband's favorite song, "Shall We Gather at the River?" She was buried in the family graveyard next to our farm, and off in the distance we could see the Little River.

The Rusk farm was well out into the country, but we were hardly isolated, being only thirty miles north of Atlanta and eight miles from the railroad that ran from Atlanta to Woodstock. The roads, deeply rutted during the rainy season, were narrow tracks in the red clay. Bridges were loose planks across heavy beams. Roswell, eight miles to the south, boasted an old covered bridge; it was always fun to go there. Transportation was by foot and by horse. I don't remember seeing a single automobile while I was a boy in Cherokee County.

Hardscrabble farming it was in those red clay hills, although down in the bottomland along the river crops grew better. My father's annual cash income during those lean years averaged a few hundred dollars. The farm yielded several bales of cotton, which brought in a few dollars. To make ends meet, he taught school seven months a year, but we grew our own food and made our own clothing. We had a few hogs, twenty to thirty chickens, two cows, and an old horse called Selim. In addition, we had ten acres of corn for ourselves and our animals and two or three acres planted in wheat, which Father harvested by hand, using a scythe and cradle. This provided grain for our bread. When short of cash, we bartered and traded for what we needed. Mother would say, "Go to the store and get me a dozen eggs' worth of sugar." We bought nothing from the store that we could grow ourselves, but we couldn't grow salt, sugar, cloth, wheat flour, and pipe tobacco. Sometimes Father would return from Roswell or Atlanta toting cartons of sweet pickles or prunes or tins of canned salmon or oysters, welcome relief from pork and other farm products. And occasionally, a can of Vienna sausages. There were seven sausages in a can and seven in the family, so everyone got one. Ever since, even while secretary of state, at any reception I always head straight for the Vienna sausages.

Basically, we lived on pork, killing the hogs with a .38 pistol right after the first hard freeze, to keep the meat fresh and the flies down. And while I don't remember eating the ears, tail, and feet, my sister Margaret said, "We ate everything but the squeal"—fatback, crackling, chitlings, bacon, smoked ham, and liver mush—which was liver, kidney, and heart all ground up. Hog brains scrambled with eggs were a real delicacy. Beef was rare to nonexistent because we had only two cows and needed the milk. We had twenty to thirty chickens, but we ate chicken only on special occasions. Sorghum syrup was our principal sweetener, and coffee was in short supply. We didn't have enough milk or calcium in our diet, and thus, most Rusks of that generation have poor teeth.

Fruits and vegetables from our garden were a godsend, fresh during the summer, canned in mason jars for the cold months but never enough of a supply to get us through to spring. We always enjoyed having new crops and plants mature because something different would turn up on our plates. From the woods we gathered walnuts, hickory nuts, chestnuts, wild berries, molypops, chinquapins ("chickapins"), wild greens, and poke salet. We had great fun hunting for wild muscadines, and sometimes we would find a "honey tree"—where bees had built their hive. To get the honey, we built a fire at the bottom, smoking the bees away, and then cut the tree down. There was very little wild game or birds in Cherokee County in those days, although we occasionally had rabbit, squirrel, and fish from the Little River. Despite times of scarcity, the Rusks never missed a meal. Mother put something on the table three times a day.

Because I was the third son, my clothes were hand-me-downs, hand-sewn by my mother. A frugal lady, she made our underwear out of cloth from flour sacks, although yard goods from Roswell or Woodstock were quite inexpensive. We wore shoes in winter and went barefoot from May through September. Father cobbled our shoes and cut our hair. For toilet tissue we used the Sears, Roebuck catalog, found in every home. We were as self-sufficient as we could be on forty acres with little cash.

The workday began before sunrise and ended at dark. We ate a solid breakfast, a big meal at noon, and a fairly light supper because we needed our energy during the day for working in the fields. Parks and Margaret, the two oldest, worked hard and helped my father in the fields a great deal, but Mother, unlike many of the Rusk wives, couldn't help in this owing to frail health. She wasn't strong enough, for instance, to chop cotton, and for that reason some women were not too genial toward her. Even so, she cared for the vegetable garden, and we younger children—Roger, Helen, and I—would help her. Being so young, I didn't pull my weight. In fact, Parks used to joke that I never worked at all. "The rest of the family did all the cotton picking," he'd complain. "Dean would sit in a basket filled with cotton at the edge of the field, making policy!" But in later years, when visiting Cherokee as a teenager, I picked cotton, pulled fodder, and shucked corn with the rest.

Like farm families everywhere, we worked together on tasks better done by groups than alone. If a man wanted to raise a barn, his neighbors helped him. Usually a group gathered for corn shucking, and women held frequent quilting parties. When a family set out to clear new ground, the neighbors would gather to help cut down trees and pull up stumps to get the ground ready for plowing. Town was a long way off, cash and things to barter sometimes were in short supply, and there was lots of lending and sharing. Borrowing was called neighboring. If you had something and your neighbor needed it, you let him have it, not waiting for him to ask. Of course, charging him would be considered "unneighborly."

On trips to Roswell or Woodstock, Father might take along a basket of fresh fruit or jars of sorghum syrup to trade or barter. With the exception of cotton, we produced little for the market. Father planted our crops more or less by the phases of the moon, as spelled out in the *Farmer's Almanac.* Having been to Davidson, Father had put aside most of the hill country superstitions. For example, I don't think he believed that beans planted in the wrong phases of the moon would "go to vines." Consequently, the neighbors might have regarded him a little "curious in the head." Even so, we Rusks shared a few quaint beliefs. We kids were always leery about the boogeymen in the woods, and during lightning storms we would always hide under a feather bed mattress, having never heard of lightning hitting a chicken.

But Father had little agricultural training, and so he paid attention to the moon's phases and did what his neighbors did. He was a smart farmer in other ways, always on the lookout for better methods. There were few improved seeds in those days and little fertilizer. We had some guano but mostly used manure from our horse and cows. We had no motorized equipment; our plow and wagon were horse-drawn. Life in Cherokee County was almost preindustrial, with no electrical appliances, no power to hook them to, and no mechanical help. Weeding, gathering the crops, pulling fodder, picking cotton, cutting sorghum cane—we did everything by hand. Father helped compensate by working exceptionally hard, and he inspired the rest of us. He took pride in his farming—had a good eye for plowing straight furrows, for example. But it was a tough, frustrating life.

Basically the only signs of twentieth-century America were rural free postal delivery—although the postman delivered our mail by horse and buggy—and a homemade telephone system that my father and some twenty neighbors built to connect their farms. They strung lines on poles and used dry cell batteries for power. To call another family, we turned a crank. Each house had a particular ring, but when the phone rang, whatever the signal, anybody else could—and did—pick up the receiver and listen in. Three long telephone rings meant "Everyone come to the phone," usually to report a fire or a mad dog coming through. With the latter, we'd follow the dog from farm to farm until someone killed it. Telephones were also useful to warn of federal government officials such as revenue agents. In Cherokee County outsiders were not welcome. As a matter of fact, we looked upon people from across the river, half a mile away, as foreigners. True foreigners, like a traveling salesman, were matters of curiosity; we followed them from farm to farm like mad dogs until they left the area.

I regret to say that in those days blacks were not permitted to live in Cherokee County or even to spend the night there. Some black families who lived in nearby Ball Ground were driven out by whites in 1912. In Forsyth County, northeast of Cherokee, there was a tradition that the sun would never set on a black man in that county, and the citizens of Forsyth County enforced it for decades. That part of Georgia, indeed much of the South, still chewed on the bitter root of Reconstruction following the Civil War.

My parents were remarkably racially tolerant for their time. My father probably learned that tolerance from his own parents. For years Grandfather and Grandmother Rusk had two former slaves living with them—a married couple named Lisa and Robert. They had been freed by Lincoln's Emancipation Proclamation but chose to remain with my grandparents. They were treated well, it seems. Grandfather and Grandmother took them to church, taught them how to read and write, and, when Lisa and Robert moved to California, corresponded with them until they died.

Although my parents firmly believed in education, we were not very concerned about national or world affairs. Our primary interest was whether the cow was giving milk, whether the chickens were laying eggs, and whether family members were healthy. What was happening elsewhere just didn't seem important to us. The only outside influence that truly affected us was the price of cotton, but we looked at that as something beyond our control, almost part of the environment.

We Rusks lived very simply. Farming was the only life our family expected to follow, and we didn't engage in self-pity or expect any help from Atlanta or Washington. That was the way people lived. We knew that we were poor, but we had a lot of pride and didn't think of ourselves as poor. We kept ourselves clean and our clothes washed. We kept our house clean as well. We scrubbed the pine floors once a week.

The day after we scrubbed the floors I always got splinters in my bare feet since wet pine "furs up" with splinters. The yard was always swept, and there was no trash lying around. Mother always planted flowers in the yard and had flowers around the house. Even after working in the fields, we never stayed dirty. Each week we had a washday for clothes. My mother's wedding present was a big cast-iron washpot; I must have helped build hundreds of fires under that pot. We would boil the clothes in the washpot, rinse them in several tubs, and hang them out to dry.

With my father's college training and mother's former teaching experience, education was very important to the Rusks. Father taught fifth grade and up at the Big Springs School seven months of the year. Called Mr. Bob, he was known as a good teacher and as one who knew the Bible from cover to cover. Neighbors liked to gather in the yard to hear him talk about his travels. We Rusk children were a part of this environment, developing even as small children a voracious appetite for reading. I don't remember many of the books around the house, although three were central to our lives: the Bible, the Sears, Roebuck catalog, and the *Farmer's Almanac.* We also subscribed to the *Christian Observer,* and neighbors came from miles around to read it. Sometimes Father brought home *Popular Mechanics,* back then a magazine dedicated to simpler things—how to make something useful out of scrap material, such as hinges out of tin cans. We just read every word of whatever we did have and traded reading material with other families.

While school in Cherokee was neither compulsory nor regular, most kids did attend until they were old enough to work, marry, or drop out. School was not held during the planting or harvesting seasons. Some students had to walk as far as five miles, even to a one-room schoolhouse. There were no standards or qualifications for teaching in those days, other than that the teacher had to be a graduate of that particular school and big enough to whip any boy in the class.

My sister Margaret and brother Parks attended a two-room schoolhouse (in the Lickskillet District) about two miles from our house, although both dropped out after the sixth grade—too busy helping Father. Roger and I were below school age during the Cherokee years, but at home we played schoolish games with each other, spelling and identifying names and places and drilling each other from Webster's "Blue-Backed Speller." I already loved learning, even at age three.

Healthwise, life in Cherokee County was somewhat precarious. Infant mortality was high; lots of children are buried in our family cemetery. There was little medical care and no antibiotics or penicillin. For sore throats my father would put soda in sorghum syrup, warm it on top of the chimney lamp, and feed it to us with a spoon. It would get all foamy, and we would swallow the mixture, which would ease our soreness. We took lots of castor oil and tonics and calomel—an all-purpose pill used for many ailments, although it simply moved your bowels. Clearing the bowels was considered good for you. There were no preventative medicines or immunizations and little understanding of what was called the germ theory of disease. Diseases like typhoid fever, pellagra, seven-year itch, and goiter were simply regarded as part of the environment in which the good Lord had put us. We kids caught all the childhood diseases—mumps, chicken pox, and measles—and my brother Roger caught typhoid fever later in Atlanta.

Religion in Cherokee County was what people today call hard-shell Protestantism. Church services were community gatherings—social events as much as religious—and everybody came. We did not have a service every Sunday because the minister often served several churches as a circuit preacher. But there was a deep religious commitment and belief. Because we were poor, we took comfort from passages in the Bible such as "It is easier for a camel to go through the eye of a needle, than for a rich man to enter into the kingdom of God."

Although Cherokee County was close to Atlanta and the legal norms of civilization, we were far enough into the foothills where a feuding tradition still existed. My uncle Jep, in a quarrel with a neighbor over a domestic triangle, was riding to Woodstock one day in his buggy and saw the other man coming down the road toward him. They got out of their buggies and started shooting at each other. Uncle Jep shot true and was charged with murder. At the trial he pleaded "unwritten law"; in those days, according to the old code, if a man tried to seduce another man's wife, killing was justified. Uncle Jep was later acquitted in court. Needless to say, strangers had to watch how they conducted themselves in North Georgia.

I had one narrow escape while living in Cherokee. I was playing in the hayloft of our barn one day and fell out of the hayloft door, perhaps fifteen feet to the ground. Fortunately I landed headfirst in a fresh pile of cow manure. That broke the fall and saved me from serious injury, but my mother said that I cried brown tears for a week. In general, with a few memorable exceptions, life on the farm was rather tame.

But it was also precarious. Even with kin living for miles around, we subsisted on a year-to-year and even month-to-month basis. That was true of almost all our neighbors, not just us. One bad crop year could spell disaster.

Disaster for our family struck in 1912. As my brother Roger

remembers it, that spring Parks and Father went to plow the bottom-land along the river. As they plowed, it began to rain. The day's work ended, Father and Parks unhooked the plow, hitched up the wagon, and rode home. It rained all summer, and the bottomlands flooded. Parks and Father could not get back to the plow until October, too late for a crop that year.

That same summer of 1912 Grandmother died. Since Father had been farming her land, he was out of a job. Again according to Roger, Father went to the estate sale without any money. And he came back with a Seth Thomas clock. Grandmother's estate had been divided up, and my father's brothers and sisters told him, "Because you got a college education, you get none of the land." That hadn't been stipu-lated in Grandmother's will, but Father, not a contentious man, ac-cepted the verdict. He also realized that without a college education, his brothers and sisters had no choice but to stay in Cherokee and farm.

In addition, Mother's health was bad and getting worse. Her housework, gardening, and raising us children were slowly killing her. Her days and evenings were constant toil—cooking, cleaning, washing, gardening, all of the burdens of mothering and homemaking. Also, Mother was sick from carrying Helen, who was born in November 1912. I think Father realized that unless he got Mother off that red clay farm, he would lose her.

So there we were with winter approaching, no corps in the ground, no job for Father, no money, and Mother sick, with Helen just born and myself not yet four. The family had little to eat except a few vegetables from the garden and was hungry for the first time. Some-thing had to change.

In desperation, Father took the train to Atlanta, where he looked for a job, first with no success. Discouraged, he wrote a letter to Mother, saying that he hadn't found work in Atlanta but would come home in any case to Cherokee County for Christmas. As he entered the post office to mail the letter, he saw a notice advertising an opening as a mail carrier. The age limit was forty-five; his forty-fifth birthday was the next day. At ten minutes to five he applied for the job, took his civil service exam, and was accepted as a substitute mail carrier at a salary of sixty dollars a month. His Atlanta roommate took a picture of him in his postal uniform, and Father sent it to us. We were so proud of him and so excited; he looked like a Confederate general. By April 1, 1913, we were together as a family in Atlanta.

Time and tide are curious. None of us knew it then, but we were fortunate. The Rusks who stayed in Cherokee County were eventually spewed out by the unforgiving land. Using guano fertilizer and contour plowing as they might, they could find no way to make a living off that Georgia clay. The Rusks' land eventually wore out and washed away. The rest of the immediate family left Cherokee County within one generation, although my brother Parks built a retirement cottage on the original homestead, where he lived until his death.

2

An Atlanta Boyhood

Atlanta in 1913 was a railroad center of perhaps a hundred thousand people, clearly not New York or Chicago, but neither was it Cherokee County. Already a connecting hub for roads and railways, a center of commerce and trade, the Atlanta of my boyhood was a hustling, bawdy place—not your typical sleepy southern magnolia town, full of opportunity compared with the quiet backwaters of rural Georgia. It was a big city to us Rusks, so lately from the country, and it took some getting used to. Even the air we breathed was different: Atlanta was heated with soft coal in those days, and soot covered the city in winter. Whenever I wore a white shirt, it was sooty by noontime.

Our first Atlanta home was a little house on Fifth Street. It has since been run over by Georgia Tech, an embarrassing admission for a professor at the University of Georgia. Even though the house was downtown, it still had an outdoor privy, a fact of some importance since Roger and Parks got typhoid fever and nearly died while we were there, no doubt from the privy.

We soon moved to West End, to Whitehall Street, along the Central of Georgia Railroad, which ran from Atlanta down to Macon. In those days West End was a modest community of residential houses and small stores about two miles from the city center. No building in West End stood higher than two stories. Our neighborhood had among other attractions a little movie house, the Shamrock, where we kids went on Saturdays for a nickel. This was in the days of silent pictures, and the Shamrock had a player piano that banged out music reasonably related to the movie.

Being on Atlanta's outskirts, West End was an important trading area for farmers who lived west of Atlanta. In those days there was a good deal of house-to-house selling. Farmers loaded up their wagons with vegetables and fruits and passed up and down the streets, selling anything from chickens to beans. One hardly needed to leave the front porch to lay in a week's groceries, even tea and coffee. The Jewel Tea Company's wagon rumbled regularly through residential areas, selling its wares. Jewel was our favorite vendor—not for the coffee but for the stick of peppermint in each pound. On the whole, life in West End was more comfortable than Cherokee County.

That life greatly stimulated our imaginations as children. We lived one half block from the number 7 fire station. The fire wagons were pulled by horses, and it was fascinating to watch the firemen train those magnificent horses. When the bell rang, the horses would leave the stables and take their places along the wagon shaft. The harnesses would fall on them from above, more or less automatically, and with the fastening of three or four buckles they were ready to go. The fire wagon had a coal-fired boiler and a steam-driven pump. That pump wagon being pulled by horses running at full gallop along Whitehall Street, with the firemen shoveling coal into the boiler and sparks blazing out of the stack, was a spectacular sight.

In the other direction on Whitehall was a switching tower for the Central of Georgia Railroad. I often climbed up into the tower and watched the switchman pull his levers and route trains through the assembly yard. Whenever coal trains came by, we kids threw rocks at the trainmen, knowing they would throw coal back at us. We eagerly gathered that coal in a bucket and took it home; a coal shortage after World War I made coal both expensive and hard to get. The policeman on his beat sometimes saw us stoning the trainmen, but he just laughed; he knew we were just trying to gather coal.

Along the railroad track was an ice-manufacturing plant, where we'd sit on the rafters, sucking ice chips, while we watched the men make huge blocks of ice. Next door was a Karo syrup plant, where we'd sit on its rafters, suck sugarcane, and smell the wonderful aromas rising from huge caldrons of boiling syrup. Farther down Whitehall was an industrial dump, where we scrounged for junk to make into toys. We never bought toys; we whittled and hammered and built our own. In our backyard we sometimes set a brick on edge and pushed it through the sand to make a track, and we were in business as a railroad. We had three huge catawba trees—similar to cottonwoods—whose many branches made superb climbing trees. They were our forts, tree houses, and sailing ships.

As with farm life in Cherokee County, at West End we lived simply by modern standards. But our lives were never drab. Every day brought a fresh adventure. We made do with what we had, and this gave full play to our imaginations. As children we all had chores to do, but Mother saw to it that we also played. We went barefoot much of the time, and it seems only yesterday that Mother would call out at dinnertime, "Supper is ready! Come wash your feet!"

We started out on Whitehall Street without electricity but were blessed with running water and a flush toilet. The ever-present kerosene lamp was with us still, at least until at age fourteen I got a job as an office boy with the Southern Electrical Supply Company a block away. There I discovered that I could buy electric fixtures and materials for factory prices, and before long, Father had wired our house. For the first time we had electric lights—no more glass chimneys to clean.

Sometime after our move to Atlanta, Father bought a model T Ford—for $298. With few license requirements back then, and not much traffic either, I started driving at age ten, so small that I had to sit on a cushion to see over the dash. Of course, on those cobblestone roads within the city and dirt roads beyond, we couldn't go very fast. How well I remember hitting forty miles an hour for the first time, with my head stuck out the window and the wind whipping past. I thought no human being could move so fast.

The railroad track along which we lived on Whitehall Street divided poor white and poor black residential areas. The blacks right across the railroad lived under terrible conditions—primitive housing, no utilities, no playgrounds or community facilities. But black children our age lived over there, and they were our friends. Each month, for twenty-nine days, we would play together in perfect fun. About once a month we'd choose up sides—cops and robbers or cowboys and Indians—and have a fight. Color was the easiest way to choose, and it was always black versus white. As we grew older, we progressed from fists to flips to slingshots to bows and arrows and finally BB guns. I once came home with a five-foot spear stuck in my earlobe. Our play became pretty rough before we finally moved apart.

Although our schools were segregated, life on Whitehall Street led to many associations with blacks. Having black playmates and living next to an all-black community taught me something about their lives. Beginning at age six, I worked as a delivery boy for the neighborhood grocer, Mr. Leatherwood, and every afternoon I hauled groceries in a little red wagon to families on both sides of the tracks. I was paid three dollars a week, and I usually took my pay in pennies; it felt like more money to me. But serving those black families—taking their orders and delivering their groceries—was an education all its own. Often my customers sat on their porches, deep in conversation, and they sometimes told me to sit on the step until they got through talking. It was then I heard what blacks said to each other when whites were not around. They didn't consider me white, because I was just a little delivery boy. What I heard bore little resemblance to what I was told on my side of the tracks.

Over the years I've heard many whites—in Georgia and elsewhere—say, "We understand black people; we've lived with them all our lives." But the truth is that white people cannot penetrate that world where blacks are all by themselves. In the "Dip"—that all-black shantytown across the tracks—they talked about the miserable shacks in which they lived, the scarcity of jobs, the racial prejudice rampant in their lives. As a boy I witnessed this first hand, heard their anger, and learned of their hopes that something could be done about it. Even at age eight, I could sense the unfairness of it all.

The general environment in West End was not only antiblack but also anti-Jewish, anti-Catholic, and antiforeign. In closely knit communities such as Cherokee County and West End, there was a strong sense of "we" and "they." Just across the street from our church—West End Presbyterian—was a Catholic church, and the stories we heard about the Catholics would curl your hair. We looked upon that church as a den of iniquity. Our resentment against Jewish children in West End flowed mostly from the fact that they got a double dip on holidays— both Christian and Jewish holidays. Attitudes in our neighborhood were typical of low- or middle-income white Protestant communities everywhere.

And I must admit that as kids we were stirred up in unpleasant ways by a memorable film called *The Birth of a Nation,* shown in our neighborhood theater. Whenever the Ku Klux Klan rode to the tune of "Dixie," with their white robes and torches, the crowd whistled and cheered and stomped their feet. The mood of West End was solidly behind *The Birth of a Nation*. We once had a boarder at our home who we suspected was a member of the mob that lynched Leo Frank, a young Jewish man charged with killing Mary Phagan; in Georgia it was a sensational case. Our boarder was gone the day and night Leo Frank was lynched, and when he came home, he showed us what he claimed was a piece of the rope used to hang Frank.

We were anti-Yankee as well. We called northerners "damn Yankees" and really meant it, still hung over from the bitter memories of the Civil War and the Reconstruction era. In those days the Republican party was still linked with Reconstruction, and whenever we said the word "Republican," we said "black Republican." I must have been fifteen years old before I saw a live Republican on the hoof. But I was fortunate; in my own family racist sentiments and other prejudices were not particularly pronounced.

More serious than regional, religious, and racial prejudice for me were class distinctions among whites in Atlanta. When I went to Boys High School in downtown Atlanta in the 1920's, some of my best friends hailed from the north side of town. Their families were members of the Piedmont Driving Club, a most selective and exclusive club. We got along fine at school, and I was accepted as a friend. It helped that the Rusk children were good in school; Roger and Helen were valedictorians of their high schools, and Helen and I each won the loving cup for best all-around student at Boys and Girls High. Because we were good students, no one could afford to look down at us. But socially I was never asked over to the Piedmont Driving Club for the dances and other events. I still tease some of my Atlanta friends that it took them forty years to invite a boy from Whitehall Street to the Piedmont Driving Club.

Economically we were better off in Atlanta than we had been in Cherokee County, but we were still poor. At one point my brothers and I had to wait two years until my father could afford to pay two dollars for a new bicycle tire. But although we were poor, we were proud poor. We knew we came from good Scotch-Irish stock, and if anyone had called us poor, we would have socked him. Our house was always impeccably clean, and Mother usually had flowers around. Some routines had not changed. In Atlanta, just as in Cherokee, every week we scoured the floors in our house. I got just as many splinters in West End as I did on the farm, from pine floors that furred up from scrubbing.

For eight years Father carried mail for the U.S. Post Office, walking an eight-mile route twice a day, rain or shine. Sometimes he came home drenched to the skin; often he soaked his feet in a tub of water after that long march. He was finally transferred to a clerk's job. Father's dream of being a minister never came true, but however disappointing he found postal work, he never quit carrying the mail. Within a year of being washed out of Cherokee County, he had built a new life for us all and enrolled us in the best elementary school in Atlanta.

We all worked as children, to help pay the family bills and to have spending money of our own. Parks and Margaret both dropped out of school after the sixth grade to work full time and help the family. Their earnings made it possible for Roger, Helen, and me to finish school. I was extraordinarily fortunate in my brothers and sisters. My sister Margaret was a mere slip of a girl who weighed less than one hundred pounds; she also was the strongest of the family, always a source of encouragement. Parks had a highly successful career in public relations and newspaper publishing, and Roger taught physics at the University of Tennessee until his retirement. My younger sister, Helen, and I were nearly the same age and very close; she became a devoted wife and mother. Parks, Margaret, and Helen preceded me in death. I treasure my memories of family and have always been grateful to my brothers and sisters—and my parents—for their help during our growing years. Whatever achievement came my way later in life, I owe to them.

I had many jobs as a boy, first selling Coca-Cola, then delivering newspapers, then groceries for Mr. Leatherwood and ice from the ice plant, all with my little red wagon. I later worked as an office boy for the electrical supply house and the Foote and Davies printing company, but with the latter, I fell victim to Georgia's child labor laws—too young to be wandering among the paper-cutting machines and printing presses.

I once saw a newspaper ad for an office boy, went downtown and applied, and found myself working for an outfit called the Knights of the Mystic Kingdom, an offshoot of the Ku Klux Klan. The Knights had a system: New members paid ten dollars to join this antiblack, anti-Jewish, and anti-Catholic program. Of this, the organizers kept eight dollars and left two dollars for the organization. Quite a stockpile of cash built up, and soon the Knights branched into other businesses. They had me running errands and delivering packages all over town. One day I discovered that I was carrying bootleg whiskey. Figuring that job was not for me, I quit.

I did get a lucky break in my senior year in high school when I was asked to be the school page editor for the *Atlanta Journal.* Each Sunday the *Journal* ran a full page of letters from correspondents in the different schools around the city. My job was to edit those letters and paste them together to make up a school page. That job paid forty dollars a month, a handsome sum in 1924. It also brought me in touch with one of the great figures in Atlanta journalism, Harllee Branch, Sr., the city editor on the *Journal*. My little desk was right under the rail behind which he sat.

A growing, industrializing turn-of-the-century Atlanta offered more than job opportunities; these were exciting years to be a boy. For example, my friends and I grew up with the automobile and the internal-combustion engine. Roger and I often sat on our front porch and tallied up the different cars that drove by. There were more different kinds of cars from today—steam-, electric-, and gas-driven—and more brands, with names like the Winston, Poetry in Motion, Austin, and Stutz Bearcat. We grew up with radio as well. We kids made our own crystal set radios by wrapping electric wire around an oatmeal box to make a coil. By scratching a cat's whisker wire over a crystal, using earphones, we could pick up a radio station. With luck we'd tune in KDKA in Pittsburgh. I heard the first broadcast of WSB in Atlanta. WSB soon began to broadcast baseball games, and whenever our Atlanta Crackers got a hit, the announcer would strike a gong—one gong for a single, two gongs for a double, three gongs for a triple, and four gongs for a home run. These gongs meant more to me than any instant replay.

Religion remained important to the Rusks. Often Father would gather the family around the fireplace while he read the Psalms in Hebrew, or sometimes chanted them in Hebrew, more or less as the original Psalms are written . . . very engrossing to us children. Our family was active in the Presbyterian Church, and every Sunday was spent in church—morning service, Sunday school, and youth meetings. We weren't allowed to play games or read the funny papers, only take walks or memorize the Bible. The Christian Endeavor—our Presbyterian youth group—with its parties, social outings, city- and statewide rallies was the "thing to do" for the children of my generation. We didn't have to be forced to attend by our parents. At age eleven I became president of the statewide Junior Christian Endeavor and drove myself all over Georgia in my father's Model T Ford to attend meetings, often making speeches about the world of Christian Endeavor.

Father once took me to see Billy Sunday, the greatest evangelist of his day. He was an early version of today's TV evangelists, but more eloquent and dramatic in his preaching. He came to Atlanta when I was ten or so, and I went to a special service held for children. It was Billy

Sunday who taught me about the Seventh Commandment—"Thou shall not commit adultery." On the speaker's platform he had a table with ten tall vases. He told a story about a little boy who played hooky from Sunday school, told a lie to his parents, and got in all sorts of trouble. As he was telling this story, Billy Sunday took a hammer and smashed a vase for every one of the Ten Commandments the little boy had broken. But he left one vase standing—the seventh vase. I had to go home and find out about the Seventh Commandment.

One of the most important things about our family was our passion for education. Consequently, with my parents' help as well as the assistance of Parks, Margaret, and Roger, I learned to read, write, and do arithmetic before I was of school age. As a result, I skipped the first grade and started school in second grade. Both parents helped with our homework; they were very patient, yet insistent that we do our best. As a fourth grader I once brought home four A's and a C in conduct. Father gave me a whipping because of that C, using a leather strap that he called Billy. Mother never used Billy on us; she used switches instead, and we'd have to cut our own.

I started at the Lee Street School. Fortunately it was the normal training school for the Atlanta school system, and that meant we had the city's best teachers. We also had fifteen to twenty teacher candidates to help out with projects and pageants. Our teachers were constantly stressing "Be somebody!" and "Do something with your lives!" My second-grade teacher, Ethel Massingale, and I corresponded until she died in her eighties. She was a wonderful teacher.

At the Lee Street School all of us learned the basics—reading, spelling, arithmetic. It was a disciplined program. Corporal punishment was still in vogue but rarely used. We marched into and out of school to the tune of military music. But the program was innovative as well as old-fashioned. For example, each year we studied a different part of the world, using geography books called *Carpenter's Readers.* One year we would use the *Reader* on Latin America, another year Africa, another year Asia, and another year Europe. Our projects and pageants were built around whatever area of the world we were studying.

Far more so than today, moral values were stressed. We learned as much about morality and the Ten Commandments at school as we did at church. Sometimes the lines were drawn rather fine. In the second grade we played the story of Sleeping Beauty, and I was cast as the prince. When it came time for me to kiss the princess and wake her up, the teacher very carefully put a handkerchief over her face for me to kiss.

Quite apart from school, five blocks away was the home of Joel Chandler Harris, author of the Uncle Remus stories. It was a children's library, and we devoured everything in it—*The Rover Boys,* the *Tom Swift* books such as *Tom Swift and His Electric Rifle, Swiss Family Robinson,* and *Robinson Crusoe,* as well as serious books about the world. The books of our youth tended to be from-rags-to-riches stories, stressing the rewards of success, virtue, and character.

For three of my seven years in grammar school, we sat in experimental open-air classrooms whose outside walls were open to the weather. Health officials, worried about tuberculosis and infectious diseases, promoted their use, thinking that outdoor schools were supposed to be healthier for children. The outdoor school was a square building with only interior walls. The outside was wide open, and we attended those classes right through winter. When it rained, we raised canvas curtains; during winter's cold we tied ourselves into thick woolen bags. In really cold weather we heated bricks at home and brought them to school, placing them in the bottoms of the bags. On cold days we hopped to the blackboard still wearing those bags. We learned to write and draw while wearing mittens, and during breaks the teachers served hot cocoa.

When I was in the fourth grade, the board of education held hearings on the open-air school. Several classmates and I testified in favor of keeping it open; we loved it! But the board closed it down, probably because—we told ourselves—it was too hard on the teachers. Interestingly I never caught cold or became sick while going to that open-air school.

Public health was nearly as primitive in Atlanta as in Cherokee County. The Spanish flu of 1919 was very severe, killing many Atlantans. During that epidemic we wore bags of asafedita around our necks. Those little bags didn't have any medical effect, but asafedita smelled so bad that folks kept their distance from those wearing them. That alone helped limit the spread of the flu.

But conditions were improving. I remember the early campaigns to eradicate hookworm; they promoted wearing shoes and taking fifty cents' worth of medicine. I was once sent home by my sixth-grade teacher for coming to school barefooted. Her pride stung, Mother wrote a frosty note to my teacher and sent me back to school the next day—barefooted! That was a little embarrassing. But when public health teams first came into the South to eradicate hookworm, they were driven out of some areas with sticks and stones. We didn't like these Yankees coming down here to get rid of what they called our "lazy worm." That criticism subsided when the health teams set up microscopes and invited people to see for themselves what hookworms actually looked like.

After seventh grade I went straight into high school, there being no junior highs in those days. Again I was fortunate. In the Atlanta school system only two schools—Boys High and Girls High—prepared young people for college. Boys High was much like the Boston Latin School, rigorously dedicated to college preparatory work, emphasizing English, mathematics, Latin, Greek, and science. This was great discipline. There was also an array of clubs, publications, fraternities, and sports teams, and all students were expected to participate. Public speaking was stressed; weekly debates were mandatory. There was a tremendous spirit to Boys High; even the homerooms had nicknames, such as Gentlemen of Leisure, Poison Gas Brigade, and Rosser's Roustabouts. Three underground newspapers—*The Bugle, The Outlaw, The Flypaper*—helped keep matters lively. By reputation Boys High was the finest public high school in the South, and 80 percent of its graduates went on to college.

I was fortunate to have attended when I did, because the Atlanta high schools were later converted to all-purpose schools. When this happened, I felt that the rigorous intellectual discipline of Boys High had been lost. Our principal, Mr. H. O. Smith, also promoted high standards. He was a Harvard man and a rigorous disciplinarian where learning was concerned. Mr. Smith would throw quite a tantrum if he came across shoddy work, but he got results.

At Boys High I was taught Greek by the finest teacher I ever had, Preston Epps. With classes of ordinary teenage boys, he really lighted our lamps and brought our minds alive by discussing with us the great questions and ideas raised by the ancient Greeks, especially Socrates, Plato, and Aristotle. One year we met at his house to read the *Odyssey* because during class we had time for only the *Iliad*. There his wife served us cookies and hot chocolate. A devoted, inspiring teacher, Preston Epps eventually became Keenan professor of classics at the University of North Carolina at Chapel Hill. He and I corresponded until his death at age ninety-four.

Boys High was Atlanta's most prestigious school, and I was fortunate to get in. I simply applied; I don't know whether it screened applicants for this citywide school. When I started there, it was a big, old red-brick building on Gilmore Street just across from the city auditorium. It was cold, dark, and drafty, but every student got a good education. As a result of that experience and my time at the outdoor school, I have developed over the years real skepticism about whether the quality of education has much to do with the luxury of the surroundings in which teaching takes place.

Upon entering high school, I joined the Reserve Offices Training Corps (ROTC). Everyone took ROTC—it was mandatory—and few complained. Steeped into the culture of the South was the notion that young men should prepare themselves for military service, in case our country ever got into trouble. We grew up believing in the traditions and values of America, were taught to sing patriotic songs and memorize patriotic speeches, and we did this without ambiguity. Robert E. Lee was one of my early heroes; our grammar school was named after him. In Georgia the military tradition was especially strong. During World War I the newspapers printed pages of figures of soldiers— German, British, French, and American—and my brother Roger and I pasted them on sheets of cardboard and cut them out. In our backyard we cut trenches three and four inches deep, thirty feet long, just like trench warfare in Europe, and shot marbles at each other's soldiers. Some of our battles lasted two weeks. When it rained, we'd make new cardboard soldiers and start over again.

I was old enough to remember World War I. In May 1917 a huge fire on Atlanta's north side destroyed one-third of the city. From West End we could see the smoke and sense the excitement and confusion. Rumors that a German plane had dropped a bomb to start the fire proved groundless. But we swallowed all the World War I propaganda about the Huns and their atrocities. Three blocks from home was the huge Candler warehouse, a military supply depot during the war years. German prisoners were interned there, and I could peek through the fence and see them working. After all we had heard about the Huns and Kaiser Wilhelm, we thought they were men from Mars. But these Germans looked like normal human beings to me; I struck up conversations with several. After the war General John "Black Jack" Pershing came to Atlanta and led a huge parade right past the Lee Street School. As Pershing rode by, my schoolteacher nearly swooned, explaining later that Pershing had looked right at her. President Woodrow Wilson came to Atlanta in his campaign for U.S. acceptance of the League of Nations, after returning from the Versailles Conference. My Lee Street classmates and I were in the crowd when Wilson passed by. I carried a placard in support of the League. I was nine years old.

In our schools we studied the Civil War at great length; we were taught that the South lost the Civil War for this reason: Lee and his men won so many battles they became too tired to win the war. With that for history, Sergeant Henry Short taught us military discipline, drill, and marksmanship at Boys High. I enjoyed ROTC and in my senior year became cadet commander of the battalion. Every year all the ROTC cadets in Fulton County high schools paraded in a mass review at Piedmont Park, and in my senior year I was chosen cadet commander of the brigade exercise.

During that ceremony I had my first in a long and occasionally tempestuous series of encounters with the press. The cadet officers advanced upon cue to present flowers to their sponsors, usually their girl friends. When I moved forward to present flowers to Ruth Boardman, my girl friend from the West End Presbyterian Church, an *Atlanta Journal* photographer tried to substitute Miss Atlanta for my sponsor. In front of this big crowd, I told him no, despite the fact that Miss Atlanta was Estelle Bradley, a soon-to-be Hollywood actress. I was sixteen.

After I graduated from high school, I immediately went to work in the small law office of Augustus Roan, who later became a judge in Atlanta. I wanted to work and save money for college. Davidson was my goal, as it had been my father's. Unfortunately, since I didn't make much beyond living expenses, I saved next to nothing. But these two years were useful anyway. Among other things, I learned how to play basketball at the local YMCA. And I actually got good enough to make the Davidson team several years later. With the emphasis that the Rhodes selection committees placed on athletics, had I not become a ballplayer, I might not have qualified for a Rhodes scholarship or found the path that the Rhodes opened to me.

3

The "Poor Man's Princeton"

After working in Atlanta for two years, unable to bank any savings, I decided if I was ever going to go to college, it had to be right away. So with more faith than cash I asked my brother Parks to drive me to Davidson College. Located twenty miles north of Charlotte, North Carolina, in rolling farm country, Davidson was then and remains today a "poor man's Princeton," of about six hundred students in my time, all male and all white, many studying for the ministry, yet all benefiting from the college's strong liberal arts and classics programs. Davidson was my first and only choice, and Parks and I arrived at the campus on a beautiful fall day in September 1927.

As I gazed over those rolling lawns, the red-brick buildings, the elms and oaks, a lump rose in my throat. All my life I had dreamed of going to Davidson. My father had been a member of Davidson's class of 1894, and even though he didn't get his degree, in his sparse conversation about his college days he had given his family an intimate picture of the place.

When I stepped onto the campus, I had fifty dollars in my pocket and, since my father had once been a Presbyterian minister, a modest scholarship. To make ends meet, I needed a job, and fortune smiled. Every four years the local bank chose an entering freshman to become bookkeeper and assistant teller, and that job came open in 1927. I was hired, and I worked at the bank every day and even Saturdays for four years, from two in the afternoon until the books were balanced for the day. I also waited on tables at a boardinghouse and, during my senior year, helped manage the student store. During summers I stayed in Davidson as a full-time bank employee.

I took ROTC at Davidson all four years under the direction of Colonel William R. Scott. He was tall, stern, handsome, disciplined, and we all adored him; he was one of the finest officers I have ever known. At Davidson, as at Boys High, ROTC was compulsory. A few students resented it, but most of us, typical of southern boys generally, regarded the military as an honorable calling. As a senior I was proud to be named cadet commander of the ROTC battalion and president of Scabbard and Blade, an honorary military fraternity.

I also played basketball for four years at Davidson, thanks to the time spent at the YMCA during the interval between high school and college. Basketball today is not at all like the game we played; we once upset the University of North Carolina 17 to 12. This was no slowdown game; both sides went all out. During those days we had a center jump after every foul shot and field goal. There were no jump shots or hook shots; everyone had his own spot on the floor, and the idea was to pass the ball around until a player got open on his spot to take a shot. The rules allowed a designated foul shooter to shoot all the fouls, and I was usually chosen.

Although only six feet one, I played center, surely one of the last midget centers in college basketball. Duke had a six-foot-five-inch center, a fellow named Joe Crosson, whom I played against for four years. We looked upon him as some sort of glandular freak, having never seen such a giant.

Athletic attitudes were different as well. Winning was appreciated to be sure, but losing was called character building. In my day Davidson teams built a lot of character. Our coach, Monk Younger, doubled as football coach and didn't know much about basketball. Returning to Davidson one fall after a summer coaches' clinic, Coach Younger sought to institute several new wrinkles, among them the intentional foul. This caused consternation among the players. Believing fouling to be poor sportsmanship, we told the coach that we would not play that way, a rather quaint attitude in comparison with the "do-or-die" competition of today.

But even for us athletes, studies came first. One year all five David-son basketball starters were Phi Beta Kappa. I myself took the regular liberal arts program with a major in political science, especially enjoy-ing Professor Archibald Currie, who taught American government, principles of law, and international law. A lawyer by training, Currie was an inspirational teacher whose courses on international law, Amer-ican foreign policy, and world events focused on the tragedy of World War I, the vain effort of Woodrow Wilson—a Davidson alumnus—to win American acceptance of the League of Nations, and mankind's first efforts—in the League—to establish an international legal authority to resolve disputes among nations.

On the whole, Davidson was an exciting place intellectually, a broadening place. But not entirely . . . I had one stultifying professor of the Old Testament who on examination day walked into class and wrote the word "Moses" on the blackboard. For the exam—the whole exam—we were to write down everything we knew about Moses.

Not even my years in government were busier. In addition to basket-ball, ROTC, working at the bank, and trying to keep up with my studies, I was president of the freshman class, active in the campus YMCA, on the staff of the yearbook *Quips and Cranks,* and an active member of Kappa Alpha fraternity, Robert E. Lee's fraternity. A typi-cal day for me was conducted at a fast trot: classes in the morning or whenever I had them, waiting on tables at the boardinghouse at lunch, on to the bank, and then, in season, across campus to basketball prac-tice. When that was over, I would take off to wait tables again at dinner. For me, Davidson was a breathless experience.

Despite the best efforts of Currie and others like him, Davidson was quite provincial. The twenties in general were quiescent years: Warren G. Harding's "return to normalcy"; isolationism; public indifference to overseas events. At Davison we had no radio, no television, and little news from abroad. Nor were the youth of my generation in a searching mode; few students challenged social values; there was little agitation for reform. We were not encouraged to think critically about the work-ings of American democracy and domestic and world events, as were the young people of later generations. This was true despite World War I and the stock market crash, the latter in my junior year. But I enjoyed Davidson immensely and was thoroughly stimulated by my experience.

Since Davidson was a church school, many of its trustees were Presbyterian ministers. Although it was one of the finest liberal arts schools in the country, social life was seriously deficient. We couldn't leave campus without permission. We were not allowed to cut classes or have cars on campus. There was an honor code to prevent cheating, a code of responsibility to define student ethics, and a student council to help enforce the rules. *In loco parentis* was taken seriously.

Davidson's trustees considered dancing immoral, even carnal, so there were no dances on campus. All our dances were held in Charlotte, about twenty miles away. And about a third of the young ladies at those Charlotte dances were women of ill repute. The trustees' idea was that Davidson could somehow "throw its arm" around those Charlotte dances and control them, but the joke around campus was "That's a long way to throw an arm."

We rarely challenged authority, but in one such attempt a committee of students of which I was a member—over the strong disapproval of my father—met with the board of trustees to petition for dances on campus. The trustees turned us down flat.

We were not even allowed to play bridge on campus, and of course, drinking was forbidden, drugs unheard of. As a member of the student council I had the job of enforcing the rule against drinking. When visiting another dormitory, I always sent a scout on ahead to advertise my arrival, to allow the drinkers time to hide their bottles. For myself, though, since I was short of both time and money, I didn't find this restrictive life too offensive.

Having worked for two years after high school, I was older than most of my classmates, and my rapidly balding "high forehead" heightened this perceived maturity. At one basketball game, after the ball had gone out of bounds, I went over to the sidelines to throw it in, and some girl called out, "You can't do that, Old Folks!" That taunt became my nickname at Davidson, along with Elijah—a hoary prophet of the Old Testament. I had dropped my first name, David, preferring to be called Dean. This, too, sometimes led to confusion. For example, when I went to meet a distinguished English lecturer arriving by train in Charlotte, I greeted him on the station platform with "I'm Dean Rusk." He replied, "Good God, man! At your age?"

To save money, I lived with a roommate, first Herman King and then Stuart Mecham, in a little room called the Crow's Nest that was attached to the armory. Our task was to fire the armory's boiler in exchange for free rent. The armory was old and ramshackle and infested with rats. A favorite pastime called for us to put cheese on a cracker or piece of bread, place it on the floor under a ceiling light, and then sit up on our beds in the darkness with rifles at the ready. When the rats came after the cheese, we'd snap the lights on and open fire.

When a delegation from the Union Theological Seminary once visited Davidson, its members were told upon arrival to go to the Crow's

Nest. Apparently they were looking for the dean of the college and someone directed them to Dean Rusk's room. One of the guests was blind, and when he was led into the "dean's room" and smelled the rich aroma and felt the dirt and sand beneath his feet, he said, "Gee whiz, what kind of college is this?" That story went all over campus. I had the reputation of doing many things well at Davidson, but housekeeping was not among them.

Davidson's primary mission was to prepare Christian leaders for the church, and I gave much thought to becoming a Presbyterian minister. We all took courses in the Old and New Testaments and memorized many passages from the Bible. In addition to Sunday church services, we had compulsory chapel every morning. Although that seemed somewhat oppressive, since a boy I had been required to go to church. I knew nothing else. At least morning chapel was a convenient time for the student body to meet, make announcements, and transact business. We often had guest speakers, with occasional moments of inspiration.

But I will admit that the religious core of a Presbyterian school did make a difference. I greatly valued the emphasis on moral and spiritual values. Davidson insisted that Davidson men meet high standards; we were expected to do our best. As a Presbyterian school it had an underlying concern about right and wrong and a conviction that some goals in life are more worthy than others. This aspiration to do well and improve one's life was part of the campus environment. Davidson clearly sought to prepare its young men for lives of service. To further this, the college hired topnotch professors to serve as our models. Davidson emphasized teaching rather than research and encouraged close faculty-student ties. We always felt welcome in the homes of our professors.

As I went through Davidson, however, I became skeptical about many traditional church views. I was, for instance, never able to reconcile the twin doctrines of predestination and free will. I gradually lost interest in questions of that sort. During my senior year, while president of the YMCA—the main religious and social organization at Davidson—I told Dean Mark Sentell that I had become skeptical about some teachings of the Protestant Church. Should I resign? Dean Sentell sensibly replied that I had been elected by the students, and any resignation would disturb them. I served out my term but abandoned the idea of the ministry and began to think about college teaching as a career, focusing on international relations and international law.

There was considerable evangelical pressure at Davidson upon nonbelievers. As a Presbyterian college Davidson made no bones about wanting to enlist its students for the church. Any student who was not "saved" was the object of much concern. Thad Brock, a football player, had not made his commitment to Christ, and we asked him to lead chapel one morning, thinking participation might help get him involved. Thad was reluctant, but we pressed, and he finally agreed. Instead of reading from the Bible, he read several passages from *All Quiet on the Western Front,* and then he said, "Let us pray." His prayer was "Oh, God, if there be a God, help us if you can."

My four years at Davidson were a tremendous educational experience, and I knew without a doubt that I wanted to go on to graduate school. Apparently I had known it a long time. My family remembers my writing an essay in high school called "What I Want to Do with the Next Twelve Years of My Life." In that essay I had aimed at graduating from Boys High, after four years, two years working in Atlanta, four years at Davidson College, then two years at Oxford University. For a young man without funds, the only way I could do graduate work was by means of a Rhodes scholarship.

If I had known about the odds against getting such a scholarship, I might have lowered my sights. But my German professor at Davidson, Guy Vowles, himself a Rhodes scholar, encouraged me. As it turned out, Vowles was also on the state selection committee that reviewed my application.

I have long been impressed with the role that accident, happenstance, and luck played in my life. My selection as a Rhodes scholar was a good example. I was called to Raleigh, North Carolina, for an interview. The review committeemen noted my proclaimed interest in world peace and equally apparent enthusiasm for ROTC and military values. They questioned me on this paradox. "The American eagle on the great seal has arrows in one claw and an olive branch in the other," I pointed out. "The two must go together. Armed force and world peace are two sides of the same coin."

Josephus Daniels, chairman of the North Carolina committee and Woodrow Wilson's secretary of the navy, frowned, looked over my application, and said, "Mr. Rusk, I see from your papers that you live in Georgia. Why in the world should we give a North Carolina appointment to a Georgian?"

I said, "Well, Mr. Daniels, I have lived in North Carolina for four years. I spend not only the school year here but summers as well. I worked in a bank in Greensboro last summer and in the bank at Davidson since my freshman year. I pay poll tax in North Carolina. . . ."

"Oh?" he said, with obvious interest. Paying that North Carolina poll tax was a complete accident. The teller of Davidson's bank was a marvelous old gentleman named Thompson whom I liked very much, and as town treasurer he collected poll tax. Just for fun, I paid him a one-dollar poll tax each year. I am quite convinced that if I had not paid that poll tax, I would not have been chosen a Rhodes scholar from North Carolina. That one-dollar poll tax turned out to be the best dollar I ever invested.

Whatever the reason, I was picked by the committee and accepted by St. John's College of Oxford University. In May 1931 I graduated from Davidson with a B.A. in political science, a Phi Beta Kappa key, and the Rhodes. My life had already changed quite a bit from my Cherokee County days, but it would change even more. In the fall of 1931 I readied to leave the South, little realizing that forty years would pass before I would live there again.

4

A Southern Yank at Oxford

I arrived in New York City on St. Patrick's Day 1931. I was twenty-two years old, and I had never been farther from Georgia than North Carolina. New York itself with its concrete canyons made an immense impression on me. Even my first evening meal in New York was memorable, because everything in the restaurant was green, including the meat. In the South green meat is usually rotten meat, but since I paid for this, I ate it anyway.

I had missed an earlier sailing for the Rhodes scholars because of a case of what Georgians call swamp fever—a touch of malaria. But I boarded the RMS *Berengaria,* a huge Cunard liner. I anticipated having to adapt to all sorts of Continental customs in England, but my education began in New York Harbor. As we passed the Statue of Liberty, all were on deck waving good-bye. A deck steward passed with a tray of ham sandwiches. "Would you like a ham sandwich, sir?" I said, "Oh, yes indeed!," took a bite, and threw it over the side—my first experience with English mustard. This rube from Georgia had a great deal to learn.

My acclimatization to Britain proceeded apace once I reached London. On one occasion when I took the underground, I spied a huge billboard portraying a picture of a stork, with its beak pointed skyward. Large letters blared GUINNESS'S STOUT KEEPS YOUR PECKER UP! And on the urinal stalls notices cautioned, in Greek, "Players with short bats should stand close to the wicket." London was a far cry from Georgia Presbyterianism.

With my ripe southern accent, I was somewhat of a biological specimen to Europeans. I quickly buffed off its worst features just to be understood. After three years I managed to lose my southern drawl and even took on a bit of an English accent. But on the voyage over an Englishwoman found out that I was from Georgia. Deciding to keep me on center stage, she said, "Oh, isn't that the place where you butcher your Negroes?"

"Oh, yes," I replied. "And we consider them rare delicacies."

At an Oxford seminar a black woman from America asked where I was from. I said, "I'm from Georgia."

Whereupon she said, "Then you can call me Annie." She was dead serious. She herself was not prepared to accept equal status with a white man from Georgia, even at Oxford.

My years at Oxford were 1931 to 1934, in an era when the sun never set on the British Empire. World War II was half a decade away. The empire, still intact, had not yet begun that massive decolonialization precipitated by a combination of Hitler, war, and changing times. Oxford in the 1930's fully reflected Britain's pride of empire. This pride was spearheaded by young Britishers of the upper classes, especially those graduates of Oxford and Cambridge who expected careers in politics or the foreign or domestic civil service or those headed for the clergy or the armed forces. The well-bred and well-educated could even choose from overseas institutions such as the Indian or the Sudanese civil service. They were expected to serve the empire. One of my Oxford friends who joined the Sudan civil service right after graduation lost his life when he plunged into the Nile River seeking to save a Sudanese from a crocodile. The crocodile got him instead.

That incident surprised no one at Oxford. It was all part of the tradition, as were the Rhodes scholarships themselves. Cecil Rhodes, who endowed the scholarships, was a celebrated imperialist, personally convinced that Anglo-Saxons were destined to rule the world. "I contend that we are the first race in the world," Rhodes once wrote. "The more of the world we inhabit, the better it is for the human race." Not all of us accepted Rhodes's view, yet under the surface most Oxonians would have admitted that the Anglo-Saxons had a special talent for leadership. The Rhodes scholarships were meant in part to prepare Britain's colonies to accept Anglo-Saxon rule.

Although the empire was stable, with traditions that seemed immutable, signs of change nevertheless were evident at Oxford in the 1930's. The older dominions such as Canada, Australia, and New Zealand were pushing for more independence. India, Malaya, and Burma were still colonies, but there, too, desires for home rule and national self-determination were emerging. Mahatma Gandhi had begun his independence movement and initiated Round Table conferences with the British government over the future of India.

In hindsight, in many ways Great Britain had built the disintegration of its empire into its very structure. When the British achieved dominance and extended their empire around the globe in the eighteenth and nineteenth centuries, they brought in their knapsacks seeds of freedom with which Britain governed itself. These little seeds of freedom later germinated. It was not possible for the British forever to have democratic rule at home and imperial rule abroad.

It was not surprising, then, that a sense of impending change, even foreboding, pervaded Oxford when I was there. Many felt that Britain was overextended and getting a little tired. Caught in the throes of the Great Depression, the country was in trouble financially; unemployment was high; its poor were suffering. Many students probed as students do for alternatives to the dominant economic and political structures. This was reflected in active socialist and labor movements at Oxford. The pacifists held many rallies on campus. Capitalism came under sharp and skeptical questioning. There was lively interest in Franklin Roosevelt and his New Deal measures.

In this period between the wars the British military was somewhat discredited and in disrepair. Antiwar sentiment was strong at Oxford; slightly more than a decade earlier an entire generation of Oxford men had gone to war and many failed to return. Almost every Britisher had lost a family member in "the war to end all wars." My English classmates rarely talked about the war, but debates at the Oxford Union, university lectures, and casual conversation all reflected this legacy of tragedy and confusion. I am personally convinced that this combination of pacifism, isolationism, and public indifference—attitudes prevalent not only at Oxford but in the Western democracies generally—contributed immeasurably to the events that led to World War II.

St. John's College was one of the oldest and most prestigious institutions among the colleges that make up Oxford. After a short adjustment period I felt completely at home there. That was fortunate because a student's social and academic life centered in his college. I applied for a degree called the Modern Greats—philosophy, politics, and economics—and plunged into study. I focused on international relations, history, law, politics, and philosophy. Indeed, Oxford supplied plenty for an inquiring mind. In addition to the fine tutors at St. John's, Oxford offered a strong lecture program which we could attend as we wished.

At the beginning of each term I looked through the university's lecture schedule with my tutors and picked those that would be helpful. The only compulsory academic appointments were weekly sessions with tutors, and the only other duties fifteen to twenty-page papers on agreed-upon topics, due each week. These the tutors critiqued for style, method, and substance. This continuous writing experience proved invaluable.

My first two years I shared an apartment with American roommates; these apartments had a common living room with separate bedrooms. It seemed that all the English boys were assigned single apartments, with no roommates. I once asked my tutor why apartments with common living rooms had been assigned only to Americans. He said, "With you Americans, there is not the presumption of homosexuality!"

Oxford's laid-back approach to education appealed to me. Students had unlimited freedom and few rules for personal conduct. Oxford said in effect, "If you want this degree, you pass that examination. You can take that examination after two years, three years, or four years; we do not care. If you pass your exam, you get your degree. If you fail the exam, you don't get it." There were no tests, no grades, no courses or terms of study except the final exam. If a student wanted to drink himself to death, Oxford let him. If he wanted to flunk out, the tutors let him fail. Oxford didn't care if we found jobs after graduation. *In loco parentis* was a concept the British left to American colleges.

Academics at Oxford were leavened by another of Oxford's quaint, incongruous traditions. While we were expected to learn and do well on our final exams, we were not to be unduly bookish. During vacations—and almost half of the Oxford year was taken up by vacations—we would cram our suitcases full of books and bone up on our studies. The trick at Oxford was to arrange your affairs so as to have time to enjoy the "Oxford life": bull sessions with students; debates and sports; dropping in on professors' homes on Sundays. We even played a fair amount of bridge although not much poker, which was regarded as an American frontier game.

Ironically, one aspect of Oxford life was denied me. St. John's was a college of the Church of England and as such held compulsory chapel every morning at seven-thirty. During my first week at St. John's the dean of the college called me in and informed me that since I was a Presbyterian, I was not particularly welcome at morning chapel. Whatever rejection I felt dissipated quickly. I had through no virtue of my own just managed to escape compulsory chapel for the duration of my Oxford life.

Oxford's relaxed pace was a welcome change. Working my way through Boys High and Davidson, I had always had to run from one commitment to another. At Oxford I first experienced some of the leisure that goes with learning. The Rhodes scholarship paid my bills, although just barely. But no one worked his way through Oxford; this just wasn't done.

The Oxford year consisted of three terms, each roughly two months long, punctuated by long vacations at Christmas, Easter, and summer. I spent most of my vacation time in Germany, then undergoing dramatic social and political change, although I also had enjoyable times elsewhere on the Continent and in England itself. I went on many shorter outings and particularly enjoyed bicycling in that beautiful Cotswold countryside surrounding Oxford. Every turn in the road brought a lovely view. I would take pictures of old churches scattered about the English countryside, often stopping at a pub for tea before biking home.

Having grown up in a strict home in the Bible Belt, for my first Easter vacation I hightailed straight to Paris, the glamour city of Europe. There I stayed in a small, dingy hotel on the West Bank. One evening as I walked around the Place de la Concorde a sleazy little fellow came up to me and said, "Do you want to buy some French postcards?"

Thinking I had been offered pornography unavailable in Great Britain or the United States, I said, "How much?"

He replied, "Ten francs."

So I gave him ten francs. He reached into his pocket, glancing around as though looking for a policeman, and handed me a little packet and ran away. When I got back to my hotel, I found pictures not of Parisian ladies but of the Arc de Triomphe, the Eiffel Tower, and the Louvre. They were French postcards all right.

I spent a second vacation living with a family on Guernsey, one of the Channel Islands off the French coast, and a third in the Lake District of northern England, in William Wordsworth country, on a reading party with perhaps ten classmates. We read in the mornings and hiked in the afternoons. During this vacation I grew my first beard, which was red and rather bushy. We had an old motorbike with us, and one day I put my lacrosse helmet on, pulled on an American sweat shirt and some baggy pants, and went for a ride in the countryside. Having stopped at a petrol station for fuel, I was filling my tank when a big limousine drove up. From the back seat a lady with a lorgnette peered at me intently, wearing a rather sour expression, and then drove off. Upon returning to camp, I found we had an invitation from the master and lady of the local manor house to have tea the next afternoon. We all were rather crummy-looking, and I decided it was time to cut off my beard.

The next day we made our way to the manor house. The hostess, of course, was that same lady in the car at the filling station the preceding afternoon. During a lull in the conversation she said, "Oh, young gentlemen, I must tell you. Yesterday I saw the most horrid creature I have ever seen in my life!" and went on to describe me in lurid detail. We all laughed, I a little nervously. Then I told our hostess that I had been the creature. It's true about the English: They are very good sports. Our hostess was most amused.

A typical day at Oxford began early. Ordinarily I was awakened by my "scout," a man named Dudley. A long-term employee of the college, each scout served eight to ten students. Dudley built a fire in the fireplace—there being no central heating—put the kettle on to boil water for tea, and served breakfast, usually eggs, bacon, and bread, in my room. Most mornings were spent in study, followed by lunch in my room, usually with friends. Downstairs there was a kitchen called the battery, where Dudley would prepare sliced ham, cheese, a roll, perhaps a piece of fruit.

Afternoons were devoted to athletics. Participation was almost mandatory. And while university teams were drawn from all over Oxford, each college had its own soccer, cricket, and rugby teams, playing fields, clubhouses, and tennis courts. On the river, each college had shells for crew racing. Whatever the sport, teams always took a tea break together around four o'clock in the clubhouse.

After athletics I returned to my quarters, showered and rested, and maybe played a little bridge or join a bull session with my fellow students. At seven o'clock, wearing coats and academic gowns, we went to the college dining hall for a formal dinner. At the end of each dining hall was a low platform called high table, at which the dons sat, always in black tie. We began each meal with a grace in Latin, given by a senior scholar. The rest of us kept a stopwatch on him, and if his grace went for more than a given number of seconds, he had to buy beer for all. Conversation was lively and animated on all subjects but one: women. If anyone broke this prohibition, he had to buy a round for all. After dinner, evenings were free for study, bull sessions, bridge, evening lectures, or other entertainment.

In addition to university competition, each college had an intensive program of intercollegiate sports. I played tennis for St. John's College but did not make the university tennis team. Had I done so, six Americans, all from North Carolina, would have represented Oxford in tennis, but an Englishman beat me out for that sixth position. I never rowed crew, but I did horse around with cricket and rugby. And although I had never played lacrosse—the game was unknown to the American South—I tried out for the university lacrosse team and made the squad. Our players were mostly American and Canadian.

I liked Oxford's approach to athletics. Our games were fiercely competitive, but there was no insistence upon winning and no professional coaches. Each year the teams themselves selected captains for the following year. Typically a captain would post an announcement for tryouts, and anyone who wanted to play on that team would show up. After some scrimmages the captain decided who would play. He did this by written invitation. For example, I would get a note from the captain saying, "Dear Dean: We are playing our next lacrosse game on such and such a day, at such and such a place. I would be glad if you could take part." If I were busy with my studies or some other engagement, I would send him a note saying, "Sorry, but I can't make it this time. Please call on me another time." If our match was in London, it was up to me to pack my gear, get myself to London, and show up in time for the game. And yet our games were highly competitive. This approach is far more wholesome than the highly organized, disciplined, pressurized collegiate sports of America. Our only training rule was the admonition not to drink more than one pint of beer at lunch the day of the game.

Oxford awarded blues instead of letters, and one could get a blue only by playing against archrival Cambridge. For my first two years we beat Cambridge handily in lacrosse. But during my third year Cambridge began importing Canadians, and I had to play left wing, opposite a huge, brawny Canuck defenseman who just beat the hell out of me. Cambridge carried the day.

The British always claimed that they had invented baseball. Just for fun, they challenged the American Oxonians to an exhibition baseball game at Lord's cricket ground in London. We Americans put together our team, and our English classmates formed a British Empire team by robbing the embassies and the crews off merchant ships in port. The British team was one man short, so my teammates lent me to them. Each player was introduced to the crowd, and I was introduced as Eric Svenson from the Yukon. By chance, I hit home runs my first two times up. The next time I came to the plate, the umpire said, "Take it easy . . . this is the only ball we have left." The American team beat us—the British and me—by the horrendous score of 25 or 30 to 2, and I had hit the two home runs for my English teammates, but the British held fast to their claims of having invented baseball.

Soon after I arrived at Oxford, my English classmates set me up for what was obviously a hazing ritual. They appointed me chairman of the Junior Common Room—the student organization—to petition the president of St. John's College for a powder room for ladies visiting the college. There were no such facilities. If you had a lady guest and she needed to withdraw, you would have to take her outside the college, across the street, down into an underground station, and put a penny in the slot of a public toilet. The president of St. John's College was Dr. James, a man in his eighties with a long, flowing white beard. We called him the Bodger. I organized my thoughts, called on him with two members of my committee, and made my speech asking for a powder room. When I got through, he glared at us and said, "What a monstrous proposal!" That was the end of that! My classmates knew precisely what the Bodger's response would be, but nevertheless, they stuck my nose into it.

The English sense of humor is more sophisticated than the American, not as bawdy as our slapstick, with fewer "tall stories." But it is extremely effective. Oxford prided itself on its eccentric traditions, offbeat characters, and good times. Dinners were especially lively, particularly among the dons who sat at high table. At Oxford it was considered infra dig—beneath dignity—to agree with anybody else, and that encouraged animated conversation. St. John's College also had a marvelous wine cellar; the dons sampled wines from all over Europe, getting the best for the college. There was lots of drinking, and despite my Presbyterian heritage, I got caught up in it. Soon after my arrival, at a party for one of my English classmates, I was handed a glass of sherry. I had never so much as touched a drop of alcohol, excepting those times when my father administered his medicinal drops of corn whiskey. I sat there staring at that glass for a long time, finally lifted it, took a sip . . . and fell from grace.

Among Oxford's delightful traditions were professors' open houses on Sunday afternoons, when distinguished visitors would have tea with faculty and undergraduates. When Mahatma Gandhi visited London in 1931 for the Second Indian Round Table Conference, he spent a weekend in Oxford with the master of Balliol College. Memorably, Gandhi brought two goats to provide his daily milk. He also agreed to spend an evening with a group of Indian students at Oxford called the Lotus Club. Each Indian could bring a non-Indian guest. My Hindu friend Eric da Costa invited me, and I quickly accepted. Over two hundred students crowded into the meeting hall. Gandhi, who had just been released from an English prison, sat cross-legged on a table, wearing only a loincloth, talking with us and answering our questions.

I remember vividly several things he told us during that dramatic evening. In talking about Satyagraha, his philosophy of nonviolence, and his hopes for Indian independence, he said, "I have always expected the best of the other fellow, including British leaders, because people try to live up to your expectations of them." But then, sitting half-naked on his little table, Gandhi added, "The British will think of me in spiritual terms. That is because of my way of life, the things I say, the way I dress. But they will forget that I have discovered the secret of power in India." And his voice became very firm. "We Indians cannot drive out the British by returning fire rifle for rifle and cannon for cannon. We simply don't have such weapons. But we can drive the British out of India by simply doing nothing. All we have to do is sit down and refuse to work for them. They cannot stay in India without our help. If we do that, just sit down and refuse to work, some of us will die, others of us may starve. But the British will have to leave." In a harsh voice that sounded like a shout, he said, "That is raw power!"

Despite his slight frame and loincloth and his philosophy of nonviolence, Gandhi was far stronger than he is usually portrayed. He was a dynamic personality, vibrant and inspiring, not at all weak or feeble. I have never forgotten that evening with Mahatma Gandhi. His remarks that night and his later acceptance of the necessity of defeating Germany and Japan in World War II made me skeptical that Gandhi was the total pacifist that others thought him to be.

Debating was another great Oxford tradition, both between colleges—I debated for St. John's—and, of course, at the Oxford Union, the world's most famous undergraduate debating society, the womb of British prime ministers. Politicians accepted invitations from the Oxford Union with alacrity—it was an honor to be invited—and debates were rather formal. The debaters wore white tie and tails. Rules mimicked those of the British House of Commons. Each week a topic was tabled for debate, usually on a serious issue. But occasionally debates were laid on just to have a good time. One of the lighter debates was "Resolved: that this house regrets Christopher Columbus," a rip-roaring affair designed to pull the legs of us Americans.

One debate I have never forgotten occurred in February 1933 in the Oxford Union. The debate topic was "Resolved: that this House will in no circumstances fight for King and Country." The philosopher C. E. M. Joad argued the motion from the pacifist side. Joad, who was, in fact, an avowed pacifist, was also suspected by some of homosexual leanings. When his opponent asked what he would do if he saw a man trying to rape his sister, Joad, in his high-pitched, squeaky voice, replied, "I would merely place myself between them." That crack brought down the house.

Joad was brilliant that evening, witty and articulate, and his patriotic opposition was rather leaden by comparison. Votes in those debates often turn on the quality of the debaters' performances rather than the merits of the issues, a factor that many people forgot. Joad carried the day; the audience voted by 275 to 153 that "This House will not fight for King and Country." Since I was both an American and a reserve officer in the U.S. Army, and because it wasn't my king and country, I did not vote on the motion. But that debate was not a trivial event. In fact, it had two serious results, one apparent and one hidden. Shortly after there arose a pacifist organization called the Oxford Movement. Further, Adolf Hitler later referred to that Oxford Union debate as a sign that Britain would not fight. It may have been one factor that encouraged him to pursue his course of aggression.

A sequel to that debate was equally memorable. In 1939, after the Nazi invasion of Poland and the outbreak of World War II, leaders of the pacifist movement in Britain—Bertrand Russell, Maude Royden, George Lansbury, and C. E. M. Joad—issued a joint statement that was widely circulated by the British Ministry of Information. It said in effect, "Sorry, chaps, but this fellow Hitler is different. Get out there and fight." Unfortunately these former pacifists were now urging young Britishers to fight without the arms, training, and preparedness which they themselves had done so much to block. In the Oxford Union that famous evening was a friend from Scotland who later, with a battalion of the Black Watch, charged German panzers with naked bayonets to help get a few more of their buddies off the beaches of Dunkirk. But in 1933 Hitler was still in the future.

Even so, the world was not at peace. In 1931, my first year at Oxford, the Japanese marched into Manchuria, hoping to seize all of

North China and secure badly needed resources. The Japanese aggression badly violated the Kellogg-Briand Pact, outlawing aggressive military action; according to the League of Nations Covenant, League members were obligated to assist China. Sensing that something very important had happened, I spent an enormous amount of time trying to follow the Manchurian crisis, not only factual accounts of the invasion but also reports of the Lytton Commission and the League of Nation's futile efforts to blunt this aggression.

In retrospect, much of this time was wasted. The Japanese seizure of Manchuria was merely one in a series of episodes that produced World War II. With a sinking heart, I watched newsreels of Chinese Foreign Minister Wellington Koo standing before the League of Nations, pleading for help from the world community, help that never came. And I remember the remark of the British foreign minister in response: "Oh, dear, I wish he would be more Wellington and less Koo!"

This was a crucial test for the League; under its Covenant, a response was clearly called for. But it failed the test, and I was terribly disappointed. This wholesale violation of international law, and the failure of the League to defend its own principles, were ominous indeed. This was repeated in 1935, after I had left Oxford, when Mussolini marched his army into Ethiopia. The world witnessed the frail figure of Emperor Haile Selassie pleading in vain to the League of Nations for help. The League discussed economic sanctions against Italy, but in America the Senate Foreign Relations Committee would not even let Secretary of State Cordell Hull state that if the League imposed sanctions against Italy, the United States would not frustrate those sanctions by insisting upon its right to trade as a neutral nation. We weren't willing to go even that far. Once again, no response from the League. Ethiopia drove the final nail into the coffin and doomed our hopes for an international response to armed aggression. Then followed the Spanish Civil War, with Franco's forces fighting to overthrow the Republican government of Spain, and Hitler and Mussolini actively siding with Franco by supplying airplanes, weapons, and personnel. Again the democracies looked the other way and pretended this was merely a conflict between Spaniards.

During this time of international turmoil I had many opportunities to travel to Germany during my Oxford vacations. My interest in Germany first developed when I was a small boy in Atlanta; the old Candler warehouse and Fort MacPherson, both within walking distance, held German prisoners during World War I. In high school I was aware of Germany's inflationary crisis, during which its citizens were forced to roll wheel barrows full of money to the grocery stores in order to buy food. At Davidson I learned that the Allies' punitive treatment inhibited German recovery from the devastation of World War I. I had also studied German at Davidson. Additionally, my mother's family had come from the Black Forest region. For sentimental reasons and a chance to hone my language skills, Germany seemed a good choice for Oxford vacations and for extended study as well.

I enrolled in Hanover University in 1933 to study German, and during my next vacation I studied economics at the University of Hamburg. I then combined Easter and Christmas vacations with a one-term leave of absence from Oxford and spent a half year in Berlin.

I was in Berlin in March 1933, when the Reichstag burned and Hitler seized power. It was a momentous time to live in Germany. The economy had collapsed; millions were unemployed; runaway inflation and high taxes impoverished many Germany families. The country struggled to meet its reparation payments required by the Treaty of Versailles. There was political chaos as well as economic. I saw Hitler's brown-shirted Nazi storm troopers rule the streets and take public platforms away from the democratic parties of the Weimar Republic. The Weimar government collapsed, and the Nazis became firmly entrenched during my time in Germany, and I saw the Nazi appeal to Germans victimized by defeat and that devastating inflation which wiped out their savings and devalued their money.

That faith was tragically misplaced. The Nazis immediately assaulted the German education system. I had gone to Berlin to study international law with Professor Bruns at the Hochschule für Politik. At our first meeting Bruns asked his students what we should focus on during the seminar. This was most untypical of German education, where by tradition Herr Professor held sway and students sat quietly to absorb the professor's wisdom. Four or five of the twenty students in Bruns's class wore Nazi uniforms. One jumped to his feet and said, "There is only one thing we ought to study, and that is the illegality of the Treaty of Versailles!" No one said a word in reply. It was appalling to see these brownshirt students take over the seminar of this distinguished professor.

I saw the destruction of German university life taking place before me. The Nazis soon took over the Hochschule für Politik and turned it into a leadership training school for the Nazi party. I was rather glad when we non-Nazis were forced to move across the street to the University of Berlin. There remnants of true university education remained.

But even there the impact of the Nazis was apparent. I once attended a lecture by a Professor Hoesch, a well-known German historian, who talked about how best to incorporate the Germans of the United States into the Third Reich. He was speculating rather wildly about future possibilities for the Third Reich in America. For example, he discussed whether it should be done through party organization within America or whether the Third Reich should demand territorial enclaves in places like Milwaukee and St. Louis. His lecture was a complete fantasy, yet he seemed serious. Obviously this professor, under pressure from nazism, was trying to please the Nazis and save his job. I was later told that he took early retirement in 1935.

The Hitler years were a terrible period for German universities; education became highly politicized and educational standards went haywire. Oddly enough, although I moved in university circles, I don't recall any Germans seriously discussing with me their own criticisms about Adolf Hitler. Whatever doubts they may have entertained, they didn't express them, at least to foreigners. They may have felt it was too dangerous, or perhaps they were taking a wait-and-see attitude toward Hitler. The Nazis burned books during this period, and I remember students hiding away their own private collections, especially titles being burned by the Nazis.

Matters went from bad to worse. There was war in the streets of Germany; Nazi storm troopers routinely broke up other people's meetings, staged their own large parades, and attacked other parades. Neither conservatives nor socialists were permitted to hold peaceful rallies and speak from public platforms. One incident in particular affected me deeply. In Hamburg one tense evening I went walking the streets looking for excitement. I didn't find any. But the next morning I woke to the news that some two hundred people had been killed in clashes between the Nazis and the socialists fourteen blocks away. I didn't look for any street excitement after that.

Yet the Weimar government continued to extend to the Nazis the normal privileges of a political party. I watched the Weimar Republic in effect commit suicide by refusing to crack down on the Nazis, who obviously wanted to destroy constitutional democracy and establish a dictatorship. Some cities were relatively quiet, but Germany as a whole—Berlin and Hamburg in particular—was a seething pot of controversy and violence. The socialists were strong in some parts of Germany, and there were many street battles. I found all this both fascinating and repulsive. Having read Hitler's *Mein Kampf,* I was aware of the possibility that Hitler meant what he wrote, and the implications were frightening.

While studying in Berlin, I lived with a German family in Neuba-belsberg, a suburb in the lake country near Potsdam. The father was a bookbinder who made a modest living. On weekends we would often cruise around the lakes in their motorboat, taking our lunches with us and stopping at small cafés for coffee or tea. I watched the effects of nazism upon this German family, an experience surely common to many Germans. I never had the impression that the mother, father, or daughters were ever caught up in the Nazi movement. But the seventeen-year-old son was crazy about motorcycles. He joined the Nazi SS motorcycle corps, I believe with no ideological commitment to Adolf Hitler, at least in the beginning. He may have acquired one as nazism progressed. This youngster served in the SS, fought on the eastern front, and survived the war. Multiply this story thousands of times, and you have the "good Germans," those who did not become Nazis themselves and did not actively support Hitler but nevertheless tolerated him. Such widespread toleration and quiet complicity let Hitler go as far as he did.

On the other hand, many German students of my generation sup-ported Adolf Hitler for idealistic reasons. They wanted to rebuild the economy and restore public morale in Germany after the terrible infla-tion of the Weimar Republic. They wanted to see Germany respected again by the nations of the world. Few believed what Hitler had written in *Mein Kampf.* In fact, at least if my friends and acquaintances were an accurate measure, most Germans had never read *Mein Kampf.* Those who had brushed its implications aside; they didn't take Hitler or his ideas seriously—until it was too late. The extent to which their idealism was betrayed is among the tragedies of World War II and the legacy of nazism.

Hitler's seizure of power affected my social life as well as my studies. Having grown up in a strict family and having attended a college where dancing was taboo, I never learned to dance. When I got to Germany, I took some lessons. Except for the Viennese waltz, all the dancing of the period was done to march music. The Viennese waltz was far beyond me; I was never light enough on my feet. On the other hand, anyone, even I, could learn the one-step. To be honest, it was a pretty dull step, but I never learned another. Anytime in the future when I was forced to dance, I always did the one-step or a variation of it, much to the dismay of my partner.

I also quit playing tennis because of Hitler. I belonged to a tennis club in Neubabelsberg which was on the estate of a Jewish landowner. The town council simply confiscated the estate, and at that point I resigned from the club.

Adolf Hitler was a genius at propaganda and a master in staging public ceremonies promoting the Nazi cause. I attended one Nazi rally, a memorial dedication to Germany's war dead, held at Berlin's Tempelhof Airfield. I watched a million people march onto Tempelhof in twenty minutes' time, a spectacular logistical performance. After they had gathered, Hitler spoke hypnotically to this mass rally. Watching him was both fascinating and repulsive as he invoked the myths of the old Teutonic culture, repudiated the sense of shame from the German defeat in 1918 and the troubles of the Weimar Republic, talked of peace even while stirring the fervor of German nationalism, and pledged the restoration of German greatness. He spoke eloquently and passionately, at times shouting and waving his arms. I learned then that the larger a crowd, the deeper its roar. The guttural roar of one million Germans shouting, "Today Germany, tomorrow the world!" was an eerie, frightening experience one never forgot.

I also committed a dangerous faux pas at the Tempelhof rally. When the bugle corps played the memorial music, I commented that the horns sounded like a flock of geese. I did not know that the word "goose" is an insult in German. Someone sitting in front of me turned around and said that I had insulted the Führer. He reported me to a brownshirt usher, who led me off and questioned me. I managed to convince him that I was only describing the strange tone of the horns.

On another occasion, Eric da Costa, my Indian classmate at Oxford who had invited me to see Gandhi, visited me in Berlin and, of course, wanted to see the sights of the city. I took him to the best show in town—a Hitler rally at the Sports Palast. At the gate a brown-shirted Nazi turned to Eric and said, "Only Aryans are admitted here." Like many Indians, Eric was rather swarthy in appearance. In my youthful brashness, I said to this Nazi, "But he is the purest Aryan in all Berlin!," as indeed he was. The brownshirt, unfamiliar with India, considered this an insult and took me to his commanding officer, who questioned me for three hours, charging that I had insulted the Führer. This chap finally concluded that I was just a crazy American who didn't know any better and let me go. I rejoined Eric, and we both sat through the rally and never gave the Hitler salute. In fact, I never gave the salute the entire time I was in Germany, even in crowds when I was the only one not saluting.

So many of us underestimated Hitler's evilness. But as an American visiting Germany, I saw only what was before me, never grasping what the Army called the big picture. In retrospect, clues were everywhere. The provisions against German rearmament were clearly being violated. I once went on a Hitler Youth camp outing; it was organized like a military operation, with young boys practicing close-order drill, doing calisthenics, running an obstacle course, and dismantling and reassembling weapons. This was no Explorer Scout outing or weekend in the fresh air of the countryside.

And American officers studying at the war college in Potsdam knew well that Hitler was rearming and violating the Treaty of Versailles. Nevertheless, many people held a wait-and-see attitude. When politicians take power, their policies are often more moderate than their campaign rhetoric. Thankful for economic recovery and admiring the order and discipline Hitler brought to German life, many German businessmen supported him. They thought they could moderate his extremism. It proved to be a great miscalculation.

Although I had been appalled by much of what I saw and experienced in Hitler's Germany, I shared this cautious, blinkered attitude. After I left Oxford and joined the faculty at Mills College, in the fall of 1934 I was invited to speak to the World Affairs Council at Riverside, California, on the subject of Nazi Germany. Fortunately no copies of that talk survive. My conclusion was "Let's wait and see what Adolf Hitler is going to do. We really don't know in what direction Germany is going to move."

Earlier in 1934 I left Germany and returned to Oxford to finish my studies. During my three years in England I developed a deep respect for that small island and its people. We Georgians remember the British with special fondness; Britain came within a hair's breadth of recognizing the Confederacy during the Civil War. Inevitably I found qualities about the British and British life that I didn't care for, some minor in character and a few major. Their living facilities, such as bath and toilet arrangements, were far too primitive for a society that had launched the Industrial Revolution. Coming from the American South, I found the absence of central heating especially objectionable. I didn't care much for the food, which in general was rather tastelessly prepared—a common student complaint. On the other hand, I recognized that most Englishmen would be appalled to eat what passes for home cooking in Georgia.

More seriously, I thought that despite their global empire, the British were relatively indifferent to the customs and cultures of other peoples. Many had a colonial attitude even toward the United States; they talked about "going out to America" as if they were traveling to the colonies. Few had any real idea what the United States was all about. They saw us as a frontier society, having taken their images of

America from our western movies. They also exhibited a superior and supercilious attitude toward other non-British people, perhaps agreeing with Cecil Rhodes that the Anglo-Saxons had a special knack for ruling the world. I have often mused that among the reasons we Americans and British did not like Adolf Hitler's master race doctrine was that we had sneaky ideas of our own about who really was the master race!

Of course, the British were somewhat testy even with each other; their class system was very evident in the 1930's. For some strange reason, commercial life had a certain taint; they called working for a living being in trade. The upper classes regarded government service, the church, and the armed forces as acceptable careers; the lower classes would do manufacturing and trading and blue-collar work. Fortunately at Oxford I was accepted as an "honorary gentleman" since Oxford undergraduates were automatically of that class.

Class differences are disappearing, although puddles of privilege are still encountered. As secretary of state on a trip to London I was visiting with our ambassador, David Bruce. When we walked into his club for lunch, the majordomo quietly told David Bruce, "I am sorry, Mr. Ambassador, but your guest is not welcome here."

David Bruce said, "But this man is the American secretary of state!"

The man said, "Well, I am sorry, but he will not be welcome here in the club."

Whereupon I laughed and said, "Well, that is not the way we do it in the Century Club in New York."

"Oh," he said, "you're a member of the Century Club! Please come in!"

Despite these idiosyncrasies, I formed a great respect for the British, beginning with my experience at Oxford. They are a people of tremendous courage and stamina, although they can be quite deceptive. The teenage son of my Neubabelsberg family, the same one who became the SS motorcyclist, visited me at Oxford after I returned. He was amazed by what he saw, these young English fellows slouching across the campus, wearing baggy slacks and old blazers, with pipes in the corners of their mouths and hands in their pockets. And he said to me with some scorn, "These people can't fight!" But they could. These differences in style, personal demeanor, that laid-back British style confused a lot of people, especially Adolf Hitler.

One of the highlights of my Oxford experience was reading Sir William Searle Holdsworth's *History of English Law.* The British have a great history, one that is crucial to our own. British parliamentary institutions developed over a period of centuries. It was the British who generated the institutional structures of human freedom; the common law, Magna Carta, the Petition of Right, the Habeas Corpus Act, the British Bill of Rights, all of which preceded our own Constitution and Bill of Rights. It was the British who worked out over centuries of hard work and sacrifice and even loss of life a way to transform the notion that "The king can do no wrong" into the notion that "If it is wrong, the king cannot do it." They succeeded in imposing upon the exercise of raw power constitutional restraints rooted in the people themselves, in the tradition of the common law, the essential fabric of British life. Holdsworth tells the story of English judges who put their arms around prisoners at the bar and, at risk to their own lives, told the king, "You cannot do this to this man!" We in the constitutional democracies owe an enormous debt to the British. It is no accident that the British Parliament is often called the Mother of Parliaments.

A day of reckoning came after three fascinating years. I took my final exams; the written portion lasted four days, and then I came before a board of examiners for the orals. At the time I feared that I had done poorly on my writtens; indeed, halfway through the philosophy exam, I tore up what I had written and started over again. But the oral examiners made such complimentary remarks about my written exams that they asked only perfunctory questions. When I reported this fine news to my dons at St. John's, they were elated. "Oh, you are a certain first!" When the results were posted, however, I found myself with a second. I later got a note of apology from the examiners; apparently the philosophy reader on the exam had gotten my paper mixed up with somebody else's. I may be the only person who ever received a note of apology from the examiners at Oxford University. But the end result, though, was welcome.

My time at Oxford had ended. I had succeeded in much and learned much. I had even managed to graduate debt-free. True, I had run up some bills, and my travels in Germany were costly, not covered by the Rhodes stipend of four hundred pounds a year. These clouds dissipated through one immensely lucky break. In the spring of 1934, while I was still in Berlin, my roommate David French had sent me a telegram reminding me of the Cecil Peace Prize competition, established by Lord Robert Cecil for the best essay among British university students on any subject dealing with international affairs.

"The deadline is next Monday morning," cabled my roommate. "Don't come back to Oxford if you don't submit an essay." So I locked myself in a hotel room in Berlin for five days and did nothing but write. I picked as my topic the relationship between the British Commonwealth of Nations and the League of Nations, having studied those matters thoroughly at Oxford. My paper advocated strengthening both institutions and a stronger role for international organizations in promoting world peace. The entire paper did not have so much as one footnote; it was a "think piece." I sent it off just before the deadline, and the damn thing won the prize, one hundred pounds. I left Oxford, and England, in August 1934, having escaped debtor's prison and with my "gentleman's second," to sail home to America.

Three decades later, as secretary of state, I returned to Oxford for an honorary degree as a Doctor of Civil Law, sharing the spotlight with Charlie Chaplin. At a dinner at St. John's my old tutor W. C. Costin, now president of the college, asked me to say a few words. "If I had known when I was here what was going to happen to me later on," I commented, "I would have been frightened, but my tutors would have been terrified."

I was influenced immensely by my studies at Oxford, my travels in Germany, and the events of the early thirties. In this tragic time I came to know individuals caught in the web of history. I will never forget, for instance, a young man I knew at Oxford, a Rhodes scholar from Germany named Adam von Trott zu Solz. Tall, handsome, charming, highly intelligent, Adam made a deep impression on his fellow classmates. Upon leaving Oxford, he joined the diplomatic service of the Third Reich. At the time we wondered about his motives because at Oxford Adam had been an articulate proponent of democratic socialism. His reasons became clear in July 1944; he was a member of the group of officials and officers—those in the Stauffenberg plot—that tried unsuccessfully to assassinate Hitler. Adam von Trott zu Solz was caught, tried, convicted, and strangled.

At the end of the war the Office of Strategic Services obtained the motion pictures of those trials. As I watched the film of his trial, I was filled with both pride and horror to see my old friend Adam von Trott zu Solz standing there before the People's Court shortly before his execution, tall and erect, telling those Nazis exactly what he thought of them and their regime. He had done what he could from the inside.

In thinking back to the thirties and my days in Europe, my mind returns always to Germany. One incident in particular speaks for the whole experience. While living with that Germany family in Neubabelsberg, I had a canoe which I paddled around the lakes. During one outing I had pulled my canoe onto a sandbank to have lunch at a lakeside restaurant. When I got back, my canoe was gone. I notified the water police, and about an hour later they pulled up in their motorboat, towing my canoe. They said to me, "Here is your canoe. We have caught the thief, and he will be punished." To my astonishment they added, "But we are fining you five marks for tempting thieves." I had not locked my canoe.

When one reviews the sad events of the 1930's in Europe, I think that the United States and Western democracies, with our pacifism, isolationism, and indifference to aggression, were guilty of "tempting thieves." For example, when Hitler marched German soldiers into the Rhineland, contrary to the Treaty of Versailles, they had been instructed to return to Germany if the French showed any sign of resistance. But the French Army did not resist. The Germans reoccupied the Rhineland. That helped build the case for aggression in Hitler's own mind. And then Hitler invaded Austria and Czechoslovakia. Finally, he attacked Poland, and this triggered World War II. This matter of "tempting thieves" is deeply embedded in the history of mankind; it poses the ultimate question, What does one do, when the armed battalions begin to march?

5

Mills College

When I finished Oxford in 1934, the United States and the world were locked in the depths of the Great Depression. I was offered several jobs overseas, but I turned them down, wanting to return to the United States. Believing that international relations was where the action was, I wrote the State Department in Washington, inquiring about the Foreign Service, and ironically—in view of my later appointments—I was politely rebuffed. Facing the prospect of returning home without a job, I wrote Frank Aydelotte, the American secretary to the Rhodes Trust, and asked him to let me know if any job opportunities came across his desk.

Shortly thereafter I got a cable from a woman named Aurelia Henry Reinhardt offering a position as an assistant professor at Mills College in California, paying a salary of two thousand dollars a year. I immediately accepted and then scurried all over Oxford, trying to find out something about Mills College; I had never heard of the place. Fortunately my roommate, David French, was from California, and he described Mills as a small women's liberal arts college of excellent reputation on the banks of San Francisco Bay. I had visions of palm trees and rolling lawns tapering off to the water's edge, where I could dangle my feet in the water. Reality was different, but every bit as good.

As president of Mills, perhaps out of financial necessity, Reinhardt habitually invited young Rhodes scholars to join her faculty. I received my offer because one of her faculty, a former Rhodes named Frank Buck, had received a temporary position at Stanford, leaving a vacancy for a year. Reinhardt got hold of Dr. Aydelotte, and I wound up going to Mills. Delighted to get a job, after visiting family and friends in Atlanta and Davidson, I traveled to California in September 1934 to teach government and international relations. It was my first trip west. The California climate and the Mills campus with its rolling hills and winding paths, eucalyptus trees and orchid meadows, Spanish architecture, and its all-women student body was an oasis to me, long immersed in the turmoil of Europe.

Previous to Mills, I had only taught soldiers as a reserve officer. I found the women of Mills a challenging contrast with GIs and better prepared, and I quickly learned that they were skeptical of soaring male generalities. They punctured my profundities with sharp questioning, wanting to know what these statements actually meant to their lives. At semester's end one student, a former court reporter, presented me with a verbatim transcript of everything I had said in that class. That humbling experience at least taught me the importance of speaking in complete sentences. I also occasionally had to write words on the black board so students could understand me; my southern drawl overlaid with an English accent mystified West Coast girls.

I taught at Mills for six years, from 1934 to 1940, and fortunately never had to write any articles or books. "Publish or perish" had not yet been firmly entrenched. I felt that professors not interested in their students and being teachers were in the wrong racket. My disenchantment with academic publishing later strengthened when I was president of the Rockefeller Foundation; so much academic writing we reviewed did not deserve to see the light of day. I concentrated on my teaching and within my first year created an interdisciplinary program in philosophy, politics, and economics, based on the Oxford system.

Aurelia Reinhardt soon promoted me to associate professor and then dean of the faculty. She told me that she made this precocious appointment—I was only twenty-seven—"to avoid confusion." The faculty at Mills were good sports about it, however, and I had a pleasant experience, often filling in for President Reinhardt during her extensive travels. She wanted to call me "Dean David Dean Rusk," but I resisted the resurrection of my first name.

Aurelia Reinhardt was an extraordinary presence at Mills—large physically, with a commanding voice, and a powerful intellect. She was the Republican national committeewoman from California, active in both local and national politics, a close friend of Herbert Hoover and Hoover's interior secretary, Ray Lyman Wilbur, former president of Stanford. She had great influence not only on campus but on the entire San Francisco Bay Area. I doubt whether Mills could have survived those rigorous years of the Depression without the special qualities of Aurelia Reinhardt. She used all her considerable talents and connections to keep Mills alive, holding the college together through sheer determination, with hairpins and baling wire, and with her indomitable sense of humor. I thoroughly enjoyed working for her.

I can recall only one moment of contentiousness. I bought a used Studebaker for forty dollars, an old gas guzzler of a car with a loose fender that rattled. In her campaign to upgrade Mills, she forbade me to park my car in front of the administration building. She wanted it off campus.

Being a young bachelor on an all-women campus created its own set of challenges. To help deal with that environment, my male colleagues on the faculty formed a Kiva, an Indian term for a lodge where men of the tribe gathered and women were not permitted. We brown-bagged our lunches, had poker games, played golf and tennis, and made annual trips to the Sierras for skiing vacations. All-male clubs are frowned upon today, but we enjoyed ours. President Reinhardt asked to join our all-male fraternity and was somewhat miffed when we turned her down.

These were happy days as well. I met my wife, Virginia, at Mills. She enrolled in two of my classes during my first year, thinking that Frank Buck, the popular and gifted professor whom I replaced while he was on leave at Stanford, would teach them. When she heard that a stranger named Rusk was substituting for Buck, she broke down and cried. But we did have common interests: Virginia was a Phi Beta Kappa, was actively interested in international matters, and had gone to Japan in the summer of 1934 with a Japanese-American exchange group. Eventually she judged me to be an acceptable pinch hitter.

In Virginia's third year, because of her interest in international affairs, I invited her to attend a conference at the University of California in Riverside during our Christmas break. To my delight she accepted, and off we drove in my secondhand Ford. Our relationship soon bloomed into a more than ordinary friendship. It wasn't easy for a young professor to court a student in a women's college in the thirties without creating a sensation. We would do things like get up at five in the morning, drive out into the countryside, cook bacon and eggs over a campfire, and drive back before everyone else had begun to stir. Or we would have dinner in a remote place where we weren't likely to run into Mills people. Our courtship was a little tricky, but we managed. We were blessed with an understanding dorm mother who gave Virginia her own key to the dorm and did not strictly hold her to the rules of the campus. She allowed Virginia, who soon became my fiancée, to leave the dorm early, but she wouldn't allow her to come in late. That wonderful woman—Mrs. Jean Bundschu—became a lifelong friend.

We did have one close call. Early on at Mills I found quarters in the home of Miss Rosalind Keep, a prim spinster who worked for Aurelia Reinhardt and was devoted to her. I ate many meals at her place and over time became branded as a "Kept man." She was equally devoted to the traditions of Mills College, especially those forbidding Mills's coeds from becoming unwitting victims of those birds of prey, unmarried professors. On our return from Riverside, Virginia and I arrived at 4:00 A.M. to find the dormitory locked. So I showed her my bedroom at Miss Keep's, invited her to spend the night there, and went down to the basement to sleep. The next morning Rosalind Keep apparently opened the door to my small apartment to check on me and saw Virginia's underthings scattered all over. She wasn't aware that I had slept in the basement. That was a moment of temporary excitement for us all.

Ruth Gillard, a Mills classmate of Virginia's, commented years later: "It became a game to decide who was making it closer to Dean Rusk; lots of Mills girls were trying for him. He was considered an "older man," and we thought an older woman would get him. All of a sudden Virginia Foisie was taking a dual major—she had been majoring in geography and then declared for social studies—and she went to Riverside with him. She was so good-looking, and whenever we queried her, she would flash her Mona Lisa smile. She never talked about Dean; in fact, they deliberately avoided each other on campus. There was never a sign or motion between them, no indication of a personal relationship—only Ginny Rusk's Mona Lisa smile. But when a classmate of Virginia's announced her engagement at a senior breakfast, the place absolutely exploded with happiness. When we asked her how she had managed, her Mona Lisa smile only deepened."

With Ginny, I was a lucky man. She was one of the most attractive girls at Mills, yet hardly a dumb blond type. Her father, born in Boston and raised in Seattle, had graduated from Harvard and became a labor relations counselor on the West Coast; her mother had attended Wellesley. Highly intelligent, Ginny made Phi Beta Kappa and was graduated near the top of her class. She had a lively interest in world affairs, and we found ourselves working together on many projects. She was a natural to be tagged research assistant for a study I was writing about a legal system that required appeals from British Commonwealth countries to be heard by the Privy Council. Exuding an air of cool elegance, this grandly talented girl just took life as it came. She appealed to me in every way.

Virginia had her own view of our courtship: "On the drive to Riverside, I was shocked to discover that Dean was only twenty-five and not in his forties; he seemed so much older. But Dean was the first eligible bachelor at Mills for years. Before he came, the youngest professor was about forty-five, so he created lots of excitement on campus. Dating a professor at a woman's college was hard on me. He was friendly to everyone, and I was extremely jealous. He didn't like that at all and almost called it off. But he was ready to be plucked. . . .

"In 1937, while getting ready to leave for Japan, Dean asked, 'Would you like to go with me?' I figured that was my proposal. That wasn't as explicit as I would have liked, but it was a proposal nevertheless; it was impossible to travel unmarried in those days."

Ginny and I married on June 19, 1937, in a small church in Seattle, Washington. Virginia's side of the church was filled with family and friends; my side had only three or four. It was raining cats and dogs outside, and I was very nervous. During the ceremony, upon prompting by the minister, in a loud voice I announced to the gathering, "With this wing, I thee wed." Fortunately the minister accepted that as authentic and didn't make me repeat it.

The year before we got married, in the fall of 1936, I began law school at the University of California at Berkeley, hoping to become a professor of international law. As I looked around the political science department at Mills and elsewhere, I found that almost none of the political scientists had legal training; most had come through the Ph.D. track. I felt that since lawyers and political scientists talk about common institutions and problems and use similar language, there would be some advantage to taking a law degree as opposed to a Ph.D. Additionally, I believed that international law would of necessity play a greater role in world affairs. Nations needed standards of law and justice in dealing with each other. Purely political considerations were inadequate in resolving disputes between nations, because they left out what was most essential—morality. Power politics pitting the strong versus the weak were an inadequate basis for peace.

With a topnotch faculty and large library, the law school at Berkeley ranked among the finest in the country. It was also about ten miles from the Mills campus. Classes at Mills ended at ten minutes to the hour, and Berkeley classes began ten minutes past the hour. I had twenty minutes to negotiate those tortuous winding roads between Mills and Berkeley in that unmuffled Studebaker with its fender clattering and banging. My principal problem was finding a place to park at Berkeley.

I took only a two-thirds load at Berkeley, since I was so busy courting Ginny, teaching at Mills, and serving as dean of the faculty. Also, throughout my time at Mills I remained a reserve officer in the U.S. Army. In the 1930's congressional appropriations were so small that we had little active training beyond an occasional two-week summer camp. We did most of our reserve training by correspondence, usually map problems refighting the Battle of Gettysburg, sent out by area headquarters at the Presidio. These were busy days, but since I had worked my way through high school and Davidson College, it was a pace I was used to.

Throughout the years at Mills the international situation worsened: Italian dictator Benito Mussolini sent his troops into Ethiopia, Hitler reoccupied the Rhineland, the Spanish Civil War broke out, and Japan's seizure of Manchuria extended into general fighting along China's coast. Long before World War II made it obvious, I felt the Western democracies had to gird themselves to ward off and end this growing momentum of aggression. Clearly, we were riding a roller coaster toward general war, and little was being done to prevent it.

I followed these events diligently and did what little I could to become involved in world events at Mills. I joined the Institute of Pacific Relations, whose West Coast branch was fortunately more moderate than the national office, and I became involved with the American Friends Service Committee, even though I had strong misgivings about the consequences of my Quaker friends' pacifism when armed battalions begin to move. We organized conferences and seminars and "peace days," and I once walked a picket line at the docks in Oakland, protesting the shipment of American scrap iron to Japan. During the Spanish Civil War Ginny and I contributed to the Loyalist cause and the American ambulance brigade, although only a token amount because we didn't have any money. But even with these efforts, I felt isolated from the real center of world events. Living an academic life on a secluded campus on the west coast of a neutral nation had its advantages, but it was frustrating as well.

Once, in my international relations class with perhaps a dozen students present, I gave full expression to my feelings about the passivity of the democracies in refusing to face up to Japanese and German aggression. I nearly shed tears before my astonished students, I felt so strongly about what was happening. We Americans had turned down the League of Nations, turned down the World Court, helped sabotage disarmament attempts, wrecked the World Economic Conference, passed the Smoot-Hawley Tariff, and done nothing in the face of German rearmament and the Japanese invasion of Manchuria. Debate between the pacifists and isolationists of the America First Committee and the activists and interventionists of the William White Committee separated the country into two opposed camps.

Then, in 1938, Hitler absorbed Austria and, the following year, moved his troops into Czechoslovakia and finally Poland. In 1940 Hitler turned west, occupied Denmark, Norway, and the Benelux countries, then marched his forces into France. When France fell, the anguish and gloom on the Mills campus were palpable. Shortly thereafter the British cartoonist David Low published his most memorable drawing, showing a British Tommy looking out across the cliffs of Dover, with his rifle held at port arms, saying, "Well, then, alone." At Mills this single cartoon drove home how bleak the future might be.

With war in Europe and U.S.-Japanese tension mounting in the Pacific, the War Department notified me in the spring of 1940 that I probably would be called to active duty later in the year. Wanting to spend as much time as I could with Virginia, who was carrying our first child, I dropped my law studies at Berkeley.

Our son David was born on October 10, 1940, and I was called to active duty two months later. Virginia and I both experienced a rollercoaster ride of emotion during those last few months of 1940, going from the euphoria of starting our family to the despair of wartime separation. But we were not alone in those emotions during those trying times.

When word got out at Mills that I had been called up for active duty, someone asked me to speak at the college's fall Peace Day. I decided to speak on mobilization. To me this was a great honor, and I prepared hard for that speech since I viewed it as a sort of valedictory, an end of one stage of my life and the beginning of the next. It was no masterpiece as far as speeches go, but someone took notes and made a transcript, and I offer it as an expression of the times and what one young Army captain felt as he packed his bags for war:

Since last Peace Day war has come—and war is spreading. The opinion of this country is already committed to one side. There is no pretense of neutrality in our sympathies . . . a moment of Allied weakness, active Italian, Russian, Japanese intervention, and we shall face a decision of historic importance. At that time or before, Mobilization Day might come. "M-Day"—out through the telegraph wires, by radio, by telephone, by mail and special messenger, through government departments and civilian draft boards, "M-Day" is an electric word, as lightning is electric. "M-Day" means sifting through the farmers, the workers, the students, the husbands, the fathers, the brothers, because war needs our best men. It means skimming off the cream, to pour it down the drain. . . .

If we mobilize, to what are we pledging our loyalties? What shall we have considered worth the sacrifice and brutality? If we know, when what is it that now stands in the way of the attainment of the things we cherish? An enemy abroad, or our own selfishness and blindness at home? If we do not mobilize and are fortunate enough to see the present belligerents make peace, what shall we be ready to offer to make the world a finer place? What concessions directed toward the prevention of a fresh outbreak? How willing to ease the suffering which had so much to do with the creation of violence among peace-loving people?

It is a serious thing to warn people of possible tragedy. I cannot predict whether we shall take up arms or remain at peace. But that is not my chief concern today. Until we begin to make our choices between better and worse, valuable and valueless, neither peace nor war has any meaning. Mobilization, therefore, means exactly what you are willing to make it mean. Last time we slaughtered twenty million men and didn't really want the things we said we shot them for. Even the academician feels justified in saying that we dare not be such brutes again.

There are many things for one person to do. What are your values? How much do you wish to bring them about? How much are you willing to do toward curbing the madness of our mutual destruction? How much can you give for things that really matter?

SECTION II

WORLD WAR II AND POSTWAR YEARS

In December 1940, a year before Pearl Harbor, leaving behind an idyllic life at Mills College and ambitions to complete law school and teach international law, my father entered public service, not to emerge for nearly thirty years.

"How did you get started in public affairs?" I asked Pop.

"I received a telegram from Uncle Sam," he told me. "It said, 'Greetings. Report for active service.' "

After training with the U.S. Army's Third Division on the West Coast, Rusk was transferred to the War Department in Washington, where he organized a new G-2 intelligence section on Asia. Reassigned as a staff officer to General Joseph Stilwell in 1943, he then served two years in the China-Burma-India (CBI) theater. Operating out of New Delhi and traveling widely throughout Asia, Rusk worked with leaders of the Allied war effort, including Lord Louis Mountbatten, Claire Chennault, General William Slim, and Generalissimo Chiang Kai-shek. Delegated major responsibilities as chief of war plans, often operating in Stilwell's absence, Rusk participated in many decisions of that distant and always difficult theater.

In 1945 Rusk was reassigned to the famous Abe Lincoln Brigade, or Operations Division, in the Pentagon, a group of Army officers who worked on occupation policies for Germany and Japan, terms of the Japanese surrender, the creation of the United Nations, and American policy requirements for rebuilding a world torn apart by global war. "We were forced by events to act as statesmen beyond our years," said my father.

When the American atomic bomb brought a merciful end to World War II but cast its horrible shadow over mankind, Dean Rusk, aware at once of the bomb's implications, followed his mentor, George Marshall, into the Department of State, the peacemaking branch of the U.S. government.

Having won the confidence of Marshall and later Dean Acheson, Rusk rose quickly through the bureaucracy. First as director of United Nations affairs, later as assistant secretary of state for Far Eastern affairs, he advised Marshall, Acheson, and President Truman on American responses to major postwar issues such as Palestine and the creation of Israel, the

Soviet occupation of Eastern Europe and northern Iran, the Communist insurgency in Greece, and the Berlin blockade. He also advised on the Baruch Plan for international control of fissionable materials, collective security and the formation of North Atlantic Treaty Organization (NATO) and Australian, New Zealand, and United States (ANZUS) Treaty, National Security Council (NSC) study number 68 and the containment policies of the Truman administration, and European recovery with the Marshall Plan.

When the North Koreans attacked South Korea on June 25, 1950, by crossing the thirty-eighth parallel, a demarcation line Rusk and another colonel had chosen in haste at a late-night Pentagon planning session in 1945, he met at Blair House with Truman and his top advisers and helped orchestrate a United Nations response. When China crossed the Yalu River in November with massive forces, a surprised Rusk helped rally American policy makers, an action some call his finest hour. He influenced how the Korean War was fought, advising on tactics and strategy, insisting throughout that both American objectives and the fighting of the war remain "limited." When Truman met with General Douglas MacArthur at Wake Island for their mid-Pacific conference, Rusk was in that small Quonset hut passing notes to the president. He later played a role in MacArthur's firing.

Even at the Rockefeller Foundation during the fifties, operating in the quiet backwaters of private philanthropy, my dad remained influential, advising Eisenhower's secretary of state John Foster Dulles, a personal friend. As foundation president he helped redirect the Rockefeller millions toward leadership training, public health and public education, agricultural productivity, and other needs of developing nations. He was also instrumental in funding agricultural research that led to the Green Revolution, vastly increasing the world's basic food crops.

Throughout these years my dad's career was a mystery to me. From 1945 through 1952 we lived in Parkfairfax, Virginia, and Pop in my eyes was just another businessman with top hat and briefcase commuting daily to Washington. He told us stories of his experiences and travels and, always, his endless procession of anecdotes. But never did he speak about the true role he played during World War II and the postwar years. As a small child I knew nothing of his activities, his rapid rise in Washington as one of the hottest talents of the postwar period, or his role as a trusted presidential adviser. My brother, David, five years older, had some inkling; reacting to press controversy surrounding Pop's "Slavic Manchukuo" speech about China in May 1951, he asked, "Is Daddy going to get fired?" We saw him drive off in the mornings and return late, often not returning for days at a stretch. "Is Daddy dead?" Dave once asked.

During the fifties, after Pop had left the State Department for the Rockefeller Foundation and moved us to Westchester County, New York, I began to sense his importance from visitors to our Scarsdale home, some of whose names would appear in the newspapers; from gazing out his office window on the fifty-fourth floor of Rockefeller Center overlooking Manhattan; from a cross-country auto trip during which Pop stopped our flathead Ford in Independence, Missouri, and I shook hands with one of his former bosses. All I remember of Harry Truman was a grinning mouthful of flashing gold teeth. I thought nothing of the fact that Pop seemed to be on close terms with him, chatting easily in shirt sleeves.

Dean Rusk's protests to the contrary, his early career was only partially related to "accident, chance, and happenstance." A born diplomat, he had the ability to befriend and work intimately with a wide variety of people, including Senator Arthur Vandenberg, Dulles, Acheson, Marshall, men who often had little use for one another. He was untouched by McCarthyism, despite having served at the vortex of Asian controversy, primarily because his ties with Republicans were nearly as extensive as those with Democrats. He was singled out not because he sought recognition or courted those in power. Obviously he climbed the ladder largely on merit, performed well at each rung, and became recognized by his peers as an able and talented man.

But according to his colleagues, there was something more than the backing of important sponsors, his exceptional abilities, and his performance as a staffer, a "perfect number two." There was also the strength of his convictions, based on a firm set of beliefs and principles, argued with a quiet but unmistakable eloquence and force that caught the attention of Marshall and Acheson and the others. Only this fully explains Dean Rusk's early achievements and makes credible his influence on foreign policy during the Truman years.

Combining the strains of Wilsonian idealism, respect for international law, and the utility of international organizations in resolving conflict, arguing that standards of morality and justice also count in decision making, instinctively preferring to take issues to the United Nations before the United States acted unilaterally, seeking to tie foreign policy to what he called "the decent purposes of the American people," Dean Rusk in his advisory role tried to steer a principled course. In general, he opposed colonialism, sympathized with the problems of developing nations, and cared deeply about the "red, black, and yellow peoples" of the world.

He argued passionately that America must honor its pledged word in its collective security treaties and alliances. He took a high road whenever possible, often to the despair of Acheson and George Kennan and the advocates of realpolitik.

After listening to a Rusk homily about the legal aspects of a problem, an exasperated Dean Acheson once exclaimed, "Damn it, Dean, the survival of nations is not a matter of international law."

"On the contrary," Rusk replied. "In a nuclear age, the survival of nations may depend upon international law."

—R. R.

6

World War II in the China-Burma-India Theater

In December 1940, one year before Pearl Harbor, Uncle Sam summoned me to active duty as a captain in the Army reserves to take command of Company A of the Thirtieth Infantry Battalion of the Third Division, then stationed at the Presidio near San Francisco. I had never commanded regular troops before, and despite years of ROTC, I have to admit I was rather green.

Our Third Division was one of only two divisions in the entire U.S. Army rated "ready for combat." This was sheer fantasy, and we all knew it. When I took command of Company A, we had 100 men in our company instead of the 225 called for by the Tables of Organization. Many of these "soldiers" were World War I veterans, too old for actual field duty as infantrymen. We had a few machine guns, and little else; during training exercises we used cardboard tubes instead of mortars. Ammunition was scarce; my company was limited to ten rounds per man per year on the rifle range. Our single 37 mm antitank gun fired a shell about the size of a carrot. It wouldn't even scar the paint of a tank. Its chief use had been to fire salutes for visiting dignitaries. In fact, the entire military establishment was rebuilding from scratch. Fearing a German cross-Channel invasion after the fall of France, the United States was sending Great Britain whatever we could scrape together— hunting rifles, shotguns, pistols—to help in defense of the British Isles. This left our own Army in a sorry condition, not that it been well supplied in the first place. In fact, when I was called to active duty, the total strength of the American Army was less than 275,000 officers and men.

And as soldiers we were rookies of the worst sort. It was a humbling experience to be part of that thin, ragged line listed "combat-ready," with the Nazis smashing their way across Europe. I once gave my company a demonstration of how to fire a 60 mm mortar. The whole company gathered around, and when I dropped a round down the tube, the recoil caused the barrel to kick skyward. One of our fellows shouted, "Jesus Christ, she's going straight up!" The entire company scattered in every direction.

Nevertheless, we conducted maneuvers as best we could, first in Marin County and later at Fort Roberts in Southern California. In the summer of 1941 we moved the Third Division from California to Fort Lewis, Washington. We trained in the rugged Olympics across Puget Sound, where Joseph Stilwell, Jr.—"Little Joe"—lost his entire company in those woods; it took us two days to find them. But my days with the Third Division were numbered. In October 1941 I received orders to report to the War Department's G-2, the intelligence section of the General Staff in Washington, D.C. My division commander protested this transfer, and so did I; I wanted to stay with my company. But the War Department persisted, and my wife, Virginia, my infant son David, and I were off to Washington. My commanding officer's effort to resist my transfer helped persuade the War Department that it had found the right man!

Had I stayed with the Third Division, I might have followed it into North Africa, up the Italian peninsula, and on the Normandy invasion. Or even more probable, to the Pacific. After my transfer to Washington, many officers in the Third Division were sent to the Philippines, where many were either captured or killed by the Japanese at Bataan and Corregidor. Those who survived had to endure the infamous Death March. In either event, it is very possible that I would not have survived the war.

But I went to Washington, and upon my arrival the War Department told me to organize a new section of G-2, the military intelligence branch of the U.S. Army General Staff. This office, commanded by Chief of Staff George Marshall, controlled all Army activities. My new section was organized to gather information and supply intelligence briefings about British-held areas in Asia and the Pacific: Afghanistan, Burma, Malaya, Australia, India, New Zealand, Singapore, and the British islands in the Pacific, a vast area of which I knew nothing. Strange are the ways of the Army. When I tried to find out why I had been assigned this, I was told that someone had run a large stack of personnel cards through a sorting machine. My card fell out for this G-2 Pacific job because I had spent three years in England, not because I knew anything about Asia.

Nor did anyone at the War Department. When I asked to see the department's files on that part of the world, a dear lady about seventy years old named Mrs. North showed me to a cabinet marked "British Asia." Inside it I found one copy of *Murray's Tourist Handbook on India and Ceylon* stamped "Confidential" to ensure that no one filched it. Apparently it was the only copy in town. Additionally, there was a 1925 military attaché report from London on the British Army in India, and finally, a drawer of articles on Asia clipped from the *New York Times*. Mrs. North had been clipping these since World War I. That was the extent of U.S. Army intelligence on British Asia.

Despite this, I passed an early test in my new position with flying colors. About my second day on the job I got a phone call from a full colonel in the War Plans Division. "Rusk, I forget," he said. "Is Indochina in South China or North China?" I straightened him out on where Indochina was, and after hanging up, he must have told his colleagues, "Boy, we get good support from those fellows down there." This appointment, indeed the whole scene, was ludicrous, of course, but the moment my feet were under that desk, I became the War Department's expert on East Asia.

To build up this intelligence section, I had to scurry all over the country, tapping possible sources of information from any quarter, from missionaries to tramp steamer captains, anyone who had spent time in the region. We found one man who was regarded as an expert on Burma since he had written a book on the country. When the Army decided that it needed a Burmese language program, we asked the Census Bureau for a list of Americans born in Burma. We were sent a dozen names like McConihan and Gillihay, all children of former British soldiers. Only one genuine Burmese appeared on the entire list. We found him in a mental institution. We fished him out and made a very successful Burmese-language instructor out of him. The ignorance of our government regarding that vast part of the world on the very eve of Pearl Harbor was astonishing in retrospect. Slowly, however, we began to overcome the past, build up intelligence, accumulate information, and establish contact with people knowledgeable about Asia.

Part of this ignorance was simply lack of money and manpower. Between the world wars the United States had almost demobilized. Our armed forces lived on a shoestring. Franklin Roosevelt once furloughed all military personnel without pay for one month. Army officers, having few troops to command, spent their time either teaching school or going to school. It was really a miracle of the human spirit that the Army officer corps produced the high leadership achieved during World War II, men like Dwight Eisenhower and George Patton and Omar Bradley. Some of these men had spent ten to fifteen years as lieutenants, struggling to raise families on $160 per month. Why they stayed with it I will never know, but I attribute some of that to patriotism.

I was as surprised as anyone by the Japanese attack on Pearl Harbor. Although assigned to keep track of British areas in Asia, I sat not far from the Japanese section of G-2 just down the hall. Both the Japanese section and my section were reasonably certain that the Japanese would attack somewhere in the Southwest Pacific on the weekend of December 5–7. But we never expected the Japanese to hit so far afield as Pearl Harbor. Both G-2 and naval intelligence had completely lost the Japanese fleet as it made its way east toward Hawaii under radio silence.

I knew none of this when I went to work at 6:00 A.M. that fateful Sunday, hoping to learn more of the whereabouts of those Japanese ships. Then came the news from Hawaii: "Air raid on Pearl Harbor. This is not a drill." My first reaction was a mixture of horror and disbelief. But I will never forget the reaction of some junior officers in the Japanese section of G-2 who went up and down the hall laughing like hell. They simply didn't believe it. With some, the news didn't register until President Roosevelt announced the attack on radio. Shortly after Roosevelt's announcement, my own chief, Colonel Compton, said, "Dean, you might want to see this memo; it is very interesting. Take a good look because you won't see it again. All the copies are being gathered up and destroyed." He gave me a memorandum prepared five days earlier by the Japanese section of G-2, listing targets in the Pacific which the Japanese might attack. Pearl Harbor was not on the list. Although G-2 failed to anticipate the attack on Pearl Harbor, by destroying this incriminating memo, it did anticipate the Roberts Commission of Investigation that followed.

Shortly after Pearl Harbor I had my first briefing with General Marshall, an experience he happily forgot. The War Department was considering an airborne landing on the island of Guernsey, in the Channel Islands off the coast of France. Marshall learned from my commanding officer in G-2 that I had spent two months on Guernsey while a student at Oxford; I had taken a suitcase full of books there during Christmas vacation to cram for exams. I was summoned to Marshall's office. Nervously I opened the door, walked in, and stood stiffly at attention. There he sat, chief of staff of the U.S. Army.

"Rusk, I hear you've been in Guernsey," said Marshall. "Describe it for me."

I prattled on about its beauty, the people, its economy, and so forth. He cut me short. "What kind of soil do they have there?"

"Well, it's rolling hills, pastureland—"

"No, not that!" he snapped. "I mean, what's the subsoil like? Is it sand? Clay? Is it rocky? Can we build airstrips?"

"Frankly, sir, I don't know."

He dismissed me with a curt "Rusk, you didn't learn very much over there, did you?"

One year after Pearl Harbor I requested overseas duty. The Army obliged by sending me to Fort Leavenworth for training in command and staff procedures. I thus became a "ninety-day wonder," received a promotion to major, and was assigned back to Washington in April 1943 to a pool of officers being prepared for overseas general staff duties. Here I languished for several months until my orders came in. I was to be staff officer to General Joseph "Vinegar Joe" Stilwell in the China-Burma-India theater.

I was mortified. When I was at summer camp in 1941 with the Third Division, General Stilwell, as the commanding officer of the Seventh Division, had paid us a visit. We prepared a dinner in his honor, and I was named master of ceremonies. I sat next to Stilwell and saw to my horror that a striptease dancer was on the evening's program and I would have to introduce her. This stripteaser was quite a stripper and quite a teaser, and the whole thing left General Stilwell even more sour than usual.

Fortunately Stilwell forgot the stripteaser in California, and when he came to Washington for consultation in 1943, I returned to CBI with him after putting Virginia and David on the train for Mills College, where they spent the rest of the war. I did not see them again until June 1945, a two-year separation. It was difficult, but it was no different from the separation endured by millions of other men in uniform and their families.

In June 1943 General Stilwell and his staff, now including me, flew to London, where Stilwell consulted with British military authorities. On the day that Stilwell was to depart for North Africa and India, the BBC unaccountably broadcast news of his leave-taking. Since the Nazis occupied France and controlled much of southern Europe, Stilwell was angered by this breach of security and delayed our departure for several hours. After taking off, we flew westward in a wide arc over the Atlantic, seeking to avoid German planes based in France. Not so long before, American fighter planes had intercepted and shot down Admiral Isoruku Yamamoto in the Pacific. We thought the Nazis might try for Stilwell in a similar way. In fact, on the very day we left for India, a British plane flying from Gibraltar to England and carrying movie star Leslie Howard went down in the North Atlantic, victim of a German fighter operating at extreme range. One can only speculate whether that German plane was in fact searching for Stilwell.

At CBI the situation was grim. The Japanese had seized Burma and cut land communication with China. Only one year earlier Stilwell had walked out in his famous retreat and made his way to India. Most of the countries we monitored in G-2 were now in Japanese hands. Burma, the Dutch East Indies, Malaya, Singapore, the Philippines, and Southeast Asia were now under Japanese control, part of Japan's "Greater East Asia Co-Prosperity Sphere." The main Allied effort was in Europe, not the Pacific. It looked like a long road back.

Our primary mission in CBI was to reopen a land route to China. We wanted to keep the Chinese in the war because they were pinning down large numbers of Japanese troops on the mainland. If the Chinese and British could not be persuaded to take on the Japanese aggressively—and quickly—those hundreds of thousands of Japanese troops could be freed for action against Admiral Chester Nimitz and General Douglas MacArthur coming across the Pacific.

But General Stilwell's job was a true "Mission Impossible." While he was to exhort the Chinese and the British in India to fight the Japanese as hard as possible, he had no significant American forces of his own to command. It quickly became clear that Generalissimo Chiang Kai-shek would not strongly commit his own forces against the Japanese because he was looking over his shoulder at the Chinese Communists and the possibility of civil war. Further, Chiang could see the Americans advancing steadily across the Pacific; they would reach China soon enough. He felt no pressure to engage the Japanese.

It was equally clear that Winston Churchill would not commit the British Army in India to serious fighting in Asia until Hitler had been defeated. That army in India was Churchill's last imperial reserve.

Made up primarily of Indian troops, it had proven itself in battle and helped hold the Middle East at a time when the war was going badly for the Allies.

General Stilwell's mission was frustrated by the attitudes of Chiang Kai-shek and Churchill. Without major American forces of his own, Stilwell was in the position of saying to both the British and Chinese, "I will hold your coats. Now get out there and fight." Irritation and disappointment were built into the very nature of Stilwell's assignment.

CBI had the lowest priority of all the theaters of operations. First priority was the war in Europe, second was the war in the Pacific with its island-hopping campaign, and finally came CBI. How low on that list of priorities is best illustrated by the War Department's appointing a young college professor as deputy chief of war plans for the entire theater. We had to make do with very little. Stilwell kept pressing for two American infantry divisions of some thirty thousand men and was finally sent one reinforced regiment of about three thousand men that later won fame as "Merrill's Marauders." There were never major American ground forces in CBI.

My job as Stilwell's chief of war plans was as much political as military. The British were the executive agents for the combined American and British chiefs of staff for Burma and India. Chiang Kai-shek was the supreme commander for China. General Stilwell was deputy to Lord Louis Mountbatten in the Southeast Asia Command for India and Burma, but also chief of staff to Chiang for China. He also commanded the American effort to keep lend-lease supplies flowing to China. I could never have drawn an organization chart for Stilwell's role—and, therefore, mine—in CBI. Because command arrangements were so complicated, we had to work on the basis of cooperation and negotiation rather than direct command.

At Stilwell's New Delhi headquarters, I was assigned to G-3, the so-called rear echelon, presided over by Frank Merrill. The forward echelon was in Chungking (now spelled Chongqing), China, under Frank Dorn. I shuffled between New Delhi and Assam in India, Chungking, and Ceylon (now Sri Lanka), where Mountbatten had set up his headquarters. Traveling in the small bombers we used for staff planes, I seemed to spend more time in the air, droning from one place to another, than on the ground.

The work was interesting, however, all the more so because Stilwell delegated so much authority to his staff. At heart he was a foot soldier who abhorred headquarters and kept himself always in the field, a superb commander of troops.

Stilwell was also impatient with the politicking of high command; that he left to me. Even as a major I wrote many of Stilwell's cables and actively participated in planning and decision making, although my rank was such that I was not noticed by the historians of CBI. The art of the matter was knowing when to go ahead and act and when to kick decisions upstairs. I was never reprimanded by Stilwell for exceeding my authority. He expected me to take charge, and I tried not to disappoint him.

We staffers made our mistakes. Looking back, I failed to educate Washington adequately on the reluctance of the British and Chinese to fight the Japanese. I also let one telegram slip out of headquarters without my knowledge. It had to do with a typhus epidemic that had struck Merrill's Marauders during the Myitkyina campaign in the spring of 1944. Many of Merrill's men were desperately sick. Our hospital at Assam, Burma, having found that it could treat typhus victims with some success by using air conditioning to lower their high fevers, cabled New Delhi about its need for more air-conditioning units. The chief surgeon replied, unbeknownst to me, "We don't have any."

When Stilwell received this cable, he sent back a stinging reply to General Dan Sultan, his deputy in New Delhi: "You and I both know where air-conditioning units are. I want them up here immediately!" Sultan was furious when he learned what had happened because we had air conditioners all over our headquarters offices. We tore those units out and sent them on to Assam, but that kind of incident does not endear staffers to troops in the field.

The China-Burma-India theater was, in effect, a large contingency effort. Building the Burma Road was like building the Alcan Highway linking Alaska with the northwestern United States. We might have needed it, but as things turned out, we didn't. Even if MacArthur and Nimitz invaded Japan, we did not know if the two to three million Japanese soldiers we thought were in China would surrender at the command of Tokyo. Thus, we needed an entry into western China to support possible Allied landings on the Chinese coast.

After the Japanese cut the Burma Road in 1942, we made extraordinary efforts to find a back-door land route to China. I flew many times over Afghanistan, Nepal, and the Himalayas scouring the terrain in search of a route. There was none. The Burma Road seemed the only feasible one.

I once climbed into a C-47 with a little bow-legged pilot from Texas and flew into the Wa country of western China to install automatic direction-finding boxes. These boxes were designed to help our pilots keep their bearings while navigating the Hump. We landed in farm fields and cow pastures, buzzing them first to see how bad the rocks were. Then we had to deal with the Wa, who had never seen white men, let alone an airplane. I had no one with me who could speak Wa, but we bargained with the people as best we could, using sign language, gesticulating, trying to gain some measure of protection for the black boxes. Those boxes were a great help to our Hump pilots.

We tried almost any scheme to gain a way into China. President Roosevelt wanted to step up lend-lease supplies to China—at least ten thousand tons per month—a nearly impossible logistical feat. When I was still in G-2 in Washington, Madame Chiang Kai-shek traveled to the United States to bolster American support for China's war effort. She spent much time in Washington, often lobbying President Roosevelt and General Marshall personally. After one White House visit we got a note from FDR saying that Madame Chiang proposed a coolie train from India over the mountains, to carry supplies into China by foot. However many Chinese coolies were needed, she would supply them, she said—one to five million if necessary. FDR's instructions were: "Go ahead and organize it." This plan, while ambitious and very Chinese, held a fatal flaw. It didn't take us long to figure out that each coolie on this three- to four-week journey through country barren of food would eat two or three times his load. So we sent a note to FDR that said in essence, "Mr. President, this is not feasible because the coolies would eat more than they could carry." FDR sent a note back that said, "Then drop their food to them by air." We had to send back another note saying, "Mr. President, if we had the planes to drop food to the coolies, we could fly these supplies all the way to China." The Allies were indeed desperate to find a route into China.

General Marshall later told me how he handled Madame Chiang's constant badgering for more war supplies for China. She was always pestering Marshall for the latest American weapons and planes, even though our own forces were in short supply. In a bottom desk drawer Marshall kept a list of surplus materials the Pentagon no longer needed. Whenever Madame Chiang presented her shopping list, he would say, "Well, that's pretty difficult, but let's see what we can do." Marshall would pull out his list of obsolete materials, turn some of these over to Madame Chiang, and she would leave, happy.

With its torrential rains, mud, and rain-swollen rivers in the wet season, dust in the dry season, switchbacks and sharp curves everywhere, the Burma Road was a fantastic engineering challenge. I drove the entire length of it once in a Jeep. Our fellows mounted armored plate on the bulldozers as protection against Japanese snipers. Building the road was heroic and a sacrificial effort, and we got lots of help from the Indians and Burmese. Eventually we pushed the road through.

In the end the Burma Road was never really used, even for supply, much less for attacking the Japanese. In the United States we had built about five thousand truck-trailer combinations to haul supplies on that road, but by the time the road opened, C-54 aircraft were available. One C-54 could do the work of sixty truck-trailer combinations. A plane could fly over the mountains of Yunnan Province in one and one-half hours, several times a day. A truck climbing through those mountains took two to three weeks to get there and on the way burned a lot more gas.

Flying the Hump made better sense logistically, too, but it was a hazardous business. A Hump pilot had only a 40 percent chance of surviving his prescribed number of missions. Before the C-46 arrived in CBI, it was even more dangerous. The older C-47's couldn't fly as high as the mountains they had to cross and had to weave their way through the passes, the crew sometimes kicking supplies, freight, and seats out the cargo door to gain altitude. When the monsoons roared out of the Indian Ocean and struck those mountains, nature went wild. We lost far more planes to weather and the mountains than we did to Japanese Zeros. The old saying was "You wished you could die and were afraid that you wouldn't." To drop three thousand feet in an instant and be blown up three thousand feet in the next was commonplace. I made that trip perhaps a dozen times, enough mountain flying to last me a lifetime.

There were lots of demands for space and tonnage into and out of China, and sometimes we made some hard decisions on what to fly. Occasionally we had to crack down on Chiang Kai-shek. Once he asked us to fly large quantities of Chinese currency across the Hump. That would have multiplied China's runaway inflation rate and made absolutely no contribution to the war effort, so we simply refused to do it.

Occasionally we caught one of our pilots smuggling gold out of China. I once shared a basha hut in Assam with a Hump pilot awaiting court-martial for smuggling. Amazed that he had been caught, he kept saying, "It's like a stab in the back! It's like a stab in the back!" Anyone flying the Hump could get rich. We were artificially supporting Chinese currency with American dollars, and it was easy to make a killing. One officer told me that if I went home without a million dollars, I was crazy.

Although the flight over the Hump was a major undertaking, it was merely the end of the trip. Just moving supplies from Calcutta to our airfields in northeastern India was a logistical nightmare of twelve hundred miles. There were large rivers to cross, such as the Brahmaputra, which in the rainy season was eight to ten miles wide. And airstrips were built on difficult terrain, often by hand in the fiercest of heat.

I was deeply involved in solving these logistical problems. Supplies shipped to Calcutta were moved by train to the airfields in Assam, along a long and winding narrow-gauge railway, but our problems included more than distance, terrain, technology, and the enemy. For decades Indians had run their trains in casual fashion. When the train stopped to take water, out came an ordinary garden hose to water the engines. That job, done in several minutes with eight- or ten-inch pipe, often required several hours with the garden hose. When crossing a river by barge, the Indians routinely drew the barge up alongside the dock and loaded the cars one at a time, crossbeam on the barge. Then they would ferry them over to the other side and unload them the same way. Had they pointed the barge into the dock, with rails running along the length of the barge, they could have loaded five or six cars at a time.

When the Indian trainmen got to their home village along the way, they stopped the train for a visit of several hours. Such practices drove us nuts, and in fact, the freight moved on that railway between Calcutta and Assam was minuscule. We finally began to operate the trains ourselves, and our shipments to Assam quadrupled almost overnight. Our fellows liked to turn on the steam and let them roll, sometimes running the trains off the tracks of this dilapidated railway.

Shipping supplies halfway around the globe to CBI was a major job, our line of communication long and hazardous. Early in the war we sometimes lost to submarines half the ships headed for CBI. Lord Mountbatten once blew his stack when, of a three-ship convoy, two ships with arms and crucially needed supplies got sunk. The surviving ship had a large shipment of chocolates.

Washington was a long way off, and the War Department often myopic. We had many misunderstandings with Washington over supplies for CBI. Being at the end of a twelve-thousand-mile supply line for a theater given lowest priority during the war didn't help. In one classic snafu, as a planner I could tell that we and the British would be returning to Burma from the north and would eventually get access to Burma's narrow-gauge rail lines. Yet the engines and rolling stock for this track were in Rangoon and other towns controlled by the Japanese. We needed engines. I cabled the Joint Chiefs, requesting small railroad engines light enough to ship by air. The chiefs just pooh-poohed this idea of "airborne locomotives." But when we retook northern Burma, there was nothing we needed more. We improvised by putting flange wheels on Jeeps. They were not the greatest, but they could pull a few cars at a time.

Another snafu concerned our carrier pigeons. Our communications company of carrier pigeons in CBI was very useful in the jungle. One day, however, Chinese troops got into the pigeon coops and made stew out of our communications. So I telegrammed the War Department: "Request a complete pigeon replacement for such and such signal company." Back came a telegram from the Pentagon saying, "Request denied. The assumption of the Tables of Organization is that the pigeons would furnish their own replacements." We hadn't told them that Chinese troops had eaten the pigeons.

Another exchange also illustrates the breakdown in communications—and common sense—in wartime. A telegram from the Joint Chiefs stated that a thousand light tanks were being loaded to ship out to CBI. We needed light tanks like a hole in the head. The terrain was so rough that armor simply wasn't relevant to the fighting. With water, soft ground, and swamps everywhere, CBI was not good tank country. Most of the fighting was done by infantrymen with rifles in hand.

I cabled back a protest saying we didn't need the light tanks; they would simply take up valuable shipping space. Yet the War Department insisted, and those tanks eventually arrived in Calcutta. There we unloaded them and put them in a big field, where they sat to rust and were picked up as scrap iron at the end of the war.

As chief of war plans I was expected to be omniscient. The signal officer, the ordinance officer, the quartermaster, and other people would customarily come in to say something like "Look, we have a long line of communication back to the United States. We need to know how long we are going to be out here in order to do our planning." In effect, they were asking me, "When is the war going to be over?"

I had to say something. Looking at them solemnly, I would intone, "You should plan on being here until April 1946." And they would go away happy.

One day an officer turned around and asked, "Oh, by the way, how do you know that it is April 1946?"

I told him, "I don't know, but I am paid to give you an answer."

Of course, I did know something about overall strategy and preparation for the invasion of Japan. April 1946 was a reasonable guess.

To retake Burma and open a land route to China, we and the British needed a common strategy, but we never achieved one until well into 1944. I suspect one reason for this tension in CBI was that Churchill simply determined that not much would happen in CBI until the situation improved in Europe. Only when Allied forces began to roll after the Normandy invasion did cooperation in CBI improve.

Churchill partially achieved his policy of delay by sending Generals Claude Auchinleck and Archibald P. Wavell, two commanders who would never take the offensive, to CBI. Although British forces carried the brunt of fighting in CBI and fought savagely at Imphal and Kohima to turn back the Japanese attempt to invade India, the lethargy at British headquarters in New Delhi was deadening. I say this while fully admitting that none of us was a stranger to the Gymkhana Club with its cricket matches, its lawn bowling, tennis, and cocktail parties.

I myself had a minor run-in with Churchill. For operations in Burma and India, American forces in CBI worked under the British chiefs of staff; in effect, this meant that we were under Churchill's command. Once Churchill ordered us to launch a long-range penetration operation into northern Burma. Three thousand Chindits were to wander about for four to five weeks, shooting at whatever Japanese they could find. We were to supply the Chindits by air. They were not assigned to capture any particular objectives.

Since this operation would have no perceptible influence on the outcome of the war, as chief of war plans I gave it the code name Pinprick. When that got back to London, out came a rocket from Churchill saying, "Change the name of Operation Pinprick to Operation Grapple." The difference between "grapple" and "pinprick" is probably the difference between Winston Churchill and myself.

There were other differences between the British and Americans in CBI. While we Americans were in CBI solely to defeat the Japanese, the British wanted to retain British rule in India at war's end. In the Pentagon, prior to my transfer to Stilwell's staff, we devised a distinctive shoulder patch for American forces to wear in CBI. The patch showed the star of India, the sun of China, and red and white stripes for the United States. Every American wore this theater-wide patch, and only Americans could wear it. We wanted Indians and other Asians to distinguish American from British forces and understand that we were there to fight the Japanese, not team up with Britain's effort to restore colonial rule in India. When General Slim asked that the patch be issued to troops under his command, we had to turn him down. We didn't want to rub Britain's nose in it, but neither did we want millions of Indians turning against us as a potential colonial master. That patch and the attitude it represented led to some friction with the British.

President Roosevelt's own attitudes on colonialism affected U.S. policy in CBI. Roosevelt strongly believed that the major colonial areas of Asia—India, Burma, Malaya, Indonesia, and Indochina—should emerge from World War II as independent nations. He pressed Churchill hard to promise that Britain would grant India its independence at the end of the war, but Churchill was very resistant. One need only to recall his famous remark "I did not become His Majesty's first minister to preside over the liquidation of the British Empire." Obviously, there was a tension between American and British objectives in CBI, and it affected everything we did: psychological warfare; our dealings with the Indians; how to present the war effort.

I believe that President Roosevelt gave up this idea of an independent Asia around the beginning of 1945. Perhaps he was growing old and sick; perhaps he was tired of butting his head against Churchill. I do know that this question arose in mid-1944, when various Frenchmen, obviously intelligence types, began to arrive in CBI, asking to be parachuted into Indochina. We knew nothing of the policy drill back in Washington. I sent a telegram reporting that these Frenchmen wanted to be parachuted into Indochina and asked for guidance on U.S. policy toward Indochina.

Weeks passed, then months. Follow-up telegrams produced no reply. Whenever one of our officers went back to Washington, he sought an answer for me. Nothing. Finally, in early 1945, the Joint Chiefs sent us a paper on the subject, "U.S. Policy Towards Indochina." The first sheet said, "The Joint Chiefs of Staff have asked the President for a statement of U.S. policy towards Indochina. The President's reply is contained in Annex A." I flipped over to Annex A, and there was a sheet of paper that said, "When asked by the Joint Chiefs for a statement of U.S. policy towards Indochina, the President replied, 'I don't want to hear any more about Indochina.' " This gap in policy—if it was a gap—lasted a full year, with far-reaching consequences.

For one thing, American indifference left matters entirely in British hands during the last year of the war and the immediate postwar period. That led directly to a British return to India, Burma, and Malaya, the return of the Dutch to Indonesia, and the return of the French to Indochina.

I recall as well with great poignancy one of the most ironic circumstances of the war. While serving as chief of war plans in CBI, I once authorized in Stilwell's absence dropping arms and American cigarettes to a Vietnamese nationalist and his band of guerrillas. The nationalist was Ho Chi Minh, and the guerrillas were the Vietminh. At that time—1944—we made common cause with anyone who would help shoot at the Japanese.

General Stilwell kept pressing the Joint Chiefs for two infantry divisions of American troops to speed up our efforts to break into northern Burma and open the Burma Road. But since the European and Pacific theaters had much higher priority, his request was denied. Stilwell was finally given a brigade of three thousand volunteers drawn from other theaters who became known as Merrill's Marauders. Gallant fighters, a motley, patchwork group organized and trained by Frank Merrill, the Marauders fought for months without rest, under the most adverse conditions. They played a decisive role in northern Burma, capturing several objectives before retaking Myitkyina, allowing us to reopen the Burma Road. With its airstrip and rail line into southern Burma, Myitkyina was an important juncture for the road into China.

I did not staff the Myitkyina operation, but I helped plan the campaign. Fortunately for the Marauders, the Japanese dug themselves in to protect the town of Myitkyina, not the airfield, and their weapons did not reach the field. The Marauders thus took the airfield first and used it for resupply before reducing Japanese resistance in the town. I landed at the airfield in May 1944, just after it was taken, when the Japanese were still holed up inside the town.

The Myitkyina campaign was an agonizing affair. General Stilwell demanded more from Merrill's Marauders than men can sustain over a period of time. Having been refused his two divisions, Stilwell had only the Marauders as a ground force, and he used them more than commanders are entitled to use such men. That has to be said. He drove them unmercifully. Weeks of jungle fighting, fatigue, and disease taxed them to the limit.

On the way to Myitkyina, the Marauders camped on a matting of dead bamboo heavily infested with rats carrying lice and ticks. Many of the men came down with typhus. They were already sick with dysentery and short of rations. Then, at the end of the long march through the jungle, they had to fight the Japanese. It was a tragic operation. Although the capture of Myitkyina was vitally important— we could not have built the Burma Road without it—the campaign destroyed a fine outfit and left a residue of bitterness among the survivors that persisted for years.

During the Myitkyina campaign, in March 1944, I received a cable from Virginia that my father had died in Atlanta. I was grief-stricken by the news. My last communication with him had not been pleasant. In an earlier letter, announcing my promotion to full colonel, I had somehow implied disrespect for my Confederate grandfather. At least my father thought so; he wrote a sharp reply and suggested that I "respect any man who fights for what he believes in." I also regretted never telling my father how I felt about him. He had never told me how he felt about me. Somehow the "Rusk reticence" discouraged our family from openly expressing our love for each other. Although a hard man to know, Father was devoted to family, a hard worker, unfailingly courteous to everyone, and one of the gentler Rusk brothers; I was very proud of him and missed him acutely. In the CBI theater General Stilwell didn't give home leave for such purposes, so I wasn't able to return to Georgia, attend his funeral, and comfort my family.

Despite his treatment of the Marauders and despite his reputation, General Stilwell's sobriquet, Vinegar Joe, was somewhat misleading. He may have had the mannerisms of a Vinegar Joe, and he looked the part, with his thin, wiry build, leathery face, fatigues, and campaign hat. In fact, he looked angry all the time; he didn't have to contort his face. Although he enjoyed his reputation for a wicked temperament, I found Stilwell to be a warm human being with great compassion, and I grew very fond of him. He was not a severe disciplinarian with his staff and tolerated incompetence longer than he should have. But I learned much from him. A laconic New Englander, Stilwell taught me not to waste words in my communiqués. "If you've got something to say, say it succinctly and then shut up," he'd remark. "Don't smother your message in a sea of words."

But there were times when Stilwell earned the name Vinegar Joe. A sardonic New Englander, he did not suffer fools gladly. A young captain fresh from the States reported to Stilwell in my presence. The captain saluted smartly and gave a brief report. As he was leaving, he said, "General, I'm sure that you and I will get along very well."

Stilwell half rose in his chair, and leaned forward, placing his hands on the desk. I could see his knuckles turning white. Stilwell's eyes snapped as he replied, "You're damn right, Captain, because you're the one who's going to do the getting along!"

His acid humor respected no rank. Once Stilwell and MacArthur tangled when some of Chennault's P-40 Flying Tigers, under CBI command, flew down to the coast and bombed some Japanese ships offshore. The line dividing CBI from MacArthur's theater in the Southwest Pacific ran along the China coast, and when MacArthur heard about this, he sent a stiff message to Stilwell complaining about this unauthorized intrusion into his—MacArthur's—theater. Stilwell sent a short cable saying, "Keep your shirt on, Doug."

Stilwell had a nickname for everyone. He called Chiang Kai-shek the Peanut, his favorite way of referring to the generalissimo. An appreciative audience, his staff encouraged him to make these smirking remarks. They should have tried to tone him down because his one-liners didn't make our job any easier. He had complete contempt for the British desire to rule India at the end of the war and clearly favored an independent India. But he greatly respected those Britishers who wanted to fight the Japanese—General William Slim and CBI Supreme Commander Lord Louis Mountbatten, for example. Officially Stilwell and Mountbatten represented differing policies, originating in Washington and London, but each knew that the other wanted to fight.

Despite his impatience and lack of diplomacy, in many ways Stilwell was the ideal man to command CBI. He had lived in China before the war and through his own experiences and studies had developed great affection for the Chinese people. Further, he respected the Chinese. He was convinced that if Chinese soldiers were properly trained, equipped, and led, they would make good soldiers. The corruption and ineptness of the Chinese government, as well as the way it mistreated its own people, infuriated him. This deep commitment to ordinary Chinese led Stilwell into many differences with Chiang Kai-shek.

But I think Stilwell underestimated the erosion that had taken place in Chinese society and political institutions as a result of fighting the Japanese for ten years before Pearl Harbor. In my opinion, it was a miracle that China even pretended to stay in the war.

Consider corruption. When the Japanese closed the Burma Road, a large stock of rubber tires lay stored in Yunnan Province. The governor of Yunnan passed a law requiring that all wheeled vehicles drive on rubber tires and then sold these tires at enormous profit. We would sent out a convoy of twelve trucks, driven by Chinese soldiers, and during the journey half of these trucks would simply disappear into the countryside. When we furnished Atabrine to Chinese troops as protection against malaria, it was our practice to place an American at the head of the chow line to shove this Atabrine down the throats of the Chinese soldiers. Otherwise, their officers would collect the Atabrine and sell it on the black market.

Cultural differences complicated our job as well. The Chinese had a fanatical sense of property. For example, we could never separate a

Chinese unit from its arms and equipment. If we wanted the Chinese to move as fast as possible from Point A to Point B, we'd ask them to leave all their equipment, saying we would fly it to them when they reached Point B. They simply wouldn't do it. We learned never to try to take anything away from a Chinese soldier.

Stilwell sometimes took unusual measures to spur the Chinese to advance. On occasion we would tell them that their food for the next day would be at such and such a point, which might be fifteen miles down the road. If they wanted their food, they would have to go down there and get it. Stilwell once ordered a Chinese unit to advance, and they stonewalled. So he took his carbine and headed down the trail toward the Japanese, all by himself. The Chinese had to trail after him as a matter of face. Despite these problems, though, most Chinese forces in Burma performed creditably.

Being a staff officer for General Stilwell was intensely political. One of my biggest challenges was working with Indian nationalists, many of whom, including Gandhi and Jawaharlal Nehru, had been jailed by the British during the war. Two of their concerns in particular were tricky to handle. The first was, When are you going to stop killing our cattle? And the second was, When are you going to start marrying our daughters?

Cattle are sacred in the Hindu faith, and the nationalists demanded that we stop killing them to feed our troops. But since our supply lines to the United States were long and crossed submarine-infested waters, it was important for us to subsist on the countryside as much as we could. We finally agreed that we would not slaughter cattle younger than twelve years old and only in screened areas where the butchering could not be observed. Our forces ate a great deal of hamburger, since cattle older than twelve tended to be tough and scrawny.

The Indian nationalists also demanded that we give our soldiers permission to marry Indian girls. We compromised by agreeing that soldiers under orders to go home would be given permission to marry within thirty days of departure. We did this even though American troops in Europe and the Pacific were not allowed to marry local people. Our reasoning was rather simple: We figured that most soldiers within thirty days of the girl back home would lose their interest in marrying local women. But to the Indian nationalists, we had accepted the principle, and that seemed to satisfy them.

We had to maintain good relations with the Indians since we were completely dependent upon them in China. They ran the trains, carried our water, hauled our food, unloaded ships, and built airstrips and the

Burma Road. Had Gandhi and his nationalists told their people not to cooperate with the Americans, we would have had to leave.

I was never exposed to ground combat in CBI, and in fact, my only "action" was rather ridiculous. About four of us staff officers were driving in a Jeep with Stilwell through some woods in Burma, and a sniper round came pinging across our hood. We stopped, and Stilwell looked at us and said, "So-and-so, you're quartermaster. You're no good for this. So-and-so, you're ordinance. You're no good for this. Rusk, you're infantry. Let's go out there and get him." So a four-star general and a thoroughly nervous colonel beat around in the bushes in Burma, looking for snipers. We didn't find any, and fortunately we didn't get any more shots.

For someone who was part of general staff, flying was the principal danger. After I had been in CBI for one year, we decided to send an officer back to Washington for consultation. All of us vied for the assignment and a chance to see our families. I tossed a coin with another colonel and lost. His plane crashed and burned on takeoff at Karachi, and all on board were killed.

Early in the war the skies over CBI were contested by Japanese and Allied planes. When Japanese Zeros came over our airfields, the drill was that every plane would take to the air, to reduce chances of destruction on the ground. I was at an airfield in western China when the red ball warning went up: Zeros were on the way. My pilot and I jumped in our C-47 and took off. As we headed north to escape, a Zero pulled in behind us. There was another C-47 aircraft about two miles to our right, and for reasons known only to that Japanese pilot, he chose to attack the other plane. By the time he shot that plane down, we had flown safely into a cloud bank. Twice in CBI I survived a fifty-fifty brush with death; I have lived on borrowed time ever since.

When all was said and done, did we in CBI serve any useful purpose? It is hard to say. To understand fully American strategy in CBI, one must remember our grim situation at the time of Pearl Harbor. The Japanese had destroyed the heart of our fleet in the Pacific, and Europe had been overrun by the Nazis. China was very important to us during those dark days, both psychologically and militarily. For our own purposes we needed to tell ourselves that this great country called China was our ally in Asia, strongly fighting the Japanese. In terms of military strategy, not until MacArthur and Nimitz came across the Pacific and actually landed in places like the Philippines and Okinawa was it apparent that we would not have to rely on China for help in defeating Japan.

Before we had much opportunity to capitalize on our effort, Allied forces had retaken the Pacific and the brunt of the war became a frontal attack on Japan. Had the war continued for a much longer period, our efforts could have been very important. But as it turned out, Japanese armies in China, much reduced by 1945, surrendered on command from Tokyo. I was compelled to conclude that our time in CBI contributed marginally at best to the defeat of Japan.

7

War's End: The Abe Lincoln Brigade

In June 1945 I flew home to Oakland, California, on a month's leave to see Virginia and David, already four years old. They were still living at Mills College, as they had been since I left for CBI in 1943. That month was joyous; we had been separated for two years, and I had missed seeing David grow up. Those four weeks had special meaning for our family.

While on leave at Mills, I received orders transferring me from CBI to the Operations Division of the War Department General Staff in Washington—the famous OPD. I was to serve in a section of the General Staff charged with long-range policy planning. Curious about my reassignment, I inquired and was told that the War Department had sent a telegram to CBI headquarters in New Delhi asking for the identity of the staff officer writing General Stilwell's cables. Stilwell had given the department my name.

At OPD I found myself among friends. Heading OPD was General George Lincoln, inevitably called Abe. A friend from Oxford, Charles "Tic" Bonesteel, who later commanded American forces in Korea, was in charge of my section. Colonels James McCormack, Ned Parker, and

Sidney Giffin, all to become generals, were among the members of this talented office. Lincoln, Bonesteel, and McCormack had been Rhodes scholars, and I had known all three at Oxford.

The Abe Lincoln Brigade, as OPD was known, gave staff backup for Army Chief of Staff George Marshall on matters coming before the U.S. Joint Chiefs of Staff and the U.S.-British Combined Chiefs of Staff. We also provided staff support for Assistant Secretary of War John J. McCloy, who was the War Department's representative on the State/War/Navy Coordinating Committee, called SWINK. We were involved in a wide range of major policy issues, and there was never a dull moment.

Our policy section was called on to give quick but informed judgments on issues of transcendent importance in rebuilding the world community following World War II, ranging from the retention of the emperor in Japan to somehow feeding the peoples of occupied countries to the launching of the infant United Nations. We were especially concerned about the demobilization of the armed forces of the Western democracies, particularly the United States, at a time when Soviet forces were at their peak and flushed with their great victory over the Germans in Eastern Europe.

We were told to "learn how to juggle several balls without losing your own." I was thirty-six at the time, the average age of OPD staffers. We were forced by events to act as statesmen beyond our years. An entire generation of young Americans, both civilian and military, played a major role in formulating American foreign policy during the immediate postwar years.

Our group helped plan the postwar occupation of Germany, the terms of surrender and the occupation of Japan, and American participation in the newborn United Nations. During World War II many policy questions were subordinated to the need for successfully prosecuting the war. Consequently, Franklin Roosevelt relied heavily upon Secretary of War Henry Stimson and Chief of Staff of the Army George Marshall for direction on foreign affairs. So much foreign policy was directly linked to the waging and winning of the war that we found ourselves dealing with issues normally handled by the State Department. The influence of the armed forces in policy making was very high throughout World War II. At SWINK assistant secretaries of state, war, and navy met regularly to coordinate policy. In the OPD we were backstopping both the civilian and the military leadership of the War Department.

I was not among those officers informed about the development of the atomic bomb. Rumors about a "Manhattan Project" involving a "big bomb" surfaced here and there, but inquiries on our part were immediately squelched. In the military we learned to keep our mouths shut and respect the "need to know" attitude. But I remember vividly when the flash came in on August 6, 1945, reporting the dropping of the bomb on Hiroshima. Upon reading the telegram, Colonel Sidney Giffin, who sat at the desk next to mine, exclaimed, "This means that war has turned upon itself and is devouring its own tail. From this time forward, there will be no sense for governments to try to settle their disputes by war."

I have never faulted President Truman's decision to drop the atomic bomb on Hiroshima and Nagasaki. In August 1945 we on the General Staff were planning the invasion of Japan. It was clear to us that taking the main islands of Japan would be a frightful affair. We planned first to launch sustained saturation bombing attacks on Japan's coast and its cities; these attacks by themselves would have killed millions of Japanese. Then we planned to invade. Millions more Japanese would have been killed then. Estimates of American casualties ranged from four or five hundred thousand all the way to MacArthur's figure of a million. We were anticipating a bloody end to the war. Truman's decision to drop the bomb should be viewed in this light. We should also remember that American B-29's killed more people in one fire-bombing raid on Tokyo than we did in Hiroshima.

In retrospect, Japan was much weaker than we realized. We might have been able to win without an invasion, with only sustained conventional bombing. But our use of the atomic bomb gave the emperor and others in the government an opportunity to bring their own military leadership under control and end the war. Hiroshima changed the political position of the military in Japan. Hardly anyone fully appreciated what the atomic bomb was, including the pilots and crews who flew the missions, until we actually saw the photos taken by our reconnaissance planes. This was an awesome weapon.

Those who say Truman used the atomic bomb for postwar political considerations, primarily to keep the Soviet Union out of Japan, may have been right, but I don't believe postwar concerns were overriding. Harry Truman wanted to end the war quickly and avoid the hideous casualties of landings on the main islands. World War II had cost fifty million dead by August 1945. General Marshall himself thought that we had to end the war quickly, before the institutions of American democracy melted out from under us. The bombing of Hiroshima and Nagasaki did in fact end the war. Winston Churchill called the atomic bomb "a miracle of deliverance." I have to agree. Until August 1945 the Japanese had not surrendered without a fight anywhere in the Pacific.

Many years later, while visiting Japan as secretary of state, I laid a wreath on the monument to the dead of Hiroshima. When the Japanese press asked me, on that occasion and other visits to Japan, if I regretted our using the atomic bomb on Japan, I told them, "I regret very deeply every casualty of that war on both sides, Japanese and American, beginning with Pearl Harbor and ending with the surrender in Tokyo Bay."

But we made a mistake with the Manhattan Project from its inception. We should have built in a political task force to consider the ramifications of using the bomb. Unfortunately those with political savvy who knew about the Manhattan Project—Roosevelt, Stimson, a few others—were too busy with the war effort to focus on the long-range implications of nuclear weapons. Such a task force might not have affected the outcome, either at Hiroshima or the arms race that followed, but at least we would have boxed the compass of all possibilities. By dropping the bomb on Hiroshima, we gave away 95 percent of the secret of the bomb simply by demonstrating that such devices could be built.

The actual surrender of Japan—on August 14, five days after Nagasaki—came sooner than we had anticipated, even with the atomic bomb. We in OPD worked feverishly for two weeks preparing formal surrender documents to get out to General MacArthur for the September 2 ceremony on the battleship USS *Missouri* in Tokyo Harbor. We also arranged terms for the American occupation of Japan and got concurrence from our allies.

A revealing moment during this time foreshadowed later difficulties with General MacArthur. After completing all that work, we put a colonel on a special plane that flew straight to Tokyo. He climbed into a small launch and motored out to the *Missouri* with the surrender documents in hand. One of MacArthur's staffers met him at the foot of the gangway, took the documents, and said, "General MacArthur says you will not be needed on board."

On another occasion well before the surrender, we had sent a colonel to confer with MacArthur, then in the Philippines. This colonel returned a week later with nothing to report. We asked him, "Didn't you have your high-level conversation with General MacArthur?"

He said, "Yes, I had one high-level conversation with him. I walked into his headquarters and stepped into the elevator, and General

MacArthur came along and stepped into the same elevator. He turned to me and said, 'You will take the next elevator, I presume.' That was my high-level conversation with General MacArthur."

Despite what these incidents may imply, POD and SWINK did influence many important decisions relating to the Japanese surrender. For example, OPD played a major role in retaining the emperor of Japan. We didn't have time to organize Ph.D. theses on the subject, but we really believed that retaining him provided our only chance for a peaceful occupation. Hirohito's position in Japanese society was such that if he called upon his people to accept the occupation, they would do it. Had the Japanese resisted the American occupation with the same fervor with which they had prosecuted the war, we would have had to land millions of American soldiers to exert control. Some in the State Department wanted to ax the emperor, but we in OPD lobbied hard to retain Hirohito. Fortunately President Truman agreed with us. That decision alone, I am convinced, opened the door for peaceful occupation.

We were also determined not to give the Soviet Union a zone of occupation in Japan. I personally wanted the United States to control every wave in the Pacific, so bitter had our experience with the Soviets been in our joint occupation of Germany and Austria in the three months since V-E Day. Additionally, we felt that since the Soviets had been in the war against Japan for only three days, they had not earned a zone of occupation. They had not been willing to cooperate in the Pacific until the last few days of the war. They had not let Jimmy Doolittle's B-25's land on Russian airfields after his famous raid over Tokyo, nor had they provided facilities for our reconnaissance planes. Manchuria, long occupied by the Japanese, dominated the Russians' psychology. They vastly overestimated Japanese strength there, and when the Russians attacked, they found that Japan's once-elite Manchurian army had been heavily depleted to reinforce Japanese positions in the Pacific. The Soviets encountered very little opposition in Manchuria, and once they had entrenched themselves, fortunately they didn't push hard for a role on the Japanese main islands.

We at OPD fully agreed with President Truman's insistence that Japan's surrender terms be kept simple and clear of complicated issues such as the fate of Korean nationals living in Japan at the end of the war. We also all agreed that Korea should emerge as an independent nation after World War II.

One episode had greater significance than we realized at the time. Widely scattered Japanese forces had to surrender, and the State and

War Departments differed over where and when American forces should accept their surrender. The State Department wanted us to accept the surrender as far north on the mainland of China as possible, including key points in Manchuria. But the U.S. Army, concerned about the future, did not want responsibility for areas where it had no or few forces. In fact, the Army did not want to go onto the mainland at all.

We finally reached a compromise that would keep at least some U.S. forces on the Asian mainland, a sort of toehold on the Korean peninsula for symbolic purposes. During a SWINK meeting on August 14, 1945, the same day of the Japanese surrender, Colonel Charles Bonesteel and I retired to an adjacent room late at night and studied intently a map of the Korean peninsula. Working in haste and under great pressure, we had a formidable task: to pick a zone for the American occupation. Neither Tic nor I was a Korea expert, but it seemed to us that Seoul, the capital, should be in the American sector. We also knew that the U.S. Army opposed an extensive area of occupation. Using a *National Geographic* map, we looked just north of Seoul for a convenient dividing line but could not find a natural geographical line. We saw instead the thirty-eighth parallel and decided to recommend that.

SWINK accepted it without too much haggling, and surprisingly, so did the Soviets. I had thought they might insist on a line farther south in view of our respective military positions. No one present at our meeting, including two young American colonels, was aware that at the turn of the century the Russians and Japanese had discussed spheres of influence in Korea, divided along the thirty-eighth parallel. Had we known that, we almost surely would have chosen another line of demarcation. Remembering those earlier discussions, the Russians might have interpreted our action as acknowledgment of their sphere of influence in Korea north of the thirty-eighth parallel. Any future talk about the agreed-upon reunification of Korea would be seen as mere show. But we were ignorant of all this, and SWINK'S choice of the thirty-eighth parallel, recommended by two tired colonels working late at night, proved fateful.

We at OPD were also involved with the four-power occupation of Germany. Because of a severe worldwide food shortage at war's end, one of our major concerns was feeding the German people, a direct responsibility of the armies of occupation. We set up a special task force, but simply keeping the Germans alive was no easy matter. Occupation zones had already been established by the time I joined OPD, and we wrestled constantly with the Russians over the occupation of Germany and the administration of these four zones. Soviet obstreperousness bolstered our determination not to let the Russians have a zone of occupation in Japan. Clearly we had made a mistake in not requiring a land corridor under Allied control in Berlin.

As an OPD staff officer I worked closely with the State Department on the newly created United Nations. Its Charter had been signed and ratified by the United States, the Soviet Union, and many countries. Its organizational meeting was scheduled for January 1946. OPD was especially interested in the makeup of the international security force to be furnished by member nations through agreements negotiated with the Security Council. As a result, I became well acquainted with State personnel working on the UN.

With the war over, my Army career was coming to an end. Before Stilwell was recalled from CBI in 1945, he recommended me for promotion to brigadier general. The Pentagon refused for the best of reasons: "We have too many generals!"

In February 1946, having been discharged from the Army, I accepted a position in the State Department as assistant chief of the Division of International Security Affairs (within the Special Political Affairs office, later to become United Nations Affairs). A wartime creation, this postwar planning office focused on the emerging world order, as World War II had completely torn apart the international community of the old League of Nations. My division chief was an old friend, Joseph Johnson, later president of the Carnegie Endowment for International Peace. Our director was a man named Alger Hiss. I was happy to get the job; working on the newly born United Nations appealed to me greatly. The appointment kept me in Washington, where Virginia had settled in; soon afterward, in March 1946, our son Richard was born.

In January 1946, during my service as assistant division chief, I accompanied Secretary of State James Byrnes to New York, where he represented the United States at the UN Security Council over the question of Azerbaijan, the first case to come before the United Nations. During the war the United States shipped lend-lease supplies through Iran to the Soviet Union. American personnel oversaw our transportation corridor in southern Iran, linking up with Soviet forces in northern Iran concentrated in the northwest province of Azerbaijan. Our understanding was that at the end of the war all Allied forces would go home. But after the war the Soviets refused to withdraw. This looked ominously like another land grab, where Soviet troops in Iran might pinch off that northwestern frontier area, turn it into a Communist stronghold, and eventually take over the entire country.

We took Azerbaijan to the Security Council. Having withdrawn U.S. forces from Iran and demobilized almost our entire armed forces, we could do little else. Eventually we were able to mobilize other governments and world opinion against the continuing Soviet presence in Iran. We fussed and we heckled, applied pressure where we could, and amassed an overwhelming majority in the United Nations against the Soviet occupation. I think Joseph Stalin reached a saturation point where keeping his troops in Azerbaijan was not worth the cost in anti-Soviet propaganda. Curiously, the Soviet Union has always been sensitive to propaganda. Thus, the United Nations passed its first test. The weight of international opinion as massed at the UN likely played a role in the Soviet withdrawal from Azerbaijan.

Some have alleged that President Truman threatened to use atomic weapons against the Soviets if they did not withdraw from Azerbaijan. I don't remember such discussions. I believe I was highly enough placed in our government to have known of such threats if they existed. But I also doubt the story for several concrete reasons. First, when the United States dropped its second atomic bomb on Nagasaki, that was the last one we had left. By early 1946 we had built only two or three more. Having learned via espionage how many atomic bombs we did *not* have, Stalin likely was in no sense intimidated by the so-called American monopoly on nuclear weapons.

More fundamentally, Harry Truman was not a man who would use nuclear blackmail. Truman's abhorrence of nuclear weapons is well illustrated by an incident during the Korean War when he was meeting with the Joint Chiefs of Staff to discuss military plans. One of the chiefs remarked, "If the Chinese enter the war, this will mean the use of atomic weapons."

Harry Truman came out of his chair, turned to the general, and said, "Who told you that?"

The general said, "That's part of our strategic doctrine."

Truman said, "You are not going to put me in that position. You'd better go back and get yourself some more strategic doctrine!"

While at the State Department, I also worked intensively on negotiations among the Big Five in the Security Council for establishing security forces called for under Chapter 7 of the UN Charter. The Charter anticipated the possible use of force by the United Nations for the maintenance of international peace. Designated in advance by member nations, these forces were to be available to the Security Council upon call and would be under the direction of a military staff committee drawn from the five permanent members.

In those early days of the United Nations we wanted to get real muscle behind the UN Charter. We had lengthy discussions with other governments and our own State and War Departments about the size and disposition of those forces and about procedures for their deployment. But it was all shadowboxing; we and the Soviets could not agree. In retrospect, I think the United States overplayed its hand. We Americans came out of World War II with much stronger naval and air forces than did the Soviets, who had only an abundance of ground forces. Our people, particularly the Joint Chiefs, wanted the American contribution to the international force to be weighted toward air and naval forces, requiring the Soviets to put up a disproportionate share of ground forces. The Russians categorically rejected any imbalance of forces. They insisted upon equality across the board: gun for gun, man for man, plane for plane, and ship for ship.

Negotiations broke down. The Soviets clearly thought that we were overreaching, as indeed, we were. Sensitive to being treated like a second-class power, they wouldn't accept the inferiority implied by the nature of UN security forces.

In retrospect, our inability to agree wasn't as tragic as it seemed at the time. With a veto in the Security Council, it was unlikely that the five permanent members would ever have worked together to employ such forces. The United Nations instead moved toward volunteer forces from middle-sized countries such as Canada, Sweden, Ireland, and Nigeria because they lack great-power status, are not feared in the world, and no one would accuse them of harboring territorial ambitions. Consequently, they make a better and more truly neutral international force. During these early years of the United Nations the United States became increasingly concerned about Soviet vetoes in the Security Council that prevented UN action. Consequently, we pushed for a greater role for the General Assembly in peacekeeping matters. With the Uniting for Peace Resolution, we tried substituting the General Assembly when the Security Council was paralyzed by a veto. But the Soviets maintained that only the Security Council could deal with such issues. And so the Soviet vetoes continue.

In the summer of 1946 I was called back to the War Department to become personal assistant to Secretary of War Robert Patterson. It was a critical assignment in that I worked on vital postwar defense questions like the desegregation of the U.S. Army, the creation of a centralized intelligence agency, which later became the CIA, and the procurement of food supplies for both Germany and Japan. We worked desperately to find enough food to prevent starvation in those two vanquished countries since it had become a direct U.S. responsibility to feed them. But because of a worldwide food shortage, we were barely able to scratch together enough food on which they could live. It was a near thing, but fortunately we found enough food.

I also continued to work on United Nations affairs. One of my responsibilities was sitting with the fifteen-nation Far Eastern Commission, which helped supervise the American occupation of Japan and the drafting of a new constitution for Japan. And it was at my urging that Robert Patterson suggested the Presidio at San Francisco as the site for the United Nations' new home. With its extensive grounds, residences, office buildings, hospital, airfield, golf course, yacht harbor, and movie house, it would have made a fantastic home for the United Nations. Secretary of State Edward Stettinius once remarked that the UN Charter might never have been written had the organizational meeting not been held in San Francisco. He may have been right. Tensions and frayed nerves were soothed by the tranquil beauty and hospitality of that great city; the very atmosphere of San Francisco probably helped move the delegates to eventual agreement.

But the United Nations preferred to locate in New York City, in part because many delegations did not relish the additional three-thousand-mile flight to San Francisco. Had jet travel been available at the time, the United Nations today might be in San Francisco. But instead of the tranquillity of San Francisco Bay, the UN today resides in the hustle and bustle of Manhattan, at whatever cost—real or imagined—to the settlement of international disputes.

Throughout this early post-World War II period, events piled one on top of the other, and our hopes for a peaceful and cooperative postwar peace eroded. But I cannot and do not accept the thesis that the United States was equally culpable with the Soviet Union for the Cold War. In the events of the postwar period the Communist world posed our primary challenge with its return to a doctrine of world revolution, supported by acts of aggression on the ground to bring it about. The Soviets disregarded the agreements negotiated at Potsdam and Yalta for postwar arrangements in Eastern Europe, and the Kremlin forcibly brought Bulgaria, Czechoslovakia, Rumania, Poland, Hungary, and East Germany into the Soviet camp. And Stalin gave a green light to the North Koreans for their invasion of South Korea as well.

During the postwar years it looked as though this mud slide of communism would continue unless stopped. The origins of the Cold War arose from this doctrine of world revolution and actions by various Communist countries to try to move that revolution ahead by force. On the basis of our experiences in the thirties, we felt that the time to stop aggression was at the beginning, before it developed a momentum. At all levels, my own included, the Truman administration believed that unless we confronted Communist aggression, the world would once again witness the sorry experience of the 1930's, when one unmet act of aggression led to another and eventually to world war.

8

United Nations Affairs

In January 1947, during George Marshall's futile mission to China to reconcile the Chinese Nationalists and Communists, President Truman asked Marshall to become secretary of state. Truman's outgoing cable came through our section, so we knew about the offer even before Marshall. Marshall accepted and upon his return from China asked me to head up the State Department's Office of Special Political Affairs (SPA), also known as the UN desk.

The UN desk was responsible for all U.S. dealings with the newly created United Nations, and heading it would have been an extremely important job. Secretary of War Robert Patterson had just offered me an Army commission and promised that when I finished law school, I would become the Army's chief expert on international law. It was a tempting offer. But with Marshall heading State, the heart of all foreign policy decision making would be there.

I opted for State, to a great extent because of George Marshall. He was the most extraordinary man I ever knew. Winston Churchill called him the "principal architect of victory" in World War II, and Harry

Truman called Marshall "the greatest living American" shortly there-after. They both were right.

Marshall had a strong influence on everyone who served with him. He was a great teacher as well. He taught us about public service and how we should conduct ourselves in public life, both by personal example and by dropping little homilies about what he expected of us. For example: "Gentlemen, don't sit around waiting for me to tell you what to do. Take some initiative. Tell me what you think I ought to be doing!" He expected everyone to perform his job well, whatever the problems. For example, soon after his appointment, Marshall was at a morning staff meeting with about fifteen of us, and someone complained about poor departmental morale. The general straightened himself up, looked around the table, and declared, "Gentlemen, enlisted men may be entitled to morale problems, but officers are not. I expect all officers in this department to take care of their own morale. No one is taking care of my morale." When word went around the department that there was no shoulder to cry on, morale at State went to the highest point that I had ever seen it, before or since.

Marshall's attitude inspired confidence in his colleagues. The old general would tell us, "Take heart!"; "Don't despair!"; "Don't fight your problems, deal with them!" During the Berlin blockade of 1948, when the United States and the Soviet Union came dangerously close to a shooting war, a colleague asked, "Mr. Secretary, how can you be so calm in the presence of such a serious crisis?" Marshall said, "I've seen it worse."

With Marshall's career and the careers of so many military leaders like Omar Bradley and Dwight Eisenhower, we shouldn't overlook their earlier service between World War I and World War II. During that time of nonpreparedness, the U.S. Army officer corps was skeletal in size, had few troops to command, no money for field training, research, and development. Army officers spent most of their time learning, teaching, and reading. The same men who gave America such brilliant leadership in World II were junior officers for ten years or more, raising their families on $160 a month. That they stayed with their profession in these lean times was a miracle of the human spirit.

George Marshall knew how to delegate responsibility. He thought that a secretary of state should do those things which only the secretary can do. If others could do something, he expected them to do it. He went home at four-thirty or five every afternoon. Of course, he had a great undersecretary in Robert Lovett, fully qualified to be secretary of state himself. But Marshall delegated massively, and if he found that he couldn't delegate effectively to a particular person, he would replace him.

Marshall tried to reduce complex problems to their simplest level. For example, when reading our memos, he expected our recommendations to be stated on a single page. We could have annexes and tabs and extra material into which he could read further, but he felt that unless we reduced our findings to one page, we had not thought seriously about the problem. It was his way of requiring us to bore into a complex issue and find the central question. Sometimes we cheated on his one-page format by using legal-length paper, by single spacing instead of double spacing, and by narrowing the margins, cramming what we could on to that page. But Marshall's insistence on brevity fostered intellectual discipline in his advisers. As secretary of state I also tried to insist on brevity, but for me, one page was too restrictive for complicated questions.

Marshall brought from his Army experience the concept of completed staff work. He wanted recommendations not only on policies to be adopted but on measures to carry them out. He wanted papers that he could simply sign, setting everything into motion. He didn't like unfinished business put before him. "Never bring me a question unless you include your proposed answer," he would say. "Because without an answer, you haven't thought enough about the question."

Marshall impressed all of us with the importance of precision, accuracy, and detail because he knew that large problems are made of many small problems. If the details of policy are not right, the larger purposes often cannot succeed. He told us, "Never agree 'in principle' because all that means is that you haven't yet agreed." That idea came from World War I, when Marshall negotiated with French authorities for operational logistics, transportation, and supplies. He often received the reply *"Oui, en principe,"* meaning "Yes, in principle." Then nothing happened.

He demanded much, an effective tool of leadership. We couldn't do a sloppy job for the old man. He always urged his associates to take more responsibility for policy, partly because President Truman had delegated enormous responsibilities to him.

Marshall was also a language fanatic. He spent hours thumbing through dictionaries, looking for exactly the right word. He didn't believe in using ten words if three would do. When I first worked for Marshall, I read him a draft reply to a letter he had received.

"Dear Dr. Brown," I began, "I have read with much appreciation your letter of March 18. I feel that—"

Here he stopped me right there. "Now wait a minute, Rusk. I didn't read his letter. You did. And I didn't appreciate it one damned bit. So let's strike that out. Let's just say, 'I received your letter.' " And then he said, " 'I feel'? I don't have feelings about matters of public policy. If I think it, let's say, 'I think it.' I don't 'feel it.' "

George Marshall was austere in his official relationships, believing that personalities should never influence how policy is decided. He always kept an arm's length distance from his colleagues and called us by our last names. Robert Lovett was Marshall's closest friend in government, but he always called him Lovett. The story is told that President Roosevelt once called Marshall George during the war, and he said, "It's General Marshall, Mr. President." Perhaps Marshall was distant because he had to relieve Army classmates during World War II when they couldn't cut the mustard of high command. I admired Marshall's practice, but when as secretary of state I tried to follow it myself, I only developed a reputation for being aloof and enigmatic.

Marshall never complimented anyone, yet after the official relationship had ceased, no one could be more generous or appreciative than George Marshall. The nearest I ever came to a compliment occurred during a United Nations meeting in Paris, France, in the fall of 1948. Early one morning I was awakened in my hotel room by the message center at the American Embassy and told there was an "eyes only" telegram from President Truman to Secretary Marshall. So I dressed and went over to the code room. The message was about Palestine and required an immediate answer. I sketched out a proposed reply and went to Marshall's quarters at the Hôtel Crillon, where I woke him about 4:00 A.M. He put on his bathrobe and slippers, read over the incoming message, read my draft reply, and made a few changes. As I was leaving, he said, "Rusk, there are times when I think you earn your pay." Since I was making only nine thousand dollars a year, his remark hardly interfered with policy. But after he left office, when I visited him in Virginia, he couldn't have been more friendly and interested in what I was doing.

During that same meeting in Paris the American delegation was housed in a small, crummy hotel not far from the convention hall. Completely gutted by the Germans for its metal, pipes, and radiators, it was as Spartan as one could imagine. Marshall's office was in a corner room, approachable through two dilapidated bathrooms. There was no rug on the floor, nothing hanging on the walls, only the barest of furniture, and a severe-looking desk, behind which Marshall sat. I once suggested, "Mr. Secretary, we ought to find you a more suitable office."

"No!" he said. "Those foreign ministers living at the Ritz Hotel who come here asking to borrow a billion dollars from the United States should see how I live."

Marshall also had a wry sense of humor. Once I flew with him from Washington to New York on a DC-3, and he pulled out a bunch of papers for me to read. "I have to speak at the United Nations tomorrow," he said, "and the department has prepared this speech for me. Look it over and see what you think." Just as I started reading, the plane hit severe turbulence. I handed the papers back to Marshall, telling him if I read the papers now, I would get sick. He said nothing and put the papers back into his briefcase. But when we landed in New York, he sent a telegram back to the department saying, "Rusk says this speech makes him sick. Get me another one!" That really made me popular at State.

Despite being a military man, Marshall was no tub-thumping militarist. At a morning staff meeting he once told us, "Gentlemen, let's not discuss this problem as if it were a military problem; that might turn it into a military problem. Military action must always be the last resort." Politically sophisticated, Marshall was a great soldier and a great civilian. He firmly believed in civilian control of the military and had enormous respect for our constitutional system.

Despite his accomplishments, George Marshall had no false sense of prestige. At a Senate committee hearing, since I was familiar with the subject of his testimony, he had me sit as the so-called expert at his side at the witness table. He told me to whisper my proposed answer to him, in response to the senators' questions. But Marshall was nearly deaf, and as the hearing progressed, he would turn to me and say, "Louder! Louder!" As my voice rose, it was picked up on the microphone and broadcast throughout the room. But he just listened to my advice and repeated to the committee exactly what I had said, word for word. That didn't faze him at all—in fact, he rather enjoyed it—although it embarrassed the daylights out of me. Marshall was a totally unpretentious man.

Marshall was clearheaded about personnel matters. Whenever his advisers disagreed about policy, we couldn't see Marshall alone; he insisted that all parties to a dispute be present. During the Roosevelt administration FDR's advisers often threatened to resign, hoping to win a presidential vote of confidence or pressure him on a policy matter.

Marshall regarded that behavior as blackmail and wouldn't allow it at State. After he became secretary of state, a senior officer of the department suggested a change of policy, then added that if Marshall didn't adopt the change, he—the officer—would have lost his usefulness and would have to resign.

"Mr. So-and-So, whether you or I work for the U.S. government has nothing to do with the merits of this question," Marshall retorted promptly. "So let's remove this irrelevancy. I accept your resignation, effective immediately. Now that this matter is resolved, if you wish to spend a few minutes discussing this issue with me, I'll hear your views." After this story got around, no one ever again pulled a "New Deal resignation" on George Marshall.

Since Marshall's day we have witnessed much guerrilla warfare in Washington by senior advisers competing for influence with the president. That wasn't a problem for Marshall because everyone knew that George Marshall was *the* adviser to President Truman on foreign policy. I know of only one case—Jewish lobbying with the White House over Palestine—where his authority over foreign policy was challenged.

Moving to State under George Marshall was a delightful opportunity for me, and I quickly accepted, succeeding Alger Hiss as head of Special Political Affairs. Later in 1947 the SPA position became an assistant secretaryship.

I was thirty-eight, rather young for an assistant secretary, and soon after acquiring the post, I received a phone call from the national director of the Junior Chamber of Commerce, who began describing the Chamber's progress on the ten outstanding young men of the year. As my chest began to swell, he said, "I wonder if you, as one of our elder statesman, would serve as a judge." People in the next room could have heard the air escape from me like a leaking balloon.

As for Alger Hiss, I worked only briefly with him. He struck me as able and intelligent and congenial with his superiors and those of his own rank. But he was a cold fish with underlings. Whatever the truth of his conviction for perjury, I was aware of nothing untoward about the man. Admittedly I had heard some "under-the-rug" rumors about Alger Hiss while I worked in the War and State Departments, but after my appointment, like an old company commander, I wanted to inventory what I was taking over. I asked State Department security for a rundown on all 227 SPA employees. Security gave everyone a clean bill of health. No one in SPA ran afoul of loyalty or security problems during the McCarthy investigations.

Clearly, Alger Hiss had not stacked SPA with questionable characters. As far as I am concerned, if in fact, Hiss was involved with the Communist party in the early 1930's, when American democracy seemed to be collapsing and many people were looking for alternatives to capitalism, he later made a clean break. But when his past overtook him during congressional investigations, he elected to bluff it out rather than admit his earlier flirtation with communism, and he got caught.

There was no doubt, however, that SPA was overstaffed. We fired memos back and forth to each other and spent most of our time reading them. Once I asked the British how many people they had in their foreign office on United Nations affairs, and they said, "Seven." I asked the Turks, and they said, "One." So I steadily reduced the size of our bureau to approximately 160 members, and we got more work done with fewer members. One does not necessarily solve problems by employing more people.

Around Washington, SPA personnel were called those UN boys with some derision, but this only inspired us to work harder. In the aftermath of global war a special atmosphere surrounded the United Nations. The human race had paid fifty million lives to draft that Charter. Our minds and hearts had been purged in the fires of a great war, and the UN Charter represented the best that was in us at the time. We had a talented group, bound together by a sense of commitment, an exhilaration rare in government, a feeling that somehow the human race was off to a fresh start. We genuinely hoped and sometimes believed that world affairs would work out for the better, although we knew even in those early days that we were going to have major trouble with the Soviet Union.

But even in our most bitter debates no delegate ever spoke scornfully of the UN Charter. All seemed compelled to try to reconcile their own positions with the Charter. This wholesome pressure on governments to bring their policies into accord with the Charter reminded me of Gandhi's remarks at Oxford. "We expect the best of the British," he said, "because they'll tend to live up to those expectations." Perhaps the Charter had a similar influence in its early days. To us "UN boys," it seemed mankind's last great hope. It remains so today.

Directing SPA was exceptionally challenging. SPA played a major role in giving birth to the United Nations; we drafted much of its organizational machinery and working procedures. Additionally, when the General Assembly convenes each September, almost every major question of foreign policy comes before the United Nations, in either general debate or committee hearings. SPA's job—and therefore my responsibility—was to backstop our UN delegation. Inevitably this drew me into almost every aspect of American foreign policy. I worked closely with the European, Latin American, Asian, African, and Middle East desks to get our delegation properly instructed.

Every month I listed on a yellow legal pad those matters with which I was concerned, one item per line. Those lists would usually run from eighty to one hundred items in a single month. When I made a new list, I threw the old one away. But some years later I found one of those old lists in a drawer, and it was fascinating to see what had happened since. Some problems had simply disappeared on their own; new problems had arisen to take their places; others had improved; a few had gotten worse. There seemed little correlation between situations that had gotten better or worse and whether we had actually done anything about them. Reflecting on my experiences in government, I think we tended then—and now—to exaggerate the necessity to take action. Given time, many problems work themselves out or disappear.

My job at SPA put me in touch with Eleanor Roosevelt, known to all of us as the grandmother of the United Nations. As head of the UN Human Rights Commission she did a brilliant job in producing the Universal Declaration of Human Rights. Eleanor Roosevelt was indefatigable, one of the hardest workers I ever saw. She often began her morning discussing UN matters with delegates over breakfast and went right through her day at full speed until midnight, when she would come home and dictate her column, "My Day." We assigned a staff officer to each member of our delegation, but to her we assigned two; one could not possibly keep up with her.

Eleanor Roosevelt and I disagreed on some issues, especially the handling of the Palestine question, but she was an eloquent and effective champion of human rights. She repeatedly took the Russian delegates over her lap and spanked them for human rights violations, and everybody enjoyed it, including the Russians. She was the UN's grandmother; people just adored her. She and John Foster Dulles were the two best vote getters we ever had. Somehow finding room in their schedules, they met with and worked hard on every delegate. In those years Dulles and Roosevelt produced overwhelming majorities on almost anything we wanted in the General Assembly.

In a peripheral sense, I also gave advice on the birth of the Marshall Plan, although it is probably fortunate that my views were ignored. The Marshall Plan evolved as a continuation of earlier U.S. efforts to feed war refugees and encourage European economic recovery. George Marshall himself deserves full credit for authorship, although the idea came from Marshall's Policy Planning Staff, directed by George Kennan. Marshall's very approach to world affairs encouraged creative thinking. "Let's not sit around in our chairs and wait for the Russians to do something," he'd say. "Let's let them worry about what we are going to do."

With the United States emerging as the only major power physically unscarred by the war, our economy was dominant in world affairs. Incredibly, in 1945 nearly half the world's gross national product was produced by the United States. We had the economic capability, and men like Harry Truman and George Marshall persuaded the American people to mobilize enormous resources with which to bind up the wounds of war and get the global economy moving forward. Although the Marshall Plan served vital American interests, it wouldn't have been possible without a strong streak of generosity in the American people.

As director of SPA and with the United Nations as my client, I was constantly looking for ways to make the UN more effective. Consequently, I thought it would be a good idea to administer the Marshall Plan through the UN; however, George Marshall and others quickly rejected this suggestion. They pointed out that if the United States proposed a plan at the General Assembly that involved only Western Europe, other countries likely would say, "Hey, we want some of that pie, too," thereby imperiling the Marshall Plan's effectiveness in Europe. Fortunately my idea was dropped like a hot potato.

I then urged that we use the Organization for European Economic Cooperation (OEEC) as the vehicle for implementing the Marshall Plan. When we first proposed the Marshall Plan, we invited not only Western European states but also the Soviet Union and its allies. Had there been Communist participation in the Marshall Plan, the OEEC might have been the best instrument around which to organize American assistance to Europe as a whole. Unfortunately the Soviets replied by walking out of the Paris meeting of European governments, dragging a reluctant Czechoslovakia and Poland with them. The Soviet walkout made it clear they were not going to play ball with us.

The Soviet bloc's refusal to participate represented a lost opportunity to ease the Cold War. I thought our offer was genuinely made. For their own reasons the Soviets turned it down. But we Americans cannot afford sanctimony. Had the Soviets accepted and become a major participant, we would have had great difficulty getting funds from Congress.

My SPA position also placed me near the center of controversy within our government over the Baruch Plan, which called for interna-

tional controls on all fissionable materials. The Baruch Plan was based
on the Acheson-Lilienthal Report, which argued that the knowledge of
how to build nuclear weapons would soon become universal and that
a nuclear arms race was inevitable unless immediate steps were taken
to prevent it. Under the plan, all fissionable materials would be turned
over to the United Nations, to be used solely for peaceful purposes.
There would be no nuclear weapons in the hands of any nation, including the United States.

In retrospect, the Baruch Plan may have asked too much of the
Soviets. We wanted them to agree to international controls after we had
already demonstrated our ability to make atomic weapons, but before
they had the ability. Our hopes for the Baruch Plan and international
controls went beyond what we Americans would probably have agreed
to had our situations been reversed. A good test of any idea is to
examine whether it is reciprocal. Had the Soviets been the first to
develop and use a nuclear weapon and had they made exactly the same
proposal, before we ourselves had cracked the secret of the Bomb, it is
most unlikely that President Truman or Congress would have accepted
it. Although I regret that we did not achieve international controls in
the 1940's, again, we cannot afford sanctimony over Soviet intransigence.

George Marshall completely supported the Baruch Plan. As a military man he understood what nuclear weapons did to the concept of
war as a means for settling disputes. Had Marshall opposed international controls, the Baruch Plan would never have gotten off the
ground. It was indeed a fleeting moment in history, a time to keep the
nuclear beast in its cage before it began to growl.

I myself argued long and hard for the Baruch Plan, even seeking
assurances from the Joint Chiefs of Staff and the secretaries of war and
the navy that the United States would indeed follow through if the
Baruch proposal were adopted and destroy its entire nuclear stockpile.
For both moral and political reasons I believed we couldn't defend the
continued existence of the Bomb. Even after talks bogged down, I
forcefully argued that we had to keep the door open and leave the
Baruch Plan on the table. To me, to do otherwise would weaken the
UN and the newly created U.S. Atomic Energy Commission. My colleagues, especially Robert Lovett, were less convinced.

There was also extensive opposition to the Baruch Plan in the
Pentagon, State Department, and Congress. The plan itself had many
booby traps, especially over verification. How could the United Nations
verify with absolute certainty that one country or another was not

building these weapons? We soon learned that the Soviets wouldn't buy international controls. If the Soviets had accepted the Baruch Plan, congressional leaders told us that Congress might have passed it. But it would have been a tough fight. Congress soon passed the McMahon Act, a nationalistic and supersecret approach to nuclear technology, which established the Atomic Energy Commission but also broke up our wartime cooperation with the British and Canadians in the development of the atomic bomb. Other winds blowing around the Baruch proposals helped sink it.

It was a great tragedy that the community of nations was unable to reach agreement on this rare opportunity to stop the arms race before it began. But our problems with the Soviet Union never gave it a chance. Distrust on both sides was running at peak heights in the late 1940's.

Nevertheless, negotiations continued in the United Nations on conventional disarmament as called for by the UN Charter. But the nearly total American demobilization after V-J Day took much steam from this idea. By the summer of 1946 we didn't have a single division in our Army or group in our Air Force rated ready for combat. Soviet armies were largely intact. It was unreasonable to think they would reduce their forces when we had already disarmed unilaterally. American demobilization resulted from surging domestic opinion and the American people's insistence that we bring our boys home. There were no bargaining chips, no linkage of our troop withdrawals with Soviet reductions. In later years advocates of unilateral disarmament argued that if the United States began to disarm, the Soviets might follow suit. They forgot the American experience after V-J Day; we have already been through that drill.

Just before I took over at SPA, the Communist insurgency in Greece and Soviet pressure on Turkey moved center stage. Since the end of the war Communist guerrillas operating from sanctuaries in Albania, Yugoslavia, and Bulgaria had threatened to overrun Greece, and the Soviets had sought to detach Turkey's two easternmost provinces and incorporate them in the USSR.

The United States became involved with Greece and Turkey rather belatedly when on February 21, 1947, the first secretary of the British Embassy in Washington notified the State Department that his country no longer had the wherewithal to support Greece or Turkey. The British decision to abandon the eastern Mediterranean put the United States in a bind: We could either commit ourselves to the defense of those countries or watch the USSR become the dominant power throughout the region.

During the next three weeks discussions within the administration and between the administration and Congress were fast and furious. I took over as director of special political affairs on March 5, the day after the first draft of Truman's speech that contained what came to be known as the Truman Doctrine was circulated for comment within the administration. I saw the speech for the first time on March 6 and by the following day was convinced that the United States should take its case to the United Nations. I made my case to Secretary of State Marshall and others on March 8 but could not get more than a passing reference to the United Nations included in the final version of the speech.

Truman delivered his speech on March 12, and he pulled out all the stops to get Congress to commit aid to Greece and Turkey, using language that suggested the United States should help any country threatened by Communist aggression. This universalist language led to a misconception; I am certain that Truman didn't want to apply this "doctrine" worldwide or make the United States the "world's policeman." What he said was part of the rhetoric needed to get congressional support for Greek-Turkish aid. In fact, when the Marshall Plan went before Congress, Senator Arthur Vandenberg told us the only way to get money was to "scare the hell out of Congress." The Greek guerrillas came to our assistance by launching a major offensive when we were in deep trouble with Congress. They withdrew after several days, but that short offensive gave us the critical votes we needed.

Within the State Department there was a lot of debate over the wording in Truman's speech. We advised him on his drafts, but when a president wants to make a speech, he sits down with his own speech writers and writes the kind of speech that he wants. Often a president—particularly Harry Truman—doesn't give a damn about what State Department bureaucrats think about his speech. That was how Truman's so-called Point Four program of technical assistance was born. On the eve of his address, Truman decided to inject more jazz into the text and perk up the language. Someone in the White House, or perhaps Truman himself, came up with the idea of providing technical assistance to the developing countries, and this became the fourth point in his speech. After he delivered his talk, we in the State Department had to scurry around and find out what the dickens he was talking about and then put arms and legs on his idea. Truman wasn't the only president to do things that way; thirty years later President Ronald Reagan's Strategic Defense Initiative was born essentially the same way.

Even though the administration disagreed with my appeal that the

United Nations be involved in the Greek and Turkish situation, Congress, and particularly Senator Arthur Vandenberg, insisted on a UN role. Indeed, Vandenberg practically made UN participation a condition for his support of the Greek-Turkish aid bill. As head of SPA I was asked to work with Vandenberg to develop the wording for the bill, and we met almost daily during April to come up with the right formula. In May Congress passed the Greek-Turkish aid bill.

But the Greek insurgency raged on and continued to present a special problem for the United Nations. The UN Charter defines aggression as "armed attack," such as the invasions of Manchuria, Ethiopia, the Rhineland, Czechoslovakia, and Poland that launched World War II. But postwar aggression tended to be more covert and indirect, with fighting by smaller units using guerrilla-style tactics. Nevertheless, believing this indirect aggression also threatened world peace, we sought to close the theoretical gap between indirect—guerrilla—aggression and direct aggression by regular armies. We wanted both recognized as violations of international law and the UN Charter. U.S. insistence on this point finally bore fruit in October 1947, when, after the Security Council deadlocked, we took the Greek insurgency question to the General Assembly. After weeks of heated debate the General Assembly called upon Greece's northern neighbors to stop assisting the guerrillas and created a special committee to investigate the situation. The United States thus played an important secondary role by mobilizing world opinion against external support for the insurgency.

U.S. aid was instrumental in helping the Greek government hold on and even make headway against the Communist rebels. Even so, the conflict dragged on into 1949. The rebels continued to get help from outside Greece, with aid from Yugoslavia being particularly important; although Tito had broken with Moscow in 1948, he had not yet abandoned the Greek Communists.

So with the Greek crisis continuing, I attended a dinner in New York in April 1949 hosted by UN Secretary-General Trygve Lie and found myself sitting across the table from the Soviets' UN representative, Andrei Gromyko. During dinner I casually volunteered the hope that our two countries could put our heads together and resolve this wretched problem in Greece. Gromyko came up like a trout after a fly. He may have known that Tito intended to close the Yugoslav-Greek border, thereby undermining the Greek insurgency, and as a result sought to salvage whatever he could for the soon-to-be-deteriorating Communist position.

But neither I nor anyone else in the West knew that, so Gromyko,

Lie, and I excused ourselves from the party for a few minutes to discuss the matter further. Gromyko and I met again on May 4, and after Dean Acheson reported my contacts with Gromyko to President Truman the following day, I was instructed to continue my meetings and learn what I could without making any commitments.

Gromyko and I met again on May 14, and it was only through President Truman's wisdom of going slow that I succeeded in stubbing my toe just slightly. Tito soon closed the border, the Rusk-Gromyko talks faded into history, and we learned once again that "diplomatic breakthroughs" aren't always what they appeared to be.

The Berlin blockade of 1948 also absorbed my energies at the UN desk. Stalin imposed the blockade in June 1948 to force the British, French, and American allies out of Berlin by denying them land access to the city. The Western allies used a dramatic airlift to keep the people of West Berlin alive until we could find some way to lift the blockade. Forcing the blockade was not a real option because of our demobilization and lack of conventional forces. But the Allied airlift kept Berlin in essential supplies—coal, food, fuel. Our pilots did a brilliant job flying around the clock, often in terrible weather, at one point taking off and landing every thirty seconds or so.

In January 1949 Joseph Stalin gave a news interview in Moscow on the Berlin issue. When we put his remarks under a microscope in the State Department, we noticed that in stating the Russians' terms for lifting the blockade, he had made no reference to the currency question—the imbalance between the West German and East German marks—an issue he claimed led to the blockade. We asked Philip Jessup to contact Soviet Ambassador Yakov Malik at the United Nations to see if this omission of the currency question was significant. Jessup found Malik having a drink at the bar in the UN's delegates' lounge. He chatted with Malik and then remarked, "Oh, by the way, I noticed that Mr. Stalin made no reference to the currency question in his speech the other day. Is there any significance to that?" Malik said, "I don't know, but I'll find out." About ten days later Malik came up alongside Jessup at the bar, where Jessup had stopped off for a drink, and said, "You asked me whether there was any significance to the omission of the currency question in Mr. Stalin's speech on Berlin. I can tell you that the answer is yes." Jessup said, "That's very interesting. What was the significance?" And Malik said, "I don't know, but I'll find out."

When Jessup reported that response from Malik, the wheels in Washington went into high gear. We gave great attention to how the blockade might be lifted. And then step by step, in the most public of all places, the delegates' lounge at the United Nations, Malik and Jessup conducted top secret talks that eventually led to the end of the Berlin blockade in May 1949. I think Stalin finally reached the point where he had extracted from the blockade all that he possibly could and found world opinion moving strongly against him. UN debate helped convince Stalin there was little to be gained in continuing the blockade.

In the fall of 1948, with the Allied airlift well under way, both the General Assembly and the Security Council met in Paris, and huge crowds attended many sessions. The meetings focused on the Berlin crisis. Philip Jessup was our principal spokesman at the council, and during one debate his lovely wife, Lois, was sitting in the audience. While Jessup was speaking, she began to knit. A French usher came down the aisle, looked very sternly at her, and said, "You must not knit! It is disrespectful to the speaker." She said, "The speaker is my husband." He straightened up and went back up the aisle. A few moments later he came down the aisle and said, "You are to knit."

Jessup was usually accompanied by our permanent UN representative, Warren Austin. On one occasion Jessup had pneumonia and Austin became ill, leaving me the senior American on the scene. We took Jessup to a leading French hospital in Paris, and the staff began treating his pneumonia with leeches—this in 1948! We got him out of there and sent him to a U.S. military hospital in Germany. With Secretary Marshall in Washington, and Austin and Jessup out of commission, we were temporarily stripped of representation. No one was qualified to represent the United States in the Security Council because only Austin and Jessup had been approved by the U.S. Senate. I asked Soviet representative Andrei Gromyko for a postponement, explaining that both of our authorized delegates were unavailable. He said, "Ah, yes. You have two delegates . . . so they can watch each other." That may have been the practice for the Soviets, but the idea was rather novel for us Americans.

As head of the State Department's UN desk I was also deeply involved in what was then called the Palestine question. Under the old League of Nations, Palestine was a mandated territory with Great Britain as the mandatory power. The end of World War II saw a sharp upsurge in demands for a Jewish homeland in Palestine. Those insisting upon such a homeland reminded the British of the Balfour Declaration issued during World War I, which promised the Jews a homeland in Palestine. By the late forties those promises had faded. The British were reluctant to move toward a Jewish homeland, possibly because of their important relationship with the oil-rich Arab countries.

President Truman, partly because the Holocaust made a deep impression upon him and partly because of domestic politics, sided with American Zionists, who were pressing hard for a Jewish state. But Truman wasn't alone in his pro-Jewish sympathies. When American and Russian soldiers finally occupied Nazi concentration camps and the carnage of the Holocaust became known, a wave of horror swept through the world community. Not only Jews but what the Nazis called the "inferior races"—the Poles, Russians, other Slavic peoples—had been slaughtered in the death camps. The Holocaust had a profound effect upon the American people. Public reaction went far beyond the Jewish community. Yet it had occurred against the background of persistent Jewish persecution in many countries over many centuries, including the United States. After the war many felt that the Jewish people ought to have their own homeland, invulnerable to state-supported persecution. Other locations for a Jewish state were discussed, but the Jews were utterly committed to a state in Palestine, their historic homeland.

With Jewish refugees by the hundreds of thousands emerging from a war-shattered Europe, President Truman pressured the British to make good on the Balfour Declaration and to permit large-scale immigration of Jewish refugees into Palestine. But the British, irritated by Truman and also worn out with overseeing a territory seething with religious conflict, resisted and in April 1947 tossed the problem into the lap of the United Nations, announcing that Britain would terminate its mandatory responsibilities on May 15, 1948, and withdraw from Palestine. The British also stated that they would accept any solution agreeable to both Jews and Arabs in the interim, a comfortable position in theory but without realism in the Middle East.

When the matter went to the United Nations, I became intimately involved with deliberations in the General Assembly, in the UN Commission on Palestine, and within the American government. The UN Committee of Inquiry finally recommended a plan calling for the partition of Palestine into separate Jewish and Arab states. It sparked a heated debate in the General Assembly, the most intense and emotional exchange I have seen in forty years of public life.

The United Nations finally adopted the partition plan, and President Truman decided to support it even though some American Zionists opposed it; they wanted more territory and better security arrangements for Israel. Others, including myself and many of my State Department colleagues, were skeptical of the partition plan. We thought that a binational state consisting of both Arabs and Jews had a better chance of surviving peacefully than separate Jewish and Arab states confronting each other within the small area of Palestine. If partition led to war between Arabs and Jews, the United States might be compelled to intervene militarily to insure Israel's survival, pitting us against the entire Arab world. The British agreed. But nevertheless, the partition plan seemed to offer a homeland for the Jews and an Arab state as well, both within Palestine, and when President Truman decided to support partition, I worked hard to implement it.

A special session of the General Assembly was called to consider the partition plan. Approaching the final vote, the American delegation counted noses, found that we were short of the two-thirds necessary to adopt partition, and estimated that if the Arab side made a simple motion to adjourn, by majority vote it could adjourn the Assembly without a decision. When Hussein Chamoun, the Arab floor leader who later became president of Lebanon, went to the podium and moved to adjourn, we muttered, "Oh, boy! Now we have had it!" But to our amazement, he added a second paragraph to his motion, to establish a new committee on the matter. That translated his motion for adjournment into a substantive question requiring a two-thirds majority, and he didn't have the votes. It was thus pure luck that we defeated his motion to adjourn.

Several weeks later we then passed the partition resolution by a vote of 33 to 13 with ten abstentions. The pressure and arm-twisting applied by American and Jewish representatives in capital after capital to get that affirmative vote are hard to describe.

Dorothy Fosdick, our liaison to the European delegations, assured us that her delegates would be on the floor when the partition vote was taken. When one European foreign minister started to walk out of the hall, she scurried up to him and said, "You cannot leave now. The vote is coming in just a few minutes." He said, "I'll be back in a moment." She said, "No, no, no, no. You must not leave. The vote could come at any moment." He said, "All right," and went back to his seat. After the vote was taken, he approached Dorothy and said, "Now, Miss Fosdick, may I go to the men's room?"

As the date for the British withdrawal drew nearer, it appeared that neither the Arabs nor the Jews would accept the partition plan. With so much resistance to partition, the withdrawal of British soldiers would surely lead to wholesale fighting in Palestine; consequently, we tried to buy more time so we could arrange a political and military standstill while we worked toward an agreement. At one point we changed our position and proposed a United Nations trusteeship for Palestine in which the United States would take over until the Arabs and Jews could work out their own solution. A U.S. peacekeeping force would keep order during the transition.

When our UN ambassador, Warren Austin, presented this idea to the Security Council on March 19, 1948, it exploded like a bomb and raised hell with the Zionists. President Truman, Secretary of State Marshall, and Undersecretary of State Robert Lovett were all out of town, and I was the hapless official who met with the press to represent the administration. The atmosphere was so thick you could cut it with a knife. I have never seen such an emotionally charged press conference. Many interpreted our latest gambit as an American repudiation of the partition plan. It eventually led to a break between us and the Soviet Union over Palestine because the Soviets had strongly supported the creation of a Jewish state in Palestine.

The White House was especially disturbed. With the Jewish lobby in complete outrage over this move toward trusteeship, President Truman's legal counsel, Clark Clifford, called Charles "Chip" Bohlen, the senior State Department officer in town, and told him to come to the White House and to bring me with him. Clifford was in a high dudgeon. It sounded like an invitation to a necktie party. During the conversation Bohlen pulled out of his folder the original green telegram sent to our delegation in New York, setting the framework by which the trusteeship plan would be aired. On that original telegram was the notation "Approved by the President. George C. Marshall." That took the wind out of Clark Clifford's sails, and he calmed down rather quickly.

President Truman may not have fully understood what he was approving, or for political reasons he may have tried to disclaim responsibility. Truman was, in fact, a little schizophrenic about Israel. Deeply troubled by the Holocaust, aware that practically every nation, including the United States, had anti-Jewish prejudice, he strongly favored a homeland for the Jewish people in Palestine, where such a tragedy could not reoccur. At the same time he agreed with Marshall that we needed a solution in the Middle East with which both sides could live, which would prevent a succession of wars between Arabs and Jews. In trying to implement his twin objectives, Truman sometimes issued contradictory instructions. That in turn contributed to feuding between the White House staff and the State Department.

I understood Truman's dilemma perfectly because I shared his schizophrenia about Israel. The Palestine question was not only emotional dynamite but baffling, ridden with contradiction. But the contradictions in American policy stemmed from the conflicting objectives in Truman's own mind, not through any deviousness by the State Department. This wasn't understood at the time. With Marshall and State working toward a long-range solution, the Zionists branded anyone not 1,000 percent behind the Zionist cause as having betrayed the president.

I was in George Marshall's office once when a delegation of Jewish leaders came to lobby Marshall on partition. Marshall sat quietly as they pressed their case, even threatening Marshall and the president with hardball tactics in the upcoming elections. Marshall had his fill, pressed a button on his squawk box, called the State Department press office, and invited any reporters present up to his office. He then told the Jewish leaders, "When the reporters get here, I want you to tell them exactly what you've told me." They quieted down and left.

Jewish pressure to the contrary, George Marshall also thought we should try the trusteeship plan and carried his recommendation to the president. Truman still favored partition but wanted to avoid war if at all possible. He agreed to support a trusteeship if partition could not be implemented. We thought we had Truman's approval for a trusteeship, and we prepared to announce it at the UN, but there must have been a misunderstanding between Marshall and Truman.

Clearly the Jewish community had its own pipeline to the White House, through White House aide David Niles and Clark Clifford and others. Not only were these back channels aggravating, but they sometimes undermined the instructions Truman gave Marshall. For example, during the September 1948 UN conference in Paris, I got a call from the code room of the American Embassy about three o'clock in the morning, telling me that an urgent "eyes only" message to Secretary Marshall from President Truman had arrived. I got dressed and walked across the street to the embassy, and sure enough, it was urgent and called for an immediate reply. So I drafted a proposed reply for Marshall, then woke him up in his apartment a half hour later. He read the incoming message, made one or two changes in my reply, and sent me back to the code room. I got finished by 5:30 or 6:00 A.M., walked into a café near the Eiffel Tower to have some breakfast, and ran into a Jewish reporter, who started asking me about the telegram Marshall had received three hours earlier. Clearly somebody in the White House had told his Jewish contacts about this telegram, and they in turn had telephoned their people in Paris. And this was an "eyes only" exchange between President Truman and Secretary Marshall!

Policy deliberations about Palestine had been tense and emotional within our own delegation in Paris as well. George Marshall left Paris early for health reasons and returned to Washington, leaving John Foster Dulles in charge. On one occasion Marshall set up a late-night teleconference with the delegation, including Dulles, Eleanor Roosevelt, General John Hilldring, and myself. It was a largely pro-Zionist group, and discussion ranged back and forth on the teletype. Then came a sentence from Marshall: "I want to know what Dean Rusk thinks."

As chief of staff I was not a formal member of the American delegation, so Marshall's query irritated some of the others to begin with. But when I made known my more moderate views, that made me about as welcome in that group as a skunk at a tea party.

Try as we might, we could not persuade the British to stay in Palestine past their self-imposed May 15 deadline. Having already been burned by the sudden British withdrawal from Greece and having to scramble to improvise a hasty Greek-Turkish aid program, we were displeased that the British would simply leave. But they were being subjected to political harassment and vicious acts of terrorism against British soldiers in Palestine by Jewish extremists, so they had simply had it with Palestine.

I personally witnessed a critical incident regarding the British withdrawal that happened a few weeks prior to the expiration of the British mandate. I was standing in the delegates' lounge at the United Nations talking with Creech-Jones, the British colonial minister, and Moshe Sharett, a Zionist leader who later became prime minister of Israel. At one point Creech-Jones said to Sharett, "We know you are going to have your Jewish state in Palestine." To my amazement, he added that the Arab Legion, Jordan's topnotch fighting force, organized by both the British and Jordanians, would move, but only into those areas designated as the Arab state of Palestine. This was an extraordinarily important piece of information for Sharett. The Arab Legion, at that moment still under British command, was the only effective military force in the Arab world that could have opposed the Zionists. Sharett immediately took off for Palestine, and I have no doubt that Creech-Jones's tip encouraged Israel to declare a provisional government at the moment the British mandate expired.

All the while the United States was wrestling behind the scenes to find a possible solution in the Middle East after the partition resolution passed in the General Assembly and after it had become clear that the Arabs would strongly oppose it. Just before expiration of the British mandate, President Truman and Secretary Marshall asked me to undertake private and discreet negotiations between the Arabs and the Zionists. Both men hoped we could at least get them to agree to a political and military standstill on May 15. We met at the old Savoy-Plaza Hotel in New York, with the Arab delegation at one end of the hall and the

Zionists at the other. From my suite halfway between, I shuttled back and forth between these two groups, trying to work out major points of contention. We made good progress except for deciding the rate of Jewish immigration into Palestine during the standstill. The Arabs strongly opposed any Jewish immigration. We finally got the Zionists to agree to not more than twenty-five hundred immigrants a month, a considerable concession under the circumstances. Feeling somewhat confident, I walked to the other end of the hall and put this figure to Prince Faisal of Saudi Arabia, who was acting head of the Arab delegation. He heard me out and said, "Impossible! Impossible! If we agree to twenty-five hundred, the Jews will simply bring in twenty-five hundred pregnant women, and that will mean five thousand!"

At that stage in the negotiations Secretary Marshall through a slip of the tongue tipped off some Washington reporters about these talks. When this happened, the talks collapsed. Both Arab and Jewish constituencies of these leaders could not accept the fact that talks were even occurring.

Matters deteriorated even further. Our delegation continued trying to find something. We now wanted a UN resolution appointing a mediator, if nothing else, to help prevent war. The British mandate was to expire at 6:00 P.M., May 14, New York time. About a quarter to 6:00 I was in my office in the State Department, and my phone rang; it was Clark Clifford at the White House. Clifford said, "The president wants you to know that a Jewish state will be declared at six o'clock and that the United States will recognize it immediately."

I said, "But, Clark, that would cut right across a standstill—what our delegation has been working for in New York for weeks—for which we already have forty votes."

He said, "Nevertheless, these are the president's instructions. He wants you to call our delegation in New York and inform them."

So I called Warren Austin, our chief delegate to the UN, off the floor of the General Assembly and told him what was about to happen. Warren apparently just said, "The hell with it," and went home. He didn't even go back to the assembly and tell the rest of our delegation.

About five minutes past six a delegate came rushing down the aisle screaming, waving an Associated Press ticker tape release at the podium and read the news: The provisional government of Israel had just been declared and the United States had given it immediate recognition. On finishing, he called on the U.S. delegation for an explanation. Sitting in our delegation at that moment were Francis Sayre and Philip Jessup. Jessup immediately left the assembly to find out what was going on.

Sayre, a lovely older man but not exceptionally quick on his feet, went to the platform, scratched his head, and said in effect, "Damned if I know." Jessup got hold of Washington, learned that this press ticker tape was indeed true, went back to the podium, and confirmed the report.

Pandemonium broke loose in the General Assembly. There was complete and utter turmoil—almost as if a bomb had gone off. Delegates were shouting at each other, and an American staff officer physically sat in the lap of a Cuban delegate to keep him from going to the podium and withdrawing Cuba from the United Nations.

About fifteen minutes past six the squawk box on my desk buzzed. It was George Marshall. He said, "Rusk, go to New York immediately and keep our delegation from resigning en masse." So I hopped on the first plane I could get and flew to New York. By the time I arrived, our people had begun to cool off. No mass resignations ensued—in fact, the mediation resolution was adopted—but it was a very tumultuous scene.

Warren Austin's decision to go home rather than return to the General Assembly was premeditated. He had decided that it was better for the American delegation to be caught completely by surprise. The other delegates had to believe that recognition was a presidential decision and that our delegation had not been hoodwinking them in recent weeks. Earlier Austin had made history at the United Nations by asking both the Arabs and the Jews to "settle their differences in a Christian spirit." But he made the right decision on May 14; the astonished reaction of our own delegation made it clear that Harry Truman's recognition of Israel had caught even the Americans by surprise.

George Marshall was among those caught off guard. Truman had pulled the rug out from under him. Some of Marshall's friends told him that he ought to resign. He said, "No, gentlemen. You do not take a post of this sort and then resign when the man who has the constitutional responsibility for making a decision makes one. You can resign at any other time for any other reason, or for no reason at all, but not that one." But Marshall reportedly told Harry Truman, face-to-face, that he wouldn't vote for him in the next election; this was one hell of a way to run a railroad.

My involvement with Palestine did not cease with American recognition of Israel. After Truman's decision we now went to work trying to obtain a cease-fire, encouraging other governments to extend recognition. Many did rather promptly, including the Soviet Union. Both we and the Soviets supported the creation of Israel, a rare instance when we were on the same side. For that reason, we didn't have to worry about conflict in Palestine escalating into full-scale war between the superpowers. Only later did the Soviets realize that since the Arabs held the United States directly responsible for the creation of Israel, if they swung to the Arab side, they would increase their influence in the Arab world. That has been their position ever since.

In retrospect, a workable solution for Palestine may not have been possible. Our attempted negotiations for a UN trusteeship were torpedoed by the creation of Israel and American recognition. Had this not happened, a UN trusteeship for Palestine under those circumstances would have required a substantial budget, and the United States would have had to pick up most of the tab, perhaps several hundred million dollars annually. It also would have required a security force, likely involving American troops. The Soviets opposed trusteeship, as did powerful groups in this country. Very few countries wanted to contribute to a trusteeship force, and the possibilities for getting this plan adopted by the United Nations were almost zero. Our last-minute negotiations were simply a desperate and futile effort to buy time.

Conflict became inevitable when the Arabs decided not to accept the partition plan. As was predicted, they took up arms to prevent the state of Israel from coming into being. Ironically, many years later the Arabs began to insist upon an Arab state in Palestine. They could have had their Arab state if they had accepted the United Nations partition resolution of 1947. But in 1948 they went to war to oppose partition. The Jews fought with great valor, finally driving hostile Arab forces out of Israeli territory. That created enormous numbers of Palestinian refugees, a problem for which the United States and the world have paid dearly ever since.

We in the American delegation and others had scoured the underbrush for every possible solution. But I think the actual creation of a Jewish state in Palestine, at the expense of Arab peoples who had lived there for centuries, was something the Arab world simply couldn't take. On November 29, 1947, the day the partition resolution passed, Prince Faisal of Saudia Arabia, later to become king, took the podium on behalf of the entire Arab world. He stood there erect and tall, a man whose honor had been insulted and his pride wounded, and he spoke with passion and clarity about this great injury that had been done to the Arab people. I have never forgotten his talk. It is not easy for Americans, living halfway around the world with an entirely different culture and historical tradition, to understand what the creation of a Jewish state in Palestine meant to Arabs who had shared that same land for centuries.

Prince Faisal said that with the creation of Israel, the Arabs were being forced to pay for the crimes of Adolf Hitler. He held the United States responsible. Those deep-seated feelings have persisted ever since. There likely would never have been a state of Israel had it not been for American support.

Relations between Israel and its Arab neighbors have been the most intractable, unyielding problem of the postwar period. I personally bear many scars from it, as have every American president and secretary of state since 1948 and many of my colleagues in the State Department. We were part of a delegation trying to carry out President Truman's instructions, but when we didn't go 1,000 percent for the Zionists, they heaped abuse on us all, especially the Middle East desk and its director, Loy Henderson. They claimed Loy and other Middle East hands were hostile to Jewish interests and an insidious element in the bowels of the State Department. Their criticism was unjust; what we wanted was simply a plan that both Jews and Arabs could live with, one that would not produce what has, in fact, happened: an almost permanent alienation between the United States and many Arabs.

We were looking for any plan that would work. If the Jews and the Arabs had come up with one, we would have bought it hook, line, and sinker.

As Loy Henderson predicted, the world has witnessed more than forty years of unceasing turmoil in the Middle East and unrelenting hostility between the United States and much of the Arab world. And the 1948 conflict was followed by additional wars in 1956, 1967, 1973, and 1982. If I were responsible for Middle East policy today, I would approach it exactly as I did in the forties and later in the sixties: on my knees in prayer.

9

Crisis
in the Far East:
The Korean War

In February 1949, after two years on the United Nations desk, I was named deputy undersecretary of state by Dean Acheson, who had replaced George Marshall as secretary of state. In this job I advised both Acheson and Undersecretary of State James Webb on policy issues, served as chief liaison officer between the State and Defense Departments, and helped coordinate the geographical and functional offices of the State Department.

Whenever my superiors were out of town, I also had to brief President Truman and represent the State Department at White House meetings. Both in this job and when I was later appointed assistant secretary of state for Far Eastern affairs at a time when Asia was in tremendous turmoil, Acheson often took me to the White House, and thus I got to know Harry Truman personally. He was an impressive man. An avid reader, he knew more about his predecessors and the traditions of the presidency than anyone I ever met. Truman told me that James Polk was his favorite president because Polk regularly told Congress to go to hell on foreign policy matters.

Truman's dry wit amused us all. Once I represented the State Department at a cabinet meeting when Vice President Alben Barkley walked in late. Barkley took his seat across the table from the president and said, "Mr. President, I am sorry to be late, but I was detained in the Senate. How are you today?"

With a wicked gleam in his eye, Truman said, "I am sorry to tell you, Mr. Vice President, that I feel just fine."

On another occasion Truman received a long and unpleasant letter from Indian Prime Minister Jawaharlal Nehru. Angry about the letter, he asked me to write a reply. When I took my draft reply and copy of Nehru's letter to the White House, Truman pulled out his own copy. I saw that he had scribbled in the margins of the original such scathing remarks as "What does he want me to do, consult Mousie Dung?" We went over the draft, and he made a number of changes. As I was leaving, he said, "Dean, is there anything else I can do for you?"

In jest I said, "You can give me your original copy of Nehru's letter."

He laughed and said, "No, I won't do that. But if you send me over your copy, I will put these same notes on it."

If his scribblings had become public, all hell would have broken loose, so I just ignored his suggestion. Ten days later I got a note from Truman saying, "Damn it, Dean. I told you to send over your copy of Nehru's letter!" So I did, and he inserted his comments and sent it back to me with a little note saying, "I want you to have this as a mimento"—misspelling "memento." Considering the hot character of that letter, for many years I paid for a safe-deposit box in which to keep it. But that little incident was entirely characteristic of Harry Truman.

One of Truman's most notable attributes was his facility for making decisions. Almost all the problems that reach a president are extremely complex, but Truman had the ability to go to the heart of a problem directly. Any tough foreign policy issue typically has dozens of secondary and tertiary questions all mixed together like a heap of jackstraws, cutting across and interfering with each other. Truman would listen to a briefing, absorb the complexities involved in the problem, and then draw back and contemplate the heap of jackstraws to decide which element in the problem was decisive. He would pick that jackstraw out of the pile, make his decision, go home and get a good night's sleep, and never look back.

Truman's ability to oversimplify a problem at the moment of decision is a trait not all decision makers have. For example, although I enthusiastically supported Adlai Stevenson's candidacies in 1952 and 1956, I wondered what kind of president he would have made. Stevenson was so intelligent and imaginative that he could always see the disadvantages of any line of action, and thus, he had difficulty reaching a conclusion. He used to complain about getting so many instructions from the State Department while UN ambassador, but I never saw anyone happier to get them.

I saw Truman operate this way—reducing complex issues to their simplest level—a number of times, but most impressively when he asked me in 1951 to head the U.S. delegation that negotiated the Administrative Agreement with Japan. That agreement dealt with the stationing of American forces in Japan after the signing of the Japanese Peace Treaty, and the bureaucracy had built up a foot-high stack of papers on everything that should go into that agreement. We went to the White House and briefed Truman on it, but after dismissing us, he called me into the Oval Office and said, "Now, Dean, don't worry about all this crap. I want you to go over there and get an agreement like the NATO agreement, one that does not discriminate for the Japanese nor discriminate against the Japanese. Those are your instructions. Go over there and get a fair agreement." So I went to Japan as head of our delegation. During the negotiations my own staff didn't always realize what I was doing, when I insisted upon a few points and gave away so many others.

Having lived long enough to become a connoisseur of American presidents, I think of Harry Truman as a great president. This little man from Independence, Missouri, had a deep confidence in the grass roots of the American people. He really did believe that the American people, at their best, are a very good people and would do what had to be done. He called upon them during the postwar years, and they responded.

There was only one matter on which I faulted Truman. He did not use the authority of his office to fight the almost total demobilization of the United States after World War II, for which we paid a terrible price. I firmly believe the American demobilization tempted Joseph Stalin to embark upon that series of adventures which started the Cold War. I was among those who expressed misgivings about this calamitous reduction of forces, but one might as well have spit in the ocean for all the good it would do. In 1945 American troops rioted in the Philippines because they wanted to get home earlier than the timetable allowed. American authorities once allotted one seat for an Indian diplomat on a military plane flying from India to Washington, and this sparked a strong reaction from congressmen who wanted that seat filled by a returning American soldier. "Bring the boys home, whatever the cost," yet strong presidential leadership might have made some difference.

I spent most of my years as deputy undersecretary of state working on Far Eastern affairs. Most of us saw Chiang Kai-shek's fall in China coming, but we were still disappointed when it happened. I saw it as a great tragedy—that the Chinese people, with their tremendous energy and potential, were now wedded to Communist ideology and allied with the Soviet Union, with which we were already having all sorts of trouble. If China were to act aggressively, clearly there would be major trouble ahead.

There was never any serious discussion of landing American forces on the mainland to support the Nationalists. The American demobilization following World War II removed that as a meaningful choice. Those of us with experience in Asia knew that even a substantial remobilization of our armed forces could do no more than hold a few port cities and have no appreciable effect upon those hundreds of millions of Chinese inland. Because of the attrition of Chinese capabilities from fifteen years of fighting the Japanese and the ineffectiveness of the Kuomintang, I do not see what the United States could have done to prevent the Chinese Communists from taking control of the mainland. For years the Truman administration sent substantial military and economic aid to the Nationalists, but to no avail. Although I had long supported sending American assistance, once it became clear that the "mandate of heaven" had passed to the Communists, I lost interest in last-minute efforts to increase this aid. I agreed with Dean Acheson that more American aid would only prolong the inevitable. If anything, Chiang Kai-shek's inability to govern and the impact of Japanese aggression, not American inaction, "lost" China.

When the Communists prevailed in 1949, their leadership targeted the United States as "public enemy number one" and tried to erase from memory all traces of more than a century of goodwill and friendly relations between the American and Chinese peoples. They even arrested and beat up Foreign Service officers in our Mukden, Manchuria, consulate, including Consul General Angus Ward. They tried to indoctrinate the Chinese people with hostility toward schools and hospitals the United States had built in China, and they denigrated other evidences of American friendship for China as well. They charged that the purpose of the Peking Union Medical College, that fine medical center built by the Rockefeller Foundation, was to allow "wicked" American doctors to practice vivisection on the Chinese. In many ways Mao Zedong's government made it clear that the United States was "public enemy number one."

In the aftermath of global war the idea that our Chinese allies had turned against us was a bitter pill for many Americans. Beginning with my own boyhood, I can remember a warm and benevolent attitude on the part of the American people toward the Chinese. We studied about China in the Lee Street School, and our church in West End maintained a missionary in China. As small boys, when playing in our backyard, we talked about digging a hole, and we knew that if we dug that hole deep enough, we would see some Chinese peering at us from the other end! There was a Chinese hand laundry two blocks away. Atlanta had special stores which sold foods, textiles, arts and crafts of China. When we were children, China was very much in our thoughts, and Americans in general were interested in that part of the world. We took some satisfaction that the United States had somehow opposed the attempts by wicked colonial powers to carve up China into spheres of influence. Our attitude was undoubtedly somewhat patronizing and involved much ignorance. We were sending missionaries to convert the heathen and teach an illiterate people to read. Nevertheless, we had a friendly attitude toward China.

As a result, our reaction to the fall of China in 1949 was that of a jilted lover. "The Chinese people have turned against us," we told ourselves. "They've become bitter and are now our enemies. How could this have happened?" This turnabout provided much of the fuel for that evil chapter in our history called McCarthyism.

After Mao succeeded on the mainland, we flirted with the idea of recognizing Communist China. We even suspended military assistance to Chiang for a time. But our prevailing attitude was, Let's wait and see how the new Chinese Communist government acts before we grant recognition. Our close ally Great Britain felt differently about the situation, Britain's ambassador in Washington, Oliver Franks, told me, and intended to face the reality of Communist rule in China by recognizing Mao's government. We both expressed regret that Washington and London would diverge on so important a matter. But then we speculated privately that our policies would come together, depending upon the behavior of Peking. If China entered the world community and acted reasonably in foreign affairs, American policy would move toward Britain's. But if China acted aggressively, Britain might move toward the United States and break relations with China.

Personally, I held no brook with those Americans who thought that the United States "lost" China; China was never ours to win or lose, but rather, Chiang Kai-shek's. The Department of State's White Paper on China, released in late 1949, made this clear. I had nothing to do with writing the paper, but I argued strongly for its public release. The historical office did an honest job, but it was unpalatable to those backing Taiwan. The Eisenhower administration later decided to write its own White Paper, hoping to "tell the truth" about the loss of China in a way that reflected poorly on the Democrats. But its paper so closely resembled ours that it never published it. The facts were simply against any such redefinition of the truth.

Nevertheless, the debate over the "loss" of China created deep divisions at home and provided at least some of the impetus for Senator Joseph McCarthy's vicious and unfounded attacks on Dean Acheson and the State Department. Alger Hiss's conviction for perjury hurt as well. Many first-rate Foreign Service officers had their careers tarnished and even destroyed by McCarthyism, for allegedly being sympathetic to the Communist cause. I worked with John Service and John Paton Davies when they were General Stilwell's political advisers in CBI, and I knew O. Edmund Clubb and many of the China hands. They were fine Foreign Service officers, entirely loyal to the United States, and their reports about China have stood history's test well. The attacks against them were wholly irresponsible. I testified in Service's loyalty hearing, and Davies as well, but to no avail. Davies could have cleared himself had he made public secret documents that would have exonerated him, but he refused to do so. Had Joseph Stilwell still been alive, his testimony surely would have cleared both men.

In any event, it was exceptionally cruel for partisan opponents of the administration to attack career Foreign Service officers when the responsibility for policy lay with their superiors. McCarthy should have gone after Harry Truman, not subordinates carrying out his instructions and policies.

Unfortunately Dean Acheson himself helped draw McCarthy's attacks against the State Department with his famous "I will not turn my back on Alger Hiss" remark in a January 1950 press conference. I helped brief Acheson for that press conference, and we all advised him that since the Hiss case was in court, he shouldn't comment on it. He seemed to accept that advice but apparently changed his mind on the elevator ride down to the press meeting. Within days McCarthy gave his infamous speech in Wheeling, West Virginia, alleging he had a list of names of fifty-three Communist agents in the State Department.

Not all the victims of the McCarthy investigations would have wound up as ambassadors to the Court of St. James's had their careers not been tarnished. Some had limited ability and would not have risen to the top of the Foreign Service under any circumstances, but this doesn't make McCarthyism any less odious or tragic, nor does it mean that Foreign Service officers became afraid to report candidly their views about policy. I did not find that to be the case. Those who rose to the top of the Foreign Service throughout this period expressed themselves freely and forcibly, whether or not their views meshed with existing policy. While the careers of some very able men were tarnished or ruined, the claim that McCarthyism stifled the Foreign Service has been exaggerated. Men like Llewellyn Thompson, Charles Bohlen, James Riddleberger, and U. Alexis Johnson never pulled their punches.

Curiously, McCarthy never laid a glove on me. I was heavily involved with China policy and could have become a target of his slander; in fact, a member of McCarthy's staff told me that they had tried hard to find something on me. But I think I escaped because of a combination of John Foster Dulles and blind luck. Once Foster Dulles hinted to me that some Republican senators had gone to McCarthy and told him to leave me alone. I had the impression that Dulles himself had warned off McCarthy.

If Dulles intervened successfully on my behalf, unfortunately he made no attempt either then or later as Eisenhower's secretary of state to defend John Paton Davies, John Service, Owen Lattimore, and others. In Dulles's defense, he didn't know them personally and had never worked with them. But many Republicans made the most of McCarthy's allegations for political reasons.

More than Dulles's possible intervention might have deflected McCarthy from me. In my dealings with senators, I tried to approach them on a bipartisan basis. I also had many friends on the Republican side, including Alexander Smith of New Jersey, Burke Hickenlooper of Iowa, and George Aiken of Vermont. I knew William Knowland when he was a memeber of the California legislature; at Mills we used to invite him to our foreign policy forums. I also called on senators individually in their offices and invited them to the State Department for dinners with distinguished foreign visitors and other official functions. While head of United Nations Affairs, I came to know the senators who served on our UN delegation. All these experiences and prior associations undoubtedly worked to my advantage during the McCarthy era.

One victim of McCarthy's attacks was Walton Butterworth, an able and patriotic assistant secretary of state for Far Eastern affairs. In March 1950, with this position open, since I thought that ongoing events in China and the Far East were extremely important, and since I'd had experience in the region and had not been tarred by McCarthy, I told Acheson that I was willing to take on FE if he wanted me to. A beleaguered Dean Acheson accepted my offer, gratefully, I think, but he never kissed me on both cheeks as he once claimed. In fact, I don't remember Dean Acheson kissing anyone on both cheeks.

My offer to change jobs amounted to a voluntary demotion, but I really thought that the policy issues involved were critically important to the United States and that in some small way, I might be able to help. Two other important personnel changes took place that spring of 1950. At my urging, we brought John Foster Dulles back as a special adviser to help build a bipartisan Asian policy, and we appointed Philip Jessup as ambassador-at-large to help on questions involving Asia.

I had strongly recommended Foster Dulles to Acheson, and when Acheson in turn passed his name to Truman, some squirt in the White House said, "Mr. President, you can't bring Foster Dulles into your administration. Look at that mean, dirty campaign he ran against Senator Herbert Lehman in New York." Truman laughed and said, "Look! You fellows don't understand politics. Of course, John Foster Dulles is going to take time out every two years to be a Republican, but between elections we want to work with him if he's willing to work with us."

I had headed the Far Eastern desk for only a few months when the Korean War broke out. On Saturday evening, June 24, 1950, Virginia and I were having dinner at Joseph Alsop's house in Washington when I received a message from the State Department that the North Koreans had invaded South Korea. Secretary of the Army Frank Pace and I left the dinner and went to our offices, leaving Alsop, our wives, and dinner guest Justice Felix Frankfurter speculating wildly about what was going on. My wife told me afterward that our journalist friend Alsop could hardly contain himself. Our ambassador in Korea, John Muccio, rendered a great service by accurately assessing the nature of the attack and immediately informing Washington. He told us from day one that the North Koreans sought to overrun South Korea when others, including MacArthur in Japan, thought it was just another border incident.

The North Korean invasion came as a complete surprise. Only four days before, I had told a congressional committee we saw no evidence of war brewing in Korea. After the attack occurred, some of our intelligence people, already bitten by Pearl Harbor, thumbed back through thousands of tidbits of information and found maybe six or seven items that seemed to point toward the invasion. They wanted to be able to say, "We warned you." That was just damn nonsense. President Truman was in Independence, Missouri, at the time and Acheson was on his farm in Virginia. And no one called my office to say, "The North Koreans are about to attack South Korea."

In any event, after reading Muccio's telegram, we immediately notified Dean Acheson, and he notified the president. We were totally preoccupied with the question, Should the United States intervene with its armed forces? I suggested to Acheson that we call an emergency meeting of the UN Security Council, believing we were obliged with any situation involving the use of force to take it first to the UN. Acheson agreed and persuaded Harry Truman. That night we woke Ernest Gross, our deputy representative on the Security Council, and he contacted Secretary-General Trygve Lie.

On Sunday and Monday I attended the meetings at Blair House with President Truman, Acheson, and the Joint Chiefs when Truman decided to intervene with American air power and naval forces and to send the Seventh Fleet into the Formosa Strait between Taiwan and the mainland and send ammunition and supplies to the South Koreans. On Friday Truman decided to land American forces. His decision was supported unanimously by his advisers. The North Korean attack seemed a direct challenge to the entire concept of collective security won at such cost during World War II. We didn't have a security treaty with Korea at that time, but South Korea had been our area of occupation, we had received the surrender of Japanese forces in South Korea, and we had occupied that area with our own forces for five years. Thus, we felt responsible for what happened in Korea and thought that our own national interests were involved in its defense.

At Blair House Truman at one point went around the table asking each person present for his views on whether or not we should intervene. He began with the junior officers present. I spoke briefly because Dean Acheson would speak for the State Department. But I reminded those present that we had a special responsibility for South Korea, that a South Korea absorbed by the Communists would be a dagger pointed at the heart of Japan, that a North Korean victory could destabilize U.S.-Japanese relations, and that it would be a serious matter for the first armed aggression following World War II to succeed. I concluded that the United States had to defend South Korea.

Militarily Truman had a difficult decision to make since the United States had demobilized after World War II and remained essentially demobilized in June 1950. Despite this, he decided to intervene, a decision I thought then and believe today was both wise and courageous. And gratifyingly, the American people and Congress supported him, at least at first. I was with Truman when he met at the White House with congressional leaders on Tuesday, three days after the attack, and they all supported him. They also agreed that the president should proceed on the basis of presidential authority, reinforced by resolutions from the United Nations Security Council, and shouldn't bother asking Congress for a resolution. Only Senator Robert Taft objected; he didn't attend the meeting, but he later said from the Senate floor, "I support what the president is doing, but I strongly object to his doing it without coming to Congress."

Truman's decision to send the U.S. Air Force to intercept North Korean armored units headed south didn't work. With a column of eighty North Korean tanks headed toward Seoul, one high-ranking Air Force officer told us, "Turn the Air Force loose and we'll stop those tanks." We turned them loose, and our planes got two or three of those tanks; the rest rolled into Seoul. MacArthur soon appreciated that we couldn't stop North Korean forces with air strikes and naval gunfire; we would have to land ground forces. On June 30, 1950, Truman authorized sending American troops to the Korean peninsula. We sent in troops who had been on occupation duty in Japan, who'd had almost no training and combat experience. We just flew these poor devils over there and sent them into combat.

Fortunately for the United States, when that handful of Americans turned up on the battlefield, the North Koreans halted for about ten days, presumably to consult with Pyongyang, Moscow, and perhaps Peking on what to do next. During that pause we reinforced our positions. Had the North Koreans kept coming, they would have driven us off the peninsula; we couldn't have landed sufficient forces to stop them.

Fortunately President Truman also decided to take the North Korean invasion to the United Nations, a decision I argued for and supported. The day after our Blair House meeting, at the administration's urging, the UN Security Council passed a resolution calling on both sides to stop fighting, and the following day it passed a vitally important resolution asking UN members to assist the Republic of Korea. At that time the Soviet Union was boycotting the Security Council, having withdrawn earlier in dispute over China's seat. To our surprise, the Soviet ambassador did not return to veto those resolutions, a tremendous oversight that allowed the UN flag to fly over the allied effort in Korea.

Many years later I asked a high-ranking Soviet official why their ambassador didn't return to the Security Council to veto the resolutions. He later told me that Joseph Stalin had personally telephoned his UN ambassador, Yakov Malik, telling him not to return to the Security Council. Apparently Stalin felt that the Chinese issue was more important than whatever might happen in the Security Council regarding Korea. He thought the United States would not react to the Korean attack and was surprised when we did.

Why did the North Koreans invade South Korea? Scholars have long debated that question, and many have focused on Dean Acheson's January 12, 1950, speech at the National Press Club in which Acheson discussed an American line of defense in the Pacific, which ran from the Aleutian Islands through Japan and into the Philippines. He failed to mention Korea or Taiwan. The day before, I helped prepare several drafts of that speech, and Acheson disliked them all. Finally he told us, "We have wasted enough time on this. I'll just go home and jot down some notes and go down there tomorrow and make a speech." True to form, Acheson spoke extemporaneously; we had no chance to flyspeck the language and consider what implications others might draw from the text. When Acheson talked about American defense interests in the Pacific, he referred to Japan, the Philippines, and other places where we had American forces. But then he added a comment that the defense of other areas would rest primarily upon the international community and the United Nations, which he said had *not* proven itself to be "a weak reed."

Acheson had justification for referring to the United Nations. Having helped resolve the Berlin blockade and the Azerbaijan crisis, the UN had not proven itself a weak reed at the time of his speech. During those years the United States and Western democracies had overwhelming voting majorities in the Security Council, and there was real hope the UN could play an effective role in resolving conflict. Unfortunately the Soviets and everyone else overlooked Acheson's UN reference. He didn't intend to brush aside everything beyond our so-called defense perimeter, but his remarks were nevertheless subject to misinterpretation. We at the department decided that issuing clarifiers after the speech would simply make matters worse. I advised Acheson to sit tight and let the matter blow over. But it didn't.

Whether or not the North Koreans invaded because they and the Soviets misinterpreted U.S. intentions remains an open question. An American businessman who dined with Soviet diplomat Andrei Vyshinsky sometime after the beginning of the war provided some evidence to support this contention. This businessman asked, "Mr. Vyshinsky, why do you think that the United States will attack the Soviet Union? You know very well that the American people don't want to attack your country."

Vyshinsky replied, "Well, we don't know what to think about you Americans. Look at Korea. You did everything you could to tell us you were not interested in Korea, and when the North Koreans went in there, you put your troops in." He added, "We can't trust you Americans."

The U.S. withdrawal of American troops from South Korea in 1949 also probably sent the wrong message to the Soviets and North Koreans, an action likely more significant than Acheson's speech. That withdrawal stemmed from a Joint Chiefs of Staff report in 1948 on the strategic significance of Korea. The chiefs concluded that in the event of general war, the United States would not want to put American forces on the Korean peninsula; therefore, we should withdraw such forces as we had in Korea. Unfortunately the chiefs did not address the question of what our response should be if Korea itself were attacked.

I strongly opposed this withdrawal. I am unsure of Dean Acheson's position; with his strong orientation toward the North Atlantic, he may not have been very interested in Korea. But because of cuts in our defense budget and the paucity of American forces in general, President Truman finally sided with the Pentagon and ordered our last regimental combat team out of Korea. We had begun to arm and train South Korean forces, but by June 1950—the time of the North Korean attack—regimental- and division-level training hadn't yet begun. The rout of the South Korean military provided ample proof of that.

Nor do I believe that only the North Koreans and the Soviets conspired in the attack. While the Soviets clearly supported the North Koreans politically and supplied arms and equipment as well as observers in the field, the Chinese may have helped plan the original attack as well. UN forces captured many thousands of North Korean prisoners during the fighting, and when they were questioned, some reported that for months before the launching of the North Korean attack, the Chinese had combed their armies in North China to find soldiers of Korean nationality or ancestry and had integrated them into North Korean units. That suggests to me that Peking was either a co-conspirator in or fully aware of the June 1950 attack.

Whatever led to the attack, Dean Acheson wanted a firsthand report on the situation in Korea, so some weeks after the attack he sent me to Pusan, where the North Koreans had compressed our forces into a tight perimeter. By the time I got there, some allied troops had arrived. The sense of solidarity among our forces was most impressive. I didn't learn much that was new, but some GIs had constructed a memorable sign that flashed by under our wing as we took off from the short Pusan landing strip: OOPS! THAT'S ALL! A sobering reminder of how tenuous our hold was, when raw troops from garrison duty in Japan were all that kept the United States from being driven off the peninsula. Their efforts took a special brand of courage.

On the same trip I also met with MacArthur in Japan. He had sent many pessimistic reports to Washington about the situation in Korea, some actually recommending withdrawal from the peninsula, and he was as pessimistic in person. I carried my report back to Acheson, telling him that our situation was grave but not without hope.

When the North Koreans first attacked, we didn't know if this was a single offensive or the opening shot in a much broader Communist offensive in Asia. Consequently, in addition to landing troops in Korea, we took other steps to deter our opponents from expanding the Korean conflict into other parts of Asia. Not knowing whether the Korean attack meant that the Chinese planned to attack Taiwan, President Truman moved the Seventh Fleet into the waters between Taiwan and mainland China and stated that our Navy would not allow any military operations in either direction. We substantially stepped up our assistance to the French in Indochina to discourage any Chinese move southward. I supported both initiatives, on the grounds that we just didn't know what was in the minds of our opponents in Moscow, Pyongyang, and Peking. Fortunately these other scenarios didn't materialize.

The intrusion of the Seventh Fleet between Taiwan and the mainland was something of a bluff. We counted thousands of Chinese junks along the mainland coast within easy sailing distance of Taiwan. To see what it would take to sink a junk, our Navy towed one out to sea and shot it up. We discovered that sinking a wooden junk with naval gunfire was one hell of a challenge: Wood floats! Had the Communist Chinese launched an invasion with several thousand junks simultaneously, we probably wouldn't have been able to stop them. We didn't have enough shells to fire a single round at each junk, much less the many shells needed to sink them.

As the American buildup at Pusan continued, it gradually became clear that the North Koreans would not push us into the sea. What was less clear was how we could break out. MacArthur pressed for an amphibious landing at Inchon, but the Joint Chiefs were highly skeptical about his plan. Nevertheless, since as a general rule Washington and the Pentagon did not second-guess their theater commanders, MacArthur went ahead, and the Inchon landings were a brilliant success.

After the September 15 landing MacArthur's X Corps, consisting of the First Marine Division and the Army's Seventh Infantry Division, retook Seoul, the capital of South Korea, and moved inland. The North

Korean invasion quickly collapsed. Following this successful counter-offensive, as United Nations forces moved northward up the peninsula, driving the retreating North Koreans before them, a controversy arose in the State Department over whether UN forces should recross the thirty-eighth parallel and possibly unite all of Korea. George Kennan and others argued against crossing the parallel; I argued in favor of crossing the parallel and helped persuade Dean Acheson, for a number of reasons.

Retreating North Korean forces were regrouping north of the parallel, and it made little sense for allied forces to mark time below the thirty-eighth parallel, with an army in the field getting ready to renew the attack. Additionally, to me, a divided Korea made little sense. We had not selected the thirty-eighth parallel as a permanent boundary; we had simply proposed it to facilitate the acceptance of the Japanese surrender. It was designed to serve a temporary military expediency. Division along the parallel made no sense economically or geographically as far as Korea itself was concerned.

Also, before the outbreak of the war, the United Nations had passed a resolution calling for the reunification of Korea and sent a special commission to help work this out. Unfortunately the North Koreans allowed this commission to operate only in South Korea. But the reunification of Korea was a United Nations objective, and this earlier resolution was reaffirmed about the same time as fighting began. Although our reasons were sound, I must admit that I was struck by this ironic turn of events—that such a tentative decision regarding the selection of the thirty-eighth parallel, made late one evening in 1945 in the Pentagon by myself and another young colonel, working hastily over a map of East Asia, could become the scene of a major act of aggression and the focus of world attention.

When United Nations forces crossed the parallel, MacArthur broke his forces into three separate fingers, which raced north toward the Yalu River, a tactic which discomfited the Joint Chiefs because of their concern over possible Chinese entry into the war. However, having had their fingers burned at Inchon and given MacArthur's formidable reputation, they were reluctant to take issue with him again. About three days before U.S. forces reached the Yalu, the chiefs finally sent him an expression of concern about the deployment of his forces, but by then it was too late. When the Chinese came across the Yalu, they were able to attack American forces piecemeal.

No one, including myself, foresaw Chinese intervention. We didn't detect any massing of major Chinese forces in Manchuria. Our intelligence did detect some movement of Chinese troops to the north, but we didn't think they were poised for a major assault. More aerial reconnaissance might have revealed the presence of these Chinese divisions, but we believed that since Mao Zedong had just seized power one year before and his regime was trying to consolidate its hold on the mainland, the chances were good that China would not come in. We were all wrong. Not a single major element of the intelligence community warned about Chinese intervention. The only real indication about the possibility of Chinese intervention came from the Indian ambassador to Peking, K. M. Pannikar, who told us that the Chinese would react if we continued to press toward the Chinese-North Korean border. Even that warning was qualified; Pannikar himself questioned its seriousness.

The possibility of Chinese intervention was discussed at the highest levels of government and was among the major issues of discussion during the October 1950 Truman-MacArthur meeting on Wake Island. I accompanied President Truman on that trip, and that long plane ride across the Pacific in two DC-4's was quite an experience. We passed over a picket line of American warships, on station every several hundred miles in case the president's plane had to ditch. I was dutifully wearing a Hawaiian shirt that Truman had given me in Oahu, one of the most outrageous shirts I ever owned. In fact, he outfitted the entire staff with those shirts. But contrary to Merle Miller's interviews with Truman in *Plain Speaking,* General MacArthur was at the airstrip and waiting at the foot of the ramp when Truman's plane landed. The idea that MacArthur deliberately arrived late and made the president's plane circle for a while before landing is simply fiction, the result of an old man's failing memory.

The meeting accomplished what it intended. President Truman and General MacArthur seemed to get along well with each other, and MacArthur showed complete respect for the president. And on the question of China, everyone was in agreement: The Chinese would not enter the war. MacArthur even predicted that if we miscalculated, American forces would simply mow them down as they tried to cross the Yalu—"the greatest slaughter in military history," he said.

That meeting went so well that at one point I became alarmed. Truman had an agenda with twelve to fifteen items to discuss with MacArthur. We met early in the morning in a little tin Quonset hut, and the president started whizzing through this agenda, covering each item quickly. It looked as though we'd finish in about thirty minutes.

Fidgeting, I passed a note to the president and suggested that he slow down, to lend a note of seriousness to the meeting. I felt that too brief a meeting would fuel the press's cynicism; it was already dubious about this mid-Pacific meeting. Truman scribbled his reply on the same note; "Hell, no! I want to get out of here before we get into trouble!" We finished the meeting promptly.

Controversy about this Wake Island meeting developed after the fact. In a little anteroom in that Quonset hut, we had asked Philip Jessup's secretary, Vernice Anderson, to wait until the end of the meeting, when she could help us draft a communiqué for the press. In that room she could hear everything that was going on. Like a good secretary, she realized that someone might want a memorandum of conversation of the meeting. So on her own initiative she took notes; we had not asked her to do so. Afterward we were delighted that she had; a complete record was useful. Unfortunately, during the hearings after MacArthur's recall, her efforts were labeled "eavesdropping" by MacArthur's staff. It was nothing of the sort. We had submitted a copy of her memo to MacArthur for his review, and he approved it.

The real failure at the Wake Island meeting was in our assessment of Chinese intentions and of our ability to handle Chinese forces if they actually intervened. On this one MacArthur and the rest of us were all wrong. On October 25 hundreds of thousands of Chinese troops began crossing the Yalu. MacArthur himself sent messages to Washington that said unless the United States declared war against China, we'd have to withdraw from the Korean peninsula. In one cable he talked about the loss of morale of his own troops, and he was clearly in a state of depression. General Matthew Ridgway, then chief of operations for the U.S. Army, told President Truman during a meeting which I attended that "when an American general loses confidence in the morale of his own troops, the problem of morale is with the general."

Among the American high command I recall our distress and anguish, realizing that we now had a new war on our hands. The Chinese clearly threatened to drive us off the Korean peninsula. But there was no mood of panic, although we carefully studied plans for withdrawal. I personally thought that MacArthur's cables themselves showed signs of panic and that he had more resources to stop the Chinese advance than he thought. Also, South Korean divisions had recovered from the impact of the North Korean attack and were becoming an effective fighting force. There was strong solidarity among the South Korean people. Additionally, as UN forces were driven southward, our supply lines became shorter and North Korean and Chinese lines lengthened.

When asked for my views, I reminded my colleagues that during the dark days of World War II we had been in tough times before and had overcome them. The United States didn't have to act like a defeated nation, I insisted, because we hadn't yet been defeated. I argued that we should turn our forces around, reject MacArthur's call for carrying the war into China, and resist demands for withdrawal. American policy was supported by the world community and was operating within the framework of the UN Charter. Great issues were at stake, and we needed to remain steadfast and determined. Dean Acheson trenchantly observed, "Mr. President, the Chinese simply must not be allowed to drive us out of Korea." Truman agreed and decided that a withdrawal from Korea was out of the question.

I strongly opposed MacArthur's desire to wage war against China, a very uninviting prospect. MacArthur also called for the systematic and sustained bombing of Manchuria with conventional weapons, and I opposed that as well. We were already bombing everything that moved between the thirty-eighth parallel and the Chinese border. We had complete air superiority, were just bombing the hell out of North Korea, and the Chinese were still able to maintain five hundred thousand men at the front. They moved their supplies at night and during bad weather when our planes could not fly. In my judgment, to extend that bombing area several hundred miles back into Manchuria would have had little effect on the war itself.

Truman's own military advisers told him that the only strategy which could possibly affect the situation in Korea would be the mass destruction of Chinese cities with nuclear weapons. That option was never seriously considered since Truman refused to go down that trail.

Only once do I recall serious discussion about using nuclear weapons: when we thought about bombing a large dam on the Yalu River. General Hoyt Vandenberg, Air Force chief of staff, personally had gone to Korea, flown a plane over the dam, and dropped our biggest conventional bomb on it. It made only a little scar on the dam's surface. He returned to Washington and told us that we could knock the dam out only with nuclear weapons. Truman refused.

In retrospect, we made one mistake that I came to regret. We restricted our military pilots to airspace south of the Yalu River and did not allow them to pursue Chinese MiGs across the border, although these MiGs were operating out of bases in China. Already facing a larger war than we wanted, we were concerned that skirmishes of American planes against MiGs and airfields in China might activate

China's mutual defense treaty with the Soviet Union. Nevertheless, I feel now that we should have allowed hot pursuit across the Yalu. Not permitting this was asking too much of our men.

Overall, even after the Chinese entered the war, I thought that we had sufficient troops in Korea to dig in, regroup, and hold. I didn't think we should expand the war, but I did think that given his pessimism, General MacArthur should be relieved. I suggested to President Truman that perhaps General Joseph Collins should assume command in Korea, allowing MacArthur to concentrate on his occupation duties in Japan.

Other issues also came to a head between President Truman and General MacArthur, particularly MacArthur's efforts to inject himself into domestic politics in the United States. His letter to Representative Joseph W. Martin, Jr., a Republican, was clearly an act of insubordination, made worse by Martin's reading the letter on the floor of the House. MacArthur's conduct became a serious issue even with our allies. As this controversy heated up, Dean Acheson strongly urged Truman to take his time and think the matter through, because firing Douglas MacArthur would raise all sorts of hell at home. During these discussions George Marshall, then serving as secretary of defense, told Truman, "Mr. President, General MacArthur is an American general on active duty. You are entitled to have the recommendation of your Joint Chiefs of Staff on this matter. I would ask them for one." Truman asked the chiefs, and they advised unanimously that MacArthur be relieved.

Truman also asked for my recommendation. I told him that he would have to relieve MacArthur on constitutional grounds, that American generals could not just refuse to obey the orders of their commander in chief. But Truman had been advised similarly by many others; I was a little fish in a situation where the president was relieving a man whom author William Manchester was to call the "American Caesar."

Harry Truman made his decision about ten-thirty one night over at Blair House. Earlier that afternoon a Washington-based reporter from the *Chicago Tribune* told us that he had a report from his home office that General MacArthur had asked the *Tribune* to save space on its front page for a major story the next day. The reporter didn't know what the story would be about. This raised the possibility that MacArthur intended to resign, beat Truman to the punch, and give the president a public blasting. General Omar Bradley and I went over to Blair House to tell the president. I think that news tip was the fuse that sparked Truman's action that night, although I think he had already decided to relieve MacArthur. He sent Bradley and me into an adjacent room, and we drafted the order relieving MacArthur.

Truman planned to send that order to Secretary of the Army Frank Pace, who was in Japan and Korea, and have Pace deliver it to MacArthur personally. But communications got screwed up, and MacArthur heard about his firing on the radio. As for myself, I had a busy night after Truman made his decision. Starting after midnight, I called the ambassadors of all the countries with troops in Korea and informed them about the firing. I got some interesting reactions over the telephone from those sleepy ambassadors, ranging from New Zealand's ambassador, who said, "Well, the little man finally did it, didn't he?" to the outrage of Philippine Ambassador Carlos Romulo, a great fan of MacArthur. Romulo was angry as hell. Most saw MacArthur's firing as we did—a constitutional issue—and were relieved that this confrontation was now behind us.

For that same reason, Truman didn't have any lasting problem with Congress, because members of Congress themselves believed strongly in civilian control of the military. Nor could they fault MacArthur's replacement, General Matthew Ridgway. Joining his troops in the front lines, with his grenades strapped over his shoulders, Matt Ridgway turned his men around and started north again.

As predicted, MacArthur's firing led to congressional hearings, his dramatic address to a joint session of Congress, and angry newspaper headlines. To his credit, Truman reminded us that MacArthur had not been back to America since World War II and hadn't received the hero's welcome to which he was entitled. He said, "I don't want anyone in my administration to interfere with the welcome he will get when he comes home." Truman predicted there would be hell to pay for a few weeks, but we should stay out of harm's way and it would all blow over. That is exactly what happened.

Truman's conflict with MacArthur was more than a clash of egos or contest of wills; Truman was concerned about the presidency. He once said, "There are a million Americans that could be president as well as I can, but goddammit, I am the president. And I am not going to turn this office over to my successor with its prerogatives impaired by an American general!" I am convinced that 95 percent of Truman's decision to fire MacArthur hinged on the relationship of the president as the commander in chief to his general and on civilian control of the military.

The furor over MacArthur's firing had begun to die down when on

May 18, 1951, I gave an after-dinner speech at the Waldorf Hotel that caused quite a stir. About eight hundred people attended the dinner, given by the China Institute, and I decided to retaliate for some of the bad language the Peking regime hurled at us. In my remarks I accused Chinese leaders of serving foreign masters and entering the Korean War to do the Soviet Union's bidding. I also charged that Mao's flirtation with the Soviets threatened the independence of China. To drive my point home, I said that the Peking regime "may be a colonial Russian government, a Slavic Manchukuo on a larger scale. It is not the government of China. It will not pass the first test. It is not Chinese."

That "Slavic Manchukuo" reference was more taunt than statement of fact, a response to Peking's rhetorical campaign. Beginning in 1949, when the Chinese Communists selected the United States as "public enemy number one," they pursued a hostile anti-American line. Occasionally we in the administration responded in kind. But the press overlooked that fact and speculated that I had announced a more militant policy toward China, even though my speech was more polemical than factual. I knew about the strong sense of "Chineseness" among the Chinese people, and I was trying to play on their sense of national pride, their feeling that they were the Middle Kingdom and the rest of the world was simply barbarians. I thought that such a taunt might encourage the Chinese to be a little "more Chinese" and less cooperative with the Soviets. I said with few words and in short sentences what the administration had been saying in much longer, convoluted sentences. Dean Acheson reviewed my speech afterward and found it consistent with what we had been saying. But the timing of my remarks was unfortunate because Acheson was about to testify before Senator McCarthy's committee, and my speech gave it ammunition for heckling Acheson.

My speech precipitated an amusing brawl between journalists David Lawrence and Arthur Krock. At lunch the next day at the Metropolitan Club they began to discuss what I had said. As their conversation heated up, they got mad at each other and actually rose at their table with balled-up fists. Friends had to calm them. When each returned to his typewriter to write his story, did they attack each other? Not at all. Each attacked me—from the opposite flank.

Some of Truman's White House advisers thought that I had politically embarrassed the president with my speech, and they sent over a memo stating that my future speeches would have to be cleared. As assistant secretary of state for Far Eastern affairs I felt that I was my own clearance officer for matters involving Asia. I stopped making speeches for a while because I refused to have my drafts edited by some White House staffer who didn't know anything about Asia. The incident blew over reasonably fast, but there was enough controversy in the newspapers that my older son, David, age ten, asked, "Pop, are you going to get fired?"

It is true that the events of the Korean War itself, with hundreds of thousands of Chinese "volunteers" pouring across the Yalu and the mounting casualty lists of Americans as the war progressed, stiffened the attitudes of many people in this country toward China, including my own. Calling upon young Americans to risk and sacrifice their lives to blunt aggression is a serious business. My speech at the China Institute, in part, reflected this hardening. Increased American aid to the Nationalists on Formosa followed, as well as our successful effort that same year to block Communist China's admission to the United Nations. The American delegation proposed a one-year moratorium on General Assembly consideration of China's admission, a parliamentary device that I helped invent.

Shortly after my speech at the China Institute, in early July 1951, peace talks began in Panmunjom, Korea, after months of hard fighting with United Nations forces and North Korean and Chinese forces stalemated in positions close to where it all started, the thirty-eighth parallel. The talks went nowhere, not surprisingly. But the manner in which the talks began was itself fascinating. At the suggestion of the State Department, George Kennan went to New York to meet privately with Soviet UN Ambassador Yakov Malik. Kennan suggested that we and the North Koreans and Chinese negotiate an end to the war on the basis of the status quo ante—return to the situation that existed prior to the North Korean attack, with Korea divided at the thirty-eighth parallel. Apparently this idea struck a spark in Moscow. Malik publicly announced the talks, and the Soviets took credit for initiating them, but actually it was Kennan on instructions from the State Department who made first contact.

In the ensuing talks at Panmunjom, I advised against public negotiations, both to prevent the Chinese and North Koreans from chipping away at our bargaining position and to give ourselves more flexibility in the talks. I also believed that the shooting war must continue until an armistice was signed, to prevent the enemy from reinforcing positions during a cease-fire.

Why did it take two years to conclude an agreement when both we and the Soviets were so eager for one as early as July 1951? President

Truman made two decisions that may have contributed to the delay, both not covered in the original conversations between Kennan and Malik. First, we would not return to the thirty-eighth parallel but would stop fighting in existing positions. That line of battle, in some places north of the thirty-eighth parallel, had some high ground preferred by our military; terrain along the parallel was less defensible. On that one, Truman sided with our military. Second, he also decided that we would not repatriate North Korean and Chinese prisoners against their will. Truman had a solid reason for this. At the end of World War II many Russian prisoners held by the Germans were returned involuntarily to the Soviet Union, and Stalin treated them badly when they got home. Some even committed suicide upon hearing they were being sent home. Truman didn't want this to happen again.

I strongly agreed with the president on both points, although we recognized that American insistence on each would prolong the negotiations. Neither was easy for the North Koreans to accept, especially our refusal to repatriate all North Korean prisoners. South Korean President Syngman Rhee also stated he would not return North Koreans who wanted to stay in South Korea. At one point he threatened to open his prison gates and let all prisoners of war go free. That would have complicated negotiations even more.

Unfortunately the Korean War also got tangled up in the Taiwan question. This was probably unavoidable since we were, after all, fighting the Communist Chinese in Korea, but it was worse than it had to be both because of the so-called China Lobby in the United States and the fraudulent offer of the Nationalist Chinese to send troops to Korea. The China Lobby, formally named the Committee of One Million, believed ardently in Chiang Kai-shek and his claim to the legitimate government of China. Henry Luce, Clare Boothe Luce, Anna Chennault, Congressman Walter Judd, and other distinguished Americans were among the lobby's more influential members. The lobby had influence on Capitol Hill, and it was a force to be reckoned with, even though it intentionally or unintentionally misrepresented the situation in the Far East.

As for Taiwan's offer to send troops to Korea, the whole idea was a fraud. Just after the North Korean invasion I received a telegram from Chiang Kai-shek that Taiwan had earmarked two divisions—thirty-three thousand—for service in Korea, but Chiang also said these divisions needed outfitting from boots to helmets, the most modern weapons, and two years of intensive training before they would be ready. From an operational point of view, this offer was virtually worthless. Indeed, some years after the Korean War, I was having a drink with a high-ranking official in the Taiwan government and Chiang's offer came up. He laughed and said, "I was the one who proposed to Chiang Kai-shek that we offer our forces for Korea." He said that everyone in the government, including Chiang, adamantly opposed the idea, but he prevailed after giving categorical assurances that Washington would reject the offer. But our refusal to take Chiang up on his offer to "unleash" his forces on Korea hurt us politically as American casualties mounted.

During the war Chiang also threatened to land Nationalist forces on the mainland to retake China. He called for American support in this undertaking, and we repeatedly refused. After the Korean War I talked with another high-ranking Taiwanese official about Chiang's idea of returning to the mainland. "What about your soldiers?" I asked him privately. "Do they want to go back?" He smiled and said, "Yes, they want to return. But as soon as they get ashore, they'll melt away and head for their own villages." There was much unreality in that raging debate over China during the forties and early fifties. We in the government were at a disadvantage, having to keep our feet grounded in the realities of that conflict while exposed to sharp, uninformed, and often partisan attack. I personally had little respect for Chiang's forces, having heard from some military friends who had trained them that they weren't very good soldiers. This contrasted sharply with the quality of Chinese troops we had served with in Burma.

The fighting and negotiating over Korea dragged on into the Eisenhower years. Despite the less than satisfactory conclusion to the war—continuing stalemate along the thirty-eighth parallel—and the continued potential for conflict that still exists, I believe the outcome of the Korean War was a success for American policy and for the United Nations. To be sure, we made mistakes, but the bottom line is that South Korea today is pro-Western, economically viable, and struggling toward democracy. Had we failed in the early 1950's, none of this would have happened.

While most of my work on the Far Eastern Affairs desk concerned Korea and China, I also became heavily involved in negotiating the Japanese Peace Treaty. John Foster Dulles and I worked closely on this project, with Dulles taking charge of the negotiations. But the 1951 UN conference in San Francisco to sign the Japanese Peace Treaty was not where the treaty came together. The real negotiations came from Dulles's traveling all over the world with briefcase in hand, negotiating in advance the actual text of the peace treaty with thirty-five to forty countries.

My job was to serve as Foster Dulles's blocking back, fending off bureaucrats who kept trying to insert trivia into the treaty. Truman wanted a simple, straightforward, and nonpunitive treaty of reconciliation with Japan, and that is essentially what we got. And at the San Francisco conference we were determined not to let the Soviets wreck prospects for a treaty by making impossible demands and repeating their performance in blocking a peace treaty with Germany. We devised some special rules of procedure which prevented the Soviets from exercising their veto. When the conference convened, any effort the Soviets or their allies made to propose amendments was ruled out of order by Dean Acheson, who chaired the meeting as host foreign minister. Acheson ruled that the first order of business was adapting the agenda. After this was done, Soviet amendments were ruled out of order because the rules of procedure declared that the purpose of this conference was to adopt the peace treaty. It took the Russians about three days to discover what was happening to them. They finally walked out, dragging Czechoslovakia and Poland with them. I don't blame them; those rules of procedure were outrageous, and I blush to think of my own role in those parliamentary maneuvers.

In accordance with the president's instructions, Dulles produced a relatively short treaty and won the support of every nation at the San Francisco conference except the Soviet Union and the Soviet bloc countries, a brilliant performance. Although Dulles and Acheson later had many personal difficulties, they were a beautiful team in negotiating the Japanese Peace Treaty. I am one of few Americans who were close friends of both Dean Acheson and John Foster Dulles. I often wondered whether each suspected this was due to lack of character on my part.

10

"The Best Job in America"

In April 1950, while still assistant secretary of state for Far Eastern affairs, I was invited to become a trustee of the Rockefeller Foundation, joining Robert Lovett, John J. McCloy, Lewis Douglas, John Foster Dulles, and others on the board. Serving on the board of a Manhattan-based multimillion-dollar philanthropic corporation was quite a jump for a Georgian from Cherokee County. The hardest thing for me about being a Rockefeller trustee was learning not to blink whenever someone mentioned a million dollars. One year later foundation President Chester Barnard came up for retirement, and to my surprise, I was asked if I wanted the job.

It was a fascinating proposition, heading one of the world's largest philanthropic foundations whose chartered goal was to "serve the well-being of mankind." And so, in spring of 1952, with the Truman administration drawing to a close, with three children to raise—our daughter, Peggy, having been born in March 1949—and tempted mightily by a badly needed hike in pay—I earned only ten thousand dollars as assistant secretary of state—I became a foundation president.

Shortly before I left the administration, President Truman called me into his office. "Dean," he told me, "you can have any job in my administration you want. Ambassador to Japan, whatever—I'd be delighted. But I will not stand in your way in taking the best job in America."

The trustees of the Rockefeller Foundation formally elected me president at their annual meeting in Colonial Williamsburg, Virginia, and the same day John D. Rockefeller, Jr., invited me to lunch at his home there. "Here come marching orders from the old man," I thought.

But I was wrong. He told me only two things: "Rusk, I never want to hear from you about the Rockefeller Foundation. It is an independent philanthropy, and I have nothing to do with it. Don't come to me with your problems.

"And don't be chained by the past," he added. "Why don't you take three or four months off, perhaps go off alone in the wilderness, and just think about how you could best use three-quarters of a billion dollars for the well-being of mankind?"

Excellent advice that unfortunately I had no chance to follow. When I became president, congressional conservatives had launched an investigation of philanthropic foundations. The Rockefeller Foundation was among those targeted, and in 1952 I was called to testify before a congressional investigating committee, headed by Representative Edward Cox, from Georgia. Cox's committee was much inspired by Joseph McCarthy. The foundation was charged with abusing its tax-exempt status and funding questionable and even subversive "anti-American" activities. To defend the foundation and especially our crucially important tax-exempt status, I and my staff had to dig into the records and study in detail virtually every grant we had made. In 1954 I testified again before a second congressional committee headed by Carroll Reece, a conservative Republican from Tennessee. His group was also investigating philanthropic foundations. Instead of ignoring the past and thinking anew, I spent these early months preparing for those hearings.

I never contested Congress's right to inquire about foundations, but these investigations were an offshoot of McCarthyism. Congressional investigators not only challenged our tax-exempt status but also tried to impose an ideological caste on the foundations. Alger Hiss had served as a foundation president—the Carnegie Endowment for International Peace—and his conviction for perjury didn't do us any good.

The irony of these congressional investigations was that the McCarthyites and their allies charged foundations, the children of capitalism, with subverting capitalism. We were incredulous that John D. Rockefeller would ever be regarded a socialist, or the Rockefeller Foundation accused with its grant making of undermining capitalism, the profit motive, and free enterprise.

But with the Cold War between the superpowers, a hot war in Korea, and citizens groping to understand America's new global responsibilities, the early 1950's were troubled times. Because foundations work at the frontiers of human knowledge, are mysterious to most people, and are often involved in highly controversial fields such as human behavior and psychology, it wasn't surprising that we were challenged in the McCarthy era, a time of public anxiety, suspicion, fear, and frustration.

The Cox and Reece committees questioned our grants to "subversive" people such as Alfred Kinsey, Paul Robeson, and Linus Pauling and to "subversive" organizations such as the Institute of Pacific Relations. In responding, I asked our critics to define what they meant by "subversive" and insisted that this standard be applied by due process of law. I said that foundations must not be held accountable for the personal politics of those receiving grants. We funded Robeson and Pauling for their artistic and scientific talent, not their politics. Foundations hunt endlessly for talented young men and women who might someday take on leadership positions, but identifying that talent is never easy. Nor is it easy to give money away wisely. Foundations must be free to make mistakes, especially when most lack staffs to investigate in detail those receiving grants. Controversy cannot be avoided if foundations do what they are supposed to do: tackle important problems. Even at this, I thought our record was admirable. Out of 28,753 Rockefeller grants, only 2 organizations and 23 individuals were challenged by congressional investigators.

The best line of the hearings came from Guggenheim President Henry Allen Moe. Hard pressed by congressional investigators over a Guggenheim grant to Linus Pauling, Moe finally leaned back in his chair and said, "Mr. Chairman, a distinguished scientist has as much right to be a damned fool in politics as anybody else!"

Despite the turbulence of McCarthyism, the investigation of foundations never generated much interest from Congress or the public. Most Americans didn't follow the hearings at all. Congressman Wayne Hays of the Reece Committee said, "If you mention the word 'foundation' in my home state of Ohio, people think of the basement of a house or a lady's undergarment." We responded to our critics as best we could and fended off threatened hostile legislation designed to revoke the foundations' tax-exempt status or assert governmental control over grant making. Fortunately the whole thing blew over.

To avoid bureaucratic stagnation, both John D. Rockefeller, Sr., and his son thought that their foundations should be liquidated after the family's third generation. Our trustees decided that the Rockefeller Foundation shouldn't liquidate just to liquidate, unless some project came along where committing all the foundation's resources and assets might make a crucial difference. For something like a way to world peace, for example, we'd have thrown everything we had into it.

However, the General Education Board, of which I was also president, liquidated during my term. That board had made many capital grants to colleges and universities and was running out of money. I visited Dr. Benjamin Mays, longtime president of Morehouse College in Atlanta, to ask whether we should concentrate the remaining funds of the General Education Board in black education. "Oh, don't do that." He smiled. "These white boys need as much education as our black boys do." We deliberately spent ourselves out of existence.

Representing the Rockefeller name and wealth led to some interesting experiences. On my first trip to Great Britain as foundation president, I was met at Heathrow Airport by several reporters. They tried to pump me about how much money I was giving away and to whom. I didn't tell them anything. But that didn't discourage one of London's more flamboyant dailies from manufacturing a story about this nice young man from the Rockefeller Foundation who had come to England with a quarter of a billion dollars and who needed ideas on how to spend it. I left London to go up-country, and when I returned to my hotel, I asked the desk clerk for my mail. "Sir, we put your mail in your room," he said with a curious smile. I went to my room, and there in the bathtub were hundreds of letters from people all across England, full of ideas on how to spend the foundation's money. We boxed them up and sent them back to New York, and our staff answered every one.

Curiously, twenty years earlier, while a student at Oxford, I once wrote as many Rusks as I could find in Northern Ireland, trying to locate relatives of the three Rusk brothers who came to America in the early 1800's. Not a response. But thanks to that reporter's story, some of those letters in the tub were from long-lost "cousins" and "relatives," and many began with the phrase "Dear Cousin Dean."

Another amusing incident occurred when the French government awarded me the the Legion of Honor, one of France's top awards. My invitation to the ceremony arrived at the home of Dr. Howard Rusk, a distant cousin and my neighbor in Scarsdale, a famed specialist in rehabilitative medicine. Through a university appointment he also bore the title "Dean," and we often got our mail mixed up. Howard forwarded this invitation to me, saying, "This is obviously for you." I sent it back, saying, "No, this one is yours." So we both wrote the French ambassador in Washington. Ten days later we each got a letter: "It was intended for both of you." Howard and I went to Washington and received our awards in the same ceremony, and we never learned for whom the invitation was originally intended.

Some lessons of foundation life came quickly. A few were painful. In reviewing proposals, I found that we had to say no about twenty times for every yes. Saying no was never easy, especially to those convinced they had worthwhile proposals, and they usually were. We also were under great pressure to fund relief programs to alleviate hunger, homelessness, and poverty at the consumer level. We tried to steel ourselves against that, despite the chronic need, preferring to spend our limited funds on the search for root causes, such as a cure for yellow fever that might help millions of people.

During the thirties and forties the joke around the foundation was that it had been "captured by the doctors," a reference to the foundation's major efforts in public health, medicine, and medical education. Foundation campaigns against the "Big Three"—malaria, yellow fever, and hookworm—had been highly successful. The foundation had also spent most of its money in the United States. After several years as president I felt it was time the foundation shifted its focus. The emergence of dozens of newly independent countries after World War II was having a major effect on the "well-being of mankind," and I believed we should spend less at home, get involved with that great mass of humanity in the Third World, and especially concentrate on public health, public education, and agricultural productivity. My memories of Cherokee County and how rural Georgia was transformed in a few decades helped convince me that the keys to Third World development lay in these areas. I also thought the foundation should focus less on original research and more on extending knowledge already gained. The Third World, where two-thirds of the world's population live, was a time bomb for the entire human race. In addition, massive resources were now being pumped by governments and international agencies into public health and medicine, and I believed the foundation could cut back in these areas.

In 1955, after many months of discussion with individual trustees, I presented these ideas to the board of trustees, which agreed. It also allowed us to dip into our capital funds and spend extra money to help get these new initiatives rolling. Although our programs in medicine and public health, natural sciences, social sciences, and the humanities continued, we channeled more funding to the developing countries in Africa, Latin America, and Asia. We also began a separate agricultural division, an effort that germinated in what was later called the green revolution. We tried to orient our programs to the needs of the emerging nations: leadership training, population control, education, resource development, increased food production, and improved health care.

Through fellowships and leadership-training grants, our biggest thrust was investing in individual talent. Most new countries came out of a colonial past, and only rarely had former colonial powers left behind educated peoples. The British developed topnotch native civil service and educational systems, but the Belgians, Dutch, French, and Portuguese did not. For example, when the Belgian Congo became independent, the entire country had no more than a dozen university graduates. Indonesia had perhaps seventy graduates in that huge island chain, populated by one hundred million people. Leadership training was our top priority, and we could have legitimately allocated all our money to it.

The Rockefeller Foundation scoured the world, looking for first-class young minds. We believed there was no better investment than people themselves. We also tried to follow up college training with laboratory equipment, books, supplies, or whatever, so graduates could hit the deck running and get on with their work. And almost always they went home. We weren't stealing talent from abroad. We tried to select people committed to working in their own countries.

In the fifties not one Third World university would have qualified for admission to the American Association of Universities—the top fifty American universities. That was understandable considering the colonial past, but this had to change. We tried to upgrade some of these universities, usually department by department; for example, we gave lots of money to the American University in Beirut, Lebanon, and the University of Ibadan in Nigeria.

Throughout, we tried to focus on "root causes." It took doctors and researchers twenty-five to thirty years to develop a cure for yellow fever, but during that time the foundation never set up programs to treat yellow fever patients. It took thirty years to make real progress in increasing the yield of basic food crops, yet we never fed people at the consumer level. We tried to focus on causes rather than symptoms.

Newly independent countries had other problems, too. Almost all lacked simple things such as libraries, and many opened their foreign affairs offices without even a reference book. So we put together "care packages" of books, including dictionaries, encyclopedias, almanacs, and atlases, and they were greatly welcomed, because the colonial powers had left nothing behind. Most of these countries had no trained diplomats, so we arranged with the Carnegie Endowment for International Peace to lay on a training program for Third World diplomats, and it was highly successful. We did the same thing for finance officers by encouraging the World Bank to begin training programs. We found that many administrators and economists of these developing countries didn't even know how to fill out applications for aid programs and Rockefeller grants.

During the 1950's the Rockefeller Foundation focused on increasing agricultural productivity in general and improving the yield of basic food crops in Latin America, Africa, and Asia specifically, with special focus on better strains of corn, wheat, rice, and blight-resistant potatoes. We knew that certain hybrids of corn and wheat grew with enormous vigor, but until the late 1950's hybrid rice was sterile. It wouldn't reproduce itself. We began a joint project with the rice-producing countries of Asia and built a facility, the International Rice Research Institute in Los Baños, the Philippines. By the early 1960's this project had helped develop the "miracle rice" of the Green Revolution, an epic success which we at the foundation found enormously satisfying. In Chapingo, Mexico, we also funded projects in wheat and corn, new strains of which contributed to the green revolution in countries like India, Mexico, and the Philippines.

We also investigated less conventional fields that potentially could expand food supplies, such as marine biology, photosynthesis, and the physics and chemistry of clouds. We continued to underwrite pure research in the life sciences for activities relating to health and food. We tried to strengthen medical and public health training, although I think our approach was too elegant. We sent young, aspiring doctors and nurses to our top medical schools, trained them on electron microscopes and the most sophisticated equipment imaginable, and then sent them home to primitive clinics. I would have preferred providing information and basic training to mothers and housewives—by whom 95 percent of all medicine is practiced—as a way of extending health care to millions of people. But that approach was slow to catch on.

With dramatic improvements in health care and food production, family planning and population control became increasingly important. We funded population studies in the United States, India, Japan, and

Formosa and began taking a strong interest in birth control, despite the fact that family planning was contrary to public policy in many countries, including the United States. Sometimes our efforts ran into cultural barriers. When visiting an Indian village to check on a family planning project, I asked the village project leader how many children he had. "Twelve," replied the proud father. "Eleven girls and a boy." When I raised my eyebrows, he said, "When I finally had a son, I became a family planner!"

Although we had mixed success with birth control and family planning, some of this foundation "seed corn" at least helped John D. Rockefeller III and others turn this country around. Rockefeller invested heavily in this effort and sought foundation backing as well. In recognition of his efforts, I nominated him for the Nobel Prize in 1968. During his term President Nixon signed a family planning bill for the United States involving several hundred million dollars. Such a bill would not have been possible during the Kennedy years.

As a consequence of the successful campaign against yellow fever, we continued to work on lesser-known insect-borne viruses, seeking to forestall potentially disastrous epidemics through mutations of viruses which had not yet attacked the human race. We supported area studies in the United States and American studies abroad, trying to build understanding across cultural barriers.

Unfortunately we were never able to work with the Soviet Union, something we badly wanted to do. We would have loved to fund cultural and scientific exchanges and various collaborative projects, but we and the Soviets simply weren't on the same wavelength regarding freedom of travel, the purposes of scientific inquiry, and issues such as academic freedom.

But we did try. In the 1950's a new wheat rust suddenly appeared in North America. That this rust didn't spread from one area like an inkblot but appeared in four places simultaneously suggested it was blown into the hemisphere by high-altitude winds, perhaps from the wheat-producing areas of the Soviet Union. We wanted to talk with the Soviets about our findings and about wheat genetics and mutating wheat rusts. But they refused, charging that we had accused them of biological warfare.

On another occasion during the 1950's the American Red Cross wanted to compare notes with its Soviet counterpart on the storage of blood plasma. The Soviets refused, saying, "The storage of blood plasma has military implications, and we don't believe you'll tell us everything you know." Our Red Cross finally convinced them that everything we knew in this field was a matter of public record. But it wasn't easy trying to deal with those people.

Interestingly, the presidency of the Rockefeller Foundation afforded me my first opportunity to meet Soviet Premier Nikita Khrushchev. During Khrushchev's tour of the United States in 1959, Averell Harriman invited me to a party for Khrushchev at his house in New York City. Most of the seventy or eighty guests were Wall Street tycoons and executives from America's largest corporations. Much of the wealth of the United States was represented at this party. I went to Harriman's by taxicab and got out about three blocks away. Although I was carrying a briefcase, I walked straight to the home and into the room where Khrushchev was standing, and no one looked into my briefcase. I could have carried a bomb, so loose was security.

Khrushchev stood surrounded by capitalists, and he seemed impressed. "You don't know what this moment means to me," he said. "At long last I am face-to-face with the people who rule the United States!" Everyone laughed, but Khrushchev was serious. He didn't make Communists out of us, and we didn't make a capitalist out of him, but we had a lively exchange.

We always tried to keep the Rockefeller Foundation out of politics. But because our charter was international in scope, and because one-third of our grants went overseas, we had close working relationships with many foreign governments. Our contacts were often better and more intimate than our own government's. Most people abroad accepted us for what we were—a private philanthropy with no political fish to fry, operating independently of Washington. Additionally, the foundation never pushed its programs. We never went where we weren't wanted. And we made clear to everyone that we kept our suitcases packed and were ready to take the next airplane home.

Being foundation president was an ideal job. It kept me involved with foreign affairs, and I traveled widely and was in close contact with the leadership of nearly eighty foreign governments. Living in New York, I was active in the Council of Foreign Relations, lectured occasionally on international issues, and participated in the Rockefeller Brothers' extensive study of American foreign relations called *Prospects for America.* I tried to keep up on the issues. Although I didn't consult with him regularly, John Foster Dulles, a good friend, invited me to Washington perhaps a dozen times to discuss policy.

One issue we discussed was Egypt's desire to build the Aswan Dam. In the mid-1950's Dulles and Eugene Black, the president of the World Bank, began putting together a consortium with private, governmental, and World Bank financing to construct the dam. I told Black that the Rockefeller Foundation could fund a study of the nonengineering aspects of the dam—its impact upon agriculture, soil conditions, and the ecology of the Nile Valley, including such exotic considerations as transmission of a snail disease. Then Dulles got mad at Egyptian President Gamal Abdel Nasser and called off the negotiations. The Russians stepped in, went ahead with the project, and ignored those nonengineering aspects—with serious and devastating problems for Egypt that could easily have been anticipated.

I had one other conversation with John Foster Dulles about Egypt—this time the Suez crisis of 1956, a painful experience for Dulles. Nasser had seized the canal and excluded Israeli shipping, provoking an Israel counterattack. Britain and France intervened in support of Israel, without consulting Washington or the United Nations. With the help of world opinion and a UN peacekeeping force, President Eisenhower forced our allies to disengage. The Suez crisis was a great misfortune, both for the United States and the NATO alliance, creating wounds within the West that took years to heal.

At the time Dulles didn't ask me to comment on Suez. But three years later I visited him in a hospital in Washington, about ten days before his death. We talked about his papers and other things a dying man has on his mind. At one point he said, "Dean, I would not have made certain decisions about Suez had I not been sick at the time." He didn't elaborate, and under those circumstances I wasn't about to ask, "Well, gee, Foster, which decisions were those?" But I was intrigued with his comment. After I returned to New York, we at the foundation thought about studying ill health among governmental leaders and how it might affect decision making. Winston Churchill, Anthony Eden, Woodrow Wilson, Franklin Roosevelt, Dwight Eisenhower, and now Dulles fell into that category. We decided that trying to isolate health from other factors involved in decision making would be impossible, that any such study would be purely speculative, and we abandoned the idea.

As foundation president I tried to delegate administrative work whenever possible, preferring to concentrate on policy and planning. Personnel matters, and some delightful situations, inevitably came to my desk. A foundation employee named John Grant once complained to me about a newly released Warner Brothers movie called *Them!*, featuring monstrous insects that emerged in the aftermath of a nuclear war. In the movie a medical doctor—also named John Grant, of the Rockefeller Foundation no less—explained how these insects survived the radioactivity and grew so huge. Our own John Grant was teased unmercifully about this nonsense. I called Jack Warner simply to urge him to be careful about using the names of real people for his movie characters. However, Warner refused to accept my phone call. He told his secretary, "Have Rusk talk with my attorney." Whereupon I told Grant that he was on his own. Grant filed his own objection and won an out-of-court settlement. Jack Warner's refusal to answer his phone cost him twenty-five thousand dollars.

One incident involved family; a cousin came to my office, visited for a while, then asked if I had ever been baptized. A Jehovah's Witness fresh from a mass rally at Yankee Stadium, he was concerned. "I've already been baptized," I told him gingerly. "As a Presbyterian." My cousin replied: "You were only sprinkled. That doesn't count." Whereupon he pulled an inflatable bathtub out of his travel bag and offered to baptize me on the spot—on the fifty-fourth floor of Rockefellar Center in midtown New York. I politely declined.

As an administrator I spent a lot of time with our trustees. When I became president in 1952, many foundation officers felt that *they* were the Rockefeller Foundation and the trustees' role was simply to approve their recommendations. I took the view that the board of trustees was the Rockefeller Foundation and, as our governing authority, was responsible for everything we did. I tried to visit each of the fifteen trustees at his home at least once a year, to review all aspects of the foundation. I involved the trustees heavily in decision making; their approval was required for every grant exceeding ten thousand dollars. It meant extra work, but they were willing to devote the time. We did away with automatic proxies and absentee voting. We wanted working trustees, not honorary trustees, and we made that clear to everyone we asked to serve on the board.

My colleagues and I had to handle proposals carefully. A common sin in the foundation world is the temptation to play God with other people's ideas. When reviewing a proposal, foundations often want to change it around and shape it along the lines of their own thinking. Robert Goheen, later president of Princeton University, once asked us for one-half million dollars for a humanities project. When he finished his presentation, one of my colleagues said, "Mr. Goheen, why don't you move this part over here?" and another asked, "What about doing it this way?" Young Goheen, then in his thirties, interrupted: "Now wait a minute, gentlemen. I am telling you what Princeton University wants to do. The only question before you is, Do you want to put some money into it? We know what we want to do." We laughed . . . and gave him his money.

While reviewing science projects, I once had some fun with my science officers, who told me about a proposal for studying why certain insects prefer some plants and ignore others. "That's easy," I said, most unscientifically. "They taste better." They gave me a rather pained look, but we made the grant. Two years later the study concluded that the "gustatory sensation plays the dominant role." In other words, some plants taste better.

I also had fun with behavorial scientists. I once spent an entire day with some members of this tribe at Arden House, Averell Harriman's home north of New York City. When asked to comment, I replied, not too tactfully, "Unless you people can tell me what you are doing in terms I can understand, I am not sure that *you* understand what you are doing." One scientist later remarked that it was a black day for the behavioral sciences when Dean Rusk became president of the Rockefeller Foundation.

Some grant requests were easy to decide. We were once asked to fund a study of the sociology of juries that involved secretly tape-recording jury sessions. We rejected that as illegal. Another group of sociologists and psychologists, for a study of hostility among children, proposed inducing hostile behavior in groups of small children. We got squeamish and rejected that as well.

There is no special expertise in applying for foundation money. Interestingly, we almost preferred proposals that had a touch of amateurism—the kind put together by a man with a dream in his heart and a gleam in his eye, who is seized by his idea and wants to give it everything he's got—as opposed to commissioned, institutional, committee-designed proposals with their slick packaging. The fancier the presentation, the more skeptical we got. What foundations most want to know is what applicants intend to do with the money, stated simply and clearly.

The work itself—dealing with top minds and fascinating enterprises all over the world—was stimulating and quietly satisfying in so many ways. Tedium was unheard of; every day brought a fresh adventure. Sometimes we tried to be a little adventuresome; in fact, we always funded a "frolic of the year" to have some fun. We funded one project on extrasensory perception, not on the grounds that anyone could prove that extrasensory perception existed but because it was impossible to prove that it didn't exist.

Another time we helped initiate a study on how we earthlings should approach a sentient being—a visitor from outer space—should one ever show up. How do we communicate with him/her/it, and what should we say? Anyone from outer space might be thousands of light-years removed from us. The study concluded that communication would be difficult, but geometry offered the best chance. Studies like these didn't offer immediate utility, but they gave us a chance to stretch our minds.

But giving away money wasn't always fun. Weighed against the pleasure of sustaining someone's hopes was the pain of not being able to help at all. My one-line declination—"We have nothing but praise for your proposal"—I had to say time and time again. But there were vicarious satisfactions as well and quiet enjoyment in the performance of others. Perhaps the most satisfying grant that we extended, at least for me, was to Preston Epps, my Greek teacher from Boys High. By this time Preston was the Kenan professor of classics at the University of North Carolina at Chapel Hill, but he had never visited Greece. All of his life he had dreamed of walking the ancient sites there, so when the chance came to send him to Greece on a possible foundation restoration project, we gave him the grant. Upon his return, he wrote a topnotch report, suggesting that we not fund the project!

During my eight years as foundation president we gave away nearly $250 million. But this was only a drop in the bucket of American philanthropy. Today the American people give to philanthropic and charitable causes nearly $80 billion a year, most of which comes from private citizens contributing small amounts to causes of their choosing. There are more than twenty thousand private and business foundations in the United States today, but combined, they contribute only about thirteen cents of the philanthropic dollar; the rest comes from people using the March of Dimes approach.

Having traveled widely, I came to appreciate this streak of generosity in the American people. Alexis de Tocqueville in *Democracy in America* commented a century ago that "being neighborly," raising a barn, and just helping out are part of the American culture. As foundation president I worked with European leaders who wanted to modify their tax laws and encourage our style of philanthropy among their own people. Unfortunately, in many foreign lands, philanthropic giving just isn't understood. For some, a philanthropic obligation can be satisfied by dropping a few pennies in a beggar's cup. Giving lots of money, even by those who had money, was rarely done.

I left the foundation with many fond memories of those whose lives we had touched. On that long list were student refugees of the Hungarian Revolution of 1956. After Soviet forces had crushed the rebellion, the foundation gave as many scholarships and fellowships as we could to Hungarian refugee students. On one trip to Vienna, where many young Hungarians had fled after the Soviet occupation, a group of these student refugees insisted on meeting with me—to thank me personally for a foundation-funded chance to rebuild their lives and finish their educations elsewhere. Their testimony that evening—firsthand evidence of what Rockefeller grants could do—was an incredibly moving experience.

I had another memorable exchange with Hungarians on that trip. I went to Budapest under the auspices of the International Red Cross to see if the Rockefeller Foundation could help rebuild a large medical center that had been heavily damaged in the fighting. I asked a Communist official to pledge that if the foundation gave expensive medical equipment to the hospital, it wouldn't be put on a train and hauled east to the Soviet Union. "I can't promise that," he said. "But if that happened, your money would be well spent. Every Hungarian in the country would know about it within twenty-four hours." When I returned to my hotel, I found a little cross of St. Stephen's, the symbol of the Hungarian resistance movement, which someone had slipped into my pocket.

Many people touched us as well. A decade before I arrived, during the Hitler years, a German scientist peered out his window and saw the Gestapo approaching his house. He hastily scribbled on a piece of paper, "I bequeath all my assets to the Rockefeller Foundation," before he was taken into custody. It was a case of mistaken identity—the Nazis were looking for someone else—but the poor fellow lost his life anyway in a concentration camp. Some years later his bequest, approximately fifty thousand dollars, was delivered to the foundation.

Had John Kennedy not tagged me for secretary of state, I would have gladly stayed at the foundation until retirement. When Kennedy offered me the post, I asked the trustees if I should take it. Several trustees had earlier asked me to remain at the foundation and not accept a job in Washington. But secretary of state was different. In fact, they insisted it was the only job I could not turn down. I really didn't have a choice; had I declined, I might have lost my job in New York! So I left for Washington—reluctantly. After eight years I knew that Harry Truman had been right: I had had "the best job in America."

SECTION III

THE KENNEDY YEARS

In December 1960 I was a freshman at Scarsdale High School in Westchester County, New York, when the name Dean Rusk began appearing in news stories as President-elect John Kennedy's possible choice for secretary of state. Characteristically, I heard of this press speculation from classmates, not from my father, who to family and friends quickly disavowed such a possibility. "I've never even met Kennedy," he told us.

Thus the news from Miami—President Kennedy's announcement in December 1961 that Pop was indeed the new secretary of state—hit me like a thunderbolt. I was astonished, I couldn't believe it, and my father felt the same way.

Pop had been in Miami, and on the way back, after stopping overnight in Washington, he took the Congressional on to New York, then rode the commuter train out to Scarsdale. He'd had two days to recover from the shock of Miami and settle his nerves. But when he walked through our front door, he remained a shaken man. All the color had drained from his face.

And so, on January 21, 1961, Rusk took the oath of office as our fifty-fourth secretary of state. He never actively sought the job, and he left his resignation on Kennedy's desk from his first day in office. Rusk had been recommended by Dean Acheson and Robert Lovett among others; most Washington insiders were delighted by his appointment. Despite his reluctance, he was far more experienced in foreign affairs than the president he was to serve. One of the best prepared secretaries of state this country ever had, my dad himself knew that he was uniquely qualified. After Kennedy had tendered the offer, Rusk called his brother Parks in Georgia and told him, "If I don't take it, all that experience will be wasted."

Despite his experience, Pop by his own admission did not perform well during the early months of the Kennedy administration. It was a rocky transition with a youthful, inexperienced president and advisers who were strangers to one another. With his war planning experience in CBI, Rusk privately opposed the abortive Bay of Pigs operation. "I knew it wouldn't work," he said of the Cuban exile brigade's landing. "But I

served President Kennedy very badly. . . . I didn't oppose it forcefully.
. . . I was too busy sitting on my little post of responsibility."

Then came Khrushchev's bullying of Kennedy at the Vienna summit,
the Soviet premier's ultimatum that the West withdraw from West Berlin,
and Rusk's determination that the United States and NATO hold firm.
"There is nothing to negotiate," said Rusk, who finally convinced his
impatient, action-oriented president. Kennedy wanted to move with
greater "vigor"; Rusk preferred quiet diplomacy. In endless talks with
Soviet diplomats, "we managed to talk the fever out of the crisis," he
said. "I simply wanted to pass this problem [Berlin] on to my successor."

Rusk's role in the Cuban missile crisis contrasted sharply with his role
in the Bay of Pigs fiasco. Working quietly behind the scenes, Rusk turned
in a "virtuoso performance," according to biographer Warren Cohen.
"We were all virtuosos," said Rusk, "including Nikita Khrushchev."
Defusing the crisis was for him a "triumph of both American and Soviet
diplomacy."

In discussing nuclear strategy and arms control, Rusk claimed that
"Khrushchev turned the key at Geneva" by opting for a limited nuclear
test ban instead of a comprehensive ban. The idea was actually floated
by Rusk and his colleagues, who allowed Khrushchev to take credit for it.
The Limited Test Ban Treaty was John Kennedy's proudest achievement; it
also sparked Rusk's deepening commitment to arms control.

Regarding the North Atlantic partnership, despite conflict with NATO
allies over the Common Market, European defense issues, and the
multilateral force, despite tensions with Great Britain over the Skybolt
missile and disagreement with Charles de Gaulle over leadership of the
European community, Rusk claimed that "NATO's very success led to
some disarray" in the sixties. In general, he thought Europe had become
somewhat "fat and lazy" in its growing prosperity. "We wanted our allies
to do more, not less, in world affairs," he often said.

Despite a strong personal interest in the Third World and the problems
of developing countries, Rusk wanted the United States to be "junior
partner" in Africa, preferring that Europe take the lead instead. "We
shouldn't play 'Mr. Big' in every African capital," he insisted, yet both the
Kennedy and Johnson administrations were drawn into the Congo crisis,
which fortunately was resolved by United Nations intervention.

Regarding China policy, Rusk described how John Kennedy, fearing a
political backlash, forbade consideration during his first term of a new
opening toward the People's Republic of China, perhaps leading to
American diplomatic recognition. "I was leaning toward a two-China

policy in 1961," Rusk claimed, despite skepticism by China specialists that American policy toward China would change while Rusk was secretary of state.

The extent of my dad's influence on Kennedy has puzzled historians and will continue to do so. As he said, "Only two men know the truth about that relationship. One is dead, and the other isn't talking." Writing few memos, sitting quietly in larger meetings, rarely informing colleagues about the details of presidential conversations, saving his advice for the presidential ear, Rusk left few tracks for history. He believed that a secretary of state should never show any blue sky with his president, that policy differences between them must remain confidential, and that failure to do so weakens an administration.

With this philosophy, Rusk worked hard to maintain confidentiality. He forbade his secretaries from listening in on phone conversations with the president and preparing memos of conversations, a long-established practice. He had both his home and office swept repeatedly for "bugs"; concerned about the FBI as well as the Russians, he once told J. Edgar Hoover, in Kennedy's presence, that if the FBI ever bugged him, he would resign and publicly state his reasons. Alarmed that cables marked "secretary eyes only" were routinely copied and distributed to various offices at State, Defense, and the White House, Rusk opened a new communications line—called Cherokee after his obscure boyhood home—and ordered that only he could have access to its cables. His passion for secrecy was so strong that after leaving office, he went back to the State Department, pulled out his copies of telephone memos of conversations with his two presidents, and threw them away.

By all accounts, the Kennedy-Rusk relationship began awkwardly, each man groping to understand the other. Although grateful for Rusk's loyalty, Kennedy was baffled by his obsession with confidentiality, for example, by Rusk's unwillingness to speak his mind freely when others were in the room, fearing that his remarks would be gossiped about around town. A mischievous White House tale, apparently spread by McGeorge Bundy, had Kennedy and Rusk alone in the Oval Office with the president asking Rusk for his views. "There's still too many people here, Mr. President," replied Rusk.

On a more serious note, Kennedy allegedly was especially bothered by my dad's reluctance to lead and his unwillingness to fight for his policy views. In turn, Rusk was confused by Kennedy's informal managerial style, the aggressive White House staff, trying to work with colleagues appointed by Kennedy who reported directly to the president, and Kennedy's habit of personally calling State desk officers and soliciting their advice.

In all accounts of the Kennedy-Johnson years, Dean Rusk remains "the silent secretary," "the quiet American," "an enigma," a "smiling Buddha," "a man without a shadow," "a man nobody knows." These labels delighted him, as did his well-earned reputation for inscrutability. When a columnist wrote that Rusk's blandness made him look like "a friendly neighborhood bartender," my dad longed to step behind a bar in Washington or New York, serve drinks, and see if anyone would recognize him.

According to most accounts, having weathered two years of crisis, with the limited test ban under his belt and a growing confidence in foreign affairs, by 1963 John Kennedy was finding his stride as president. Rusk was finding his way as well, his relationship with Kennedy improving. Less ad hoc in style, Kennedy by mid-1963 had learned the wisdom of operating primarily though his secretary of state. Columnists were writing about the "comeback of Dean Rusk" rather than speculating about his imminent departure. All this was shattered by an assassin's bullet in Dallas, Texas.

Had Kennedy lived and been reelected in 1964, he might have named a new secretary of state. Rusk had told the president-elect at Palm Beach that he could serve only one term. In 1964 I was wounded by headline accounts of Kennedy's alleged dissatisfaction with my father. Pop told me of Kennedy's reaction when he offered to resign in 1963, in advance of the 1964 election.

"No, I want you to stay on," Kennedy had told him. "I like your guts, and I don't have many people around here with any guts." After passing on this story, Pop made me pledge I wouldn't use it, which twenty years later I disavowed.

While interviewing my dad for this book, I pressed hard for his feelings about John Kennedy and his reaction when he heard about the assassination.

"We were alone with our thoughts," said my father, who, along with fellow cabinet officers, was high above the Pacific on a jet headed for Tokyo. After twenty minutes or so, Rusk called the group together and began discussing what came next.

"What were your thoughts during those twenty minutes?" I asked him.

"I never tried to put into words my thoughts about Kennedy's death."

"But, Pop," I protested, "that is what we have to do now." I kept pressing him.

"What do you want me to do?" he said. "Slobber all over the place?"

"Yes," I told him.

He never did.

But on November 23, one day after the assassination and just after my father's jet had returned to Washington, my sister, Peggy, walked into our living room and found Pop in tears. He once told me that he had "liked Kennedy immensely." Perhaps the highlight of his eight years in office took place at Runnymede, England, where, representing the United States, he spoke briefly but eloquently about his slain president, with Jacqueline Kennedy and Queen Elizabeth as witness. While in Georgia, whenever asked for a memento of his years in office, my dad always passes on a copy of his remarks at Runnymede.

—R. R.

11

The First
Hundred Days

After a new president is elected, one favorite pastime of the American press is to speculate on the makeup of his cabinet. John Kennedy's election was no exception, and gradually by December 1960 my name had begun to be tossed about as a possible choice for secretary of state.

I paid little attention to this speculation. I had never met John Kennedy, and I had not been active in Democratic politics beyond rather casual membership in the Democratic Club of Scarsdale, New York. Anything more would have been inconsistent with my job as president of the Rockefeller Foundation. Consequently, I thought it unlikely I would be selected.

In fact, I knew so little about John Kennedy and his group that when I received a telephone call from Sargent Shriver, I thought the call was from a Kennedy military aide. How could it be that the president-elect would delegate so junior an officer to make his telephone calls?

Kennedy and I first talked in early December 1960 during a Rockefeller Foundation trustee meeting in Colonial Williamsburg. Just weeks after the election Kennedy was staffing his new administration and seeking the advice of many. During our meeting Rockefeller trustees Douglas Dillon and Chester Bowles were called by the president-elect. Then the phone rang for me. "Why on earth is Kennedy calling me?" I wondered out loud.

"He wants you to be his secretary of state," Bowles replied.

I picked up the phone. Kennedy said that he was busy staffing his new administration and wanted to see me. The next day I found myself sitting with him in his Georgetown home. On the table before us was a copy of an article titled "The President" that I had written for *Foreign Affairs.* In this article I argued the case for a strong president, served by a secretary of state who would remember that he was an adviser to the president. Kennedy had apparently read the article.

For nearly two hours we talked about various candidates for secretary of state and what qualities make a good secretary of state. We both liked David Bruce, and I also suggested Robert Lovett, who had been George Marshall's undersecretary of state and later served as secretary of defense. We spoke at length about Senator William Fulbright. Kennedy liked Fulbright but was concerned that since Fulbright had signed the Southern Manifesto on Civil Rights, his appointment might be opposed by the Democratic party's liberal wing. I told Kennedy that if he surrounded Fulbright with perhaps Adlai Stevenson at the United Nations and Chester Bowles as undersecretary of state, their presence would prevent strong liberal opposition to a Fulbright appointment.

The only name that Kennedy brushed aside was Adlai Stevenson. He rejected Stevenson quickly and without explanation. I never knew why. Stevenson's role at the Democratic Convention in Los Angeles may have irritated Kennedy, or perhaps he felt that since Adlai had been the Democratic standard-bearer in 1952 and 1956, he might as secretary of state somehow upstage Kennedy.

My own name never came up. This just confirmed what I previously had thought, so when I returned to New York, I told my colleagues to forget the rumors and resign themselves to the fact that they would have to put up with me for a while longer.

The next day Kennedy called and offered me the job. "Now wait a minute, Senator," I said. "We didn't talk about that at all. There are a lot of things we should discuss before you make that decision."

"All right." Kennedy chuckled. "Come on down to West Palm Beach tomorrow morning, and we will talk it over."

So I flew to Florida in the early morning and was ushered into the living room to wait for Kennedy. There on the table sat a morning

Washington Post with a big black headline, RUSK TO BE SECRETARY OF STATE. Kennedy walked in and saw that headline and blew his top. "Did you talk to anybody?" he demanded. I told him no, except for my wife, Virginia, and I was sure she hadn't said anything to anyone. Kennedy then called Philip Graham, the publisher of the *Washington Post,* and gave him hell for this page one story. I could hear only one side of the conversation, but apparently Graham told Kennedy that the president-elect had told him about the appointment the night before. I heard Kennedy explode, "But that was off the record!"

After that inauspicious start Kennedy and I sat down to talk about how foreign policy should be made. He asked for my thoughts on the course of U.S. policy since World War II. I told him that as far as I was concerned, it was a remarkable success. We came out of the war with enormous power, frittered it away with our precipitous demobilization, but then gradually rebuilt our strength commensurate with our responsibilities. I told Kennedy that although the United States had made some mistakes and suffered some disappointment, postwar U.S. foreign policy showed restraint, responsibility, and generosity. We did not try to set up an American empire, and American power had been harnessed to the rather simple and decent purposes of the American people. I told Kennedy that I strongly supported the United Nations, NATO, and collective security and thought we should try to normalize relations with Third World countries and find areas of agreement with the Soviet Union even though fundamental differences existed between us. Kennedy asked if I felt qualified for the job. I told him that he would have to judge that himself. "Previous experience will help, but there is no way to be adequately prepared to become secretary of state."

Kennedy smiled and said, "How do you think I feel?"

At one point Kennedy asked, "Is there anything about you that I should know before we announce your appointment?" I told Kennedy that I had been in the political center my whole life and that I had no concerns on that account except for criticism from the extreme left and the extreme right, which never bothered me. I also told him that during the Democratic Convention in Los Angeles I had sent a telegram to Averell Harriman, head of the New York delegation, telling him to stop being a damn fool and come out in support of Adlai Stevenson.

He laughed and told me that was not what he meant at all. "Is there anything about your personal life?" he asked, wanting to know if I had any skeletons in my closet.

I told him I didn't have any. "Senator," I asked in return, "is there anything I ought to know about you before I take this job?"

He laughed again but volunteered nothing!

I also told Kennedy that under no circumstances could I serve for more than one term. Financially I was operating on thin ice and could not support my family for more than four years on a secretary of state's salary. I was taking a pay cut from sixty thousand dollars per year as foundation president to twenty-five thousand dollars as secretary of state, and with one child in college and two headed that way, so little money would disappear fast. There were also hidden official costs of becoming secretary. For example, I had to buy striped pants, a silk top hat, a long tailed morning jacket, a gray vest, white tie and tails, and a vast array of other formal clothes. Fortunately the Internal Revenue Service called these tax-deductible as "official costumes."

Additionally, I told Kennedy that if he offered me the job, my resignation was on his desk from the day we took office. I felt the purpose of the secretary of state was to serve his president, and the moment that the president felt the secretary did not, the secretary should go.

At the end of our discussion Kennedy told me he still wanted me as his secretary of state. And so it was.

Kennedy never explained why he chose me, and I never asked. The Washington rumor mill suggested that Dean Acheson and Robert Lovett both recommended me strongly. In any event, I never sought the job, nor did I ask anyone to write a letter or make a phone call on my behalf. Having seen what Dean Acheson and George Marshall and others had gone through, I didn't really want the job. I was happy as president of the Rockefeller Foundation and could have stayed there until my retirement. Ironically, I probably wanted to be secretary of state less than any of my predecessors, but I wound up serving in the office longer than anyone else in American history except Cordell Hull.

Any cabinet officer must surround himself with good people. Of course, the president actually makes the appointments, but he usually goes along with the preference of his cabinet officers. In the State Department at least twenty positions as well as all ambassadorships are presidential appointments, and I got to work on these positions immediately. I strongly urged Kennedy to appoint Adlai Stevenson ambassador to the United Nations, believing he would be an admirable representative for the United States. I also recommended Chester Bowles for undersecretary of state, having known him as a congressman and trustee of the Rockefeller Foundation. Kennedy called both men during our meeting, and both agreed to serve.

Kennedy's sales pitch to Stevenson surprised me. Remembering how Kennedy had brushed aside any notion of Adlai as secretary, I was concerned that he would be cool toward Stevenson at the UN. But his call quickly dispelled my concern. Kennedy really laid it on Stevenson, telling him how critical the UN position was, how only Stevenson could handle it the way Kennedy wanted it done, and so on. After he described Adlai's expected role in the administration, I wondered what would be left for Kennedy and myself. Poor Adlai had no choice but to accept.

With so much to do and so many people to see, I lost fifteen pounds in the three weeks after Kennedy appointed me. The flurry of activity reminded me of John Foster Dulles's reaction in 1952, just after President Eisenhower appointed him secretary of state. Foster Dulles called me in New York and asked me to see him that same day. When I got there, I could see that he was shaken by the appointment even though he and everyone else had expected it. He told me he almost would have preferred being a White House staff officer making policy instead of administering the entire State Department and being responsible for relations with over one hundred countries.

The transition from Eisenhower to Kennedy went rather smoothly, in good part because of the gallant efforts of Christian Herter. Herter was severely crippled by arthritis but nevertheless carried out his duties as outgoing secretary of state during the waning days of the Eisenhower administration. He kindly provided me with an office, a small staff, and access to important cable traffic. Sometimes Herter invited me to comment on specific problems, but I always reminded him that Kennedy refused to allow any of us incoming officers to comment on decisions taken during Eisenhower's final days. "Mr. Secretary," I told him, "it's still your show."

I, of course, underwent an extensive FBI investigation to become secretary, and as part of that, I filled out a long questionnaire on loyalty and security issues. One question read, "Have you ever tried to overthrow the government of the United States by force or violence?" I answered no. The next question was "Has any member of your family ever tried to overthrow the government of the United States by force or violence?" I answered yes. The next line stated, "If the answer is yes, name them." So I put down the names of my two grandfathers without explaining further. That threw the examiners into a tizzy until they figured out that both my grandfathers had fought for Robert E. Lee and the Confederate Army in the Civil War.

The Senate quickly reviewed my lurid past and confirmed my appointment by voice vote. Lack of personal wealth may have reassured them. At one point Senator George Aiken of Vermont questioned me about my connections with the Rockefeller family, Chase Manhattan, and Standard Oil. He asked if I had divested myself of all securities.

"Senator," I replied, "I have never held securities in corporations."

"What do you do with your money?" asked Aiken.

"I begin, sir, by paying taxes."

Having never expected to become secretary of state, I had no personal staff or "team" to take with me to Washington. This made the move difficult, especially for Virginia. Much of the burden of that hectic period in late 1960 and early 1961 fell upon her, but she handled it wonderfully. She found our family a home, moved our household belongings from New York to Washington, made all the arrangements for our children to finish school, and took up the full-time duties of a cabinet officer's wife. Public life is tough on the wives and children of those whose names are in the headlines. The job of secretary of state often called for fifteen- and sixteen-hour days, including diplomatic dinners in the evening. Virginia and I ate at home with the family about once a month during my eight years as secretary of state, and the children essentially grew up on their own.

At any rate, we were in Washington, more or less settled in, and I was ready to begin my new job. Thirty-three years after leaving Cherokee County, I knew a thing or two, but my "real learnin' " was just about to begin. As I began my first days in office, I thought back to a letter I had written John Foster Dulles in 1953 at the end of his first hundred days as secretary. The letter was a long and unsolicited commentary on his performance as secretary of state as I saw it. I offered him my views "as a friend who wants nothing more than to see your complete success in the toughest of all jobs." I likened his job to that of an airplane pilot:

The secretary of state flies a four-engined plane. He draws his power and support from (1) the president, (2) the Congress, particularly the Senate, (3) the Department of State and the Foreign Service, and (4) the public, with emphasis on the press. The secretary can fly his plane on three engines and . . . for a considerable time with two, as did your predecessor [Dean Acheson]. But at least two motors must be in good shape. . . . It goes without saying that if all four motors are sputtering, trouble is ahead. It doesn't make life any easier to discover that sometimes the four motors don't want to move in the same direction.

I then commented on the condition of Dulles's four motors—his relationship with President Eisenhower, problems in Congress posed by the Republican right wing, lingering unrest by "your troops" in the department following Truman's departure—and offered some hints about dealing with the press. Boldly I also suggested several areas where Dulles could improve his piloting.

Little did I know that only eight years later I would experience my own first hundred days as secretary of state, and I am not too proud to admit that my own performance during that critical learning time was also less than perfect. I had told President Kennedy at West Palm Beach that no one was fully qualified to be secretary of state, and that was surely true of me.

During the early weeks of Kennedy's presidency many of us senior advisers sat on our own little posts of responsibility and did not look at problems from the broad perspective in which a president must see them. Another difficulty that we faced was than many of us were strangers to each other and to President Kennedy as well; I was not the only cabinet officer who first met Kennedy in December.

I believed that cooperation between departments was particularly important. I developed this belief way back during the Truman administration when Louis Johnson became secretary of defense. Johnson knew that I had lots of friends in uniform and that I worked for maximum communications between State and Defense. Johnson didn't like that, wanting to be in complete control of the Pentagon and its relations with the Department of State. He insisted that every communication between the two departments go across his desk. Once I heard a knock on my office door. A distinguished-looking general stuck his head in and said, "Are you Dean Rusk?" I nodded, and he said, "I'm General Burns. May I see you a minute?" I invited him in. He said, "I've just been given a new job by the secretary of defense."

"Oh, what's that?"

He said, "Secretary Johnson told me to protect the Pentagon against that fellow Dean Rusk over in the State Department, so I thought that I ought to come over and get acquainted." General James H. Burns and I became good friends.

I resolved that the mistrust that led General Burns to my doorstep would not take place under the Kennedy administration. Actually, Robert McNamara, Kennedy's secretary of defense, and I developed a very effective working relationship. But not in time for our first crisis. Early on we did not give Kennedy the best advice we could have.

On April 17, 1961, a brigade of some fourteen hundred anti-Castro Cuban exiles, organized, trained, armed, transported, and directed by the Central Intelligence Agency, landed at the Bay of Pigs to overthrow Fidel Castro. CIA advisers assured the brigade that Castro's own men would defect, that the landings would inspire a popular uprising against

Castro's regime, and that American forces would back them up in case of trouble.

The exile force made it to the beaches, but the landing was opposed. The men fought bravely while their ammunition lasted, but they were quickly surrounded by tanks and twenty thousand Cuban soldiers. Two of their freighters containing vital ammunition, food, and medical supplies were sunk by Castro's planes, and President Kennedy forbade U.S. forces to go to the brigade's assistance. Castro's troops crushed the brigade in less than three days. The general uprising never took place, and Castro arrested two hundred thousand Cubans in Havana alone. Throughout the island he rounded up anyone suspected of underground connections.

The circumstances leading to this fiasco are well known. When Castro first seized power in 1959, he was supported by most Americans, relieved that former Cuban dictator Fulgencio Batista's repressive rule had finally ended. Soon afterward Castro even visited Washington and talked about replacing the Batista regime with a constitutional democracy, based upon free elections. Americans at first wanted to work with Castro. In fact, there is some classic television footage of Castro walking out of then Vice President Richard Nixon's office and Nixon putting his arm around Castro and saying, "We're going to work with this man."

However, the relationship soured, and Castro angered Eisenhower even more by demanding that the U.S. Embassy in Havana reduce its staff to eleven people within forty-eight hours. After asking Kennedy and myself through Christian Herter if we wished to advise him on whether to break relations with Cuba (we chose not to), Eisenhower broke off relations on January 3, seventeen days before the Kennedy inauguration.

During the transition State Department briefers warned me there was something I should learn about Cuba as soon as I took office. On January 22 I found out about the Cuban exile brigade training for an invasion of Cuba. I later learned Kennedy had received a briefing on the brigade in November, but I doubt he ever endorsed it or opposed it. He and I never discussed it before our January 22 meeting.

In subsequent briefings I discovered that the CIA had begun to train the Cuban exiles in Guatemala in 1960. They planned to launch a conventional assault and establish a foothold close to main population centers. The exile group was described as having a broad political base made up of liberal democrats, not just Batista followers. The CIA also believed that defectors from Castro's armed forces and other anti-

Castro Cubans would join the brigade after it landed and trigger a popular uprising to overthrow the Castro regime. If the brigade did not succeed in the invasion, it would fall back into the hills and conduct guerrilla operations.

CIA planners may have remembered that Castro's own movement started small but eventually overthrew Batista. We had heard of widespread disillusionment in Cuba and had seen a steady stream of refugees fleeing the island. This gave us the impression that many Cubans did not like Castro and would do something about him if the opportunity arose.

Within his own administration President Kennedy received divided advice. White House aide Arthur Schlesinger, Jr., wrote a stiff letter of opposition, and Undersecretary of State Chester Bowles strongly opposed it as well. I reported Bowles's opposition to Kennedy, but I did not give him the memorandum Bowles gave me since Kennedy had let us all know he didn't like having a bunch of memos shoved at him. Vice President Lyndon Johnson appeared skeptical about the operation, but he didn't attend many of our meetings on it; he seemed to think the invasion was a harebrained scheme that could not succeed. William Fulbright, chairman of the Senate Foreign Relations Committee, also opposed the invasion and told the president so. But other key congressional leaders were not consulted because we feared leaks. Ironically, more congressional consultation might have helped Kennedy avoid a serious mistake.

President Kennedy nevertheless decided to proceed, primarily on the advice of Allen Dulles and Richard Bissell at the CIA. The Joint Chiefs of Staff also supported the operation, but I am convinced they never looked at the plan as professional soldiers. They figured that since the whole show was a CIA operation, they would just approve it and wash their hands of it. Had the Joint Chiefs been responsible for the operation, my guess is they would have expressed serious reservations; for example, they would have spotted the great gap between the brigade's small size and its large objectives.

I myself did not serve President Kennedy very well. Personally I was skeptical about the Bay of Pigs plan from the beginning. Most simply, the operation violated international law. There was no way to make a good legal case for an American-supported landing in Cuba. Also, I felt that an operation of this scale could not be conducted covertly. The landing and our involvement would become publicly known the moment the brigade started for the beach. We didn't grapple with that reality at all. Finally, having never seen actual evidence that

Cuba was ripe for another revolution, I doubted that an uprising would spring up in support of this operation.

But I never expressed my doubts explicitly in our planning sessions. With large numbers of people sitting around the cabinet room talking with the president, I felt that my role was to penetrate weak points and raise searching questions about assumptions taken for granted. Although I expressed my opposition privately to President Kennedy, I should have made my opposition clear in the meetings themselves because he was under pressure from those who wanted to proceed.

I should have pressed Kennedy to ask the Joint Chiefs a question that was never asked. Kennedy should have told the chiefs, "I may want to invade with American forces. How many men would we need to conduct the operation ourselves?" I am sure that the chiefs would have insisted upon sustained preliminary bombing and at least two divisions going ashore in the initial landings, with full backup by the Army, Navy, Marines, and Air Force. In looking at the chiefs' total bill, Kennedy also would have noted the extraordinary contrast between what our professional military thought was needed and the puny resources of the Cuban brigade.

Having been both a colonel of infantry and chief of war plans in the China-Burma-India theater in World War II, I knew that this thin brigade of Cuban exiles did not stand a snowball's chance in hell of success. I didn't relay this military judgment to President Kennedy because I was no longer in the military.

Only once during these planning meetings did I venture military advice. When we first sought acceptable landing sites in eastern Cuba, I suggested that if the brigade actually invaded, it should land immediately east of our base at Guantánamo Bay. That way, if the brigade ran into trouble, we could rescue it from Guantánamo, or if the brigade succeeded, we could support it. But the Joint Chiefs rejected this, not wanting to compromise the virginity of Guantánamo by getting it mixed up with this operation. They moved the landing site much farther west to the Bay of Pigs.

The Joint Chiefs may have had the better argument because had the brigade landed next to Guantánamo and failed, we might have been forced to withdraw from the base as well. There would have been great international pressure upon us to cede the base to Cuba had we involved Guantánamo in the landings.

I am not sure which specific arguments convinced Kennedy finally to authorize the invasion. An overriding concern for him might have been the chance to overthrow Castro's regime. Cuba's move toward communism had been a deep shock to the American people, posing a real threat to the stability of other Latin American countries. Thus, Kennedy may have felt the operation worth the risk, if success meant a non-Communist Cuba and a loyal member of the Organization of American States (OAS). Cuba's focus on Marxist revolution was unsettling the hemisphere.

Yet Kennedy was clearly troubled by the operation, and I am sure that he saw the difficulties. His judgment to proceed was very much razor-edge, a closely balanced decision. It would have been very difficult to disband the brigade, already organized and trained.

In retrospect, if I had mounted a campaign within the administration and pulled together Secretary of Defense Robert McNamara and the Joint Chiefs and others, I might have blocked the invasion. But I found that kind of activity distasteful, in terms of the relative positons of the president and his senior advisers and the advice to which he is entitled. To me, such actions would have been like conspiring against my president. Kennedy knew of my doubts. Yet in replaying and re-thinking everything, I wished that I had pushed my reticence aside and organized resistance to the invasion or at least insisted that the Joint Chiefs come clean with an honest, professional, military judgment regarding its probability of success.

And so the invasion went on as planned, and it ran into trouble from the beginning. Early Saturday morning, April 15, Cuban exile pilots flying prop-driven B-26's took off from an airfield in Nicaragua and attacked Castro's air force on the ground in Cuba. The raid damaged only a few planes. Equally ominous, the CIA cover story that the raid was the work of defectors from Castro's own air force fell to pieces when one B-26 made an emergency landing in Key West, alerting the American press. Not only did the raid fail to knock out Castro's air force, but it warned him that further action was imminent.

Early Monday morning, April 17, the exile force of fourteen hundred men reached the beaches at the Bay of Pigs after a difficult landing. The brigade met stiff resistance on the ground, and there was no popular uprising. Castro's few T-35's raised havoc during the first two days, strafing the brigade on the beaches and sinking two supply ships. Sometime during this period, with the invasion suffering from inadequate air support, Richard Bissell and Charles Cabell of the CIA came to my office and asked my permission to launch a second B-26 strike against Cuban airfields. They claimed the second strike had already been authorized. My impression was that this had not been part of the plan, although I wasn't sure because I never had a written copy of the plan.

I told them I couldn't authorize that strike. They persisted, and I invited them to call President Kennedy and ask him personally. They elected not to do so but later claimed that had that strike gone ahead, Castro's planes would not have hit the landing ships.

That was nonsense. A handful of obsolete B-26's could not have provided air cover for the landing or destroyed Castro's entire air force, as small as it was. Even if American planes had flown the mission, as some were advocating, a sustained and systematic operation would have been required; we didn't even know where Castro had hidden all his planes.

The Bay of Pigs invasion was an obvious blunder. The news of this disaster and the subsequent loss of life hit Kennedy hard. It also shook his confidence in people for whom he had great regard. It increased his tendency to be skeptical of everything he was told, a healthy attitude for any American president. I was especially concerned over what damage it would do to the administration and Kennedy's relations with Congress and our NATO allies.

Kennedy himself refused to deny his responsibility, as some White House aides suggested he do; some even hinted to the press that Kennedy was only carrying out an operation planned and organized by President Eisenhower. This infuriated Kennedy. We had had a full chance to review the operation and make our own judgment, and he wasn't going to dump the failure on Eisenhower. He immediately held a press conference and took full responsibility. But some others, Chester Bowles, for example, went around Washington after the Bay of Pigs, telling reporters, "Oh, this was a terrible mistake . . . a great mistake. . . . I tried my best to prevent it." When this got back to the president, it cooked Chester Bowles's goose with John Kennedy. He deeply resented any lack of solidarity in his own administration over this debacle. He remarked that "success has many fathers, but failure is an orphan," and he did not like it when some of his own people abandoned ship.

Although I deeply regretted not forcefully opposing the Bay of Pigs, as far as the rest of the world was concerned, I didn't let any blue sky show between me and the president. My opposition was not known even within the Department of State. Many of my colleagues, including Chester Bowles, believed that I favored the invasion. But when it came time to close ranks with the president, that I did.

Despite my poor performance in advising Kennedy, our relationship came away strengthened. He really appreciated personal loyalty in a disaster of this magnitude. Two years later, in the summer of 1963,

I suggested to the president that with the 1964 elections approaching, he might want to make a fresh start with someone else as secretary of state. He said, "Hell, no. And don't bring that up again. I like your guts, and I don't have many people around here with guts." And on another occasion, on a 1962 trip to Great Britain with President Kennedy, we had dinner with Prime Minister Harold Macmillan at Chequers, his official home in the country. After dinner, when Macmillan was about three sheets to the wind from drinking highballs, he lurched up to me, put his arm around my shoulder, and said, "Rusk, I have got to know you better. Jack tells me that you were opposed to the Bay of Pigs, but after it happened, you acted as though you had planned it yourself."

As for the Bay of Pigs disaster itself, General Maxwell Taylor and Bobby Kennedy conducted a postmortem on everything we did wrong—and that was just about everything. Error one was the timing. We had just taken office, and we weren't ready as a team to evaluate so serious a plan. We were just getting to know each other, and Kennedy had not established his own methods of administration. He should have turned to his secretaries of state and defense and said, "I would like a recommendation from you fellows on this." But he kept talking to all sorts of people, including junior staff officers, as though we were equals in the responsibilities we carried. Once, after a press conference in the State Department auditorium, Kennedy and some others came up to my office to discuss the Bay of Pigs operation. There were seven or eight people around the table, some of them very junior, and yet he went right around the table, asking each one to give his views on the operation. I was the only one to express any reservation. I never again took part in that kind of session.

Error two concerned the CIA's playing games with Kennedy. I am completely convinced that at no time did the president ever consider using American forces at the Bay of Pigs. Some in the CIA might have thought that if the brigade got ashore and ran into trouble, Kennedy would have to send Americans in support. The brigade itself thought so. Both completely misread the president.

A third problem was that those proposing the operation also provided the information upon which the "go, no-go" decision was made. The CIA told us all sorts of things about the situation in Cuba and what would happen once the brigade got ashore. President Kennedy received information which simply was not correct. For example, we were told that elements of the Cuban armed forces would defect and join the brigade, that there would be popular uprisings throughout Cuba when the brigade hit the beach, and that if the exile force got into trouble,

its members would simply melt into the countryside and become guerrillas, just as Castro had done. When that moment arrived and the
brigade found itself sinking, we were told that the men had no guerrilla
training and that such an idea was infeasible.

Undoubtedly much of the CIA's intelligence came from biased
speculation by Cuban exiles anxious to topple Castro and return to
Cuba. Because intense secrecy surrounded the operation, I myself could
not consult my own Bureau of Intelligence and Research at the State
Department, from which I might have received different information
about conditions inside Cuba. Secrecy was so tight that I did not even
discuss the operation with my senior colleagues in the State Department. So few people analyzed the plan that the talents and resources
of the government were not brought to bear.

None of this means that I impugn the motives of the CIA planners;
they were high-minded, dedicated, and loyal. But I do think they got
caught up in the enthusiasm for this project and made intelligence
estimates based upon wishful thinking. They may have been enticed by
the prospects of overthrowing the Castro regime in Cuba, a dramatic
stroke. They may have remembered the CIA's earlier actions in Guatemala and thought this operation would be as simple. But I thought the
operation was too pat, their answers to probing questions too glib. Their
commitment distorted their judgment.

John Kennedy himself supported the CIA's insistence upon total
secrecy for obvious reasons; anything less would have compromised the
entire operation. This may have been an error. Castro had probably
infiltrated the brigade with his own people and knew more about the
plans than Kennedy's senior advisers. The extreme emphasis on secrecy
also concentrated responsibility for the entire operation in CIA hands.

This secrecy has also made it difficult for historians to reconstruct
the Bay of Pigs operation, particularly its planning, because very little
was put on paper. Dulles, Bissell, and others proposing the operation
briefed us orally. Sometimes they handed out papers, but the papers
were always gathered up after the meetings. Because we weren't allowed to study the plan, we never had a precise understanding of what
was to happen.

The Kennedy-Taylor Report also established that considerations of
international law were simply brushed aside when the final invasion
decision was made. No one asked the State Department legal adviser
or the Justice Department to prepare a brief on the proposed operation.
The entire U.S. role in the invasion clearly violated international law,
as spelled out by the UN General Assembly's definition of aggression.

Of course, we rationalized that should the invasion succeed, it would be self-legitimizing if Castro were run out of office and a new Cuba had come into being. Yet we were troubled by what we were doing. Conducting this operation covertly did not give us the chance to mobilize overt support that we might have gotten from other nations in the hemisphere or from the American people. Conceivably, with success, we could have overcome OAS objections. I believe that after the disaster, our Latin American neighbors were appalled more by the invasion's failure than by the invasion itself. Most Latin American governments would have been delighted to see the landings succeed. Had a new government taken over in Cuba, most would have promptly recognized it. But they could not support a failed operation.

The United Nations was another matter. Inevitably the operation came before the UN, and Adlai Stevenson had a hard time justifying it, given the general attitude of member naitons toward covert actions. Although he hated every minute of it, Stevenson performed brilliantly at the UN. He had not been fully briefed ahead of time and was embarrassed by events. At one point I unwittingly contributed to the confusion. We received reports that several Cuban planes had defected to Florida, and I passed that word along to Adlai. Then I found out that these "defections" had been staged; the planes had been rigged by the CIA to land in Florida as if they were Cuban planes. I was misled, and in turn I misled Adlai; that kind of thing just made the whole operation an unholy mess. But he did a brilliant job of advocacy with a weak theoretical case. Had Adlai been consulted about the Bay of Pigs, I have no doubt that he would have sharply opposed it. His opposition might have made some difference.

President Kennedy had named Stevenson to the United Nations with the understanding that he would help formulate foreign policy. With Adlai in New York, that proved difficult in practice. His participation throughout his tenure at the UN was less than he would have liked, and there were times—certainly the Bay of Pigs—when he fretted over "not being in on the takeoffs as well as the crash landings," to borrow Senator Arthur Vandenberg's expression.

The Senate Foreign Relations Committee conducted its own post-mortem of the disaster. At one executive session, not among my more pleasant appearances before that committee, I remember testifying that among our concerns was the possibility that Cuba might eventually become a missile base for the Soviet Union. This was in spring of 1961, two and one-half years before the Cuban missile crisis.

In analyzing the mistakes of this first-class disaster, we learned our lessons the hard way. But we learned quickly, and there was not much chance that we would fall into that kind of trap again. The sharp contrast between our handling of the Bay of Pigs and our later handling of the Cuban missile crisis reflected many lessons learned at such cost in the spring of 1961.

Despite our setback, we continued to grapple with the problem of Castroism in the hemisphere. Longer-range efforts not relating specifically to the Bay of Pigs operation came to fruition in 1962 at the Organization of American States conference in Punta del Este, Uruguay. At that meeting the OAS expelled the Castro government from participation in hemispheric affairs and declared that Marxism-Leninism was incompatible with the institutions of the Western Hemisphere. The vote was not unanimous, but we got the necessary two-thirds to isolate Castro.

Following the Bay of Pigs, the CIA tried harassing Cuba with various dirty tricks. I vetoed some as being foolish or unproductive. For example, the CIA once proposed contaminating shipments of Cuban sugar with a chemical to render the sugar inedible by the time it reached foreign ports. I thought that was just damned nonsense. Covert action against Castro by Cuban exiles was discontinued while we were negotiating the release of the brigade, seized after the abortive invasion, but this was resumed after Castro released the prisoners.

As for assassination plots against Castro, I didn't know any existed until the Church Committee hearings in 1975, long after I had left office. On one occasion Llewellyn Thompson, my representative on the interdepartmental 303 Committee, which reviewed CIA activities, mentioned to me jokingly that some junior person at a meeting had said something about the assassination of Castro. Tommy and I both laughed and agreed that it should be knocked out the window, and it was knocked out of the window as far as we were concerned. We simply didn't take it seriously. Where authorization for the assassination plots against Castro and other foreign leaders came from as disclosed by the Church Committee hearings remains a complete mystery to me.

I have always marveled that the Bay of Pigs fiasco did not inflict greater damage upon the Kennedy administration than it did. We survived that episode better than we had any right to expect. The international community and the United Nations could have really nailed the United States for violating international law. But most governments were sorry that we had failed; regret, not outrage, seemed to mark their reactions.

The Bay of Pigs disaster was one hell of a way to close out my first hundred days as secretary of state. Sometime after the tragedy my secretary, Phyllis Bernau, who had been John Foster Dulles's secretary, quietly came into my office and laid on my desk a copy of the letter I had sent Foster Dulles eight years earlier. That letter has since become a chain letter for incoming secretaries of state; just for fun, in January 1969 I sent a copy to President Nixon's Secretary of State William Rogers.

12

Showdown over Berlin

Even as the Bay of Pigs fiasco unfolded in Cuba, a more serious foreign policy crisis was brewing in Berlin. The Kennedy administration was not the first to come into conflict with Moscow over the little isolated outpost of the West. Indeed, throughout the postwar period Berlin had been a bone in the throat of the Soviet Union, a little island of freedom in the middle of a Communist world. The contrast between West and East Berlin was a continuing embarrassment to the Soviets and East Germans and a threat to totalitarian society. The flow of refugees fleeing East Germany to the West, including many professional people, became a flood by 1961, a virtual hemorrhage. Berlin itself was an infectious city to neighboring East Germany, with its robust economy, Western-style affluence, and political freedoms.

Berlin had long been a bone in my throat as well, beginning when I was a Pentagon staff officer involved with the four-power occupation of Germany at the end of World War II. As head of United Nations Affairs, I also worked on lifting the Berlin blockade in 1948. In retrospect, it was a great mistake when the United States failed to demand a land corridor for West Berlin at the European Advisory Commission talks in 1945. Our ambassador to the talks later said that he did not press for a corridor because he didn't want the Russians to think we mistrusted them. Of course, the purpose of diplomacy is to make agreements where the issue of trust does not arise. At the end of the war we pulled our forces back from large areas of Germany to comply with those 1945 agreements, and the rest is history.

Shortly after the Kennedy administration took office, I warned the president about renewed Soviet pressures on Berlin. I believed that Khrushchev might decide to test the new president, and the Soviets also wanted formal recognition of a divided Germany. Additionally, Khrushchev in early January delivered a rather aggressive speech on wars of national liberation. All told, since the West was so exposed in Berlin, it was a logical place for Khrushchev to turn up the heat.

I wasn't the only one concerned about renewed Soviet pressure on Berlin. In early February I met with the West German foreign minister, who expressed similar fears as well as uncertainty about the depth of the new administration's commitment to defend Berlin. I assured him that the Kennedy administration recognized the importance of Berlin and West Germany and was fully committed to the defense of both.

Just after this, on February 17, the Soviets told the West Germans that unless a comprehensive peace treaty to terminate the Allied occupation and four-power administration was signed, they would sign a separate peace treaty with East Germany. West Berlin, the Soviets said, would become a demilitarized "free city," and the East Germans would take over from the Soviets control of all air and land access routes to Berlin. The Allies would then have to negotiate with East Germany new terms of access.

For the next several weeks the Berlin situation simmered as Kennedy, National Security Adviser McGeorge Bundy, McNamara, and I dealt with Cuba, the Congo, and Laos. But the Berlin problem did not go away. From my perspective, Berlin was all the more dangerous because President Kennedy wanted to travel to Europe and while there, if possible, meet with Khrushchev. I was nervous about this, and although I didn't recommend flatly against it, I saw the glare of publicity that accompanies a summit as something that could not help our position in Berlin.

Traditionally secretaries of state are skeptical about negotiations at the summit. I don't object to courtesy visits in which leaders get acquainted and shake hands and perhaps agree to start negotiations. But there is simply not enough time at a summit for the careful, precise negotiating that makes for genuine agreement. For example, a summit that lasts six hours must be cut in half for interpretation and in half again for equal time, and that leaves each head of state one and one-half hours. Additionally, an American president at the summit is under pressure from the news media and the public to produce results, whereas the Soviet chairman is not under that same pressure. Secretaries of state are inclined to believe that summits are courts of last resort that should not come into action very often. Chills still run up my spine when I think of what might have happened if Khrushchev and Kennedy had met face-to-face during the Cuban missile crisis. I firmly believe that negotiations conducted quietly behind the scenes, not in the atmosphere of a football stadium, are more likely to succeed.

Yet there is something about the chemistry of being president that causes presidents not to agree with secretaries of state on the value of summits. Presidents are inclined to think that if they could just sit down with that other fellow, maybe they could work things out. So against my urging, President Kennedy concluded he should meet with Khrushchev, and in mid-May a summit was set up for Vienna in early June 1961. And even worse than the summit itself, there was no agreed-upon agenda, a sure prescription for disaster.

Thus, we went to Austria, supposedly a neutral country. In Vienna huge crowds greeted Kennedy everywhere he went. On one occasion, while I was riding with the president through those beautiful Viennese streets, with these huge crowds cheering and shouting, Kennedy interrupted our high-level policy conversation and told me with a laugh, "You know, Rusk, you're a hell of a substitute for Jackie."

Kennedy's welcome in Vienna contrasted sharply with Khrushchev's. The Soviet leader drove through nearly empty streets, greeted by stony silence. I even felt a little sorry for him. To this day I remain convinced that this contrast nettled Khrushchev and added to his jealousy of Kennedy's youth. Several times during the summit he referred to Kennedy's youth, and he never meant it as a compliment.

At the summit Khrushchev began with a long ideological screed about communism and the inevitability of the world revolution. When he got through, Kennedy said to him, "Well, Mr. Chairman, you're not going to make a Communist out of me and I'm not going to make a capitalist out of you, so let's get down to business." Some of our Kremlin watchers, George Kennan among them, thought that Kennedy made a mistake by not answering Khrushchev with his own ideological reply. I sympathized with Kennedy; so much time is wasted on fruitless ideological recitation.

But once the two did get down to business, they made some headway on Laos and set some guidelines that helped us establish the Laos accords of 1962. However, when the discussion turned to Berlin, the conversation became very rough. At one point Khrushchev said to Kennedy, "We are going to negotiate a new agreement with East Germany, and the access routes to Berlin will be under their control. If there is any effort by the West to interfere, there will be war."

Diplomats almost never use the word "war"; they always talk about "gravest possible consequences" or something like that. But Kennedy went right back at him, looked him in the eye, and said, "Then there will be war, Mr. Chairman. It's going to be a very cold winter."

Clearly at the Vienna summit, held only two months after the Bay of Pigs fiasco, Khrushchev set out to intimidate this new, young president of the United States. The experience sobered and shook Kennedy. He stood head to head with Khrushchev in their verbal duel, but for the first time he felt the full weight of Soviet pressure and ideology. It was a brutal moment, and Kennedy was clearly startled that Khrushchev would try to roll over an American president. What bothered Kennedy even more than the Berlin issue itself was that Khrushchev would even make such an attempt.

Khrushchev also presented us with a formal aide-mémoire setting December 1961 as the deadline for a peace treaty. If one were not signed by then, the Russians would go forward on their own. But how serious were the Russians? My own belief was that if the Soviets went public with their demands, they were deadly serious, and on June 10 my worst fears were confirmed: The Soviets published the aide-mémoire.

We now had a real crisis on our hands, and we spent much of the rest of June preparing a detailed U.S. and Western position on Berlin. No one favored conceding anything to the Soviets, but we differed on how to approach the issue. Dean Acheson, whom we called for advice, advocated a building up of NATO and U.S. nuclear and conventional forces to demonstrate Western resolve. He also wanted an allied ground probe along the autobahns if the Soviets tried to cut off access. Adlai Stevenson wanted a buildup of NATO and U.S. nuclear and conventional forces to defend our rights in Berlin, but he also wanted progress on resolving other Berlin issues. My own position, supported by Bob McNamara and our outside consultant Henry Kissinger, was to talk the question to death. I saw nothing that we could negotiate. We already had a Berlin policy, and it had stood firm for fifteen years. It was the Russians who wanted a new policy, who wanted to change the status quo. The Berlin problem could not be solved in my view, but neither did I want it to deteriorate into war. I also advocated passing the problem on to the United Nations.

When we returned to Washington after the Vienna summit, we drafted a specific response to Khrushchev's aide-mémoire and within a week or ten days at most delivered it from the State Department to the White House. There our draft response died. Martin Hillenbrand, who worked on the Berlin task force, told me years later what happened: After getting no response from the White House, State inquired where the draft was and got only embarrassed evasions. Finally someone admitted he had lost the draft. We immediately sent over another copy, and again there was dead silence from the White House. Then we were told to our amazement that the second draft had been locked up in the safe of another White House staffer who had gone on a two-week vacation, and no one could get into the safe. The State Department had already circulated that draft to the British, French, and Germans. At that point White House aides were trying to cover their tracks with Kennedy, who was getting impatient with me because of State's alleged delay. The whole mess got blamed on the State Department.

Hillenbrand further told me that after we resurrected the missing draft and everyone took a shot at it, the White House decided it was too dry and factual. Ted Sorensen, Kennedy's special assistant and speech writer, redrafted it, filling it with flowery language that read like an inaugural address but was totally unacceptable for a diplomatic note. This led to further delays as the exciting adverbs and purple prose were toned down. Aware of Kennedy's irritation over the delay, Hillenbrand and his colleagues sent a memo to the president, gently implying that the ball had been bobbed in the White House. Hillenbrand told me that he suspects that memo was also diverted; Kennedy never mentioned it.

Meanwhile, in early August, I flew to Paris to meet with the French and British in an effort to coordinate our response. I didn't believe in full-scale negotiations—seeing little to negotiate—but thought we and the Soviets could hold "exploratory talks" to see if there was a basis for negotiations. Trying to draw four governments together on the precise language of a common policy is never a simple matter. But we agreed that West Berlin was vital to the integrity of NATO and the safety of Europe as a whole and that negotiations with the Soviets were acceptable, but only if our positions were well prepared and didn't insist on preconditions.

During the summer, in response to Khrushchev's ultimatum, Kennedy asked for significant increases in our defense budget, called up selected National Guard and Reserve units, and began beefing up our forces in West Germany and West Berlin. I supported the buildup but urged that we do so quietly and not declare a national emergency. In talks with our NATO allies, we reached solidarity on the importance of defending Berlin. We agreed that our presence was vital not only to the health and well-being of the people of West Berlin but to the entire NATO alliance. The West quickly demonstrated to Khrushchev that it was serious about the defense of Berlin.

But Khrushchev and the East Germans saw Berlin in a different light. Many years earlier Winston Churchill spoke of an Iron Curtain stretching from the Baltic to the Black Sea. Berlin was a hole in that curtain. After the Vienna summit we thought the Russians and East Germans would have to do something to stanch the flow of people fleeing East Germany through that hole. By 1961 this steady emigration had become a flood: doctors, engineers, scientists, skilled workers; in July alone thirty thousand East Germans, a hemorrhage that was bleeding them white.

I was at a baseball game on August 13 when I was informed the East Germans had begun to build a barricade and to string barbed wire between East and West Berlin, the first step in what eventually became the Berlin Wall. This move caught us by surprise, but we soon determined that the East Germans aimed the Berlin Wall at their own people, not the people of West Berlin. They were not trying to keep anyone out, but rather to keep their own people in. It was a startling demonstration of the nature of Communist society.

We quickly decided that the wall was not an issue of war and peace between East and West; there was no way we would destroy the human race over it. By and large, even though we often thought their actions despicable, what Eastern European regimes did to their own people was not an issue of war and peace between East and West. So we did not seriously consider knocking the wall down. Had we done so, either we would have had an immediate confrontation with Soviet forces or they simply would have moved the wall back fifty or one hundred yards and started again. How far into East Germany would we go to keep knocking down walls? Some of our critics wanted us to threaten general war over the wall, but if you take that first step by military means, then you must think of the second, third, and fourth steps.

But the Berliners were terribly disturbed seeing this wall go up, this hideous scar that now divided their beautiful city and broke off contact between East and West Berliners. Although we weren't going to give up West Berlin because of that wretched wall, the wall created a psychological problem that we had to deal with. We had to separate the understandable psychological reaction to the building of the wall from the safety and security of West Berlin. We lodged a firm protest with Moscow over the building of the wall; I called it a "confession of Communist failure"; and President Kennedy sent fifteen hundred additional troops to West Berlin over the autobahn. He also sent Vice President Johnson to Berlin and later visited Berlin himself.

With the West's position in hand, President Kennedy felt that the time had now come for negotiations with the Soviets on Berlin. I still believed that we should talk with the Russians only to see if a basis for negotiations existed and, I hoped, to talk some of the fever out of the crisis. The British agreed, but the French and Germans were hesitant. French President Charles de Gaulle refused to participate in discussions with the Soviets, believing there was no basis for any new agreement on Berlin that would be acceptable to the West. He relied wholly on his conviction that the Soviets would not seize Berlin by force because he felt they knew it would result in general war. He didn't think they wanted war. We were less certain, because Khrushchev had a well-earned reputation for impulsiveness and had gotten himself way out in front on a major commitment. Berlin was always vulnerable militarily; the city was more than one hundred miles inside East Germany; token contingents of British, French, and American soldiers were surrounded by overwhelming Warsaw Pact divisions. To Khrushchev, West Berlin was a tempting target.

The Germans, meanwhile, were willing for us to have talks but were biting their fingernails, fearing we might make vitally important concessions on West Berlin. German Chancellor Konrad Adenauer always took a hard line on "German issues," but I often wondered how deeply he meant it. He always insisted that we proclaim our support for German reunification, but I never felt Adenauer wanted reunification. Germans themselves were nervous as cats about negotiating with the Soviets, and Adenauer was suspicious of anything that smacked of an agreement with the Russians. He feared and resented Slavic pressure against Western Europe. Not trusting the Russians, he felt negotiations with them were meaningless, and he resented any agreement that didn't somehow improve the "German question."

Although I occasionally became irritated with the old chancellor, I could never remain angry with him. He was a great figure in German life who had brought Germany out of a terrible war onto a sound democratic footing. But he lived in a world of shadows and needed constant reassurance about the loyalty of the Americans to NATO and to Germany. John Foster Dulles had had to give him assurances every few months about American support, and I was expected to as well. Adenauer had a great affection for Dulles and used to remind me of it often. Every time I called on him, he would spend the first ten minutes reminiscing about the "good old days of John Foster Dulles." I found this rather amusing because I had known Dulles well, and Dulles had told me about the problems he had with Konrad Adenauer.

Despite this French and German hesitancy to talk, we and the British felt that we ought at least to meet with the Soviets. After all, Khrushchev had issued an ultimatum. We were operating against a deadline. Although we could not see any basis whatsoever for a fresh agreement on Berlin in the face of Russian demands, British Foreign Minister Alec Douglas-Home and I decided that we could talk just as long and just as repetitively as Gromyko. We may have surprised Gromyko—he wasn't used to Western long-windedness—but we just talked and talked. We repeated ourselves and made the same arguments over and over again. We even began to refer to our different positions by numbers; we'd say to Gromyko, "That is argument number four. Should we go over it or should we just pass on to another subject?" Even in this stale exercise we were taking some of the steam out of the crisis.

Throughout this period we maintained that there were three non-negotiable elements in any Berlin settlement: West Berliners must retain their political freedom, the United States must retain its forces there, and the West must have free civil and military access to the city. We met with Soviet Foreign Minister Andrei Gromyko in late September and October and reiterated these points. We also suggested that East Germany conclude an agreement with the Soviet Union recognizing the four-power agreement on access to Berlin. For his part, Gromyko stated that the USSR would delay its December deadline if the United States was serious about negotiations.

These negotiations were not easy. Gromyko started off with the same hard language—"there will be war"—that Khrushchev used at Vienna. At one point I finally told him, "Now Mr. Gromyko, if you want war, you can have it in five minutes. All you have to do is start it. But if you don't want war, then we'd better talk about this further." On another occasion, as the Soviets continued to drop chaff in the Western air corridors leading to Berlin and practiced other forms of harassment, Alec Douglas-Home gave Gromyko unshirted hell. He verbally hit Gromyko between the eyes by turning to him and shouting, "This harassment has got to stop! This must stop! You must not and cannot do this!" Although he kept his poker face, I think even Gromyko was startled by the intensity of Douglas-Home's remarks. The harassment stopped shortly afterward. Additionally, Douglas-Home and I repeatedly told Gromyko point-blank, with as much conviction as we could muster, "Berlin is *not* vulnerable because the United States, Great Britain, and France are there!" In our making that statement, what stood behind our words—Western preparedness and resolve—greatly influenced how those words were perceived by the Kremlin.

Both at Vienna with Khrushchev and later with Gromyko, we also stressed that the Soviet Union could not give to East Germany what it did not possess—namely, control over allied rights in Berlin. As victorious powers in World War II, Britain, France, and the United States were in Berlin on the same basis on which the Soviet Union was in East Berlin and East Germany. We also insisted that the Soviets not interfere with allied access to Berlin.

Then, on October 17, the first day of the Twenty-second Congress of the Soviet Union's Communist party, Khrushchev withdrew his deadline for a new German peace treaty. The Berlin crisis was over, but the Berlin problem remained.

We still had to work on solidifying NATO's position. Thus, at the NATO foreign ministers' meeting in Paris in December 1961, all the foreign ministers except France's Maurice Couve de Murville were unanimous that talks with the Soviets should continue. At one point we got locked up over the word "negotiations" in the final communiqué; Couve simply would not allow its use in the text. We spent most of the day on that single word, and I finally cornered Couve in a corridor and asked him why he did not telephone de Gaulle, clear the way, and go along with the majority. He said, "One does not telephone President de Gaulle." I later learned that in fact, he had talked with de Gaulle on the telephone and had had his instructions confirmed. As a result of that experience, I told my NATO colleagues that thereafter I would not spend more than fifteen minutes on a communiqué. If it took longer than fifteen minutes, I would absent myself from their deliberations.

Soviet harassment of Western access to Berlin, particularly air traffic, began again in February 1962, but the Soviets still evidenced a desire to talk. From March 11 to 27 I talked almost daily with Andrei Gromyko at the Eighteen-Nation Disarmament Conference in Geneva. We accomplished nothing, but neither did the situation worsen; again, our long talks may have helped defuse the crisis. Shortly before I left Geneva, Gromyko suggested that the new Soviet ambassador to the

United States, Anatoly Dobrynin, continue the discussions. Dobrynin and I discussed Berlin from mid-April to late May, and I must say I became rather good at saying the same thing over and over in different ways.

Berlin continued percolating and may have been a precipitating factor behind the Soviet decision to install missiles in Cuba later in 1962. And on occasion a sense of crisis returned. As late as September 1963 Soviet forces harassed the American military's access to Berlin on the autobahn, over the issue of tailgate inspections. To me, issues involving Berlin have always reminded me of the dance of the gooney birds on Wake Island—much posturing on both sides. Each event is loaded with symbolism, and issues such as the height of the tailgates on trucks and whether or not we would lower them for Soviet guards took on absurd political significance. We were as much concerned that the Soviets might try to nibble us to death with minor incidents—known as slicing the salami—as we were with more dramatic actions. After all, it was Khrushchev who said, "Berlin is the testicles of the West. Every time I want to make the West scream, I squeeze on Berlin." That was far too apt a metaphor.

There are two postscripts that must be added to the 1961–62 Berlin crisis. I accompanied John Kennedy on his trip to West Berlin in June 1963, and we were awed by these tremendous masses of West Berliners surrounding Kennedy, stretching as far as the eye could see. Their response to Kennedy was unforgettable. I stood with Konrad Adenauer during Kennedy's speech, when Kennedy told that huge crowd, *"Ich bien ein Berliner."* Afterward I asked him, "What did you think of this today?" Adenauer said, "I am worried. Does this mean that Germany could have another Hitler?" Kennedy himself wondered if he had perhaps gone too far in stirring up the emotions of the people of Berlin; the response was overpowering.

That Berlin was a crisis of the highest order was underscored by a conversation I had with Khrushchev at the Black Sea in August 1963. After the signing ceremonies for the Limited Test Ban Treaty, Khrushchev invited me to visit him at his dacha. It was my fourth meeting with Khrushchev; on all occasions he impressed me as a shrewd, impulsive, ebullient, highly intelligent man, a dedicated Communist, and a great patriot of Mother Russia. But during our talks at the Black Sea, Khrushchev drew me aside with only his interpreter and told me something that still chills my blood.

"Mr. Rusk," said Khrushchev, "Konrad Adenauer has told me that Germany will not fight a nuclear war over Berlin. Charles de Gaulle has told me that France will not fight a nuclear war over Berlin. Harold Macmillan has told me that England will not fight a nuclear war over Berlin. Why should I believe that you Americans would fight a nuclear war over Berlin?"

That was quite a question, with Khrushchev staring at me with his little pig eyes. I couldn't call Kennedy and ask, "What do I tell the son of a bitch now?" So I stared back at him and said, "Mr. Chairman, you will have to take into account the possibility that we Americans are just goddamn fools." We glared at each other, unblinking, and then he changed the subject and gave me three gold watches to take home to my children.

At the time I was often asked what my hopes were for resolving the Berlin crisis. I said, "I hope to be able to pass this problem along to my successor." This we were able to do—without war and without sacrificing the integrity and safety of West Berlin. In 1971, one decade later, President Nixon negotiated a constructive new four-power agreement on Berlin, East and West Germany recognized each other, and both joined the United Nations. The "Berlin problem" remains, but it is not the same flashpoint of violence and confrontation among the great powers that it was during the sixties.

13

The Cuban
Missile Crisis

Berlin was a festering problem
that perplexed several U.S. administrations, but the Kennedy administration had the unfortunate luck to experience the most dangerous
crisis the world has ever seen, the Cuban missile crisis. The superpowers
were at each other's throats, national interests and national pride were
publicly at stake, and neither side at first showed any willingness to
back down. But we managed to come through and survive the crisis,
an achievement that I've always viewed as a triumph of both American
and Soviet diplomacy.

The crisis began slowly enough. During the spring and summer of
1962 we received quite a few reports about offensive missiles in Cuba,
mostly from Cuban refugees. We checked out every rumor that we
could and concluded that these refugees had seen surface-to-air antiair-
craft missiles (SAMs). The business end of a SAM missile lying on its
launcher looks like one hell of a missile.

That same summer Senator Kenneth Keating of New York took up
the cry, charging that strategic missiles were in Cuba. But Keating
would not share with us any of his alleged sources so we could check

them out. Reconnaissance overflights and on-the-ground espionage within Cuba yielded little new information.

On Sunday, October 14, a U-2 reconnaissance plane flying over San Cristóbal in western Cuba photographed what was clearly a ballistic missile complex under construction. Fortunately for us, the Soviet complex had exactly the same configuration as similar sites in the USSR itself. This allowed us to identify the missile site quickly, and I remain convinced that had the Kremlin used a different deployment pattern, we might not have identified the site until the missiles were ready to fire. We would have been confronted with a fait accompli.

The U-2 film was processed on October 15. That night I was at a party when I received a call from Roger Hilsman, assistant secretary of state for research and intelligence, about the damning pictures. I immediately knew that we had a major crisis on our hands. On the military side, Soviet missiles installed in Cuba could destroy our Strategic Air Command bases with almost no advance warning; missiles coming from the Soviet Union at least gave us fifteen to twenty minutes to get our planes airborne.

The political consequences of missiles in Cuba were equally bad. If we allowed deployment of Soviet missiles just ninety miles off our coast, American credibility would have been destroyed, and there would have been a devastating psychological impact on the American people, the Western Hemisphere, and NATO. As for domestic politics, the Kennedy administration would have been discredited. Clearly the missiles would have to go. The question was how to remove them.

By midnight on October 15 all of President Kennedy's senior advisers knew about the photos. McGeorge Bundy thought it best not to awaken the president, arguing that the best preparation for him would be a good night's sleep. Briefed on the impending crisis when he awoke, Kennedy immediately formed an ad hoc group called the Executive Committee of the National Security Council (ExComm) to advise him. The ExComm had sixteen members, including McGeorge Bundy, Bob McNamara, Maxwell Taylor, Douglas Dillon, Bobby Kennedy, Paul Nitze, George Ball, Llewellyn Thompson, John McCone, Ted Sorensen, Dean Acheson, Lyndon Johnson, and myself. And I guarantee that if each wrote his own account of the Cuban missile crisis and ExComm deliberations, there would be sixteen different stories, each true from the author's perspective.

At our first meeting we talked about the military and political implications of missiles in Cuba and formed working groups to examine our options. They included bombing the missile sites, invading Cuba, and forcing the missiles out by the so-called quarantine plan. A fourth task force chaired by Llewellyn Thompson studied possible Soviet responses. The one alternative we didn't examine was doing nothing. All agreed that the missiles were simply unacceptable.

Although I realized the missiles would have to be removed, I didn't commit myself to any policy line or join any task force at first, although I consulted with all. Others were more vocal—notably Paul Nitze and Maxwell Taylor, who argued for an air strike to destroy the missiles. Bob McNamara and George Ball opposed an air strike, and McNamara even argued that Soviet missiles in Cuba did little to change the strategic equation.

As secretary of state I felt that I should hold myself in reserve and hear all points of view before giving my recommendation to the president. Also, President Kennedy and I decided that we would continue to meet our public appointments since we did not want the crisis to become public until we had decided on a course of action. He thought that even to reveal the presence of Soviet missiles in Cuba might spark demonstrations, peace groups marching in the streets, perhaps a divisive public debate that could have misled the Soviets. Critics would cry, "Soviet ICBMs can already hit the United States. Why get so excited about missiles in Cuba?" We worried that premature disclosure could lead to panic and confusion and even a mass exodus from our cities. It would have passed policy initiative to the Soviets; there's no telling what might have happened. So I kept to my schedule and had Undersecretary of State George Ball sit in for me at many meetings. Fortunately security held, and events moved too fast for an adverse public reaction.

Remarkably for a "leaky" administration, security remained tight. Everyone knew this was one hell of a crisis and refrained from shooting his mouth off about it. Fortunately security was not so tight as during the Bay of Pigs fiasco eighteen months earlier. Then only Kennedy's top people were involved. This time, in addition to the ExComm, we immediately drew in a broad range of talented people and resources within the government. For example, my State Department intelligence researchers were fully involved.

The atmosphere at our ExComm meetings was extremely serious, but I would not call it emotional. Although this was the worst crisis we ever faced, most of us had been there before. The emotion that Bobby Kennedy portrayed in his book The Thirteen Days and that was reflected in the television program "The Missiles of October" was unique to Bobby; this was his first major crisis. His brother set the tone for us all, however. Throughout, John Kennedy was cool as a cucumber. That alone—keeping his cool—was JFK's greatest contribution in the crisis.

Quite apart from ExComm and task force meetings, much private consultation took place. I talked at great length with Bob McNamara, Llewellyn Thompson, George Ball, McGeorge Bundy, and Bobby Kennedy. Our one-to-one consultation probably had more to do with the successful outcome of the crisis than formal action taken by working groups and the ExComm itself. I worked closely with Thompson, former ambassador to the Soviet Union and our in-house Russian, because the Soviet reaction to whatever we did would be the crucial factor in the crisis. In fact, Tommy Thompson was the unsung hero of the crisis. His deep understanding of the Russians helped us predict Khrushchev's probable reactions.

During the first week we further refined our policy options. I intentionally took no position at first because I did not think that was my appropriate role. Instead, I raised many questions. For example, on Thursday, October 18, I argued against a surprise attack, pointing out that world opinion would turn against us because we didn't first try diplomatic avenues and because an air strike would inevitably kill Russian advisers, perhaps causing Khrushchev to react impulsively. Later that day I stated that if the Soviets had not stopped working on the missile sites by October 23, we should announce our intent to attack and destroy the sites the following day, telling Khrushchev that any response on his part would mean war. These were not contradictory positions; I was probing the strengths and weaknesses of both options.

Throughout the first week we debated possible courses of action, likely Soviet responses to each, international reaction, and the role of international law. The Justice Department thought we should invoke the doctrine of self-defense in whatever action we took. Our State Department legal office didn't think we should broaden the doctrine of self-defense in that fashion since nobody had fired a shot and we were not under attack. We recognized that Cuba could legally obtain defensive weapons, as laid out in the Rio Treaty and the OAS Charter, as long as they did not threaten peace in the Western Hemisphere. But the Rio Treaty and the Charter also provided another way: The OAS Council could declare the missiles a threat to the peace and call on Cuba to get rid of them. I pressed hard for this, and we decided to use the OAS approach.

Some ExComm members, Dean Acheson, for one, wanted to brush legal matters aside, but I argued that a nation's legal case greatly influences public opinion and the attitudes of other governments. I reminded my colleagues that among the problems facing the British, French, and Israelis in the Suez crisis of 1956 was that they had not presented a feasible "theory of the case." They did not give anybody anything to support. I also pointed out that we had brushed aside legal issues during the Bay of Pigs and had been burned badly. The legal case was very important.

Legal issues also led us toward a naval "quarantine" instead of a "blockade." In international law a blockade can mean a number of things, but over the years the blockade concept had become rigid and developed all sorts of barnacles. A blockade was hard to apply in strict accordance with international law. To shed the barnacles and allow for maximum flexibility, we hit upon a new term, "quarantine," partly because no one knew exactly what a quarantine meant. Ironically, this created problems since our Navy insisted the quarantine was a blockade. Bob McNamara had to ride herd on the Navy in implementing the quarantine.

We were uncertain whether the Soviets were on to our discovery of the missiles. Soviet Foreign Minister Andrei Gromyko in particular added to our uncertainty. On Wednesday, October 17, I hosted a long-scheduled dinner for Gromyko at the State Department, and during our long after-dinner talk, Gromyko let on nothing about the missiles. President Kennedy met with Gromyko the next day and gave him every opportunity to confess knowledge of Soviet missiles in Cuba. At one point Kennedy even read from transcripts of his own press conferences, stating that the appearance of such weapons in Cuba would create a very grave situation. Gromyko kept a poker face and did not respond, but his interpreter came up out of his chair as though he were wired, suggesting that he understood the significance of Kennedy's words.

As Kennedy talked, he had before him a stack of pictures of the missile sites, but he decided not to show Gromyko the pictures since we still hadn't decided on a course of action. Gromyko asserted that the Soviet Union had shipped only defensive weapons to Cuba. Here lay some ambiguity. To the Soviets, since these weapons were allegedly emplaced for the defense of Cuba, they could be called defensive. From our point of view, since they could hit almost all of the United States, they were offensive in character. However, to have shown Gromyko the pictures might have given the Soviets an opportunity to issue an ultimatum, which would have made things much more difficult to resolve.

We thought long and hard about each option, and curiously enough, each working group came back with good arguments as to why its own line of action was unsatisfactory. But gradually Bob McNamara, McGeorge Bundy, Bobby Kennedy, and I reached a consensus that a naval quarantine was the best course of action. Because it was a nonviolent response, we could more easily win international support in the United Nations and hemispheric support from the OAS, under the Rio Treaty. It would also allow Khrushchev more time to sort out his own options. If a quarantine did not work, we could move to an air strike or invasion. Others, the Joint Chiefs in particular, had reservations about a quarantine and still wanted to begin with an air strike, despite doubts that the Air Force could knock out all the missile sites.

Another dissenter was Adlai Stevenson, who wanted to take the matter directly to the United Nations. Adlai was unfairly criticized for this and in some accounts was charged with advocating a "Munich" and "selling out to the Russians." But John Kennedy did not take that view; he pointed out that representing the UN and making such proposals were Stevenson's job and that we were fortunate to have him at the UN.

After five days of deliberation it was time to decide. On Saturday morning, October 20, President Kennedy asked me as the senior person to begin the meeting with a recommendation. I had written on a small piece of paper "a naval quarantine" of Cuba, listed my reasons why, and added, "We should not suppose that this will be an inconsequential action. This will produce a crisis of the gravest importance." I read my note aloud and offered it to the president. But he didn't want anything in writing from that meeting, so I kept it. It is now in the State Department archives, only a small piece of paper.

Bob McNamara spoke next and supported a quarantine. Kennedy then asked Lyndon Johnson for his comments. Johnson told the president, "You have the recommendation of your secretary of state and your secretary of defense. I would take it." Kennedy did.

Having made his decision, President Kennedy decided to inform the American people in a 7:00 P.M. television address the following Monday, October 22—eight days after a missile site was first photographed. Ted Sorensen wrote the draft, but McNamara, Bundy, and I all worked with him in crafting a carefully constructed speech.

Two hours before Kennedy went on television, he called about thirty congressional leaders to the White House for their first briefing about the missiles. They were as shocked as we were. The facts spoke for themselves. Kennedy told the group we would respond with a naval quarantine. One elderly senator just groaned and fell over on the table with his head in his hands and stayed there for a while.

When it came their turn to talk, some senators, William Fulbright and Richard Russell in particular, pressed hard for an immediate strike on Cuba. Nevertheless, at meeting's end the group supported Kennedy, and despite their misgivings, neither Fulbright nor Russell publicly questioned the president's decision. Equally important, no one present questioned whether Kennedy had constitutional authority to initiate a quarantine. No one suggested that Kennedy come to Congress for authorization. In fact, one senator told me upon leaving, "Thank God I am not the president of the United States!"

An hour before Kennedy's speech I met with Soviet Ambassador Dobrynin in my office, gave him a copy of the president's speech, and told him we knew about the missiles and what we planned to do. Dobrynin aged at least ten years right before my eyes. He reacted as a man in physical shock. "This is a terrible situation," he said. "A most unfortunate thing for us to do." Judging by his reaction, I assume that Dobrynin didn't know about the missiles.

President Kennedy's speech went well, and now the entire world recognized the gravity of the crisis. One hour after the speech I met in the State Department with the ambassadors of over sixty nonaligned countries, showed them the photographs, and reviewed the steps that President Kennedy was taking. After that meeting about forty ambassadors lined up to shake my hand and wish us well.

Following the president's speech, I met with the press corps at the State Department; in fact, I talked with the reporters daily. That was a special week for the press; the reporters were tired, scared, and haggard, and they more or less leaned on me for support. In turn, my having to support them helped me to support myself. The press handled the missile crisis very well and was remarkably calm; there was little investigative or sensatinalized reporting that week. Reporters, like us, realized we'd be lucky to survive the crisis.

I stayed at the department very late the night of Kennedy's speech, not arriving home until 2:00 A.M. I went to sleep and woke up four hours later as daylight broke. With sunlight streaming through the windows, I thought, "Ah, I am still here. This is very interesting." Khrushchev had not immediately responded with a nuclear strike. This was serious business, but perhaps it wouldn't be fatal.

Later that morning we launched a diplomatic effort to win international support for the quarantine. Earlier we had asked Deputy Under-secretary for Political Affairs Alexis Johnson to prepare a diplomatic plan of action. Alexis put together a complex package involving close consultation with Western Hemisphere governments, NATO states, and also the United Nations. He did a superb job.

On that Tuesday Dean Acheson flew to Europe to line up French support. Acheson had wanted an air strike but nevertheless agreed to brief French President Charles de Gaulle. Acheson told de Gaulle, in essence, "Here is the situation, and this is what President Kennedy feels he must do." At the end of the conversation Acheson said, "Mr. President, I have with me the aerial photographs of the missile sites. Would you like to see them?" De Gaulle replied, "No, Mr. Acheson. The United States would not deceive me on a matter of such great importance. Tell President Kennedy he must do what he has to do. And if this leads to World War Three, France will be with the United States."

The British, by comparison, were somewhat skeptical until they saw the aerial photographs. Right away they urged Kennedy to release them. Some people in our intelligence community did not want them released because they didn't want the Russians to know of our espionage capabilities. But Kennedy wisely decided that this intelligence consideration was less important than the overall problem of credibility and publicized the photos. After that NATO support throughout the crisis was solid.

Adlai Stevenson presented our case brilliantly at the United Nations. He had pushed the UN option so strongly at earlier ExComm meetings that some of our members feared Adlai would be a little weak-kneed. This fear was totally unfounded.

Although we took the missile crisis to the UN, we knew this alone would not get the job done. With their veto, the Russians could postpone discussion and action in the Security Council until the missile sites became fully operational. Nevertheless, although the Cuban missile crisis was directly resolved between Washington and Moscow, it was very important that the Security Council take it up. Prolonged discussion lessened the chance that one side would lash out in a spasm and do something foolish. The UN earned its pay for a long time to come just by being there for the missile crisis.

In another prong of our diplomatic effort, seeking support from our Latin American neighbors, on Tuesday, October 23, we met in an all-day meeting with the OAS. I worked closely with Edwin Martin, assistant secretary for Latin American affairs. All twenty OAS members voted in favor of a resolution demanding that the Soviets withdraw all offensive missiles from Cuba. They also authorized the use of force individually or collectively in a limited blockade. We were delighted with the vote. I am convinced the overwhelming support we received from the international community—and Castro's neighbors in particular—helped persuade Khrushchev to withdraw the missiles. Support came willingly at that Tuesday morning OAS meeting in Washington;

I didn't have to twist arms or bludgeon anyone. OAS members believed Soviet missiles in Cuba were dangerous for the hemisphere and something had to be done about it.

The Soviets' initial reactions to Kennedy's speech worried us. They denied the missiles were offensive and condemned American "aggression." They continued to build their missile sites as twenty-five Soviet ships moved toward the quarantine line. The Soviets officially rejected our quarantine on Wednesday, October 24, and sent submarines to join their cargo vessels.

We imposed the quarantine very carefully, looking for maximum flexibility. Since it affected only offensive weapons, we allowed ships engaged in normal trade and not carrying weapons to go on to Cuba. We let a Soviet tanker through the blockade because it appeared to hold nothing but oil, and for our first boarding and inspection, we stopped a ship from another country rather than begin with a Soviet ship. At one point we moved our naval forces closer toward Cuba, reducing the radius of our blockade line from five hundred miles out to something less, to give Soviet ships steaming toward Cuba—and the Kremlin— more time. The crisis was building, and how it would end was unclear.

The moment of truth would not come until we stopped Soviet ships that carried missiles. Fortunately we never got that far since on Thursday several ships we suspected of carrying missiles stopped dead in the water, then turned around and headed back to the Black Sea. When we heard this news, I said to my colleagues, "We are eyeball to eyeball, and the other fellow just blinked."

That phrase came from a childhood game we used to play in Georgia, where we would stand about two feet apart and stare into each other's eyes. Whoever blinked first lost the game. It is not an easy game to win. That someone in the room leaked that remark to the press really infuriated me, the only leak in my eight years as secretary that could have been calamitous. Here in the middle of the crisis, where any consideration of face or prestige might make a considerable difference, I thought it incredibly stupid that a colleague leak that remark.

The television program "Missiles of October" misrepresented our reaction in the ExComm when the Soviet ships turned back. The filmmakers had people jumping around and clapping, as if their high school team had just scored a touchdown. That was not the mood at all. It remained very serious business. We knew that the missiles already in Cuba had to be taken out and that the Soviet buildup was continuing. We still had a most dangerous crisis on our hands.

Because of the missiles, we continued to build up our conventional forces in case an invasion became necessary. Florida was about to sink into the sea with the weight of military power we had assembled. Khrushchev could count sixteen American troopships steaming through the Panama Canal on one day, headed for Florida. We knew that Soviet missiles were on the verge of becoming operational, with intelligence predicting the sites would be finished possibly by Saturday, the twenty-seventh, and definitely by Sunday, the twenty-eighth. We would be ready to invade by Tuesday, the thirtieth, and could have launched an air strike sooner to prevent the sites from becoming operational.

In studying the Soviet deployment, I am convinced the missiles were brought into Cuba at the very end; that made them difficult to detect. The Soviets brought in all that equipment, everything prefabricated, even the concrete covers for the cables running from radar sites to firing positions. It was a superb technical job. We could see an empty cow pasture grow toward a missile site day by day, and we went down some blind alleys. One site we studied carefully for a couple of days turned into tennis courts.

Even though Soviet ships had turned around, time was running out. We made this very clear to Khrushchev. Earlier in the week Bobby Kennedy told Ambassador Dobrynin that if the missiles were not withdrawn immediately, the crisis would move into a different and dangerous military phase. In his book *Khrushchev Remembers,* Khrushchev states that Bobby Kennedy told Dobrynin that the situation might get out of hand in the United States and the military might take over. Khrushchev either genuinely misunderstood or deliberately misused Bobby's statement. Obviously there was never any threat of a military takeover in this country. We wondered about Khrushchev's situation, even whether some Soviet general or member of the Politboro would put a pistol to Khrushchev's head and say, "Mr. Chairman, launch those missiles or we'll blow your head off!"

On Friday, the twenty-sixth, came encouraging news; Alexander Fomin, the top Soviet intelligence officer in the United States, asked ABC's State Department correspondent John Scali to see if we would issue a public promise not to invade Cuba if the Soviets removed their missiles, pledged never to reintroduce them, and allowed UN inspectors to verify their removal. I gave Scali a note stating that we thought this could be worked out but that time was short. I told Scali to tell Fomin that our reply came from "the highest levels."

Kennedy also received a long message from Khrushchev, which we all believed bore Khrushchev's personal stamp. The letter encouraged us since Khrushchev obviously realized how grave the crisis was and indicated he wanted to avoid war, even implying that he might withdraw the missiles if we pledged not to invade Cuba. But its distraught and emotional tone bothered us, because it seemed the old fellow might be losing his cool in the Kremlin.

The next day, Saturday, we got another long message from Khrushchev, but this one was clearly a collective effort, a foreign ministry type of letter. It raised the red herring of U.S. Jupiter missiles in Turkey and offered to withdraw Soviet missiles in Cuba for our Jupiters in Turkey.

Those Jupiters had long been a problem for us. When Kennedy took office, he had on his desk a very negative report from the congressional Joint Atomic Energy Committee criticizing deployment of Jupiters in Turkey and Italy. The Eisenhower administration had built these medium-range missiles without knowing what to do with them. They could not be based in the United States since they couldn't reach the Soviet Union. So Eisenhower, casting about, managed to persuade both the Turks and the Italians to accept some missiles, and there they sat. The Jupiters were badly obsolete, and we even joked about where they might go if we fired them. They were also vulnerable. In Turkey any casual traveler with a .22 caliber rifle could shoot holes in the missiles from the adjacent highway and put them out of action.

Soon after taking office, Kennedy and I discussed the matter and decided we should withdraw the missiles. But during a Central Treaty Organization (CENTO) meeting in Ankara, Turkey, in spring of 1961, I had a walk in the garden with Selim Sarper, Turkey's foreign minister. I raised the question with him, and he expressed great concern. His government had just convinced the Turkish Parliament to appropriate money for the Turkish costs of putting those missiles in, and it would be very embarrassing to go back so soon to Parliament to say the missiles were being dismantled.

Second, he said that Turkish morale would be seriously affected if the Jupiters were withdrawn without substituting another weapons system such as Polaris submarines in the Mediterranean. But these submarines were not going to be available until spring of 1963.

I came home and discussed this fully with President Kennedy. He disliked further delay but understood the Turkish point of view. Also, we couldn't withdraw the missiles without consulting NATO. But reports that Kennedy blew his top during the Cuban missile crisis because the Jupiters were still in place were simply untrue. We regretted the Jupiters were still there because if we had destroyed the missile sites in Cuba, the Jupiters were likely targets. Early in the crisis, to discourage this kind of swap and lessen the threat the Soviets felt from the Jupiters, Kennedy ordered American personnel to remove their warheads and to do so conspicuously so the Soviets would see this.

All this occurred before Khrushchev's second letter of Saturday, October 27. In framing a response, the president, Bundy, McNamara, Bobby Kennedy, and I met in the Oval Office, where after some discussion I suggested that since the Jupiters in Turkey were coming out in any event, we should inform the Russians of this so that this irrelevant question would not complicate the solution of the missile sites in Cuba. We agreed that Bobby should inform Ambassador Dobrynin orally. Shortly after we returned to our offices, I telephoned Bobby to underline that he should pass this along to Dobrynin only as information, not a public pledge. Bobby told me that he was then sitting with Dobrynin and had already talked with him. Bobby later told me that Dobrynin called this message "very important information."

Later Dobrynin brought back to Bobby Kennedy a memo of conversation recording their exchange on the Turkish Jupiters, implying that we had made an official agreement. That memo was returned to Dobrynin as inappropriate in the circumstances.

Although most people credit Bobby Kennedy, actually Llewellyn Thompson came up with the idea of how to respond to Khrushchev's linking American Jupiters in Turkey to Soviet missiles in Cuba; Tommy suggested we simply ignore the second letter and respond to the first. Bobby got the credit because he proposed it at the ExComm meeting, but it was Thompson's idea.

It worked. We ignored the second letter entirely, picked up on Khrushchev's feeler in his first letter about an American pledge not to invade Cuba if the Soviets withdrew their missiles, and attributed the idea to Khrushchev. That was the key that defused the crisis.

There is a postscript to the saga of the Jupiter missiles. Neither Kennedy nor I, nor anyone on the ExComm with the exception of Adlai Stevenson and John J. McCloy, thought a missile trade with the Soviets wise because it smacked of blackmail and could set a dangerous precedent. Nevertheless, Kennedy clearly didn't want the Jupiters to impede the removal of the missile sites in Cuba and perhaps lead to war with the Soviet Union, since the Jupiters were coming out in any event. That Saturday night—October 27—the president remained troubled, and so did I; what would we do if Khrushchev refused to accept what Robert Kennedy had discussed with Dobrynin? We needed a final option, and instinctively I thought of the United Nations.

I suggested to Kennedy that he let me telephone Andrew Cordier, then at Columbia University, and dictate to him a statement which would be made by Secretary-General U Thant at the United Nations, proposing the removal of both the Jupiters and Soviet missiles in Cuba. I had known Andrew Cordier for many years in New York, and I trusted him. During his years at the UN he was known as an expert parliamentarian. He sat next to the president of the Security Council during all the debates. He also had ready access to U Thant.

Kennedy readily agreed. U Thant was in a better position to make this proposal than we, because the Soviets could more easily respond to a United Nations plea. From the U.S. point of view, the Jupiters were a red herring—they were coming out—and responding to U Thant wouldn't have been a serious concession on our part. The swap might have created strain within NATO, but a temporary disruption of the alliance or our relations with Turkey was preferable to war.

Kennedy never decided in advance to go to the UN; it simply gave him an additional option if the Soviets didn't withdraw their missiles. I called Cordier, and he quietly took the message. Cordier was to put the statement in the hands of U Thant only after a further signal from us. Fortunately we never had to send that signal.

The crisis ended as quickly as it started. On Sunday, October 28, Khrushchev announced from Moscow that he would withdraw the missiles under UN supervision. He simply announced it in a public broadcast, which made good sense because time was such a factor.

Fortunately we never saw nuclear warheads on Soviet missiles or launchers ready to fire. We thought their warheads were on ships coming through the Strait of Gibraltar when we imposed the quarantine because these ships were the first to turn back. All of us agreed that we couldn't allow the missile sites to become operational; it could have become an entirely different ball game if they had.

As the crisis wound down, President Kennedy said he didn't want us to gloat about a diplomatic victory. If Khrushchev wanted to play the role of peacemaker, let him. Kennedy didn't want to make life any more difficult for Khrushchev than it already was.

There were plenty of tense moments during the crisis. An American U-2 reconnaissance plane was shot down by a Soviet SAM missile fired from Cuba. I heard a rumor that Castro himself pulled the trigger that fired the SAM. But Kennedy kept his eye on the main play and didn't let the plane's loss alter our deliberations.

In a sense, Khrushchev reciprocated our restraint when one of our Alaska-based airplanes flew to the North Pole on a routine weather mission. Apparently, in turning for home at the Pole, the pilot locked on to the wrong star and soon found himself over Siberia. Fortunately he had the good sense to radio his base in clear English and say, "Hey, I think I'm lost. I may be over Siberia. For Christ sake, tell me how to get home!" The Soviets scrambled their fighters, listened to his chatter, decided that he was indeed lost, and didn't shoot him down.

We never knew why Khrushchev thought that he could put missiles in Cuba without a strong American reaction. Kennedy's failure to follow up the Bay of Pigs landings with American forces may have suggested to Khrushchev that our young president would not stand up in a severe crisis. Khrushchev may have thought that even a 20 percent chance of success would be worth taking, had the Soviets been able to complete the missile sites. We had some indication from a top-ranking Russian after the crisis that the Soviets wanted to get those missiles into Cuba secretly and quickly and then, after our November elections, use the Cuban missiles as additional leverage with us on Berlin.

Possibly Khrushchev put missiles in Cuba as a shortcut to nuclear parity with the United States; we did have superiority over the Russians in missiles at that time. Or perhaps Khrushchev was genuinely concerned about Cuba's security. After all, there was the Bay of Pigs and afterward a series of pointless "dirty tricks" pulled on Castro by the Central Intelligence Agency and Cuban exiles. Yet Khrushchev should have realized that deploying missiles in Cuba was too threatening and destabilizing for the United States meekly to allow this to happen. My guess is that Khrushchev had more than Cuba on his mind—probably Berlin.

The aftermath of the missile crisis was most interesting. Dean Acheson had opposed the quarantine strategy; he wanted an immediate air strike on Cuba. After the quarantine had proven successful, he said, "It was just plain dumb luck." Of course it was dumb luck. We were lucky; the Russians were lucky; the whole world was lucky. But I would hasten to add, you can give yourself a chance to be lucky. Acheson overlooked that.

Although nuclear war was avoided and the missiles were withdrawn, the Cuban missile crisis was not an unqualified success for U.S. policy. To begin with, the crisis could have been avoided. If we had more clearly explained our opposition to any potential stationing of Soviet nuclear weapons in the Western Hemisphere, Khrushchev probably would have never tried. Additionally, because many saw the crisis as a "victory" for the United States, shortly after their "humiliation" the Soviets decided to build up their missile forces. When factoring in lead time for research, production, and deployment of these weapons, much of the Soviet buildup we saw in the 1970's came from decisions taken in 1963. Soon after the Soviets withdrew their missiles, a senior Russian official told John J. McCloy in New York, "Well, Mr. McCloy, you got away with it this time. But you will never get away with it again."

A clear loser in the missile crisis was Fidel Castro. The attempt to station Soviet missiles on Cuban soil consolidated opinion in Latin America that Castro posed a real problem to the hemisphere itself, not just to Washington. His regime was closely linked to Moscow, and this meant the intrusion into the hemisphere of an extra-hemispheric force, violating not only the Monroe Doctrine but the hemispheric charters that multilateralized the Monroe Doctrine. The fear of a "second Cuba" became an issue for all.

After the missile crisis, Castro's influence in Latin America dropped to almost zero. Despite the earlier Bay of Pigs disaster and continuing economic and social unrest in Latin America—supposedly fertile ground for communism—Castroism as an exportable commodity from Cuba to the rest of the Americas seemed a dead issue. When Che Guevara went to Bolivia, hoping to export revolution, the Bolivian peasants didn't sign on. Castro's ability to monkey around with his neighbors became greatly diminished. When he was caught red-handed landing men and arms on the coast of Venezuela in 1964, the OAS foreign ministers imposed upon Castro all the sanctions that are available under the Rio Pact, with the exception of the use of armed force. But at this meeting they said to Castro that if his subversion continued, they would not exclude the possible use of armed force.

Despite the tension, there were occasional moments of humor. Once George Ball, Dean Acheson, my security agents, Gus Peleusos and Bert Bennington, and I were taking my personal elevator from the State Department garage to my seventh-floor office. As it was grinding its way up, I told Ball and Acheson, "You know, the only decent advice I have had this past week has come from these two fellows," pointing to Gus and Bert. Bert, an ex-lineman for the Pittsburgh Steelers and a hefty, gruff-spoken type, retorted, "The reason for that, Mr. Secretary, is that you have surrounded yourself with nothing but dumb fucks!" George Ball blushed moderately, Dean Acheson turned a scarlet red, and the American secretary of state was in near collapse with his best laugh of the week.

Another light moment came compliments of my younger son, Rich. During the sixties "raiding" was a favorite teenage pastime. A raid usually took place at night, and a family that had been raided would awake to find its house, trees, yard, and car draped with toilet paper or pelted with eggs, flour, and the like. Rich, as a "cabinet kid," had built-in advantages. Whenever he raided his friends, they would spend the next morning cleaning up their property, but when they raided the secretary of state's house in return, a story ran in the *Washington Post* or *Evening Star* saying VANDALS ATTACK DEAN RUSK HOME.

Midway through the Cuban missile crisis, as my son tells the story, one of his football teammates known as the Greek decided to stage a raid. We had security men with automatic weapons living in our basement at the time. Early one morning Rich's friend began crawling across our front lawn, dragging a heavy black satchel. My security agent Jim McDermit opened the front door and stepped outside, but the Greek dived into some bushes and fortunately was not seen. Jim went back inside. The Greek resumed his crawl and left on the front porch a satchel filled with bricks and a large alarm clock ticking away. On the satchel was the lettering "Black Russian." I walked by it on my way to work. Jim spotted this for a prank but nonetheless called in some bomb disposal experts. I got a chuckle out of the exercise, but if Jim had spotted Rich's friend, the outcome could have been tragic.

During the crisis my security men lived round the clock in the basement of our Spring Valley home to maintain communications and—if the horn sounded—evacuate me and my family to shelters in West Virginia. Having lived through the missile crisis, I am convinced that government leaders, if called upon to evacuate, are simply not going to say good-bye to their colleagues and possibly their own families and then board a helicopter and whirl away to some cave.

Even if we did, and if the president and secretary of state survived a nuclear attack, the first band of shivering survivors who got hold of them would likely hang them from the nearest tree. We can't suppose that a government which had allowed such a thing to happen would be allowed to function after the strike occurred. This whole program of evacuating top officials in a nuclear crisis is nonsense.

I've never been impressed with the case for civil defense against nuclear attack. Americans simply are not the kind of people to dig themselves underground. We're more inclined to say, "The hell with it. We're not going to live that kind of life." These shelters offer only a temporary existence at best. When I became secretary of state, the Republicans had just completed a brand-new State Department on C Street. Amid the Kennedy administration's renewed emphasis on civil defense in the months prior to the signing of the Limited Test Ban Treaty, I rode the elevator to the basement to look at the fallout shelter in our new building. It was the size of an ordinary living room. Even government didn't take civil defense seriously.

Anastas Mikoyan, the Soviet deputy premier and a first-generation Bolshevik, gave us another lighthearted—and fascinating—afterthought. Mikoyan was sent to Cuba just after the missile crisis to pacify Fidel Castro. The withdrawal of the missiles deflated Castro's prestige and made him something of a laughingstock in Latin America, and he was furious. Mikoyan stayed almost two weeks, during which time his wife died in Moscow and he did not even go back for her funeral. He came through Washington on his way home and told one of our people, "You know, that fellow Castro is crazy. He kept me, Mikoyan, waiting for ten days without seeing me. I finally told him that if he didn't see me the next morning, I was going home and he would be sorry. He finally saw me. That Castro is crazy."

Mikoyan also said, "You Americans must understand what Cuba means to us old Bolsheviks. We have been waiting all our lives for a country to go Communist without the Red Army, and it happened in Cuba. It makes us feel like boys again!"

After the crisis ended, John Kennedy gave each of the ExComm members a small desk calendar with the thirteen days of October highlighted. I have that calendar still, and whenever I glance at it, I remember a question that haunted me throughout the missile crisis and since. The question actually comes from the Westminster Shorter Catechism of the Presbyterian Church, which I had to memorize as a small boy growing up in Atlanta. It reads, "What is the chief end of man?" The catechism gives a theological answer: "To glorify God and to enjoy Him forever."

During the early days of the crisis, before Kennedy's speech to the nation, as I drove through the streets of Washington and saw people walking on the sidewalks and riding in their cars, not knowing what was going on, and as I thought about my own family, equally ignorant, I could not help remembering that question. It really asks, "What is life all about?" And I realized that this first of all questions had become an operational question before the governments of the world. Above all else, the Cuban missile crisis drove that home, and I found that very sobering. This crisis did raise the ultimate question, What is life all about?

14

Nuclear Strategy, Arms Control, and the Test Ban

The Cuban missile crisis drove home to all of us in the Kennedy administration that a nuclear exchange would be an unspeakable calamity. We had been to the abyss, had peered over the edge, and were most unsettled by what we had seen. Few of us were novices about nuclear strategy; Kennedy and his senior advisers, myself included, had received many briefings before the missile crisis.

The first—on the effects of a nuclear war—came shortly after our assuming office. That lengthy briefing was an awesome experience. Long aware of the power of nuclear weapons, I was surprised nonetheless by the magnitude of destruction that a full-scale nuclear war would bring. Every aspect of life would be affected. More than one hundred million Americans would die in the first salvo. Adverse effects included serious climatic change; even in 1961, long before Carl Sagan's nuclear winter thesis, we knew that neither superpower could tolerate the effects of nuclear weapons. To see it all laid out vividly confirmed Khrushchev's warning "In the event of a nuclear war, the living would envy the dead." After the briefing ended, Kennedy led me back to the

Oval Office. As we walked through the door, he had a strange look on his face. He turned to me and said, "And we call ourselves the human race."

President Kennedy clearly understood what nuclear war meant and was appalled by it. In our many talks together, he never worried about the threat of assassination, but he occasionally brooded over whether it would be his fate to push the nuclear button. From the early days of his administration, he lived through crises where he looked down the gun barrel of nuclear war.

Wisdom on nuclear matters stems from a clear understanding of what these weapons can do. Every president, every Soviet general secretary, the head of state and senior advisers of every nuclear power should go through a detailed and exhaustive briefing on the effects of nuclear war. Perhaps the UN could establish a five-member committee, composed of Americans, Chinese, Britishers, Frenchmen, and Russians, to brief political leaders everywhere. At the very least, leaders ought to understand what they are talking about when they discuss nuclear war.

If any of us had held doubts, that 1961 briefing convinced us that a nuclear war must never be fought. Consequently, throughout the Kennedy and Johnson years we worked to establish a stable deterrent and to get a handle on the arms race.

We began by changing our thinking on military strategy. By 1961 Eisenhower's policy of "massive retaliation," in which the United States would respond to any kind of attack with immediate use of nuclear weapons, had become outmoded. Earlier, massive retaliation had appealed to both NATO and the United States since the West could not match the Warsaw Pact's conventional forces. Reliance on nuclear weapons meant we could get by on the cheap. "A bigger bang for the buck" it was called.

During the first year or two of the Eisenhower administration, massive retaliation may have made sense as a deterrent, but by the mid-fifties, as the Soviets developed intercontinental bombers and missiles, a full nuclear exchange became an operational possibility. From that time forward American presidents had to face a new possibility: virtual destruction of the United States. That fact changed the basis of our foreign relations. It injected more caution and prudence into policy and led to attempts to build diplomatic bridges with Eastern Europe and find points of agreement with the Soviet Union.

By the time we took office, massive retaliation was outdated. So, too, was NATO's "trip wire" or "plate glass" doctrine, in which NATO would use nuclear weapons as soon as fighting started with Warsaw

Pact forces. The rhetoric of plate glass and trip wire was not believable even to NATO's European heads of state; they knew that a decision to use nuclear weapons would turn their countries into piles of ashes.

We in the Kennedy administration felt that a "balanced forces" strategy was more appropriate. Strong conventional forces gave us the option of a "flexible response" and even added credibility to our nuclear deterrent. A strong conventional NATO defense forced the Soviet Union to disclose its intentions and delayed any U.S. decision to use nuclear weapons. Thus, flexible response raised the nuclear threshold.

Flexible response remained linked with deterrence. We hoped, as before, if Soviet or Warsaw Pact forces were to attack the West, their leadership—and ours—would stop in their tracks and ask, "Now wait, where are we going here? Are we really going to destroy each other and the human race?" Having never seen any intention of a Warsaw Pact invasion of the West or any deployment of Warsaw Pact forces positioning to launch such an attack, I seriously doubt it will ever occur. If this happened, however, their forces would soon encounter American tactical nuclear weapons in the field. No American president could sit by and allow the Soviets to capture those weapons, and the Russians know it.

Because of our deployment of tactical nuclear weapons and the Warsaw Pact's superior conventional forces, the United States has never renounced possible first use of nuclear weapons. I personally think that the United States is committed to a second strike only, after we have received nuclear weapons on our own soil. Under no circumstances would I have participated in an order to launch a first strike, with the possible exception of a massive conventional attack on Western Europe. The Constitution does not authorize an American president to destroy the nation.

Flexible response had its problems. Our NATO allies, enjoying the protection of the American nuclear umbrella and getting by "on the cheap," were reluctant to undertake the added costs of building up conventional forces. It also struck some NATO members that our change in strategy meant a weakening of American support for NATO. They claimed we were prepared to allow conventional war in Europe but sought to avoid the threat of major destruction to our own country.

Charles de Gaulle in particular argued this point and used it to press ahead with France's own nuclear program, the *force de frappe*. Several times de Gaulle told me that France must have its own nuclear capability and not rely on someone else. If the Warsaw Pact attacked, "First there would be the battle for Germany. Then there would be the battle

for France. I want to have my forces ready for the battle for France."
He did not accept the idea of a NATO forward defense in Germany.
He was motivated by a mystical concept of France. Like any patriotic
Frenchman who had lived through those terrible chapters of French
history in World War II, he wanted to restore France's position among
the nations of the world. To de Gaulle, that meant having nuclear
weapons.

While boasting about a French nuclear striking force, a French
diplomat once observed that "the *force de frappe* . . . could be aimed
at any azimuth"—in other words, toward any point on the compass.
In response I asked, "Should we Americans take that statement into
account with the targeting of our own weapons?" He smiled rather
tightly and let the matter drop.

On another occasion a French reporter asked me, "Well, Mr. Secretary, don't you think that France should have a few nuclear weapons
which they can fire, to ensure the firing of the American nuclear force?"
I said, "Look, my friend, you are not talking about the real world. If
you're asking me, 'Do I think France should reduce itself to a cinder
pile in order to insure the firing of American nuclear weapons?' at least
you're in touch with the real world. Your question makes no sense,
standing alone."

Another difficulty with flexible response developed as the Kremlin
fielded its own battlefield nuclear weapons. It became probable that if
we used small nuclear weapons, the Soviets would, too, and further
escalation would almost inevitably occur. As far as I can tell, there
would be no way to stop it. A full-scale Soviet attack on Western
Europe would bring in both American conventional and nuclear forces
and lead to all-out nuclear war. Anyone who thinks escalation can be
controlled once nuclear weapons are used is living in a dreamworld.

But paradoxically, linking nuclear weapons to the defense of Europe
reduces the chances that conventional or nuclear weapons will ever
have to be used to defend Europe. Indeed, as secretary of state, under
no circumstances would I have supported an order to use nuclear
weapons first with the possible exception of blunting a massive Warsaw
Pact attack on Western Europe. In fact, with that single exception, I
believe the United States is committed to second use only, after we have
received nuclear weapons on our own soil.

At bottom, however, throughout the wide range of our foreign
policies in the sixties, I was struck by the irrelevance of nuclear weapons
to decision making, despite their unimaginable power. Nuclear weapons tie chains around the countries that possess them. Countries like

Burma, Uruguay, and the Central African Republic aren't influenced by our nuclear bombs. They know we're not going to drop one of them, whatever the dispute. Weapons that can never be used don't translate into political influence.

Most of Kennedy's advisers had this perspective and shared Kennedy's own abhorrence of nuclear war. Thus, the president with Congress's approval established the Arms Control and Disarmament Agency (ACDA) during his first year in office. ACDA was under the general guidance of the secretary of state, but nevertheless independent of the State and Defense Departments. The continuing Berlin crisis, the awesome destructive power of modern weapons and the speed with which they could be delivered, the momentum of the arms race itself and the fears and instability it alone creates, the possibility that some mistake or miscalculation could create a spark that could plunge the world into disaster brought into even sharper focus the urgency of arms control and the need for this agency.

ACDA was critically important in helping us focus our arms control policies. Before ACDA's creation, arms control was handled within the State Department, by personnel often borrowed from other agencies. I believed that a separate agency to coordinate the efforts of State, Defense, the Atomic Energy Commission, Congress, and NASA would be a better way to go; such an agency would help us arrive at a national arms control policy, using a full-time professional staff. I thought that disarmament was too complex a field to be addressed on an ad hoc basis by borrowed staff.

Kennedy named William Foster to head ACDA, a fortunate choice; Foster and I, old friends from the Truman years, had the same general views toward arms control. We really wanted to make progress. Foster carried the rank of undersecretary of state and as such had considerable leeway to cut across departments and agencies on behalf of a unified policy. An energetic and committed leader, he pushed so hard that he often collided with the Joint Chiefs. Their relationship became very touchy. But without Foster's persistence, we might not have had the Limited Test Ban or Nonproliferation Treaty.

We also established a Committee of Principals to work on arms control and related issues. The committee's members were the secretary of state, secretary of defense, chairman of the Joint Chiefs of Staff, the ACDA director, the CIA director, and the national security adviser. This was not a committee where the principals sent substitutes. We personally attended all meetings and worked hard. Bob McNamara and I frequently discussed arms control in our weekend meetings as well.

Thanks to McNamara, a staunch believer in arms control, I never had to arm-wrestle the Joint Chiefs on this score. McNamara took care of all disputes with the chiefs inside the Pentagon. And the chiefs always participated in our discussions.

Within the department itself, with the exceptions of Far Eastern Affairs and the European desk during the Berlin crisis, no single bureau received more of my time than ACDA. Bill Foster or one of his colleagues attended our morning staff meetings, I read all of ACDA's papers, and I talked daily with Foster or his able deputy, Adrian Fisher. As secretary of state I had overall responsibility for arms negotiations, for the instructions sent to our negotiators, for insuring that they spoke for the United States government with our internal differences resolved and all parties—State, Defense, ACDA, the Joint Chiefs, and the White House—on board. What I said flowed from meetings of the Committee of Principals; fortunately we agreed on the necessity of arms limitations.

Always, arms control stood among the top three items on our foreign policy agenda. Both the Kennedy and Johnson administrations were absolutely determined to negotiate limits to the arms race. Constantly before me was Bernard Baruch's vivid statement before the United Nations on nuclear disarmament: "We are here to make a choice between the quick and the dead."

On taking office, the Kennedy administration was engulfed in one crisis after another: Khrushchev's ultimatum at Vienna and the Berlin crisis, Communist aggression in Laos and Vietnam, and the dangerous missile crisis. Despite these events—and to some extent because of them—Kennedy and his senior advisers felt it was too late in history for two nuclear superpowers to pursue a policy of total hostility toward each other. Consequently, we searched for areas of possible agreement on large matters or small, agreement which might broaden the base of common interest between our two countries and reduce the range of issues which could lead to violence. At home Kennedy formed the Arms Control and Disarmament Agency and the Committee of Principals. Abroad we and the Soviets began talks that ultimately produced in the sixties a hot line agreement, a Limited Test Ban Treaty, two outer space treaties, a civil aviation agreement, a consular agreement, the Nonproliferation Treaty, and preliminary talks for the Antiballistic Missile Treaty concluded by President Nixon in 1972.

We kept negotiating quietly behind the scenes with the Kremlin. We also involved Congress. Our goal: to take a bite out of this nuclear impasse wherever we could find an opportunity. Whenever talks bogged down, we didn't fuss publicly over Soviet obstinacy or search for public relations advantages. We just kept at it, with unlimited patience, conscious of our joint and primordial responsibility for slowing an arms race that threatened the survival of the human race. Our strategy paid off—in arms control agreements with the Soviets that helped make the world a little safer.

But we also realized that nuclear weapons do not fire themselves. People do. We believed the nuclear weapons competition itself taxed the ingenuity and patience of decision makers. The more sophisticated, instantaneous, and complex these weapons systems become, the more difficult it is for frail human beings to control them. Acting on these views, with characteristic energy and foresight, Secretary of Defense Bob McNamara worked to improve safeguards on nuclear weapons, developing permissive action links—PALs—and other procedures to lessen the risks of accidental use. He encountered resistance from the Joint Chiefs, who felt these safeguards would slow our launch capability. Since I always believed we are committed to a second strike, actually to absorb nuclear destruction on our territory before counterattacking, slowing our launch capability didn't bother me in the slightest.

Like McNamara at Defense, I tried to modernize State for decision making in a nuclear age. One new wrinkle derived from my travels. When we stopped at Air Force bases for refueling, I tried to make a point of visiting our pilots on ready alert as well as the operators who scanned radar screens for long hours. In their tedious duties lay the safety of the Western world. We in Washington felt a special empathy for those men.

The Strategic Air Command impressed me during these visits. At SAC headquarters near Omaha, Nebraska, I saw that huge underground room with its screens, displays, and communications showing the location and readiness of the American and Soviet militaries. With officers on duty at every station, it was a scene that conveyed unimaginable power. During my tour someone pushed a button and some sixty nuclear firing centers came on-line instantaneously. It occurred to me that if they had that kind of communications to fire nuclear weapons, we ought to have similar communications to prevent their being fired. Back at the State Department, my colleagues and I lobbied Congress for money to build an operations center in the department.

PALs and improved communications centers were important, but they were only part of the control package. An early success with the Soviets occurred on the heels of the Cuban missile crisis. During the final stages of the crisis, when time was running out, we and the Soviets began to talk via public broadcasts. There simply wasn't time to route messages through embassies, to encode and decode via diplomatic channels. Because communicating by public statement isn't appropriate crisis behavior, we established the hot line, a teletype communication between the operations room in the White House and a similar room in the Kremlin. When one party wishes to make a call, it alerts the other. Officials convene at their respective teletype machines, then begin the transmission of messages with interpreters at both ends for instant translation. Designed for rare use, the hot line first came into play—by the Soviets—during the June 1967 Six-Day War.

Over time we improved the hot line by placing a clock on each end, showing the time of day in the other capital. During the Six-Day War the Russians got us up at 3:00 A.M., which quickly became something of a bore. During quieter times operators keep up a constant chatter to ensure that the hot line is operational. They exchange poems and stories of all sorts. Andrei Gromyko once asked me, "What does it mean when your people say, 'The quick brown fox jumped over the lazy dog'?"

Before the hot line, we had reached another understanding with the Soviets. For a long while they had called at the United Nations General Assembly for "general and complete disarmament," an approach we regarded as sloganeering and nonproductive. We preferred arms limitations that focused on more specific and obtainable objectives such as a limited test ban. "General and complete disarmament" was simply a pipe dream. It lacked substance. There was no way to put arms and legs on it. Utopian concepts are no framework for negotiations.

In the summer and fall of 1961 Soviet UN Ambassador Valerian Zorin and Kennedy's arms control adviser John J. McCloy hammered out a "joint statement on agreed principles." These principles did not lead directly to arms agreements, but they did enable us to adopt the Soviet position and get it off the table.

With that out of the way, we could get down to serious talk. During the Eisenhower administration the United States and Soviet Union discussed a comprehensive test ban treaty, and the Kennedy administration resumed talks quickly. Both countries were testing nuclear weapons, but given crises in Cuba and Berlin, we saw little prospect early in Kennedy's term for an arms agreement. Indeed, talks with the Soviets over a comprehensive test ban broke down in part because we couldn't agree on how to verify a ban on underground shots. Nevertheless, both countries continued to observe an informal moratorium on testing. I urged that the United States honor the moratorium and not be the first to resume testing. However, in August 1961 the Soviets undertook a massive testing program in the atmosphere. In a matter of weeks they set off dozens of blockbusters—huge, dirty bombs with massive fallout.

When they broke the moratorium, we faced a question: whether to resume testing. I supported resumption for military reasons; we couldn't continue an indefinite suspension while the Soviets went ahead. In the early 1960's both countries were developing nuclear technology at a lively pace. Failure to resume testing would have given us problems with Congress and the American people. Arms control requires reciprocity; we couldn't indulge in unilateral actions. I also felt that the hazards of radioactive fallout from atmospheric testing, although worrisome, were minimal compared with the potential risks caused by misunderstandings about our purposes and military strength.

As for underground testing, we and the Soviets disagreed over verification. The Joint Chiefs insisted on more verification than the Soviets would accept. Russian xenophobia and passion for secrecy, attitudes that go back to the czars, also impeded talks; the Soviets adamantly opposed on-site inspections. To overcome that, we wanted to locate little seismic black boxes in strategic points of the Soviet Union to help distinguish between underground tests and ordinary seismic events. We asked for eight boxes first, then seven; the Soviets would allow only three. Because the Soviet Union is so huge, we didn't think three were enough. The difference between seven and three made a comprehensive ban impossible, and negotiations locked up over it.

Throughout these negotiations I felt that the United States could not accept an underground ban without on-site inspections. Our government had to assure its own people that a total ban was being observed. Yet throughout the sixties the Soviets adamantly opposed on-site inspections. The issue was thorny because they look upon verification as a unilateral concession we demand of them. Consider the cultural differences, however. Russia can get information about us from congressional testimony, technical journals, and published reports. The Soviets are helped by an American government that does not know how to keep its mouth shut. To get intelligence not available on the open market, the Soviets used a little dash of espionage. In dealing with the Soviet Union, we faced a country in which large areas are off limits to foreigners, a government that keeps its mouth shut, and a closed society where surveillance is difficult to conduct. The Soviets did not need the kinds of verification we insisted upon.

Nevertheless, for us, verification remains essential both to monitor compliance and to maintain public support for arms agreements. Particularly in democratic societies, lack of knowledge over what the other side is doing could produce political storms of fear and suspicion leading to demagoguery that ultimately would undermine the entire structure of arms control. Verification is the means by which the politics of hate and fear can be kept under control.

As secretary of state I would have supported eliminating nuclear weapons if verification capabilities would have permitted it. If someone could have shown me then or now how to verify against hiding warheads away in salt mines in Utah, Siberia, and the Yunnan Province of China, I would propose zero nuclear weapons tomorrow morning. The American people are far less safe today than we were before these weapons were invented.

With Soviet opposition to on-site inspection and unwillingness to allow more than three seismic boxes, a comprehensive test ban was a dead issue. I personally saw another problem with a comprehensive ban: A ban on all testing might have led to dismantling our atomic laboratories and research teams, whereas the Soviet Union could more easily maintain these capabilities. Our own military was loath to give up testing existing missiles and warheads; without occasional proof-testing of our inventory, doubts might set in about the reliability of our weapons and lead to political turmoil. Stalemated on verification, we needed a new approach.

With this in mind, during the summer of 1962, at meetings of the Principals, I questioned the wisdom of continuing to insist upon on-site inspections and seven boxes. Why not propose an atmospheric test ban instead? It made no sense for our delegation at Geneva to press for a comprehensive ban. Kennedy agreed; a limited test ban was better than no ban at all.

But it takes two to tango in international negotiations. Throughout late 1962 and early 1963 we had no luck moving the Soviets toward a limited test ban. Khrushchev had his own problems with the Chinese, and in the wake of the Cuban missile crisis, he may have assumed that he couldn't move too far too fast. On our part, we gradually formulated our own conception of a Limited Test Ban Treaty during early 1963.

By May I thought everyone was on board with the limited test ban concept, but just as we were finalizing our proposal, the Joint Chiefs demurred. I was indignant; they had had over two years to object to a test ban and a full year to examine the limited test ban idea. Kennedy had approved the proposal, the Principals had all agreed that the risks of an unrestrained arms race outweighed the risks of a test ban, and Averell Harriman was leaving for discussions in Moscow in a month and we needed a position. Several days before Harriman's scheduled July 15 departure, the chiefs again declared they couldn't support a limited ban. I told the chiefs their time for review had passed.

Ironically, given Soviet obstreperousness in past talks, Khrushchev was the one who turned the key at Geneva that led to a limited test ban. Perhaps in response to discreet hints from our side, in early June he intimated to British Prime Minister Harold Wilson that the Kremlin might find a limited ban acceptable. On July 2, just thirteen days before Harriman's departure for Moscow, Khrushchev publicly called for a limited test ban outlawing nuclear explosions in the atmosphere, in outer space, and underwater. He suggested that we leave an underground testing ban for later.

A boat trip with Soviet Ambassador Anatoly Dobrynin might have played a small role in this. One evening in June 1963 Dobrynin and I went down the Potomac on the presidential yacht and spent several hours discussing arms control. Dobrynin and I badly wanted a treaty, and he might have communicated the seriousness of the administration's intent—and interest in a limited ban—back to Moscow.

Test ban negotiations and Soviet-American relations in general were greatly assisted by President Kennedy's speech of June 10, 1963, at American University. In his remarks, with an eloquence that only John Kennedy could muster, he asked the superpowers to move beyond ideology, bring an end to the Cold War, and recognize our common interests. I wish I could claim authorship of that speech, but I only read over the final draft. That speech was pure Kennedy.

Averell Harriman and his negotiating team flew to Moscow as scheduled on July 15, and ten days later Harriman had our treaty. Parties to the Limited Test Ban Treaty agreed "not to carry out any nuclear weapon test explosion . . . in the atmosphere, underwater, or in outer space, or in any other environment if the explosion would cause radioactive debris to be present outside the borders of the state conducting the explosion." We couldn't have sent a better man than Harriman; negotiating this treaty was his finest hour.

Back in Washington, news of Harriman's achievement excited us all, especially John Kennedy. Throughout the negotiations Kennedy exercised strong presidential leadership, a prerequisite for successful arms negotiations. He drew enormous satisfaction from the test ban's passage. He met frequently with the Committee of Principals, followed the negotiations closely, and mastered its detail. No one questioned his commitment. In a memorable United Nations speech he once referred to the threat of nuclear holocaust as a "sword of Damocles hanging over the human race by a thread." He called the test ban "not the millennium . . . but an important first step . . . a step toward peace—a step toward reason—a step away from war."

As a measure of Kennedy's enthusiasm for the treaty, he sent a prestigious delegation, including key senators and myself, to Moscow for the signing ceremonies. Throughout the sixties we kept senators fully briefed on arms negotiations and actively solicited their views, believing that involving them in all stages of negotiations, including treaty-signing ceremonies in Moscow, would enhance prospects for ratification.

When our delegation arrived in Moscow, nobody paid any attention to us as we moved through the city's streets. Two days later someone in the Kremlin passed the signal. Everywhere we went, crowds gathered to cheer and applaud. With the snap of a finger, the whole atmosphere changed. The Soviets have a remarkable ability to drum up public support or squelch protest. Some years later, during a demonstration outside the American Embassy, one of our officers asked a Soviet security man, "How long is this going to last?" The Russian looked at his wristwatch and said, "Sixteen more minutes."

Khrushchev himself was immensely pleased with the treaty. He threw a huge reception in the Kremlin, where we met among other Russians all the members of the Politboro and high officials of the Russian Orthodox Church. Amid the festivities, my wife, Virginia, and I visited Leningrad and were taken on a guided tour through the Hermitage Museum. We saw that remarkable art collection ranging from the czars' treasures to French impressionistic paintings. The Soviets placed Picasso's "Dove," the original painting, which had become the symbol of communism's peace movement, at the end of the tour. They asked me to sit in a chair under the painting to have my picture taken, but I politely declined.

Leningrad's "mayor" drove me around the city, pointing out the sights. Leningrad had been restored to its old classical beauty. At one point I turned to him and said, "I am so glad that I came because Leningrad is not what I expected to find."

"Don't mind," he replied. "Dean Rusk is not what I expected to find either!"

We both laughed. I think he expected horns and a forked tail or something.

The entire trip was especially poignant for me: the beauty of Leningrad, a private visit for Virginia and me with Khrushchev at his Black Sea villa, and, of course, the test ban signing, a source of elation to us all. One must live through dark times with the Russians to savor fully a moment like this. It was the first arms control treaty actually negotiated after eighteen years of talks between Moscow and Washington.

During our visit to his Black Sea villa Khrushchev played the perfect host to Virginia and me. On one occasion he began to speak of the bravery of the Russian people. "Mr. Chairman, you don't have to persuade me," I said. "We know the Russian people are brave." And then I recalled the defense of Leningrad during the German onslaught, defended by the men, women, and children of that city for over three years, under the most terrible conditions, one of the great epics in the history of warfare. When I glanced at Khrushchev, he had tears in his eyes. In that same conversation I asked why an old Bolshevik like him so often quoted the Bible. He told me about an old Russian priest, his first teacher as a small child. He had learned his Russian largely from the Bible. He obviously had great affection for and endearing memories of this old Russian priest.

At another point Khrushchev led me on a tour of his villa. He showed me his outdoor swimming pool, then pushed a button, and out slid a hangarlike cover, converting it into an indoor pool. Then we went into a small gymnasium, where Khrushchev and I picked up badminton rackets and batted a bird back and forth, without a net. The floor had no lines, because it was covered by a Persian rug. I complimented him on his badminton game, and he said, "It takes practice. It takes practice." The press made much of this "East-West contest" and reported that I had lost the match. The rotund Khrushchev was surprisingly agile; in a pinch, however, I believe my tennis background would have carried me to victory.

Despite heated opposition to arms control from some quarters, we sensed that most Americans supported the limited test ban. Americans are a peaceful people, isolationist at their core, not wanting territorial gain or wars of conquest, certainly not eager to destroy anyone with nuclear weapons. After the signing of the Limited Test Ban Treaty, John Kennedy got firsthand evidence of this when he toured the western states, talking about peace and the need for arms control. He was buoyed by the response; his overtures seemed to strike a responsive chord everywhere. Our experience in the sixties proved that a large majority of Americans will follow presidential leadership and support arms control in preference to the dangers, costs, and uncertainties of an unlimited arms race.

During Senate debate on the limited test ban, I testified on behalf of the treaty. This time the Joint Chiefs supported the treaty, in exchange for four safeguards: a vigorous underground testing program, continued maintenance of our atomic laboratories, improved detection devices, and a readiness to resume atmospheric testing if the Soviets ever began testing. On every point I supported the chiefs. From the viewpoint of foreign policy, I felt that we needed these safeguards and underground tests.

Limited though it was, the partial test ban was a great achievement. At the time it seemed a practical step toward limiting the arms race, and it likely slowed it somewhat. An additional benefit of the treaty was its environmental impact; since testing stopped, strontium 90 has practically disappeared from the atmosphere.

More fundamentally, after the Cuban missile crisis, it was important to demonstrate that the United States and Soviet Union could coexist. The test ban required careful and extensive negotiations, but we and they did sign a major agreement on the heels of the most horrendous crisis the world has seen. The Limited Test Ban Treaty opened the door to future agreements, a broadening of trade and exchanges, increases in American and Russian tourism, and a general lessening of Cold War tensions. Such is the legacy of what President Kennedy felt was his proudest achievement.

15

Managing
the Alliance

Our successes with the hot line agreement and Limited Test Ban Treaty meant a lot to us, but at the same time we could not ignore the continuing U.S.-Soviet confrontation in Europe. Try as we might, we could not cut through the Gordian knot of a military buildup in Europe. As a result, throughout the Kennedy administration and on into the Johnson years, NATO and Western Europe occupied much of my time. Although the very success of European recovery and NATO has in recent years tended to take Europe off the front pages and even led to the impression that European matters are somehow less important to the United States, we should not forget that as recently as 1961–62 we had a major crisis over Berlin that threatened general war.

But that war never came, nor has any other broken out on European soil since 1945. Much credit is due NATO for countering the Soviet threat to Western Europe. NATO has stood firm as a barrier to Soviet expansionism and helped normalize relations within Europe. War today between France and Germany is unthinkable.

Ironically, NATO's very success has led to some dissatisfaction with it. Some say NATO threatens the Soviets, and others say the Soviet threat has diminished so much NATO is no longer needed. Ironically, whenever the word "NATO" is mentioned today, the next word that usually follows is "disarray." This despite the fact that NATO has brilliantly achieved the purpose for which it was founded; no member of NATO has been subjected to attack since 1949.

Yet it is only natural that new generations of Americans and Europeans do not automatically accept their fathers' and grandfathers' answers over how best to assure the security of Europe. Nevertheless, they cannot avoid the questions, If not NATO, then what? What's the alternative? Conceivably they may find a better scheme for the defense of Europe. NATO did not come down from the mountaintop on tablets of stone. It was put together by living, breathing human beings grappling as best they could with the issues of their day following the bitter experience of the Second World War. If there is a better alternative, let's move to it. Then again, the search for an alternative to NATO might lead to a rededication to NATO and the principle of collective security.

Throughout my years as secretary of state, there never was any real question about the American role in the alliance; the United States was expected to lead. And even though NATO's primary purpose was and is to provide for the defense of Europe, managing the relationship between fifteen sovereign states is often ticklish, and I frequently became involved in NATO affairs.

But leading the Western Alliance is rather tricky; a leader cannot lead unless others are willing to follow. Europeans often called for American leadership and yet refused to follow us when we tried. This situation did not exist immediately after World War II, when we were serving up the Marshall Plan and its military handmaiden, NATO, and lots of dollars for recovery. Then American leadership was automatic and taken for granted. But with Europe politically stable and economically healthy in the sixties, when attack from Eastern Europe seemed less of a threat, leadership of the alliance became more complex as Europeans became more assertive, nationalistic, independent, and ingrown with domestic concerns.

Even so, throughout the Kennedy and Johnson years, we tried to provide leadership on specific issues. But even though some European allies called for American leadership in general terms, I didn't see much point in stepping out front and then looking around and saying, "Gee, where is everybody?" I once asked Belgium's foreign minister Paul Henri Spaak, who was then pressing us to counter French President

Charles de Gaulle's opposition to European unity, "All right, my friend, if we lead, will Belgium follow?" He blinked at me and said, "I don't know whether we will or not."

Western European reticence was particularly irksome during consultation over alliance policies. With the significant exception of Britain, rarely did our European allies ever take the initiative to inject their own views into the policy-making process of the U.S. government or the NATO alliance. More often than not the Europe of the 1960's tended to sit like a pouting dowager, waiting to be persuaded after we decided upon policy. During the sixties I once counted the initiatives taken by members of NATO to raise issues for discussion in the NATO Council. The United States had a ten-to-one lead over the rest combined. These European governments knew where the State Department was and our embassies; they had our addresses. Rather than take advantage of many opportunities to make known their views, all too often they confined their input to carping about decisions we had already made.

We had other difficulties with the alliance as well. Europe had drawn into itself and was not playing the global role it should. As unfortunate as this was, it was also quite understandable. Decolonialism had been quite a shock to both France and Great Britain, and when they had been stripped of their overseas colonies, their tendency to become "little France" or "little England" was very pronounced. There grew up in Europe a strong feeling of isolationism, in the sense that Europe would look after its own affairs and not pay much attention to the rest of the world. The United States was far too lonely as a world power. We wanted to have others associated with us, and a unified Europe could play that role.

But Europe in the sixties had become comfortable and fat, somewhat lazy about its international responsibilities. We heckled our European friends to build up their defense budgets and contribute more to NATO, to spend more on foreign aid, and especially to become more involved in Africa, that vast continent only twenty minutes' flying time from Europe. In general, we wanted Europe to do more rather than less on the world scene. But we were unsuccessful in stimulating our allies to do this. Had Europe reached out, life would have been much easier for the United States in the sixties. At a NATO foreign ministers' meeting, I once commented that NATO's area of responsibility stretched from continental Europe to the Bering Strait. My colleagues looked at me as if I were a man from Mars.

We also had major difficulties with the alliance over nuclear issues.

When the Kennedy administration took office in January 1961, Western nuclear capabilities included tactical nuclear weapons in Western Europe under two-key (U.S. and host-country) control; obsolete U.S. Jupiter and Thor missiles in Great Britain, Italy, and Turkey; the U.S. strategic retaliatory force consisting of bombers (mostly B-52's and B-47's), the new Minuteman ICBMs, and Polaris submarines; a British nuclear force centered on the aging V-bombers; and an emerging French nuclear capability tied to aircraft. We faced two issues: To what extent did we want an independent nuclear Europe, and what should we do to replace the Thors and Jupiters.

These questions became more urgent in the summer of 1960, when Paul Henri Spaak, then secretary-general of NATO, and General Lauris Norstad, the supreme commander of NATO, told the U.S. NATO delegation that American monopoly over nuclear strategy and planning in the alliance was no longer acceptable. They said the Europeans had become restive over being left out of nuclear planning and wanted to become full partners in the decision making. In response to this, the Policy Planning Staff studied the problem of NATO nuclear cooperation. Its report of August 1960 recommended the creation of a NATO multilateral force (MLF) based in Polaris submarines manned by multinational crews under the command of the supreme allied commander in Europe. Secretary of State Christian Herter carried this proposal to the December 1960 NATO foreign ministers' meeting.

When President Kennedy took office, we realized the MLF proposal had resulted from a European initiative and felt it was up to the Europeans to follow through. Both publicly and privately we told our allies that we would welcome any proposal they developed. President Kennedy made clear the U.S. position in his May 17, 1961, speech to the Canadian Parliament in Ottawa, and I reiterated the president's statement at the December 1961 NATO foreign ministers' meeting in Paris. But nothing happened. Finally, our European friends in effect said, "Now look, you're the nuclear power. You have all the information. Why don't you propose one to us?" So we devised a specific multilateral force concept as a "for instance," as something that could be done.

We formed a task force to work up the idea and present it to our allies. Because of the opposition of Admiral Hyman Rickover, some members of Congress, and some of our military to sharing submarine technology, the original idea of a multinational submarine force became a surface vessel force. But new problems arose when the task force developed an enthusiasm for the MLF that went considerably beyond

President Kennedy's and mine. Task force members became theologians for the MLF, committed themselves fully to it, and pressed our government to throw its full weight behind it. In their zealotry they forgot it was simply a sample idea of what might be done to create a NATO nuclear force. Such a desire might meet the desires of our allies for greater participation in nuclear matters. If our allies didn't want it, the president didn't want to ram it down their throats. President Kennedy was never that sold on the MLF, and neither was I. We were content with the status quo. If our allies had embraced the MLF enthusiastically, we would have gone forward with it. But when they failed to agree, Kennedy and I more or less lost interest in the MLF.

Bob McNamara was caught in the middle; he became more of a proponent than I did, because as secretary of defense he was responsible for working out the details. The MLF looked like a viable force from his point of view, with all these reasonably invulnerable surface vessels with missiles that could reach the Soviet Union. It seemed a workable plan. But Bob's commitment did not go beyond the attitude of his president.

What ultimately doomed the MLF was the inability of the Europeans themselves to unite behind the multilateral force. We knew Charles de Gaulle, with his commitment to *la gloire française* and French nuclear forces, would never accept it, but we could have gone ahead without France. However, the British were also cool to the MLF; they were not excited by the prospects of a German finger on the nuclear trigger. Nor did they want to dilute their own status as a nuclear power; the MLF would have incorporated into a NATO force the basic structure of the British nuclear force. The Germans were basically for it but fretted that we were unable to deliver the British. We didn't want to pressure the British because again, the MLF was put forward in the interests of our allies. We felt our European friends must reach agreement on the MLF without pressure from us. Throughout, the Italians and Belgians were uncertain how they felt about it.

We again reiterated our willingness to consider any proposals from Europe. The British came up with something called the Allied Nuclear Force, a modified version of MLF, which also failed to take hold. We did establish a nuclear planning group inside NATO which went a long way toward satisfying our allies' desire to be included in nuclear planning and strategy and to share nuclear materials and information. So there was a positive outcome to the MLF imbroglio.

But frankly there was considerable reservation within our own government about the MLF's sharing nuclear weapons. We would never allow control to move outside the United States, and in all these discussions we always reserved a veto on the actual firing of American nuclear weapons. We were willing to allow consultation and consider various voting schemes in which we had a majority vote, where our vote would be essential before nuclear weapons could be used. With that condition, it wasn't easy for our NATO allies to share real power regarding American nuclear weapons.

For the same reasons, we respected British and French autonomy over their own nuclear forces. I was less concerned than some about the British or French pursuing their own defense strategies or even firing their weapons independently of the American nuclear force. I didn't believe that either government would be willing to risk turning their countries into piles of ashes by firing their nuclear weapons at the USSR or anyone else.

The Soviets vigorously opposed the MLF since it would put the Germans near the center of a nuclear decision. This is one issue on which the Soviets are always passionate: Germany must never control nuclear weapons. Given their horrendous experiences with Germany in the twentieth century, the Russians see German access to nuclear weaponry as an issue of war or peace. Interestingly, I believe the MLF caused the Soviets to take greater interest in the nonproliferation arms control talks of the late sixties.

By the time Lyndon Johnson became president, there was resistance to the MLF both within the alliance and on Capitol Hill. We let it wither on the vine, and it died a natural death. Congressional leaders, already skeptical about sharing nuclear weapons, wouldn't support the MLF unless it was welcomed with open arms by our allies.

The MLF also became entangled with American-British defense policies on nuclear weapons. They dated back to the Manhattan Project itself when British, Canadian, and American scientists worked closely together to build the atomic bomb. The British played an especially key role in the Manhattan Project. Yet in 1948 Congress initiated and passed the McMahon Act, which ended that cooperation. We Americans simply drew into a cocoon on nuclear matters and cut the British and Canadians out. The British felt they had been shortchanged by the McMahon Act, and I don't blame them.

But in March 1960 the United States and Great Britain agreed that the United States would develop a bomber-launched missile, the Skybolt—a new air-to-ground missile that could be armed with nuclear warheads—and would sell one hundred to Great Britain in exchange for the British allowing us to use the Holy Loch naval base in Scotland for U.S. nuclear submarines. Unfortunately the Skybolt development program did not go well, and by November 1962 Secretary of Defense Bob McNamara had all but decided to cancel it. Bob reported that Skybolt was too expensive, was redundant as a weapons system because of the development of new Polaris and Minuteman missiles, and had failed its test flights. He felt it simply wasn't worth pursuing. He told British Defense Minister Peter Thorneycroft that Skybolt was in trouble. Bob and I both felt it was primarily a military matter with only incidental political overtones. Even so, Bob warned me it would cause some trouble with the British.

That was the understatement of the year. For some reason, Thorneycroft did not prepare his own cabinet and Parliament for Skybolt's cancellation, so when we later announced the end of the program, it hit like a thunderclap in London. It became a major issue because Britain's continued role as a nuclear power was in Britons' minds closely related to Skybolt. I was quite surprised by the turmoil. I personally think British surprise and outrage were somewhat contrived, to strengthen their bargaining position for concessions at the December 1962 Nassau meeting between President Kennedy and British Prime Minister Harold Macmillan. The British wanted American-made Polaris missiles for their nuclear submarines. My net impression was that either the British handled the cancellation of Skybolt rather awkwardly since they knew long before Nassau that Skybolt was in trouble, and it was their responsibility to prepare British public opinion for its cancellation; or they handled it brilliantly, to increase pressure on us to give them Polaris.

British paranoia over Skybolt may also have been fostered by some in our bureaucracy who wanted to use the Skybolt cancellation to pressure the British to give up an independent nuclear force. Neither John Kennedy nor I ever intended to go in that direction, at least in part because our relationship with Britain on nuclear matters left much to be desired, and some of us had a guilty conscience over it. Nevertheless, our MLF enthusiasts saw the possible transfer of Polaris technology to the British as potentially reducing British incentive to join the MLF. However, those in our administration who wanted to kill the British independent nuclear deterrent didn't speak for the United States government. Both President Kennedy and I felt the British were grown men and women who could make their own decisions and determine what best served their national interests. I never pressed my British colleagues to give up their nuclear force, to join the MLF, or to obtain Polaris submarines; whatever they chose, that was their decision as far as I was concerned.

I didn't attend the Nassau conference and later was criticized for not going. But I had already scheduled the annual dinner for the entire diplomatic corps at the State Department before the Nassau meeting was arranged, and I didn't want to snub the entire diplomatic corps over one bilateral meeting, so I sent Undersecretary George Ball in my place. Additionally, I had a pretty good idea how the Nassau conference would turn out. I was content with the agreement reached. Predictably the British asked for an alternative to Skybolt; Polaris missiles were an obvious choice. I knew that if the British wanted American cooperation in the nuclear field, they would get it, and I favored Britain's getting Polaris missiles if it wanted them. I believed we owed the British cooperation in nuclear matters because of their wartime cooperation in developing the atomic bomb, and I advised John Kennedy accordingly.

The British could have proceeded unilaterally with Skybolt. We would not have objected. But they would have run into the same technical problems that we did. It soon became apparent to the British that Skybolt wouldn't work and they had to find another weapons system.

The Skybolt affair was a painful, regrettable—and temporary—disturbance in U.S.-British relations. In the sweep of postwar history, it was "no big deal" and certainly not worth all the attention it received at the time. Some claimed that the Skybolt affair nearly brought down the British government, but I frankly do not believe it. And even had that happened, it would have been a self-induced fall. British leaders knew that Skybolt was headed for the rocks, and the responsibility for informing their government and public belonged to them.

In a perverse way, the Skybolt affair served de Gaulle's purposes since he used the Nassau agreement to block British entry into the Common Market. Harold Macmillan told us as early as April 1961 that Great Britain desired to enter the Common Market. We were pleased with that prospect. It is true that the United States and Great Britain had a "special relationship" growing out of World War II, when Winston Churchill and Franklin Roosevelt led their respective nations to victory over the Axis powers. Two decades later we hoped that if Britain joined the Common Market, it would take into Europe that special relationship with the United States. Perhaps our special relationship could be expanded into Europe itself. We were rather miffed, therefore, when President de Gaulle used that special relationship as an excuse for vetoing British membership.

Throughout 1962 de Gaulle played his hand close to the vest on

British entry into the Common Market. During the spring and summer some felt the French president would support the British bid, but most believed de Gaulle either hadn't made up his mind or would oppose British entry. Then, in the wake of the Nassau agreement, de Gaulle on January 14, 1963, flatly vetoed British participation, arguing that the Nassau agreement made clear that Britain was more tied to the United States than to Europe. But to me, Nassau was only an excuse. De Gaulle's agenda aimed at establishing a European continental system led by France.

Should we strongly support British entry or sit quietly on the sidelines? Most of my European colleagues felt that a spirited American push would only stir up French resistance and further complicate relations among Europeans. Taking their advice, I suggested to Kennedy that we should respond calmly to de Gaulle's veto. His claim that Great Britain would be merely a running dog for the United States inside Europe was patently ridiculous. Other schemes designed to substitute for a Common Market without British participation, such as free trade areas involving Britain, the United States, and other countries in Western Europe and Latin America, looked far too complicated to me. I believed that we'd just have to wait for de Gaulle to leave the scene before progress could be made on European unity and the expansion of the Common Market.

Not all my colleagues were equally relaxed; George Ball in particular wanted to launch a frontal assault on de Gaulle. Ball was a great Europeanist, strongly in favor of European unity, NATO, and the transatlantic partnership, and he considered de Gaulle a major obstacle to everything he stood for. But neither President Kennedy nor later President Johnson allowed a high-profile response to de Gaulle's obstructionism.

De Gaulle himself was a most extraordinary man, but what can a mere mortal say about Charles de Gaulle? I had many talks with him in the sixties, but I would hardly call them diplomatic exchanges. Talking with de Gaulle was like crawling up a mountainside on your knees, opening a little portal at the top, and waiting for the oracle to speak. When in Paris, I usually paid him a courtesy call at his office in the Élysée. I always began by conveying the greetings of my president, and he always reciprocated by extending his good wishes to the president. Then he would say, *"Je vous écoute,"* meaning "Well, Mr. Secretary, I am listening." He rarely volunteered a subject of his own for conversation. There was never any give-and-take; de Gaulle gave us pronouncements from on high, but never any real discussion. He was there, he would listen—"*Je vous écoute*"—and then he would bid you good-bye.

I can't say that I enjoyed my talks with Charles de Gaulle, but I always found them fascinating. "My personal tragedy is that I have respect only for those who stand up to me," he would say. "But those persons I find intolerable." I once caught his attention after hearing his persistent doubts of American willingness to live up to our NATO commitments. I said, "Mr. President, the United States will do whatever France allows us to do."

De Gaulle was always sensitive about matters he felt were France's business and not ours. Once he became icily furious when I raised with him the question of the French base at Bizerte in Tunisia, a matter of great controversy at the time. We felt that France ought to come to terms with Tunisia over the base. He took my comments as outrageous interference in a matter wholly French, said Tunisia was none of our business, and insisted we stay out of it. Usually polite officially and always dignified, de Gaulle never conveyed personal warmth. I have no doubt that de Gaulle, as the only surviving member of the Big Four of World War II—with Stalin, Roosevelt, and Churchill all dead—looked upon the rest of us, including John Kennedy, as mere boys.

Indeed, de Gaulle did render great service to France and to the West in the postwar period. Any patriotic Frenchman who lived through those dark chapters of World War II was, of course, affected by France's humiliation and passionately interested in restoring the position of France in world affairs. This was central to de Gaulle's attitude and to his success as a politician. I firmly believe that de Gaulle's outlooks were based less on personal vanity than his mystical concept of France, the France of Joan of Arc, Louis XIV, and Napoleon.

This outlook once led him to propose to President Eisenhower a three-nation *directoire* of France, the United Kingdom, and the United States, to guide the destinies of the Free World. Eisenhower turned that down, not because of France but because he was not prepared to nominate the United States for such a presumptuous role. After all, we had to consider the views of Canada, Germany, Japan, Brazil, Mexico, and many other countries both in Europe and outside the continent. De Gaulle repeated his proposal to President Kennedy, and for the same reason, Kennedy turned him down. We were prepared to consult with de Gaulle and his government on all matters, but it wasn't consultation he wanted as much as our acknowledgment of a special position for

France. De Gaulle never forgave us. Some years later we asked for his cooperation on another issue, and he said, "I told you how you could have the cooperation of France and you rejected it. Now it's too late."

De Gaulle could be great in moments of crisis, as with Kennedy on the Cuban missile crisis, and very petty at other times. When we landed U.S. Marines in Santo Domingo in the Dominican Republic in 1965, he blasted us strongly. Privately he asked us, "Won't you please move your Marines four blocks and protect the French Embassy as well?" We did, but he never thanked us. In fact, he continued to berate us publicly.

But it was over the idea of European unity that John Kennedy and I had our most serious confrontations with de Gaulle. Since World War II the United States had supported European unity, believing that what had worked for the United States of America would be good for Europe and that greater political and economic cohesion in Europe would help block Soviet expansionism while serving our own interests. However, when I was secretary of state, I was advised by several NATO foreign ministers that we should keep our mouths shut and not react to de Gaulle. De Gaulle felt that France should be the spokesman for Western Europe. I once told de Gaulle that we found it difficult to deal with Europe when there really was no "Europe"—rather, fifteen separate nation-states and individual members of NATO. I meant only that sufficient cohesion did not exist for us to deal with Europe as a whole. De Gaulle responded with a classic Gaullist observation, "Well, what is Europe?" He said, "Here is France, at the very heart of Europe—the heart and soul of European culture. Then," he said, "there are the Benelux countries." And with a gesture of contempt he waved them aside. Then: "Psshhh! There is Italy." Another scoff. "Psshhh! There is Germany. We have to respect German economic power. . . . But Germany must be kept in its place!"

Then he said, "And what about the British? But the British are not Europeans. They are Anglo-Saxons!" In de Gaulle's eyes, Britain was fatally infected because of its close relationship to the United States. Thus, to de Gaulle, France was Europe. That kind of thinking complicated the cause of European unity, blocked the expansion of the Common Market for at least a decade, and certainly plagued the lives of us diplomats.

Ironically, had President de Gaulle thrown himself into the leadership of the European movement and promoted transatlantic cooperation, he would have become the spokesman for Western Europe. But the very tactics that he adopted to build up the position and prestige of France frustrated his central purpose. Rather quickly the Kennedy administration reached a point where we simply did not care what de Gaulle thought except on those matters over which he held a veto. We learned to proceed without him.

It was hard to work with Europe during the de Gaulle era. I talked often about this with de Gaulle's foreign minister, Maurice Couve de Murville. I believe that in 1961 and 1962 Couve de Murville was trying to modify de Gaulle's entrenched opposition to European unity and salvage what he could out of NATO and transatlantic cooperation; he had been a strong NATO man in the past. But Couve de Murville gradually became fully Gaullist in character and played de Gaulle's line to the hilt, having no real alternative if he wished to remain as foreign minister.

De Gaulle must have been a severe taskmaster. During Kennedy's visit to Paris in April 1961, we met in de Gaulle's office one morning. The French prime minister and foreign minister came in after we had arrived, and I watched with amazement as the prime minister walked up to de Gaulle, gave a little schoolboy bow, clicked his heels, and presented himself much like a cadet at St. Cyr. The foreign minister did the same thing.

De Gaulle's extreme views culminated in France's withdrawing from military cooperation with NATO in 1966. He insisted that NATO headquarters and American troops be moved out of France, despite the logistical nightmare for NATO. He never did like American military commanders in key NATO positions, and he felt that the United States dominated the alliance too much. France's voice was not listened to, in his view. He told President Kennedy in 1961 that there would never be another French soldier in Southeast Asia. From that point on de Gaulle for all practical purposes withdrew from the Southeast Asia Treaty Organization (SEATO). Personally, I believe he also began thinking in 1961 of withdrawing France from NATO.

When President de Gaulle decided to quit NATO, President Johnson was determined to do everything that de Gaulle asked us to do, simply as a matter of dignity, and get our forces out of France before the deadline. But de Gaulle's request went down hard in Washington. In fact, Johnson insisted that I ask de Gaulle, "Do you want us to move American cemeteries out of France as well?" I carried out my instructions. De Gaulle, very embarrassed, had nothing to say.

Yet de Gaulle constantly questioned the sincerity of the American commitment to NATO. Being an extreme nationalist himself, he just couldn't conceive that one country would accept major injury in defense of another country. Perhaps he was merely predicting French behavior if an ally was attacked. In the event of an attack by the Warsaw Pact, he talked about the battle of Germany being followed by the battle of France, as if the French would hold their forces in reserve until the Soviets reached the Rhine. De Gaulle's fears were unfounded; I am convinced the United States would have waged even nuclear war to protect Western Europe.

At best, Charles de Gaulle was difficult to deal with and always unpredictable. During the Kennedy years, with tensions over Algeria at their peak, de Gaulle himself faced a possible military coup d'état; his situation was very serious. At one point he called upon the women and children of France to block the highways and the airstrips to help prevent a coup. In the midst of this turmoil President Kennedy wrote him a personal message saying, "We are thinking of you during these difficult days. If there is anything we can do to be helpful, please let us know." I heard that de Gaulle was infuriated by this message; the idea that John F. Kennedy thought he could do anything to help Charles de Gaulle in France! A few years later France had trouble over balance of payments and the devaluation of the franc during a severe economic crisis. President Johnson, never one to miss a chance, wrote de Gaulle, "We are thinking of you during these difficult days. If there is anything we can do to help, please let us know." This time de Gaulle was most appreciative. He even asked Johnson's permission to make that message public. So how do you deal with a fellow like that?

16

Africa
and the Congo

While Europe remained the central theater of U.S.-Soviet confrontation during the Kennedy years, Third World issues became increasingly important. Sometimes this created tension not only between the United States and the Soviet Union but also between the United States and its Western European allies. Nevertheless, during the Kennedy administration our European allies and we had an unspoken division of labor in the Third World, especially in Africa. Some Western European nations had been colonial powers in Africa, understood Africa better, and had a superior entrée to African countries. Consequently, they concentrated much of their foreign aid there and took the lead in Africa. During the Kennedy and Johnson years about 75 percent of Africa's foreign aid came from Western Europe, the rest from the United States.

This arrangement suited me since I always looked upon the United States as the junior partner in Africa. Yet this attitude of mine irritated some State Department colleagues and particularly our ambassadors to African countries; they believed that the United States should play "Mr. Big" in every African capital. When I tried to calm them down, some in State's African Bureau concluded I was indifferent toward Africa. This was untrue; I just felt that the informal division of labor we had with our Western European allies was the right way to proceed in Africa.

This was all done as a matter of conscious policy, not accident. We could not do everything in the world, and we needed to establish priorities. Our assistant secretary of state for African affairs, G. Mennon Williams, didn't like his area of the world assigned a lower priority, so U.S. African policy became a matter of debate between us.

Soapy Williams was one of the best assistant secretaries for African affairs this country ever had. He was hardworking, knowledgeable, loyal, and always considerate, but we disagreed on the role the United States should play in Africa. Naturally he wanted us to put our best foot forward in Africa and send more foreign aid. But we were pinched for funds, and his position did not prevail.

One point that Soapy and others raised was that as secretary of state I never visited Africa. To be sure, Africa was not high on my list of priorities, but in truth I could never find a way to visit just a few African countries without creating resentment in the others.

Even so, the Kennedy and Johnson administrations could not ignore Africa. The United States had no security alliances with African states, reflecting a general feeling that the African continent was not as vital to U.S. security as, say, Europe or Latin America. But we wanted to limit Soviet influence in Africa as well as our own. Both Kennedy and Johnson believed our African policies should support decolonialization and the emergence of the African states and offer assistance to those new nations.

One of our first African problems concerned Portuguese colonialism in Angola. Two months after taking office, we faced an important vote in the UN Security Council calling for Angolan self-determination. It was right to support the resolution, submitted by the Afro-Asian bloc, but some at State believed that since Portugal was a NATO ally and granted NATO forces access to air and naval facilities in the Azores, we should not anger Lisbon. In short, they wanted us to oppose the resolution.

I strongly recommended to the president that we support the resolution. The United States had to demonstrate that we opposed colonialism in fact as well as in rhetoric, and supporting the resolution was one way to do this. I was pleased that Kennedy accepted my recommendation, somewhat less pleased that he then dispatched me to Lisbon to see the Portuguese dictator, Antonio Salazar, to explain the U.S. vote. I met with Salazar at his palace, in a room in which the curtains were drawn and the lights dim. He seemed very distant, almost ghostlike, and removed from reality. I failed utterly to convince him that colonialism was a thing of the past. At one point he said, "I cannot give Portugal's African colonies what I cannot grant to my own people." It was an eerie experience.

Another problem that we faced in Africa—and elsewhere as well—was how to react if a country began to move politically and economically closer to the Soviet Union and became anti-American. We came head to head with this problem in Ghana. President Kennedy wanted to improve U.S. relations with Ghana's leader, Kwame Nkrumah, in part because Nkrumah was a leader in the nonaligned movement. In late June 1961 we pledged to provide Ghana with twenty-five million dollars to help it build a dam and hydroelectric plant on the Volta River. Unfortunately Nkrumah also sought the support of the Soviet Union, received Soviet assistance, sent Ghanaians to the Soviet Union for training, and supported many Soviet bloc positions in his speeches and at the United Nations. We were particularly galled by his denunciation of the United States at the Belgrade meeting of nonaligned nations.

All this led Kennedy to delay his final decision on the dam. The project came up for review at a National Security Council meeting in December, and several people, including Robert Kennedy, tried to kill it. I disagreed with Bobby, arguing that because we had already given our word that we would fund the dam, we had to honor that commitment. The consequences of breaking our word would be felt all across Africa. I remembered when John Foster Dulles became angry with the Egyptians during negotiations on the Aswan Dam and cut off American participation; the result was greater Soviet presence in Egypt and greater Egyptian anti-Americanism. To cut off aid we had pledged would be an act of petulance, misunderstood all over Africa. Maybe I am old-fashioned, but when the United States pledges its word, that's a very important thing. We should avoid situations where our pledged word is not taken seriously. Fortunately John Kennedy decided to continue our assistance.

Our major problem in Africa was the outbreak of civil war in the newly independent Republic of the Congo. Belgium, long the colonial master of the Congo, decided with breathtaking speed to grant the Congo its independence in June 1960. Few Congolese were trained to accept governing responsibility, no more than a dozen university graduates, no indigenous police force to maintain law and order and internal security. The absence of effective leaders meant it was hard for the

Congolese themselves to give effect to the policies they wanted to adopt. Congolese independence soon turned into chaos.

In cynical moments I always suspect that some Belgians decided to turn the Congo loose so precipitously, hoping that in the ensuing chaos mineral-rich Katanga Province would secede, become an independent state, and grant favorable concessions to Western mining interests. This almost happened, but the Congo ultimately managed to retain its territorial integrity.

Trouble in the Congo began days after independence. By mid-July 1960 fighting and mutiny had broken out in the Congo's army, and public disorder spread, reportedly threatening the lives of European settlers in the Congo. Belgium sent troops allegedly to protect lives and property. The new country's president, Joseph Kasavubu, reacting to the return of Belgium forces and the breakdown of civil authority, requested that the United Nations put a peacekeeping force into his country to prevent civil war. The UN responded, but conditions in the Congo continued to deteriorate.

The situation was made even more sensitive because of the Soviet Union's involvement. When the Congo began to fall apart in July 1960, Kasavubu and his prime minister, Patrice Lumumba, requested help from all: the United Nations, the United States, and the Soviet Union. President Eisenhower faced an urgent problem: how to restore public order and permit the withdrawal of Belgian troops, without leading to internal collapse in the Congo, civil war, and foreign involvement.

Eisenhower rejected any direct superpower intervention, preferring to support the UN presence. But the Soviets, UN resolutions to the contrary, poured material and personnel into the Congo to establish what they hoped would be a foothold in the heart of Africa. Secretary-General Dag Hammarskjöld stated that each Soviet Ilyushin aircraft flight was bringing in political agents as well. When the Soviets refused to halt these activities, the United Nations Command closed major airfields in the Congo to all but UN traffic. Shortly thereafter President Kasavubu ordered the Soviet and Czechoslovak embassies to close, and several hundred Russians and Czechoslovaks were forced to leave the Congo.

The United Nations blocking of this Soviet takeover scheme prompted the Soviet Union to declare political war on Dag Hammarskjöld and begin its futile campaign for a "troika directorate" that would replace him with three secretary-generals and effectively handcuff the United Nations. The Communist bloc refused to finance any part of this UN operation to restore political stability to the Congo.

By the time the Kennedy administration took office in January

1961, the Congo was on the verge of disintegration. Kasavubu remained as president in Léopoldville (now Kinshesa), but he headed a weak and divided government. In Katanga Moïse Tshombe declared that that mineral-rich province had seceded. In Stanleyville (now Kisangani) the pro-Communist Antoine Gizenga set up his own self-proclaimed Congolese government. Meanwhile, Kasavubu imprisoned the pro-Soviet Patrice Lumumba.

The situation was a mess. When I reviewed U.S. Congo policy with President Kennedy in early February, I saw no easy solution, but I nevertheless made three recommendations to the president: that the UN peacekeeping force be given power over all military forces in the Congo; that Kasavubu be encouraged to broaden his government to include Lumumba elements but not Lumumba; and that the UN play a greater role in running the country until peace was restored. As I saw it, the UN had to stop the Congo from disintegrating and at the same time help an independent government emerge that could govern the country.

Things only got worse when, on February 13, Patrice Lumumba was killed, allegedly by agents of Tshombe. Kasavubu had passed Lumumba to Tshombe for "safekeeping," but under Tshombe's "protection," Lumumba was instead assassinated. A crisis was again at hand.

Kennedy warned the Soviets not to intervene in response to the death of their protégé, and I supported him. I also believed the UN had to play an even greater role, and often I found myself in contact with Ralph Bunche, who controlled the UN peacekeeping force. Bunche and his international force performed yeoman service in easing the crisis following Lumumba's death. Within a few months the crisis had passed. UN forces also put down Gizenga's insurrection in Stanleyville.

But the Katanga problem remained. We opposed Moïse Tshombe's efforts to have Katanga secede from the Congo for the same reasons we opposed altering any political boundaries in Africa: First, most African nations opposed any boundary changes, and second, if existing political boundaries were altered to take into account tribal, cultural, and religious background, the whole continent would have split up into hundreds of tiny principalities. However, Tshombe had some important external support. Belgium mining interests represented by the Union Minière supported secession and put lots of money into a pro-Katanga campaign; some American senators also took up the cause of a "free Katanga." Tshombe also had support from an army of mercenaries, mostly Belgians, South Africans, and Rhodesians.

I myself had misgivings about whether the UN should get involved in Katanga for the simple reason that I doubted that the UN force could succeed militarily. It was a conglomerate of national units, had very thin supply and logistical backup, and no permanent general staff or military command structure. Ralph Bunche had to run the operation out of his vest pocket from UN headquarters in New York City. I thought the UN force might easily get its nose bloodied by Tshombe's forces and his mercenaries, and I expressed my reservations—and Kennedy's—to UN Secretary-General Dag Hammarskjöld. He replied rather sharply and accused us of siding with the Katanga rebels, a controversy I especially regretted when, in September 1961, Hammarskjöld was killed in an airplane crash in the Congo while trying to negotiate a cease-fire. His untimely death not only complicated peace-keeping efforts in the Congo but saddened me immensely—and the international community as well.

Hammarskjöld was a fine UN secretary-general who took the Charter as his Bible and fought hard for the United Nations, however the chips might fall. The coffee table in Hammarskjöld's office was a famous institution. If two nations quarreled, he called representatives of both nations around his table and scolded, cajoled, and pleaded with them to try to work out a solution. Superpowers got the same treatment as smaller countries; he gave us Americans unshirted hell whenever he felt we deserved it.

But by early December the situation had deteriorated to the point where I believed military action was necessary, in conjunction with negotiations. The UN landed its largest-ever peacekeeping force, with fifteen countries contributing troops. We decided to provide air and logistical support but not troops, trying to keep the superpowers out of central Africa. This UN Congo mission became costly for us because some countries would participate in the peacekeeping force only if we subsidized their efforts, and these bills mounted. We had quite a time getting Congress to approve a hundred-million-dollar loan to help the UN finance the operation, because of strong pro-Katanga sympathy in the Congress. But the alternative to this UN effort was to acquiesce in Katanga's secession and risk a civil war that would likely result in a great-power clash.

Under an Indian commander, United Nations troops quickly scattered Tshombe's forces and succeeded in imposing United Nations and Congolese government authority and preventing the secession of Katanga. Diplomatically, later in December, Tshombe signed an agreement in which he accepted the authority of the central Congo government.

But even this did not end the Congo crisis. Tshombe once again began to defy the central government in 1962, and only after more fighting between UN troops and Tshombe's forces was Katanga finally integrated into the Congo in January 1963. I was preoccupied with other issues during this period, and the task of coordinating U.S. policy with our allies and the UN fell to George Ball.

The Congo became an issue once again in 1964, when Simba rebels revolted against government authority and seized several hundred Caucasians, including a number of American citizens, as hostages in Stanleyville. With the help of President Jomo Kenyatta of Kenya and President Julius Nyerere of Tanzania, we tried first to free the hostages by negotiation, but these talks proved futile. Consequently, we began to think of a possible rescue mission by Belgian paratroopers, transported by American planes. I was closely involved with its planning.

While we were discussing this operation with the Belgians, their foreign minister, Paul Henri Spaak, left a cabinet meeting in Brussels to telephone me. He said, "I am meeting with our cabinet. We would like to know the American view on this matter."

I said, "We are prepared to do whatever you want to do. If you wish to commit your paratrooper battalion, we will make our planes available and do everything possible to make the operation a success. If you decide not to try a rescue, we will understand."

He paused and then said, "Do you mean that the great United States of America is leaving this decision to Belgium?"

I said, "Yes, that is exactly our position."

Spaak said, "That's incredible. No decision affecting Belgium has ever been made in Belgium before."

The Belgians made their decision, and on November 24, 1964, twelve U.S. C-130's dropped 545 Belgian paratroopers into Stanleyville to rescue the hostages, all with the full knowledge of the Congolese government. The operation was a success. We estimated that when the shooting started, the rebels would melt away pretty fast, and in fact, they did. The Belgian paratroopers were first-class; we had complete confidence in them. While this wasn't a formidable military challenge, it was risky for the hostages; could the paratroopers get there fast enough to keep the Simbas from shooting the hostages?

When the paratroopers appeared, the Simbas started firing wildly. One American missionary named Paul Carlson was killed while scaling a wall. Our own consul general, Michael Hoyt, one of the hostages, said that if the paratroopers had arrived ten minutes later, most of the hostages would have been killed. They all had been herded into a public square in Stanleyville, and these doped-up Simbas were firing tommy guns all over the place. It was touch and go and had to be handled quickly; had these Simbas gotten any word through a news broadcast or leak that a rescue mission was being contemplated, they might have killed the hostages. We did not consult with Congress prior to the rescue, and we kept the Congolese president nearly under house arrest in his own capital so he couldn't tell anyone. Secrecy was vitally important.

Our efforts to support President Kasavubu yielded mixed results. Kasavubu himself was deposed in November 1965 by General Joseph Mobutu, who promptly established a military dictatorship with himself in control. That was not what we had worked for.

But on the positive side, we had supported the UN's successful efforts to hold the Congo together and to prevent the secession of Katanga. Only the effort to develop a broadly based national government had failed. And we at the same time had prevented the Soviets from gaining a major position in Africa.

Political instability continued. Later in 1964, after the rescue in Stanleyville, some six hundred foreign mercenaries who had been working for the Congolese government rebelled and seized control of an area in the eastern Congo. This was interpreted by the Congolese people as a white plot against the Congo, creating antiwhite furor all over the country. Our ambassador told us that to forestall racial bloodshed, the United States or some important predominantly Caucasian country must publicly demonstrate its solidarity with the Congolese government. We also heard that some Congolese were calling for mass meetings all over the Congo, saying things like "Bring your machetes with you, because there will be some business to take care of after the meeting."

To us that sounded like a possible massacre of Europeans and Americans in the Congo. To help fend this off, we cooked up a plan to send three American C-130 transport planes to help the government and allow it to say publicly, "Look! We are being supported by the United States against these white mercenaries."

We flew those planes to Ascension Island in the Atlantic to get them closer to the area, and Lyndon Johnson asked me to talk to Senators William Fulbright and Richard Russell about possibly sending them into the Congo. Both Fulbright and Russell strongly opposed it, and I reported their opposition back to Johnson. But the situation continued to deteriorate, so Johnson ordered the planes in. The Congolese government broadcast on radio and drove sound trucks around the cities calling attention to this American assistance, and tensions quieted down. But both Fulbright and Russell got up on the Senate floor and blasted us for having sent the planes.

Consider the press conference that would have followed had Johnson not sent the planes and if there had been a massacre of whites in the Congo. Question from a reporter: "Did you know that this massacre was coming, Mr. President?" "Well, we had been warned that it could happen." Reporter: "What did you do about it?" "We didn't do anything about it." Reporter: "Did anybody suggest anything that you could do about it?" "Well, our ambassador wanted us to send three transport planes." Reporter: "Why didn't you?" "Senators William Fulbright and Richard Russell didn't think it was a good idea." The immediate reaction would have been, Who in the hell is running the U.S. government?

I remain convinced that we pursued the proper policies in the Congo. Later some people criticized the Kennedy and Johnson administrations for getting involved with the wrong people in the Congo, but frankly I am not one who thinks that political leftists are automatically good guys and rightists the bad guys. There were many different political groups in the Congo, and the ones we supported via the UN appeared to us to have the best opportunity to bring about an independent and unified Congo. We believed that what happened in that large, diverse, and complex country in the heart of Africa was important to the rest of Africa. The problem—and it is not a problem unique to the Congo—was finding people who could organize and lead a government. That was the missing piece in the Congo then, and in many places that remains a problem today.

17

China Policy

In May 1961, in a long, private talk, I asked President Kennedy if he wanted the State Department to explore possible changes in China policy. He wanted to know what the ramifications of change were, so the president and I sketched out some options: Recognize both Chinas, the so-called two-Chinas approach; work quietly behind the scenes for reconciliation between Peking and Taipei; and sit tight and await future developments.

Kennedy's interest in exploring China policy derived in part from a resolution passed by Congress several years earlier that strongly condemned any recognition of Communist China and any change in Nationalist China's UN seat. My own interest in China was triggered by many memories: heading Far Eastern Affairs during the Truman administration; the Korean War; wartime service in CBI; intense study at Oxford of the Japanese invasion of Manchuria; even boyhood recollections of missionaries serving in China and school projects.

Despite my long involvement with China, I had no "Rusk plan" to give Kennedy on China. I did lean toward a two-Chinas approach, even though both Chinas probably would have rejected it. I also believed that

Peking would eventually receive a UN seat regardless of what we did. Kennedy and I agreed that American China policy in the year we took office, indeed for many years, did not reflect Asian realities.

Ironically, considering my interest in probing a two-Chinas approach in 1961, during the Truman years I had helped invent the parliamentary device by which we kept the People's Republic out of the United Nations and maintained a seat for the Republic of China on Taiwan. We also managed to refer the issue of substituting Peking for Taipei's seat to a commission, and the General Assembly voted to postpone its consideration for the duration of the session. When that succeeded, I thought at the time it might last four or five years. I was astonished to find this gambit intact in 1961 and further astonished that it lasted until the Nixon years, when the UN General Assembly finally seated mainland China.

Not surprisingly, Kennedy ruled out any changes in our China policy. With his razor-thin victory in the November elections—he used to attribute his win to "Cook County, Illinois"—he felt he lacked a strong mandate from the American people. Consequently, he was very cautious about selecting issues on which to do battle. And any change in China policy would have been one hell of a battle. In fact, just before Dwight Eisenhower left office, he told Kennedy that although he would support him on foreign policy in general, he would strongly oppose any attempt by the new administration to recognize Peking and seat mainland China at the United Nations.

Also, such contacts as we had with Peking were not promising. Simply put, the Chinese Communists didn't seem interested in improving U.S.-Chinese relations. As far as Kennedy was concerned, then, adopting a more realistic China policy became a future task, not a present one. Fearing the issue might divide Congress and the American people, he decided the potential benefits of a more realistic China policy didn't warrant risking a severe political confrontation. He could have been cut to ribbons politically by the China Lobby, the Republicans, and many members of Congress. We would have had great difficulty implementing a two-Chinas policy.

I agreed with Kennedy's reasoning and his conclusions, and I told him so. But as I was leaving the Oval Office, he called, "And what's more, Mr. Secretary, I don't want to read in the *Washington Post* or the *New York Times* that the State Department is thinking about a change in our China policy!" I went back to the department, and when Adlai Stevenson, Chester Bowles, and others would drop by to talk about China and especially their hopes for a two-Chinas policy at the

UN, I stonewalled them and played the role of the "village idiot." I didn't tell them about my talk with the president because I would have read about *that* in the *Washington Post* or the *New York Times*. Nor did I initiate any new studies on China policy; in that leaky Kennedy administration even that would have gotten to the press.

Stevenson and others wanted us to offer Peking U.S. recognition, even knowing that Peking would likely turn it down. That type of initiative would have pleased Stevenson—and our critics at home as well—but discomforted our Asian allies, such as Japan, South Korea, Nationalist China, and Thailand. I felt there was little to be gained in making an empty gesture beyond pleasing our domestic critics. Had there been any evidence that a change in China policy would have produced significant results internationally, Kennedy might have considered it. But Kennedy and I both agreed we shouldn't stir things up. Even so, had Kennedy lived and been reelected in 1964 with a strong mandate, I am sure he would have eventually reopened the China question.

Personally my own view was that two Chinas had in fact emerged from World War II and the postwar turmoil. But American policy was unavoidably locked in on Taiwan for both historical and policy reasons. American recognition of the Republic of China on Taiwan as the "government of all China" was somewhat artificial, but if we simply transferred diplomatic recognition from Taiwan to Peking and if the Chinese Communists were unwilling to recognize Taiwan, that was equally artificial. We never recognized Taiwan as the government of all China; it was simply the only Chinese government we recognized. But because neither China recognized the other, that left little room for maneuver.

Many people, myself included, toyed with the idea of recognizing the People's Republic of China in the late 1940's, but that idea died on November 26, 1950, when tens of thousands of Chinese "volunteers" poured across the Yalu River to join battle with MacArthur's Eighth Army. At the end of the Korean War, with the anti-Communist Chinese sentiment the war had built up, the China Lobby backing Taiwan, and congressional opposition, no president could have narrowed the gap with Peking even if he had wanted to. The Korean War hardened American attitudes toward Peking; it certainly hardened mine.

After the war ended, President Eisenhower had continuing problems with the People's Republic over the offshore islands of Quemoy and Matsu and several minor crises. But happily there followed a period of calm. In late 1955 Secretary of State John Foster Dulles invited me to Washington. He asked me to approach Senator Walter George of Georgia, then chairman of the Senate Foreign Relations Committee, to inquire discreetly if George would back a new China policy. I readily agreed. We then discussed the outlines of a new policy: In exchange for a UN seat and eventual American recognition, I hoped for an agreement that recognized Taiwan's right to exist as an independent nation, that Communist China would cut off aid to North Vietnam, that India be substituted for Nationalist China at the UN Security Council, and that Japan also be allowed a UN seat.

Dulles seemed to agree. But nothing came of this project. Shortly after our meeting, Governor Herman Talmadge of Georgia announced that he would run for George's Senate seat in 1956. George then decided he would not run for reelection. Under those circumstances, Dulles concluded that George would not take on such a difficult and controversial issue, and the effort was abandoned.

Although President Eisenhower strongly opposed recognition and a UN seat for the People's Republic, Foster Dulles was clearly tempted by the two-Chinas approach despite the political difficulties. In fact, just before he became secretary of state, he had me review an article that he wrote for *Life* magazine in which he advocated, among other things, a two-Chinas approach. I felt that in 1953 it was a fish that wouldn't swim, and I urged him to delete the idea, which he did.

Had Dulles broached a two-Chinas policy in 1953, or had we together moved forward with his Walter George initiative in 1955 and then received both presidential and congressional backing, I believed the two-Chinas initiative would have received extensive international backing. But both Chinas would have rejected it. We could not have forced it upon them. The one issue upon which both Peking and Taiwan have always agreed is that there is only one China, and Taiwan is part of China.

At one point I asked Taiwan about a two-Chinas approach, and it categorically dismissed it. Peking would have refused as well. After our original discussion of the China question, it became essentially a dead issue as far as the president and I were concerned. Kennedy's reluctance to reopen the China question was strongly reinforced by our experience with the Laos accords of 1962. We made many concessions to get an agreement, far more than the Eisenhower administration would have allowed, but we got no performance on those accords from North Vietnam. Kennedy was bitterly disappointed, and this undoubtedly influenced his attitudes on China.

In the Johnson years additional barriers cropped up that discouraged new initiatives. Chief among them was the Vietnam War. Peking clearly urged the North Vietnamese to press for victory in South Vietnam and backed this up by supplying weapons, munitions, and advisers. Peking also tried to block efforts to end the war. It opposed efforts to take Vietnam to the United Nations and joined Hanoi in claiming that Vietnam was not a problem for the UN. Their attitude led Secretary-General U Thant and others to agree that the UN would waste its time involving itself with Vietnam. Several times we quietly counted noses and found we lacked nine votes even to place Vietnam on the Security Council's agenda. Similarly, the Chinese blocked reconvening the Geneva Conference, a peacemaking body which could have helped. China's attitude on Vietnam alone precluded recognition.

A second barrier was Mao Zedong's infamous "Great Cultural Revolution"—a ferocious internal power struggle pitting old-line Communists, youthful Red Guards, the military, workers, professionals, and intellectuals against each other. Beginning in 1966, the Cultural Revolution raised havoc not only within China but with Chinese diplomacy. Throughout the late 1960's the State Department didn't even know to whom we should address our letters. At one point the Red Guards called for the burning of my counterpart, China's Foreign Minister Chen Yi, which I thought an exceptionally bad idea.

Throughout most of the Kennedy and Johnson years we nevertheless maintained a channel of communications with Peking via a series of bilateral meetings in Warsaw. These talks began in Geneva in the mid-1950's, then moved to Warsaw; in reality, the United States probably had more contact with the People's Republic than did many governments who recognized Peking. But these talks failed to improve relations, as we had hoped. Among other things, Washington continuously proposed exchanges (reporters, scholars, scientists, students, ordinary tourists, cultural groups, sports teams, meteorologists); offered improved varieties of plants to expand agricultural production; and more, all to no avail.

The Chinese continually insisted that there was nothing to discuss until the United States agreed to surrender Taiwan, despite the fact that Taiwan was never ours to surrender. This sterile impasse for decades blocked better relations with mainland China. Peking never accepted that China had been divided by civil war and that Taiwan had a right to its own existence. Repeatedly, we heard that unless we abandoned Chiang Kai-shek and surrendered thirteen million Taiwanese, we couldn't do business with Peking. Peking further insisted that we withdraw all American forces from Asia. So, despite the fact that we always had channels of communication open, neither side liked what the other said. Throughout these years no initiative by the People's Republic to help resolve our mutual differences and build better relations ever came across my desk. All told, by January 1968, when the Chinese suspended the Warsaw talks, 134 bilateral negotiating sessions had taken place, and not once did the Chinese propose an initiative to improve relations. Despite this barren impasse, I felt talks were better than no talks at all and was disappointed when the Chinese broke them off.

I myself had only infrequent contacts with the Communist Chinese. The most memorable occurred in May 1961 at a meeting on Laos in Geneva, where I encountered Chinese Foreign Minister Chen Yi and his delegation at a reception. Seeing Chen Yi, I remembered a famous—and unfortunate—incident when John Foster Dulles had refused to shake hands with Zhou Enlai at an international meeting. So I walked up to Chen Yi, greeted him, and offered my hand for a handshake. Startled, he stepped back, turned to his colleagues, and spoke in rapid Chinese. Finally he smiled and shook my hand, and we exchanged pleasantries. Earlier I had discreetly inquired whether he wished to meet privately with me, but he refused. For the record, when the United States signed the Laos accords, to which the People's Republic was a signatory, I stated that our signing implied nothing with respect to recognition.

In my talks with Soviet Foreign Minister Andrei Gromyko, several times I tried to enlist Soviet help in our problems with China. Gromyko never responded. Excepting Nonproliferation Treaty talks, the Soviet Union never discussed China with us, neither its China problems nor our China problems. A witty retort from Gromyko set the tone early on. When Kennedy took office, two Americans were being held prisoner in the People's Republic. We tried to get them back, without success. I finally told Gromyko about these Americans and asked if his government would intercede and encourage Peking to release them. "You will have to do that yourself," he said. "But as you know, we don't have diplomatic relations with the People's Republic," I said. Whereupon Gromyko replied, with a tight little smile, "Then take it up with Chiang Kai-shek!"

I never raised that issue with Chiang, but I met with him many times about other issues. My acquaintance with Chiang Kai-shek extended back to World War II and the CBI theater; of course, I saw him more frequently as secretary of state. I usually saw Chiang in Asia; he rarely visited the United States, preferring to send in his place Madame Chiang, a charming and skillful substitute. He was always a thoughtful host when I visited Taiwan.

On one of my trips Lyndon Johnson asked me to give Chiang a Bulova clock as a gift. This clock operated on a tuning fork, a new principle of timekeeping from our space program, and it bore appropriate inscriptions to Chiang from LBJ. I flew to Taipei and mentioned this gift to someone in our embassy. He turned pale and warned, "You must never give a timepiece to a Chinese! That means his time has run out!" With Chiang's view of his own importance, that would have been quite an insult, and we scurried to find a more appropriate gift.

I had mixed feelings about Chiang Kai-shek. He did a remarkable job bringing China through the thirties and World War II. It was miraculous that anything resembling China even survived two decades of warfare. Unfortunately he had illusory ideas about his own position in world affairs, Taiwan's role, and developments on the mainland. He genuinely believed a second revolution on the mainland would someday restore him to power. Because he lived in the past, it wasn't easy to do business with him. In the sixties we worked primarily with his cabinet. Chiang was out of touch, a remote, almost ghostly figure, and I never came to know him well.

I will never forget my final meeting with Chiang Kai-shek. During this last call—in 1968—he remained true to form and retold his long story about representing the government of all China and how he would one day return to the mainland and resume his rightful place—with massive American support, of course. When he finished, I said, "Mr. President, there are only two hundred million Americans and there are eight hundred million mainland Chinese. I can assure you that we Americans are not going to bleed ourselves white in fighting a conventional war against China."

Chiang, misinterpreting what I in fact meant—that the United States would not help him regain the mainland—turned on me almost in a fury: "You must never, ever think of using nuclear weapons against China."

Suddenly it was clear that his "Chineseness" was more important than being Chiang Kai-shek, ruler of all China. So I then told him, "Well, Mr. President, you have your answer." But I was gripped by his response. Again, it illustrated what had vastly impressed me in CBI, the strong "Chineseness" of the Chinese people.

Throughout the Kennedy and Johnson years we in government received severe criticism for our unimaginative "Cold War" approach to China. Perhaps some of this criticism was deserved, but during those eight years Peking was a militant, aggressive power. Peking sent men and arms across the northeastern frontier of Burma, attacked India, sent agents into northern Thailand, and, of course, sent massive supplies and arms to North Vietnam. At one point Chinese engineers were building a road through Laos, aimed at Thailand. Communist China even broke with the Soviet Union over how militant to be in support of world revolution; the Chinese preached extreme militancy, while the Soviets urged caution. And when you add to that mix the fact that China was interested in improving relations only if we abandoned Taiwan, any approach other than what was adopted would have been impossible.

I did try to signal Peking's leaders that we were not interested in a conflict with them over Vietnam or anything else. In March 1966 I gave a speech on our China policy to a subcommittee of the House Committee on Foreign Affairs, saying that the United States did not intend to attack China, sought expanded unofficial contacts with China, intended to continue the Warsaw talks, and was ready to negotiate arms control and nonproliferation issues. I said there was nothing eternal or immovable about American China policy; we had to avoid assuming that current hostility meant unending and inevitable hostility. But I also stressed our commitment to Taiwan, our refusal to allow Taiwan's expulsion from the United Nations, and our determination to help countries in Asia threatened by Peking.

On May 10 Zhou Enlai declared that China would not provoke a war with the United States, but it would defend itself if attacked and would carry the war to the aggressor without regard to boundaries. This was fine with us, for we had no intention of attacking China. Throughout the rest of 1966 we continued to tell the Chinese that we sought better relations with them and had no hostile intent toward them.

Even though we didn't recognize the People's Republic, we recognized its importance. There was no way to ignore the Chinese; only a decade earlier we had fought them in Korea. "Let China sleep," Napoleon once said, "for when she awakes, the world will tremble." Despite the problems posed by Taiwan and recognition, we tried to base our Asian policies on the fundamental reality of China's presence during both the Kennedy and Johnson administrations.

On at least one occasion this got me into trouble with the press. At a press conference in October 1967 someone asked me what I thought about China's future twenty years from then. I answered with three simple facts: "One, we face the prospect of a billion Chinese; two, they'll be armed with nuclear weapons; and three, no one knows what their policy is going to be twenty years from now." James Reston of the *New York Times* wrote a column charging me with dragging up the racism of the "yellow peril." There was nothing racial about what I said, just three statements of fact. I complained to Reston, who wrote a semiapology and then buried it in one of his columns. My remarks weren't racially inspired at all . . . and I suspect Reston knew it. They were a simple reminder that China would inevitably play a major role in the world's future, but what that role was we had no way of knowing.

For whatever it is worth, my October 1967 remarks proved accurate: There are now a billion Chinese, they do have nuclear weapons, and no one in 1967 could have predicted the course of events that has transformed China since. Few would have thought then that within two decades billions of American dollars would be invested in China, Americans would be touring China, and thousands of Chinese students would be studying in the United States. I enthusiastically applauded President Nixon's historic trip to China, although when I recalled my own scars from the Truman years and how Republicans had savaged the Democrats over China, I thought the Grand Old Party got off easy. Any Democratic president visiting Peking would have been torn to pieces by the Republicans, likely with Nixon himself leading the way.

I also enthusiastically endorsed President Jimmy Carter's success in normalizing relations with the People's Republic. And in the years since, I have mused over my Oval Office meeting with John Kennedy shortly after he took office. Could we have begun the process of rapprochement then, more than a decade earlier? Kennedy and I decided in 1961 that we could not.

Today a certain euphoria pervades much of the public's perception of U.S.-Chinese relations. This could be as unfortunate as the hostility that infected relations during the 1950's and 1960's. We might remember that while Chinese and American interests may sometimes coincide, they are not identical. Indeed, they may at times be opposed.

This was driven home to me in a humorous way during Chinese leader Deng Xiaoping's visit to Atlanta in 1979. For some reason Deng asked me to call on him, and we met in his hotel suite. Early in the conversation I said, "Mr. Vice Premier, I know that your colleagues in Peking have a six-inch-thick file on me, telling what a terrible person I am. I want you to know that I am more interested in the next thirty years than the past thirty." He replied, "Mr. Rusk, we don't have a file on you." Then he laughed like hell—and invited me to visit him in Peking!

During our conversation I asked him what China really wanted from the United States. "That's simple," he said. "Your science and technology." But lest we Americans become too paternalistic in our new relationship with the People's Republic, as we were with the China of old, we should remember Deng Xiaoping's remarks to an Atlanta audience during that same trip: "You Americans must always remember that China remains the Middle Kingdom. There are the Chinese and there are the barbarians. And you," he said, pointing to the audience, "are among the barbarians."

18

Death of a President

John Kennedy never got a chance to change U.S. China policy or pursue other initiatives he may have contemplated for a second term. Had Lee Harvey Oswald not snuffed out Kennedy's life on November 22, 1963, I firmly believe that Kennedy would have made a great president. After a rough shakedown cruise we had learned to work together as a team and were developing momentum. I was impressed with Kennedy's growth in office, how quickly he learned on the job, and his spirit. He enjoyed being president and thrived on challenge. I never heard Kennedy talk about the burdens of the presidency. When events didn't go his way, he rarely complained and never indulged in self-pity. He took success and failure in equal stride; I was as impressed with his performance after the fiasco of the Bay of Pigs as by any of his accomplishments.

An extremely intelligent man, Kennedy had an extraordinary memory and retained most of what he read and heard. A speed reader, Kennedy could read a report nearly as fast as he could turn the pages; he took briefing very fast and had an insatiable curiosity about the world. His mind was constantly at work, spinning over ideas and policy. He involved himself with details that most presidents would leave to their staffs.

Yet John Kennedy was in no sense an overwhelming personality. There was no "Kennedy treatment" comparable with the "LBJ treatment," perhaps because Kennedy was too skeptical for that, too skeptical about himself as well as other people and ideas.

Kennedy was more cautious than many people realize. Sobered by the narrowness of his victory, he selected carefully the issues over which to battle politically, particularly with Congress. Sometimes he disappointed his colleagues by not fighting for every issue that came before him. He used to tell us, "If you are going to have a fight, have a fight about something. Don't have a fight about nothing."

I had instant access to John Kennedy twenty-four hours a day, something I later enjoyed with Lyndon Johnson as well, although I tried not to abuse it. Intermediaries never came between us. White House operators and staffers always put through my calls. The layering of the later Nixon White House just didn't exist under Kennedy or Johnson; it was inconceivable to us.

Despite my near total access to Kennedy, our relationship was always official, never personal. I was not a member of his family or social circle, and I did not play touch football up at Hyannis Port or get pushed into Ethel Kennedy's swimming pool at Hickory Hill. President Kennedy always called me Mr. Secretary, never Dean. At a White House dinner once I sat next to Jacqueline Kennedy. She turned to me and said, "You know, it is very significant that my husband always calls you Mr. Secretary." I wasn't sure what she meant, but I shared George Marshall's view that those carrying official responsibility should have an arm's length relationship with each other. Personal relationships should not enter into the consideration of public policy. Certainly Kennedy and I had some differences in style and temperament, and we came from wholly different backgrounds, but in foreign policy we were on the same wavelength on most issues.

John Kennedy was an impatient fellow who didn't waste time. I learned to speak precisely to the point at hand, then shut up and go back to my office. Kennedy was especially impatient with people who talked too much and easily bored. Distinguished foreign guests or heads of state liked nothing more than to come to the Oval Office to deliver lengthy and often well-rehearsed remarks. Listening to these, Kennedy often started his rocking chair going and tapping on his teeth with his fingernails, sure signs to me that we should cut the visitors short and get them talking business. I myself had hundreds of discussions with

Kennedy, but our conversations were always business; we never fanned the breeze or exchanged small talk. I had far more leisurely conversations even with George Marshall, a very austere man, than with Kennedy.

Kennedy's team was new to public administration. His people for the most part had never negotiated anything with a foreign government, had never made a decision involving foreign affairs, or taken their lumps for unfortunate decisions, although there were outstanding exceptions like Douglas Dillon and Averell Harriman. Early in the Kennedy years we in the State Department tried to impress upon our White House counterparts the importance of diplomacy, the rules of protocol, the process of negotiation, the role of the United Nations and international law, but it was a rough go. Fortunately National Security Adviser McGeorge Bundy understood these concerns, but there were others in the White House who did not. Often I argued a more cautious line than Kennedy's White House advisers, and frequently I suggested that we not take on every problem in the world as if it were our problem, but many of Kennedy's staffers and the president himself favored a more activist approach. "Vigor" was the word of the day. The Kennedy administration, all of us, had a bias toward taking action, even when doing nothing might better serve American diplomacy and our national interest.

All three presidents I served—Truman, Kennedy, and Johnson—had lively senses of humor, but Kennedy's was the best. He used his humor and sardonic wit on everyone, including himself and his family, so we all took his barbs in good grace. He also used his humor to lighten up serious and even grave situations. When we met on that Saturday morning before his televised speech to the nation about Soviet missiles in Cuba, he entered the room, looked around the table, and said, "Well, gentlemen, today we are going to earn our pay."

All three of my presidents were good family men. I saw many evidences of Kennedy's affection for his family; he was very proud of Jacqueline and thoroughly enjoyed his children, who were in and out of the Oval Office. Those wonderful pictures of John-John hiding under his dad's desk were not staged. I walked into the Oval Office one morning before Kennedy had finished breakfast, and as I sat there waiting, Caroline, then three or four years old, came out from behind a screen at the end of the room and said, "Mr. Secretary, what is the situation in Yemen today?" I heard someone tittering behind the screen, and it was John Kennedy. He had put her up to it.

Many myths have been inspired by this fascinating man, some not flattering to his presidential stature. Stories have emerged since his death about his sex life, but during the hundreds of times I saw the man in a great diversity of situations, never once did I hear or see anything that caused me to speculate about his personal life. Whatever these stories about John Kennedy, and I was only his secretary of state and not his chaperon, if there was anything to hide, he hid it well.

Kennedy had an Irish temper, which he usually kept under control. A rare exception occurred during Indonesian President Achmed Sukarno's visit to Washington. During their presidential talks Sukarno kept diverting the talk to Gina Lollabrigida and other sex symbols. Kennedy felt that was very unpresidential; he didn't like it at all. Adding insult to injury, shortly after Sukarno went home, he invited Jacqueline Kennedy to visit Indonesia. I vetoed that myself and never forwarded the invitation to the White House. Kennedy was further displeased when I later told him his wife had received an invitation from this international lecher.

I cannot shed any light on Kennedy's physical problems. Not once did I hear him complain about his back or any physical pain, nor do I think he was under any form of sedation. By my observation, Kennedy's "impairments" never interfered with his being president. I found him able for duty at all times.

Of John Kennedy's many fine qualities, I most respected his courage. His performance during the Cuban missile crisis particularly impressed me. We have never had a crisis as dangerous as that one, and yet the calm way in which Kennedy handled that crisis filled me with admiration. He was as cool as a block of ice during those thirteen days of October, carefully weighing the dangers of each policy option and making the decisions that led to its resolution.

He also had views about policy not fully shared by some of his advisers. For example, take that famous sentence in his inaugural address "Let every nation know, whether it wishes us well or ill, that we shall pay any price, bear any burden, meet any hardship, support any friend, oppose any foe to assure the survival and the success of liberty." Even though some of the so-called Kennedy people tried to brush that sentence away as rhetoric after his death, it was a sentence characteristic of John Kennedy. He really believed it. In fact, by the choice of his family those words are engraved on his tombstone at Arlington. And when the British gave an acre of ground at Runnymede to the American people in memory of John Kennedy, they chose those same words for his stone marker. They weren't just campaign rhetoric or inaugural oratory, but words that reflected Kennedy's approach to problems affecting the United States and its vital interests.

Throughout the Kennedy years the press often speculated about my imminent departure as secretary of state, caused in some measure by my formal relationship with him. I was always relaxed about such a possibility, having in effect laid my resignation on Kennedy's desk from the first day we took office. In the summer of 1963 I did tell Kennedy that if he wanted a new man for secretary of state in preparing for the 1964 elections, it was all right with me. But Kennedy told me that he wanted me to stay on and not to bring resignation up again.

Kennedy never intimated to me that he wanted me out. In any event, I had told him that for financial reasons I could serve only one term. His brother Bobby felt differently, however, and undoubtedly wanted a different secretary of state. My differences with Bobby may have begun when he realized I served John Kennedy as president of the United States, rather than out of personal commitment to the Kennedy family. I was never one of the "Kennedy people" and never made the effort to become one. My difficulties with Bobby over State Department appointments stemmed in part from this. He didn't think all of the appointees were true Kennedy people. And Bobby was right. I chose people for their professional ability, not their political commitment. Worse yet, Bobby wanted a commitment to the whole Kennedy clan, not just his brother. To his credit, John Kennedy never let his brother's attitudes affect his own assessment of people; JFK's concern was over whether or not someone could do his job.

On November 22, 1963, six members of the cabinet, including myself, were flying to Japan for a joint meeting with the Japanese cabinet. About an hour west of Hawaii the captain of the plane brought me a one-line flash message from the wire services that President Kennedy had been shot in Dallas. I asked Pierre Salinger, on board as Kennedy's press representative, to call the White House on the plane's radio and confirm this. When Salinger received confirmation, I told the pilot to turn around and head back to Hawaii. Then word came that Kennedy had died. I announced this on the plane's loudspeaker to everyone on board, saying, "Ladies and gentlemen, we have received official confirmation that President Kennedy is dead. I am saddened to tell you this grievous news. We have a new president. God bless our new president and our nation." I was stunned; I didn't know what else to say. No one did. We sat for perhaps fifteen to twenty minutes in complete silence, each person alone with his thoughts, contemplating privately the tragedy that had occurred. There were many tears on that plane; to be on an airplane halfway across the Pacific and learn that our president had been killed, especially that president, forever marked us all.

Gradually we pulled ourselves together and gathered in the forward

"Forty Acres and a Mule." Born in a wood-frame house built by his father, Dean Rusk never forgot his humble beginnings on a red clay farm in Cherokee County, Georgia. "We were poor," said Rusk. "But if anyone had called us poor, we would have socked 'em!" *Dean Rusk Collection, University of Georgia (DRC)*

Dean's father, Robert Rusk (standing, far right), was one of eleven children and the only member of his family to attend college. His brothers and sisters stayed on as farmers in Cherokee and were "eventually spewed out by the unforgiving land." *DRC*

Robert Rusk at Davidson College. Forced by a throat ailment to give up the ministry, Rusk found a mail carrier job and moved his family to Atlanta in 1913. Rusk carried the mail for twenty years, stabilized the family income, and sent his children to Atlanta's best public schools. *DRC*

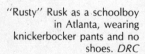

''Rusty'' Rusk as a schoolboy in Atlanta, wearing knickerbocker pants and no shoes. *DRC*

A "breathless experience" at the "Poor Man's Princeton." With more faith than cash, Rusk worked his way through Davidson College, played center on the basketball team, became president of the YMCA, and cadet commander of the ROTC, and was graduated Phi Beta Kappa. His impressive record helped him win a Rhodes scholarship in 1931, fulfilling a goal first dreamed in boyhood. *DRC*

Having arrived at Oxford, England, in 1931, Rusk played lacrosse (standing, third from left) and won his "blue" against archrival Cambridge. He studied international relations, history, law, politics, and philosophy, spent his vacations in Nazi Germany, and witnessed first hand Hitler's terrifying rise to power and the West's indifference to totalitarianism and aggression. His experiences in the thirties and in the world war that followed were formative for Rusk and an entire generation of American policy makers. *DRC*

Returning in 1934 to mid-Depression America, Rusk hired on with Mills
College, an all-women school in Oakland, California, where for six years
he taught political science and history; was named dean of the faculty at
age twenty-six, "to avoid confusion," said the college president; and
courted Virginia Foisie, one of his students. *DRC*

"It wasn't easy for a young professor to court a student in the thirties," Rusk confessed, but he managed, marrying "Ginny" in 1937. "This grandly talented girl . . . appealed to me in every way." *DRC*

A family gathering to meet the bride: from left to right, sister Margaret; brother Roger; Roger's wife, Helen; their daughter, Carolyn; brother Parks; Park's wife, Sally; Father; Dean; Mother; Virginia; Richard Orr; sister Helen Orr. *DRC*

"In the field with 'Vinegar Joe'" (Rusk at far right). Called to active duty as a reserve Army officer in December 1940, Rusk first served at the War Department in Washington, then in 1943 became a staff officer for General Joseph Stilwell in the China-Burma-India theater. Rusk served in CBI for two years, survived two near-fatal airplane incidents, witnessed the brutality of modern warfare, and once, in supreme irony, personally authorized an airdrop of American cigarettes and supplies to Ho Chi Minh and his Vietminh guerrillas, then fighting with Americans in common cause against the Japanese. *DRC*

"Driving a Jeep in CBI." Rusk designed a distinctive shoulder patch for Americans in CBI. With the star of India, the sun of China, and red and white stripes for the United States, the patch reminded Asians and Britons that the Americans were in CBI to fight the Japanese, not to restore British colonial rule. *DRC*

"New Delhi." Operating in the wake of the irascible Stilwell, Rusk needed all his diplomatic skills to smooth the ruffled feathers of British, American, Indian, and Chinese leaders, and his incisive cables caught the attention of superiors in Washington. In June 1945 Rusk was reassigned to the famous "Abe Lincoln Brigade" in the Pentagon, Army officers who worked on American policy requirements for rebuilding a world torn apart by global war. *DRC*

"Fending off the press." Handpicked by Secretaries of State George Marshall and Dean Acheson, Rusk rose in the bureaucracy, first as director of United Nations Affairs and later as assistant secretary of state for Far Eastern Affairs during the Korean War, becoming an important adviser in postwar decision making. "I was one hell of a staff officer," says Rusk. *DRC*

From the left: Christian Herter; Dean Rusk; Dean Acheson. After the "fall" of China and with McCarthyism at its height, Rusk volunteered for Far Eastern Affairs. He was an ideal lightning rod. "We kissed him on both cheeks and gave him the job," said Dean Acheson. *United Press International (UPI)*

As president of the Rockefeller Foundation from 1952 to 1960 Rusk spent evenings and weekends at home in Scarsdale, New York. With son David (far right), he helped coach son Rich's elementary school football team. The hardest thing about the Rockefeller job? "Learning not to blink whenever someone mentioned a million dollars." *DRC*

"Christmas in Washington." From the left: Rich; David; Virginia; Dean; Dave's Argentine wife, Delcia; Peggy. Vowing to protect his family's privacy, when a persistent reporter stuck his foot in the front door to get a "Christmas with the Rusks" story, Rusk stomped on it and watched him hobble off down the sidewalk. *DRC*

President-elect Kennedy announces his choice for secretary of state to the press. Although unknown to the American public, Rusk was highly recommended by former policy makers and became John Kennedy's surprise choice for secretary of state. The two men had never met. *Department of State, Visual Services Section (DOS)*

A superb staffer whose greatest strength was the lucid articulation of a problem, called the "perfect number two" by friends and critics, Rusk had a quiet, nonassertive manner as secretary that at first confused and disappointed Kennedy. Their relationship improved after a rough shakedown cruise, the Bay of Pigs fiasco, and the Berlin crisis. *DRC*

With Defense Secretary Robert McNamara, advising the president. "The Kennedy years were not Camelot; they were years of crisis," said Rusk. "John Kennedy himself would have been the first to kick any notions of Camelot out the window. He was too skeptical for sentimentality." *DRC*

"Bob McNamara and I hit it off right from the start." Vowing to avoid acrimony at the top, Rusk worked hard to iron out differences with his colleagues, often meeting with McNamara on weekends for long, private talks. "Our discussions were infused with the thought that we were all trying to serve the same president." *DOS, DRC*

Rusk wanted to serve frog legs at a luncheon for Soviet Foreign Minister Andrei Gromyko and was warned not to. "You have very wise advisers," cracked Gromyko. Rusk's long intimate conversations with Gromyko and Soviet Ambassador Anatoly Dobrynin helped defuse superpower tensions during the crisis-ridden sixties. *DOS, DRC*

"The most fascinating foreign leader I ever met," said Rusk of Nikita Khrushchev, here bantering with Rusk during signing ceremonies in Moscow for the Limited Test Ban Treaty. *UPI/Bettmann Newsphotos*

Invited to Khrushchev's Black Sea dacha, Rusk played badminton with his Soviet host on a Persian rug. "Khrushchev was surprisingly agile," said Rusk of their match, billed by the press as an "East-West contest" that Rusk "lost." "In a pinch," claimed Rusk, "I think my tennis background would have carried me to victory." *UPI/Bettmann Newsphotos*

"He was the perfect host to Virginia and me," said Rusk. Yet during this same visit Khrushchev and Rusk had a bloodcurdling exchange over Berlin. *DRC*

While mothering two teenage children, Virginia Rusk worked as hard as
her husband, attending national day celebrations, representing Rusk at
social functions, and helping Foreign Service wives and foreign diplomats.
All the while she was sick with multiple sclerosis, undiagnosed until she
left Washington. Focusing on Third World diplomats, she and her
husband used flash cards on each other, seeking to learn their names.
Murillo Diplomatic News Photo Service

"A few words for a security guard." Rusk's Cherokee County roots, sense
of humility, and habit of visiting all levels of the State Department
endeared him to his secretaries, security men, junior colleagues. "The
word spread very quickly: 'Hey, this is a super guy!' " remembers
security agent Gus Peleusos, when the "gunslingers" came face-to-face
with their new boss. *DOS, DRC*

Rusk never campaigned for top office, offered to resign repeatedly, and wanted to serve only one term. But after the trauma of the Kennedy assassination Rusk couldn't refuse Johnson's request to stay on. "I probably wanted that job less than any other secretary of state, said Rusk. "The irony is, only Cordell Hull served longer in office." *White House Photo*

"The most complex, powerful personality I have ever known," said Rusk of LBJ. "It was the strength of his convictions more than the 'LBJ Treatment' that made him so persuasive. He really believed in what he was trying to do." *White House Photo*

President Johnson and Rusk greeting South Vietnamese leaders Nguyen Cao Ky and Nguyen Van Thieu at Honolulu in February 1966. Despite misgivings over Western colonialism and having witnessed in CBI the limitations of American power in Asia, Dean Rusk led his Truman administration colleagues into French Indochina and laid the seeds for America's thirty-year war. Rusk questioned the wisdom of a SEATO Treaty, negotiated during the Eisenhower years. But after it was signed and ratified, he advised his presidents to honor it. *DOS, DRC*

To the dismay of aides, Rusk discontinued his visits to South Vietnam when he discovered that American helicopters and crews were used as decoys to draw enemy fire whenever he traveled in-country. *DOS, DRC*

Until spring 1965, fearing he might have picked "a losing horse," Rusk agonized over whether the United States should commit combat troops and bomb North Vietnam. "But my doubts were registered only as questions, never as opposition to policy," said Rusk. "I never advised Kennedy or Johnson to withdraw." *DOS, DRC*

Testifying before Congress. Rusk claimed that both the Kennedy and Johnson administrations consulted freely with Congress about the war. Of his congressional critics? "I wish more had simply said, 'We've changed our minds,' rather than misrepresent what both we and they had actually done." *DOS, DRC*

Rusk regarded Senate Foreign Relations Committee Chairman William Fulbright as "an instinctive maverick" and tangled repeatedly with his congressional opponents, yet remained on good terms with many. After leaving office, he offered to campaign for Wayne Morse when the Oregon senator's patriotism was questioned because of his antiwar views. *DOS, DRC*

Years later Rusk admitted to mistakes but never changed his mind about the war. "I have not apologized for my role, for the simple reason that I believed in the principles underlying why we fought that war. There is nothing I can say now that would diminish my share of responsibility. I live with that, and others can make of it what they will." *DOS, DRC*

New York cartoon of Dean Rusk in a cook pot, being poked by Fulbright, was Rusk's favorite cartoon. "Too bad he functioned best as 'cornered rat,' " said one critic. *Gib Crockett,* Washington Star *(March 13, 1968)*

'THE HOTTER THE FIRE THE TOUGHER HE GETS!'

During Rusk's visit to Uruguay a man ran out of the crowd and tried to spit on him. "He was so scared that he didn't have any spit," recalled Rusk. "But the photographer dubbed into his negative a huge blob as big as my fist." *Associated Press*

To my friend and alter ego george Ball as proof that we look at things alike!
Dean Rusk

Despite this quip, Rusk greatly respected George Ball for his courageous and eloquent opposition to Vietnam decision making. *Reprinted courtesy of George W. Ball*

New Yorker cartoon, Dean Rusk being hanged in effigy by college students. Shaken by the Tet offensive of February 1968, aware that Americans were tiring of the war, Rusk played a quiet insider's role in persuading President Johnson to de-escalate the fighting, call off the bombing of North Vietnam, and move to the negotiating table. Even Defense Secretary Clark Clifford was unaware of Rusk's efforts. *Drawing by D. Fradon;* © *1965 The New Yorker Magazine, Inc.*

"It's encouraging to see they're interested in what's going on off campus."

The family cemetery in Cherokee County. Exhausted after eight years in Washington, Dean Rusk came home to Georgia in 1970 to teach international law. Said Rusk upon his return to academic life, his true love: "After a thirty-year detour I finally made it." *DRC*

Breakfast at Willie's Place. Welcoming the anonymity of private life, when accosted by an elderly woman at the Atlanta airport as someone she had seen before, Rusk replied, "Hoss Cartwright of 'Bonanza.'" *Leanne Turner, School of Journalism, DRC*

"From pariah to professor." Relishing teaching and invigorated by his contact with young people, Dean Rusk built a new life for himself in Georgia. During seventeen years as John Sibley Professor International Law, he gave 750 talks about foreign affairs and world peace to groups throughout Georgia and the South, including young schoolchildren, "my toughest audience." *DRC*

cabin. We spent the rest of the flight back talking about what we could do to help keep the government going; Kennedy had died, but the nation lived, and we knew that Kennedy himself would have insisted that this tragedy not paralyze the government. I called George Ball, then acting secretary of state back in Washington, and asked him to investigate what foreign policy problems would arise from Kennedy's assassination. Ball confirmed that the procedures and arrangements dealing with the death of an American president in office—Kennedy had not been our first—were going forward.

We landed in Hawaii in the middle of a full military alert. No one knew what lay behind Kennedy's death. We had communicated with Lyndon Johnson, who was still in Dallas, asking whether he wanted us to come to Dallas or Washington, and he told us to return to Washington. So we took on additional fuel and made a nonstop flight from Hawaii to Washington.

Upon arrival, I slept a few hours, and then Lyndon Johnson called me to the Executive Office Building. Under such circumstances, cabinet officers customarily tender their resignations to the new president, freeing him to form his own government. I offered to resign, but Johnson urged me to stay on, saying that it was my duty to do so. He intended to continue the policies of the Kennedy administration. We all needed to pitch in and keep the country going during this moment of great tragedy. Under those circumstances, I could not refuse the president.

My greatest concern during that long return flight home and in the assassination's aftermath was whether or not Kennedy's murder had international ramifications. Was it a conspiracy involving the Cubans or the Russians? We just didn't know.

After our return to Washington, I helped with the arrangements for receiving guests and heads of state who came from all over the world to attend Kennedy's funeral. Some I met at the airport. Frequently I had to work out matters with the Kennedy family and with President Johnson. We were especially concerned about French President Charles de Gaulle's personal security during the Kennedy funeral. Political tensions were high in France, resulting in threats to his personal safety. We wanted to have him driven from the White House to the funeral service, but he refused, saying, "No, I shall walk with Mrs. Kennedy." So this towering figure walked through the streets of Washington to the memorial service, near Mrs. Kennedy and next to the tiny emperor of Ethiopia, Haile Selassie. We breathed a genuine sigh of relief when de Gaulle returned safely to Paris.

Jacqueline Kennedy won my admiration that November day. She

set an example for us all and helped the nation through that experience. She was a lovely First Lady. I am certain at times she found the role of First Lady quite burdensome, but she tried to carve out as normal a life as possible for her two small children. Those were hard years for her, and when she married Aristotle Onassis, I sent her a note wishing her happiness; Jacqueline Kennedy had earned it.

Our embassies overseas recorded an astonishing reaction to Kennedy's death. Africans walked through the bush fifty miles to our nearest consulate or embassy to say, "I did not know President Kennedy, but he was my friend. I came to say that I am sorry." The same thing happened in Asia, South America, and elsewhere. It reminded me of the death of Franklin Roosevelt. In April 1945, on the day Roosevelt died, I walked through a crowded Indian city, wearing an American uniform. Upper-class Indians gave me their folded-hand salute as I passed by, and the beggars and urchins on the street reached out to touch me, not begging. They reached out of sympathy. Such emotion was repeated manyfold when John Kennedy died. When I met President Charles de Gaulle at Dulles Airport, I thanked him for coming to Kennedy's funeral. He said, "Don't thank me. The people of France demanded that I come."

Our friends abroad grieved with us over President Kennedy's assassination, and to their credit, even our adversaries didn't try to make much capital out of his death; it saddened them as well. Indeed, I was told that Chairman Nikita Khrushchev burst into tears when he heard of Kennedy's death.

During the weeks after Kennedy's death, in his desire for continuity, President Johnson went out of his way to keep in office as many Kennedy appointees as were willing to serve. He kept Kennedy's entire cabinet, all the ambassadors, almost every presidential appointee. He asked Kennedy's White House staff to remain with him, but some for their own reasons decided to leave. Lyndon Johnson was determined to create both the appearance and fact of continuity. He did this effectively and, from my vantage point, with full consideration for the feelings of the Kennedy family and staff. William Manchester's book *The Death of a President* badly misrepresented this alleged feud between the Kennedys and Lyndon Johnson. I was actively involved with the funeral, and whenever a question arose, I asked Sargent Shriver, who spoke for the family at that time, what he thought we ought to do. He usually said, "Whatever the president wants." When I asked LBJ about something, he usually said, "Whatever the family wants."

The Kennedy years engendered much sentimentality and are remembered as an idealistic period in American history. It is worth remembering, however, that these years were filled with crisis. There was no Camelot in the early 1960's, and John Kennedy himself would have been the first to kick such notions out the window. He was too skeptical for sentimentality. Most of the Camelot literature that was written after his death, and the anti-Camelot literature that followed, had little to do with the John Kennedy that I knew.

Although I never formed a close personal friendship with Kennedy, I liked him immensely. He had a delightful personality, was fun to work for, and he was a stimulating man with whom to discuss foreign policy. He had an extraordinary capacity to enlist the enthusiasm and interest of both young and old for politics and public service, and he tended to set all of us around him on fire.

In May 1965, eighteen months after Kennedy's death, the people of Great Britain dedicated an acre of ground at Runnymede, the field where the Magna Carta was signed by King John and all the British lords in 1215, in tribute to our late president and as a gift to the American people. Lyndon Johnson asked me to represent the United States, and I flew to Britain with Jacqueline Kennedy to receive this memorial from Queen Elizabeth. This honor was a moment of great emotion for me and a highlight of my eight years as secretary of state.

In giving my remarks, my voice almost broke over a line I had borrowed from the war memorial at Edinburgh: "At the going down of the sun and in the morning, we shall remember him . . ."

With his respect for our British heritage, Kennedy himself would have loved this gift at Runnymede, a little piece of which every American now owns; it reflected so sensitive an understanding of the man himself.

I accepted that acre on behalf of the American people, with the joy and sadness which shall forever mark those of us who knew this extraordinary man John Fitzgerald Kennedy.

SECTION IV

THE JOHNSON YEARS

Four days after President Kennedy was assassinated, Dean Rusk wrote his new president a letter of resignation, which Lyndon Johnson declined. "I want you to remain secretary of state as long as I am president," said Johnson. Pop's hoped-for one term quickly became two terms. This extension was not discussed with family. My dad believed in democracy, but he ran our family like a benevolent monarch and made the command decisions.

With his eldest son in college and Peggy and me headed there shortly, Pop's financial worries continued. He confided to a reporter that when his bank balance read zero, "I'll have to find a job." After reading the newspaper story, a well-endowed "little old lady" from a midwestern state instructed her attorney to include a care package of five thousand dollars in her will.

"I tried to talk her out of it," her lawyer explained to a surprised Rusk. "I told her there were better causes than supporting you. She replied, 'You're right. Like hiring a new attorney.' " Upon her death a grateful Rusk deposited the five thousand dollars. But when a wealthy Scarsdale, New York friend of a friend offered to match his twenty-five-thousand-dollar salary as secretary of state until 1968, to enable him to finish office without incurring debt, he declined. "In my position, I just can't accept that kind of money," he wrote.

Lyndon Johnson and my dad liked each other. "Our official relationship was reinforced by personal friendship," said my father. "I love that Dean," Johnson told friends, more bluntly. Two southerners in a town overrun by the eastern establishment, both born and reared in poverty, sharing common values as well as boyhood memories, they became fast friends. Unsure of himself in foreign affairs, Johnson relied heavily upon Rusk. Two weeks after taking office, Johnson announced that the State Department would be the "central force" in foreign policy decision making.

My dad was untroubled by Johnson's less admirable traits. Reportedly LBJ was rough on staff but never on Dean Rusk; the respect between them was too deep. "Johnson was in awe of your father," George Ball explained. "The most complex man I have ever known" was all my dad would allow, when confronted with tales of Texas-size excesses; he respected LBJ enormously.

"A reticent and dour man from Cherokee County was never able to tell Lyndon Johnson what I really thought about him," he wrote Lady Bird Johnson after her husband's fatal heart attack in 1972. "I regret not trying a little harder. My respect for him as a president was matched by my love for him as a human being, but I suppose I thought it presumptuous to express the latter."

There were many evidences of their friendship, easily visible to family. With colleagues, LBJ was an inveterate giver of gifts, tokens, LBJ lighters, personalized pens, etc. One arrived on our doorstep at Christmas; I unwrapped the package and found inside . . . a small bust of LBJ. He had sent it to our family as a Christmas present. My dad laughed uproariously. Yet he quickly intervened when I headed for our basement shop, where I intended to drill a hole in the sculpture's base, tap some threads, and mount the presidential bust on the hood of our car.

Despite the fact that Vietnam decision making increasingly monopolized the energies of the Johnson administration, much was accomplished in foreign affairs. Crises arose and were weathered: American intervention in the Dominican Republic in 1965 gave way to an OAS peacekeeping force and a return to constitutional government. More than one hundred crewmen of the intelligence ship USS *Pueblo* were returned safely after being seized by North Korea in an act of international terrorism. A decade of relative calm in the Middle East exploded in violence in 1967 with the Six-Day War, in which a swift Israeli victory helped forestall superpower confrontation. Rusk's interest in the United Nations remained strong; every September he attended the opening ceremonies of the General Assembly in New York and met personally with every head of state and foreign minister. His interest in the Third World and the problems of developing countries continued. However, with government spending rising as the result of inflation, Johnson's Great Society programs, and an escalating Vietnam War, Rusk had to fight tooth and nail with congressional critics to keep American foreign aid programs funded.

Rusk's long, intimate talks with Soviet Foreign Minister Andrei Gromyko and Soviet Ambassador Anatoly Dobrynin reflected and perhaps contributed to a growing rapprochement between the superpowers, marred by the Soviet invasion of Czechoslovakia in 1968. Following the Limited Test Ban Treaty of August 1963, American and Soviet negotiators helped conclude the Outer Space Treaty and Nonproliferation Treaty and did most of the groundwork for the Seabed

Arms Treaty and Antiballistic Missile Treaty, both concluded during the Nixon years. Rusk enthusiastically supported these agreements and was heavily involved.

"Dean Rusk never got the credit he deserved for arms control," said his executive secretary, Ben Read. "He really worked on them, even the details. Bill Foster and Adrian Fisher [from the Arms Control and Disarmament Agency] regularly attended his morning staff meetings, and arms control was always on the agenda. They were constantly on the phone with him."

At the Rusk home the Johnson years were no different from the Kennedy years; such were the demands of office that for all practical purposes we lost our father for eight years. It is hard to convey how totally the job consumed him. Up at 7:00 A.M., home late at night, he worked Saturdays and even Sundays. He never took vacations; the nearest thing to it was a ten-day rest at George Ball's place in Florida "to recover from the flu." His staff found that he had taken only twelve days off in eight years in office. Preferring to stay on the job in Washington, he quickly set new records for travel both at home and overseas, far surpassing his predecessors.

Pop was home for dinner perhaps one evening a month. But even when home, he could never relax; the phone was always ringing, and often his special assistants or couriers brought him messages. He was in overdrive all the time. When using the telephone, which in the modern world often substitutes for visiting, my dad had time only for business. When I moved away to college, all our phone calls were abruptly cut short, something I resented until years later, when I learned that he had treated his presidents the same way. Walt Rostow told me that he once saw Lyndon Johnson holding a telephone receiver at arm's length, staring at it with a pained expression. "He did it again!" Johnson shouted. "He hung up on me before I was through with him." Johnson had Rostow relay the rest of the presidential message.

At the same time, despite his chaotic life in Washington, Pop tried to remain a father. On his rare evenings at home I sometimes coaxed him into a game of chess despite his fatigue. We'd set up the pieces, and although he was a good chess player, during the sixties I'd beat the tar out of him. My dad taught me to drive; somehow he made time for that. Occasionally he'd drive one leg of the way to a canoe trip, up to Harpers Ferry, West Virginia, or somewhere along the Potomac. It was my dad who rescued my buddies and me after our legs gave out on a fifty-mile hike along the Chesapeake and Ohio barge canal.

But there were limitations. For example, only twice in three years did he come to see my high school football team, the second time arriving only to see me lying unconscious on the field, my final play as a senior. When Delcia, my brother's wife, had her first child in 1967, Pop went to visit her at the hospital, walked into her room, and found someone else there. She had checked out two days earlier.

That was life with Father in Washington, D.C. In some respects it was no different from before. I had always hungered for his attentions, yet in Washington his remoteness and reserve were compounded by an impossible job. With his constant traveling and time at the office, we didn't expect much fathering from Pop during the sixties. Only once do I recall being upset by his absence. He was leaving the house as I roared up in our 1957 Ford Fairlane, and in passing, he said, "Oh, by the way, I'm going to Asia for ten days. I'll see you when I get back." That scene was repeated many times; but for some reason, something welled up from the depths, and his teenage son, a husky footballer, went to his room in tears. "What the hell kind of life is this anyway?" I thought. During the sixties we kids "grew up like weeds," in my dad's words, for which he often apologized. But he was involved in vital work, and Pop had warned us in December 1960 that family life would suffer in his new job. We took pride in his achievements, agonized with him over his "disappointments," kept up with his travels and activities through the media, and relished those snatches of home life with Pop.

—R. R.

19

LBJ Takes Over

Lyndon Johnson entered office well prepared for the presidency. Although he sometimes deprecated his own competency in foreign affairs, he was very well informed. He brought great talents and a rich experience to the Oval Office. As Senate majority leader during the Eisenhower years he had been deeply involved with the major issues of the fifties and with legislation affecting foreign and defense policy.

Early in the Kennedy administration I had assigned a Foreign Service officer to Vice President Johnson, to serve as his liaison with the State Department and to keep him fully informed about foreign policy. Johnson's liaison officer got the daily intelligence reports, the flow of incoming and outgoing telegrams, and the daily wrap-up of activities from the State Department, and he was always available to the vice president for consultation. The idea for this liaison officer was mine, but Johnson fully embraced it.

Johnson took his vice presidential duties seriously. He frequently sat with us at meetings of the National Security Council and the cabinet. Whenever matters of critical importance were discussed, Johnson was there. I had many informal talks with him. He absorbed briefings in expert fashion and with his powerful intellect went directly to the heart of issues under discussion. President Kennedy frequently asked him to travel abroad and consult with foreign leaders on issues of major, not merely cosmetic, importance. He visited some twenty-five countries and for each trip was thoroughly briefed to talk business with his foreign hosts. As vice president Lyndon Johnson was well exposed to foreign policy and he knew what President Kennedy was trying to accomplish. Johnson never represented himself as an expert on foreign policy, but as both president and vice president he kept closely in touch with developments.

Some Kennedy staffers and press reporters needled Johnson while he was in the Kennedy White House; indeed, the favorite indoor sport in Washington is to make fun of a sitting vice president. Hubert Humphrey had an uproarious routine that he often used on himself. When giving a speech, Humphrey sometimes referred to four or five former vice presidents whom we have long since forgotten as "those great Americans." Then he compared the vice president's seal with the president's seal, pointing out that the vice presidential eagle had only one arrow in its claw, compared with three for the president's eagle, and that his eagle's wings were drooping rather than upraised.

In comparison, Lyndon Johnson rarely joked about the impotency of the vice presidency. But it always impressed me that this man of such enormous energy and drive had the capacity even to act as a true vice president, always deferring to John Kennedy and exhibiting restraint and consideration. For a man whose instincts were to take control and lead, this must have taken immense self-discipline. President Kennedy respected that, and I never heard Kennedy or Johnson say a disparaging word about the other, even in private conversation, while they served together in the administration.

Lyndon Johnson was a man of great complexity and easily the most powerful personality I have ever known. He was a driven man, a president in a great hurry, partly because he never knew from one day to the next if he would still be alive the following day. Johnson had had a massive heart attack in 1955, and at one point his blood pressure had dropped to zero and he had been given up for dead.

Johnson was a highly intelligent man. When the scholars dig deeply into those thirty-five million items in the LBJ Library, they will be surprised by the evidence of his sheer intelligence. LBJ hid that intelligence from a lot of people with his southern accent and his cornpone stories. Yet in sessions when even the most complex and technical matters were discussed, Johnson grasped all that was involved, and he never missed the key issues before him. George Ball's assessment of Johnson was correct: LBJ suffered not from an inadequate education but from the belief that he had one.

As president Johnson had an all-consuming commitment to the job. He knew that he had not been the electorate's first choice, and he tried to compensate for that by doing everything he could to be a good and even a great president. Johnson was a severe task master, demanding of his colleagues and personal staff. He was also demanding of Congress and the American people. But he was most demanding of himself. Many of us worried about whether he would work himself into another heart attack, but he stubbornly refused our admonitions to slow down. He worked from early morning late into the night, often taking reading to bed with him. That reading sometimes kept him up until two in the morning or even later. There was so much to do and so little time.

Johnson had a great gift for persuasion, fueled by the famed "LBJ treatment" and his own native intellect. Taller than most men, LBJ used his height to advantage. He would draw close to his target, look down at him, stick a finger in the man's chest, and launch a barrage of extravagant language to make his point. Johnson was the most dynamic man I ever knew, simply overpowering at times. And he knew where his opponent's vulnerable points were, when to appeal seductively, and when to apply pressure. Fortunately LBJ never used the "treatment" on me; he never had to!

Johnson could use his intellect to influence people because he did his homework and thought about each issue he planned to act on. That allowed him to talk effectively with whomever he came into contact. I saw him in meetings with businessmen and labor leaders, members of Congress, in the cabinet and with foreign dignitaries, and with all, he had a gift for persuasion. In meetings, whether one on one or in groups of two to three hundred, he was the most eloquent, convincing person I had ever seen in my life. LBJ used his share of tricks to move people, and, of course, the "treatment," but it was the strength with which he held his convictions more than gimmickry that made him so effective. He really believed in what he was trying to do.

However, for some strange reason, when Johnson got before the television cameras at press conferences, he froze up. We could never get LBJ to loosen up before those little red eyes of the TV cameras. He was not nearly as effective on television as Kennedy, or Ronald Reagan in later years, and this hurt his relationship with the American people. Unfortunately for LBJ, John Kennedy on television was a hard act to follow. Kennedy was incredibly relaxed before the cameras, partly because he prepared hard and knew his stuff. Frequently I took briefing books to Kennedy that the State Department prepared for his news conferences. Early in his administration his political handlers recommended that on at least half the questions he simply say, "No comment." But Kennedy would have none of that: "No comment, hell! I'm having a press conference, and I've got to say something!"

But I never understood why Lyndon Johnson, who was so alive and vibrant at all other times, was so wooden before the cameras. Maybe he lacked confidence on policy matters and worried that he might make a mistake in responding to questions. He never realized that he knew more about policy than any of the reporters before him and that if he used his own judgment, he would come out all right. He was even wooden when he gave toasts at state dinners in the White House. He stood behind his podium and telePrompTer even then, refusing to improvise. His stiffness before the cameras remains a mystery to me.

LBJ's reputation for crudeness was overplayed by the press, and undoubtedly he was sensitive to this. Reporters were unmerciful in breaking through his personal privacy. Once LBJ simply got fed up with this badgering and, after his abdominal surgery, showed the press his scar. Reporters blew that into the crudest thing a president ever did, and yet he was only trying to accommodate them. And Lyndon Johnson used those cornpone lines and stories out of West Texas, for instance, quoting that old saying "Even a blind hog can find a few acorns if he roots around long enough." On the eastern seaboard that sounds pretty crude. Yet Lyndon Johnson was not a crude man; he showed impeccable manners when the occasion demanded it or when dealing with other chiefs of state.

Johnson was also portrayed as a skilled political manipulator, which was true enough. Unfortunately this led to the impression that he was a man without integrity. Johnson was a very complicated man, no doubt about it. But in my own relationship with him and in our dealings over foreign affairs I found him true to his word.

With his domestic program, Johnson understood that passing it would require Congress to act as a corporate body, on behalf of the national interest. To get 535 members of Congress to act with the necessary consensus requires continual persuasion and adjustment of view. Some people call that "wheeling and dealing." Much of it is necessary to prevent those impasses that are built into the very structure of our constitutional system.

Some of Lyndon Johnson's attitudes on policy were almost visceral;

they seemed to come from his gut. Whereas John Kennedy's approach on issues such as civil rights was often intellectual, Lyndon Johnson's just gushed out of him like lava from a volcano. After Johnson no longer had to worry about being elected senator from Texas, he could afford to let his real attitudes about civil rights come to the front.

Johnson often quoted former Supreme Court Justice Hugo Black, who said after he left the Court, "No lawyer had to tell me that 'separate was not equal.' I've known that 'separate was not equal' all my life." Johnson felt the same way. His views on civil rights and human rights were basic to him and rooted in his experiences in growing up in Texas and teaching Mexican-American schoolchildren. He was almost a driven man on the subjects of civil and human rights and helping the poor. He had genuine compassion for his fellowman, and this compassion, coupled with his leadership and knowledge of Congress, led to the most extraordinary legislative session in American history.

No American should ever forget that remarkable evening of March 15, 1965, when President Johnson addressed a joint session of Congress on the voting rights and civil rights bills. After recalling his days as a youth in West Texas and a schoolteacher in the late 1920's, he said, "It never occurred to me in my fondest dreams that I might have the chance to help the sons and daughters of those students and to help people like them all over the country." And then, looking directly at the members of Congress and pointing his finger right at them, with eyes that bored into the consciences of us all, he said, "Now I have that chance, and I mean to use it. And I hope you will use it with me." Then he talked about his hopes and dreams for the country. In my opinion, it was the finest speech of his presidency. His remarks were not the product of intellectual exercise or political calculation; they were a volcanic eruption from the innermost being of his soul, which erupted when the responsibility for leadership finally became his own.

On issues other than civil rights, Johnson had deep feelings about his objectives. His goals were always bold ones; he never thought in small terms or chose modest objectives.

Loyalty was another Johnson trait. He never cut up one colleague in the presence of another. He supported colleagues and joined with them whenever they were subjected to criticism. He insisted upon loyalty in return, however. Yet I found President Johnson to be considerate of his cabinet officers and protective of their positions. He didn't go behind their backs to their respective departments to give instructions to subordinates without their knowledge. He believed in the chain of command, delegated extensively, and operated through the cabinet officers themselves. He had some blue-chip cabinet officers, some very strong individuals, but he was never jealous of them and never tried to diminish their stature. He believed that a strong cabinet meant a stronger administration.

Not all his cabinet relationships were successful. Lyndon Johnson had a troubled relationship with Bobby Kennedy, from the earliest days of the Kennedy administration. I don't know all the elements in that relationship, but I assume that Bobby Kennedy had not wanted Johnson to become vice president. The traumatic experience of President Kennedy's assassination itself created a wound between Bobby Kennedy and Johnson that never healed.

I also had my share of "Bobby problems." They began during John Kennedy's administration but worsened after LBJ took over, through absolutely no fault of Lyndon Johnson. When John Kennedy was in the White House, he and I had a clear understanding about Bobby's dabblings in foreign policy matters. After Bobby had intruded into State Department dealings on several occasions, I finally expressed my concern to Kennedy, and the president responded, "Well, let Bobby have his say on these matters because he is very much interested in them. However, if he ever gets in your way, let me know and I'll take care of it."

It is difficult to speak frankly about a man who met the same tragic end as his brother, but my impression of Robert Kennedy was that he was not a true liberal. Basically he was conservative in his outlook, and I derive this primarily from his attitude on many personnel problems that arose in government. He was ruthless about people. I had the impression that Bobby Kennedy's liberalism did not fully emerge until he himself began to run for public office.

When Lyndon Johnson became president, our problems resurfaced, I am sure, because Bobby's presidential brother was not there to exercise a restraining hand.

Not all of my disagreements with Bobby were over foreign policy. Once Bobby invited me to join a fifty-mile cabinet hike along the Chesapeake and Ohio canal towpath. He registered disapproval when I declined.

"Bobby," I said, "when you were still wearing diapers, I was a captain of infantry. I have done all my hiking. In any event, if I had taken a company out for a fifty-mile hike without adequate preparation, I would have been court-martialed." His opinion of me didn't improve.

Bobby also believed that Lyndon Johnson had the wrong secretary of state. In 1968 LBJ called me into his office and told me, amid gales of laughter, that Bobby had told him that if LBJ took my resignation and appointed Bill Moyers secretary of state, then he—Bobby—would not run for the presidency. On Johnson's side, one source of tension was Johnson's belief that Bobby wanted to be president. Not only was that personally irritating, but Johnson didn't think that Bobby Kennedy was qualified for the job. On that point I agreed with Johnson. John Kennedy was an exceptional man, but the Kennedy brothers were not triplets. I felt that Bobby lacked the personal qualities, experience, maturity, depth of commitment, and ability to lead this country as president. Moreover, Johnson believed that Bobby Kennedy would reach out for his job, and sure enough, Kennedy ran against him in 1968.

Interestingly enough, Bobby Kennedy once volunteered to President Johnson to go to Saigon as our ambassador to South Vietnam. I vetoed that on the grounds that this country could not take another Kennedy tragedy, and Saigon duty was just too dangerous. Ironically, in terms of what later happened to Bobby, he might have been safer there than in the United States.

In personal terms, although I admired and respected both men greatly, I was closer to Lyndon Johnson than to John Kennedy; our official relationship was reinforced by personal friendship. We often reminisced about our southern upbringings and rural pasts, and occasionally we'd argue over which one of us was born in the smaller house. Our pasts were very similar, although there was a considerable difference between the hill country of West Texas and the red clay hills of North Georgia.

I saw President Johnson a great deal more than I saw President Kennedy. The growing fighting in Vietnam made that inevitable. He and I occupied the same foxhole together for so long, and when you are in a foxhole with somebody, you get to know him rather well. There were many sides to his personality, and I came to know most. Lyndon Johnson was a natural ham actor, and he loved to pull out his tall stories and put on a little act. His impersonations of Dean Acheson testifying before Congress were outrageously funny. He acted out the tall, patrician, immaculately dressed figure of Dean Acheson with his bristling mustache, entering a Senate committee room with his nose in the air and twitching as though he were smelling a skunk. Johnson's public sense of humor inclined more to slapstick and storytelling, but in private he was a very funny man.

Lyndon Johnson had a great lady at his side. Although Lady Bird stayed away from our policy discussions and meetings, I have no doubt that she was an important influence on her husband and a great source of strength. She was a hard worker, indefatigable, a good hostess to visiting VIPs, an agreeable and sympathetic guest when she and the president traveled abroad. The burdens that fall upon a First Lady are very heavy, and Lady Bird carried them to the queen's taste.

Although some would not agree, I found Lyndon Johnson to be a man of great personal kindness. He was always ready with words of encouragement and appreciation. Family problems, illness, or fatigue of his senior colleagues always found a sympathetic ear in Johnson. He was also a compulsive giver of gifts. I am a smoker who prefers to light cigarettes with book matches rather than a lighter, and every time LBJ saw me struggle with my matches, he gave me an LBJ-inscribed lighter. The next time he would forget that he had already given me one; I have a dozen LBJ lighters around my house.

Lyndon Johnson is remembered almost solely in terms of the Vietnam War and whether he did too much or too little in that tragic struggle. With the passage of time, Americans and surely historians will take a broader view and weigh such developments as the consular and civil air agreements with the Soviet Union, the Nonproliferation Treaty, the Outer Space Treaty, the East-West trade bill, the beginnings of the SALT talks, and many other initiatives aimed at building the peace. On the domestic side, his Great Society legislation permanently changed the American landscape. Despite the tragedy of the Vietnam War, he was a good president, and in many respects, a great president. It was his unfortunate fate to have been a wartime president.

I don't know anyone except for the men and women who were actually carrying the battle and their families who agonized more over Vietnam than Lyndon Johnson. We could never break him of the habit of getting up at five in the morning and going down to the White House situation room to check on the latest casualty figures from Vietnam, each one of which took a little piece out of him. To his credit, as painful as it was, he did not divorce himself from the tragic news and growing unpopularity of the Vietnam War. He used many sources and channels of information to keep in touch—political leaders, newspaper editorials, Congress, network news, opinion polls—and he telephoned many people personally to check on public attitudes. He stayed involved, and he realized after the Tet offensive that Americans at the grass roots were turning against the war.

There was so much that he wanted to do, and in so much of that Vietnam was in the way. It was a problem that he inherited, and he could not resolve it while he was president. But Lyndon Johnson was at heart a man of peace. In his last State of the Union message to Congress, his final sentence was "But I believe that at least it will be said that we tried." He tried indeed, with reckless disregard for his own life.

In the final chapter of *The Vantage Point,* reflecting upon his return to that ranch along the Pedernales River in West Texas that he loved so much, Johnson wrote, "I knew that I had given it everything that was in me." As time passes, I think the American people will increasingly acknowledge that the "everything" that was in Lyndon Johnson was a great deal indeed.

20

Arms Control Under Johnson

Lyndon Johnson believed in arms control, but he lacked Kennedy's effervescence and contagious enthusiasm for it and never took a strong personal interest in it. He supported the Arms Control and Disarmament Agency (ACDA) and allowed us to move ahead with arms control initiatives, but his heart and soul were first with his Great Society and after that with Vietnam. But by temperament, if Johnson saw a good deal could be made with the Soviets, he was ready to strike one.

After we concluded the August 1963 Limited Test Ban Treaty, arms control advocates in the Kennedy administration had invested so much effort on the test ban that we needed to recharge our batteries, to consider what came next. Consequently, a lull ensued in arms negotiations with the Soviets.

But the lull was short-lived. During the Johnson years arms control moved forward on a broad front. Controlling the spread of nuclear weapons was one of our highest priorities. Indeed, this need had been clear since the dawn of the nuclear age. In the months after Hiroshima, the United States believed that even one nuclear power was too many, and with the Baruch Plan we tried to remove nuclear energy from military competition. Tragically it was never adopted, and by the early 1960's five countries had joined the nuclear club. In the Kennedy administration we hoped that the limited test ban would discourage further proliferation, but we were only partially successful.

In the early 1960's the search for peaceful uses of the atom had intensified and nuclear power plants were operating and under construction in many countries. Because nuclear reactors produce plutonium that can be separated and diverted into weapons production, an international system of safeguards to discourage proliferation and regulate fissionable material became increasingly important.

In January 1964 Lyndon Johnson outlined a program to stop the nuclear arms race in a message to the Eighteen-Nation Disarmament Conference in Geneva. This message suggested that safeguards be created for international transfer of nuclear materials intended for peaceful purposes and that the nuclear-capable countries also submit their nuclear power plants to inspection.

Discussions on nonproliferation and other nuclear safeguards continued at the Eighteen-Nation Conference for the next year, but even though most countries supported it and UN nonproliferation resolutions passed resoundingly, no agreement was reached. Then, in August 1965, we tabled a draft nonproliferation treaty that prohibited transferring nuclear weapons to any country not having them, and we asked nonnuclear nations to allow the International Atomic Energy Agency (IAEA) to inspect their peaceful nuclear energy programs.

Despite widespread support, three years passed before a Nonproliferation Treaty became reality. One of the biggest stumbling blocks was the multilateral force then being discussed by the United States and NATO. The Soviet Union strongly objected to the MLF or any plan for sharing nuclear weapons with NATO countries, especially West Germany. The prospect of a West German finger on the nuclear trigger was a *casus belli* for the Soviets. Although we insisted that the United States would never relinquish final decision over the firing of such weapons—we weren't going to give that away to anybody—we eventually dropped the MLF entirely when NATO failed to get behind it and when alliance sharing seemed to threaten prospects for a Nonproliferation Treaty. This cleared the way with the Soviets.

Despite problems created by the MLF, both superpowers worked closely on the Nonproliferation Treaty. Both recognized that as more governments developed a nuclear capability, fissionable material and weapons might someday fall into irresponsible hands. The Cuban missile crisis sobered us all; we learned that nuclear weapons enslave as well as empower.

Both superpowers really got behind the Nonproliferation Treaty. Because we and the Soviets basically were on the same wavelength, I didn't get actively involved in the talks. ACDA head William Foster and others handled most of the negotiations for the American team.

But frankly I was less enthusiastic about the Nonproliferation Treaty than other arms control measures, not because it was a bad treaty but because I just didn't think it would be very meaningful. With mainland China developing a nuclear capability, I questioned whether countries in China's shadow, such as India and Japan, could pledge never to develop nuclear weapons and whether they should depend entirely upon the American nuclear umbrella. Some of my colleagues exaggerated my coolness toward the Nonproliferation Treaty because of my habit of boxing the compass on questions like these. Countries bordering Mao's China had a harder time saying, "We'll never go nuclear," and I wasn't convinced the United States should insist they do so.

Nevertheless, even with my doubts, I always supported the Nonproliferation Treaty, and I never changed my mind about the desirability of nonproliferation. But I doubted that nonproliferation could become truly global, and I doubted whether every country could or should sign the treaty.

There were other problems. Two nuclear powers, France and China, refused to have anything to do with nonproliferation. More ominously, the very countries we most wanted to ratify the treaty— South Africa, Israel, Brazil and Argentina, Pakistan and India, among others—didn't come aboard. What happened was entirely predictable. Regardless of membership, the Nonproliferation Treaty doesn't stop a country from developing the bomb. Nuclear weapons can be developed without nuclear tests, and in fact, no country has failed to explode a nuclear device in its first test.

At least fifteen to twenty countries have made or have the capacity to make nuclear weapons today. What holds them back is not the Nonproliferation Treaty but whether they will commit the money and resources to developing nuclear weapons and whether they want to complicate their foreign relations by going nuclear.

We were especially concerned about the Israelis. If they ever developed and deployed nuclear weapons, nuclear proliferation in the Middle East could not be far behind. Fearful of this, we repeatedly urged Israel not to be the first country to introduce nuclear weapons into the

Middle East. If they did, we told them they'd lose the United States and the protection of our nuclear umbrella. The last time I saw Israeli Foreign Minister Abba Eban, he gave me the usual assurance: "We'll not be the first." But as he was leaving my office, he turned and said, "But we won't be the second!" Israel has never openly tested or announced a nuclear capability, but I am quite certain it is at least eight and three-fourths months pregnant and could produce nuclear weapons on very short notice.

Negotiating the final treaty was quite a task. By its very nature—because it tries to eliminate the spread of nuclear weapons—the Nonproliferation Treaty discriminates against nonnuclear countries, and nonnuclear countries understandably sought a quid pro quo. We found one in the preamble to the draft treaty, which stated that nuclear powers should make a maximum effort to limit and reduce the number of nuclear weapons. Nonnuclear nations insisted that we take that clause out of the preamble and make it binding as an operational part of the treaty. Under that pressure, we and the Soviets moved that clause to Article Six of the treaty, agreeing to make a serious effort to limit and reduce our nuclear arsenals.

We also had quite a fight over Nonproliferation Treaty safeguards, inspection procedures to discourage the shipment of fissionable material and critical technology to other countries. When we made our first Nonproliferation Treaty proposal in August 1965, we didn't require safeguards for nonnuclear countries. They were later added, with my support. However, some of our allies, especially France, wanted loose controls. I think Charles de Gaulle was less concerned about the danger of proliferation than he was personally offended by the thought of participating in negotiations in which "second-class countries" were present. He also thought proliferation was inevitable and couldn't be stopped.

As the negotiations unfolded, ACDA head William Foster and Glenn Seaborg of the U.S. Atomic Energy Commission pushed hard for mandatory safeguards with enforcement provisions. I felt mandatory safeguards wouldn't fly. No international body has enforcement authority, and trying to put real teeth in the International Atomic Energy Agency wouldn't have worked. Pushing for tough safeguards would have scared off many countries that otherwise signed the treaty. As it was, nonnuclear countries already believed the treaty discriminated against them, so I argued that voluntary compliance was the only way to go.

I also felt the United States could not ask nonnuclear countries to accept what we were unwilling to accept, so I urged that we place our own peaceful nuclear facilities but not our weapons laboratories under IAEA safeguards. This idea caught on and became part of our draft treaty, and today all other nuclear powers accept IAEA scrutiny of at least some of their peaceful nuclear facilities.

The Nonproliferation Treaty was finally signed in July 1968, but the Soviet march into Czechoslovakia in August 1968 delayed Senate ratification until March 1969, three months into the Nixon administration. Had we tried to move faster and arm-twisted the nonnuclear countries, fewer would have ratified. In any case, more than 130 countries eventually ratified the treaty, most very quickly.

Unfortunately many prime targets of the Nonproliferation Treaty refused to climb aboard. The nonsignatories—Brazil, Argentina, Israel, Egypt, India, Pakistan, South Africa, and others—make an ominous list. In addition to the six acknowledged members of the nuclear club, fifteen or twenty others could become nuclear if they committed their resources, engineering, and talent to that effort. The treaty helped slow the pace of proliferation, but so did other factors. Nonnuclear countries have learned, along with the superpowers, that the possession of nuclear weapons puts chains around a country as well as bestows unimaginable power. A nuclear country knows two things: that it would receive intolerable destruction if it attacked another nuclear power and that it would wear the mark of Cain for generations to come if it ever attacked a nonnuclear country with nuclear weapons.

The Nonproliferation Treaty also led indirectly to other U.S.-Soviet negotiations. For example, it encouraged both superpowers to study carefully the possibilities of a nuclear strike or an accidental launch from another country. Our talks led to lengthy discussions, an agreement in 1971 to reduce the risks of accidental nuclear war, and eventually "crisis reduction centers" negotiated during the Reagan years. It is inconceivable to me that either government would allow someone like Muammar Qaddafi of Libya to cause the superpowers to fire their arsenals and destroy each other and virtually the entire human race. This just won't happen.

Another arms control treaty initiated during the Johnson years was the Outer Space Treaty, one of the smoothest arms negotiations ever conducted. The treaty was proposed by the United States and Soviet Union in June 1966 and signed in December, six months later. Eighty-one countries signed it within that first year. A delight to negotiate, it was one of my favorite arms control treaties.

To appreciate the treaty fully, it is necessary to recall how we have thought about space in different eras. Consider the sharp contrast between how we now think about outer space and how we thought about it in the 1950's, when the space age began. Shortly after I joined the Rockefeller Foundation in 1952, we asked four or five universities if the United States should examine the political and legal consequences of man's entry into space. Their reaction was one of colossal indifference. Indeed, my good friend Philip Jessup, then teaching at Columbia University and wise on other matters, told us "the future is not the business of the university," even though the laboratories of his own university were hurling us into the future at a breathtaking pace.

Then, in 1957, came Sputnik, and universities across the country scrambled for funding for space research, scientific and technical training, and thinking about the future. Sputnik was about the size of a basketball and issued only an occasional beep as it orbited the earth, but it threw consternation into American society. A few months after Sputnik we launched Explorer 1, the Soviets then orbited a man in space, and the question of how man should enter space—the same question we had raised so unsuccessfully in 1952—was given immediate attention by the United Nations. The General Assembly established the Committee on the Peaceful Uses of Outer Space and, in October 1963, adapted unanimously a far-reaching resolution about man's entry into space, specifically calling upon nations not to station weapons of mass destruction in orbit or on celestial bodies. That eventually became the Outer Space Treaty of 1967.

Consider what had occurred. Within ten years of Sputnik's launch the nations of the world had declared that outer space was to be a vast arena of scientific research and peaceful cooperation; that astronauts and cosmonauts were the "envoys of all mankind," entitled to assistance from anyone in a position to help, exploring space for the benefit of the entire human race; that nations venturing into space were required to report all findings bearing on the safety of astronauts; that the moon and other celestial bodies could be used only for peaceful purposes and couldn't be appropriated as national territory; and that weapons of mass destruction could not be orbited in space, nor could military bases be built in space.

The language of the treaty itself, with such phrases as "recognizing the common interest of all mankind in . . . the exploration of outer space for peaceful purposes," explains why we felt uplifted in spirit. This treaty applied the beginnings of international law and the principles of the United Nations Charter to man's activities in space. With its passage, the human race had faced the issue squarely and come up with reasonable, hopeful, intelligent, civilized approaches to the problems posed by man's entry into space.

The treaty permitted certain passive uses of outer space for military purposes, such as satellite photography, which I supported. Satellite reconnaissance helps both countries monitor arms agreements; indeed, the Soviet Union finally acknowledged in the SALT 1 Treaty that satellite photography was an appropriate means of national detection. Before SALT 1 the Kremlin held that satellite reconnaissance violated Soviet sovereignty.

One reason I supported the Outer Space Treaty was that space had always fascinated me, even as a child. My brother Roger started an astronomy class at Tech High School in Atlanta, and our Boy Scout troopmaster, an astronomy buff, would let us kids get under one end of his telescope and stare up at the stars. With me, outer space was somehow associated with the Bible, teachings such as "The heavens declare the glory of God; and the firmament showeth his handiwork." By looking at the stars, one is overwhelmed by the immensity and beauty of space. As secretary of state I enjoyed meeting our returning astronauts and the celebrations held in their honor; some of their pictures hang on my wall; they were genuine heroes to me along with millions of Americans. The idea of being shot into space in a capsule was most impressive. Helping negotiate a treaty to regulate man's entry into space capped a lifelong fascination with space.

There was also a pragmatic reason for the space treaty: Sometimes our scientists didn't know what would happen when we did something in space. Before the limited test ban, President Kennedy received a request from our military for permission to explode a nuclear weapon far out in space on the inner edge of the Van Allen belt. I asked if this would have any effect on the Van Allen belt, and Kennedy put the question to his scientific advisers. Their reply began, "The following is a negotiated scientific conclusion . . ."—a sure sign they didn't know. After that opening qualifier, they said, "There should be no effect," so the president authorized the shot.

Two days after the shot the same advisers told us, "Sorry, we were wrong—by a factor of two thousand!" The shot had indeed affected the Van Allen belt; it created another one!

And there were other examples. Once we exploded a device that scattered millions of little metallic needles in space to test communications. After a loud outcry we discontinued the program. In another project someone came up with the idea that we station giant reflectors in space, thereby eliminating night. Howls of protest buried that idea.

As a member of the National Aeronautics and Space Agency's (NASA's) Space Council I helped plan American ventures in space, further stoking my enthusiasm for an outer space treaty. I was especially interested in future projects for NASA after a successful landing on the moon. We anticipated cutbacks in NASA funding once that goal was achieved, and rather than disband NASA's extraordinary collection of managerial and scientific talent, I suggested that it take on such projects as searching for alternative energy sources or improving civil aviation. One project I helped veto was a manned flight to Mars. That two-year round trip would have cost an estimated two hundred billion dollars, and I felt that decision ought to be made by a future generation, not ours.

With the Outer Space Treaty we really thought we had achieved something of lasting importance. Outer space would be reserved for international cooperation. The last thing we wanted was the militarization of space. With that treaty we hoped that man would never put weapons into orbit. Outer space would be a place of peace, somewhat like Antarctica. I suggested that an Apollo crew carry a United Nations flag and plant it alongside the American flag on the moon, but that idea came a cropper in Congress.

In comparison with the Outer Space Treaty, the Seabed Arms Control Treaty was much harder to negotiate. Talks began in the spring of 1968, shortly after the UN General Assembly established an ad hoc committee to find ways to reserve the seabed for peaceful use. The idea was to prohibit weapons of mass destruction on the seabeds outside territorial waters. Because the oceans constitute over three-quarters of the earth's surface, I found a spatial limitation—like the Antarctic and outer space treaties—greatly appealing.

Not everyone agreed. When the administration began to discuss a seabed ban at a meeting of the Committee of Principals, the Joint Chiefs of Staff argued against it. Our conversation went something like this:

"Do you have any weapons on the deep seabed now?" I asked them.

"No."

"Are you doing any research and development about the possibility of having such weapons?"

"No."

"Do you have any plans for placing such weapons on the deep seabed in the future?"

"No."

"Well, then, what are your objections?" I asked.

"We might want to develop those weapons sometime in the future."

Insisting that the ocean floor might someday be a good place to deploy nuclear weapons, the Joint Chiefs argued that it wasn't in the national interest to narrow the range of possible deployment of those weapons. That was too remote and too theoretical for my tastes; ocean-based bombs would do nothing to increase our security. Both the United States and Soviet Union had the capability of destroying themselves many times over. Why move to higher levels of destructive capability by adding still another environment for nuclear weapons?

The experience—and others like it—made me more sympathetic by the late 1960's to President Eisenhower's warnings about "unwarranted influence . . . by the military-industrial complex." I had noticed how people in government are often hypnotized by the sight of a man in uniform. Unfortunately, back then, because of the Joint Chiefs' influence in Congress, if the chiefs opposed an arms control agreement that required a two-thirds Senate vote for ratification, that measure was in trouble.

Resistance by the Joint Chiefs on arms control could be broken through only by a president and by secretaries of state and defense determined to assert civilian sway over the military and push hard for arms control. That was one reason we kept in close touch with Senator Richard Russell, chairman of the Senate Armed Services Committee, and others in Congress. Even during the Truman years I witnessed unfortunate intrusions by the Joint Chiefs on policy making. For example, the chiefs persuaded their Senate allies to delay ratifying the Japanese Peace Treaty, against President Truman's wishes, until Truman concluded an administrative agreement about stationing U.S. forces in Japan.

During the seabed negotiations the Soviets pushed for complete demilitarization of the seabed, calling upon all states to use the ocean floor exclusively for peaceful purposes. We favored a more limited ban, prohibiting the placement of weapons on the seabed only. I supported the military in its preference for a limited treaty because by the late 1960's the United States had installed listening devices on the ocean floor that could pinpoint the location of Soviet submarines, a capability we didn't want to give up.

Both countries eventually adopted the American version, but time ran out on us again. The Seabed Treaty was finally approved in May 1972—another initiative incubated during the Johnson years that came to fruition under President Nixon.

Perhaps the most important arms control issue during the Johnson years concerned antiballistic missile (ABM) defense systems—missiles, targeting devices, guidance and tracking radar used to destroy incoming hostile strategic missiles or their warheads before they reach their targets. Long before President Johnson met with Soviet Premier Aleksei Kosygin in June 1967 at Glassboro, New Jersey, we had done our homework in Washington on ABM defense systems. Under the leadership of Robert McNamara, we began studying the feasibility and long-range implications of ABMs. We were skeptical that antiballistic missiles would work at all, and the more we looked, the more we realized that if we and the Soviets began building antiballistic missile systems, inevitably both sides would multiply their offensive weapons so they could saturate and penetrate ABM systems. McNamara and his whiz kids, with their charts and statistics, made a convincing case. Bob was a formidable proponent of arms control, unusually forceful for a secretary of defense. With his prodding during the sixties, the Joint Chiefs themselves began to appreciate the futility of a nuclear arms race and took a stronger interest in arms control, even though they often sought to delay or weaken arms agreements.

President Johnson wanted to meet with Kosygin, who was in the United States visiting the United Nations, to discuss arms control and other matters. However, Johnson didn't want to go to the UN and Kosygin was unwilling to meet in Washington. We suggested an Air Force base not far from the UN, but Kosygin turned that down. Johnson then called Richard Hughes, the governor of New Jersey, and asked him to pick a site between Washington and New York. Hughes suggested the president's house at Glassboro State College, and when we proposed that to Kosygin, he accepted.

The Secret Service then moved in and completely gutted the president's home and installed new furniture and air conditioning. It even emptied the freezer of vegetables and fruits that the president's wife had canned. And forgot them. The food thawed out and spoiled, breaking the poor lady's heart. She handled everything else but broke down and cried over that. As partial compensation, we left the air-conditioning units in the house after the summit. Moving an American president about the country or traveling abroad is an incredible operation, somewhat akin to docking a battleship without tugs, and Glassboro was no exception.

Before the Glassboro summit we briefed Johnson to the gills about ABMs. At the summit itself he really gave Kosygin the "LBJ treatment" about limiting ABMs. At one point he said, "I'll have Robert McNamara in Moscow next Wednesday morning at nine o'clock. Will you see him?" It was quickly evident that Kosygin hadn't been briefed on ABMs and lacked authority to discuss them. At one point he said, "How can anyone object to defensive weapons?," a remark I call the "naiveté of the first look."

The Russians went home, did their staff work, and eventually came to the same conclusion we did: ABMs would simply accelerate an arms race in offensive weapons. Finally the Soviets appeared interested in some type of treaty, but a year had already passed since Glassboro, and time was running out on the Johnson administration.

Consequently, I pushed hard for a treaty. I was convinced that the costs of deploying ABMs were ruinous, that bold steps were necessary to bring the arms race under control, and that we could not quibble over details as we had done so many times before.

We prepared during 1968 a proposal that banned the deployment of ABM systems beyond a token few, prohibited the construction of additional ICBM launchers, set a fixed number of launchers for inter- mediate- and medium-range missiles, and outlawed all mobile offensive missile systems. Additional missile-firing submarines and surface ships were also banned.

We decided not to seek a ban or set restrictions on multiple independ- ently targetable reentry (MIRV) vehicles because of verification prob- lem with MIRVs—to find out which missiles had MIRVs, you needed an inspector with a screwdriver to take the cover off each nose cone and count the warheads underneath—and because the Joint Chiefs opposed banning MIRVs, even though none was yet deployed. Throughout this effort I became increasingly impatient with the Joint Chiefs' cautious- ness and their instinctive resistance to arms control. By this time Bob McNamara had left the administration and I had to deal more directly and forcefully with the Defense Department. But it wasn't the Joint Chiefs that prevented us from going forward; it was the Soviets.

Throughout the sixties I generally opposed linking arms control measures to other problems because linking one problem with another and then another requires a comprehensive solution across the range of our total relationship. Arms negotiations are difficult enough without dragging every Soviet-American problem into the same basket. Arms talks are of transcendent importance and should stand alone.

Unfortunately sometimes linkage is inescapable. On Wednesday morning, August 21, 1968, we and the Soviets were all set to announce simultaneously in Washington and Moscow that President Johnson would go to Leningrad in early October to open strategic arms limita- tions talks. But on Tuesday night, just before the announcement, Soviet tanks rolled into Czechoslovakia. I was testifying before the platform committee of the Democratic party when an aide came down the aisle and handed me a note informing me of the invasion. One learns to view apprehensively notes hand-delivered in the midst of speeches and social engagements. Excusing myself, I returned to the State Department.

There I telephoned Ambassador Dobrynin to protest the invasion, telling him that the Soviet action was like throwing a dead fish in the president's face. I insisted that Dobrynin telephone Moscow immediately and tell the Soviets not to announce Johnson's upcoming trip the next morning because that would have been interpreted worldwide as the United States' condoning the Soviet march into Czechoslovakia. Only three weeks earlier Dobrynin had told me no invasion was planned; I assumed that the ambassador himself had not been kept informed by Moscow.

Interestingly, Anatoly Dobrynin told me months later that the arms control talks and the Czechoslovakian invasion were on separate tracks at the Kremlin and never considered together. I was skeptical about that since the Soviet Politboro undoubtedly makes decisions of such magnitude and the Politboro is pretty small.

I was deeply disappointed by the postponement of LBJ's trip to Leningrad. It put all arms control, including a MIRV agreement, on the back burner, a delay with tragic consequences. Had we concluded an arms agreement in 1968, MIRV technology might have been brought under control. Despite the delay posed by the Soviet move into Czechoslovakia, President Johnson tried to restart these talks in October and November. But the Soviets wanted to wait for the new administration. By the time the Nixon arms control team got its ducks in a row, it was November 1969, and not until then did strategic arms limitation talks (SALT 1) actually begin.

Richard Nixon and Leonid Brezhnev concluded the ABM Treaty in May 1972. Under the treaty, ABMs were limited to two sites in each country, later reduced to one site: theirs around Moscow and ours protecting a missile site in the Midwest. Ours is entirely in mothballs. Unfortunately MIRVs remained unrestricted, and they spiraled out of control; the horse had cleared the stable. Because counting warheads was virtually impossible, arms negotiations became far more complex; future agreements had to focus on delivery systems—missiles in silos, submarines, bombers—weapons that can be counted with accuracy. Nevertheless, the ABM Treaty was a vital step forward, and to have helped with its conceptual groundwork in 1967 and 1968 was most rewarding.

Not all arms control initiatives worked out. One idea that went nowhere was joint reductions in American and Soviet defense budgets. In theory, each side would voluntarily reduce its budget in parallel with the other, bypassing the need for a formal agreement. I wanted to create a committee of experts to recommend how to proceed with joint reductions. At one point the Soviet Union even proposed reductions of up to 20 percent of each country's defense budget. But two developments defeated it. First, we could never get the Russians to tell us what went into their budget. They were so tight-lipped about it that their own people were starved for information. Soviet diplomatic personnel occasionally asked members of the U.S. delegation for basic information about the Soviet military because their government refused to tell them. Without figures, we could never compare their budget with ours. And second, our talks with the Soviets occurred when an escalating Vietnam War called for increased rather than reduced defense expenditures on the American side. Vietnam occasionally hampered American arms control efforts, and this was a clear example.

We also had little success encouraging other countries to pursue arms control. Third World countries frequently charge the United States and Soviet Union with not living up to their disarmament pledges under the Nonproliferation Treaty, but there is another side to the story. In my opening speech at the Geneva Conference on Disarmament in March 1962 I called upon Third World countries to limit the arms race in their own regions and cut military expenditures and not just harangue the superpowers. My appeal fell on deaf ears. Third World nations in general exhibited colossal indifference and refused to do anything themselves about arms control.

Between sessions at Geneva the Nigerian foreign minister approached me in a corridor and in a rather chesty fashion said, "Well, Mr. Secretary, if we can get you and the Soviets to begin disarming, then my country can buy arms more cheaply!" For years we tried to get India and Pakistan to limit their arms buildup and made no headway there either.

There are special reasons for this indifference. At least fifty Third World countries are ruled by military dictatorships. And the military simply won't cut back on defense spending, much less participate in disarmament. At times, as disappointing as our own record may be, I've felt that the only two countries interested in limiting their own armaments were the United States and Soviet Union. At the United Nations all countries happily voted for disarmament resolutions, but only as these measures applied to the great powers. Few showed the same interest in curbing their own arms races with their neighbors or in settling the disputes that gave rise to them.

Fortunately there were exceptions. During the late sixties Mexican Foreign Minister Antonio Corillo Flores spearheaded an effort to declare Latin America a nuclear-free zone, culminating in the Treaty of Tlatelolco. Under the treaty each participating country renounced the right to acquire nuclear weapons and station them on its territory. The signatories further agreed to place their domestic nuclear facilities under the jurisdiction of the International Atomic Energy Agency and submit to enforcement provisions. We supported this treaty, thinking it might give our Latin American neighbors greater peace of mind, but the talks were complicated by their wanting to include U.S. territories in the Caribbean. We were willing to include the Panama Canal Zone in the treaty and to include Guantánamo Bay if Cuba joined the treaty; we didn't want to include Puerto Rico and the Virgin Islands. Jimmy Carter decided to include these territories as well, and Ronald Reagan agreed, ratifying that part of the treaty in 1981.

In a related development we tried again to establish direct commercial air service between the United States and the Soviet Union, a project begun during the Eisenhower years. Negotiations remained snarled during the Kennedy and Johnson administrations, but in 1968 we finally succeeded; both countries worked out the fine print on a civil aviation agreement that allowed Pan American and Aeroflot to make direct flights between Moscow and New York. Apparently traffic was so light that Pan American's new route was not profitable, but at least it was an opening—and another small improvement in Soviet-American relations.

On the whole, our record on arms control under Lyndon Johnson was respectable. While we didn't accomplish everything we set out to do, progress was made. In reviewing the accomplishments of the Kennedy-Johnson years, I claim only one for myself: that with the agreements negotiated and our constant talking with the Soviets, my colleagues and I helped add eight years to the time since a nuclear weapon has been fired in anger.

21

Building a Better East–West Relationship

Arms control is generally the centerpiece of the cooperative side of U.S.-Soviet relations, and rightfully so. For nearly a half century the two superpowers have had the capacity to obliterate each other and mankind in the process, so it is only proper that arms control capture the spotlight whenever significant steps forward can be achieved.

But the emphasis on arms control should not obscure the fact that even in the absence of arms negotiations, Washington and Moscow interact in a variety of ways. This was true in my day, even more so today.

For example, beginning in the fifties, the United States and Soviet Union had discussed the need for an agreement on consular rights and practices. Neither side, however, got serious about these talks until late 1963. Then, after seven months of sometimes intense negotiations, we and they finally signed a consular agreement on June 1, 1964. The agreement was rather straightforward, creating additional consulates in both countries, defining the rights of American and Soviet tourists, and offering fair treatment under American and Soviet law for any offense.

The Consular Convention, small though it was, ran into strong opposition in the United States. Some senators felt that no agreement was desirable with the Russians. FBI head J. Edgar Hoover claimed that building additional consulates in America would increase Soviet espionage capabilities. His strong opposition hurt our chances in the Senate. President Johnson could have directed Hoover to stand down, saying, "I expect all officials of this administration to support this treaty," but he didn't—testimony to Hoover's extraordinary and even dangerous independence as intelligence czar. Hoover later calmed down when we pointed out that his objections were tantamount to admitting that his FBI couldn't handle the security risks posed by additional consulates. In March 1967 the Senate finally gave its consent. Problems continued with Americans traveling in the Soviet Union, but the agreement was a big help.

Our experience with the consular convention—a relatively simple agreement that took years to conclude—and, in fact, all our negotiations underscored the difficulty of dealing with the Russians. Winston Churchill once called the Soviet Union "a riddle wrapped in a mystery inside an enigma." Many, including Churchill, have negotiated with the Soviets, but I don't know any who could truly be called expert at it, certainly not myself. The cemeteries of Washington are filled with the tombstones of so-called Kremlinologists who came to town beating their breasts, saying, "I know how to deal with the Russians. Just let me at them."

The Soviets are tough negotiators, extremely stubborn, persistent, and unyielding in their positions. We Americans are characteristically agreement-oriented and too quick to strike bargains. All this gives the Soviets a negotiating advantage.

Soviet positions can be utterly untenable, such as Khrushchev's outrageous ultimatum to Kennedy at Vienna and his attempt to install Soviet missiles in Cuba. And because of Soviet ideology, they see any nation that stands in the way of their "world revolution" as an aggressor. They say we were the aggressors in Korea, Berlin, and Southeast Asia despite the evidence; they claim that NATO is the aggressive power in Europe despite the fact that NATO is a wholly defensive alliance incapable of waging offensive war.

There is a certain rhythm to negotiating with the Soviets. Talks seem to follow three stages. In stage one, they start off tough and demanding, hard as nails, and harshly ideological. Americans, always impatient and in a hurry to conclude agreements, are tempted to pick up their briefcases and go home. In stage two, little hints or openings begin to appear, suggesting that progress might somehow be possible. With luck, we arrive at stage three, where the serious work of drafting an agreement begins. It takes patience, persistence, and a great deal of sensitivity to what you're hearing from Soviet negotiators to get anywhere with them. One has to study their inflections carefully and occasionally probe to see where they might lead. They are more reluctant than we to initiate proposals, preferring, like Charles de Gaulle, to avoid the role of "demander" or asker. They prefer that we make the proposals so they can whack away at them.

Moreover, in talking with the Soviets, one had the feeling there were uninvited ghosts at the table. In our bilateral talks they often seemed to be looking over their shoulders at China, a nation of a billion people, armed with nuclear weapons, with whom they share a long frontier. What might appear to Americans to be a reasonable balance between the United States and Soviet Union requires something extra because of China.

From the Soviet perspective there is also the problem of British and French nuclear forces, growing steadily in recent years. The Russians care little what nationality of missile might descend on them, again requiring something extra because of Britain and France. We resist, but the Soviet position is entirely rational.

Negotiating arms agreements with the Soviets is particularly difficult because both we and they come at arms control as at a bank balance; each side each wants an extra margin in its account. Because the nuclear forces of both countries are asymmetrical and difficult to compare, this leads to prolonged negotiations and jockeying for position.

The history of U.S.-Soviet arms negotiations is a long and lugubrious story. For years the Soviets proposed "general and complete disarmament," as though we could reach utopia in short order if everyone would just lay down his arms. Yet the Soviets often resisted the partial steps needed to take us there. In my day the Kremlin's far-ranging proposals for across-the-board reductions were not practical and could never be achieved. We knew the Soviets would never withdraw the Red Army from Eastern Europe without losing control of that area, and with China's masses on their eastern frontier they would never demobilize. To move ahead with arms control, we had to fit their broadside approach to the American preference for taking one step at a time.

Among the special problems of negotiating with the Soviets is that because American democracy gives off a multitude of signals, the Soviets strain to determine our official views. With so many conflicting voices, confusion is bred in Moscow and other foreign capitals. Americans also pressure their negotiators to conclude agreements, pressures spared Soviet negotiators because of their totalitarian system. In addition, arms control advocates in this country sometimes urge our government to disarm unilaterally, outside of agreements with the Soviet Union or anyone else. Twice in my lifetime I have seen the consequences of such unilateral disarmament: during the thirties and after V-J Day. Both were disastrous.

In addition, every four years we go through a national grand inquest in our search for a president. This is the most solemn political and constitutional duty we citizens perform, but it is also a quadrennial silly season, during which we say foolish things about each other, to the confusion of friends and adversaries abroad. Nikita Khrushchev once said to me, "It is very difficult to deal with the West because someone is always having one of those damned elections," and I fully sympathized with him. Surely, considering the totality of information flowing out of the American government and the media, there were times when the Soviets would question whether the words of the president and the secretary of state represented official policy.

The Soviet Union's closed society presented us with a different problem. During my many talks with Dobrynin and Gromyko they never once discussed personal relationships among members of the Politboro. We knew little about Soviet leaders themselves and how they reached decisions. Occasionally Dobrynin suggested we make certain concessions "to encourage those in Moscow who want better relations with the United States." We used a similar ploy: "Yes, we would agree to this, but we'd have a hard time getting Congress to accept it."

In my conversations with Soviet diplomats I often tried to clarify to them the workings of American democracy. Many of my talks with Gromyko and Dobrynin were what I called "pointless talks." We talked not to resolve a particular problem or reach a specific goal but to create a broader basis for understanding each other's societies. Yet negotiations between countries are always negotiations between people, albeit people with different backgrounds. Over the years I came to know my Soviet counterparts rather well.

Andrei Gromyko was a unique personality. I first met him in the 1940's, when he was Soviet ambassador to the United Nations and I headed our United Nations desk. I had many talks with him then and later, of course, as secretary of state. We met and discussed issues at many locations, at opening sessions of the UN General Assembly, Geneva conferences, the signing of the Limited Test Ban Treaty in

Moscow, the tenth anniversary of the Austrian State Treaty in Vienna, and at the Black Sea when I visited Khrushchev. We came to know each other on a first-name basis.

Despite superpower rivalry, we managed to develop a relationship based on mutual respect as professional diplomats. Occasionally, in representing the views of his government, when Soviet policy was deceptive in character, Gromyko would "lie" from our point of view, such as failing to confess to President Kennedy about Soviet offensive missiles in Cuba. In all other respects I regarded him as a true professional. After our talks, when we agreed on what we would say to the press, he always abided by those guidelines. Occasionally I told him things on a confidential basis. Gromyko always honored those confidences. Normally staff and note takers were present at our talks, but occasionally we retreated into a corner, just the two of us, to talk with real intimacy about policy. Had those exploratory talks been officially recorded, our conversations would have been considerably stifled.

Gromyko and I never shouted or traded insults. We always treated each other with impeccable courtesy. For example, if I wanted to send him a note about some unpleasant matter, I would begin: "The Secretary of State of the United States presents his compliments to the Foreign Minister of the Union of Soviet Socialist Republic and acknowledges receipt of his communication of such and such a date." Then, in measured and correct terms, whether the issue was Berlin or Laos or whatever, I might tell him to go to hell. I would end my note with the expression "Accept, Excellency, the assurances of my highest consideration." That formality has a purpose: to reduce the impact of personality upon relations between nations. There's wisdom in the cool conventions and tedium of diplomacy. To that same end President Johnson would not let us criticize any foreign leader by name, whether it was Khrushchev, Charles de Gaulle, or Mao Zedong, not wishing to inflame difficult relationships with personal invective. LBJ wasn't responding to my coaching; he probably learned that in the Senate.

Gromyko, tagged "Great Stone Face" by the media, didn't give away much with facial expression in our negotiations. He did have a sense of humor, although on the heavy side. At one bilateral luncheon at the United Nations I thought of serving him frog legs, one of my favorite dishes. My advisers warned me off, suggesting beef or a more conventional dish. During the meal I told Gromyko that I had wanted to serve frog legs but was warned not to by my advisers. "You have very wise advisers," he said in his thick Russian accent, without cracking a smile.

Over the years Gromyko taught me a lesson or two about the Soviet penchant for security. Once, while president of the Rockefeller Foundation during the fifties, I crossed the Atlantic on the British liner *Queen Elizabeth* when Gromyko was on board. The captain invited us both to his quarters for cocktails before dinner. When the captain's steward brought Gromyko's drink, a security man stepped forward to taste it, right at the captain's table. When word of this incident spread, the crew became so infuriated over this insult to their captain that they threatened to throw Gromyko over the side.

This Soviet caution was entirely routine. Throughout the postwar years any high Russian official offered a drink at a cocktail party or reception would hand it first to his security man. This happened even at parties the Soviets gave for each other! When Nikita Khrushchev traveled to the United States in 1959, his party went from Washington to New York on a special train. Once the train got rolling, the menfolk ordered drinks. All were sampled by Russian security men. Mrs. Gromyko had ordered a Coca-Cola, and when it arrived, no one stepped forward to sample it. She looked around the car at Khrushchev and the others and said, "You do not care if I die?"

Gromyko, briefed to the gills, always knew the Soviet position and was always tough. But when Moscow signaled that agreement was desired, he'd look hard for a road to agreement. He was basically a technician rather than a political leader, and he survived many years of political strife in the Soviet Union partly because he remained a foreign policy specialist.

Over the years Gromyko mellowed and matured, grew in sophistication, and came to understand the United States thoroughly. Further, he gradually accumulated influence of his own as a member of the Politburo, until he became all but irreplaceable. The Soviets keep their best people in the same jobs. Gromyko served alongside nine American presidents and fourteen secretaries of state.

Gromyko spoke excellent English; in our talks it failed him only once. After a United Nations meeting in New York, I had lunch with him, and over preluncheon cocktails we discussed the expressions in various languages for intimate conversations: "heart to heart," as we Americans say, "tête-à-tête" as the French say, "before four eyes," as Germans call it. Then somebody naughtily whispered the phrase "eyeball to eyeball," and there was some nervous laughter because the Cuban missile crisis was still fresh in our minds. We finished our drinks and began lunch. By custom, Russians begin with a toast. Gromyko rose, vodka glass in hand, and said, "We're very glad to have you with us, Mr. Secretary, and I am looking forward to talking with you balls to balls." We Americans managed to control ourselves, although Gromyko's interpreter nearly died.

Gromyko could take a gentle ribbing. On one occasion former General Omar Bradley, board chairman for the Bulova Company, gave me a new Accutron watch as a test model. It operated by a tuning fork vibrating in a magnetic field, a new concept of timekeeping developed in our space program. I liked it and gave one to Gromyko as a gift. While unwrapping the box, he asked, "Do you mind if I show this to our engineers?" I said, "I've already taken care of that." I had given him a watch with an open face, exposing all its gears and inner workings; his engineers wouldn't even have to pull off the cover. He looked at it and laughed.

I once told Gromyko something that in retrospect probably would have been better left unsaid: that from the Soviet point of view, Joseph Stalin made a great mistake at the end of World War II. If Stalin had invested ten years in genuine peaceful coexistence, he would have faced a disarmed and isolationist America. But instead, he embarked upon adventures which forced the United States to rearm and play a greater role in world affairs. Said Gromyko: "Very interesting."

Although I admired Gromyko's professionalism, we didn't become friends in any personal sense. Gromyko was not a man to engage in pleasantries. But at a party just before the Nixon inaugural, when Gromyko knew I was leaving office, he drew me aside, referred regretfully to my retirement, and spoke warmly about our long association. Although Gromyko and I had often sat in opposing foxholes and tossed grenades at each other, I respected him as a professional Bolshevik diplomat of considerable ability.

I spent a great deal of time with Ambassador Anatoly Dobrynin as well. An outgoing man by Soviet standards, sociable, civilized, and well read, like Gromyko, he developed a real understanding of the complexities of American democracy. When John Kennedy took office, the Soviets guessed that an ambassador with Dobrynin's temperament and personal style would be more effective than his predecessor, Mikhail "Smiling Mike" Menshikov, a cold warrior of the old school. Dobrynin was a great asset to the Soviets in his twenty-four years of service as ambassador.

Shortly after I became secretary of state, I asked Dobrynin to use the basement entrance of the State Department and come up to my office on my private elevator, so that we might meet more informally and so newsmen wouldn't swarm all over Washington, trying to find out what we were talking about. Dobrynin appreciated those intimate talks, as I learned in the years since. I was rather miffed when Secretary of State Alexander Haig revoked this arrangement during the Reagan presidency. Instead of telephoning Dobrynin in advance and asking him to come to the regular diplomatic entrance, State Department security blocked Dobrynin's car as it headed into the basement, had it back out, and drive around to the main entrance. Television cameras recorded the entire incident. That was highly embarrassing to Dobrynin, an affront that American diplomacy could do without.

As with Gromyko, Dobrynin and I kept our relationship on an official basis. But even so, it was evident that he understood the United States as few Russians did. Even with his understanding, however, I still do not know to what extent his superiors in Moscow listened to him when he sent back his reports.

U.S. and Soviet efforts to understand each other during the 1960s did not lead to harmony or the avoidance of crisis. When the Soviets invaded Czechoslovakia in August 1968, we responded as strongly as we could, taking into account the geopolitical and strategic reality of the situation. President Johnson, like President Eisenhower during the Hungarian Revolution of 1956, realized the United States could not assist any Warsaw Pact country with military forces without automatically engaging in general war with the Soviet Union. NATO is by design a defensive alliance, with no capability for launching offensive operations. Although we in the West are obviously sympathetic to the Hungarians, the Poles, and the Czechs, what happens in Eastern Europe has never been an issue of war and peace between us and the Soviet Union—however ignoble this sounds.

Yet the administration didn't ignore the Soviet invasion of Czechoslovakia. With tension mounting before the invasion, we strenuously protested Soviet efforts charging "Western imperialists" with stirring up unrest and trying to overthrow socialism in Czechoslovakia. I told Ambassador Dobrynin that this war of words looked like a pretext for moving Soviet forces into Czechoslovakia. He denied it. After the invasion I again strongly protested. And we, of course, refused to allow the strategic arms limitations talks to begin.

Shortly after the invasion itself Soviet Chairman Leonid Brezhnev claimed a Soviet right to intervene in any Communist country to insure that it remained Communist—the Breshnev Doctrine. This sounded like a pretext for Soviet moves against other Warsaw Pact countries such as Rumania and Yugoslavia, and we responded with quiet talks of our own. We even discussed with the Yugoslavs their weapons and ammunition needs if they were attacked and needed outside supply.

Two months after Brezhnev's pronouncement, in a speech before the United Nations General Assembly, I addressed some penetrating questions to Soviet Foreign Minister Andrei Gromyko, sitting before me in the audience, about this so-called doctrine. Brezhnev's claim that "the sovereignty of each socialist country cannot be opposed to the interests of world socialism" was a threatening and pernicious contribution to international law.

"Does this mean," I asked, "that the U.N. Charter . . . is powerless to shield smaller states within the Communist bloc from invasion and domination by the Soviet Union in the name of the 'class struggle'?"

I pressed Gromyko on what the doctrine meant with respect to the UN Charter, the national sovereignty of states, the concept of peaceful coexistence, and the independence of member nations of the United Nations. Gromyko sat quietly.

I thought mine was an important speech. The TV networks thought otherwise. At the beginning of my talk six youths in the public gallery stood up to protest the war in Vietnam. And this is what the networks ran. Other than a few inane sentences, they covered nothing important about my speech. Anonymous news managers back in studios had chosen the dramatic rather than the important. We ran into this problem all the time.

However, at a UN reception after my speech, several delegations from the Eastern European countries found a way to thank me for "making our speech."

The Czechoslovakian invasion marred five years of improving relations between the superpowers as well as arms control. It reminded us all of the tension in U.S.-Soviet relations, the crises of the postwar years, and the fact that American efforts to improve relations can go only so far.

To understand American policy in the sixties, to understand it today, we must remember these past forty years. How tragic that American and Soviet wartime collaboration in defeating Adolf Hitler had dissolved so rapidly! Almost before the ink was dry on the surrender documents of the worst war in history, the world was once again divided into two armed camps.

The Soviet Union suffered horribly in World War II. Twenty million of its citizens died. The whole world recognized the magnitude of such sacrifice. And the Soviets honored the enormous Allied effort required to defeat Germany. But even during the war there were strains. In Russian eyes, the Allies were slow to open a second front in the West, and they were not fully appreciative that we were sending massive supplies to Russia through submarine-infested waters. We had our own grievances; for example, the Soviets would not allow our planes to land at their airstrips during deep-penetration raids into Germany or allow General James Doolittle's B-25s to land on Soviet fields after his famous raid on Tokyo in 1942. The Russians were late entering the war against Japan, yet insisted on full consideration of their claims for a zone of occupation on the Japanese island of Hokkaido. Serious differences also emerged over how to handle a defeated Germany.

I was insulated from problems with the Soviets while serving in the China-Burma-India theater, but my transfer to the War Department General Staff in June 1945 put me in the thick of it. And I regret to say that we Americans may have played a major role in the beginning of the Cold War, but not the one revisionist historians allege. If, in fact, the United States bears coresponsibility for the Cold War, I find our responsibility in self-imposed weakness rather than in belligerency.

Most Americans remember from history or direct experience the sad story of the 1930's, when my generation, because of unilateral disarmament and unwillingness to take a stand against Hitler, was led down the path into the catastrophe of World War II, a war which could have been prevented. But most have forgotten what happened after V-J Day. The United States and its Western allies demobilized totally, almost overnight. By the summer of 1946, scarcely a year after war's end, we did not have a single Army division or Air Force group rated ready for combat. The ships of our Navy were being put into mothballs as fast as we could find berths for them. Those that remained afloat were manned by skeleton crews. We left vast stocks of war matériels overseas, not even bothering to ship them home. For fiscal years 1947, 1948, and 1949, our defense budget came down to a little over eleven billion dollars a year, groping for a target of ten billion.

This was dangerous business, and we definitely paid a price. With our precipitous, unilateral disarmament, we in the West tempted Joseph Stalin to intolerable temptations through our own weakness. We forgot Stalin's famous reply to Churchill's remark about the views of the pope on a certain question. Said Stalin: "The Pope? How many divisions does he have?"

So after the war, when Stalin looked out across the West and saw the Allied armies melting away, what did he do? He tried to keep Azerbaijan, the northwest province of Iran, which became the first case before the United Nations Security Council. He demanded two eastern provinces of Turkey, Kars and Ardahan. He supported Communist guerrillas going after Greece, operating out of sanctuaries in Albania,

Yugoslavia, and Bulgaria, thinly disguised as "civil war." He contemptuously brushed aside his wartime commitment to give the peoples of Eastern Europe some say in their political future. He had a hand in the Communist coup d'état in Czechoslovakia, under the shadow of the Red Army. Counting on economic chaos as his ally, he tried to extend Soviet dominion into Western Europe. In 1948 he blockaded Berlin, denounced the quadripartite control machinery for the occupation of Germany, and incorporated East Germany within the Soviet bloc. He instructed his delegation at the United Nations to exercise the veto repeatedly. He precipitated a serious crisis by blockading access to Western occupation zones in Berlin. In June 1950 he gave the green light to the North Koreans to go after South Korea. In 1956 came the ruthless suppression of Hungary.

In the 1940's Stalin took no serious interest in the Baruch Plan, calling for the international control of fissionable materials and outlawing nuclear weapons for any country, including the United States. He broke off talks for a billion-dollar loan from the United States. He turned down Secretary of State George Marshall's invitation to participate in the Marshall Plan and in walking out of those talks, dragged a very reluctant Poland and Czechoslovakia with him.

Against this background, the meaning of the Cold War becomes clearer. We did not declare it; we alone cannot end it. The Cold War results from the Soviet bloc's announced determination to extend its "historically inevitable" world revolution by every available means. The Soviets disguise their intentions and actions as "scientific principles." They speak of the irresistible spread of ideas. But they fail to show a single instance where people have voluntarily embraced communism through free elections.

Some may look upon me as a dinosaur of the Cold War, but these are the facts. Revisionist historians can write until their pens run dry of ink, but these—the adventures of Joseph Stalin—were the events that started the Cold War. These confrontations came about through Soviet initiatives. We were disarmed. The Americans had gone home. Not until 1950 did we begin to build up our armed forces. The implications of the past for American policy are clear. The simple fact is that the Cold War will end when those who declared it decide to abandon it.

Our experiences with the Soviets during the Kennedy and Johnson years—dangerous crisis over Berlin and Cuba, then five years of relative calm, marred by Czechoslovakia in 1968—drove home another point. Even when the two superpowers are "eyeball to eyeball" and locked in crisis, there are frequently solid contacts at lower levels. And the opposite is true: When our relationship is good, in some areas tension remains. Public opinion about U.S.-Soviet relations tends to swing back and forth like a pendulum between something called "détente" and the "Cold War." Such sloganeering misses the point. Both elements have been involved in our relations since World War II. Despite many crises, numerous agreements have been reached. Our relations have never been as good as "détente" or as bad as the "Cold War."

Underpinning our relationship is a simple fact: The United States and the Soviet Union share a massive common interest in the prevention of all-out nuclear war. No one in his right mind either in Washington or Moscow would deny that. Similarly, the word "détente" means nothing more than the persistent, continuing search for possible points of agreement on matters large or small, which can broaden the base of our common interests and reduce the range of issues on which violence might occur. Détente does not mean that fundamental differences between us and the Soviets have disappeared. Unfortunately, talk of détente during periods of calm tends to create a false sense of euphoria among the American people.

Despite the ups and downs of our relationship, whatever we think of the Russians, whatever they think of us, despite the litany of Soviet misdeeds during this postwar period, despite anger and suspicion on both sides, we must realize that anger standing alone has no future and that at the end of the day we and they must sit down at the negotiating table and find some way to live together on this planet. That's the bottom line. We have to set aside our frustrations and continue to try.

On the whole, I am optimistic regarding U.S.-Soviet relations and greater cooperation between the superpowers. Not for half a century has a nuclear weapon been fired in anger, despite many serious and even dangerous crises since 1945. We have learned during these forty-five years that the fingers on the nuclear trigger are not itchy, waiting for a pretext on which to fire these dreadful weapons. The United States has taken nearly five hundred thousand in dead and wounded since the end of World War II in support of collective security, without firing a nuclear weapon. This is no guarantee for the future, but it is a good platform upon which to build and an antidote to the Doomsday talk with which our young people are being battered.

We have also learned that Soviet leaders have no more interest in destroying Mother Russia than we have in destroying America. Both we and the Soviets share a massive common interest in the prevention of nuclear war. We also share a primordial obligation to the entire human race because we are the only two nations that if locked in mortal conflict could raise a serious question about whether this planet could any longer sustain the human race. It follows that Washington and Moscow bear a special responsibility for world peace and the survival of mankind. That is the bottom line, the place where we begin and end with Soviet-American relations.

In times of crisis with the Soviets, we must take care not to play games of "chicken" with each other, to see how far one side can go in a particular adventure without crossing that lethal threshold. Down that path lie miscalculation and misjudgment, even catastrophe. We should also watch the level of rhetoric between Moscow and Washington. If words become too vitriolic for a sustained period of time, there's always the chance that one side or the other could begin to believe its own rhetoric.

Those of us who served with Chinese forces in Burma during World War II were both frustrated and amused by the Chinese refusal to surround a Japanese force. They cited an ancient Chinese military doctrine, first set forth by Sun-tzu several hundred years before the birth of Christ: "Never completely surround an enemy, or he will fight too hard. One must always leave him a route of escape."

Sun-tzu's doctrine takes on special meaning in a nuclear world. I do not believe we shall ever have nuclear war through a rational and deliberate decision by any government to launch one. Nor do I believe that a full nuclear exchange will start by accident or because of the fabled "psychotic pilot." Existing safeguards are extremely thorough, and I am confident they will hold. But nuclear war is just possible if a leader and his advisers find themselves driven into a corner from which they see no escape, where they lose all stake in the future and elect to play the role of Samson and pull the temple down around themselves and everyone else at the same time. For that reason President Kennedy went to great pains during the Cuban missile crisis to try not to drive Mr. Khrushchev into that kind of corner, to allow him the chance to withdraw Soviet missiles peacefully. We must never give our adversaries a reason to play Samson.

Past arms agreements with the Soviets remind me of a dam that stretches halfway across a river. Unless we can finish the job, the same volume of water will flow, in different channels. With the arms race already reaching the edges of insanity, if we already have more than the planet can tolerate, any fourth-grade schoolchild can ask, "Why build more?" The only rational purpose of nuclear weapons is to ensure that no one else will use them against us. That purpose could be achieved with 10 percent of present stockpiles.

Although we and the Soviets must find ways to limit this insane arms race, we can do so only by agreements binding upon both sides. I remain opposed to unilateral disarmament. It is true that the extent of nuclear "overkill" today is so vast that minor differences in numbers of weapons have little meaning in military terms. Henry Kissinger once asked, "What in heaven's name is nuclear superiority?" Winston Churchill once said of the concept of overkill, "What's the point in making the rubble bounce?" A small fraction of the weapons in existence can produce unbearable results for any country.

But what concerned me as secretary of state was the perceptions in other leaders' minds about what these numbers mean. If the numbers become out of balance, if one side believes it has nuclear superiority, it might take certain risks without fear of opposition. To avoid this, the numbers must be kept in some kind of balance. Unfortunately the arms race itself contributes to instability and perceptions of fear and suspicion.

So what do we do with the Soviets, and how do we ease superpower tensions and curb the arms race? Raymond Fosdick, a former president of the Rockefeller Foundation, used to speak of the "infinity of threads that bind peace together," such threads as cultural and scientific exchanges, tourism and travel, trade, joint space missions. Big things like world peace are made up of a lot of little things, and if the little things are put right, then big things have a chance. We and the Soviets must cast threads across the chasm that divides us. Little by little, stitch by stitch, we and the Soviet Union can weave a structure of peace.

In thinking about our troubled relationship, looking back over my eighty years, I am confronted by a great mystery and cannot begin to suggest an answer. I am convinced that the peoples of the Soviet Union, and, indeed, people everywhere—Europe, China, Africa, the United States—prefer peace to war. How is it that this universal yearning for peace at the grass roots is not translated into better relations among governments? During the Truman years, with a bitter debate in progress in the United Nations Security Council, Soviet Ambassador Andrei Gromyko and our own ambassador, Warren Austin, were going at each other hammer and tongs over the Berlin blockade. A friend of mine was sitting next to Mrs. Gromyko in the audience. At one point my friend asked, "What do you think of these proceedings?" She said, "These men are playing such childish and dangerous games."

22

Crisis in the
Dominican Republic

The April 1965 crisis in the Dominican Republic that led to U.S. intervention had its roots in the collapse of the Trujillo regime four years earlier. For more than thirty years Leonidas Trujillo had run a brutal dictatorship, much like Batista's regime in Cuba. Trujillo's rule was especially obnoxious. Its human rights record was deplorable. The Trujillo family operated the Dominican economy like its own private cow, milking off vital resources to Swiss bank accounts and safe havens abroad. Decades of Trujillo rule had left the economy impoverished.

Trujillo was a rogue in foreign affairs as well. During the fifties the Organization of American States imposed sanctions against the Dominican chief for trying to assassinate the president of Venezuela. Trujillo had blackmailed visiting American politicians by planting cameras and recording devices in their hotel rooms and catching them in compromising situations. On one occasion we sent the CIA into the Dominican Republic to try to recover the pictures and recordings from Trujillo's files. Trujillo was a thoroughly nasty fellow, and we in Washington shed no tears over his demise in May 1961.

The State Department learned of Trujillo's assassination before it was announced in Santo Domingo, the Dominican capital. President Kennedy was in Paris, so I called Pierre Salinger, Kennedy's press secretary, and told him that we had received word that Trujillo had been killed. I asked Salinger to tell the president, but I cautioned him to keep it confidential, especially since Trujillo's son Ramfis was also in Paris. I feared that if the younger Trujillo heard the news from Salinger, he might think the United States had had something to do with killing his father. However, in a press conference before the news became public, through some slip of the tongue Salinger mentioned Trujillo's assassination. I gave Pierre Salinger hell over that.

In the ensuing weeks I urged that we take active steps aimed at preventing the Trujillo family from regaining power and continuing dictatorial rule. I hoped that this long-suffering country could somehow have elections and come up with leaders who would respect the wishes of the Dominican people. Elections to find a successor to Trujillo were finally held eighteen months later, on December 19, 1962, and Juan Bosch emerged the winner. We brought Bosch to Washington, wined and dined him, assured him of our support, and tried to help him get off to a good start. Bosch talked about political reforms and constitutional government and was obviously more socially concerned than Trujillo. But unfortunately he had zero governmental and administrative experience, and he surrounded himself with people who knew even less about running a government than he did. A former writer, Bosch neither sought advice nor welcomed it when it was offered. Three of Bosch's closest friends in the hemisphere, Luis Muñoz Marín of Puerto Rico, Rómulo Betancourt of Venezuela, and José Figueres Ferrer of Costa Rica, assured us of Bosch's good intentions but at the same time cautioned us, "Juan Bosch is a poet and a dreamer . . . he isn't capable of organizing a government and running a country . . . he won't last a year." We tried to persuade Bosch to turn to his three friends for help, but he wouldn't do it.

On September 25, 1963, the Bosch government was overthrown in a coup d'état and eventually replaced by a three-man civilian junta, headed by former Foreign Minister Donald Reid Cabral. Bosch went into exile in Puerto Rico. We recalled our ambassador. President Kennedy cut off economic aid, refused to appoint a new ambassador, and withheld diplomatic recognition, actions that I approved. Despite our disappointment with Juan Bosch, we were unhappy that a military junta had overthrown a man elected by popular vote. I thought we should suspend American aid, to be sure it wasn't gobbled up and sent off to Swiss banks by these generals.

But life—and government—have to go on. By late fall 1963 President Kennedy was considering getting back actively into the Dominican scene, with a view to influencing developments there. It fell to President Johnson, three weeks after Kennedy's assassination, to reverse course, to extend recognition, and resume economic aid, and he named W. Tapley Bennett as ambassador.

Had Kennedy lived, I believe he, too, would have recognized the Wessin government. In their general approach to Latin America and the Dominican situation in particular, I didn't see dramatic differences between Kennedy and Johnson.

The Dominican situation, and many others involving political turmoil, put the United States in a delicate spot—namely, should we recognize a dictatorship or a government that comes to power via a coup d'état? Many people confuse diplomatic recognition with support, but that is not what diplomatic recognition means; it simply means that the United States recognizes a government. In fact, if the United States subscribed to President Woodrow Wilson's somewhat holier-than-thou doctrine that dictatorships or any governments coming to power through unconstitutional or illegal means shouldn't be recognized by the United States because they don't represent the expressed wishes of their own people, the United States in my day would have found itself without relations with most Latin American countries. We normally recognized a new government when it was clearly in control, after we had waited to see how neighboring states felt about it.

Throughout the next year the situation in Santo Domingo deteriorated. The junta pledged to hold elections in fall 1965, but a worsening economy—the price of sugar fell below three cents a pound—political infighting, and the regime's own lack of popularity led to general disorder by spring of 1965. Army officers, some loyal to Juan Bosch and some with their own ambitions, attempted a coup d'état on April 24, 1965, and fought to gain government control. At first, government forces headed by General Elias Wessin y Wessin were expected to put down the rebellion, but in the crunch Wessin seemed to lose his nerve. At a crucial moment on April 28, his troops failed to press the attack. Anarchy descended on Santo Domingo, roving gangs fought in the streets for control, and more than two thousand Dominicans, mostly civilians, were killed. These gangs included *tigres*—young men armed with machetes and weapons taken from government arsenals, which had been broken into. Guns were passed out indiscriminately, even to eight- and ten-year-olds.

In that turmoil the heads of the armed forces and the police both told us they couldn't accept responsibility for the safety of American and foreign nationals. Our embassy reported that public order in Santo Domingo had completely broken down.

Facing this rapidly deteriorating situation, Lyndon Johnson dusted off a contingency evacuation plan prepared earlier under the instruction of President Kennedy and moved ships from the Atlantic fleet into Dominican waters. On April 27 a discouraged group of rebel leaders, led by rebel Provisional President José Rafael Molina Urena, came to the American Embassy in Santo Domingo. Under pressure from government forces and assuming the battle was lost, they asked Ambassador Bennett to negotiate a settlement—in essence to rescue them from the consequences of their own actions in starting the fight. Bennett refused their request for mediation, not wanting to involve the U.S. government directly in the dispute. I think Bennett did the right thing; with so much chaos, it would have been premature for us to assume responsibility for any negotiation.

The following day Bennett cabled from Santo Domingo with a disturbing message: Approximately one thousand Americans had gathered at the Embajador Hotel to prepare for evacuation and, while there, had been harassed by armed thugs, who lined them up against the walls and sprayed tommy-gun fire over their heads and all over the hotel. Fortunately no lives were lost, and Bennett didn't recommend American intervention at that time. Late that same day, after the Agency for International Development office had been ransacked and sniper fire directed against the embassy, Bennett cabled that American lives were again endangered and urged that we land the Marines.

Bob McNamara, McGeorge Bundy, President Johnson, and I were at the White House when Bennett's cable arrived. With the total collapse of Dominican civil authority, and with neither the armed forces nor the police taking responsibility for the safety of our citizens, we decided to send help. On that same day, April 28, President Johnson ordered the landing of five hundred U.S. Marines and the next day ordered sixteen hundred more ashore from our naval task force. I strongly agreed; the evacuation of foreign nationals from the small port at Haina, west of the city, had begun, and five hundred Marines were too few to take on the jobs that needed doing.

In rapid succession President Johnson met with congressional leaders to discuss the operation. We also called an urgent meeting of the Organization of American States. OAS ambassadors were scattered all over Washington, at dinner, out of town, at concerts, and so on, and we couldn't schedule a meeting until nine o'clock the next morning. The meeting was somewhat heated. We anticipated instinctive opposition to any form of American intervention in Latin America, especially a landing of Marines, and we got it. Ellsworth Bunker explained our case and our reasons for moving quickly, but to a skeptical audience. Some delegates sharply criticized us.

In retrospect, I think we erred in not insisting upon meeting that same evening, even if we had to meet at midnight, because we were later severely criticized for not taking this issue to the OAS as quickly as possible. But early reactions were largely instinctive; as the crisis developed and more information became available, many OAS representatives and their governments back home came to support our intervention, although usually quietly, rarely publicly.

On April 29 President Johnson ordered the Eighty-second Airborne from Fort Bragg, North Carolina—eventually some twenty-two thousand men—to reinforce our Marine contingent and help with the evacuation. We landed the Eighty-second for several reasons. First, we didn't know whether the fighting and chaos would spread to other parts of the country and whether the Marines would have to form rescue teams and go after pockets of Americans isolated in the countryside. Fortunately that wasn't necessary, as the political turmoil was confined largely to Santo Domingo. Second, we established a security zone about sixteen miles long around the Dominican capital to try to contain the fighting and prevent arms from being sent to other areas of high tension. Having to patrol that long corridor and provide security for the airfield and evacuation centers required a large force. Without reinforcements, the smaller Marine contingent could have been challenged not only by armed bands inside Santo Domingo but by elements of the Dominican armed forces outside the city. We also thought that effecting a cease-fire might require placing American troops directly between the two contending groups. Third, we couldn't have our men on duty twenty-four hours a day; we needed shifts.

And finally, we also sought to prevent a dictatorship of either the left-wing or right-wing variety. This last point requires clarification. After the Marines landed, critics of our action charged that we landed American forces to prevent Juan Bosch from returning to power. This is simply untrue. Our Marines went ashore to protect American and foreign nationals, and the Eighty-second didn't go in until we heard talk in Santo Domingo about prospects for a bloodbath and another dictatorship. Only then did we try to work a broader solution. Had rebel forces been only from Juan Bosch's own party, whatever our doubts about Bosch's administrative abilities, we were prepared to accept his return to the presidency. But various groups of armed ruffians roaming the streets of Santo Domingo, who were directly involved with extremist groups, including the Communists, were a different matter. With a complete breakdown of public order and with extremists of all persuasions on the prowl, we felt we had to act. But we emphatically did not act to prevent Juan Bosch from returning to power.

In any event, United States forces and the inter-American peace force that later landed in Santo Domingo evacuated some five thousand people and distributed emergency food and medical supplies throughout the Dominican Republic. I don't think the Johnson administration overreacted. The presence of a large force discouraged challenges to the Marines and the Eighty-second Airborne, smothered the disorders and kept them from spreading, and helped restore public order.

The evacuation of foreign nationals went smoothly. Emanuele Clarizo, the papal nuncio and dean of the foreign diplomatic corps in Santo Domingo, strongly supported our action and thanked President Johnson effusively for helping with the evacuation. The French gave us hell throughout this Dominican action but privately were glad to see us there. Charles de Gaulle, through his ambassador in Santo Domingo quietly asked us to extend our troops four blocks to pick up the protection of the French Embassy. We also evacuated French citizens along with other foreign nationals since the French ship dispatched to rescue them unaccountably never found the port of Haina. After we did, we received not a word of thanks from de Gaulle nor any slackening of criticism from Paris.

If there was a mistake in the crisis, it was the way in which we presented our actions to the American people and the world. Before the president's April 28 speech justifying the landing of the Marines, I urged that we broaden our approach beyond saving American lives and stress the importance of preserving free institutions. But the president disagreed, partially because that approach involved the Organization of American States and we hadn't yet taken the Dominican situation to the OAS or had time to coordinate a common policy. Both the CIA and the American Embassy reported a growing Communist strength in the rebellion, and Ambassador Bennett estimated four thousand in three separate factions. But some of us felt the president should wait until the dust cleared and we knew more accurately the extent of Communist participation. I doubted, for example, that Communists had taken over the rebellion or that a small number of Communists would play a decisive role. The president, however, decided to stress the Communist threat. We knew that a small but highly disciplined group could seize power in the midst of confusion and have a political influence far beyond their numbers. This had happened before in Cuba in 1959, in Petrograd in 1917, and in Germany in the 1930's.

In his speech the president gave in to some hyperbole, as was the Johnson manner, for example, when he spoke of "headless bodies lying in the streets of Santo Domingo." We had heard reports of such, but this statement was challenged by our critics. Johnson called Ambassador Bennett personally, said that he didn't like having his credibility questioned, and told Bennett, "For God's sake, see if you can find some headless bodies." It may sound grotesque, but Bennett came up with some grisly photographs which proved the point. LBJ was never a man to understate his case.

I was equally concerned, perhaps more than the president, about a Trujillo-style dictatorship taking power. Had General Wessin and his military leaders regained their nerve and moved effectively to quash the rebellion, the Dominicans could easily have wound up with another right-wing dictatorship.

From where I sat, the Dominican crisis involved two distinct phases. In phase one President Johnson landed Marines for the limited purpose of protecting and evacuating American and foreign nationals. Then, after the Marines got ashore, phase two: Various Dominicans from many political factions, including the secretary-general of Bosch's own party, came forward and told us there was pure chaos inside the capital, with a half dozen armed bands fighting each other for power. Nobody was in control. Even leftist groups disagreed on whether to unite under Juan Bosch's banner and try to return him to power. Colonel Francisco Caamano Deno, Bosch's main representative in Santo Domingo, refused to go into certain parts of the downtown area because of the danger. According to some reports, Communist elements were heavily involved, some reportedly armed. Bands of men under nominal control of the so-called rebel colonels had broken into police stations and armories, armed themselves, and begun fighting each other over control of the city.

In the days preceding our intervention, the Dominicans we talked with agreed that unless a cease-fire were put into effect and order restored, widespread civil fighting and perhaps even civil war would ensue, followed by a possible dictatorship of the left—a Castro type—or the right—a Trujillo type. Neither appealed to us because, among other things, both had been rejected by the hemisphere. The Organization of American States had imposed sanctions upon Trujillo for tinkering in the internal affairs of Venezuela and upon Castro for numerous activities in Latin America, including landing men and arms on the coast of Venezuela in 1964. Indeed, at Punta del Este in January 1962 and again in 1964 the OAS declared by more than a two-thirds vote that Marxism-Leninism was not an acceptable political system in the Western Hemisphere. Thus, the nature of the regime inside the Dominican Republic was not just a Dominican affair; it involved principles upon which the OAS was founded; it had international ramifications.

On May 15 McGeorge Bundy, Cyrus Vance, and Assistant Secretary of State for Latin American Affairs Thomas Mann went to Santo Domingo to try to negotiate a broadly based interim government, more or less politically neutral, that would preside over national elections and let the Dominican people choose their new leadership. One key concern was finding someone who could form a government acceptable to the military that would also allow free elections. It was difficult to find people willing to stick their necks out and run for office because their safety was threatened by armed bands prowling the streets of Santo Domingo.

Unfortunately our mission itself became divided, with Bundy and Vance wanting a strong role for Juan Bosch in the interim government, and Mann vigorously opposing Bosch. Mann wanted categorical assurances that there'd be no Communist participation in the new government, but neither Bundy nor Vance demanded categorical assurances. I supported Mann's position. As for Bosch himself, I hoped his views would be represented in an interim government, but I didn't favor Bosch's playing a leading role. He had already proven himself unable to run the country. If the Dominican people really wanted Bosch, they could return him to power in general elections.

LBJ sided with Mann in this dispute. I was skeptical about McGeorge Bundy's selection to this team, as I would have been about any member of the White House, because his presence involved the White House directly in the outcome. But in any event, the Bundy mission was rapidly superseded by the OAS commission. Ellsworth Bunker was the American representative on this commission.

That commission helped organize an OAS peace force with troops from six Latin American countries—Brazil, Costa Rica, El Salvador, Honduras, Nicaragua, and Paraguay—joining U.S. forces on the island. The commission went on to negotiate an interim government to hold elections. Ellsworth Bunker did a beautiful job.

Despite some friction over our landing of the Marines, most OAS countries supported the creation of an inter-American peace force and an OAS commission to negotiate a new interim government that would hold elections. A two-thirds vote was required, and there was no undue pressure on our part to get those votes. Speaking for at least one of the holdouts, the Mexican ambassador told me privately that the United States had taken a necessary action. "But don't ask Mexico for formal approval or public endorsement. Just go ahead and do what has to be done."

For the upcoming elections, Juan Bosch was on the ballot, but he didn't return to the Dominican Republic to campaign until the final weeks. He spent his time in Puerto Rico instead. Concerned about his safety, perhaps with reason, Bosch wanted security forces to escort him during his campaign and asked the U.S. government to provide them. We refused. Bosch had sharply criticized American actions, but privately he seemed to want our stamp of approval for his candidacy. Had Bosch exercised more courage, returned to his country, actively campaigned, and taken his chances, he might well have been reelected.

After considerable agony, elections were finally held; on June 1, 1966, more than 1.3 million Dominicans, in a record turnout, went to the polls and this time elected Joaquín Balaguer as president, giving him 57 percent of the vote. A former president of the Dominican Republic under Trujillo, although never associated personally with the corruption and brutality of the Trujillo regime, Balaguer was highly respected by the Dominican people as a moderately conservative politician and an experienced administrator. He also had personal courage—enough to campaign in that election. We welcomed his selection. Those elections were closely watched by many people including the American and foreign press, members of Congress, and OAS representatives from eighteen countries; the elections won widespread praise for their fairness.

In retrospect, on the basis of the information available to us in spring of 1965, I would support landing the Marines once again. We did the right thing when we evacuated American and foreign nationals, helped prevent a bloodbath in Santo Domingo, helped foreclose a left-wing or right-wing dictatorship, and arranged for free elections. Admittedly, the Dominican crisis was confusing; the personalities themselves were unknown to me—I had met Juan Bosch only once—so it was hard for me to assess the situation personally. Of necessity I relied heavily on Ambassador Bennett and later Tom Mann to sort this out. Tap Bennett drew much criticism for his role, but I found his handling of the situation first-class, considering the circumstances in which he was operating and the information that he had. The Dominican crisis moved fast, and Bennett had to rely on his instincts at times, but he did a great job.

The Dominican crisis of 1965 was a confusing situation, complicated by a complete breakdown of public order and threats to the safety of hundreds of American citizens. Decisions had to be made, and made quickly. But events turned out well.

I have no regrets about the United States' role in the Dominican crisis. The outcome reflects what we were working for. The Dominican people emerged with an elected president, a constitutional democracy, and a stable government that reflected many of Juan Bosch's attitudes. Unfortunately the United States paid a price; Twenty-six Marines and Eighty-second Airborne troops were killed, as were several thousand Dominicans in the civil fighting around Santo Domingo. Also, we spent lots of money keeping the country afloat during the unrest. But we operated with general hemispheric support, brought the Marines home ahead of schedule, and helped the Dominicans avoid the tyranny of a Trujillo or a Castro and continue on a constitutional path. Their country has had stable—and constitutional—government for over two decades.

23

The Six-Day War

During the Kennedy years and up until 1967 the Middle East presented few major problems for me as secretary of state. Relations between Israel and its Arab neighbors were relatively quiet, still coasting along on the modus vivendi reached after the Suez crisis of 1956, and none of the several Arab versus Arab disputes except for the Yemen civil war escalated into open warfare.

Early in the Kennedy administration the president and I decided we would not go into the region with some sort of American "peace plan" and try to sell it to both sides. This decision was the result of both the relative quiet in Arab-Israeli relations and my own experiences during the Truman years, when during negotiations I got kicked in the shanks by both the Arabs and the Jews. Anyone who works for peace in the Middle East inevitably gets clobbered by both sides. During the Kennedy and Johnson years the United States maintained strong support of Israel, but this was part of a broader regional policy: that the United States supports the political independence and territorial integrity of all Middle Eastern states.

That in fact had been U.S. policy throughout the post-World War

II era. But it is often overlooked that we have tried to pursue relations in the region as evenhandedly as possible, despite our close friendship with Israel. That friendship admittedly created difficulties for the United States in the Arab world, but during my tenure as secretary, and before and after as well, we have tried to work with all Arab states. We succeeded with some and failed with others. For example, our good friend Saudi Arabia opposes the existence of Israel, but both we and the Saudis are able to say, "We know that we disagree over Israel. Let's admit that difference, put this problem into a corner, and try to work instead on the rest of our relationship."

Our efforts to be evenhanded yet provide for Israeli security didn't always work, and sometimes we were sharply criticized, especially by the Arabs. For example, because Arab nations had built up their armaments throughout the fifties and we wanted Israel to be strong enough to fend off possible attack, in 1962 we sold Hawk air defense missiles to Israel, our first major sale of sophisticated weaponry to the Israelis. We at State were concerned about Arab reaction to the sale, but since Hawks were basically defensive weapons, we did not strongly oppose the sale. We simply pointed out that there would be sharp reaction from the Arab world, and indeed, there was. During the Kennedy years we also supplied arms to Jordan and Saudi Arabia, so this helped the Arabs take the Hawk missile sale in stride. Under Kennedy we did not get into such sensitive and provocative matters as selling Phantom jets to Israel, as we later did under Johnson; that stimulated a far sharper Arab reaction.

We tried hard to improve our relations with Nasser and Egypt, but to no avail. Nasser was unpredictable and exceptionally difficult to work with. Whenever our ambassador or a private emissary, such as Eugene Black or John J. McCloy, met with Nasser, he found himself talking with a reasonable man. Yet whenever Nasser got in front of his own people, he lost his head, started screaming, and said the most outrageous things, swept by the emotions of the crowd and the peculiar fanaticism of the Middle East.

Nasser wanted to unite the entire Arab world under his leadership. I never favored Nasser's kind of Arab unity, partially because he tried to base his program on hostility to Israel, but primarily because his Arab neighbors wouldn't buy it. Regimes such as Jordan, Saudi Arabia, Libya, Tunisia, and Morocco didn't want Nasser's leadership over a unified Arab world.

On one occasion, in June 1962, President Kennedy approved a three-year Food for Peace program for Egypt that was worth several hundred million dollars and fed at its height up to 40 percent of Egypt's people. We didn't expect Nasser to bow, scrape, lick our boots, and say, "Thank you, Uncle Sam," but we did expect him at least to moderate his virulent criticism of the United States. Instead, he got up before those big crowds in Cairo and shouted such things as "Throw your aid into the Red Sea!" Nasser's fiery speeches persuaded Congress to move to do exactly that, and Congress called me on the carpet about our Egyptian food program.

I testified against cutting off food aid to Egypt, thinking that most Egyptians would see through Nasser's crazy rhetoric and have a more favorable attitude toward the United States than would otherwise be the case. One Arab foreign minister told me, "We have strong, almost violent views about Israel, as far as our government is concerned. But if you want to know what ordinary people in the Arab world think of America, they remember the hospitals, the schools, such institutions as the American University in Beirut. Relations between American and Arab peoples are still good. Don't assume that every Arab hates the United States." But I could not persuade Congress, which slowed our food aid to Egypt to a trickle.

We Americans must never underestimate the deep sense of injury and bitterness which Arab peoples feel about the very creation of the state of Israel. One Arab leader told me, "The West has made the Arabs pay for the crimes of Adolf Hitler." The territory now called Israel has been overrun historically by many people—the Assyrians, Babylonians, Greeks, Romans, Ottoman Turks, Egyptians, and the British. The idea of going back two thousand years to find legal title for Israel was just too much for the Arab world to swallow. Arabs have lived on that ground for centuries. Only in the last ten to fifteen years have some Arabs finally accepted Israel's right to exist.

Most Arabs do not understand the United States' relationship with Israel. Israel is not an American satellite, and it has shown this time and time again. For example, in 1962 Israel launched a raid against Syria in retaliation for a Syrian-supported terrorist action against Israel. We were not consulted about the Israeli raid. We felt that the Israeli response was totally disproportionate to the original act of terrorism and that it could potentially lead to general war. Adlai Stevenson, McGeorge Bundy, and I persuaded John Kennedy that the United States should vote for the Security Council resolution condemning Israel for this action. The beginning of the 1967 war also illustrated Israel's independence.

That Israel is not an American satellite is a point many Arabs unfortunately miss. But the opposite is true as well: The United States is not an Israeli satellite, a point that Americans sometimes miss. The United States shares important interests with Israel, but Israeli and American interests are not identical.

Every president beginning with Harry Truman has affirmed American support for the independence and territorial integrity of Israel, and clearly those affirmations have had the full support of Congress. But we and the Israeli's have never signed a treaty of alliance. It is my impression that Israel was never interested in such a treaty because that would imply an obligation upon Israel to try to coordinate its policy with us. The Israelis prefer to gamble on doing things their own way, in the expectation that we will follow along.

Unfortunately some people in the American Jewish community and other U.S. supporters of Israel share this attitude; they look upon anything less than an all-out pro-Israeli stance by the State Department and the U.S. government as betrayal. This began during the Truman years. Every U.S. president and secretary of state since then have dreaded a great debate on precisely this issue, the degree to which the United States should align itself with or oppose Israeli policies. A debate over this issue would be vicious and ugly; all sorts of latent anti-Semitism—always present on the American scene—would creep out from under the rocks. For that reason, Washington has often shown great patience with Israel publicly, while behind the scenes our objections and differences are sharply expressed. We always feared that official differences stated publicly could lead to eye-gouging debate.

Fortunately the Middle East was generally quiet up until 1967; the most severe tension during the Kennedy years was not between Israel and the Arabs but between Arabs themselves, for example, Egypt's threatened attack on Saudi Arabia and the very difficult problem of the Yemen.

Of all the world's problems, the Arab-Israeli conflict has been the most stubborn, intractable, and unyielding. Its root causes go back centuries, and the emotions that it generates are awesome. It often even prevents Arabs and Jews from recognizing where their interests coincide. For example, when I was president of the Rockefeller Foundation, we talked with Arab and Jewish scholars about establishing a joint institute of Semitic studies, on the theory that both peoples are Semites and interested in Semitic studies. We thought about locating this institute on Mount Scopus, an area that both sides claim. The foundation would have funded it, and I felt the Israeli government would have backed it. But the Arabs just turned us down flat. We couldn't even muster enough harmony to build a cooperative educational institute in the Middle East.

In reviewing American policy toward Israel and its Arab neighbors, we must remember that the United States itself never had a "plan" for the Middle East. When the British put the issue of Palestine before the United Nations in 1946, they said that they would accept any solution that was agreeable to both Jews and Arabs. In a sense, that became the American position. We didn't have a formula that we were trying to sell to both sides. We were ready to accept any solution that Israel and its Arab neighbors could agree upon. We were just trying to prevent war in the Middle East and promote peace in the area.

All the same, we knew that the Arab-Israeli conflict would continue to fester unless the Palestinian refugee and territories problems could be somehow resolved. These problems worsened following the 1967 war, but they were bad enough before that conflagration.

As secretary I made several attempts to work through both problems, but without success. In 1961 Joseph Johnson, the president of the Carnegie Endowment for International Peace, began negotiating with Israel and its Arab neighbors on the refugee issue. I was fully involved with this initiative, which sought to close the refugee camps and resettle the Palestinian refugees.

After discussing the Palestine refugee impasse with several Arab foreign ministers, I had the impression that if an international authority interviewed the refugees in these various camps confidentially, perhaps in some sort of "confessional booth," and asked them the question, Where would you like to be living ten years from now?, many would choose not to be in Israel. If a list of possible areas for resettlement included Israel, Jordan, Lebanon, Syria, Egypt, Brazil, the United States, Australia, countries far removed from Palestine, I believed that many would choose to leave. Palestine would not be on that list because there was no Palestine. This plan allowed refugees to live wherever they chose. A refugee who wanted to go back to his home in territory that had become Israel had the choice of going back to Israel, not returning to Palestine. My hunch was that refugees choosing to live in Israel would be so few in number—we guessed no more than 10 percent—that Israel could readily accept them. I knew that Israel would accept a certain number, at least two to three hundred thousand, although we never finalized a figure. Obviously Israel would never agree to accept the entire two million refugees because that would change the very character of Israel and create major security problems for them.

This solution required two things: money and international cooperation. I am confident that we could have mobilized enormous sums of money to assist in resettlement, but international cooperation was more difficult to arrange. Indeed, the initiative failed because Arab leaders themselves did not want Palestinians to have this choice. Arab states refused to agree to any resettlement figure that was reasonable; instead, they wanted Israel to keep almost all the Palestinians. Some of my Arab friends later told me that Arab extremists threatened to tell the camp refugees that if they elected anything other than to stay where they were, they risked having their throats cut.

This "Joseph Johnson-Rusk plan" failed primarily because the Arabs were unwilling to agree to any figure for the return of Palestinian refugees that was within Israel's capacity to accept. They wanted Israel to take all who wanted to go back, without regard to number; Israel was unwilling to make any open-ended commitments as to numbers. But I still think this approach—allowing each refugee a private and secret choice as to where he wants to live—has promise for an eventual settlement of the Palestine issue.

During a United Nations meeting before the June 1967 war, I tried my hand at peacemaking when I proposed an eight-point program to the Egyptian foreign minister. I merely hoped to find some basis—any basis—for further negotiations. I don't remember any specifics; my "plan" is buried somewhere in the archives of lost hopes for the Middle East. The Egyptians turned it down flat. Had I presented it after the Six-Day War, they might have looked upon it more favorably.

What I do remember of my abortive proposal concerns Jerusalem. Muslims, Jews, and Christians look upon Jerusalem as a city essential to their religions and traditions; the city of David, Christ, and Muhammad, the center of three great religions. They all claim to worship the same God. Yet whenever they sit down to talk about Jerusalem, they ball up their fists and get ready to kill each other. I thought that one way to get around these hatreds might be to create a system of governance and administration for Jerusalem so complicated that no one could understand it, much less fight over it. I suggested splitting the city among the three religions, with religious authorities in charge of some shrines and hotel facilities, perhaps Israel in charge of the police, Jordan running the utilities, and Egypt controlling public services. Because feelings were so intense, we wouldn't even address the issue of sovereignty, just leave it floating in air to be resolved in the future. However, this approach never had a chance.

Considering the tensions and hostilities inherent to Arab-Israeli relations, eleven years of relative peace between 1956 and 1967 were welcome indeed. But it was a situation too good to last. In the spring of 1967 several Arab states took some actions that increased the military threat to Israel. Their leadership organized a joint command among the Arab armies. They also stepped up their holy war propaganda against Israel, eliciting a strong response from Tel Aviv. The Soviets, maneuvering to improve their own position in the Arab world, stirred the pot of crisis when they stimulated anti-Israeli attitudes among Arabs, increased their weapons sales to Arab countries, applauded the creation of a united Arab command, and spurred Jordan and Syria into signing defense agreements with Egypt.

Moscow also circulated a false report that Israel had mobilized its forces along the Syrian border. Israel offered to bring the Soviet ambassador to the border to verify that no mobilization had taken place, but he refused to go. Syria appealed to its Arab brothers for help, and on May 14 Nasser mobilized Egypt's armed forces and moved them into the Sinai. Two days later he asked UN Secretary-General U Thant to withdraw UN peacekeeping forces along part of the common border between the Sinai and Israel.

Without even consulting the Security Council or the General Assembly, U Thant made two decisions, and they were both disastrous. First, he decided that the United Nations could not keep forces in any country that did not want them. And second, he decided that if part of these forces were to be withdrawn, all would have to leave. Had U Thant at least taken Nasser's demand to the Security Council, we'd have had several weeks to try to stabilize the situation and work something out. As a matter of international law, it is perhaps true that United Nations forces cannot stay where the host government does not wish them to stay. But on the other hand, those forces were stationed there by UN action. We felt that U Thant ought to have at least referred this matter to the UN, and we were both upset and alarmed when on May 18 he withdrew the entire UN contingent from the Sinai.

This put Nasser in a difficult position, or so he claimed. Nasser later told us that with the complete withdrawal of UN forces as opposed to the partial withdrawal he had requested, he found his forces at the Sharm el Sheikh, at the tail of the Gulf of Aqaba, unopposed by a UN buffer force, with Israeli ships passing through the Strait of Tiran. "What could I do?" he later told us. "These were Israeli ships. I couldn't let them pass. I had to close the Strait of Tiran." In my mind this was a feeble excuse, but he nevertheless closed the strait, a reckless provocation. This *casus belli* for Israel also challenged President Eisenhower's commitment, made at the time of the 1956 Suez crisis, pledging

American support to keep the strait open if Israel withdrew from the Sinai. Nasser's closure of the strait played a major role in provoking the June 1967 war.

We tried to defuse the crisis by asking about fifteen maritime powers that used those waters if they would sign a joint declaration that the Strait of Tiran was an international waterway through which shipping must move. Most said that they would, although some were surprisingly lukewarm about it. We realized that a declaration would mean very little to Nasser, so we examined forcing the Strait of Tiran with a naval task force. We asked those same countries if they would join up, but volunteers were few. Great Britain and the Netherlands indicated they might, and Australia later signed on.

Forcing the strait would have required a major military operation since the Sixth Fleet in the Mediterranean was on the wrong side of Suez. We would have had to send the fleet around the Cape of Good Hope and through the Indian Ocean. And conducting a naval operation in those narrow waters might have meant bombing Arab airfields to assure the safety of our fleet.

In the midst of these discussions, Bob McNamara and I met with eighty or ninety senators and representatives. Somewhat to our surprise, they unanimously opposed our unilaterally reopening the Strait of Tiran by force. They said this should be left to the United Nations. However, the UN didn't have a naval task force. Bobby Kennedy, then a senator from New York, told McNamara and me, "I don't know what you fellows in Washington think about the attitude of my Jewish friends in New York, but they don't want any part of this."

The Israelis were aware of this congressional opposition and the lack of response from the maritime nations. One thing the Israelis have is good intelligence. If any other country ever penetrated the American government the way they did, we would probably break relations with them. I suspect this domestic and international opposition to forcing the strait helped convince the Israelis that they were on their own.

Since the Soviets had been egging on the Arabs, we were somewhat surprised when in late May the Soviets became greatly concerned that war might break out. Possibly their own military intelligence had given them the same prognosis that our Joint Chiefs had giving us: If a war started, Israel would win quickly and the Arabs would suffer a stinging defeat. So we and the Soviets began to discuss how we might help cool off the tension. The Soviets thought they had a commitment from their Arab friends not to make the first move, and after our May 26 meeting with Israeli Foreign Minister Abba Eban and Premier Levi Eshkol's

May 30 assurances, we thought we had a similar commitment from Israel. At least we and the Soviets exchanged these assurances with each other.

Meanwhile, in the Middle East events continued to unfold. On May 26 Abba Eban came to Washington, where President Johnson and I urged restraint upon him in the strongest terms. LBJ also told him that Israel would not be alone unless it acted alone. Four days later, on May 30, Premier Eshkol assured Johnson that Israel would wait for as much as two weeks for international action to open the Gulf of Aqaba. Jordan's King Hussein flew to Cairo on May 30, signed a joint defense agreement with Egypt, and allowed an Egyptian to take command of Arab forces in Jordan. Egyptian and Iraqi troops moved to Jordan the same day. On May 31 Nasser announced that his vice-president, Zakarya Mohieddin, would visit Washington on June 7. We in Washington thought that with the Egyptian vice-president's June 7 trip and Levi Eshkol's May 30 assurances that Israel would not move for two weeks, we had a good chance to de-escalate the crisis.

It was not to be. On June 5 Israel struck. The Soviets were outraged by the Israeli attack and immediately lit up the hot line, the first time it ever was used. It took some hard persuading to convince them that we were as surprised by the Israeli attack as they were. Fortunately they believed us and didn't hold us responsible for the outbreak of the Six-Day War.

At one point during our exchange the Soviets hinted that if the Israelis attacked Syria, they would intervene with their own forces. We sent a message back that this would be a very bad idea. President Johnson immediately ordered the Sixth Fleet to the eastern Mediterranean to discourage Soviet military intervention. Fortunately the Israelis stopped at the Golan Heights.

In six days Israeli forces, well trained, well equipped, well led, and extremely motivated, won a stunning victory. Even our own Joint Chiefs were surprised; before the war started, they estimated it would take Israel ten days to win. They missed by four days. The problems for us were rendered easier with an Israeli victory than an Arab victory. At least we were spared the spectacle of the Israelis being driven onto the beaches, the nightmare which we and the West all fear. American intervention in that case would almost certainly become necessary.

But we were shocked as well, and angry as hell, when the Israelis launched their surprise offensive. They attacked on a Monday, knowing that on Wednesday the Egyptian vice-president would arrive in Washington to talk about reopening the Strait of Tiran. We might not have succeeded in getting Egypt to reopen the strait, but it was a real possibility. Ironically, later that summer Nasser told one American he had no problem with reopening the strait. Had he told us that on June 1, there probably would have been no Six-Day War.

We desperately wanted Egypt to reopen the strait, thinking this alone would greatly ease tension. During any Middle East crisis the Arabs' "holy war" attitude is matched by the Israeli's fears of apocalypse, but from our side, all we sought was an open waterway and peace. Lyndon Johnson emphatically urged the Israelis to stay their hand. We all felt that way; to my knowledge, Israel had no undercover encouragement from the United States to start the war.

But in all fairness to Israel, considering the major Arab mobilization, the movement of sizable Egyptian forces into the Sinai, the formation of an Arab high command, the Jordanian-Egyptian Treaty, the movement of Iraqi and Egyptian units into Jordan, and the stepping up of the Arabs' holy war propaganda, if the Israelis had waited for the Arabs to strike first, their situation could have been very grim. I don't think highly of the doctrine of preventive self-defense, because it is too easily abused. But if there ever was a justification for preventive action, the Six-Day War might have been the case for it.

We tried hard to persuade King Hussein of Jordan not to become embroiled in the fighting, but he said, "I am an Arab and I have to take part." As an Arab he felt honor-bound to assist Egypt, especially since Israel had struck first. I think we could have gotten the Israelis to stay their hand, but Hussein insisted on getting into it. It was one of the sadder moments of this crisis because it certainly was not in Jordan's interests to attack Israel, then lose the West Bank and the old city of Jerusalem.

When the fighting started, we tried to get an immediate cease-fire. The Israelis seemed willing even on that first day. But for some strange reason, the Arabs and Soviets attached lots of conditions to a cease-fire; they wanted to link it with a withdrawal of forces and in effect settle the entire problem of the Middle East. That was wholly unacceptable to Israel, and a cease-fire was stalled for six days. Had we gotten a cease-fire on that first day, the Egyptian Air Force would have been destroyed and Israeli columns might have moved thirty or forty miles into the Sinai, but there would have been no fighting with Jordan and no Israeli occupation of the West Bank, the Golan Heights, the entire Sinai peninsula, and the old city of Jerusalem. Arab leaders and their Soviet friends badly served the Arab cause by complicating and thereby delaying an immediate cease-fire.

American relations with the Arab world fared badly during and after the war. President Nasser accused the United States of participating in the air raids that knocked out the Egyptian Air Force in the first twenty-four hours of the war, a false accusation, but he broke diplomatic relations with us nevertheless. Many other Arab states followed suit. Israeli planes were flying four and five sorties daily, and I think Nasser was overwhelmed; he had never seen so many planes. Soviet intelligence ships were operating alongside American ships in the Mediterranean, and surely the Soviets told the Egyptians that American carriers were not launching planes during this period.

We also lost ten American lives when, on June 8, the fourth day of the war, the U.S. communications ship *Liberty* came under air and naval attack. We were meeting with President Johnson in the White House situation room, considering the implications had the Soviets or Egyptians attacked the ship, when we received word from Tel Aviv that Israeli forces were responsible. That didn't please us, although an Israeli attack on *Liberty* was far easier to deal with. But I was never satisfied with the Israeli explanation. Their sustained attack to disable and sink *Liberty* precluded an assault by accident or by some trigger-happy local commander. Through diplomatic channels we refused to accept their explanations. I didn't believe them then, and I don't believe them to this day. The attack was outrageous.

What followed was just as bad. For twenty years, since the creation of Israel, the United States had tried to persuade the Arabs that they needn't fear Israeli territorial expansion. Throughout the sixties the Arabs talked continuously about their fear of Israeli expansion. With the full knowledge of successive governments in Israel, we did our utmost to persuade the Arabs that their anxieties were illusory.

And then following the Six-Day War, Israel decided to keep the Golan Heights, the West Bank, the Gaza Strip, and the Sinai, despite the fact that Israeli Prime Minister Levi Eshkol on the first day of the war went on Israeli radio and said that Israel had no territorial ambitions. Later in the summer I reminded Abba Eban of this, and he simply shrugged his shoulders and said, "We've changed our minds." With that remark, a contentious and even bitter point with the Americans, he turned the United States into a twenty-year liar.

After the cease-fire finally went into effect, the conflict moved to the United Nations. Our UN ambassador, Arthur Goldberg, handled those negotiations with great skill. They eventually culminated in Resolution 242. When Goldberg was appointed, his critics charged that his being a Jew would prevent him from establishing working relations with Arab countries. But his sense of fair play was tested thoroughly during these talks. Arthur Goldberg was a superb negotiator.

Resolution 242, passed by the Security Council in November 1967, called for an end to hostilities and said that every nation, including Israel, had a right to live in peace. It also called for freedom of navigation through all waterways, a just solution for the Palestine refugee problem, and Israeli withdrawal from most territories occupied in the June fighting. Resolution 242 did not settle all issues, but it provided an agenda for peace in the Middle East. It seemed a good balance at the time, and both Arabs and Israelis reluctantly accepted it.

Unfortunately both sides have departed from 242 in important ways. There was much bickering over whether that resolution should say from "the" territories or from "all" territories. In the French version, which is equally authentic, it says *withdrawal de territory,* with *de* meaning "the." We wanted that to be left a little vague and subject to future negotiation because we thought the Israeli border along the West Bank could be "rationalized"; certain anomalies could easily be straightened out with some exchanges of territory, making a more sensible border for all parties. We also wanted to leave open demilitarization measures in the Sinai and the Golan Heights and take a fresh look at the old city of Jerusalem. But we never contemplated any significant grant of territory to Israel as a result of the June 1967 war. On that point we and the Israelis to this day remain sharply divided.

This situation could lead to real trouble in the future. Although every president since Harry Truman has committed the United States to the security and independence of Israel, I'm not aware of any commitment the United States has made to assist Israel in retaining territories seized in the Six-Day War. If another war breaks out over the territories, Washington will face a hard decision.

But the Arabs have not been blameless with respect to Resolution 242 when they insist upon an Arab state of Palestine in the West Bank. Resolution 242 did not imply this. It anticipated that the West Bank would be returned to Jordan. Ironically, a separate Palestine could have been created in 1948 had the Arabs accepted the partition plan. Instead, they went to war to prevent it.

Because of the refugee and territory problems, I am quite pessimistic about the prospects for peace in the Middle East. I hope events will prove me wrong, but the intractable nature of the divisions between Jews and Arabs and even between moderate and extremist Arabs almost defy solution. They involve deeply human passions, the holy war psychology of the Arabs and the sense of apocalypse of the Jews. These issues do not lend themselves to solution by compromise and negotia-tion. Public emotions run so high that governments in the area are almost helpless; even dictatorial Arab regimes as well as Israel's demo-cratic government are influenced by these deeply held passions.

Neither side is ready to make the concessions necessary for genuine peace. I don't believe the Arabs are willing to accept Israel's right to exist as a nation, nor is Israel prepared to make the necessary territorial concessions. I don't believe peace is possible until Israel agrees to withdraw from all territories seized in the June 1967 war.

I never knew anybody in our government, including myself, who felt he had the answer to peace in the Middle East. When both Jews and Arabs are convinced they're speaking for God, that makes for a tough negotiation. I've been at the table when Arabs quoted the Koran while Jews quoted the Book of Moses. And I couldn't say, "Oh, come on now, don't give me any of that stuff!"

American policy in the Middle East faces deadlock. The Camp David accords were the only positive step taken in forty years, and full credit should go to Anwar Sadat, Menachem Begin, and certainly Jimmy Carter. But the process is long and tedious. I am not optimistic about any quick peace in the Middle East. Perhaps the best we can hope for now is simply an absence of war, a restless, seething status quo that is neither peace nor war. If we can do that, avoid a major outbreak in fighting, and keep both sides in contact with each other, perhaps future generations might be able to muster more compassion and wisdom than we were able.

24

The Pueblo Affair

On January 23, 1968, in international waters off the Korean coast, North Korea seized the USS *Pueblo*, a state-of-the-art intelligence-gathering ship. The *Pueblo* was surrounded by a North Korean subchaser and three motor torpedo boats, fired upon, and boarded. One American sailor was killed in the attack, and three were wounded; Commander Lloyd Bucher and his entire crew of eighty-one men were taken captive.

When news of the *Pueblo* seizure reached us, we boxed the compass for possible responses. A rescue operation was quickly ruled out. The *Pueblo* was secured in Wonsan Harbor, North Korea. A rescue was not operationally feasible. Military responses were weighed: retaliatory strikes against North Korea with air power and naval gunfire, interdicting coastal shipping, mining Wonsan Harbor or other North Korean ports, and blockading North Korea. We considered seizing a North Korean merchant vessel in retaliation, but after looking all over the world for a North Korean ship to capture, we could find none. The North Koreans had coastal vessels only, no oceangoing ships.

Some advisers argued strongly for military action, but a military response seemed unpromising to me. Should we sacrifice additional American lives simply to strike at the North Koreans and vent our anger? In retaliation, the North Koreans might have executed the officers and men of the *Pueblo* or begun land operations against South Korea, or both. We certainly didn't want another Asian war on our hands. And any air or naval operations we undertook would have been endangered by four or five hundred Soviet-made MiG fighters based in North Korea. It would have taken us three to four weeks to mobilize sufficient air power to deliver such strikes without heavy American losses.

Other options were discussed. One senior presidential adviser wanted to lure a Soviet intelligence ship into South Korean waters and then have South Korean naval vessels seize it as counterhostage. He claimed that approach offered perfect "symmetry" for the taking of the *Pueblo.* I resisted that idea, saying that the only symmetry about a South Korean seizure of a Soviet intelligence ship would have been its equal outrageousness. Surely we wouldn't improve a nasty situation by dragging in the Soviet Union.

We quickly concluded that our first priority must be the safe return of our officers and men. We ourselves had ordered the *Pueblo,* an undefended vessel, on that mission. We were relying on international waters for their protection, and that protection proved illusory. Our primary duty was to get them out of North Korea.

Publicly and privately we demanded the immediate release of the ship and its crew. To underline American resolve, President Johnson called to active service nearly fifteen thousand reservists, sent 372 additional fighters and transport planes to our bases in South Korea, and mobilized a large armada in the Sea of Japan. The president also did this to deter any possible North Korean attack on South Korea. We asked the United Nations Security Council for a resolution condemning the North Korean action, and we offered to refer the entire matter to the United Nations or World Court. We were willing to abide by a third-party decision, but the North Koreans weren't interested in any negotiations or third-party intervention, at least at first.

We were admittedly in a bind. Few options lay open to us. Lives were at stake. Wanting the freedom of the *Pueblo*'s crew, we had to act and speak prudently. Throughout months of its captivity, we made no inflammatory speeches about the *Pueblo.* In diplomacy many situations are better resolved if decision makers work behind the scenes and keep their mouths shut in public. After the *Pueblo* was captured, I often quoted from Ecclesiastes 3:1–7, "To every thing there is a season . . . a time to keep silence, and a time to speak. . . ."

At one point the North Koreans threatened to put our men on trial as war criminals. We strongly objected to that, and the Soviets might have advised the North Koreans against that as well. Had the North Koreans started executing our men, that would have changed the nature of the crisis and of our response. North Korea would have paid dearly.

Our position was also complicated by initial uncertainty about whether the *Pueblo* had entered North Korean territorial waters. Bob McNamara and I appeared on "Meet the Press" shortly after the seizure, and Bob commented that the administration couldn't be absolutely certain about the *Pueblo*'s route and whether it went within the twelve-mile limit until we talked to Captain Bucher and read the ship's logs. Bob's remarks gave rise to considerable controversy about where the *Pueblo* was, but he was simply telling the truth. Bucher was under orders to stay in international waters on this mission, but errors in navigation could have been made.

The North Koreans forced Bucher to plot the *Pueblo*'s "route" prior to its seizure, insisting that he include locations within Korean territorial waters. In plotting the course, Bucher included several positions on dry land, many miles inland. He also plotted other positions suggesting that the *Pueblo* would have had to travel at enormous rates of speed, far exceeding the capabilities of naval craft. The North Koreans picked up none of these anomalies. Bucher's publicly released "log" of the *Pueblo*'s route was a clear sign to us that the entire message was a phony. Despite the controversy over whether the *Pueblo* had violated North Korea's twelve-mile limit, we decided against releasing Bucher's deceptive log, fearing recriminations against him and his crew. We worried that American journalists would find these discrepancies, but fortunately they missed their scoop.

We did know beyond doubt that the *Pueblo,* when seized, was outside North Korean's claimed twelve-mile limit and in international waters. Indeed, even if the *Pueblo* had at some time entered North Korean waters—navigating in unfamiliar seas on a dark night, the *Pueblo* possibly could have slipped across that line—North Korea could not legally have seized it. Under international law, a country cannot seize another country's ship. Under laws adopted in 1958, a coastal nation can demand that a warship leave its territorial waters, but it does not have the right to board it, much less open fire and physically seize it. On several occasions during my tenure, Soviet warships broached our three-mile limit, and we didn't seize them. We simply required them to depart.

Although we didn't know why North Korea had seized the *Pueblo,* we feared that North Korea would move against South Korea, possibly believing that the United States was tied down in Vietnam and would not respond. During 1966 and 1967 the North Koreans had sharply increased their infiltration of South Korea, sending teams of saboteurs to destabilize the South. Only two days before the *Pueblo* seizure, a North Korean assassination squad came within a few hundred yards of President Park Chung Hu's residence, the famous Blue House raid. The South Koreans were furious about this attempted assassination of Park, and we genuinely feared the outbreak of a second Korean War. South Korean ground forces were more than a match for North Korean, but the latter had clear superiority in the air, with their large contingent of Soviet MiGs.

We were, in addition, dealing with a lawless country. Since World War II, North Korea had behaved like a pluperfect bastard, even with other Communist states; neither the Soviet Union nor China had much influence on North Korea or much leverage in this crisis. North Korea was and remains a renegade nation, indifferent to world opinion, disrespectful of international law, and a source of contention for its Asian neighbors.

All things considered, I was not optimistic about negotiating a quick release for the *Pueblo*'s crew. Eventually we began painfully slow private talks at Panmunjom. Bucher and his men were treated harshly, and under the pressure of coercion, some members of the crew signed letters of confession claiming that the *Pueblo* had violated Korean waters on a spy mission. We discounted these so-called confessions and statements; they were made under duress. The men of the *Pueblo* found ways of signaling hidden messages. In one group photo taken by the North Koreans, half of the men had their middle fingers extended in a gesture familiar to Americans. The wire services sent that picture all over the world. When the North Koreans discovered they had been had, they beat the Americans severely; the prisoners had assured their captors that the extended middle finger in American culture was a peace symbol.

Opening talks at Panmunjom were intensely hostile. North Korea charged that the *Pueblo* had entered Korean waters and that the United States planned to attack North Korea. Finally, in a bizarre windup of the whole affair, we concluded an agreement that led to the release of the crew. North Korea had demanded from the beginning that the United States sign a confession of guilt, taking full responsibility for violating Korean waters on a spying mission. The North Koreans wanted our signature on a piece of paper; eventually we told our negotiators to sign a confession and simultaneously add the line "We are instructed to inform you that there is not one word of truth in the above." For some reason, the North Koreans accepted that and released our officers and men.

I was totally surprised and completely delighted by this bizarre end to an eleven-month crisis. The deal was roughly equivalent to the kidnapping of a child, in which the parent offers a hundred-thousand-dollar check to the kidnappers for ransom, saying, "By the way, I am going to stop payment on this check at the bank." And the kidnappers accept that and return the child. I have never understood why North Korea accepted this arrangement.

Possibly North Korea believed that since they had milked this incident for all it was worth, it was time to terminate it. Or perhaps they felt they had gained a propaganda advantage with our signature on this "confession," despite the fact that we simultaneously repudiated it. Caring little for world opinion, with state control of their own media, the North Koreans could distribute this alleged confession and distribute it to their own populace without the American repudiation. In any event, this bizarre diplomatic maneuver ended the crisis. Our men returned safely, but not our ship. As far as I know, the *Pueblo* is still tied up in Wonsan Harbor.

After the crisis ended, Lloyd Bucher and some of his officers faced a naval court of inquiry for surrendering their ship without firing a shot. Bucher was convicted, but I believe he made the right decision. Had he headed his ship away from Korea and steamed at full speed to get out of the area, possibly the North Koreans would have called off their attack. More likely, Bucher would have had his ship shot out from under him, with the loss of his crew.

I have often wondered what the hearing officers themselves would have done had they been in Bucher's shoes. It is an easy matter for officers sitting in a courtroom to act gung ho about Bucher's surrendering the *Pueblo*. Our Navy wasn't even close enough to pick Bucher's crewmen out of the water if the ship had made a run for it and been sunk. Secretary of the Navy John Chafee later overturned the court of inquiry's critical finding, and wisely in my opinion, on the grounds that the responsibility for this fiasco should be borne by all, not just Lloyd Bucher and his crew.

The Johnson administration later conducted its own investigation of the *Pueblo* affair, concentrating in part on the intelligence damage resulting from the loss of highly sophisticated equipment. We studied the necessity for conducting missions like the *Pueblo*'s and concluded they served a useful purpose. For example, they could pick up radio traffic between military headquarters and various units, most of which is not encoded. Had North Korea been moving its forces south, preparing to attack South Korea, the *Pueblo* could have monitored that activity.

But in the *Pueblo* affair we learned the hard way that we could not rely upon international waters to protect espionage vessels incapable of defending themselves. *Pueblo*-type ships were decommissioned after the *Pueblo* seizure. We now assign such missions to destroyers and other naval craft that can fight back. And we now keep American naval and air units close enough to lend support in case of trouble.

Intelligence-gathering missions such as the *Pueblo*'s last voyage were a necessary part of the world of the sixties; today, with the development of high-resolution satellite photography and other remote sensing capabilities, such missions are not as important. The need for intelligence quickly raises questions about how to gather it. Missions such as the *Pueblo*'s were routine, a junior-level matter. I rarely was asked to authorize them. Occasionally, more sensitive intelligence-gathering missions did cross my desk. I once vetoed a plan to send an American submarine into Soviet waters in search of fragments of a recently fired Soviet missile. I ruled against it, deciding I'd rather not have the information if it took those means to get it. Both we and the Soviets regularly tested air defense systems by lighting up the other's radar stations. Our planes would charge toward the Soviet coast and then turn off at the last minute, hoping to activate Soviet radar so we could plot the location of their stations. The Soviets did the same with us. To me, that type of gamesmanship was not worth the danger. I tried with some success to cut back on those activities; we lost some fliers near Murmansk because of this monkey business.

The seizure of the *Pueblo*, like many acts of terrorism in which hostages are taken, quickly raised the question of priorities. We felt that our primary obligation was to the officers and men of the *Pueblo*; there was unanimity within the administration on that point. But once you make that decision, other possible lines of action are taken away. Striking back and bombing targets don't get your people back; they almost guarantee their deaths. In the *Pueblo* case one man had already been killed and eighty additional lives were at stake.

In an age increasingly threatened by international terrorism, far more so today than the 1960's, the *Pueblo* affair taught us that patience and negotiation can work. We could have mounted a more forceful response. But when contemplating action, the policy maker must consider not only the first step but the second, third, fourth, and fifth steps. A wrong response by us could have led to the execution of Bucher and his crew and even a second Korean War.

In the framing of policy responses to terrorism, broader ideas come into play. Americans are somewhat handicapped in such contests because the United States is a civilized country. We should not instinctively react in anger when crises arise. International terrorists and renegade nations such as North Korea and Iran take advantage of that, to some extent. Further, in responding to terrorism, we cannot ourselves become terrorists. When the Iranians seized the American Embassy in Teheran, it was fortunate that we did not seize the Iranian Embassy in Washington and imprison its inhabitants. We are not that kind of country or that kind of people.

25

The Third World
and Foreign Aid

From the beginning of the Kennedy administration and continuing into the Johnson years, we made a deliberate effort to improve relations with Third World countries by abandoning the old Eisenhower-Dulles approach that neutralism and nonalignment were immoral. We really weren't bothered by Third World countries that refused to take sides in the Cold War and line up with the West. We believed that any country that was independent and secure, concerned about the needs of its own people, and cooperative in the international arena helped the interests of the United States. Consequently, we set out to improve our relations with Third World leaders such as General Abdel Nasser of Egypt, Ahmed Ben Bella of Algeria, Kwame Nkrumah of Ghana, Sukarno of Indonesia, and Sékou Touré of Guinea.

Despite our best efforts, we didn't always succeed. Some of these fellows were just plain rascals, and others occasionally had their own larger designs for their area of the world. Sometimes our overtures were misinterpreted. For example, when we tried to improve relations with India, the Pakistanis became very suspicious; likewise with Nkrumah's

African neighbors when we sought closer relations with him. Nkrumah wanted a united West Africa with himself as its leader, and some Africans feared we intended to support him. We ran into similar difficulties with Nasser because of his desire for Arab unity and with Sukarno because of his designs on Malaya.

Another reason we tried to improve relations with Third World countries was the lingering presence of colonialism. Even though colonialism's days were numbered, some European states—for example, Portugal in Angola and Mozambique and the British in Rhodesia—retained their colonies. We knew these anachronisms had to end, but the colonial powers were our allies in NATO. This created problems for us in the Third World, problems that we tried to overcome with good relations with Third World states.

Also contributing to tensions between the United States and the Third World was the "North-South" problem, the conflict between the rich and the poor. During my tenure as secretary the average per capita income throughout Africa was about thirty cents per day. There was only one doctor for every seventeen thousand Africans, about one twenty-fifth of the ratio in the United States. Infant mortality in tropical Africa ran as high as one child in four, ten times the American rate. Illiteracy ran at 85 percent. The average African farmer produced only 4 percent of his North American counterpart.

When these countries broke their colonial bonds, in their campaigns for independence, Third World leaders often told their people that misery, grinding poverty, illiteracy, and poor health were caused by their colonial masters. When the colonialists went home, conditions would improve. Yet after independence these new nations faced those same problems. Prime Minister Nehru told me once how easy it was to lead a revolution and how difficult to build a nation. The leaders of the developing countries had the hounds of hell barking at their heels; they could not escape the "revolution of rising expectations." Modern communications taught Third World peoples that poverty, misery, illiteracy, and malnutrition were not inevitable, that living conditions were better elsewhere and could be improved. People everywhere were awakening from the stagnation of centuries, and they were less inclined to regard poverty, oppression, and squalor as the law of nature. They were determined to have for themselves and their children more and better food; housing fit for human habitation; better schools, sanitation, and medical care; and honest and responsible government.

This pressure led many struggling countries to demand transfers of wealth from rich countries to poor, to resort to authoritarian or dictatorial rule, or to turn away from human rights in other ways. All of these attempted solutions to poverty created tensions between Third World states and the United States. But one issue I've never been too concerned about in the Third World, and particularly in Africa, is "ideological penetration." My hunch is that if Americans, Soviets, Chinese, and foreigners in general would keep their fingers out of the Third World, the peoples of these regions would listen to what everyone had to say, smile politely, shrug their shoulders, and then go off to run their own lives and their countries however they saw fit. Even today, for example, I believe that at some point the Ethiopians and Angolans are going to regurgitate the Russians and Cubans, both foreign elements to Africans.

But just because Third World nations may prefer to go their own way doesn't mean that the United States should abandon or ignore them. The United States must remain involved, as we have throughout the postwar years. Our foreign aid started in 1938 with military aid to China. This small beginning soon became the great wartime weapon of lend-lease. Before the war was over, the United States began a program of international relief known as UNRRA (United Nations Relief and Rehabilitation Administration) to war-ravaged nations. Much of the UNRRA effort was simply providing food to the war victims of Europe and Asia. From relief we moved on to the Truman Doctrine, in which the United States assisted Greece and Turkey in fighting Communist insurgencies, and from there to economic assistance, culminating in the Marshall Plan, one of the most dramatic and successful assistance programs in history.

In the postwar period the United States provided foreign assistance on a scale unprecedented in history. As we provided that aid, we discovered that its purpose multiplied to include military aid against agression, funds for economic growth and development, political advantage, and so on. But in our noblest moments we discovered that with foreign aid we had embarked upon nothing less than an attack upon mankind's ancient enemies: want, sickness, ignorance, and hopelessness.

For years, then, foreign aid has been a fundamental instrument of U.S. policy. From the days of the Greek-Turkish aid program and the Marshall Plan, foreign aid has helped build stable economies, stimulate economic growth, and assure the Free World security from aggression and subversion. The record of success is remarkable. Western Europe today is prosperous, free, and independent. Economic aid has ended in twenty-six countries. Many former aid recipients are now providing assistance to other nations. In fact, as of 1987, one former recipient of U.S. foreign aid—Japan—became the leading donor of foreign aid, ahead of even the United States.

Foreign aid must include military assistance; after all, the United States does face formidable military threats. But the primary task of foreign aid—and American foreign policy—is to help build a decent world order. National power is not a matter of arms alone. Strength comes from education, fertile acres, humming workshops, and the satisfaction and pride of a free people. A vibrant society is not vulnerable to subversion. National defense is easier when there is something worth defending.

Admittedly, it is easier to sell foreign aid to the American people and Congress whenever U.S. interests are threatened, and more often than not the threat of communism has been used to justify aid, both economic and military. For example, during consultations over an upcoming appropriations request for the Marshall Plan, Senator Arthur Vandenberg advised us, "If you want this kind of money, you'll have to come in here roaring." He had in mind the threat of Communist aggression and subversion in Europe, and roar we did. But the roaring was discordant; it confused our purposes, misrepresented our motives, and impaired our execution. Foreign aid would be just as compelling if there were no Soviet bloc, no People's Republic of China, and no doctrine of world revolution.

We shouldn't underestimate the threat of communism—it is a real threat—but foreign aid has purposes more solemn than combating communism. Said George Marshall, in testifying for the plan that ultimately bore his name: "Our policy is directed not against any country or doctrine but against hunger, poverty, desperation, and chaos." When we look back over the aid programs of recent decades, it seems we have lost sight of Marshall's words. Our aid has been a reaction to crisis and rapidly changing events, and the original Marshall concept has been blurred.

After World War II, at a time when our minds and spirits had been purged in the fires of a great war, the American people made a major effort to bind up the wounds of war and get the world economy started again. We came up with major resources for that purpose—the Marshall Plan and Point Four Program. True, we came out of World War II as the only major power physically unscarred by the ravages of that war. Yet during the Korean War we maintained the Marshall Plan with a gross national product about half of what it is today. We were putting more than 3 percent of our gross national product into foreign aid. Such aid served our national interest, but it could not have been possible without the generosity of the American people. But this earlier commitment has slackened. When I was secretary of state, my efforts to win congressional approval of our foreign aid requests—averaging one-half of 1 percent of our GNP—were like pulling teeth.

One trouble with foreign aid is that it has no real constituency in American politics. No politician thinks he will win votes at home by voting for foreign aid. In fact, members of Congress can win votes by opposing aid. Herman Talmadge ran against Senator Walter George of Georgia on foreign aid, and not once as a senator did Talmadge vote for anything that even resembled it. He's not the only one.

During the sixties Congress really dug its heels in on foreign aid, with people like Bill Fulbright leading the way. Congress disagreed with the administration on how much foreign aid we should give, the priorities we should focus on, and whether foreign aid had to be used to buy American products. A disregard of and even selfishness by other countries toward U.S. economic problems also fueled congressional discontent with foreign aid. For example, in the early 1970's, when the United States was having balance-of-payments problems, West Germany resisted offsetting the foreign exchange burden of our stationing American troops in Germany.

A prominent German friend once asked me, "What can we Germans do about it?"

"You've repaid the loan portions of the Marshall Plan," I said. "Why don't you now repay the grant portions of the Marshall Plan?"

"That is unthinkable!"

I reminded him that it wasn't unthinkable for us Americans in the late 1940's to make those grants. My German friend returned to West Germany and mentioned this idea in the German parliament. He told me later that he was treated like a skunk at a tea party.

In my eight-year tenure as secretary of state I personally testified before congressional committees thirty-two times on behalf of foreign aid. That meant four times a year, once before each house for appropriations and once again for authorization. Each committee wanted a new speech on foreign aid, and each wanted me—the secretary of state—to appear. I found that I couldn't give thirty-two different speeches in support of foreign aid without boring the hell out of my audience. The first few times weren't so bad, but trying to say something interesting about foreign aid thirty-two times was quite an assignment!

Secretary of State George Shultz once summarized the case for foreign aid in two sentences: "The United States cannot be prosperous if two-thirds of the world is in abject misery and poverty," and "This country cannot be safe and at peace if two-thirds of the world is in turmoil." In saying that, Shultz said it all; the rest is window dressing. Foreign aid is an insurance policy.

The presidents whom I served as secretary of state had strong commitments to foreign aid, but both were rather ambivalent about fighting to get aid money from Congress. Only rarely did John Kennedy or Lyndon Johnson use the White House to push for foreign aid; both expected their cabinet officers to take primary responsibility for getting legislation for their own departments through Congress. I had to carry that ball myself, along with the directors of the Agency for International Development and other agencies.

Yet Kennedy was very interested in the Third World and the problems of developing countries. Intellectually he recognized that assisting these countries and trying to improve relations with them were something we had to do. Kennedy's commitment to foreign aid came out of his mind; it didn't derive from his experience. Although he had been raised a rich man's son and had no firsthand experience with poverty, fortunately Kennedy could understand and empathize with the problems of the poor.

While Kennedy's approach to foreign aid was rhetorical and intellectual, Johnson's approach was emotional. He knew poverty and underdevelopment first hand growing up in Texas, and when he became president, he felt the time for sloganeering was over. LBJ wanted to get things done. During his first week as president LBJ asked me what programs the Alliance for Progress had in place. I gave him a rather vague State Department kind of answer, full of generalities. He jumped all over me, saying, "I don't mean that! I mean, what are we doing? What are we actually doing? What's going on down there in Latin America?" After Johnson became president, U.S. funding under the alliance increased rapidly. Johnson wanted us to get the job done. He kept pressing us to "Get on with it"—housing projects, schools, agricultural projects, and so on. He would say things like "It's not rhetoric that counts; it's performance. It's what we actually do that counts."

LBJ was especially interested in the Western Hemisphere. He used to tell us, "This hemisphere is our home. This is where we live. These people are our neighbors. If we can't make it work here, where we live, how can we expect to make it work anywhere else?" Supposedly begun by the Kennedy administration, the Alliance for Progress had its groundwork actually laid during the Eisenhower administration by

Douglas Dillon and Milton Eisenhower. The Kennedy administration put a new label on it and launched it with great fanfare, and the alliance meant a lot to LBJ. He left office disappointed that more was not accomplished for and with our Latin American neighbors.

At the same time Johnson didn't just want to throw money at problems. At one time he insisted that he personally approve and review aid projects exceeding ten million dollars. His preference for action stood in bold relief in his reaction to a food crisis in India in the late 1960's. India had two bad monsoons in a row and developed serious food shortages. In reviewing this problem, we concluded that the Indian people could not be fed unless India itself did a great many things which it was not doing. For example, if one Indian state had a food surplus and a neighboring state had a food shortage, surplus food did not move to the deficit state as it would in the United States. The Indian government refused to allocate rolling stock to move food around the country. There were other problems: India spent no government funds for fertilizer plants and few funds for food storage. India lost almost 20 percent of its food stock each year to the effects of improper storage: mildew, rot, rats, and other pests.

President Johnson was appalled. To my dismay and against my advice, he sent Secretary of Agriculture Orville Freeman to warn the Indian minister of agriculture that unless the Indian government implemented the reforms Johnson wanted to see, the United States would stop shipping food aid to India. India at first didn't believe Freeman, but then Johnson stopped the ships.

Freeman and the Indian minister then worked out a remedial program, whereupon Johnson started the food ships sailing again. Since his admittedly heavy-handed intervention, India has been in a much stronger food position. Nevertheless, Indians still talk about this "outrageous" American intrusion into their domestic affairs.

Seeking to encourage a broader approach to economic development and growth, the Kennedy and Johnson administrations shifted the emphasis in foreign aid away from big, dramatic capital-intensive projects like dams, steel mills, and football stadiums to public health, public education, and improved agricultural productivity. The earlier focus on industrialization had gotten out of hand, and agriculture, education, and public health were being neglected. We based our thinking on the American experience with development, when our country was still young with large undeveloped areas of its own. Lyndon Johnson and I, among others, had witnessed a dramatic transformation in the lives of family and neighbors in our home counties, through this powerful combination of public health, public education, and increased productivity.

As we learned in the Rockefeller Foundation, in some countries there was simply no awareness of the germ theory of disease. While traveling through India in the fifties, I saw villages where the water supply was a tank maybe ten feet in diameter and waist-high, located in the center of the village. A barber would be shaving one of his customers; next to him a woman would be washing the family clothes; next to her another woman would be dipping for drinking water; and then there'd be a cow standing with its front legs over the wall—all using the same tank. Sickness, disease, illiteracy, and a lack of public education and modern hygiene greatly hampered efforts to increase agricultural productivity.

Both with our own experience and in watching what happens in the Third World, we learned that development encompasses an entire society. In the early days of the Green Revolution, plant geneticists, plant pathologists, and agronomists all worked to improve food production in underdeveloped countries. They soon discovered that agricultural experts alone could not get the job done. Transportation, education, communication, literacy, research, fiscal and tax policy, public administration, export/import policy, the social standing of agricultural scientists, the landholding system, a working legal system, and social order all played roles in increasing agricultural productivity.

In planning aid programs, both at the Rockefeller Foundation and State Department, we constantly had to remind ourselves how interrelated the problems in the developing world were. Experience was a hard teacher, and many mistakes were made, much time and money wasted.

Another error we made was drawing too categorical a line between what we call the developed countries and the developing countries. We set a per capita annual income figure as the breakpoint; those below it were considered developing while those above were developed. This implied that somehow the responsibility for assisting development belonged to the developed countries. If the United States has any obligation toward such countries as Argentina, Venezuela, and India, surely they in turn have an obligation toward such countries as Paraguay, Ecuador, and Burma. Concern about development should be shared by all.

And some have. For example, Mexico has helped by accepting trainees from other countries in its corn and wheat development center, its graduate school of agriculture at Chapingo, its fine children's hospital, and its Institute of Cardiology in Mexico City. Mexico also ships thousands of tons of improved seed to countries all over the world.

We also made a great mistake when we told Third World peoples, "It takes two or three centuries to develop a modern economy. You can't do this too fast." In fact, development has occurred rapidly in some societies. Many older Americans grew up under primitive conditions in underdeveloped regions of our own country; they remember the days when typhoid, malaria, pellagra, goiter, and other diseases were common and considered simply part of the environment which Providence had given us.

When I was a boy in Georgia, only two American farms in a hundred had electricity. Fifty years ago hookworm and malaria were rampant in the South. The rural Georgia of my youth was certainly underdeveloped; we enjoyed few of the benefits of modern science, technology, medicine, public health, or education. My father was the only one of eleven brothers and sisters to go to college. Three of his five children went to college. All of his grandchildren went to college. What happened to our family and what happened to Cherokee County have happened all over America. It can happen elsewhere as well.

The astonishing economic growth and capacity of the United States present us with some heavy responsibilities. In 1968, my final year in office, our gross national product equaled that of the NATO countries and Japan combined; it was twice that of the Soviet Union; ten times that of mainland China; ten times that of Latin America. Our foreign assistance for fiscal year 1968, including the Peace Corps and contributions to the International Development Association and the Inter-American Development Bank, totaled about six-tenths of 1 percent of our gross national product. If we are negligent about the needs of the rest of the world, we could easily find ourselves regarded as a voracious, rapacious nation calling upon everyone else to feed our own economy, widening the gap between Americans and peoples abroad. We cannot accept so stark a contrast between the future we would ask for ourselves and the future to which others aspire. If we are not to become isolated from others, we must be willing to engage in their problems, help share their burdens, and be a caring, helpful nation. Those who would like to forget the rest of the world must face the fact that there is no place to hide. I reject the argument that we cannot afford to pay more than sixth-tenths of 1 percent of our GNP—our current rate—for foreign aid. I reject it profoundly.

In the final analysis the United States sends foreign aid because it serves vital national interests. Indeed, one of the basic lessons of this century is that our national security is inextricably bound up with the freedom and economic and social progress of other nations. As they become prosperous, so, too, our own economy and security benefit. Seen in this light, "national interest" isn't Machiavellian, hard-boiled, or selfish; it encompasses the lives and welfare of ordinary people around the globe.

We also send aid overseas because it is right to do so. Throughout the world people are in need of food, shelter, education, health care, and jobs. Self-interest alone is not the essence of foreign aid. We need no other reason to support it than the profound and overriding fact that to do so is right.

It is right because people abroad need help, and we are in a position to help. Children become sick, and we have the medicines to save them. Millions are illiterate, and we have the means to help educate them. In many countries farmers barely scratch a living from the soil, using their primitive tools and techniques, and we have the technical skills and equipment to help them grow more food and live like human beings.

Inevitably there are disappointments. My congressional critics often demanded that nations receiving foreign aid have efficient economies, thriving free-enterprise systems, and full-fledged democracies before we should aid them. They also expected Third World nations to modernize quickly. But the purpose of our aid today, as was true in the sixties, is to help move these countries toward democracy, freedom, and efficiency. These are not preconditions to our assistance; rather, they are the objectives of our assistance. It is precisely because these countries lack the attributes of a developed free society that we give aid in the first place.

We shouldn't let political upheavals, crises, our irritation with a few Third World leaders, and our impatience with the slow pace of development obscure real progress being made around the globe. The successes of foreign aid far outweigh the defeats: Children are being fed, inoculated against disease, educated for the future; hospitals, dams, schools, and roads are being built; and, perhaps most important of all, the peoples of Africa, Asia, and Latin America can look to the future with hope. Their children are not doomed to lives of poverty. Economic growth and development can occur.

26

The United Nations

Reflecting my interest in the Third World and the problems of developing countries, I had the privilege of participating in seventeen annual meetings of the United Nations General Assembly. My first was with the UN's birth in San Francisco in 1945, and my last eight were as secretary of state. Perhaps the United Nations has fallen short of the high hopes entertained at its founding, but I personally have never lost my enthusiasm for the UN. My service as one of Harry Truman's "UN boys," heading the United Nations desk in the late 1940's, was among the most fulfilling and exciting times of my life.

During my years as secretary of state I spent two or three weeks every September in New York at the opening session of each year's UN General Assembly. Prime ministers and foreign ministers from around the world descend on the UN for the "general debate" that takes place each opening session. I tried to meet with as many leaders as I could, often eighty to ninety each trip.

I always tried to follow protocol for these meetings. If a foreign minister was senior to me in service, I called on him at his office;

otherwise, I invited him to my office. I found these bilateral talks extraordinarily useful, because for each I had to go through a big book of briefing material on that man and his country. Those briefings and our talks were very informative, a refresher course on the entire world. Personal relationships should not play much of a role in diplomacy, but I wanted to meet the man we were sending cables to and get some impressions of him, and for him to meet me. Particularly with newly independent countries, where politics tends to be personalized and personalities make an enormous difference, I think this approach may have helped.

We in the State Department took the United Nations seriously during the Kennedy and Johnson administrations, probably more so than any administration in the last four decades. We readily brought issues such as the Congo crisis, the Cuban missile crisis, conflict in the Middle East, and the Six-Day War to the United Nations. We didn't always get what we wanted, but we at least made the effort.

Not everyone in the Kennedy and Johnson administrations was as wedded to the United Nations as I was, but then most other senior officials had not had my past experience with the UN. Having emerged from the most terrible war in history, we who helped launch the UN felt deeply that the paramount task for all mankind was "to save succeeding generations from the scourge of war." The question was, How could that best be accomplished?

To me and others, the answer was clear: collective security. But even before the UN Charter was finally ratified, we realized that collective security could not be found in common action by the permanent members of the Security Council and that the UN's main mission of preserving the peace would be frustrated. Joseph Stalin pressed what became known as the Cold War, and the shadow of a paralyzing veto fell upon the Security Council, that body responsible for maintaining international peace and security. By mid-1945 we had learned that we could not expect cooperation from the Soviet Union at the United Nations. The UN Charter presupposes unanimity among the five permanent members of the Security Council in maintaining peace. Instead, we tried to bypass that lack of unanimity and strengthen the UN by supporting international activities not subject to veto: the war relief programs; the work of the General Assembly and specialized agencies. We tried to create a United Nations military force and international controls of atomic power under the Baruch Plan, but we and the Soviets failed to agree.

In the early days of the United Nations most of its members voted with the United States. To charge the Soviets then with abusing their veto was a red herring because we had sufficient votes in the Security Council to defeat any resolution we did not like without having to employ our own veto. I once chided Soviet representative Andrei Gromyko for his country's long string of vetoes. "There will come a time," he replied, "when you Americans will use the veto as much as we Russians." He was right.

One of the most significant changes in the UN has been the vast increase in its membership. When it was first organized, the UN had 51 members. Architects planning the UN headquarters building were told to plan for 60 members, with a possible expansion to 75. When I became secretary of state in 1961, the UN already had nearly 100 members. Today it has 159 members.

Not all of this expansion has helped. At least thirty-one current UN members are microstates—nations with populations less than a million. In the General Assembly a nation such as Vanuatu has the same voice and vote as the United States, the Soviet Union, or China. This imbalance between voting power in the General Assembly and influence in the real world tends to undermine the UN's authority. Had those of us who drafted the UN Charter anticipated this explosion of small states, we might have created a bicameral body, something like a Senate and House of Representatives. We discussed creating associate memberships for the smaller countries, in which they would have full opportunity to state their views on the UN floor but wouldn't vote or pay dues. But by that time countries like Iceland and Luxembourg were already charter members and would have nothing to do with such a plan.

We were both surprised and disappointed by the postwar disintegration of the colonial empires into so many tiny states. We hoped there would emerge regional groupings such as a West Africa confederation, an East Africa confederation, a West Indies confederation, and so forth. But these areas broke up into small fragments.

Today nations representing 10 percent of the world's population and less than 5 percent of the financial contribution to the UN now cast two-thirds of the votes in the General Assembly. This can sometimes lead to strange situations. For example, when the Maldive Islands joined the UN, their seat remained vacant for a long time; they couldn't afford to maintain a delegation in New York, even though the General Assembly paid travel costs.

This proliferation of smaller and newer nations has changed the UN. Many newly independent countries, now members, don't remember the circumstances that led to the UN's creation. They didn't even exist when the Charter was drafted. They rarely address the broader issues of war and peace; they involve themselves only on issues that affect them directly. This has weakened the UN's willingness to take a stand on conflicts that threaten world peace.

The way that the UN is set up, much depends upon the secretary-general. I had the highest regard for Trygve Lie and Dag Hammarskjöld because they took the UN Charter as their Bible. Hammarskjöld was exactly what we wanted a secretary-general to be: strong, forceful, and utterly committed to the UN Charter. The United States had no misgivings about a strong secretary-general because the Charter was consistent with American purposes and ideals. That was not by accident, because we Americans played a major role in drafting the Charter in 1945; we wanted a Dag Hammarskjöld! Since Hammarskjöld's death, however, no secretary-general has been as effective or had the same passion for the Charter.

Hammarskjöld's forceful leadership in the Congo crisis prompted the Soviets to come up with their famous "troika proposal"—that there be three secretary-generals, one each from the socialist, capitalist, and nonaligned worlds. Under the Soviet plan, the three could act only in unison. The troika proposal flew in the face of everything known about effective administration. Khrushchev's idea that the world was divided into three "blocs" was also pretentious; there was only one bloc in the United Nations which took its orders from a single authority, that of Mr. Khrushchev's. We managed to beat back his three-headed directorate, but the Soviets pressed hard and succeeded in watering down the role of the secretary-general.

Partially as a result, those who followed Hammarskjöld have not been nearly as effective as he was. For example, I thought U Thant was a weak secretary-general because he didn't attach himself to the Charter and say, "Here is where I stand. These are the principles I am fighting for." In my experience, it was awfully hard to know where he stood or even what he had said in our talks.

Whatever the capabilities of the secretary-general, given the present membership, the General Assembly will pass some resolutions that will annoy the hell out of us. But most of these resolutions are not binding, and we ought to be able to live with them. But it is important that the United States send ambassadors to the United Nations who understand the purposes of diplomacy and who also will work at their jobs. Even my good friend Adlai Stevenson, always sympathetic to the Third

World, devoted little time to actually working with the delegates of Third World countries. He didn't cultivate individual delegates the way a John Foster Dulles or an Eleanor Roosevelt did.

Unfortunately some of our more recent ambassadors acted as if they were trying to score points in a high school debate. For example, during the Carter administration the General Assembly barely passed a resolution stating that Zionism was a form of racism. Our delegation could have easily defeated that resolution, with the effort one would expect of an American delegation and our ambassadors abroad. It appeared that our ambassador preferred to milk the issue rather than defeat the resolution. We can't take that kind of approach at the UN and expect to get anywhere. He preferred to box delegates' ears rather than try to work with them.

During my forty years of public life the United Nations proved itself useful on many issues. Admittedly it has fallen short of the far-reaching hopes that many entertained for it in 1945, and it has not banished war, but the world organization has helped us overcome crises of desperate danger these past four decades. The UN has had many notable successes in the postwar years. UN-sponsored negotiations and task forces have backed peacekeeping operations in Indonesia, Greece, Palestine, Kashmir, Korea, Trieste, Suez, Lebanon, Laos, the Congo, West New Guinea, the Yemen, and Cyprus. Not all were successfully resolved, but in every case UN intervention helped reduce conflict. In carrying out its peacekeeping mission, in its own fumbling, stumbling way, this much-maligned institution on New York's East River has helped keep smaller wars from spreading into larger wars. The UN has also helped move along the historic process of decolonialization, which is reflected in the growth of its membership from 51 nations to 159.

And the UN helped in superpower confrontations as well. During the Cuban missile crisis, with the United States and Soviet Union at each other's jugular veins, it was terribly important that the Security Council was in place to hear the world community discuss and debate this crisis and give the superpowers more time to cool off. In that crisis alone the United Nations earned its pay for a long time to come. Despite obvious failings and frustrations, our investment in the United Nations has paid off.

In short, the United Nations has not ushered in the millennium. But it has laid the foundations for a world community through a wide range of international institutions. Some, such as the World Bank and the International Monetary Fund, have grown into powerful, mature organizations; others are still finding their way. Some accomplish undramatic but important tasks such as working out common technical definitions and allocating frequencies for radio transmission. Others have humanitarian tasks such as the elimination of malaria and the inoculation of millions of children against crippling diseases. It was due to the United Nations that smallpox has disappeared from the human race. This took cooperation among nations with the deepest kinds of differences. Still others work in new fields such as worldwide weather reporting. Over the years the United Nations has created a framework for conducting the world's business on the basis of voluntary cooperation among sovereign states.

Within this family of UN organizations the United States cooperates with most countries of the world. Despite Soviet obstructionism, the veto, threats to the peace, severe budgetary problems, the passions of old problems such as colonialism, the inexperience of new members and the inertia of old ones, despite its inadequacies and the parochialism of all its members, I am convinced that the United Nations and its family of more than one hundred agencies are utterly indispensable in today's world.

Among the UN's problems is that its work gets very little attention. Today somewhere in the world American delegates are attending anywhere from twelve to fifteen multilateral intergovernmental meetings on subjects ranging from the control of nuclear weapons to the control of hog cholera, mostly under the auspices of the United Nations. They get little press attention because—"no blood, no news"—they aren't exciting enough to be newsworthy. The international community conducts an enormous amount of work every day, most of which goes unreported.

The global nature of modern problems—hunger and famine, overpopulation, the threat of conventional and nuclear war, destruction of the environment, the energy crisis and depletion of nonrenewable resources—will increasingly force nation-states to work together and take international institutions such as the United Nations seriously. We Americans cannot even solve many of our national problems without an international effort.

The United Nations is the symbol and substance of the kind of world which the United States seeks to build. Its Charter contains an expression of our deepest national ideals. Despite the frustrations of this postwar period, I believe that the American people will remain faithful in their support of the United Nations and that their purposes will continue to be the purposes and principles defined in the UN Charter, particularly the preamble and Articles 1 and 11.

I am convinced those sections accurately and succinctly reflect the hopes and values of the American people. I believe the UN Charter describes the kind of world we hope will come into being. That Charter was drawn up at a time when the human race was engaged in the greatest bloodletting in history, when our hopes were lifted by the prospects and necessity of peace, when we sat down quietly and dared to think about what kind of world we needed to "save succeeding generations from the scourge of war."

The basic principle that we chose to achieve a lasting peace is stated in Article 1 of the UN Charter: "To take effective collective measures for the prevention and removal of threats to the peace, and for the suppression of acts of aggression or other breaches of the peace, and to bring about by peaceful means, and in conformity with the principles of justice and international law, adjustment or settlement of international disputes or situations which might lead to a breach of the peace."

This is the central, overriding, abiding purpose of the United Nations. These words represent the lessons drawn from World War II and the events which led up to that war. They are the lessons on which we must build to prevent World War III. An enormous price—fifty million lives—was paid for those lessons. We must find ways to bring them to life, to give them strength, to nourish and cherish them, day in and day out, because the days of learning lessons from war are over.

SECTION V

VIETNAM

My father is brutally honest about his role in the decision making on Vietnam. He takes full responsibility for it. There is candor, confessions of error on tactical matters, and an unspoken sadness that it ended so badly. However, his private views as an old man in the 1980's barely wavered from his official views as secretary of state two decades earlier.

There are some inevitable lapses between my father's on-the-record views on policy in the sixties and his memories twenty years later. The year 1968, most climactic in American history since the Civil War, was a "blur" to him. "I was bone-tired," he said, and he survived it on a daily diet of "aspirin, scotch, and four packs of Larks." He confessed, "I don't remember too much of what happened that year," and the transcripts of our interviews reflected his gaps. I worked hard to reconstruct 1968 for him, seeking to trigger his memory.

One lapse is especially misleading. Years later, referring to the Tet offensive of February 1968, which overran much of South Vietnam and shattered American confidence, Rusk said: "I realized that many Americans were losing heart in the war effort and that if we couldn't tell them when the war would be over, we might as well chuck it." Had Dean Rusk been willing to "chuck" the war effort after Tet and in the waning months of the Johnson administration, a negotiated settlement might have been obtained in Paris. But the facts suggest otherwise. In the policy review after Tet, he told me, he "might have had some influence" on President Johnson's decision and speech of March 31, announcing a bombing halt, the sending of 18,000 troops rather than the 206,000 Westmoreland had requested, and a renewed interest in negotiations, although "only LBJ could make those decisions." Still, to the despair of Averell Harriman, Cyrus Vance, and American negotiators in Paris, there was no "chucking" of basic American objectives: the seating of the South Vietnamese government at the talks and the withdrawal of North Vietnamese forces. With Hanoi fearful of a Nixon victory in the November elections and suddenly eager to talk, a chance to cut American losses, negotiate a withdrawal on terms no worse than those negotiated in 1973, and end the war in 1968 may have been lost.

Beneath the confidence of his official views, my father had undergone an agony of indecision prior to the spring 1965 buildup. Dean Rusk wouldn't confess to "agony," but others have told the tale. Warren Cohen, in *Dean Rusk,* spells out how Rusk, fearing the United States was committing itself to a "losing horse," resisted the introduction of U.S. combat forces, the bombing of the North, and the Americanization of the war. "Cohen made me into too much of a good guy," my dad insisted. "My doubts were registered only as doubts rather than opposition to policy." But my brother, David, said that Pop had told him he had opposed the bombing of North Vietnam, saying it would only strengthen Hanoi's determination to prosecute the war and rally the support of their people. "I have spent all my professional life," he told Dave, "dealing with the differences between the promise and the performance of air power."

My mother remembered an agony of indecision as well, describing how in 1964 Pop sat by himself for long periods of time, both at home and at the office, "obviously lost in thought" about the biggest decision of his career. That same year McGeorge Bundy wrote a memo to President Johnson, explaining that "it's almost unheard of for Dean or Virginia to give any sign of weakness, so that when I hear from both of them my ears go up like a beagle's. Your secretary of state very much needs a rest. Twice in the last week he has spoken to me about nightmares, and once about his doctor telling him that he must have time off soon. Last night I sat next to Virginia Rusk, and she is deeply worried about him. . . . I think you should send him away for a solid ten days."

And I myself often walked into the living room of our Washington home and saw my dad stretched out on the floor.

"What's the matter, Pop?"

"My gut hurts," he'd tell me. "I'm just trying to relax." That pain in the gut was chronic, never diagnosed despite dozens of physical exams and the best medical advice he could get, and it persisted into old age. In Georgia the stomach pains were almost disabling. They had begun in the months prior to the American buildup in Vietnam in 1965.

But once the decision was made to intervene, there was no turning back for my father, and he played a major role in all the subsequent decisions to land the Marines at Da Nang, begin bombing North Vietnam, send American troops into combat, and commit American prestige to the defense of South Vietnam. He was deeply involved in the many efforts—"peace feelers," bombing halts, bilateral and third-party talks—to negotiate a peace, and he believed these efforts ultimately failed because of an "incompatibility of objectives in Hanoi and Washington." That failure of diplomacy was a "searing experience" for him and everyone involved. He played a major role in the climactic events of 1968: the Tet offensive and the policy review that followed, President Johnson's decision to de-escalate the fighting, and the Paris peace talks, which tried and ultimately failed to end the war.

In our talks my dad spelled out his regrets, what the "lessons of Vietnam" were for him, what issues were vital, and why he supported the war so tenaciously. He questioned whether gradualism was the proper strategy to employ, also whether a democratic society could fight and sustain a limited war. He readily admitted to two mistakes: overestimating the patience of the American people and underestimating the tenacity of the North Vietnamese. Sensing an opening, seeking to dip beneath his official views, for one of the few times in our project I challenged him.

"Why were the North Vietnamese so tenacious, Pop?" It was really the central question of the war.

He attributed their tenacity to Communist ideology, Hanoi's fanaticism, the social controls and discipline a totalitarian society has over its populace.

"Do you really believe what you are saying?"

"Yes, I do," he replied.

Yet the North Vietnamese had withstood every weapon in the American arsenal except nuclear, had been bombed with seven times the total tonnage of explosives dropped in World War II, and had fought for thirty years with no sign of quitting. To many observers, including many Americans who fought them, NVA regulars were the finest infantrymen the world had ever seen. That the North Vietnamese finally prevailed over a superpower was one of history's epic experiences; theirs had been a national effort, involving their entire populace. Short of blowing them off the face of the earth, how could we have defeated such a people?

"Why did they keep coming?" I asked him. "Who were those people? Why did they fight so hard?"

These were questions for which he had no answers.

"I really don't have much to offer on that, Rich," he finally said. Both of us were emotionally drained.

I turned off the tape recorder. There would be no *mea culpa*. Inadvertently I was asking my father to do what I had done in the late 1960s. As a Marine reservist whose Syracuse, New York, tank battalion was never activated for Vietnam, and as a student at Cornell University, I tried doggedly to believe in American policy until the war's relentless illogic made this impossible. Not wanting to volunteer for Vietnam, unwilling to embarrass my father by joining an antiwar movement that was appearing all around me, unable to stop the war, unable to take part, caught between love for my father and the growing horror of Vietnam, I had begun to question the premises and assumptions that underlay my dad's thinking. All this led to an emotional and psychological journey that ended, one year after he left office, in psychological collapse.

"You had your father's nervous breakdown," a psychologist told me seventeen years later. And he explained how sons take responsibility for their fathers and occasionally try to shoulder their burdens and take some of the blame for their actions, in the same way that fathers feel responsible for their sons.

"I did my thinking on Vietnam before we went in," my dad once told me. "Throughout, I believed in the principles that underlay our commitment to South Vietnam."

What choice did he have, once the buildup had begun and the coffins started coming home to small towns all across America? What choice did he have, this decent, humane father of mine to whom the sanctity of human life was every bit as important as the principle of collective security?

"Once American troops were committed, there would be no turning back." That was the essence of Dean Rusk's advice on Vietnam. And thus began the process by which "one dead American begets another dead American begets another dead American," according to David Halberstam.

"I was never one to dwell upon the past," my dad told me. With this reticent, reserved, self-contained, emotionally bound-up father of mine from rural Georgia, how could the decision making have gone any differently? His taciturn qualities, which served him so well in negotiating with the Russians, ill prepared him for the wrenching, introspective, soul-shattering journey that a true reappraisal of Vietnam policy would have involved. Although trained for high office, he was unprepared for such a journey, for admitting that thousands of American lives, and hundreds of thousands of Vietnamese, might have been lost in vain.

Why did we Americans fight that war? There were few markets at stake, no vital strategic interests, no military bases, and, for Dean Rusk, no hidden purposes. For Pop, it was just as he said.

"There was the pledge [SEATO]. We had given our word."

—R. R.

27

Roots of the American Commitment

Every story has a beginning; my involvement with Vietnam began in the China-Burma-India theater during World War II. As chief of war plans for General Joseph "Vinegar Joe" Stilwell I once authorized a drop of arms and American cigarettes to a Vietnamese nationalist named Ho Chi Minh and his Vietminh guerrillas in Indochina. Ho was a shadowy figure to us. None of my New Delhi colleagues had met him, but we all knew of his struggle against the Japanese. The Office of Strategic Services (OSS), that extraordinary combination of bluebloods and thugs that ran clandestine operations for the Americans in World War II, was helping Ho Chi Minh and supplying agents. I was in close touch with the OSS's small liaison group attached to Stilwell's headquarters in New Delhi.

Our OSS agents thought highly of Ho Chi Minh, and in the hurly-burly of the war any enemy of Japan was our friend. We helped anyone willing to shoot at the Japanese. I knew nothing of Ho's political leanings, and I am not sure anyone else did, either. But even if I had known he was a Communist, it wouldn't have mattered. After all, the Soviet Union was a major ally.

The future of American policy toward French Indochina first became an issue for me in mid-1944, when various Frenchmen, obviously OSS types, arrived in India asking to be parachuted into Indochina. None of us knew what Washington's policy drill was, so I sent a telegram back to the States telling of these Frenchmen and asking for a statement of U.S. policy.

Weeks passed, then months. Finally there came FDR's reply: "I don't want to hear any more about Indochina." Consequently, we had a gap in policy toward the region for a full year, with perhaps major consequences for the history of Southeast Asia.

After Roosevelt's death President Truman was so preoccupied with problems arising from the occupation of defeated Germany and winning the war against Japan that lost in the shuffle were FDR's postwar plans for Asia: that colonies such as India, Burma, Indochina, Indonesia, and Malaya emerge from World War II as independent nations. Very likely, we could never have imposed decolonization upon our allies immediately after the war; but except on rare occasion, we never made the effort, and when we did try, we failed. For example, we urged Churchill to return Hong Kong to China after Hong Kong was retaken, but Churchill thumbed his nose at us and sailed the British fleet into Hong Kong Harbor. There were limits to what we could do.

We were also limited in what we could do after the war. Following the war, French participation in both the Marshall Plan and the North Atlantic Treaty Organization was indispensable. This meant that Indochina stayed on the back burner. Good Franco-American relations were vital to the success of the Marshall Plan and NATO, and we could not allow those relations to be disrupted over Indochina.

We did undertake one or two halfhearted attempts to influence France to grant Indochina its independence, but we could have done better. In both law and diplomacy there is a substantial difference between rape and seduction, and I was convinced then and am convinced today that while we could not have forced France's hand, we could have seduced it more forcefully. Sharp arguments frequently broke out within the State Department, especially between the European and Far Eastern bureaus. In this debate, because of the fear of Russia, the imperative of NATO, and the critical role of France in rebuilding Western Europe, the Europeanists usually prevailed. They had Dean Acheson's support as well. Basically a "North Atlantic man," Acheson was a superb secretary of state, and yet he really didn't give a damn about the brown, yellow, black, and red peoples of the world. He wanted full cooperation with the French.

Roosevelt's instincts during the war were right. Colonialism was dead. These great areas in Asia had to become independent. Throughout this period, whatever policy we adopted, I believed that the countries of Indochina would eventually emerge as independent nations. But how and when should the United States encourage this trend? While I was entirely sympathetic with Dean Acheson that we must work with France, I hoped that Indochinese independence would develop in stages. The creation of associated states would be an important first step. Given the weakness of the French governments of the late 1940's, we believed that we could not publicly demand that France leave Indochina. Had we been as rough with France over Indochina as we were with the Dutch in Indonesia, we could easily have brought about the fall of a succession of French governments.

Fortunately we did make progress in Indonesia; I was a midwife of Indonesian independence, working closely with Secretary of State George Marshall on that issue. During a critical stage, Marshall told the Dutch prime minister, "You Dutch can't stay in Indonesia. You would bleed yourselves white if you tried, and you'd still have to get out." That military judgment by our World War II chief of staff really impressed the Dutch. They simply didn't have the muscle to stop Indonesian independence; indeed, the effort would have taxed the resources of any country. Indonesia's peoples, in the late 1940's, numbered some eighty million, scattered among dozens of islands and stretched over three thousand miles. Military occupation was nearly impossible.

Despite our success with the Dutch in Indonesia, sharp controversies remained within the department over Indochina. At one point Acheson insisted that Far Eastern Affairs, meaning me, restrain its views. As an officer of the government I had already acquired what my wife calls an "infinite capacity to adjust to the inevitable," and I followed Acheson's instructions; I had no trouble remembering he was my boss. By 1949 American support of anticolonialism in Southeast Asia was giving way to developments elsewhere: We were strongly influenced by instability in Europe, the Berlin blockade of 1948, and the recent Communist takeover of China.

The weak French governments of the late 1940's and early 1950's also complicated the picture. Not one was politically strong enough to withstand the domestic criticism sure to be triggered by relinquishing Indochina, but on the other hand, if we pressed the French too hard, they might throw up their hands and say, "All right, Uncle Sam, we are leaving. Indochina is now your baby." The British did exactly that in Greece. We had our hands full in the late 1940's, and we didn't want Indochina in our basket.

But frankly I never thought that the French would stay indefinitely in Indochina. Whatever our policy, whatever the French did, I believed the countries of Indochina would inevitably emerge as independent nations.

We did press the French to move toward a political settlement in Indochina, encourage home rule, allow nationalist forces in Southeast Asia a chance to work out their own solutions, and eventually work toward complete independence. In fact, France split Indochina into three "associated states"—Cambodia, Laos, and Vietnam—that remained within the French Union. But it didn't help matters when the French diverted some Marshall Plan aid to Indochina for military purposes. This further added to the tension since such use was far removed from the purpose of the Marshall Plan. In any case, this delay of Indochinese independence gave Ho and other Communists a chance to rally and align with authentic nationalist forces, and nationalism drove the Vietminh rebellion.

Harry Truman did not take a strong personal interest in Southeast Asia until the Korean War started in June 1950, and even then, his interest in the region—as was State's—was piqued mostly by the growth of Chinese military assistance to Ho Chi Minh's forces and by concern that China might take over its neighbors to the south. Chinese aid was not large during the early 1950's, perhaps a few hundred tons a month in 1951 and 1952, but it nevertheless showed us that the Chinese were interested in and involved with Ho. Chinese intervention in Korea showed that Mao would use his "volunteers" outside China. We were thus naturally concerned he might look to the south as well. In fact, after the Korean War began, we were no longer concerned about France's diversion of Marshall Plan aid to Indochina. We even increased Marshall Plan aid to France specifically so more French support could go to Indochina. We were concerned that the Korean War signaled the onset of a major Communist onslaught in Asia and perhaps beyond.

By the early 1950s I had become convinced of the strategic, political, and economic importance of Southeast Asia not only to the United States but to other countries in the western Pacific, and I argued for continuing American economic and military assistance to the region.

I left government service in January 1953, when the Eisenhower administration came into office, and consequently am not familiar with the inner workings of U.S. policy toward Indochina during the next eight years. But I tried to stay abreast of events, particularly those surrounding the battle of Dien Bien Phu and the Geneva negotiations on Indochina, both in 1954, and the creation of the Southeast Asian Treaty Organization (SEATO) in 1955.

Concluded hard on the heels of the disastrous French defeat at Dien Bien Phu, the Geneva agreements contained obvious seeds of future trouble. Large numbers of Vietnamese were told they had to relocate, Vietnam was split into two parts with its future dependent on an election to be held in two years, and the North was controlled by a militant Communist regime. It seemed inevitable that North Vietnam would become a center of aggression against the rest of Southeast Asia. Rather than stamp American approval on an agreement confirming the Communist nature of North Vietnam, John Foster Dulles walked out of the conference. The United States did not sign the 1954 accords, although Dulles's representative, Walter Bedell Smith, issued a statement that the United States would consider any attempt to upset those agreements by force a threat to the peace.

The Eisenhower administration was also sharply divided over the course to take in Indochina. We outsiders could almost plot the temper in Washington by the whereabouts of John Foster Dulles. When he was in Washington, the possibility of American intervention seemed to increase. But when Dulles was traveling, President Eisenhower's innate caution often asserted itself. In the aftermath of the French defeat at Dien Bien Phu in 1954, Eisenhower decided not to send American troops or air power to assist the French, and I believe that was the right decision. I was intrigued with an idea floating around Washington of moving American troops into the Red River delta of North Vietnam to repair roads, improve communication and transportation, and help rebuild North Vietnam. But in retrospect, an American presence, however helpful and well intentioned, wouldn't have stemmed the tide of communism in North Vietnam.

Some confusion surrounded the U.S. role at Geneva and our unwillingness to live with the agreements signed there. The passage of time has done little to clear it up. But when we look back on the record of the 1950's, American decisions not to intervene militarily, not to sign the agreements, and then to support the government in South Vietnam seem defensible. Ho Chi Minh was clearly a Vietnamese nationalist, but he was a nationalist with an appetite. Throughout his life he made clear that he wanted Vietnam to gain control over Laos and Cambodia as well as South Vietnam, even though Laotians and Cambodians sharply resented those ambitions. Ho was clearly determined to bring all of what had formerly been French Indochina under his control. Given the international climate of the 1950's, U.S. policy makers also could not overlook the fact that Ho had allied himself with the Soviet Union and with China, even though in retrospect he may not have been under control of either.

With Ho's expansionist tendencies, the terms of the negotiations at Geneva raise the interesting question of why Ho signed them. I suspect that one or more parties to the conference, perhaps the Soviets, Chinese, or maybe even the French, said to Ho Chi Minh in effect, "Go ahead, you're going to get what you want in the long run anyway. Reunification elections are supposed to be held in 1956, and regardless, you'll still have the strongest military force in Indochina." After the elections of 1956 were not held, and after President Ngo Dinh Diem was relatively successful in establishing his Saigon regime, Ho Chi Minh might have felt betrayed by those who earlier made under-the-rug suggestions that Indochina was eventually his for the taking. These developments may have helped trigger his decision to go after South Vietnam.

U.S. dissatisfaction with the Geneva agreements played a major role in the creation of SEATO in 1955. For a host of reasons, at the end of World War II and throughout the late 1940's and early 1950's, the Truman administration thought it unwise to involve the United States in security treaties on the Asian mainland. President Truman thought we should stay offshore, largely because of our own experience in Asia and the experiences of colonial powers before, during, and after the war. The Japanese in China, the British in India, and the Americans in CBI had never been able to impose their will upon the masses of Asia.

Purely military considerations weighed heavily against alliances on the mainland. America had demobilized after the war. We were short of forces. During the Truman years some of us felt that the United States must not try to bluff its way through the obligations of a mutual security treaty. If the United States entered a treaty, it must make good on its promises. By staying offshore with our alliances, we could involve American sea and air power with great effect; thus the ANZUS Treaty and our agreements with Japan and the Philippines. The Joints Chiefs themselves were not enthusiastic about taking on additional commitments in the Pacific. For example, although they considered Taiwan strategically important to the United States, they furnished no military support for its defense. In 1950 the chiefs told the State Department, "You've got to defend Taiwan with diplomatic means."

We also thought that if the United States aligned itself with some but not all nations in Southeast Asia, the American presence would become a divisive element within Southeast Asia. We believed the United States should wait until the entire region developed a security consciousness, and then this country could stand behind the region as a whole. For all these reasons, the Truman administration did not push for a Southeast Asia treaty.

But the Eisenhower administration saw things differently. In 1955, believing that the situation in Asia had changed, President Eisenhower drew up security treaties with South Korea, Taiwan, and the countries of Southeast Asia—with Thailand and the Philippines as signatories of the SEATO Treaty, and South Vietnam, Laos, and Cambodia as proto-col states—extending an American collective security pledge to the Asian mainland. SEATO was a comprehensive pledge, accepting re-sponsibility for the security of the protocol states, even though they didn't sit at the conference table or have a vote on matters affecting SEATO.

Although I was out of government and watching only from the sidelines, I thought the SEATO Treaty was a mistake. Of course, we in the Kennedy and Johnson administrations made our own decisions on Vietnam, and events of the 1960's remain our responsibility, but I think the die for American commitment to Southeast Asia was cast in 1955. When the United States signed that treaty, SEATO became the law of the land and linked South Vietnam to the general structure of collective security.

I was amazed, even dismayed, by the casual way the Senate ratified the SEATO Treaty. Senate debate was limited, and unlike the NATO case, there was little public discussion. No one really stopped to think what an American commitment to collective security on the Asian mainland might mean. Nevertheless, there was no way that anyone in the Senate could have voted for that treaty—it passed 82–1—without realizing what it was. In Article IV each party recognizes that "aggres-sion by means of armed attack in the treaty area would endanger its own peace and safety, and agrees that it will in that event act to meet the common danger in accordance with its constitutional processes." Article IV binds each party separately; it doesn't require a collective finding. Nor could there be any doubt about what the United States believed itself committed to in the event of a North Vietnamese assault on the South. When testifying before the Senate Foreign Relations Committee, John Foster Dulles specifically stated that Article IV cov-ered an armed attack "by the regime of Ho Chi Minh."

The mid-fifties was the era of "massive retaliation," a "bigger bang for a buck" doctrine that did not require ground forces but relied instead on American strategic naval and air power and the threatened use of nuclear weapons. With massive retaliation backing up our treaty obligations, we may have entered SEATO "on the cheap," without fully recognizing the price we might have to pay to back up our treaty pledges.

We in the Kennedy administration knew before we took office that we would have to deal with Indochinese affairs. It was evident that the situation was deteriorating, especially in Laos. The day before Kennedy's inauguration, on January 19, 1961, four of us—Robert McNamara, Clark Clifford, I, and President Kennedy—met with Dwight Eisenhower for a final conference. In that session Eisenhower offered Kennedy only two specific pieces of advice in foreign affairs: the first, don't extend American recognition to Red China, and the second, put American troops into Laos, "with others if possible, alone if necessary." He told Kennedy that he himself had not taken that action because he regarded Laos as a long-term problem best left for the incoming president. Eisenhower's advice contrasted sharply with his cautious approach to Indochina during the French crisis there. Nevertheless, that was his advice.

In 1961 the situation in Laos was dire indeed. North Vietnamese and Pathet Lao forces were close to victory, supported by a Soviet airlift in their drive to take over the country. We looked long and hard at the Laotian situation, and the more we looked, the more forbidding was the prospect of landing American troops. Laos is landlocked. The terrain did not lend itself to military operations, and communications and logistics with the United States would have been most difficult. More important, the Laotians themselves were a gentle people, with little interest in killing each other. When only Laotian forces were on the battlefield, a few explosions made one whale of a battle; there were rarely serious casualties. We heard that the two conflicting sides in Laos once left a battlefield to attend a water festival. After ten days they went back to the battlefield. In a later incident King Vatthana Savang called his top officials and nobles to the royal capital of Luang Prabang for funeral services to bury his father. Knowing that Pathet Lao and North Vietnamese forces were only about thirty-five miles away, our ambassador cautioned the king, "Your Majesty, is it really safe to gather all your top people for this occasion? These forces could easily move in and seize you." The king said with much conviction, "They won't do that! I am burying my father!"

Because of the weakness of Laotian armed forces and the Laotians' own gentle nature, we concluded that an American stand against Communist aggression in Laos would have been frustrated by the Laotians themselves. I opposed committing American troops to the defense of Laos. Rather than land American troops, Kennedy and I agreed that we should try for a political settlement. We entered negotiations with North Vietnam at the Laos conference of 1961–62, under the co-chairmanship of Great Britain and the Soviet Union. Our hope was that everyone would get out of Laos—we, the French, the North Vietnamese, and so on—and let the Laotians manage or mismanage their own affairs. We wanted an agreement that produced a neutral but independent Laos, an "island of peace" in Southeast Asia that would be a buffer zone between North Vietnam and its neighbors.

And we made concessions. We agreed to a coalition government in Laos made up of right-wing, neutralist, and Communist elements. We agreed that the International Control Commission (ICC) comprised of Canada, Poland, and India would supervise the settlement. We accepted Souvanna Phouma, a neutralist, as the Laotian prime minister, even though he was clearly the Soviet candidate and not our own. And after two long years of negotiations, conducted brilliantly by Averell Harriman, we concluded the Laos accords in July 1962.

Unfortunately the North Vietnamese failed to observe them. They went ahead with their effort to take over Laos, violating the agreements in many ways. They wouldn't let the coalition government operate in those areas held by Vietnamese forces and wouldn't let the International Control Commission monitor those areas. The North Vietnamese continued to use Laos as an infiltration route into South Vietnam, and they refused to withdraw their own forces from Laos.

The failure of North Vietnam to honor those Laotian accords was a bitter disappointment for John Kennedy. Its impact upon him has been greatly underestimated. The presence of substantial numbers of North Vietnamese troops in Laos was clearly contrary to international law, and their activities destroyed the civil war aspects of the Laotian conflict. The Laotian accords were quite acceptable to the United States had they been complied with.

When it became clear that North Vietnam was flouting the accords, we sought British and Soviet pressure on Hanoi. However, the Soviets would not go along, fearing that pressure would simply drive North Vietnam into the arms of China. That triangular relationship more or less neutralized Soviet influence on North Vietnam.

The United States continued to comply with the Laos accords of 1962. We pulled American personnel out of Laos and did our best to cooperate with the ICC. As a matter of policy, we were prepared to pull out of Laos entirely and let it become a neutral buffer state between North Vietnam, Thailand, and Cambodia. We didn't step up clandestine activities in Laos until after it became apparent that North Vietnam was not complying with the agreements. Given North Vietnam's intransigence, I fully supported the decision to step up U.S. covert activities.

Then Laotian Premier Phoumi Nosavan insisted that American activities inside Laos be conducted covertly and not be publicly acknowledged. Phoumi was generally supportive of our actions but didn't want to tie his own hands to them. We complied with his wishes, although our covert role later got us in trouble with the press and the American people when these activities became known. We didn't want to acknowledge publicly what we were doing, both because of Phoumi's position and because we knew that Hanoi would not acknowledge its own illegal activity. All in all, another contribution to what later became known as the credibility gap. Even after repeated violations of the accords, first by North Vietnam and then by the United States, we worked hard to preserve the accords if only in appearance. They were an excellent framework for a future Laotian settlement, and we gave them up with great reluctance.

Deteriorating conditions in Laos increased pressure on South Vietnam. At the time Kennedy decided not to put American troops in Laos, he told us, "If we have to fight for Southeast Asia, we'll fight in South Vietnam." The South Vietnamese seemed far more willing to defend themselves, and with South Vietnam accessible by sea, our supply lines were simpler. American air and naval power could readily be brought to bear in South Vietnam. Diplomacy had not worked in Laos. North Vietnamese troops and guerrillas were on the march, prepared to shoot at all who stood in their way. Should we get out of their way or shoot back? That was the question posed by the collapse of the Laotian accords.

John Kennedy never questioned that Southeast Asia was vital to American security. His only question: Where should we fight if we had to fight? His decision: South Vietnam.

During the late 1950's, then, the United States was openly supporting the Diem government and making good progress in helping them build a viable South Vietnamese state. Many of us thought that the "two Vietnams" solution was workable, just the way the two-Germanys, two-Koreas, and two-Chinas solutions were proving to be. No one was too concerned that the reunification elections scheduled for 1956 had not been held; after all, neither the United States nor South Vietnam was a party to the Geneva accords that sanctioned the elections, and no one had figured out a way to hold fair elections anyway.

Starting in 1959, possibly over concern that South Vietnam was becoming a viable state, Ho Chi Minh began to infiltrate men to the South to undermine the Diem regime. At first these infiltrators were southerners who had moved north during 1954 and 1955 under the relocation terms of the Geneva accords, but by 1960 infiltrators included northerners: And the numbers had increased as well.

When John Kennedy took office, the United States had no more than 685 military advisers in South Vietnam, the number permitted under the 1954 Geneva accords. By agreement with the French, the Eisenhower administration had substituted American advisers for French, and even though neither the United States nor South Vietnam ever signed the 1954 accords, the Kennedy administration decided to stay within the accords' constraints regarding advisers.

In those years American advisers were primarily supply, communications, and ordnance personnel who advised the South Vietnamese on the use of American equipment supplied under our military assistance program. We were clearly and openly supporting the Diem government and making good progress in building a viable South Vietnamese state.

By early 1961 the optimism of the late 1950's had waned. After it became apparent that the limited American assistance effort would not do the job, President Kennedy secretly ordered 500 Special Forces and other military advisers to South Vietnam. As far as I know, this was the first time the United States went above the 685-man limit, but since North Vietnam was already violating the agreements and we had not signed them, we didn't feel bound by them.

All this happened in May, just after the Bay of Pigs fiasco and before the Vienna summit with Khrushchev. Conditions in Laos and South Vietnam continued to deteriorate. In October, wanting a detailed report by people he trusted, President Kennedy sent White House military adviser General Maxwell Taylor and National Security Council assistant Walt Rostow, McGeorge Bundy's deputy, to Vietnam to assess the situation. We all had great confidence in Taylor, a broad-minded counselor with a brilliant military record.

Shortly before the Taylor-Rostow mission arrived in Saigon, South Vietnamese President Ngo Dinh Diem asked for U.S. combat troops and declared a state of emergency. After meeting with Diem, in an "eyes only" report to President Kennedy, Taylor recommended stepping up American military assistance to South Vietnam in a "limited partnership," that American pilots and helicopters fly South Vietnamese troops into battle, and that six thousand to eight thousand American combat troops be sent to Vietnam under the guise of a flood-control mission to stiffen the South Vietnamese further. He also cautioned that additional troops might be needed.

I was in Japan when I received a copy of Taylor's recommendations. On November 1, 1961, I cabled President Kennedy, stressing that the decision to put U.S. military forces in Vietnam was a portentous decision, that the road ahead was exceptionally difficult, and that we should not make such a commitment unless we were prepared to see it through. I also questioned what there was to support in South Vietnam. The critical part of my cable read as follows:

Since General Taylor may receive first full report prior to my return, believe special attention should be given to the critical question whether Diem is prepared to take necessary measures to give us something worth supporting. If Diem unwilling to trust military commanders to get job done and take steps to consolidate non-communist elements into a serious national effort, it is difficult to see how a handful of American troops could have decisive influence. While attaching greatest possible importance to the security of Southeast Asia, I would be reluctant to see the United States make major additional commitments of American prestige to a losing horse.

Other considerations also led me to send this cable. We were in the middle of negotiations over Laos at the time, and I feared that sending U.S. troops to Vietnam might jeopardize the talks. A low level of North Vietnamese infiltration and the ongoing Berlin crisis increased my reluctance to make additional commitments to South Vietnam.

My cable of November 1 later surfaced in the *Pentagon Papers,* giving rise to speculation that I had been an early dove among Kennedy's advisers. But I didn't necessarily oppose sending combat troops to Vietnam; I just wanted Kennedy to realize that this was truly a fateful decision with enormous consequences. I also didn't want us to go gung ho into Southeast Asia until we saw how the Laos agreements worked out.

I was sympathetic to the recommendations of the Taylor-Rostow mission, although I preferred sending military advisers openly, rather than a thinly disguised flood-control effort. I was skeptical about trying to provide that kind of cover and felt that if we wanted to send troops, we ought to be straightforward about it. But I agreed with President Kennedy's decision to increase our assistance.

Ten days after my Japan cable, Secretary of Defense Robert

McNamara and I gave President Kennedy another memorandum stressing the importance of an American commitment to South Vietnam:

The loss of South Vietnam to Communism would not only destroy SEATO but would undermine the credibility of American commitments elsewhere. Further, loss of South Vietnam would stimulate bitter domestic controversies in the United States and would be seized upon by extreme elements to divide the country and harass the administration. . . .

The United States should commit itself to the clear objective of preventing the fall of South Vietnam to Communists. The basic means for accomplishing this objective must be to put the Government of South Vietnam [GVN] into a position to win its own war against the guerrillas. We must insist that the government itself take the measures necessary for the purpose in exchange for large-scale United States assistance in the military, economic, and political fields. At the same time we must recognize that it will probably not be possible for the GVN to win this war as long as the flow of men and supplies from North Vietnam continues unchecked and the guerrillas enjoy a safe sanctuary in neighboring territory.

We should be prepared to introduce United States combat forces if that should become necessary for success. Dependent upon the circumstances, it may also be necessary for United States forces to strike at the source of the aggression in North Vietnam.

At first blush it may appear that I had changed my mind between November 1 and November 11, but this was not so. In my cable from Japan I pointed out the seriousness of introducing American troops; in the November 11 memorandum I stressed the importance of Vietnam and why we might have to send those forces. Throughout this period I believed that we had to help the South Vietnamese without adopting the war as our own. We also had to encourage Diem to broaden his political base. Of Kennedy's advisers, only George Ball opposed a gradual increase in support. Disagreement among my colleagues existed over how fast we should build up our effort, but not over the commitment itself.

Contrary to views expressed later, the Kennedy administration did not "drift" into its commitment to South Vietnam. President Kennedy, his other top-level advisers, and I gave Vietnam our full attention. I don't think we were naive. We knew that tough days lay ahead, although none of us except George Ball guessed how tough indeed they would be.

From the very beginning of the Kennedy administration we spent long hours boxing the compass of all options regarding South Vietnam, but to my recollection, we never seriously considered the option of outright withdrawal and allowing South Vietnam to be overrun by the Communists. We took for granted that the United States had a treaty commitment to South Vietnam and that South Vietnam's security was important to the security of the United States. We also took for granted that if we failed "to take steps to meet the common danger," our network of collective security treaties throughout the world might erode through a judgment made by the Communists that these treaties were a bluff. At no time did we say to ourselves, "We will put in X number of men but no more. If the other side continues to escalate, then we'll just pull out." At no time did we think that the American people would not support an effort to prevent Southeast Asia from going Communist.

North Vietnamese violation of the July 1962 Laos accords strongly influenced our decision making on Vietnam. In late 1961 we had perhaps a thousand U.S. servicemen in Vietnam; when the Laos accords were signed, perhaps six thousand. With any semblance of North Vietnamese adherence to the accords, we could have entertained the idea of a neutralized South Vietnam. In view of Hanoi's wholesale violation of the accords, we didn't believe Hanoi would accept a neutral South Vietnam. We were convinced that such an arrangement would have solved nothing, resulted in Hanoi's takeover of all Vietnam, and created continuing problems for Laos, Cambodia, Thailand, and perhaps the rest of Southeast Asia. That was the way I saw it in the early sixties, and nothing that has happened since suggests to me that this view was wrong.

As President Kennedy increased our advisory role from 685 administrative and logistical personnel to 18,000 military advisers between 1961 and 1963, the United States gradually committed itself to the security of South Vietnam. We undertook this buildup in stages, and I agreed with and supported the early decisions and the later ones as well.

To be sure, the situation in South Vietnam in the early 1960's was grim, but to some extent my views were affected by my own experiences and memories of other dark situations that worked out for the better. Ten years before, American and South Korean forces had been driven into a tiny perimeter around Pusan. The situation looked extremely grim. General MacArthur at one stage recommended that we withdraw from the Korean peninsula. In World War II, three months after the Japanese attack on Pearl Harbor, Allied resistance was collapsing all over the globe. German armies had attacked Russia, Rommel was driving through North Africa toward Cairo, and the Japanese had destroyed our fleet at Pearl Harbor.

Having lived through dark times before, I was not willing to yield to pessimism in Vietnam just because the outlook was bleak. And I discouraged that kind of thinking by my colleagues, except at the very highest levels, believing that those kinds of policy reappraisals would inevitably leak to the press and cast doubt on the sincerity of the American commitment. Had this happened, pessimism could easily have become a self-fulfilling prophecy.

President Kennedy hoped that economic aid and advisory support would enable the South Vietnamese to handle North Vietnamese aggression themselves, without the direct involvement of American combat troops. He did not want to Americanize the war or send large numbers of U.S. forces to help South Vietnam deal with what was then a relatively low level of infiltration from North Vietnam. When this infiltration increased and conditions in South Vietnam continued to deteriorate, we still hoped to limit our role to an advisory nature. Throughout the Kennedy years and the first year of the Johnson administration, we tried to help the South Vietnamese do this job themselves. This approach had worked in combating Communist guerrillas in Greece.

For me, the issue at stake in Vietnam was collective security. In 1961 the United States had a treaty commitment to South Vietnam and forty-two other allies. The integrity of the American commitment to collective security involves the life and death of our nation. When an American president makes a commitment, what he says must be believed. If those opposing us think that the word of the United States is not worth very much, then those treaties lose their deterrent effect and the structure of peace dissolves rapidly. If the president cannot be believed, we will face dangers we've never dreamed of.

By 1962, when we were considering whether to build up American forces in Vietnam, the United States had just come through two dangerous crises. We had in our minds this question: What might have happened had Nikita Khrushchev not believed John Kennedy during the Berlin crisis of 1961–62 or the Cuban missile crisis of October 1962? There could easily have been general war.

The credibility of an American president at a time of crisis and the fidelity of the United States to its security treaties are not just empty matters of face and prestige. They are pillars of peace in a dangerous world. When John Kennedy took office in January 1961, the SEATO

Treaty was part of the law of the land. That treaty linked South Vietnam to the entire structure of collective security, created at such painful cost in the postwar period. In Vietnam I felt our honor as a nation was at stake. Honor is not an empty eighteenth-century concept or a question of one prince's being offended by a neighboring prince. This word, "honor," is a matter of the deepest concern to the life and death of our nation. When the president of the United States makes a commitment, it is vitally important that what he says is believed. When both my presidents said, "Gentlemen, you are not going to take over South Vietnam by force," I felt we had to make good on that pledge.

As we gradually stepped up our presence in South Vietnam during 1962 and early 1963, my concern about the political situation there continued to rise. I saw no way to help improve South Vietnam's military position unless President Diem began governing more effectively.

I had met Ngo Dinh Diem once before in 1957, when I was president of the Rockefeller Foundation. Diem had inquired about agricultural assistance. We did not fund his project, but I was impressed with him. He seemed to be a genuine nationalist, an experienced and successful leader, and dedicated to his country. Diem helped reconcile dissident sects within South Vietnam and presided over growing economic prosperity. He impressed me as being a doughty fighter, committed to the independence and security of South Vietnam. We appreciated his staunchness.

But in the early 1960's President Diem lost touch with his own people. For reasons we never quite understood, Diem came to rely upon his brother Ngo Dinh Nhu and his wife, Madame Nhu, rather unsavory characters who appealed to Diem's darker instincts. Also, Diem was very suspicious of anyone who did not support his views, so he permitted no "loyal opposition" in South Vietnam; political opponents were treated harshly. His regime became increasingly repressive, and he alienated Buddhists, students, and elements of the armed forces. Much of this may have been due to the activities of his brother Nhu and Madame Nhu, but clearly Diem lost the support of his people. I hoped that Diem would get rid of his brother, ameliorate his repressive policies, and get on with the job of governing South Vietnam. We tried unsuccessfully to persuade Diem to remove the Nhus from government and at one point urged Diem to send his brother as the South Vietnamese ambassador to Washington, where we could keep an eye on him.

Failing to convince Diem to end his repressions of the Buddhists and broaden his base of political support, we held up economic assistance, protested through diplomatic channels, and had our ambassador, Henry Cabot Lodge, pursue a policy of aloofness in his relationship with Diem as a sign of our displeasure. But our actions had little effect. We didn't want to be positioned as supporting Diem's repressions of the Buddhists, and yet cutting back on American aid may have encouraged those contemplating a coup d'état. We were on the horns of a dilemma.

In the summer of 1963, as the Nhus' private army brutally crushed Buddhist opposition, a lively debate broke out within the administration over whether the defense of South Vietnam could succeed with Diem in power. Some elements within the administration—including the CIA, United States Information Agency (USIA), State Department, our Saigon embassy—and some *New York Times* reporters felt we ought to nudge Diem into retirement or even conspire with other elements in South Vietnam to bring about a coup d'état. I was personally repelled by Diem's repressive rule but uncomfortable with talk about trying to replace him, thinking this was not a decision for Americans to make. In any event, coup d'états don't always produce better leadership.

But it was clear in the wake of the Nhus' brutal suppression of the Buddhists that the Nhus would have to go if Diem's government were to survive. What to do if Diem refused to part with his brother was less clear.

On August 24, 1963, on a Saturday when President Kennedy, Robert McNamara, and I were all out of town, Undersecretary of State George Ball, Assistant Secretary of State for Far Eastern Affairs Roger Hilsman, Undersecretary of State for Political Affairs Averell Harriman, and White House specialist for Vietnamese affairs Michael Forrestal drafted a cable to be sent to our ambassador in Saigon, Henry Cabot Lodge, that said in part: "U.S. Government cannot tolerate situation in which power lies in Nhu's hands. Diem must be given chance to rid himself of Nhu and his coterie and replace them with best military and political personalities available.

"If in spite of all of our efforts, Diem remains obdurate and refuses, then we must face the possibility that Diem himself cannot be preserved."

George Ball called me on an open phone and in rather guarded tones read me the cable. I thought George told me Kennedy agreed with this cable. I later learned that Kennedy had said, "I will approve it if Rusk and McNamara approve it." But at the time, thinking Kennedy's approval restricted my own freedom of action, especially in dealing with such a sensitive matter on an unclassified phone, I gave my concurrence. I added one provision: that we continue to furnish assistance to the South Vietnamese even if the Saigon command structure broke down.

When Kennedy, McNamara, and I returned to Washington that Monday—August 26—we looked at this cable and realized that it went further than we wanted to go. At that time the United States had only a small presence in South Vietnam. We did not have the power to sustain Diem if the Buddhists, students, the armed forces, and his own people were determined to get rid of him. Nor did we have the power to unseat him if he had the support of his people. In any event, I felt that it was not up to Americans to decide whether Diem should stay in office; that was a matter for the people of South Vietnam.

We had a rather stormy meeting at the White House that Monday. I more or less summed up the general confusion by observing that if the situation in Vietnam didn't change, we would be heading toward a disaster, but at the same time we couldn't encourage a coup. After some reflection we realized that our Saturday cable was precipitous, and we took steps to pull back on it, in effect withdrawing our authorizing Lodge to encourage a coup. We did not want to be a prime mover in any coup d'état.

The cable was not entirely a bolt from the blue, as the issue that prompted it—political turmoil in Saigon—was under lively discussion in Washington. But the Saturday cable was a snafu to which we all contributed. We should never have sent so important a cable without meeting separately on it and all of us flyspecking the text.

Three days later Ambassador Lodge cabled back his objections to withdrawing American support for a coup: "We are launched on a course from which there is no respectable turning back, the overthrow of the Diem government. There is no turning back because U.S. prestige is already committed to this end in large measure and will become more so as the facts leak out. In a more fundamental sense there is no turning back, because there is no possibility in my view that the war can be won under a Diem administration."

Lodge proposed that aid to Diem be halted, that this was the signal awaited by the generals to launch the coup, and that its outcome would depend "at least as much on us as on them."

My own position remained what it had always been: that the real problem was the Nhus more than Diem and that they had to go. I sent a cable back to Lodge asking for his views about whether the Nhus could be somehow removed from office with Diem staying on, and

Lodge said it couldn't be done. Even after I got Lodge's response, it seemed to me that the situation was not that clear-cut, nor would a coup likely improve it. But I strongly believed that Diem had to reconcile with the Buddhists, who amounted to 95 percent of the population. And if he did not, the end of his regime was in sight, however the end came. I didn't feel that the United States could acquiesce in Diem's repressions of the Buddhists.

With my thinking that our support for a coup had been withdrawn, the situation in Saigon continued to percolate through September and on into October. A flurry of cable activity in early October stressed that the United States did not want to encourage a coup. But then, on October 6, President Kennedy cabled Lodge that "the United States will not thwart a coup." Lodge later claimed that was his green light to move ahead.

While I don't remember all the details of this cable traffic or any effort by Washington to encourage a coup, we definitely wanted to follow the coup planning to know what was going on. There were lots of cables between Washington and Saigon during this period, routed through the State Department. I believe I read them all. I doubt there was back-channel communication between Lodge and Kennedy that I didn't know about. My impression remains that after the August 24 cable we took steps to withdraw authorization for encouraging a coup d'état, that we wanted to keep tabs on developments but not actively promote or be involved in a coup.

Obviously there were discrepancies between how I saw the situation in Saigon from where I sat in Washington and what various Americans were doing on the streets in Saigon. Some of our people may have encouraged the generals to undertake a coup d'état. I have some doubts as to the precise role which President Kennedy played. I talked often with Kennedy during these weeks, and I wanted the United States to keep a distance from this turmoil in Saigon because our commitment to South Vietnam would require us to pick up the pieces and try to work with whatever leader and government emerged. It may be that Ambassador Lodge at times pumped up the generals or otherwise fudged on our desire not to commit the United States to a coup. I can only recall my own participation, and even this is sketchy.

I cannot vouch for what various Americans in our mission might have said to various South Vietnamese in the weeks preceding the November coup. If they pledged American support in overthrowing Diem, they did so without authorization from the president and secretary of state. I am convinced that when the South Vietnamese generals moved to overthrow Diem, it was their show—their judgment that he could no longer run the country and their decision to remove him. I personally believe that opposition forces generated by President Diem himself and his repressive policies led to his downfall. In situations involving personal jeopardy, when plotters make what John Locke called the "appeal to God" and put their own lives on the line, the United States is a long way off.

Clearly, Henry Cabot Lodge was more supportive of a coup than we were in Washington. Lodge was a man of great stature, a take-charge type accustomed to exercising authority. That was why we sent him to South Vietnam. He was on the scene, and I encouraged my colleagues to delegate heavily to him. And necessarily so—during political confusion in foreign capitals, Washington cannot call the shots. Accounts that Lodge may have played a more active role in the coup than we wanted don't surprise me. But even if this happened, his ability to influence events was limited because the real decisions were in the hands of the South Vietnamese generals.

We did tell Cabot Lodge to try to insure Diem's safety in the event of a coup. When Lodge heard the coup was under way, he telephoned Diem and offered to make arrangements for his safe departure from the country. But in hopes of finding military units that would support him, Diem rebuffed this offer, was captured and killed. Had we been as actively involved in the coup as others suggest, we could at least have prevented Diem's death.

We all were shocked by the news of President Diem's assassination. President Kennedy had a grudging appreciation for Diem and realized that he faced massive difficulties in trying to rule his country. Vice President Johnson was especially disturbed by the assassination, having met with Diem personally in Asia. He thought Diem's overthrow was a great mistake. I myself was deeply distressed but hoped that his successors would bring greater unity to the country.

The immediate result of Diem's downfall was positive since South Vietnam no longer had public demonstrations in the streets and civil chaos in Saigon. General Duong Van Minh's ascension to power led to widespread rejoicing in Saigon and much of South Vietnam; he had become a national hero by resisting the Japanese occupation during World War II and was popular with the people.

But the bloom soon wore off; one coup followed another in rapid succession. South Vietnam had repeated changes of government after the Diem assassination. Almost every political leader had his own party, and the military itself broke up into small cliques that were unable to act as a cohesive group. The generals were unable to subordinate their personal ambitions to the war effort, and I resented this enormously. I sometimes wondered if this reflected the French political tradition where every politician has his own party. This lack of social cohesion that most Western democracies enjoy gave reality to the question I raised in 1961, What is there to support? That problem continued to plague our efforts.

Constant turmoil in Saigon adversely affected American aid; each change of government narrowed the base of officials available for administrative duty. When the generals moved against Diem, officials who worked for Diem were considered ineligible for posts in the new government. That pattern repeated itself with each coup. We pressed all kinds of programs upon the South Vietnamese to improve agriculture, public health, and education and to help broaden the base of political support. We strongly encouraged the regime to implement these programs—I remember one count of forty-two—but this profusion was simply beyond the administrative capability of the South Vietnamese government. It didn't have the muscle to put them into effect.

Three weeks after Diem was killed, President Kennedy was assassinated in Dallas. As American involvement in Vietnam continued to escalate in subsequent years, the question inevitably arose about whether John Kennedy would have followed the same policy course that Lyndon Johnson did. This question became all the more important when, sometime after Kennedy's death, his appointments secretary, Kenneth O'Donnell, and Senator Mike Mansfield both commented that Kennedy had told them that he was planning to withdraw American troops from South Vietnam in 1965, following the elections of 1964.

Despite his frustration over Vietnam, I do not believe John Kennedy came to any such decision. I say this for two reasons, one unimportant reason and one critical. First, I talked with John Kennedy on hundreds of occasions about Southeast Asia, and not once did he ever suggest or even hint at withdrawal. This by itself is not conclusive, since for reasons of his own, Kennedy possibly didn't want to confide in me his future plans for Vietnam.

The important reason is that had he decided in 1963 on a 1965 withdrawal, he would have left Americans in a combat zone for domestic political purposes, and no president can do that. Neither Kennedy nor any other American president could live with himself or look his senior colleagues in the eye under those conditions. Had Kennedy said that to Bob McNamara or me in 1963, we would have told him, "If that is your decision, Mr. President, you must take them out now." John

F. Kennedy was the kind of man who would have seen that point immediately. Kennedy liked to bat the breeze and toss ideas around, and it is entirely possible that he left the impression with some that he planned on getting out of Vietnam in 1965. But that does not mean that he made a decision in 1963 to withdraw in 1965. Had he done so, I think I would have known about it.

Actually there was a period of optimism in the summer of 1963 when we thought the war was going well and we could begin to think of withdrawing American advisers. Unfortunately that optimism was based partially upon faulty reporting from the Diem regime about progress in the countryside. We compounded our intelligence problems by relying too heavily upon President Diem and his advisers. To my regret, Bob McNamara even publicly discussed bringing some troops home. But when we sent our own people into the countryside, we discovered the situation was less hopeful than we had thought.

Had Kennedy lived to witness the future in Southeast Asia, he might well have decided to withdraw from Vietnam. Kennedy's statements suggest that he might have stayed the course as well. In 1956, then senator from Massachusetts, Kennedy said that South Vietnam's independence was "crucial to the free world." In a news conference in September 1963, two months before his death, he summed up what he called "a very simple policy" in regard to Vietnam: "We want the war to be won, the Communists to be contained, and the Americans to go home. That is our policy. I am sure it is the policy of the people of Vietnam. We are not there to see a war lost."

President Kennedy's attitude on Vietnam should be derived from what he said and did while president, not what he may have said at tea table conversations or walks around the Rose Garden. That also is the standard by which his advisers will be judged, the standard by which public servants should always be judged. Kennedy strongly felt that the United States had a commitment to South Vietnam, that the security of Southeast Asia was important to the security of the United States, and that we could not let aggression in Asia develop a momentum that might threaten peace elsewhere. That was his policy, and the so-called Kennedy people who have portrayed him in a different light have missed the point.

28

America
Goes to War

When Lyndon Johnson became president in November 1963, he wanted to establish a sense of continuity from the Kennedy administration to his own in both domestic and foreign policy. Thus, Johnson made do with the same force levels— seventeen to eighteen thousand men—that Kennedy had sent to South Vietnam. Kennedy's policy clearly aimed at maintaining the independence of South Vietnam, Laos, and Cambodia, and Johnson's intended the same. For the first year and one-half of his presidency, Johnson pursued Kennedy's policy of providing military advisers and economic assistance, but expecting the South Vietnamese to deal with their own insurgency.

Throughout the early months of the Johnson administration we all were troubled by the chronic instability of South Vietnamese politics following Diem's assassination. Despite continuing political problems in Saigon, we had no choice but to support the regime in power. We all hoped for a stable government to evolve there, but with the continued North Vietnamese infiltration and our commitment to SEATO, we never gave serious consideration to withdrawing.

On August 2 and 3, 1964, we received reports that the USS *Maddox* and USS *C. Turner Joy,* American destroyers operating in the Gulf of Tonkin off the coast of North Vietnam, had been attacked by North Vietnamese torpedo boats in two separate incidents. Neither destroyer was hit. There is no doubt that the first attack took place, but we more or less brushed that aside as possibly the action of a trigger-happy local commander. Some doubt existed about whether a second attack ever occurred, but when we heard reports of a second attack, that raised the possibility that Hanoi might have decided to challenge the American presence in the Gulf of Tonkin.

I wasn't on the decks of those American destroyers that evening, but at the time, on the basis of the information available to us, we in Washington thought the second attack had occurred. The captains of those destroyers thought their ships had been attacked, and most convincing to me, our intercepts of North Vietnamese radio transmissions suggested that the North Vietnamese thought a second attack was in progress. The Republic of Vietnam today celebrates August 2—the day of the Tonkin Gulf attacks—as part of its national war effort against the Americans, so whatever happened that night in the Tonkin Gulf, evidently it takes credit for it now.

Lyndon Johnson was not looking for a pretext to launch retaliatory raids or escalate the war. Had he wanted a pretext, we could have used the first attack. Our two destroyers were on intelligence-gathering missions in international waters, and the American Navy had a right to operate in those waters. North Vietnam was using coastal waters to infiltrate men and arms into South Vietnam; from our point of view, this conduct was contrary to international law. South Vietnam under the doctrine of self-defense was trying to block this infiltration and mount retaliatory raids of its own—a secret operation called 34-A, supported by the American Navy. But the destroyers attacked in the Gulf of Tonkin were on intelligence-gathering missions, not participating in South Vietnamese actions along the coast. It is entirely possible that the North Vietnamese thought that our destroyers were involved in these 34-A raids and in blockading operations along North Vietnam's coast to stop their infiltration of the South by sea. But even if Hanoi thought this, it isn't valid to call the exercise of self-defense a provocation.

After the second attack President Johnson called together about thirty congressional leaders, briefed them on what had happened, and told them about the retaliatory air strikes he intended to order. He then reminded them of President Truman's experience with Senator Robert Taft at the outbreak of the Korean War. Despite congressional assurances that Truman should respond to the North Korean invasion without seeking Congress's authorization, Taft had attacked Truman publicly.

Lyndon Johnson's memories of that experience were the real genesis of the Tonkin Gulf Resolution. Shortly after becoming president, Johnson told us, "If we stay in South Vietnam much longer or have to take firmer action, we've got to go to Congress." Various drafts of what eventually became the resolution circulated around the State Department long before the actual attacks occurred. But when the time came, we put aside those drafts, worked with the members of the Senate Foreign Relations Committee, and put together a streamlined version.

Having told congressional leaders about the Taft episode, Johnson asked if this was an appropriate time for a congressional resolution on American policy toward South Vietnam. The leadership, with near unanimity, urged him to go ahead but keep it short; it would be passed promptly and with a strong vote. Indeed, the Tonkin Gulf Resolution, in which Congress declared its support for the United States' willingness to come to the assistance of those protected by the SEATO Treaty, including the use of armed force "as the President shall determine," was passed rapidly: 88–2 by the Senate and 416–0 by the House.

The resolution was simply worded, and there was no question about its meaning during the floor discussion. One senator asked Foreign Relations Committee Chairman William Fulbright if this resolution would permit dispatching large numbers of American forces to South Vietnam. Fulbright said he hoped it wouldn't be necessary to take such steps, but if this proved necessary, the resolution would allow it. Fulbright's views were those of Lyndon Johnson's; both men hoped there would be no escalation of the war. At the close of Secretary of Defense Robert McNamara's testimony, Fulbright told me privately that this was the best resolution of its sort he had ever seen presented to the Senate. I never forgot Fulbright's remark. He was all for it at the time. He urged the Senate to give it immediate and unanimous approval.

Senator Wayne Morse opposed the resolution as an unwarranted delegation of the war powers of Congress, warning of its far-reaching implications. But he was nearly alone. When some members of Congress later changed their minds about the war, they tried to throw a cloud on the resolution itself and the way we had presented it. But I have no doubt that they knew exactly what they were voting for. It was simply stated, and the floor discussion brought out all relevant aspects. Some later complained, "We didn't anticipate sending a half million men to South Vietnam," but neither did Lyndon Johnson.

I never worried about the constitutionality of the Tonkin Gulf

Resolution or about subsequent actions based upon its authority. If Congress can declare war, surely it can take measures short of declaring war that fall within its constitutional powers. I felt the Tonkin Gulf Resolution was not congressional evasion of its war powers responsibility, but an exercise of that responsibility.

Because of political turmoil in South Vietnam, continued fighting, and the Gulf of Tonkin incidents, Vietnam became a major issue in the 1964 presidential campaign. Lyndon Johnson followed a two-track policy, reaffirming the American commitment to South Vietnam but also opposing American involvement in a larger war. His Republican opponent, Barry Goldwater, implied that if elected, he would escalate the war in order to win. Johnson won the election by a landslide. It is entirely possible that Hanoi may have thought, "Aha! President Johnson defeated Senator Goldwater, and Johnson said that he does not want a wider war in Southeast Asia. Maybe we can widen the war and the Americans won't do anything about it." In any event, after the election North Vietnam began sending units of its regular army into South Vietnam. It was only after this North Vietnamese escalation that Johnson decided to meet this additional effort.

Throughout the war the term "escalation" was largely reserved for the American side. Many people overlooked the fact that our own "escalation" was a direct response to escalation by North Vietnam. President Johnson was later attacked for sending U.S. combat troops to Vietnam despite his campaign pledges not to "send American boys to fight in an Asian land war." But if one views the totality of his remarks during that 1964 campaign, he did not mislead the American people. He constantly reaffirmed our commitment and never suggested that we intended to abandon South Vietnam.

Other critics later alleged that the Johnson administration came to a consensus in the fall of 1964 to land American troops and begin bombing North Vietnam. This allegation is not true. There cannot be a consensus on a decision of that magnitude that does not include the president and the secretaries of state and defense, and neither Bob McNamara nor I was ever a party to such a decision.

Admittedly we did discuss bombing North Vietnam, as one of a series of options always being examined. But although I recall such discussion, I know of no decision taken before February 1965 to bomb North Vietnam.

What was my advice on sustained bombing of North Vietnam? As Lyndon Johnson accurately portrayed in *The Vantage Point* (page 123), "Rusk opposed air attacks and sustained reprisals in August, September, and December 1964." I believed we should persevere with our policy of advising and assisting the South Vietnamese and playing for the breaks, rather than risk a major escalation if one could be avoided. At this stage, in late 1964, the stakes were high enough that we couldn't simply withdraw, but neither did I want us to go all out in fighting a guerrilla war. Unless the South Vietnamese themselves could carry the major burden, I didn't see how we could succeed. My conviction that the war would be won or lost in the South also led me to oppose U.S. retaliation against North Vietnam in response to the November 1 Vietcong attack against Bien Hoa air base and the December 24 Vietcong bombing of an American billet in Saigon.

As 1965 opened, the military situation in South Vietnam was dire indeed, and we didn't know how far the North Vietnamese would go. They continued to infiltrate men and supplies to the South. At a White House meeting in January 1965, with the war going poorly, McGeorge Bundy and Robert McNamara argued for a much stronger use of American power to force a change of Communist policy or to achieve a negotiated withdrawal, saying that "the time has come for harder choices." I did not agree with this. President Johnson later wrote, "Rusk knew that things were going badly" and "he [Rusk] did not claim that the deterioration could be stopped." McGeorge Bundy accurately described my position in a January 27 memo: "What Rusk does say is that the consequences of both escalation and withdrawal are so bad that we simply must find a way of making our present policy work. This would be good if it were possible. Bob [McNamara] and I do not think it is."

On February 7, 1965, the Vietcong attacked a U.S. installation at Pleiku, killing seven Americans. In retaliation, President Johnson ordered air attacks against North Vietnamese barracks and staging areas. I did not participate in this decision authorizing the first retaliatory bombing attacks against the North. I had just returned from Winston Churchill's funeral in Great Britain and had come down with a bad case of the flu. After a stint in the hospital I went to George Ball's place in Florida to recuperate; that's where I was when the decision was made. Although I had some reservations about the bombing raids, I did not oppose them.

Soon after these retaliatory raids, President Johnson authorized regular bombing attacks against North Vietnam. This campaign, called Operation Rolling Thunder, sought to punish North Vietnam for attacking the South and also was intended to help South Vietnamese morale and instill a greater willingness to fight.

With the increased fighting and continued infiltration, in February 1965 I supported a limited bombing of North Vietnam, believing that we should do whatever was necessary to sway the battle in South Vietnam, including bombing infiltration routes in Laos and Cambodia as well as North Vietnam. I made my own views clear in a "no distribution" memo to the president on February 23, in which I urged that the United States take every possible action "to throw back Hanoi's aggression without a major war if possible" and that air strikes against the North "be directly linked to specific events in South Vietnam . . . so that the responsibility for major escalation will continue to rest with the other side." In the same memo I also stated that "I would favor the immediate stationing in Da Nang of a Marine battalion combat team, to be promptly reinforced to a brigade if the security situation calls for it." Additionally, the memo shows that I favored increased U.S. naval action against coastal infiltration, continued air action against the enemy in South Vietnam, and possible use of our most sophisticated conventional weapons systems. Clearly I was not a dove.

The beginning of all my thinking in this memo, and indeed throughout the Vietnam decision making, was that the United States must help the South Vietnamese repel aggression from the North. I never thought that we should cut and run or that we should renege on our pledged word to assist those covered by the SEATO Treaty if they were subject to attack. For me, that was fundamental. Some felt we had more freedom of action under the SEATO Treaty and collective security. I did not.

I was convinced we had to do everything possible to throw back North Vietnamese aggression, without a major war if possible. We couldn't accomplish that result without the risk of major escalation. But I thought that risk had to be taken.

Although I supported bombing North Vietnam, from the beginning I was skeptical about claims that the bombing of North Vietnam would have dramatic effect on the battlefields in South Vietnam. The North Vietnamese needed only two hundred tons a day down those jungle trails to keep their troops in the South supplied with what they could not take from the land. Given bad weather and rugged terrain, we were never completely able to interdict by air the small amount needed for resupply. I was skeptical about bombing targets farther north, especially in the Hanoi-Haiphong area, because these operations would have little impact upon the battle in the South.

My general attitude toward the bombing of the far North and the Hanoi-Haiphong area reflected my impressions from the Korean War.

We bombed everything in North Korea from the thirty-eighth parallel to the Yalu River, had complete air superiority, and yet, even with this effort, we were not able to prevent the North Koreans and the Chinese from maintaining an army of five hundred thousand men at the front. They moved their supplies at night and during bad weather, and it was never possible to choke off their supply routes.

Hanoi and Haiphong's strong air defenses also took a costly toll on men and planes. Our slow-flying B-52's were sitting ducks for North Vietnamese fighter planes and missiles. I did advocate their use along the Ho Chi Minh Trail and also, oddly enough, because of their extraordinary accuracy, for close support of ground troops. But we in the State Department never thought we could cut off North Vietnamese infiltration and supplies by bombing. We could at best slow them down; perhaps with Rolling Thunder it took two months instead of two weeks for a given amount of supplies to arrive in South Vietnam.

Nor did we at State think that our Air Force could bomb North Vietnam—a primarily agricultural society—into submission. Had North Vietnam been a highly organized, industrial society, other targets would have presented themselves. I was always ready to suspend the bombing of the far North and the Hanoi-Haiphong area if there were any chances for negotiations.

Through prisoner interrogation we later found that the bombing made life extremely difficult for the North Vietnamese. The bombing of the Ho Chi Minh Trail slowed down infiltration, helped South Vietnamese morale, and helped maintain congressional support for our policy. We would have had great difficulty keeping that support if we hadn't been willing to bomb infiltration routes. Even so, I never felt that air power would be decisive. Perhaps this reflected my bias as an ex-captain of infantry, but in Vietnam as elsewhere, the infantryman with his rifle remained the queen of battle.

About the time of Rolling Thunder, on March 6, we also sent two battalions of U.S. Marines into Da Nang to defend the air base there. I supported this decision, having recommended several weeks earlier that this step be taken. But I wasn't convinced that a Marine landing at Da Nang for defense of our air base signified a major change in our commitment to South Vietnam.

On April 1, realizing that the bombing of North Vietnam would not stave off the collapse of South Vietnam, President Johnson authorized the deployment of two more Marine battalions and an air squadron. Also, he changed the mission for the Marines "to permit their more active use."

Within the administration we debated how to announce this change in mission. The president preferred not to release his April 1 decision publicly. His directive read as follows: "[We] should minimize any appearance of sudden changes in policy. Any official statements on these troop movements will be made only with the direct approval of the secretary of defense in consultation with the secretary of state. The President desires that these movements and changes should be understood as being gradual and wholly consistent with existing policy."

Although some considered this a significant change in policy, to me this was more of a change in detail. The basic policy remained unchanged: to assist South Vietnam in protecting itself against aggression. I had no problem with U.S. forces protecting air bases. Even in a defensive role, troops have to patrol aggressively and take on anyone trying to shoot at them. Nor did I try to persuade Johnson to announce this change.

Even with the combination of Rolling Thunder and additional limited U.S. troop deployments, the military situation continued to worsen. President Johnson's determination to keep American forces to an advisory role and within the limits established by President Kennedy gave way to new developments. In early 1965, following our November 1964 elections, the North Vietnamese began to send regiments and divisions of their regular army into South Vietnam. With this escalation, President Johnson faced a situation that President Kennedy never had to face: Do we let North Vietnam overrun South Vietnam, or do we try to stop it?

By June 1965 increased North Vietnamese escalation was threatening to cut South Vietnam in two, through the highlands area, and win the war. For us the options were "fish or cut bait." We had to make a major effort or concede defeat. I could see that our gradual response was not working.

At a July 1 meeting at the White House, attended by President Johnson, McGeorge Bundy, Robert McNamara, Assistant Secretary of State for Far Eastern Affairs William Bundy, George Ball, and myself among others, I put my reservations aside and advised the President to send an additional hundred thousand men. I told Johnson that we must not allow North Vietnam to impose its will on South Vietnam. I hoped we could do this without a large war, but we had to risk a large war if that was necessary. I argued that the integrity of the U.S. commitment was the principal pillar of peace in the world, that the Communist world might draw the wrong conclusions that could lead to world war if we reneged on our commitments, and that as long as the South

Vietnamese were prepared to fight for themselves, we had to help them. I also argued that once we sent troops, the United States was in South Vietnam for the duration and there was no turning back.

During this and other meetings Undersecretary of State George Ball sharply disagreed, comparing the American effort with France's tragic experience. He predicted defeat, presented his case with great force and eloquence, and compelled our attention. I agreed that the road ahead would be difficult but pointed out an important difference between us and the French: France tried to reassert colonial rule; we were helping defend South Vietnam from North Vietnamese aggression. I don't think any South Vietnamese thought that the United States was trying to establish an American colony or win control of South Vietnam. To me that difference was decisive.

Others presented their views, but in the end Lyndon Johnson decided to expand the American presence in South Vietnam, with the strong concurrence of his secretary of state. Our force levels climbed rapidly in response to increasing North Vietnamese escalation. When Johnson won the 1964 election, we had fewer than 25,000 men in South Vietnam. In July 1965 we had 75,000 troops. By November, one year after the election, we had 165,000. This occurred because of the changed situation in South Vietnam and what we thought it meant for world peace, not because of some long-planned secret desire to escalate.

Once American ground forces were committed to a combat role, I preferred leaving tactical decisions to our military commanders in the field, believing that Washington was too far away. We couldn't tell them how to handle their battalions and regiments. In general, I supported General Westmoreland and our professional military, sometimes overriding the military judgments of my State Department colleagues. But we in Washington did discuss overall strategy and the use of our forces. Some felt Westmoreland's search-and-destroy tactics were too aggressive and costly in American lives. I disagreed. The purpose of search and destroy, in addition to actively going after Vietcong and North Vietnamese forces, was to keep their battalions and regiments at a distance from South Vietnam's cities. Westmoreland did not want to adopt a passive strategy and simply wait for the enemy to pick and choose villages and cities to attack. Had this happened, we would have had to fight a series of urban house-to-house battles, even more costly to American lives and South Vietnamese civilians caught in the crossfire. The cost of retaking those towns and cities occupied by the Vietcong and North Vietnamese during the Tet offensive illustrates what might have flowed from inactivity. The idea behind search and destroy was to catch enemy units in the countryside, where artillery, naval gunfire, and air support could be used more effectively and with less disruption than if we waited until they came into the cities.

We debated tactics at considerable length, considering, for example, an enclave strategy that called for the defense of a limited number of key cities along the coast. I believed that idea was a prescription for losing the war, since if we held a few enclaves and allowed the North Vietnamese and Vietcong to overrun the countryside, South Vietnam would be divided.

I personally think that General Westmoreland and our military command in general were unfairly criticized for how they chose to fight the war. I know something about the decisions made in the last half century to commit American military forces to combat; on no single occasion were those decisions made on the initiative of our military. In our system the duty of our armed forces is to carry out the missions assigned to them by constitutional authority. Karl von Clausewitz, the patron saint of many in uniform, emphasized that the mission of the military is determined by national authority and not by the armed forces. Five American presidents, with the advice of their secretaries of state and defense, committed the United States to the defense of South Vietnam. Our military cannot be faulted for this.

Drawing upon our Korean experience, I did advocate integrating American Army units with South Vietnamese—an idea that went nowhere. In 1950 we sent General Douglas MacArthur seven divisions and told him, "That's all you're going to get." Working with that ceiling, MacArthur integrated American supply, logistical, even combat units with tens of thousands of South Koreans, right down to rifle squads. His policy of using "Katusas" (Koreans attached to the U.S. Army) wherever possible not only fleshed out our own ranks but left behind a corps of tough soldiers for the South Korean Army.

I pushed hard for making full use of the South Vietnamese, primarily because of my belief that the war would be won or lost by them, but lost this argument within the administration. Bob McNamara told me that he had too many problems with the Joint Chiefs and didn't want to push it. General Westmoreland didn't want to use South Vietnamese either. I once specifically asked him about using Vietnamese truck drivers to deliver supplies to our forces. He said, "We can't have American forces relying on Vietnamese." Without South Vietnamese help, we had to do everything ourselves, creating an enormous administrative and logistical tail behind our combat forces.

Certainly Vietcong infiltration of South Vietnamese forces created a security problem—Westmoreland was constantly worried about Vietcong infiltrators—but that doesn't quite explain it. There's both a tradition and an institutional bias in the American military to want to do everything with our own forces. After V-E Day the British were ready to send their navy to the Pacific to join the war against Japan, but our Navy resisted. We had to do it ourselves. That military mind-set—"this is our job, and by George, *we're* going to do it"—and that unwillingness to use South Vietnamese in direct support of American units cost us dearly in manpower requirements for the war.

In retrospect, one mistake we made was not having a unified command. Our military always talked about unity of command, but we never achieved it. The battle inside South Vietnam was under the command of General Westmoreland, the bombing of North Vietnam was under the command of CINCPAC (commander in chief, Pacific) in Hawaii, and the B-52's remained under the operational control of the Joint Chiefs of Staff in Washington. In addition, Westmoreland did not have direct command of South Vietnamese or other allied forces such as the South Koreans and the Australians. The Joint Chiefs of Staff gave CINCPAC in Hawaii orders for the war effort, which were in turn relayed to Westmoreland in South Vietnam. I thought the intervention of CINCPAC was an unnecessary level of command that fueled bickering over priorities and resources.

Another unfortunate consequence of these split commands was that each headquarters thought it could win the war by itself. CINCPAC thought bombing the hell out of North Vietnam would do it. That psychology didn't always coordinate with Westmoreland's needs in South Vietnam. We should have had a single command, so that all allied forces could concentrate on the primary mission of keeping North Vietnam from overrunning South Vietnam by force. I raised this with Bob McNamara, but again, because of other problems with the Joint Chiefs, he didn't want another.

Relationships between our military and political commands were cumbersome. On the military side, as noted, the chain of command came from Westmoreland in Saigon back through CINCPAC in Hawaii to the Joint Chiefs of Staff. On the political side the ambassador was the president's in-country representative, responsible for all aspects of the American presence in Vietnam, including the military. This relationship was hard to manage and could be worked out only by the personalities involved. Although our command relationships were confused in theory, fortunately Ambassador Ellsworth Bunker, Generals William Westmoreland and Creighton Abrams, and the rest worked effectively together.

We discussed turning Vietnam into a theater of operations, as we had done for World War II, and concentrating all authority in the theater commander, with the ambassador as the political adviser. We decided against that because such an arrangement might have downgraded the Vietnamese role and Americanized the war even further. Also, the Koreans, Australians, South Vietnamese, and other allies might not have liked an "American warlord" running the war.

During the Johnson years the principal decisions about Vietnam were made at the Tuesday luncheons. Present were the president, the secretaries of state and defense, the chairman of the Joint Chiefs of Staff, the CIA director, and the national security adviser. We discussed all aspects of Vietnam policy—military, political, economical, and psychological. I don't believe there were serious problems of coordination in Washington. The Pentagon kept closely in touch with political matters, and the State Department with military concerns. President Johnson's personal assistant, Robert Komer, helped coordinate what was called the other war—political-economic-psychological aspects. I don't claim that coordination was perfect, but it wasn't as bad as has been suggested.

Because the South Vietnamese carried the brunt of the fighting, the idea that we Americanized the war was somewhat misleading. Our news media naturally concentrated more heavily on what American forces were doing and often overlooked South Vietnamese operations. At the peak of the war the South Vietnamese had 800,000 men under arms. If we had been similarly mobilized, we would have had more than 9 million men in uniform. The South Vietnamese military suffered more than 220,000 deaths in comparison with 57,000 American deaths. We Americans played a big role, but no one can honestly say that the South Vietnamese did not fight and die for their country.

From the beginning we wanted to enlist other members of SEATO in the defense of South Vietnam. With the exception of France, we had strong political support from the ministers of the SEATO countries; they were unanimous on supporting our effort politically. But we had only partial success in getting help on the ground.

In their first meeting in 1961 French President Charles de Gaulle told President Kennedy that there would never be another French soldier in Southeast Asia. For all practical purposes, de Gaulle's pledge meant that France had seceded from the Southeast Asia Treaty Organization. Pakistan was not interested in providing assistance to South Vietnam because from its point of view, SEATO was designed to contain India.

Because of problems in Malaysia, a general withdrawal from world affairs after Suez, and domestic opposition, the British gave only lip service to SEATO and decided against coming to the defense of South Vietnam. A British Commonwealth division had served with great distinction in Korea, and we would have welcomed a British flag flying in Vietnam. Its absence was keenly felt. After I left office, I once asked Denis Healey, former British minister of defense, "What if the American reaction to an act of aggression under NATO protection was the same as the British reaction under SEATO?" Healy called my query an "indecent question."

On another occasion at a NATO foreign ministers' meeting, my German, British, and French colleagues expressed misgivings about the U.S. effort in Vietnam and concern that we might someday neglect Europe. I told my colleagues, "You cannot expect the United States to be a virgin in the Atlantic and a whore in the Pacific." I reminded them that Britain and France shared our treaty commitments in Southeast Asia and that the United States, as a two-ocean country, had to treat its commitments in the Pacific with the same seriousness as those in the Atlantic. I deeply regretted the unwillingness of Britain and France to "take steps to meet the common danger," believing that the erosion of commitment to collective security in the Pacific posed a significant threat to NATO.

The principal concern about North Vietnamese aggression came from the nations of Southeast Asia: Australia, New Zealand, Malaysia, the Philippines, and particularly Thailand. Prince Wan of Thailand once told me that the United States should think of Thailand as a "golden bell" that would be shattered by fighting inside Thailand. He said that Thailand can be defended only from outside its borders, and because of that, his country had practiced a policy of accommodation for centuries, bending with the winds of change. Prince Wan warned that Thailand's security depended upon the security of Laos and Cambodia and South Vietnam and that if a serious Communist insurgency or attack were to develop against Thailand, he could not predict the outcome.

Fortunately the regional members of SEATO took the threat of North Vietnamese aggression seriously. South Korea sent approximately two divisions of troops, who fought effectively in Vietnam. Thailand concentrated its efforts against guerrillas operating in its northeastern regions. Australia, New Zealand, and the Philippines all sent troops. But frankly we had hoped for more.

Throughout the rest of 1965 and the next two years most critics of the Johnson administration's Vietnam policy were the so-called hawks, not the doves. Many Americans, members of Congress included, wanted us to use maximum force against North Vietnam. We made a deliberate decision to keep the war as limited as possible and not build up a war fever in the United States. We didn't parade military units through big cities or have beautiful movie stars sell war bonds in factories, as we had done during World War II. In a nuclear world it was too dangerous for an entire people to grow too angry. We may have made a mistake. Fighting a limited war is tough on the men and women carrying the battle and tough on the home front as well. We were asking our countrymen to support in cold blood what our men in uniform were having to do in hot blood in Southeast Asia. Yet behind that problem was the ever-present threat of general war and escalation into a nuclear war.

Our conduct of the war and especially the bombing of North Vietnam were influenced by the possibility of Chinese intervention. If anyone had asked me in 1963 whether we could put five hundred thousand American soldiers in South Vietnam and bomb almost every military target in North Vietnam up to the Chinese border without bringing in the Chinese, I would have been hard pressed to say yes. Yet with our policy of gradual response, at no time did we present Beijing and Moscow with a major change in the war that forced them to decide whether or not to intervene. As the North Vietnamese escalated, so did we. However badly it otherwise may have served us, gradual response helped limit the war to Vietnam. We downplayed the importance of our own military actions for the benefit of the Chinese and Soviets, not wanting to provoke them into responding. We often described increased bombing, more American troops, and more aggressive actions on our part as consistent with past policy. This was true, in the sense that our policy never changed: to prevent North Vietnam from taking over South Vietnam by force.

We never tried to deceive the American people; we only wanted to avoid a wider war. Our statements exacted a price—criticism for not being more explicit about tactical changes in policy, even though such measures were part of our general policy of defending South Vietnam.

Our China specialists stated almost unanimously that if we sent American ground forces into North Vietnam, the chances of Chinese intervention were high, and for that reason I strongly opposed U.S. ground operations against North Vietnam. An American offensive against North Vietnam would likely have triggered Hanoi's mutual security pact with China and brought Beijing in. We watched for potential mobilization of Chinese forces, avoided bombing territory adjacent to China, and tried to avoid threatening the Chinese or leaving our intentions unclear, as had been done by General MacArthur's advance to the Yalu. The possibility of Chinese intervention definitely influenced how we fought this war.

Limited wars are difficult for a democracy. The requisite combination of firmness and restraint is hard to maintain because the American people, to their credit, are impatient about war. But moving to new levels of violence is no guarantee of ending conflict quickly. However unpopular limited war may be—and Korea and Vietnam did little to enhance its attractiveness—it is worth remembering that the alternative to limited war is unlimited war. One does not have to fear that in any craven sense. But one must have total respect for what unlimited war means to the survival of the human race. I could have told President Johnson that we could invade North Vietnam with American forces and that the Chinese would not come in. He might have taken my advice. Had the Chinese intervened, I could have picked up the phone and said, "Sorry, Mr. President, I was wrong." But Johnson would have had no one to phone.

We never seriously considered using nuclear weapons in Vietnam. From a purely tactical point of view, there was no way to control the fallout from such weapons; it could have spread eastward to Japan and the Philippines or westward to China and the Soviet Union. More important, there weren't any nuclear targets in North Vietnam. We could have destroyed Hanoi and Haiphong with conventional weapons had we so desired. But we tried to conduct the war without deliberately attacking civilian populations. One military memorandum discussed American ground forces invading North Vietnam and opined that such an invasion in the eye of the memo writer would not "bring in the Chinese." But the memo continued, asserting, "But if they do come in, that will mean nuclear war." In a memorandum the clause looked like fine print. But such a sentence pops off the page at an American president.

Whenever we boxed the compass of all conceivable lines of action, the so-called nuclear option was occasionally on the list. Researchers coming across such documents delight in such lists and inevitably blow them out of proportion. Eight American presidents in this nuclear age have resolutely rejected the "nuclear option." Despite the enormous costs and frustrations of Vietnam, the Kennedy, Johnson, and Nixon administrations chose to fight that war with conventional means, and eventually lost the war rather than "win" it with nuclear weapons.

Our restraint unfortunately also led to American casualties. A major unwritten story of Vietnam concerns the additional casualties Americans took trying to observe rules of engagement designed to protect civilian life. During the Korean War the State Department played little role in target selection for American bombing, but in Vietnam strikes against North Vietnam were approved during President Johnson's Tuesday luncheons, at which State played a role. At these luncheons we selected strictly military targets; the overriding criterion was the avoidance of civilian casualties. The Tuesday lunch group also determined the direction of attack for aircraft. On my conscience are those times—more than I care to remember—when we asked our pilots to fly their missions the "hard way": to attack targets by more heavily defended routes but routes which would reduce the risk of civilian casualties. We did this knowing that American lives would be lost.

After the first full year of American bombing of North Vietnam, Hanoi claimed five hundred civilian casualties. Without minimizing those deaths, that figure showed that our planes, which flew thousands of missions, were not out to bomb civilians. Indeed, had we wanted to kill civilians, we could have bombed Hanoi into ashes with conventional weapons, and there wouldn't have been any Hanoi for Jane Fonda, Ramsey Clark, and Harrison Salisbury to visit. We could have bombed the dikes south of Hanoi and ruined much of North Vietnam's rice production, but we didn't do it, because it was not our purpose to wage war against civilians. We also observed rules of engagement designed to protect civilians during ground operations and took additional casualties. The massacre of Vietnamese civilians at My Lai was not representative of American war conduct. Our careful selection of bombing targets partially reflected a fear of Soviet and Chinese intervention, but it also reflected the basic humanitarian aspects of American character.

29

The Frustrations of Negotiations

Shortly after he became president, Lyndon Johnson called Defense Secretary Robert McNamara and me into the Oval Office. He told McNamara, "Your mission is to ensure that North Vietnam does not seize South Vietnam by force." Turning to me, he said, "Your mission is to bring about a peaceful settlement of this situation at the earliest possible moment."

As events proved painfully obvious, McNamara, General Westmoreland, and our fighting men in Vietnam were far more successful—until the fall of Saigon in 1975—in achieving their mission than we in the State Department were in achieving ours. Our inability to negotiate a peaceful end to the war was an immensely frustrating experience and exceedingly painful to everyone involved.

In retrospect, considering the incompatibility of objectives in Hanoi and Washington, the failure of negotiations was almost inevitable. During my eight years as secretary of state I cannot recall a single initiative from North Vietnam that could genuinely be called a peace initiative. There were many peace initiatives, but they always came from the United States or third parties, never from North Vietnam. The frequency of our bombing halts and probes for negotiations might have misled Hanoi to think that we were irresolute and ready for peace at any price. But in defense of our negotiating efforts, other crises such as the Berlin blockade of 1948 and the Korean War had been resolved by diplomacy.

We took many initiatives ourselves, far more than were ever revealed publicly, beginning with President Kennedy's talk with Khrushchev at Vienna in 1961. We appreciated the efforts of the Canadians, Poles, Rumanians, Hungarians, Soviets, and others, both official representatives and private citizens, to find a basis for talks. Despite the absence of formal talks until 1968, we were never out of contact with the North Vietnamese.

The North Vietnamese listened to what we had to say but never sent anything back on the return channel except a harsh reiteration of their "Four Point Program," which they insisted must be the sole basis for peace in Vietnam. Originally proclaimed by Hanoi in April 1965, the Four Point Program was quite deceptive; the third of those four points required the imposition of the program of the National Liberation Front upon all South Vietnam. To us this meant that Hanoi was never interested in talking seriously about peace.

What was Vietnam all about? To stated the answer simply, Hanoi sent thousands of trained men, including more than fifty regiments of the North Vietnamese Regular Army, to impose its will upon the South Vietnamese by force. Hanoi had more than forty thousand troops in Laos contrary to the Laos accords of 1962, an estimated twenty thousand troops in Cambodia despite the protests of Prince Norodom Sihanouk, and Hanoi-trained guerrillas in northeastern Thailand.

The United States had a clear and direct commitment to the security of South Vietnam against external attack. This commitment was based upon bilateral agreements between the United States and South Vietnam, upon the SEATO Treaty, upon annual actions by Congress in providing aid to South Vietnam, upon the policy expressed in congressional action such as the August 1964 Tonkin Gulf resolution, and upon the solemn declarations of three American presidents. Not just South Vietnam and Southeast Asia were at stake; so, too, were the integrity of the U.S. commitment and the importance of that commitment to peace around the globe.

In short, war broke out in Southeast Asia because Hanoi and Peking supported and committed acts of aggression beyond their own borders. The American negotiating position was very simple: They had to stop this aggression, take their troops home, let the South Vietnamese work out their own future, honor the Laos accords of 1962, and cease the infiltration of men and arms into neighboring countries. I was often criticized for stating these goals too simply. Yet the most fundamental issues are often quite simple. There could have been peace in Southeast Asia if North Vietnam had been willing to live at peace with its neighbors.

We didn't ask Hanoi to surrender an acre of ground or a single soldier. We didn't try to destroy North Vietnam, invade its territory, nor did we support or encourage a South Vietnamese attack on North Vietnam, nor did we seek to change the regime in Hanoi or its affiliations with the Communist world. We didn't want bases or permanently garrisoned American forces in South Vietnam. Lyndon Johnson was willing to schedule withdrawal of our forces if Hanoi would schedule the withdrawal of its. We were not in South Vietnam for economic reasons. After I left office, I heard that we defended South Vietnam because of oil. I never heard of oil in Vietnam while I was in office.

One of our first efforts to find a formula for peace used the good offices of J. Blair Seaborn, the chief Canadian delegate to the International Control Commission on Indochina. I strongly supported Seaborn's efforts to help us reach agreement with Hanoi.

Beginning in June 1964 and extending until August 1965, Seaborn made five trips to Hanoi. On his first, on the eve of the American buildup, he carried a carrot-and-stick offer from us: If Hanoi would stop its assistance to the Vietcong and withdraw its forces, the United States would withdraw from South Vietnam and extend economic assistance and diplomatic recognition to North Vietnam. We also warned that if our offer was not accepted, we would undertake naval and air attacks against North Vietnam. Seaborn returned to Hanoi in August, just after the Gulf of Tonkin incidents. He told North Vietnamese Prime Minister Pham Van Dong that the United States held Hanoi accountable for subversion in South Vietnam and that unless the North Vietnamese stopped their aggression and honored the Geneva agreements of 1954 and 1962, they would "suffer the consequences." Representing our views, Seaborn warned the United States would visit "great devastation" on North Vietnam and said that "U.S. patience is growing extremely thin."

Following each of his trips, Seaborn reported that Hanoi was uninterested in talks based on American terms. North Vietnamese Prime Minister Pham Van Dong countered our position, declaring that unless the United States withdrew from South Vietnam and the Vietcong joined in a coalition government in Saigon, American attacks against

North Vietnam would spread the war "to the whole of Southeast Asia." He told Seaborn to return with fresh proposals and said "there was nothing to negotiate about."

Throughout Seaborn's travels American policy could have gone either way. We were building up our forces but reluctantly; we wanted a negotiated end to the war. We hoped for a sign that would have made our military effort unnecessary. We conveyed to the North Vietnamese exactly what we would do if their aggression did not end. Unfortunately the North Vietnamese thumbed their noses at Seaborn's overtures. Seaborn represented our views faithfully and performed a valuable service. We regretted that his repeated trips to Hanoi did not produce results.

During Seaborn's shuttle another story about negotiations broke, one that wrongfully led to embarrassment and even scandal for the United States. In the fall of 1964 UN Secretary General U Thant, believing that Hanoi and Washington misunderstood each other's resolve and that a negotiated settlement was possible, sought to arrange secret talks between the two governments. According to U Thant, Hanoi "agreed" to meet in Rangoon, Burma, for opening discussions.

We found no proof of such an initiative, and Hanoi itself later denied telling U Thant that it was willing to conduct secret talks. We believed that U Thant's channel for this initiative was the principal Soviet representative in the United Nations Secretariat, who we suspected worked for the KGB. We didn't know if he represented his government in stating that Hanoi would be willing to meet in Rangoon or if he might be conducting a clandestine operation for propaganda purposes.

Our skepticism rose when U Thant never gave us a copy of any message that he sent to or received from Hanoi about a meeting in Rangoon. We never had anything in writing on which to make a judgment. U Thant was so insistent upon utter secrecy that we respected his request to handle this on a word-of-mouth basis. All we had were U Thant's guarded hints that if we would go to Rangoon, Hanoi would join us there. He kept us in the dark about this whole initiative.

Additionally, other sources cast doubt on the authenticity of this "initiative." Either Blair Seaborn or the North Vietnamese themselves, I don't remember which, told us that Hanoi was not interested in talks. And later a Burmese official in Rangoon confirmed that there had been no approval from Hanoi. Consequently, in the absence of any solid evidence about the Hanoi "initiative," we didn't respond for five months. Finally our UN ambassador, Adlai Stevenson, told U Thant that Washington had learned that Hanoi was not interested in talks.

On February 24, 1965, disappointed with the American reaction, U Thant told his story to the press. "I am sure . . . the American people, if only they knew the true facts . . . , would agree with me that further bloodshed is unnecessary," he said. "In times of war and hostilities, the first casualty is truth." But whatever his motives, we felt U Thant had grossly misrepresented the situation.

Possibly U Thant himself was the victim of misinformation or simply wishful thinking, but frankly, I thought he had lied like a sailor. I never had much respect for U Thant's integrity. He probably knew he never had a message from Hanoi that pointed toward peace. Sometimes intermediaries will say things to each side that go beyond the facts, hoping that somehow this will get the two sides together. Perhaps he was trying to find a face-saving device for us to get out of Vietnam. But we weren't trying to save face; we were trying to save South Vietnam.

Immediately following this episode, I had several talks with Soviet Foreign Minister Andrei Gromyko, and he never indicated awareness that Hanoi wanted to meet with us in Rangoon. Had this been a Soviet initiative, Gromyko would have said something about it. He and I talked often about Vietnam. I also asked Soviet Ambassador Anatoly Dobrynin to check into this affair, and on his next trip home Dobrynin talked to his colleagues in the Foreign Office, searched the records, and reported back to me that there had never been a message from Hanoi. He also said that the Soviet official in the secretariat had no instructions to say anything to U Thant. As Dobrynin speculated, perhaps their man had made a casual remark at a cocktail party, one U Thant seized upon without having anything concrete upon which to build.

The fallout from U Thant's misrepresentation damaged U.S. prestige and added to our so-called credibility gap. It also led to disagreement between Adlai Stevenson and me over whether Hanoi had provided any basis for talks. Desperate to find a way toward peace, Adlai was impatient with me and didn't think we were being responsive. Our conflict was rather sharp. Stevenson publicly took a position fostered by U Thant which, as far as I was concerned, was just a cock-and-bull story. But in an interview, published in *Look* just after he died in July 1965, Adlai did allow that "it was never very clear with whom the talks were supposed to be held, and about what."

There is one last epilogue to this entire unfortunate incident. In October 1966 Lyndon Johnson and I visited U Thant in his United

Nations office in New York. According to U Thant, as reported by David Kraslow and Stuart Loory in *The Secret Search for Peace in Vietnam*, LBJ allegedly "sat in that very chair and said he had never heard" of the alleged fall 1964 Hanoi initiative.

I remember no such statement, but if that is U Thant's story, either U Thant or Lyndon Johnson did not tell the truth. I prefer to think it was U Thant because Johnson was kept up-to-date on these developments. I briefed him specifically on this so-called Rangoon Initiative.

Late in 1965, we received rumors of another North Vietnamese peace feeler, this time from Hungary. It, too, proved fraudulent. In a speech at the United Nations, Hungarian Foreign Minister Janos Peter declared that North Vietnam would agree to talks if we stopped the bombing. He told me the same thing a little later in the presence of Janos Radvanyi, the Hungarian chargé d'affaires who later defected to the United States and is now a professor at Mississippi State University, and added that the talks would be in Budapest. Just before Christmas, I called Radvanyi to the State Department to give him some negotiating points, which we later released as our fourteen-point program for peace in Vietnam during the thirty-seven-day bombing pause that same December. Those fourteen points are worth recalling:

1. The Geneva agreements of 1954 and 1962 were an adequate basis for peace in Southeast Asia.
2. We would welcome a conference on Southeast Asia or on any part thereof.
3. We would welcome "unconditional negotiations."
4. We would also welcome "unconditional discussions."
5. A cessation of hostilities could be the first order of business at a conference or could be the subject of preliminary discussions.
6. Hanoi's four points could be discussed along with other points which others might wish to propose.
7. We wanted no bases in Southeast Asia.
8. We did not desire to retain U.S. troops in South Vietnam after peace was assured.
9. We supported free elections in South Vietnam to give the South Vietnamese a government of their own choice.
10. The question of reunification of Vietnam should be determined by the Vietnamese through their own free decision.
11. The countries of Southeast Asia could be nonaligned or neutral if that was their choice.

12. We preferred to use our resources for the economic reconstruction of Southeast Asia rather than for war. If there was peace, North Vietnam could participate in a regional effort to which we would contribute at least one billion dollars.

13. The president said that "the Viet Cong would not have difficulty being represented and having their views represented if for a moment Hanoi decided she wanted to cease aggression. I don't think that would be an insurmountable problem."

14. We said publicly and privately that we could stop the bombing of North Vietnam as a step toward peace although there had not been the slightest hint or suggestion from the other side as to what it would do if the bombing stopped.

We summarized our position by saying, "We have put everything into the basket of peace except the surrender of South Vietnam."

Before I met with Radvanyi, Soviet Ambassador Anatoly Dobrynin had told National Security Adviser McGeorge Bundy that if we stopped bombing for two or three weeks, the Soviet government would have time to contact Hanoi and see if something could be arranged. President Johnson was skeptical—in May 1965 we had stopped bombing for six days, but after we saw no indication of any desire by Hanoi to begin talks or to slow infiltration, we started bombing again—but even then, acting on my recommendation and the advice of others, President Johnson ordered a bombing halt that eventually stretched for thirty-seven days.

Johnson also sent Averell Harriman, G. Mennon Williams, Arthur Goldberg, Hubert Humphrey, and other emissaries to 145 countries on a "Christmas peace offensive" to explain American objectives in Vietnam and ask for help in bringing North Vietnam to the conference table. I cabled our ambassadors, saying that the pause could be extended if North Vietnam made any move toward peace. Hanoi, as usual, called our effort a "deception."

I wasn't optimistic that the pause would lead to peace, but I had pushed hard for this bombing halt and for extending it beyond the traditional Christmas cease-fire. I hoped that something might come from the Hungarian probe. That Dobrynin was involved had special significance, if the Soviets were willing to resume their role as cochairman of the Geneva Conference and use whatever influence they had to change Hanoi's attitude.

Unfortunately all this came to naught. The State Department

pressed Budapest continually throughout the bombing halt and never got anything concrete in return. After Janos Radvanyi defected to the United States, he told me that Peter was never in real contact with Hanoi and that they had no encouragement from Hanoi on the points Peter was raising. Radvanyi told me that before his defection, at a meeting he tried to convey the duplicity of Peter's dealings with me by using facial expressions. He couldn't speak openly, as he was accompanied during our talks by an embassy staffer who he believed was a member of the Hungarian secret police.

As for the Soviet involvement, we eventually learned that the Kremlin never intended to push Hanoi too hard toward settlement, for fear of driving Ho into the arms of the Chinese.

With this thirty-seven-day bombing pause and peace offensive, LBJ had taken a big step toward encouraging talks. Now he became thoroughly disillusioned. North Vietnam used the bombing halt to pour men and supplies into South Vietnam. After thirty-five days Ho Chi Minh announced in a radio broadcast that he wouldn't respond to the pause, and two days later the president resumed the bombing. Thinking that we had gone the last mile, I favored resumption.

The failure of the thirty-seven-day pause to bring about any movement toward negotiation made a lasting impression on Lyndon Johnson because from that time forward he was skeptical that bombing halts could accomplish anything. He may have felt that he had been badly advised to proceed with the thirty-seven-day pause. It was a calculated risk, but because Dobrynin recommended it, I felt it was worth a try.

I also recommended other bombing halts, for example the weeklong February 1967 bombing stoppage, but each time it only resulted in stepped-up North Vietnamese infiltration of men and supplies down the Ho Chi Minh Trail. Only after the Tet offensive of 1968, when it became apparent that Americans at the grass roots had begun to turn against the war, was Lyndon Johnson convinced that stopping the bombing was a good idea. The bombing halts were easy for me to support, because I believed the bombing of the far North wasn't worth the cost in men and planes. But because of the increased infiltration and past experiences, Lyndon Johnson resisted the halts.

During the second half of 1966 another peace initiative, the Marigold Initiative, lived its strange life. Janusz Lewandowski, the chief of the Polish delegation to the International Control Commission, went to Hanoi in June 1966, claimed to have met with Ho Chi Minh, and then met in Saigon with our ambassador, Henry Cabot Lodge. Lewandowski said that North Vietnam agreed to talks if the United States would stop bombing and agree to have the National Liberation Front take part in peace negotiations. This would have been a major change in North Vietnam's position since Hanoi would have abandoned its insistence that the NLF's program be put in place in South Vietnam.

Unfortunately Lewandowski's position was specious. He thought Hanoi would talk on the basis of his stated position, and he never could produce anything more concrete than his own reinterpretation of Ho's position. If Lewandowski was being sincere, and I had my doubts, he was trying to put together an agenda for talks based on long-range goals acceptable to both sides and to rely on further negotiations to determine how an agreement would be reached.

Despite this strange procedure, I overcame my own skepticism and told Lodge to get Lewandowski to spell out what Hanoi had in mind. We wanted to find out to what extent Lewandowski was acting upon Hanoi's specific instructions. For example, what was Hanoi willing to do in exchange for the suspension of American bombing? We told the Poles to tell Hanoi that we would talk on the basis of Lewandowski's points, although they would need clarification and further discussion. In private talks we were always willing to discuss anything Hanoi brought up. The Poles objected strenuously to our request for clarification because they wanted us to buy categorically their interpretation of our position. I don't know what message the Poles eventually sent, but in any event Hanoi refused to talk.

We were ready to go to Warsaw and begin talks, but the Poles couldn't produce any North Vietnamese. Lewandowski simply didn't reflect Hanoi's views. This was later confirmed by Janos Radvanyi, who told us that Lewandowski was a Polish intelligence agent acting on his own and that the Marigold Initiative was a sham.

Talks continued between us and the Poles through the last half of 1966, but throughout the Marigold exchanges we never received a single authoritative statement from Hanoi. All this while the Vietcong and North Vietnamese shelled and rocketed cities in South Vietnam. I visited Saigon while this initiative was under way, and the day before I arrived, the enemy attacked the airfield where I landed. During my stay the enemy tried to blow up the bridge on the main road leading northwest out of Saigon. But when the Poles said to us, "Your bombing is terrible. It prevents talks from starting," we stopped bombing around Hanoi and Haiphong for an extended period, not starting again until early December. However, that made no difference either. The Poles could never produce any North Vietnamese.

In early December we resumed raids around Haiphong while discussions continued between Polish officials and the U.S. ambassador to Warsaw about where talks could begin. In mid-December our planes staged more raids, creating dissension at State and elsewhere about their timing and whether we had allowed events to get out of hand and disrupt the possibility of talks.

Personally, I wasn't surprised by the raids; we had discussed them at the Tuesday luncheons. I may have failed to report these discussions to my colleagues within the department, leading to some confusion. But the December raids on targets around Hanoi were planned, not accidental. The truth is, we simply doubted the authenticity of Marigold; after six months of talking with the Poles, we hadn't received any confirmation from the North Vietnamese that they wanted to talk.

Nevertheless, after we started to bomb again, the North Vietnamese, the Poles, and others charged that the talks collapsed because of our bombing of Hanoi. In my view, there was nothing to collapse.

When the mid-December bombings took place, I was in the Far East and sent President Johnson an "eyes only" cable that expressed a different concern. I told the president that the intensity of our bombing around Hanoi when viewed in conjunction with the Marigold operation might create the impression that we were trying to throw a monkey wrench into negotiations. To quote the cable, I warned President Johnson that "we are in danger of being trapped into a situation where the Poles or Soviets could cause us grievous harm by a charge that there was a serious effort by Hanoi toward peace and that we rejected it by intensified bombing." This is, in fact, exactly what happened, and we received another black eye for an effort undertaken in good faith on our part even though there was never any concrete response from Hanoi.

We made another good-faith effort to set up negotiations with the North Vietnamese in early 1967, this time the so-called Phase A—Phase B proposal discussed in talks in London between British Prime Minister Harold Wilson and Soviet Premier Aleksei Kosygin. These talks roughly coincided with the February Tet bombing pause. Unfortunately the Phase A—Phase B effort also ended in acrimony.

Phase A—Phase B was simply a device to get around North Vietnam's insistence that negotiations could not begin until the United States stopped the bombing of North Vietnam. In Phase A we offered to stop the bombing as a first step, provided we had assurances from the North Vietnamese, either private or public, that they would enter Phase B talks and take reciprocal action leading toward de-escalation. In other words, we wanted to know what would happen if we stopped bombing. No one was able to tell us. Phase A—Phase B was an attempt to negotiate around that impasse.

Since Great Britain and the Soviet Union were cochairmen of the Geneva Conference, we urged Wilson to bring up Vietnam with Kosygin, hoping that perhaps the Soviets could bring their influence to play on Hanoi. Before talks began, we sent Averell Harriman's special assistant, Chester Cooper, to London to brief Wilson about the American negotiating position. During the talks Wilson discussed the Phase A—Phase B proposal with Kosygin on the basis of what Cooper told him.

Kosygin expressed interest in the idea, and when he asked for a written version of the American offer, Cooper prepared a draft, saying that the United States "would stop bombing as soon as we are assured that infiltration from North Vietnam will stop." Cooper sent a cable with this formula to Washington for approval, but after a day no response came. Interpreting silence as approval, Cooper and Wilson went ahead and presented the draft to Kosygin. I don't know why we delayed responding to Cooper's cable. Perhaps we were unable to get to the president. But Cooper had a right to think that the message he drafted for Kosygin was consistent with his original instructions. I believe Johnson was upset when he heard Cooper's draft had already been sent to Kosygin because he felt he hadn't had a chance to review the text and suggest changes. The president did not have a close relationship with Harold Wilson and was skeptical about whether Wilson would accurately reflect his views. This underlying mistrust probably didn't help matters.

Additionally, while the London talks were under way, Johnson on February 8 sent a personal letter to Ho Chi Minh, pledging that the United States would stop its bombing "as soon as I am assured that infiltration into South Vietnam by land and by sea 'has stopped.'" Two days later Johnson saw Cooper's draft message and realized it was inconsistent with his letter to Ho. Johnson ordered me to cable Cooper that Hanoi would have to stop infiltration before we stopped bombing on a permanent basis. Johnson's change did not withdraw the Phase A—Phase B offer but simply affirmed that we expected something in return for an American halt to the bombing; we wanted the North Vietnamese to reduce infiltration and fighting before we stopped the bombing.

I don't recall my exact advice to the president. The change in verb tense from "will stop" to "has stopped" triggered controversy; it was a position that Hanoi had rejected many times. I would have preferred Johnson's changes to be minimal, so it would be least embarrassing to Wilson; I may even have argued with the president on some of those changes. But Lyndon Johnson was the action officer and had the final say.

Cooper, Wilson, and Kosygin considered this a major change in the U.S. position, but personally I don't think the change was that big a deal. Had Hanoi been seriously interested in talks, this kind of misunderstanding could have been ironed out. It could have resulted in a serious initiative, had there been any response from Hanoi, because of the involvement of the British and Soviets, cochairmen of the Geneva Conference. At any rate this was perhaps as close as we came to setting up talks before 1968.

I cannot assign fault for the mixup on the U.S. and British side to anyone. It was just one of those things that sometimes happen. Wilson and Cooper thought they were proceeding along lines of policy approved in Washington, and President Johnson wanted to review whatever message went to Kosygin on such an important matter. It was an unfortunate slip of communication. Predictably those who wanted to see the war end on the basis of peace at any price held us responsible for the breakdown in the talks.

Again, the failure of the thirty-seven-day bombing halt in 1966 to bring about negotiations was a major factor in Lyndon Johnson's thinking. North Vietnam took advantage of that bombing halt to initiate a massive buildup, and in February 1967 our intelligence reported that two North Vietnamese divisions were just north of the demilitarized zone and ready to move south. Johnson feared that if we extended our Tet bombing halt, the North Vietnamese would take advantage of us just as they did a year earlier. Consequently, we reworded the Phase A—Phase B proposal and began bombing again on February 14.

Despite the mixup over Phase A—Phase B, I believe the Soviet Union tried on this and other occasions to play a helpful role in negotiating an end to the Vietnam War. The Soviets had played a key role during the Korean War in getting talks under way at Panmunjom, and both we and the Soviets worked hard to negotiate the Laos accords of 1962. It was my impression they would have preferred to see Hanoi comply with those accords. When we got no performance out of North Vietnam, we pressed the Soviets to put the heat on Hanoi to comply with them. But it seemed that Moscow was unwilling to exert real pressure on Hanoi, for fear of driving the North Vietnamese into the arms of the Chinese.

That pattern repeated itself throughout the Vietnam War. At Glassboro, New Jersey, in 1967, Lyndon Johnson and Aleksei Kosygin wrote a joint message which Kosygin promised to send to Hanoi. But that message made little difference to the North Vietnamese. In the competition between Peking and Moscow, the North Vietnamese were able to elbow some wiggle room for themselves. The Soviets came to realize that they really couldn't play a decisive role, that Hanoi was largely out of their control. Concerned about their relations with the rest of the Communist world, they never took positions not already agreed to by Hanoi. They referred our suggestions to Hanoi simply as messages from the United States and occasionally implied that if we stopped the bombing or de-escalated the fighting in some way, good things would happen. Their influence was quite limited. But I disagree with those who think that the Soviet Union wanted us bogged down in Vietnam. I think the Soviets came to realize the importance of an American presence in some of these divided countries, perhaps even in Germany and West Berlin.

Between peace initiatives that became publicly known and others that remained private, we were never out of contact with the North Vietnamese. Although we did not maintain diplomatic relations with North Vietnam, we occasionally dropped off messages for them at embassies in capitals where they were represented. They usually returned those messages to us, allegedly unopened, but we knew the contents had been read. All sorts of people also visited Hanoi in those days—representatives of other governments, private citizens, public officials—and if these people heard something in Hanoi they felt was significant, they would come back eight months pregnant with peace. For some, trying to negotiate an end to the war became a race for the Nobel Peace Prize. Yet when we checked these "peace feelers" out with Hanoi, there was nothing to them.

With many peace initiatives, especially when we talked with the Poles, Soviets, Hungarians, and other intermediaries, they seemed to think that the problem was to find a face-saving way for the United States to get out of South Vietnam. That became a little frustrating, because, again, we in the Kennedy and Johnson administrations were not trying to save face; we were trying to save South Vietnam.

The North Vietnamese might have agreed to face-saving devices by which the United States would abandon South Vietnam. But the bombing halts, peace initiatives, the well-intentioned efforts of many intermediaries ran up against the hard fact that Hanoi never abandoned its plan to unify all Indochina by force. Whenever we halted the bombing, whether for six days or thirty-seven days, there were always those who said, "If you only stopped the bombing a little longer, some good might have resulted." We halted the bombing permanently in 1968 to initiate the Paris peace talks, and North Vietnamese negotiators remained as implacable as ever.

Our interest in pursuing any possible leads to negotiations may have helped convince Hanoi that we were interested in peace at any price. Had North Vietnam been convinced that the United States was un-equivocally committed to South Vietnam and that we were going to see it through, Hanoi might have decided to negotiate a settlement on terms less than the reunification of all Vietnam by force. But instead the North Vietnamese judged that if they stayed with it, American public support for the war would collapse and that they could win on the home front in the United States what they couldn't win on the ground in Vietnam. Perversely, our interest in peace feelers and negotiations may have encouraged them to make that decision.

In retrospect, without my wishing to sound bitter, the North Viet-namese had little incentive to negotiate an end to the war. Well into 1966 they thought they could take South Vietnam by force. But by 1966 the United States and its allies had established a military position in South Vietnam which the North Vietnamese could not possibly have overrun. From a strictly military point of view, our men in uniform achieved their objective: to prevent North Vietnam's forcible takeover of South Vietnam. But in late 1966 and early 1967 Hanoi began to hear signals coming out of the United States. For example, if we had heard of fifty thousand demonstrators in Hanoi calling for peace, we would have thought the war was over, and we probably would have been right. One of our problems was that they could see two hundred thousand people marching on the Pentagon. And it was difficult trying to set up negotiations with those who are quoting your own senators back at you.

Americans opposed to the war, whatever their motivations, how-ever sincerely they may have wanted peace, in effect said to Hanoi, "Now, just hang in there, fellows, and you will get what you want politically even though you cannot win it militarily." Hanoi's persist-ence was incredible; I don't understand it, even to this day. The North Vietnamese suffered enormous casualties. But they were never willing to negotiate anything that we could call peace.

My mistake was not that I misread the strength of the North Viet-namese but that I underestimated their tenacity. As had happened in Korea, Berlin, and other crises in this postwar period, I believed the time would come when the North Vietnamese would find the job ahead of them too tough, come to the table, negotiate at least a cease-fire, and call off their aggression.

Of all those advising John Kennedy and Lyndon Johnson, George Ball was the only senior officer in government who flatly and unequivocably said, "I think what we are doing in Vietnam is a mistake." No one else came into my office, dug his heels into the rug, and said, "Mr. Secretary, I don't like this policy."

We never doubted where George Ball stood. He earned the respect and affection of both Kennedy and Johnson by the courage and eloquence with which he opposed the war. Although we all had a duty to support the president once a decision was made, before any decision a president ought to have the widest range of viewpoints available. Ball basically felt that our policy would not work, and he believed its costs were out of proportion to our obligations elsewhere. Like Dean Acheson, Ball was a strong North Atlantic man. He felt that Southeast Asia was peripheral to American interests. I disagreed, arguing that what happened in the Third World was important to our long-range interests. I also felt strongly about the United States' fidelity to our security treaties. George was not as worried if the United States failed to make good on the SEATO Treaty. We disagreed over the war, but I greatly valued his views.

At times I insisted that President Kennedy hear Ball's views directly, not channeled through me. Lyndon Johnson always sought Ball's views. We all appreciated his willingness to press his case privately within the administration, which he did with great force and eloquence. When the decisions did not go his way, he didn't try to undermine the administration by gossiping with journalists or going public with his views. The way he dissented earned our respect, and that was the key to his influence. Vietnam was but one issue; Ball fully supported the administration on hundreds of other issues, and I believe that's why he stayed on despite his profound differences on the war.

Others at State and within the administration had doubts about the war. Why they didn't express their misgivings remains a mystery to me. Several people resigned and later attributed their resignations to Vietnam, but while they were in office, they didn't say a word.

This held true as well for the cabinet. At most cabinet meetings Lyndon Johnson asked Bob McNamara and me to comment on Vietnam, and then he would go around the table, asking each cabinet officer, "Do you have any questions or comments?" Everyone sat silently. As soon as he left office, Ramsey Clark went all the way to Hanoi, but while he was attorney general, he wouldn't lean eight inches to his left to whisper in my ear, "I don't like what you are doing."

Vietnam raised difficult questions for some of my colleagues. Our Vietnam policy had been made by the president and Congress, the constitutional authorities of the government. The duty of those working for the executive branch is to take their direction from officials elected to give them direction, within the Constitution. It is one thing for public servants to raise questions and propose alternative views about policy, but it is another thing entirely to let those questions diminish their support for policy. I was sensitive on that point. It's not for civil servants or the bureaucracy to decide that the president is wrong, or bureaucracy's job to undermine presidential policy. There is a delicate line between raising questions about policy and failing to support the policy. When the president has decided what policy shall be, an officer should either support that policy or resign.

30

Tet, Policy Review, Paris Peace Talks

Most wars have a turning point, a key battle or series of engagements that are decisive. North Vietnam's Tet offensive of 1968 was the turning point of the American involvement in Vietnam. Up until Tet our military kept North Vietnam from overrunning the South, even though hard fighting continued. Politically, although support for our policies was eroding, we still had the support of Congress and the country.

But after Tet things changed. Even though American and South Vietnamese forces dealt the North Vietnamese a shattering military blow, the Tet offensive unleashed a tidal change in American opinion about the war.

Late in 1967, as prelude to the Tet offensive, the North Vietnamese laid siege to the Marine outpost at Khe Sanh and made a major effort to take it. Because of the French defeat at Dien Bien Phu, Khe Sanh assumed a symbolic importance beyond its actual value. Lyndon Johnson attached great importance to the defense of Khe Sanh and ordered our military to hold it. In that effort, American air power devastated the surrounding area with bombing more intense than any before in the history of warfare. Pinpoint bombing by high-flying B-52's made a moonscape of that entire area, and the North Vietnamese suffered terrible losses. I was not heavily involved with this campaign, but I, too, hoped that we could hold Khe Sanh.

While the fighting at Khe Sanh continued, in the weeks before Vietnam's Tet holiday on January 31, intelligence warned us that the Vietcong and the North Vietnamese were getting ready for a major effort. We were aware that something was coming, but the timing and strength of the Tet offensive surprised us. We didn't think the enemy would launch an offensive in the middle of the Tet holidays, any more than we would have expected Americans to launch a major offensive on Christmas Day. Many South Vietnamese soldiers were on leave to be with their families, but fortunately American soldiers were on duty and able to respond.

On January 31, while the siege of Khe Sanh continued, about seventy thousand North Vietnamese and Vietcong troops attacked over a hundred cities, villages, towns, and military bases throughout South Vietnam. In Saigon alone over four thousand North Vietnamese and Vietcong troops invaded the Cholon district, Saigon's Chinatown, and a Vietcong suicide squad attacked the U.S. Embassy.

The battle raged throughout the country for two weeks, except in Hue, where Communist forces retained control for a month, and everywhere enemy losses were enormous. After desperate fighting and much gallantry, American and South Vietnamese forces drove the enemy out of Hue and other strongholds and back into the countryside. The Communists failed to hold a single town, and more important, they failed to receive any popular support. General Westmoreland estimated the North Vietnamese and Vietcong lost fifty thousand men to our two thousand.

Tet was a major military victory for allied forces, but it quickly proved to be a political loss. In the days and weeks after the offensive, opinion remained divided within the administration and the nation at large over the meaning of the Tet offensive. From a purely military point of view, it reminded me of Germany's Battle of the Bulge in World War II—a last-ditch offensive. North Vietnamese strategists committed all their available manpower, apparently hoping that their offensive would spark a general uprising among the South Vietnamese people, but this did not occur. For us and our South Vietnamese allies, these were indeed rough days, and we suffered substantial casualties. The Tet offensive severely disrupted the pacification program in the countryside, and South Vietnamese forces were drawn back to defend provincial capitals, towns, and populated areas, leaving much of the countryside exposed to the enemy. But overall the Tet offensive was a severe military setback for the enemy. He took terrible losses.

And yet what was a striking military defeat for Hanoi was turned into a brilliant political victory in the United States because of Tet's effects upon the American people. How that came about is a very interesting question. The media's portrayal of the Tet offensive was certainly a factor. In *Big Story,* Peter Braestrup contrasted the events of Tet with their reporting back in the United States, raising compelling questions about the role of the press in wartime. When the networks broadcast footage of Vietcong sappers inside the walls of the American Embassy in Saigon, the inevitable impression was that the American effort in South Vietnam had simply gone to hell. The real truth was more complex.

After the Tet offensive, at a Friday backgrounder for newsmen, ABC correspondent John Scali asked what I thought was a loaded "no-win" kind of question. In responding, I asked him rather pointedly, "Whose side are you on?," startling both Scali and the reporters present. Contrary to the rules of backgrounders, that remark was reported and given national coverage; the media treated the remark as if I had raped the vestal virgins. When Scali later became our ambassador to the United Nations, I had good fun reminding him that he was going to be asking many people, "Whose side are you on?"

At our backgrounder, I felt I had asked Scali an appropriate question. If the United States failed in Southeast Asia and if this led to aggression elsewhere, there might not be any television networks or newspapers. The press had no vested interest in American failure in Southeast Asia, and yet some media reported our setbacks with far more enthusiasm than they reported our achievements. As secretary of state I never felt that I was refereeing a distant international dispute. My client was the United States of America, and my job was to represent the interests and policies of my country. I always felt that I was "on our side." If that question made the press uncomfortable, I am not entirely surprised in view of its performance in covering Vietnam.

In the weeks and months following Tet, many Americans at the grass roots, quite apart from protesters and college demonstrators, reached the conclusion that if we could not tell them when this struggle would end, we might as well chuck it. From public opinion polls, word of mouth, media reports, and our own observations, we received increasing evidence of a significant change in the mood of the country. Realizing that support for the war was waning, we intensified our efforts to negotiate an end. I felt that somehow we had to work toward either a negotiated settlement or, in the absence of a settlement, a de facto reduction of the American effort.

To defend our policy and help bolster public support, on March 11, 1968, I testified before the Senate Foreign Relations Committee in hearings broadcast live to a national audience. I had long wanted to testify before Fulbright's committee about the war. But in 1967 President Johnson had forbidden me to appear in public session because of negotiations already under way with Hanoi. He thought the timing was bad, and the last thing he wanted was a televised row over Vietnam. I offered to appear in executive session, but Fulbright wanted to grill me about Vietnam policy in televised hearings. But he and I both knew that if the State Department wanted foreign aid money that year, I would eventually have to appear. I finally showed up in March, and this time all the senators were in their seats, half with pancake on, ready for the show. For two days of solid testimony—nearly twelve hours' worth—not a word was said about foreign aid. It was all about Vietnam.

Viewers watching the hearings probably thought that those senators were trying to cut my liver out. But when the hearing was over, we went into a back room and had drinks together. Senator Albert Gore of Tennessee, who had roughed me up during the hearings, wrote me afterward and said, "Dear Dean; I've been looking over my mail on your testimony, and I thought you'd like to know that you won! The mail is running about three to one in your favor!"

Other trends and forces had been at work as well. After the Tet offensive had run its course, President Johnson invited the Joint Chiefs of Staff and General Westmoreland to report on the situation and their upcoming military requirements. Westmoreland subsequently submitted a bill for 206,000 more troops, a request that was, in effect, invited by President Johnson. Although this was only a contingency figure, it would have involved billions of dollars of additional defense expenditures, mobilizing national guardsmen and reservists. In effect, a national emergency would have been declared.

Personally I believed that the 535,000 Americans already serving in Vietnam, plus the much larger forces of the South Vietnamese and other allied forces, were fully adequate to deny military victory to the Vietcong and the North Vietnamese. I advised against sending another 206,000 men.

On February 28, 1968, Lyndon Johnson had formed a committee to consider the Joint Chiefs' report and Westmoreland's 206,000 troop request; he also named Clark Clifford to chair the committee. Clifford had just replaced Robert McNamara as secretary of defense. I attended only the first meeting because it was apparent that this group was not going to recommend sending another 206,000 men to Vietnam. In addition to me, Lyndon Johnson and Clark Clifford both opposed the troop increase. We were concerned about the status of our strategic reserve because we had begun calling some of these forces for duty in Vietnam. We even drew some key personnel out of NATO in Europe. I was more relaxed than the others about this because I felt that American forces serving in Vietnam constituted a strategic reserve. If a crisis developed elsewhere, we could readily redeploy them.

But at the same time I believed we should take additional steps to try to increase the possibility of negotiations. At a meeting held on March 4 to discuss the Clifford committee's report, I suggested to President Johnson that as an alternative to major reinforcements, we consider halting the bombing in those areas of North Vietnam not directly involved in the battle in the South. I suggested to the president that he insert the following passage in an upcoming speech: "After consultation with our allies, I have directed that U.S. bombing attacks on North Vietnam be limited to those areas which are integrally related to the battlefield. No reasonable person could expect us to fail to provide maximum support to our men in combat. Whether this step I have taken can be a step toward peace is for Hanoi to determine. We shall watch the situation carefully."

Given Hanoi's adamant refusal to consider negotiations unless we stopped bombing all of North Vietnam, I wanted an unconditional halt to bombing the northern regions of North Vietnam, especially the Hanoi-Haiphong area, which had cost us many planes and pilots. I wanted our bombing to concentrate primarily on the demilitarized zone and surrounding territory—staging areas, infiltration routes, and those areas directly related to the battlefield—thereby giving tactical support to our Marines and soldiers. I opposed a total bombing halt because we owed it to our men in uniform not to allow the North Vietnamese a free ride down the Ho Chi Minh Trail. Worsening weather from the upcoming monsoon would reduce opportunities for bombing in any case. Limiting our bombing to areas around the demilitarized zone (DMZ) and to tactical air support was a major initiative, which I hoped we might parlay into talks with Hanoi.

Rather than make a major diplomatic effort to begin talks or stage another peace offensive with our ambassadors flying all over the world, I urged simply taking the action—a partial but extensive halt—and waiting for Hanoi's reaction. If Hanoi failed to respond, as seemed entirely possible, we could resume bombing. I felt we shouldn't embroider the halt with "conditions" or "assumptions."

"Get on your horses and let's get something ready," the president replied. During March we prepared a plan for cessation of bombing north of the twentieth parallel. Although a bombing halt would help rally public opinion and demonstrate once again our genuine interest in negotiations, I believed Hanoi probably would insist on a total halt before beginning negotiations. Yet no president could endanger American troops along the DMZ by stopping all the bombing. We faced a clear dilemma, and I was not optimistic that our initiative would lead to talks.

I don't think President Johnson actually made a decision on the partial halt until a day or two before his March 31 speech on Vietnam. Earlier drafts of his speech didn't include the bombing halt proposal; when drafting presidential speeches, we never inserted initiatives that the president hadn't fully accepted. It is theoretically possible that always sensitive about leaks, especially of forthcoming decisions, Lyndon Johnson had decided in favor of the halt earlier in March and not shared that decision with me. General Westmoreland's request for 206,000 additional troops had leaked to the press, and that really set off LBJ. But I was not aware of any presidential decision to proceed with a bombing halt until just before the March 31 speech.

I am also persuaded the president decided on the halt at the last minute for two other reasons. First, Johnson was very skeptical about bombing halts. Over the past three years bombing halts had produced nothing except intensified infiltration by the North Vietnamese. After Tet LBJ remained disenchanted, although he realized that Americans at the grass roots were tiring of the war. Only then did he become more amenable to a pause.

Second, on March 25 and 26 a group of senior statesmen and former officials—whom Dean Acheson used to call "sons of bitches from out of town"—met again at the president's invitation to advise him on Vietnam. The group included Acheson, George Ball, John J. McCloy, McGeorge Bundy, Douglas Dillon, Cyrus Vance, Arthur Dean, General Omar Bradley, General Matthew Ridgway, General Maxwell Taylor, Robert Murphy, Henry Cabot Lodge, Abe Fortas, and Arthur Goldberg. I valued their input, not only because of their great experience but because most had not been involved in the daily decision making on Vietnam and now were somewhat removed from its detail and theology. I thought LBJ's asking them to convene was a good idea, however the chips might fall.

At their first meeting in October 1967 the "wise men" felt almost to a man that we were on the right track in Southeast Asia. Yet when that same group met after the Tet offensive, they were not nearly so sure that we ought to proceed; most felt that we ought to make the best peace that we could.

Dean Acheson, in particular, had changed his mind, saying that we ought to cut our losses and bring the war to a conclusion. Others had undergone a similar change. Acheson had been a hawk, strongly supporting our policy and the need to persevere. Because of Acheson's great experience, we had called upon him before. We did not take his advice on the Cuban missile crisis because he wanted to begin with an air strike. He opposed the quarantine, calling that action too weak. During the Truman years Acheson had been strongly criticized by many Republicans for being "soft" on communism. My guess is, after he left office, he overreacted to that earlier criticism by being extra hard-boiled. His advice on other occasions was rather hawkish. He had never been secretary of state when a full-scale nuclear exchange was operationally feasible, and this, too, may have influenced his thinking.

But because of his earlier support, Dean Acheson's change of heart—and that of the others as well—deeply affected Lyndon Johnson. The political tides had clearly moved against the war when Dean Acheson abandoned ship.

On March 28, Clifford, Rostow, William Bundy, and presidential speech writer Harry McPherson came over to my office to review the draft of the president's upcoming speech. It proposed 15,000 additional troops for Vietnam, much smaller than Westmoreland's requested 206,-000 men, and said nothing about a bombing halt or a peace initiative. As we reviewed it, Clark Clifford expressed strong misgivings about its tone and substance. He wanted to soften the language and stress negotiations. Halfway through the meeting, following vigorous discussion of options facing the president, I suggested that a second draft be prepared, incorporating many of Clifford's ideas. I also inserted a paragraph outlining a bombing halt north of the twentieth parallel, which I had intended to add quite apart from Clifford's expressed views:

Beginning immediately, and without waiting for any signal from Hanoi, we will confine our air and naval attacks in North Vietnam to the military targets south of the 20th parallel. That parallel runs about 75 miles south of the cities of Hanoi and Haiphong. North Vietnam's military reaction to this change in our bombing programs will determine both our willingness to confine it—and the reasonableness of our assumption that they [the North Vietnamese] would not take advantage of a complete bombing halt during the course of negotiations.

I added the partial halt not knowing what the president's final decision would be, although I thought he was moving in that direction. The fact that he hadn't snapped at such suggestions in earlier talks suggested he might go along with a halt, despite our earlier disappointments. But on a decision of such momentous importance, with so many conflicting views, I didn't want to hem him in by providing only one speech draft.

Afterward Clark Clifford expressed surprise that I went along with his suggestions. Clifford had argued persuasively, but I found even more persuasive the increasing evidence that Americans were losing heart in the war effort. The second draft's moderation pointed toward negotiation more so than the first draft. Reports that Clifford and I had a sharp confrontation in the post Tet offensive decision making have been sharply exaggerated. I simply had come to realize with Clifford that many Americans had changed their minds about the war. There was nothing insincere about my backing a partial bombing halt, as Clifford at first had suspected. I wasn't trying to appease public opinion. Clifford and I simply came together on what we must do.

During this March 28 meeting I also instructed William Bundy to draft a cable notifying Ellsworth Bunker, then our ambassador to South Vietnam, that the president had approved a partial bombing halt. We had earlier sent this proposal to Bunker for his reaction; he thought the South Vietnamese could live with a partial bombing halt but not a total halt. I wanted Bundy's cable to Bunker—drafted at our session—to be ready to go if the president approved it.

William Bundy and I visited the White House later that evening, and I met alone with the president. Believing we ought to maximize our chances for discussions that might lead to the end of the war, I advised him to use the second draft and announce a partial bombing halt, although I remained skeptical that the halt would lead to peace. President Johnson told me to send the cable to Bunker announcing a partial halt. Two days later, on March 30, the State Department cabled the news to our embassies. That same day I left for Wellington, New Zealand, for a SEATO meeting.

On March 31, in his speech to the nation, Johnson went with the partial halt and the revised speech. He declared that the United States would sharply curtail the bombing of North Vietnam, and that he had approved a 13,500-man troop increase—much smaller than Westmoreland's 206,000-man request. He also proposed peace talks with North Vietnam. At the end he announced that he would not run for reelection. On each point I thought he made the right decision.

My guess is, Lyndon Johnson made his final decision only when he saw and approved the second draft. I may have influenced Johnson somewhat, but suggestions that I played a decisive role in this decision have been exaggerated. Only LBJ could play the decisive role—and he did.

In the final speech draft Undersecretary of State Nicholas Katzenbach, acting in my absence, recommended changing the language from halting all bombing "north of the twentieth parallel"—which is what the president had decided upon—to saying that the bombing would end in North Vietnam "except in the area north of the demilitarized zone, where the continuing enemy buildup directly threatens allied forward positions." Although I had left for New Zealand, I was aware of and had approved Katzenbach's change, and I bear some responsibility for the controversy that followed. On April 1, one day after the president's speech, American planes struck targets just south of the twentieth parallel, prompting charges that we had misled the public in describing the no-bombing zone. American planes never again bombed targets north of the nineteenth parallel, although the administration never announced that as policy.

Although I was not consulted about Johnson's decision not to run, I was not surprised by it. In 1967 he talked with me about withdrawing not because of Vietnam but because of health. We discussed other men in public life who had become ill: We talked about President Eisenhower's heart attack, Woodrow Wilson's paralysis, Franklin Roosevelt's increasing age and illness, and the fact that no vice president had ever succeeded to the presidency and then run for two full terms. He never said this categorically, but I think Johnson was primarily concerned about his health. Lady Bird Johnson stressed health as well and encouraged him not to run.

When Johnson made his March 31 speech, I was in Wellington, New Zealand, attending a SEATO meeting. During my flight to New Zealand the White House called to alert me about a "final paragraph" that had been added to the March 31 speech. I knew what it was—Johnson's withdrawal statement—and it came as no surprise. All my advice to Johnson during this period was based on my view that the

American people were tiring of the war, and we needed to get some talks started with North Vietnam as an alternative to further escalation of the war. Johnson was determined to move toward peace, and I think his withdrawal helped.

On April 4, five days after the president's speech, Hanoi announced it would send representatives to begin talks. Perhaps licking their wounds from the Tet offensive, the North Vietnamese probably sensed that we, too, would come to the bargaining table in a weakened position. The timing was propitious for both sides.

Four days later President Johnson, our negotiators, Averell Harriman and Cyrus Vance, William Bundy, and I met at Camp David to prepare. Beyond wanting the North Vietnamese to move promptly to substantive talks, our basic negotiating position remained consistent. We wanted the North Vietnamese to agree to a cease-fire, accept the South Vietnamese regime at the conference table, negotiate a mutual withdrawal of American and North Vietnamese forces, respect the demilitarized zone, stop attacking South Vietnamese cities, release American prisoners of war, and comply with the Laos accords of 1962. The president and I didn't discuss fallback positions or easing terms in those original instructions, preferring to modify them as events unfolded. We were concerned that leaks could undercut our position if the negotiations proved long and difficult and that our negotiators, operating under enormous pressure, might move to a fallback position too quickly.

Averell Harriman—my personal choice as well as the president's—headed our delegation for the Paris talks. Harriman was a superb troubleshooter. He knew how to deal with the Soviets and had done a great job in negotiating the Laos accords and Limited Test Ban Treaty. He was ably seconded by Cyrus Vance, who had done valuable work for us in the Dominican Republic and Cyprus. Vance also knew his way around a negotiating table. President Johnson had enormous confidence in Vance; because of Vance's Pentagon background, Johnson was more comfortable with a Harriman-Vance team than if State alone had been represented.

A number of my colleagues in the State Department were just as qualified as I to be secretary of state and would have gladly taken the job, Averell Harriman among them. He might have been John Kennedy's choice had he been fifteen to twenty years younger. Yet Harriman was probably younger in spirit than any man in Washington. He worked harder than men half his age. Despite his accomplishments and aristocratic upbringing, I always found Harriman easy to work with. Although he had been a member of Franklin Roosevelt's cabinet and former ambassador to London and Moscow, his vast experience never led to vanity. Harriman took on whatever chores needed doing.

While Harriman was traveling in Europe, I once called to tell him that President Johnson wanted to name him assistant secretary for Far Eastern affairs. "Of course!" he said. "Whatever the president wants." Thirty minutes later he called back. "Well, as you know, Dean, I am a little deaf. Which assistant secretary did he want me to take?" I repeated, "Far Eastern affairs." He said, "All right." He hadn't even understood which post he had accepted in our first conversation.

Despite his forceful views and independent mind, Harriman was a disciplined negotiator who stayed within his instructions. He never went around town backbiting the administration. However difficult or hopeless a situation, Averell Harriman never despaired or stopped trying. Those qualities were tested to the limit by the Paris talks.

I was somewhat naive in thinking that Washington and Hanoi could conduct meaningful talks. We had great difficulty simply getting under way. Troubles began over selecting a site. Hanoi turned down Geneva, Vienna, New Delhi, Jakarta, Rangoon, everything we proposed. In a maneuver with Lyndon Johnson as well as Hanoi, I deliberately left Paris off our list of acceptable sites. Had our list included Paris, Hanoi would have turned it down. Lyndon Johnson probably would have as well; he was not enthusiastic about Paris because he feared Charles de Gaulle's hostile attitude toward the war might negatively influence the talks. But despite Johnson's reluctance, we agreed on Paris. I knew that LBJ would have to accept Paris if the North Vietnamese accepted it as a site. And Paris proved a good choice; the French did everything possible to facilitate the talks.

Once a site was selected, the talks bogged down quickly over substantive issues. Hanoi wanted a total and unconditional halt to our bombing and what it called "all acts of force" against North Vietnam. Insisting upon reciprocity in exchange for a halt, President Johnson wanted the North Vietnamese to respect the DMZ, stop infiltrating men and supplies, stop attacking South Vietnamese cities, and specifically explain how they would reduce the level of fighting if we called off the bombing.

The simple truth was we didn't know how they would react if we stopped the bombing, and Hanoi refused to tell us. This wasn't a problem of diplomatic technique; there were many ways for Hanoi to signal its intentions. We knew that if we stopped bombing in exchange for expanded talks, the North Vietnamese would simply go ahead with the war in South Vietnam.

Our position never included withdrawal from South Vietnam regardless of the consequences. We didn't want a repeat of the Laos accords of 1962, where we got a good agreement on paper but no performance by North Vietnam. We weren't willing in 1968 to accept any formula in which the Americans withdrew from South Vietnam yet allowed North Vietnamese troops to remain; that was tantamount to surrender.

Despite the shock of the Tet offensive, our policy throughout 1968 remained close to what it had always been. The United States continued to support South Vietnam, preventing North Vietnam from seizing it by force. We hoped to negotiate an end to the fighting. By spring of 1968 we genuinely felt that the impact of the Tet offensive on the North Vietnamese, coupled with our own perceptions about the attitude of Americans on the home front, might open up new possibilities.

But it didn't work out that way. Throughout April, May, and June 1968, the North Vietnamese, even in their weakened state, continued to attack in the South, including the cities. Despite this offensive and the lack of progress in the Paris talks, I advised the president not to resume bombing. In July, however, the frequency of attacks dropped dramatically. We weren't sure if this was due to exhaustion or if Hanoi was trying to send us a signal, but Harriman and Vance were convinced the lull in the fighting was politically significant. They requested a complete bombing halt of North Vietnam, arguing that the cutback in North Vietnamese activity would continue. Harriman was convinced that progress in the Paris talks would come only if we stopped all bombing of North Vietnam.

I buried my doubts and supported their proposal, encouraged that Hanoi had dropped its demands for South Vietnam's complete adherence to the NLF's program and thinking we should test the water to see if this "lull" was significant. But the president rejected a total halt, remembering past experience and believing that Hanoi would use another halt to flood men and supplies into South Vietnam. He ordered our limited bombing to continue.

I doubt this was a "missed opportunity for peace," however. Throughout 1968, although physically present at the table in Paris, the North Vietnamese made no substantive contribution toward a negotiated settlement. They remained adamant in formal talks, as with all those private contacts throughout the Johnson years. Through the summer of 1968 and into the fall there was never any sign that Hanoi wanted peace in Southeast Asia on any terms other than its own: an unconditional halt to the bombing, the withdrawal of all American forces, and a North Vietnamese takeover of South Vietnam, Laos, and Cambodia.

The talks deadlocked over whether the National Liberation Front and the Saigon regime would be represented at the conference. Also at issue, although we had scaled our bombing down considerably, was North Vietnam's insistence that we stop the bombing entirely for the talks to proceed. We had wanted Hanoi to state publicly how it would respond to a bombing halt. To circumvent the obstacle of reciprocity, we told the North Vietnamese that a complete halt involved what we called three "facts of life." In secret sessions we insisted that if we stopped all the bombing, North Vietnam would have to accept South Vietnam at the conference table, not violate the demilitarized zone so that the bombing halt wouldn't endanger American forces south of the DMZ, and refrain from attacking South Vietnamese cities. We also told the Soviets, "Please tell your friends in Hanoi that we are concerned about these 'facts of life,' we told them. "We're not calling them 'conditions.' We're just saying that no president can stop the bombing while American troops are in combat unless these three things occur."

Instead of haggling indefinitely over the separate status of the NLF and South Vietnamese, we proposed an "our side-your side" formula whereby both North Vietnam and the United States could have whomever they wanted on their side of the table.

I remained skeptical about not only Hanoi's willingness to observe the main elements in our proposal but even its willingness to take part in expanded talks. However, on October 27, 1968, Hanoi told us that if we stopped bombing, expanded talks could begin in Paris on November 2 and all three of our assumptions would be realized within a week. This pledge met the American formula. Hanoi's acceptance of South Vietnam at the conference table was a vital breakthrough. Bunker met with South Vietnamese President Nguyen Van Thieu to get his approval.

On October 31, 1968, one hour before Washington, Hanoi, Saigon, and the National Liberation Front were publicly to announce the start of expanded talks, South Vietnamese President Thieu, after meeting with his cabinet, backed out. He reportedly was nervous about the presence of the Vietcong at the negotiating table and where such negotiations might lead. Thieu presented new demands. He wanted all procedural issues to be agreed upon first and a firm assurance that

Hanoi would both de-escalate the war and negotiate directly with his regime. Changing his mind, he also refused to accept seating the NLF as a separate delegation.

Also, Thieu was gambling that he could get a better deal from Richard Nixon than he could from either Lyndon Johnson or Hubert Humphrey. Thieu may have had reasons for thinking that. Throughout his 1968 presidential campaign Richard Nixon implied that he had a plan to end the war, but when asked what it was, he would tap his coat pocket as if something were there and say he didn't want to interfere with the Paris talks. We appreciated his not wanting to interfere, but I am not certain his staffers held to his desires. Late in the campaign, perhaps nervous about the prospects of a settlement, some Nixon backers reportedly encouraged Thieu to hold out in the talks.

I never had any evidence that Richard Nixon himself was involved, but rumors abounded that Spiro Agnew and Anna Chennault had contacted the South Vietnamese. I never got to the bottom of it, but because the evidence was so sketchy, I did tell Lyndon Johnson that I didn't think he should go public with this.

Although Thieu wanted to delay talks until after our presidential election, he also had trouble convincing his own colleagues to negotiate. Some were adamantly opposed to the Paris talks. Consequently Thieu's problems in Saigon compounded his differences with us.

Unfortunately tension developed between Washington and the American delegation in Paris over Saigon's refusal to participate. This tension was partly built in: Harriman's job was to get on with the negotiations, and Ellsworth Bunker's was to obtain Thieu's participation. Obviously the United States had great leverage with the Thieu regime, having underwritten much of South Vietnam's war effort and economy. Some of our people wanted to use American aid as a trump card to force Thieu to the table, but I believed that kind of leverage isn't always decisive. You can't put a yes in a man's mouth if he insists on saying no.

For that reason, I advised against trying to force the South Vietnamese to acquiesce to talks. My view was that we Americans, whatever our influence, could not make a regime act against its will. Ellsworth Bunker couldn't name a South Vietnamese delegation, tie its members into an airplane, and fly them to Paris in handcuffs when Thieu gritted his teeth and refused to participate. Harriman seemed to think we could order Thieu to Paris. But as we had learned with Diem in 1963, the United States couldn't make and unmake governments in

South Vietnam. We could advise, persuade, cajole, pressure, and occasionally threaten, but at the end of the day, especially during the Paris talks, when the very survival of South Vietnam was at stake, those decisions had to be made by the South Vietnamese themselves. Despite our substantial military presence and economic leverage, we couldn't force decisions upon them.

At a Tuesday luncheon on October 29 I tried to take a long-range view of the problem: "President Kennedy said we would make a battle there to save South Vietnam. That set us on course. We lost 29,000 men and invested $75 billion to keep South Vietnam from being overrun. We must be careful not to flush all this down the drain. But we do have a right to expect cooperation from the South Vietnamese. . . . If the problem in Saigon is only a matter of timing, we should set a time convenient to them."

But there was another side to the problem; we couldn't let Thieu's refusal sabotage the Paris talks. Having already agreed to expanded talks, we had to proceed even though the South Vietnamese were unwilling to come to Paris. We had quite a fight with Thieu and faced the prospect of a choice between withdrawing American forces and abandoning South Vietnam or trying to get Thieu's cooperation. However, we did have a convenient tool with which to pressure Thieu: the negotiations themselves. Thus, on October 31, as scheduled, President Johnson announced a complete halt of air, naval, and artillery bombardment of North Vietnam effective the next day; also, he announced that expanded peace talks would begin in Paris on November 6 and noted that South Vietnam was "free" to attend. Finally, in early December, Thieu agreed to send a delegation.

After more delay the talks soon degenerated into haggling over the shape of the negotiating table, and little was accomplished in the remaining weeks of the Johnson administration. We hoped until the end that an agreement might be possible, but it was not to be.

I cannot fault Ellsworth Bunker in his unsuccessful effort to get Thieu on board. He warned us that the South Vietnamese would be difficult. With Bunker, as with Harriman, we had sent our best; Ellsworth Bunker was one of the finest diplomats this country ever turned out.

Disingenuously Thieu claimed that Bunker never kept him adequately informed on the Paris negotiations, even though Saigon kept a liaison officer in Paris. Thieu's charges were without substance. We had delegated heavily to Bunker, telling him to use whatever instruments of persuasion and pressure he felt necessary to get South Vietnamese participation, but Thieu simply filibustered, awaiting a change of administrations.

Thieu's absence and last-minute objections were extremely annoying, but the main problem continued to be North Vietnam. Hanoi bore responsibility for the lack of progress from April to October by insisting upon an unconditional bombing halt and refusing to seat the South Vietnamese. In addition, Thieu had every right to be suspicious of Hanoi's purposes in the Paris talks. North Vietnam had broken the Geneva accords of 1954 and the Laos accords of 1962. The North Vietnamese signed both without any intention of complying with them.

The Paris talks were hard on all of us but especially on Averell Harriman. He had been a supporter of U.S. policy throughout most of the Vietnam decision making, and his efforts to negotiate a settlement were frustrated by the impasse resulting from Hanoi's adamancy and Washington's insistence upon reciprocity. There were times when Harriman's suggestions went further than the president and I wanted to go. During the summer he advocated a phased withdrawal of American troops that might have left North Vietnamese soldiers in place in South Vietnam. That, to me, was outright surrender. But I cannot fault Harriman or our team in Paris. They tried their best to move difficult negotiations forward under circumstances heavily complicated by the attitudes of both the South and North Vietnamese.

As the Paris peace talks dragged inconclusively toward the Nixon inauguration, President Johnson realized that he was not going to wind up the Vietnam War before he left office. He told us that he wanted a smooth transition and that he didn't want to make any major decisions that should be made by the incoming administration. He preferred leaving President Nixon a full range of options. By January 1969 the United States had established a military position in South Vietnam that North Vietnam could not overrun, the Paris peace talks were under way, and we had gone a long ways toward building up South Vietnamese forces. With little substantive progress during nine months of Paris talks, we thought the new president should make his own decisions for the future since he had been chosen by the American people to do just that.

When we turned responsibility over to the incoming administration, I had supposed that any new president would have to move as promptly as possible to get us out of Vietnam. I was surprised that President Nixon took five years to end our involvement. I sympathized completely with what he was trying to do—leave something behind that made sense from the American point of view—but in terms of continuing the war, I felt that the American people had made that decision in a nationwide election.

Unfortunately two things we could not turn over to the Nixon administration: a unified Congress and a unified people. Although some hope for South Vietnam's survival existed at the end of 1968, the simple truth was that the American people were tiring of the war. President Nixon's secret guarantees of future assistance to President Thieu, without the support of Congress and the American people, really weren't his to give. He no longer had a mandate for continuing the war.

The Paris peace agreements of 1973 were in effect a surrender. Any agreement that left North Vietnamese troops in South Vietnam meant the eventual takeover of South Vietnam. We knew this from North Vietnam's failure to comply with past agreements. If in 1961 President Kennedy and his advisers had had the 1973 agreements to look forward to, we wouldn't have made the effort. We could have had peace at any time on the basis by which we finally pulled our troops out in 1973. Our basic position throughout the Johnson years was that any settlement must require the withdrawal of North Vietnamese forces. I cannot fault the Nixon administration for negotiating the 1973 agreement—President Nixon had no alternative—but no one should have expected Hanoi to comply with that kind of agreement. And as history has shown us, once again it did not.

31

A Vietnam Retrospective

Since leaving office in January 1969, I have been offered many chances to present a *mea culpa* on Vietnam, but I have not availed myself of those opportunities. I thought the principal decisions made by President Kennedy and President Johnson were the right decisions at the time they were made. I supported their decisions. There is nothing I can say now that would diminish my share of responsibility for the events of those years. I live with that, and others can make of it what they will.

I have not apologized for my role in Vietnam, for the simple reason that I believed in the principles that underlay our commitment to South Vietnam and why we fought that war. As a private citizen I believe in those principles today. The withdrawal of American troops did not bring genuine peace to Southeast Asia.

As a so-called senior statesman I have not tried to play the role of grandstand quarterback or participate actively in postmortem discussions of our Vietnam policy. We all made mistakes of judgment and decisions we came to regret. There is blame enough. But I feel that I owe my primary allegiance to my two presidents, to the men and women we sent to South Vietnam, and to the cause they tried their best to serve.

Could the Vietnam War have been won? I think so, if we could have maintained solidarity on the home front and if we could have accepted "winning" as defined by the Kennedy and Johnson administrations: preventing North Vietnam's takeover of South Vietnam by force.

Personally I hoped and expected the North Vietnamese would realize that they could not overrun South Vietnam militarily and that when they came to this realization, we and they would find some way to conclude the war, negotiate a cease-fire, and work toward a political settlement along the lines of the status quo ante. But they were encouraged to stick it out, and they eventually got it all. However, I am convinced that our men in uniform carried out their mission: to prevent North Vietnam from seizing South Vietnam by force. It wasn't until we pulled our forces out and Congress cut off supplies that North Vietnam overran the South.

Had this not happened, Vietnam would still be divided in the fashion of the two Koreas and the two Germanys, and it would not have emerged as the strongest military power in Southeast Asia. Cambodia would probably still be under the rule of Prince Sihanouk, who, however unpredictable, was devoted to his people. Laos might have fallen under Communist domination unless special arrangements were negotiated at the time of a Vietnamese settlement, but the Laotians would be muddling along in their Laotian way. We wouldn't have witnessed hundreds of thousands of refugees fleeing Vietnam, genocide in Cambodia, or erosion in American support of collective security regarding conflict in Central America, the Middle East, and elsewhere. A peace of sorts, better than what resulted, would have settled over Indochina and Southeast Asia, and although we Americans would be licking our wounds as we did after Korea, we would have recovered from the experience more rapidly than we have.

In spite of Hanoi's reliance on division in this country, I don't conclude that Americans should refrain from lively and even boisterous debate on foreign policy. Questions of war and peace must be freely and fully discussed. Nor do I believe that government should try to stifle dissent. If confusion both at home and abroad is a by-product of this debate, that is a price we pay for democracy.

The Nixon administration had an unfortunate habit of associating dissent over Vietnam with treason. The Kennedy and Johnson administrations tried to steer clear of that. The many critics of our Vietnam policy were not unpatriotic. I never thought of them in that light. Nor were members of Congress who supported our policy initially and later changed their minds. I never challenged our antiwar critics' constitutional right to dissent, but I wish more of them had simply said, "I've changed my mind," and not scurried around, misrepresenting what both they and the administration had actually done.

I have served at both ends of military command—receiving orders in the China-Burma-India theater during World War II and giving orders for Vietnam in the sixties. In some ways it is more difficult to give orders, although you can't tell veterans that. But whether issuing orders or receiving them, I have deeply regretted every casualty on all sides of every war fought in my lifetime, beginning with World War I. To me, war is the principal obscenity of the human race; it is horrible in every respect. But in making decisions or obeying them, I had a duty to perform. It was that sense of duty—that someone must do this job and make those decisions—and also my full belief in the principles that underlay our policies that sustained me as secretary of state.

On a trip to South Vietnam in 1966 I visited a hospital in Saigon where badly wounded American soldiers were being treated. As I walked through the wards, an Army nurse, a captain or major, stared long and hard at me, with a look of undisguised hatred. She didn't say a word. She didn't have to. From the look on her face she clearly held me responsible for what happened to those men. I never forgot the look on that nurse's face.

Every casualty takes a little piece out of those who carry command responsibilities. After all that had happened in World War II and the postwar years, it was a great tragedy to ask young Americans to undertake this fighting. It is at such times that a decision maker relies on what he truly believes. Decisions that commit men to battle are not made casually. We in the Kennedy and Johnson administrations thought long and hard about every decision. We did not drift into commitment to South Vietnam, and we did not enter the war thoughtlessly.

The overriding problem before us in Southeast Asia was the same problem that all mankind faces: how to prevent World War III. The principal lesson I learned from World War II was that if aggression is allowed to gather momentum, it can continue to build and lead to general war. That is why we drafted the United Nations Charter and the collective security treaties of the postwar period. If I thought there was no connection between the events in Southeast Asia, the broad structure of world peace, and the possibility of a third world war, I might have advised differently on Vietnam. But in Southeast Asia, and in that pattern of aggression practiced by North Vietnam, I saw what I thought were the seeds of conflict for future war.

Will history validate my views? Historians won't be able to make those judgments for another two or three decades. In any case, I won't be around for history's verdict, and I am perfectly relaxed about it. I do hope that the events of the next twenty and thirty years will move so positively in the direction of a durable peace that future historians will say, "President Kennedy and President Johnson and those fellows Rusk and McNamara overdid it. What they did wasn't necessary at all."

Whatever views they might hold about the war, all Americans owe a great debt to those who carried the battle. I myself would hope that none of our men and women of Vietnam feel that they were engaged in a shameful enterprise. They served at the behest of constitutional authority, on issues perceived to involve war and peace and the survival of the human race. They have nothing of which to be ashamed.

Foreign policy decisions are almost never drawn between black and white, good and evil. In the real world, good principles often contradict each other, sometimes collide, and always compete for influence in final decisions. Presidents and their advisers frequently have to choose among unpleasant alternatives since easy questions are handled farther down in the bureaucracy, long before they get to a president.

Decisions like those of Vietnam have within them dozens of secondary questions. Out of that profusion of elements, a president must find the decisive factors. In Vietnam the decisive issue was the fidelity of the United States to collective security and its treaty commitments and the implications of that fidelity for world peace.

Considering the importance of the issues at stake, it is unfortunate that they were trivialized with the term "domino theory." I never used that term myself, thinking that we should not turn to games of wooden blocks that children play on living-room rugs. When I left office in January 1969, there were thousands of North Vietnamese in Laos, tens of thousands in Cambodia, and more than one hundred thousand in South Vietnam. Every week men trained in North Vietnam and armed and supplied by North Vietnam were moving into northeastern Thailand. Every week men and arms were moving across the northeastern frontier of Burma out of China. Every week bands of saboteurs crossed the thirty-eighth parallel from North Korea into South Korea. I didn't have to look for dominoes. I had only to look at what was happening on the ground. The theory involved was not the domino theory but the theory of the world revolution.

I draw no satisfaction out of the course of events in Indochina since the U.S. withdrawal, but at least those who opposed our Vietnam policy during the sixties can now see for themselves what we were trying to avoid. Indochina is now ruled by the men in Hanoi. Since leaving Washington, I have never referred to postwar developments to help justify past policy. Why keep these sores of Vietnam open? We must learn from our experience, but we must also put the war behind us.

Outside of Indochina, in the rest of Southeast Asia, the American stand in South Vietnam probably encouraged economic growth and political stability among the ASEAN (Association of Southeast Asian Nations) members. During the late 1960's an Indonesian general told me that the abortive Communist coup d'état in Indonesia in 1965 might have succeeded had it not been for the presence of American forces in Vietnam. He felt our presence helped prevent the communization of Indonesia. And in Thailand the U.S. presence in the region helped the Thai government meet and cope with the Communist insurgency in the Northeast. The recent prosperity of non-Communist Southeast Asia may flow from the American stand in South Vietnam. Nowhere is the momentum of regional cooperation more evident than in eastern Asia and the western Pacific. A variety of regional associations have taken root; cooperative projects in education, agriculture, transportation, and communications abound.

What of my own role in America's Vietnam experience? Some scholars have speculated that in advising my two presidents, I resisted the introduction of American combat forces, the "Americanization" of the war, and the bombing of North Vietnam. That is not correct. What I tried to do was make sure that we acted without illusion and understood the seriousness of our decisions. I knew that tough times lay ahead, and I raised many questions along the way. Some of my questions and memos found their way into the *Pentagon Papers*. More will emerge as information is declassified. But my doubts were registered only as questions, never as opposition to policy. I never advised either president to withdraw from South Vietnam.

I agreed with both President Kennedy and President Johnson on the major decisions. John Kennedy was right to increase American advisers beyond the U.S. Military Assistance Advisory Group limits of the 1954 Geneva accords and to increase advisers throughout his term. I agreed with Lyndon Johnson's decision to launch retaliatory strikes after the

August 1964 Tonkin Gulf incidents, to begin bombing North Vietnam in February 1965, and to land Marines at Da Nang shortly thereafter, and I supported the buildup that followed. I supported the military in their use of antidefoliants, napalm, and antipersonnel weapons.

I did have misgivings about bombing targets in the far North, including the Hanoi-Haiphong area, and I raised those objections at the Tuesday luncheons. I never thought it was worth the cost in American lives and airplanes. When the decision was made, I tried to keep the bombing restricted to genuine military objectives, and I fully supported the bombing of the Ho Chi Minh Trail and the areas north of the seventeenth parallel, in efforts to stop the infiltration of men and supplies into South Vietnam. To me, the war would be won or lost in the South.

As secretary of state I made two serious mistakes with respect to Vietnam. First, I overestimated the patience of the American people, and second, I underestimated the tenacity of the North Vietnamese. They took frightful casualties. In relation to our own population, their total casualties throughout the war were roughly equivalent to ten million American casualties. I thought North Vietnam would reach a point, as happened with our adversaries during the Korean War and the Berlin blockade of 1948, when it would be unwilling to continue making those terrible sacrifices, come to the conference table, and either negotiate an end to the war or make some concessions we could live with, perhaps postponing a final settlement for another day. After the Tet offensive of January 1968, which was a severe military setback for the Vietcong and the North Vietnamese, I thought Hanoi might come to the conference table and call the whole thing off. I was wrong.

My other mistake was overestimating the patience of the American people. As a people we Americans are very impatient about war, and God bless us for that. Americans, as do ordinary people at the grass roots in every country, strongly prefer peace and abhor war. The trouble is, in a democracy this yearning for peace gets full expression, offering opportunities for totalitarian regimes to misinterpret American policy and underestimate what we are prepared to do.

Our impatience with war can lead to unfortunate outcomes, as George Marshall once pointed out to me when we were traveling together after World War II. I asked Marshall what was really in the minds of the Americans in their argument with the British over whether to reenter Europe through Normandy or through the southern Mediterranean and the Balkans, what Churchill called the "soft underbelly of Europe." Marshall said that the United States had to get the war over with as soon as possible, before the very institutions of our democracy melted out from under us and we could no longer sustain the war effort. Our educational system was running down; our professions were drying up; our industrial system wasn't meeting the essential requirements of the American people; we were running out of capital stock; all because our society was wholly committed to mobilization. He and FDR believed that going in through Normandy was the quickest way to end the war and that we couldn't prolong the war for postwar political purposes, as Churchill wanted to do with the southern approach.

With this American impatience, we knew that gradualism—our policy of restraint—would run into problems. Using American power with restraint and fighting a limited war in Vietnam were a tough proposition, hard upon the home front and hardest of all upon our men and women in the field. Fighting that kind of war requires a special devotion to duty.

But we had tried this approach before and it had worked; indeed, we had to make it work to avoid slipping into general war. Since the end of World War II, in no small part because of the overarching threat of nuclear weapons, the United States had consistently tried to use just enough military force to accomplish the mission at hand.

The examples are numerous. When Soviet forces tried to stay in northern Iran, we didn't resort to military force. We took that case to the United Nations Security Council; we pressed, complained, and demanded; and we finally winked the Soviets out of Iran. When Communist guerrillas went after Greece, operating out of bases in Albania, Yugoslavia, and Bulgaria, we did not open up hostilities against those three countries. We gave as much help as we could to the Greeks, who eventually took care of their own problems, with an assist from Yugoslavia's defection from the Warsaw bloc. When Stalin blockaded Berlin, a reckless act that brought the superpowers close to war, we used an airlift to keep the people of West Berlin alive until we and the Soviets finally negotiated the end of the blockade. After the Chinese crossed the Yalu, MacArthur wanted to go to general war against China, but Truman said no. When his military advisers told Truman that only the destruction of Chinese cities by nuclear weapons could affect the fighting in Korea, Truman again said no. Especially in a nuclear age, when general war would mean catastrophe, the United States has tried to use its enormous power with restraint. Fighting a limited war and placing restraints on the use of American power are hard on a democratic people. And yet there is a certain grandeur to American policy in this postwar period, to our record of restraint, to our insistence that we were not going to let things slip out of control.

In all these crises we tried to take whatever action was necessary to blunt aggression and restore peace, without sliding down the slippery slope into general war. That effort required discipline and self-restraint and prudence; it also required a special gallantry by our men in uniform, who did their professional duty without the support of a democratic people whipped up for general war. During this postwar period, in any number of crises, we could have had general war anytime we wanted one. With Vietnam, in the late 1960's we were losing on the average one hundred men a week. We could have lost ten thousand a week or a hundred thousand a week. We could have knocked out three hundred million people in the first hour.

We used this same approach in our responses to aggression in Southeast Asia. All we were trying to do was deny North Vietnam's effort to take over South Vietnam by force. We weren't trying to conquer North Vietnam or seize its territory. The Johnson administration didn't mine Haiphong Harbor, bomb downtown Hanoi, destroy the Red River dikes, or invade North Vietnam with American forces. We never contemplated using nuclear weapons. Tactically American military operations often took the offensive, but strategically we were on the defensive. We were trying to prevent something from happening. We did not want to do any more than was necessary to defend South Vietnam. We responded gradually to increasing effort by North Vietnam. Our own actions were usually taken in response to its initiatives. That always left the North Vietnamese the opportunity to decide that if they just did a little more, we would eventually do less.

Was gradualism the best way to proceed in South Vietnam? Could we have prevented further North Vietnamese escalation had we landed more American troops sooner? No one can answer this, but had President Kennedy committed one hundred thousand men in 1962, as soon as we learned that North Vietnam was violating the Laos accords negotiated that same year, if he had pushed in a stack of blue chips at the very beginning, it is just possible the North Vietnamese would have realized we were serious. They realized it eventually when we had one-half million Americans in South Vietnam, at great cost to us and them. But our gradual response possibly encouraged North Vietnam to speculate that we did not intend to stay the course.

Since we wanted to limit the war, we deliberately refrained from creating a war psychology in the United States. We did not try to stir up the anger of the American people over Vietnam, and we did not have military troops parading through our cities or put on big war bond drives. Neither did we send movie actors around the country, whipping up enthusiasm for the war. We felt that in a nuclear world it was just too dangerous for an entire people to become too angry. There's too much power in the world, and it's too dangerous for great nations to get too mad. With nuclear weapons in our arsenal, we didn't want to chance letting things get out of hand. We tried to wage this war as "calmly" as possible, treating it as a "police action" rather than as a full-scale war. This may have been a mistake. And we never tried to use the government's power to reverse the war's growing unpopularity. Perhaps this, too, was a mistake.

We learned from our Vietnam experience that no president can pursue a policy committing American soldiers to combat for very long without the support of Congress and the American people. When enough people change their minds, then policy changes. Yet it is quite revealing to review the extent to which Congress supported the war. Congress demonstrably turned against the war only in the last months of the Johnson administration and continued on this path during the Nixon and Ford administrations by rescinding the Tonkin Gulf Resolution and passing the War Powers Act over President Nixon's veto. But until these actions, congressional support for our Vietnam policy was steady.

Up until 1967 our principal congressional opponents had been hawks, who pounded the table and demanded tougher action against North Vietnam. But when the Johnson administration decided not invade North Vietnam, not to obliterate Hanoi, and otherwise refused to enlarge the war, many hawks in Congress became doves. They told us, in effect, "If you're not going to fight this war our way, we might as well get out."

In my congressional appearances over Vietnam, I was instructed by President Johnson never to promise Congress advance consultation on exact numbers of troops. Johnson considered that his decision as commander in chief. Several times committee members tried to get me to promise advance consultations for further troop increases, but I couldn't promise that because the president wouldn't let me. But I also agreed with Lyndon Johnson; I don't think a committee of 535 members can run a war.

Some called Vietnam an abuse of presidential power, claiming that the Kennedy and Johnson administrations led the nation blindly into Vietnam. I disagreed. So, too, did Arizona Senator Barry Goldwater, who, during floor debate on the War Powers Act in 1971, became fed up with congressional whining about how the president had exceeded his authority and bypassed Congress. In a speech on the Senate floor, Goldwater said that Congress had been involved up to its ears in the war. He spelled out line, chapter, and verse each specific action taken by Congress, beginning with Senate ratification of the Southeast Asia Treaty Organization in 1955. He said the implications of the SEATO Treaty were well understood when Congress ratified it with only one dissenting vote. He pointed to the Tonkin Gulf Resolution, which the Senate approved 88–2 and the House approved unanimously. He observed that Senator Fulbright was asked whether the resolution gave the president authority to take whatever action might be necessary to defend South Vietnam, even if such action might lead to war, and Fulbright answered, "That is the way I would interpret it." Goldwater reminded his colleagues that in 1966 Senator Wayne Morse moved to rescind that resolution, and on a motion to table, only five senators supported his position. Goldwater listed twenty-four separate appropriations actions on which Congress held hearings, debated the issues, and signaled its support by approving funds for the war effort. Concluded Goldwater: "It would be a malicious falsehood to use the tragedy of Vietnam as the fulcrum of a war against the executive branch by a Congress which was wholly involved in the policies it now questions."

Long before the Tonkin Gulf Resolution, we met regularly with key committees of Congress. When the transcripts of these executive sessions are finally published, the record will show that little was withheld from Congress about Vietnam during the Kennedy and Johnson years. For two years Lyndon Johnson invited the entire Congress to the White House in small groups for full briefings on Vietnam and to hear their questions and comments. Johnson probably consulted with Congress more extensively than any other president.

We did consider asking Congress each year for a fresh vote on the Tonkin Gulf Resolution. I wanted an annual vote and advised President Johnson to that effect. But when Johnson asked congressional leaders, they advised him not to do it. They said the resolution would pass, but with a smaller majority than the first time. "Live with the one you've got," said the leadership. So we decided not to resubmit it. In retrospect, that was probably a mistake. Perhaps members of Congress didn't want to face that vote. But we should have gone to Congress every year for an up or down vote on Vietnam following the Tonkin Gulf Resolution, so that we would know with certainty what the views of Congress were. I would have preferred a direct vote on the war itself, rather than have antiwar members of Congress wage guerrilla war with amendments. I would have respected Congress's wishes if at any point it had passed a resolution saying, "Let's get out of Vietnam."

To get that up or down vote, we could have sought a congressional declaration of war, but we decided against it. Formal declarations of war have gone out of fashion in the post-World War II era because they make situations more rigid and make it harder to resolve conflict informally, as we did to end the Korean War and the Berlin blockade. Furthermore, from the viewpoint of Congress, a declaration of war vastly increases the constitutional powers of the president, for taking action in wartime emergency that we normally don't allow in peacetime.

Whenever Congress passed appropriations bills for the war, President Johnson tended to view this as endorsement of our policy. I didn't agree with him. Bill Fulbright was right in saying that it is one thing to disapprove policy; it is quite another to withhold appropriations from soldiers in the field getting shot at.

Because Vietnam ended badly for American policy, an architect of that policy is not the best one to assess whatever good might have come from our commitment to Southeast Asia. But even so, other capitals remember that the United States of America went halfway around the world, sacrificed nearly sixty thousand dead, hundreds of thousands of wounded, and vast resources to meet its commitment to a small country. We did "take steps to meet the common danger," as we pledged to do if those protected by SEATO were attacked. I suspect that leaders in other capitals, when contemplating fresh adventures, might say, "Now wait a minute, comrades. We've got to be a little careful here, because those damned fool Americans just might do something about it." If future events ever lead to a conviction that the United States will not respond to acts of aggression, the world would face risks to peace more severe than we've ever seen.

Should the United States have made a stand in South Vietnam? Undoubtedly Presidents Kennedy and Johnson might have decided differently with the full benefit of hindsight—but that opportunity never comes. History will make its own judgment, but I personally believed the American commitment to South Vietnam was the right decision and have never changed my mind.

There are many questions about Vietnam that should be carefully studied by the State and Defense Departments, war colleges, and colleges and universities around the country. We must reflect long and hard on that experience. The conclusions we draw will have a considerable bearing on our approach to the future. But at the end of the day there is one overriding question which future generations must address, a question they cannot avoid: How can we foster and create durable world peace?

My generation of students was led down the path into the catastrophe of World War II, which could have been prevented. We came out of that war thinking that collective security was the key to the prevention of World War III. It was written strongly and plainly into Article I of the United Nations Charter, reinforced by the Rio Pact in this hemisphere, by NATO across the Atlantic, and by certain treaties across the Pacific.

In the aftermath of Vietnam I can understand why support for collective security has eroded. First, new generations have arrived on the scene who did not experience and cannot remember the events of the postwar years, when we built the United Nations, the Marshall Plan, NATO, and the entire postwar structure of collective security. Like any new generation, they won't take answers automatically from an older generation. Second, the American people have taken almost five hundred thousand casualties in dead and wounded since the end of World War II in support of collective security. And it has not been very collective. We put up 90 percent of the non-Korean forces in Korea, 80 percent of the non-Vietnamese forces in Vietnam. If my cousins in Cherokee County were to say to me, "Look! If collective security means fifty thousand American dead every ten years, and it is not even collective, maybe this is not a very good idea." I have profound respect for that reaction. But that still leaves young people today with the question, If not collective security, how will you prevent World War III? If not NATO, then what? What do you put in its place?

John Kennedy, Lyndon Johnson, and their secretary of state did not ask the Senate to approve additional collective security treaties. We had a basketful already, and we didn't want to take on additional responsibilities. Yet through our most solemn constitutional processes—Senate confirmation of negotiated treaties—we determined that certain areas of the world—the NATO countries and Europe, the Western Hemisphere, and certain countries in the Pacific—are vital to the security of the United States. Perhaps we should review those treaties periodically and make up our minds all over again, because nothing is more dangerous than a security treaty this country doesn't mean. What would foreign capitals think about the fidelity of the United States to its treaty commitments? If we don't regard an attack on Turkey or Norway as an attack on the United States, we had better watch out, because that is exactly what the NATO Treaty says.

There is nothing more disastrous to the prospects for peace than confusion on questions of war and peace. People no longer read the UN Charter with the realization that contained in those articles are the lessons of World War II and the events leading to it and that it cost fifty million lives to write that Charter. They do not read the UN Charter with the reverence with which we drafted it, with a prayer on our lips, knowing that this time we simply cannot fail. They cry, "We cannot levy more taxes for foreign aid," but the alternative to funding those programs really means stopping the effort to build peace in the world. Of course, Americans do not like to pay taxes, and it is always easier to cut foreign aid than domestic programs. However, without peace, there is no world left for us.

When I see sharp reductions in a prudent foreign aid budget, mobilization of protectionist interests to interfere with liberal world trade, pressures to withdraw our forces from NATO, or hear the arguments opposing the Vietnam War, I wonder if we don't need a great debate all over again either to reaffirm collective security and American participation in world affairs or to find something better to put in their place. I would welcome something better, but I am desperately concerned that we'll find something worse by inadvertence, inattention, laziness, or a withdrawal into "Fortress America."

The idea of collective security did not come down from the mount on tablets of stone. It was drawn up by living, breathing human beings who wrestled with the problems of their day, against the background of bitter experience. They had the same potential for error and mistaken judgment that accompanies all human endeavors.

What effect will our Vietnam experience have on collective security? This is a question that each generation must answer for itself. They won't take answers from an old duffer like me, and it is well that they won't, because each generation must find its own answers to the major problems of its times and to the overriding question, How do we best organize for peace?

But young people today cannot avoid the question. I hope in so doing, they don't reject the mistakes of their fathers only to adopt the mistakes of their grandfathers.

How the story turns out depends partly upon what kind of people we are. The American people are now in the process of deciding. Collective security as defined in the United Nations Charter and drawn in our mutual security treaties does not call upon the United States to

be the world's policeman. We can be selective in our overseas commitments. In those treaties we have undertaken specific responsibilities to
specific countries that come into effect only under specified circumstances. My view is that we should take those responsibilities seriously.
But that does not mean that we are responsible for whatever happens,
anywhere in the world. It means that we should not enter into a security
treaty without full recognition of its consequences; otherwise, we
weaken the entire structure of collective security. On the basis of our
Vietnam experience, one thing is for certain: The days when the United
States will go it alone on a major overseas commitment are over.

SECTION VI

MAKING FOREIGN POLICY

"T he secretary of state flies a four-engine plane," my dad wrote John Foster Dulles in May 1953. In making foreign policy, he "draws his power" from the president, Congress, the Department of State, the media, and the public. "He can fly his plane on three engines, and for a considerable time, with two," Rusk warned. "But at least two motors must be in good shape or there is serious trouble . . . and if all four motors are sputtering, trouble is ahead." In January 1961 Rusk found himself piloting that plane. Eight years later, with three motors sputtering and only one engine pulling hard—his relationship with the president—he touched down. Or pancaked in, rather. For 1968 was a tough year for Dean Rusk, the Department of State, and, indeed, the ship of state.

Although pilot error may have been involved, Rusk did operate with a preflight checklist. It included a strong sense of what the secretary of state's job requires, its place in the constitutional system, and how a secretary should conduct himself. After leaving Washington, he often talked about the office itself and how the different ingredients of making foreign policy relate to one another.

"At least one-third of my time," he estimated, was devoted to testifying before Congress and meeting with its members. "It takes enormous amounts of time to make the system work." Even his critics concede that he was good with Congress, adept at building bipartisan support for foreign policy. His skills and rapport helped sustain congressional support for Vietnam policy until 1968.

Rusk had a love-hate relationship with the press, the instrument by which he communicated with the American people. Called the "silent secretary," he was more voluble than most, holding many press conferences and backgrounders, and he was respected by the press, if not a media favorite. He was no headline grabber, and his chief objective as secretary was to "get foreign policy off the front page and back to page eighteen."

He explained: "There are times when a secretary of state must say nothing at considerable length." Yet he enjoyed fencing with the press, especially the "media giants" who had varying techniques for getting the story. Even in his old age, although feigning irritation, he loved having journalists ring his telephone.

Gathering information and reading intelligence reports, vitally important to decision making, consumed much of his day as secretary. Unable to "pierce with accuracy the fog of the future," swamped by too much information, at other times laboring with insufficient information, Rusk was fascinated by the role of intelligence in decision making. He had rich experiences with his presidents, the Central Intelligence Agency, J. Edgar Hoover and the FBI over contradictory intelligence assessments, unauthorized leaks, wiretapping, and CIA covert operations.

Although born and raised in the South, Rusk also had strong convictions about civil rights and human rights. He believed our track record on both influenced American foreign policy. He tried to improve living conditions for foreign diplomats in segregated Washington and to promote blacks within the State Department. He was also the administration's strongest witness on the Civil Rights Act of 1964. When asked if he "favored Negro demonstrations," Rusk told a shocked committee chairman, Senator Strom Thurmond, "If I were denied what our Negro citizens are denied, I would demonstrate." My father's views on civil rights were tested in a personal way in 1967, when my sister, Peggy, married Guy Smith, a black American. There was some parental unhappiness—only eighteen, Peggy was changing colleges to get married, and her husband was leaving for Vietnam to fly helicopters—but if race was an issue, it went unexpressed. Leaving the chapel, my dad was photographed wearing a grin from ear to ear, a picture that went around the world. "Just two people in love" was all he would say.

Rusk's dealings with the White House and the executive branch involved more than whispering into John Kennedy's or Lyndon Johnson's ear. He and his colleagues at State had to interact with the National Security Council, White House staff, Defense, Treasury, and other departments and agencies in the executive branch to create foreign policy. Although the Nixon, Ford, Carter, and Reagan administrations that followed were rife with feuding and bureaucratic skirmishing, Rusk worked to avoid these. "Our discussions were infused with the thought that we were all serving the same president," he said.

Finally, running the State Department was no easy chore for this "perfect number two," who had only limited administrative experience as foundation head, college professor, and staff officer. According to the accounts of the Kennedy and Johnson years, Rusk ran the State Department much the way he ran his own family: uncomfortable with asserting leadership: delegating to others the details of administration:

encouraging his colleagues to "fill up their own horizons of responsibility." His colleagues said that he lacked Dean Acheson's "killer instinct"; he couldn't be a son of a bitch when the situation demanded; he was notoriously poor at disciplining those who needed it and providing direction to others stumbling in a climate of pure freedom. Although he was highly respected, his penchant for privacy exasperated assistant secretaries and others in the pipeline who needed to know his thinking but often did not.

Yet those same colleagues genuinely liked my father and enjoyed working for him. His office staff—secretaries, security men, and personal assistants—adored him. "He really was the quintessential gentleman," said Andy Steigman, a personal assistant. He took a personal interest in the lives of his staff, often inquiring about family matters.

"Your father would ask, 'Who's heard from Jim? How's his baby?' " said Gus Peleusos, of a fellow security agent whose blue baby had to be watched constantly. "Other officials would not even have known who Jim was, or the Jims of this town—people who for the heavies were just ciphers." When visiting an American embassy abroad, my dad usually met with the entire staff, not just the ambassador, to tell them personally how much he appreciated their work. When refueling at Strategic Air Command bases, he often talked with pilots in the ready rooms and with radar technicians, thanking them for their vigilance. At the State Department, Pop loved to wander into the code room or file room or cafeteria, places that rarely see an American secretary of state, to shake hands and let people know that their work was important and that he cared.

"He would walk into the most obscure offices," said Gus, "and say, 'Hello. I'm Dean Rusk.' And people would go 'bong.' It's a wonder he didn't give somebody a heart attack. There was none of this, 'The secretary is coming. Everyone stand at attention!' He would just walk in."

"A gentleman beyond compare," said his secretary Jane Mossellem. "One of the warmest men I've ever met. If profanity was used, he would stop the offender and apologize to us." Jane and other secretaries used to take notes of his conversations with Lyndon Johnson. Rusk discontinued this practice partly because he didn't want his secretaries exposed to presidential profanity.

When my parents left the State Department on Pop's final day, special assistant Harry Shlaudeman accompanied them down the elevator and walked them to the C Street entrance. "The lobby was jammed," said Harry. "There were hundreds, many of them ordinary working people—file clerks, custodians, secretaries. The applause for him was something that no other secretary of state has ever had. It was chilling . . . spine-tingling.''

One final impression as a son: In view of Pop's chaotic schedule—fourteen-hour days, seven-day weeks with no vacations—where was there time for long-range planning, for quiet reflection, for reconsidering the directions of foreign policy as well as operational detail? Always chasing fires, dealing with one crisis after another, my father admitted that the toughest thing about his job was trying to keep up with the intelligence flow, that mass of reports and information that came across his desk. And then, for each problem that came to his desk, he would have to absorb everything that he could, make his decision, let his mind go blank, and then reload for the next decision. "I would have to do that twenty-five to thirty times a day," said my dad, a process he called "mentally exhausting."

Rusk's executive secretary, Ben Read, the "official bottleneck" in the State Department's secretariat, filtered everything that went to him: cables; phone calls; personal callers; reports. As Rusk's alter ego he was intimately involved with the decision making.

"Your father was enormously disciplined in the way he absorbed information," said Read. "But we were always struggling, . . . always dealing with kaleidoscopic situations that we saw imperfectly and incompletely, particularly at times of crisis. We were terribly concerned with the limitations of our vision and understanding of the events transpiring before us."

My father's preference for operational concerns probably made things worse. "We can think only in action," he often told his colleagues, quoting Dean Acheson. Not a reflective man, to the despair of policy planners he usually returned their longer-range studies with a quip: "How will this affect what we do tomorrow morning at nine o'clock?" But obviously the demands of his schedule contributed.

"Dean would try to schedule Saturday morning meetings on matters like population problems or on countries not on the front page, like Indonesia," said Ben. "Yet it was hard to do, because everything pushed him toward the crisis of the moment."

According to Ben, my father tried to delegate as much as he could, but some things couldn't be delegated. Congressional committees wanted to hear the secretary of state, not an assistant secretary. Only he could properly represent the United States at many diplomatic functions; a stand-in would breach protocol.

"Dean would say that ninety-five percent of the department's work gets handled at levels below his office," continued Ben. "And he was right. Yet the five percent that only he could do sometimes approximated ninety-five percent in importance."

He tried to do it all. Although his office had a machine that could sign his name, he even spent an hour each Saturday personally signing autograph requests after several collectors had complained that machine-signed signatures were not authentic. "They were part of my constituency," he explained. "You've got to be considerate of the American people when you hold a job like that." For eight years he tried to do everything and accommodate everyone.

"Your dad would look at his schedule," said Gus, "discover that he had twenty minutes of free time, stick his head out a side door, and say, 'I'm going to take a nap. Wake me up in eighteen minutes.' By the time I hit the light switch on my way out the door, he would be asleep in his chair. In eighteen minutes I would open the door and say, 'It's time, Mr. Secretary.' He would get up, splash a little water on his face, and meet his next appointment."

I didn't spend much time with my dad at his office, and I didn't personally witness all this. But I recall what it looked like at home, and I especially recall how it ended. The pictures tell the tale, show the lines etched into his face. He ran out of steam his final year in office. "I was bone-tired," he admitted. His colleagues called him an "incredible stoic, durable beyond belief," and he lasted eight years. As his son I know something about the price he paid in mental and physical exhaustion and broken health. In carrying those responsibilities and working that kind of schedule, was there a price paid by American foreign policy as well?

—R. R.

32

Advising
the President

When I became the United States'
fifty-fourth secretary of state in January 1961, I took office under our
thirty-fifth president. I also served the thirty-sixth. Since I left office in
1969, we have had seven more secretaries of state and five more presidents. A little arithmetic suggests that being secretary of state is a
hazardous occupation.

Every secretary of state should memorize the often forgotten first
sentence of Article II of the Constitution: "The executive power shall
be vested in a President of the United States of America." And it should
be framed and hung on the wall of the White House mess as a daily
reminder to all who work there.

A secretary of state serves at the pleasure of the president; his
resignation implicitly is always on the president's desk. The president
must in turn give thought to arrangements that make it possible for a
secretary of state to carry out his responsibilities.

Dean Acheson once remarked, "In the relationship between the
president and the secretary of state, it is imperative that both understand at all times which one is president." Sometimes secretaries of state

forget that, James Byrnes, for example. His boss, Harry Truman, was the wrong president to be forgetful about. Byrnes paid for his forgetfulness with his job. Other secretaries, such as William Jennings Bryan and Cordell Hull, had independent political bases and therefore more leeway, but even then their independence was constrained by the underlying constitutional relationship.

Nevertheless, I think cabinet officers should have some independence in their relations with the president. The Dutch have an interesting practice. When someone joins the Dutch cabinet, from that moment on he is guaranteed a year's pay if he leaves office. This "go to hell fund" gives Dutch cabinet officers some breathing room.

In my own case my willingness to leave office brought me an extra measure of independence that I otherwise may not have had. I never sought or campaigned for the job and I didn't fight to keep it, and both my presidents knew that.

I never had any problems communicating with my presidents. There was a constant flow of communication between us, through meetings at the White House, phone calls, written memoranda, position papers, and personal conversation. But some of my colleagues in the State Department complained that I was too reticent, that they never knew what I thought about policy. Two things influenced this. The first I copied from George Marshall, the habit of wanting to know what your colleagues, including junior ones, think about a matter before you make up your mind. At meetings in the department I did not begin by stating my views. I preferred to listen to others. I didn't want my own views echoed in their replies.

Second, I did not disclose to my colleagues the details of presidential conversations. When I advised the president, I presented the department's views as best I could, but when the president's decision went against the recommendations of the department, I would come back, implement that decision, and see that it was carried out. I did not want my colleagues to score me on how hard I fought for a State Department policy position. My job was not to fight for State's views on policy; my job was to help find and implement the best foreign policy for the United States.

An effective relationship between the president and his secretary of state requires confidentiality. There should be no blue sky between them on foreign policy issues. As President Kennedy once said, "Domestic questions can only lose elections. Foreign policy can kill us all." A president is entitled to his secretary of state's support for the decisions he makes. Without that support, domestic critics and foreign governments can seek divisions within the administration to weaken policy. If the secretary of state disagrees with a presidential decision, he has only two choices of action: support the president, or resign.

Concerned over confidentiality, I rarely wrote memos on policy issues to my two presidents. As a result, I will not be a favorite of historians. Most advice I gave to my presidents was transacted orally. I did send to the president for his evening reading a one- or two-page summary of the decisions and actions we took each day and what we planned to do the next day. These daily reports helped keep him informed and kept us in touch with each other. They also kept him safe from being surprised by the press and gave him a chance to ask for more detail on matters that interested him.

When I took office, I found by accident that a secretary in my outer office routinely stayed on the phone and listened to my talks with the president, made little memoranda of those calls, and circulated them around the department. I put a stop to this practice, a holdover from the Eisenhower administration, and installed a private phone in my office connected directly to the White House.

Knowing what to take to the president and what to include in his reading was part of the art of being secretary of state. That art began with the assistant secretaries; they, too, had to decide what to handle themselves and what to send upstairs to me.

Disagreements inevitably emerge between secretaries of state and presidents over foreign policy for two reasons. First, presidents are in very different political positions from secretaries. Secretaries of state try to deal with foreign policy in terms of the national interest, but presidents must also take into account the domestic political situation.

Harry Truman once told us, "I want to hear from you fellows on matters of foreign policy, but I don't want you to base your views upon political considerations. In the first place, good policy is good politics. In the second place, you fellows in the State Department don't know a damned thing about domestic politics. And I don't want a bunch of amateurs playing around with serious business."

Secondly, foreign policy is very diverse. This diversity virtually guarantees that no two individuals, no matter how well matched, will see every issue the same way. Disagreement is built into the job. My presidents and I had our share; for example, my differences with Lyndon Johnson over food aid to India. But when disagreements occur, a secretary of state must remember who has the authority for making decisions for the executive branch.

Bureaucratic skirmishing among State, Defense, the National Security Council, the White House staff, and other agencies involved with American foreign policy works its toll. The NSC has greatly complicated the secretary of state's role as chief spokesman on foreign affairs. When President Truman established it, the NSC considered only questions assigned by the president or cabinet members of the council. There was no general NSC involvement in foreign affairs. The council focused on specific issues on which papers were prepared and circulated throughout the government. President Eisenhower developed the NSC into a complex machinery of groups and subgroups. Robert Bowie, Eisenhower's State Department liaison to the NSC, once told me that only one afternoon per week was not taken up with NSC staff meetings.

My impression when we took office in 1961 was that the NSC had become muscle-bound with too much machinery, too many meetings, too much wasted time. Kennedy swept most of that away. Kennedy's NSC began with the president and secretaries of state and defense, the chairman of the Joint Chiefs of Staff, the national security adviser, and the CIA director putting their heads together periodically on major issues. National Security Adviser McGeorge Bundy had perhaps a staff of dozen people, allowing him to avoid the evils that come with bigness. Bundy's NSC existed to facilitate the president's participation in the foreign policy process. It organized the massive stream of business and papers that came to his office, helped with scheduling, travel abroad, and speech writing.

Bundy's was a lean and trim operation. I could not spend my day scurrying back and forth to the White House, carrying papers and memoranda. We sent those papers to Bundy, who organized them, highlighted and underlined key points, and identified critical questions and decisions for the president's attention. He also insured that the president reacted on time and checked with the various departments to see that presidential decisions were executed.

I looked upon McGeorge Bundy and his successor, Walt Rostow, as allies rather than competitors. They and their assistants greatly assisted the State Department in presenting issues and preparing papers and speeches for the president. I once tried to get Bundy transferred to State, but Kennedy decided that he couldn't spare him.

We worked so closely together that I regarded the National Security staff at the White House as almost another wing of the State Department. We had many joint meetings and often came up with combined recommendations for the president. Competent people served on the White House and National Security Council staffs, none more competent than Bundy himself. A man of great ability, wherever he was put in the executive branch, he was bound to influence affairs. In our relationship he always dealt honorably with me, and I never detected any backbiting, behind-the-scenes maneuvering, or trying to influence decisions without my knowledge. Articulate, a skilled draftsman, he was invaluable to his presidents. And Walt Rostow also performed admirably as Bundy's replacement. He was more prolific than Bundy and not as succinct, but Rostow tightened up and eventually became an efficient national security adviser in all aspects of a difficult job.

Unfortunately, under recent administrations, national security advisers or members of their staff have interposed themselves between the president and a cabinet officer. Our operation was not that way. During the Kennedy and Johnson administrations such interference happened only rarely. Bundy and Rostow were extremely conscientious. Whenever they advised the president directly on policy, they asked me to comment on their proposals. Bundy and Rostow strengthened relationships at the top rather than circumvented them; they were not divisive.

To help keep lines of responsibility clear, I told my colleagues that if a White House staffer called and said, "The White House wants this," or, "The White House wants that," my colleagues were to ask, "Who in the White House?" Unless it was the president, my view was that I spoke for the president. I refused to allow White House staffers to break into the chain of command.

However large it has now become, the modern NSC operation is no substitute for the Department of State and the Foreign Service. The national security adviser does not conduct relations with other governments. He neither meets regularly with Congress nor coordinates foreign policy with other agencies and departments of the executive branch. The head of the NSC holds no press conferences, makes no speeches around the country explaining and defending administration policy. He does not go to the United Nations or meet with foreign ministers. He doesn't bear a two-hundred-year tradition of being the president's principal spokesman on foreign policy. He is in a very different position from a secretary of state, who does all of the above. More than any other person in government, the secretary of state shares the awesome constitutional and public responsibilities of the president in foreign affairs, and he must be recognized at home and abroad as the one who has the full confidence of the president.

During the Johnson years Tuesday luncheons were, in fact, meetings of the National Security Council. Typically those luncheons would include the president, occasionally the vice president, the secretaries of state and defense, the chairman of the Joint Chiefs of Staff, the CIA director, and the national security adviser, all statutory members of the NSC. We didn't call these luncheons NSC meetings because if we had, twenty-five or thirty staff people would have lined the walls.

Quite a bit of important business took place in the Tuesday luncheons. Formal NSC meetings really didn't lend themselves to wide-ranging debate and discussion since far too many people attended these meetings, thereby increasing the possibility of leaks. Also, a president and his cabinet officers shouldn't debate each other in the presence of others. Those differences could easily be leaked to the press.

The minutes of those Tuesday luncheons summarize discussion and conclusions reached. They do not reflect the lively debate between us. There was lots of give-and-take; everyone present knew that he could speak freely and wouldn't read about it in the *Washington Post* the next morning. Johnson discovered that this group knew how to keep its collective mouth shut.

At cabinet and National Security Council meetings I spoke with some reticence since I sought to maintain confidentiality in my advice to the president. Arthur Schlesinger wrote in *A Thousand Days* that in those meetings I sat like an old Buddha, seldom saying anything. He was right, because when forty and fifty people were in the room, especially people like Schlesinger, I kept my mouth shut; I always wondered how secure our conversations were in Schlesinger's presence. Typically I would either see the president ahead of time or pass him a note that asked him not to make a decision until I talked further with him after the meeting. I did not want the content of my discussions and possible differences with the president circulated around the Georgetown cocktail circuit.

There were times when I had trouble with Arthur Schlesinger. Not content with his life in the East Room with the social secretaries, Schlesinger liked to play a role in policy matters. He wrote a strong and sensible letter opposing the Bay of Pigs and helped keep Adlai Stevenson on the team during that fiasco. On other matters he was less helpful. For example, a question arose over whether the Italian government should shift toward the left and build a broader coalition of political parties. Schlesinger wanted the United States to use some pressure and nudge the Italians in that direction. However, our ambassador in Rome, Frederick Reinhardt, and I felt that this was not our job. I stonewalled Arthur, believing "an opening to the left," as Schlesinger called it, was a matter for the Italians to decide. They later made their move and indeed shifted to the left, but not because of American pressure.

Schlesinger was a fifth wheel in decision making. As the White House intellectual in residence he often made his views known, darting in and out rather like a hummingbird. Once I was talking with President Kennedy when Schlesinger walked in and made some wild-eyed proposal. Kennedy thanked him, and as Schlesinger left the room, the president turned to me and said, "There are times when Arthur is very interesting in the Rose Garden." But Kennedy liked to chew over ideas and have that kind of person around. As such, Schlesinger played a useful role.

Sometimes secretaries of state also clash with secretaries of defense. Fortunately, though, that never became a problem between Bob McNamara and myself. Remembering Defense Secretary Louis Johnson and the bitter feuding between State and Defense during the Truman years, I sat down with Bob McNamara for a long talk on the first day we took office. I told Bob that the safety of the American people was a primary object of American foreign policy, and therefore, as secretary of state I would be supportive of national security. He told me that the primary mission of the Defense Department was to support our foreign policy and he would be as helpful as possible. We agreed at that first meeting to encourage contacts between our two departments at all levels. At the time over three hundred Foreign Service officers (FSOs) were graduates of the war colleges, and at least that many military officers and Defense Department civilians had graduated from training programs at State. We thought this cross-fertilization would help both departments understand each other's problems. This contrasted markedly with State-Defense relations under Louis Johnson, who insisted that every communication from the State Department come across his desk. That made for an impossible relationship.

Bob McNamara and I hit it off right from the start. We insisted upon cooperation and worked hard to obtain it. We had our differences, and on rare occasions we took those differences to the president. But Bob and I met nearly every weekend for long talks, usually in my office, where we tried to hammer out our differences. That led critics in the Pentagon to assert that Bob listened to me too much, and critics at State to assert that I listened to Bob too much. But our frequent talks led to common positions on many issues. Also helpful was the fact that Bob handled his problems within the Pentagon; for example, I never had to wrestle with the Joint Chiefs of Staff. With McNamara as defense secretary, there was never any question who ran the Defense Department.

We did have some disagreements, but we also agreed that it was best for the United States if we not go public with them. Both of us recognized that national security policy and foreign policy merged into an indivisible whole. Bob was a good colleague, wholly committed to finding the best national policy for complicated issues.

One area where McNamara and I never saw eye to eye was in his heavy reliance on statistical methodology; sometimes he tried to reduce to numbers certain factors and values that I believed could not be quantified. By 1967 we had also begun to disagree on Vietnam; as the war intensified and he began to oppose it, we for the only time during our tenure lost communication with each other. At the same time, even though he apparently came to believe that we could not win the war, I do not remember him ever saying to me, "Dean, we cannot possibly succeed in what we are attempting to do in Vietnam."

Underneath all his talk about numbers, Bob McNamara was a very compassionate man. The death, destruction, and misery of Vietnam just ate away at him. He agonized over that war.

I am rather proud that an inquisitive and diligent press was unable to generate any stories of feuding between Bob McNamara, McGeorge Bundy, his successor, Walt Rostow, and myself—those at the top levels of government. We spent a great deal of time talking things over, in discussions infused with the thought that we were all trying to serve the same president.

We fully realized that honest men and women can disagree about the complex problems of a tumultuous and contradictory world. But we did not let those differences come between us. Guerrilla warfare among top government advisers is simply too dangerous in the modern world.

33

Administering Foggy Bottom

President Kennedy had organized himself as a senator and candidate, but not until well after his election did he organize himself to be president. He did not bring a large staff into government with him. His cabinet appointments included a number of total strangers, including myself, and, to his credit, few cronies. Because he was not organized to be president at the time of his election, the search for talent in his administration was a never-ending affair.

I faced the same problems as I staffed the Department of State. Not having anticipated becoming secretary, I had not built up a coterie of personal assistants in whom I had complete confidence. In addition, beginning with the sixties, we began to lose that generation of Americans who had taken an active part in foreign affairs over the previous twenty-five years. Age had taken its toll on the Robert Lovetts and Dean Achesons. Our men were largely new men, relatively young and untested by experience, a point brought home vividly once while the cabinet was discussing prospective candidates with President Kennedy for a high-level job. Someone objected to one man, saying that he was too young. We all laughed when we realized that the candidate was older than the president himself.

I was particularly surprised at how few of the truly qualified wanted to enter public service. All sorts of reasons rule against public service: low pay; long hours; loss of privacy. But both administrations I served fared well.

One of those we were fortunate to get was Henry Cabot Lodge. Although the Republican vice presidential standard-bearer in the bitter 1960 campaign, Lodge told me early in the Kennedy years that he still had some public service left in him and would be available if I needed him. But he wanted a tough, challenging assignment; he didn't want an easy job. I remembered his offer and eventually sent him to South Vietnam as our ambassador, a tough enough job for anyone. Lodge had heart trouble at the time; both his offer and subsequent service were most gallant. But Henry Cabot Lodge was a rare breed. A shocking number of people will not drop what they are doing, make the sacrifices necessary for public service, and actually pitch in and help.

I did wrestle with the White House staff and occasionally President Kennedy over ambassadorial appointments. In our time about 70 percent of our ambassadors were Foreign Service officers, and another 15 percent were professionally qualified although not career FSOs in the usual sense—such men as David Bruce, Edwin Reischauer, and Lincoln Gordon. Then there were always 10 or 15 percent who were old-fashioned political appointments, and among these we always picked up a few dogs. If I lost my wrestling match with the president over one of these political ambassadorial appointments, I tried to surround that person with highly competent Foreign Service officers to save the neophyte from error. The United States doesn't need ambassadors of no experience, those who know nothing about overseas trade or how to write a diplomatic note, negotiating with foreigners. But I and every other secretary of state must leave the president some wiggle room because he has his own problems, very often on Capitol Hill, and these political ambassadorial positions are one way he takes care of them.

Although the key positions in the State Department are presidential appointments, for the most part John Kennedy and Lyndon Johnson let me name the people I wanted. I had problems, however, with Bobby Kennedy on personnel because Bobby wanted dedicated "Kennedy people" in those jobs. Most Foreign Service officers had no personal attachment to John F. Kennedy or the Kennedy family. George Ball, George McGhee, and Harlan Cleveland, for example, were longtime

Democrats and loyal to the president, but not Kennedy people to suit Bobby's tastes. Fortunately John Kennedy took a broader view. On key appointments I managed to prevail.

Overall, few applications for appointments to the State Department and the ambassadorships came through political channels. Most political appointees weren't very interested in the top posts like Rome, Paris, London, and Tokyo because there they have to work too hard. Neither were they interested in the far-off, smaller posts where dysentery is the order of the day. Many of these smaller posts tend to be dull, uncomfortable, even dangerous. Political appointees preferred nice little countries like Switzerland, Denmark, and Ireland. Once Ireland's foreign minister said to me rather wistfully, "Mr. Rusk, do you think the United States will ever send us an ambassador with whom we can talk foreign policy?"

John Kennedy took office with much fanfare about being his own secretary of state. Because of Article II of the Constitution, this is inevitable. Yet a president cannot be his own secretary of state in any real sense, the job of the presidency is simply too big.

In fact, even a secretary of state cannot run U.S. foreign policy by himself. He must delegate the overwhelming bulk of decision making to hundreds of Foreign Service officers, authorized to act on his behalf. The world has become so complex in the postwar years that junior officers in the State Department now make decisions which before World War II would have been made by the secretary.

Fortunately the secretary of state is backed up by a professional diplomatic service second to none in the world. It is fashionable for new boys surrounding a president to regard the Foreign Service with a mixture of suspicion and derision. The Foreign Service does not share their view that the world was created at the last presidential election or that a world of more than 160 nations will somehow be very different because we elected one man rather than another as president. But at the same time the Foreign Service must ensure that the wishes and policies of the president and secretary of state are carried out. That process is very complex, but the system works.

During my eight years 2,100,000 cables with my name signed to them went out from the Department of State to our embassies and other governments all over the world. Of these 2,100,000 cables, I saw fewer than 1 percent. The rest were written and sent on the basis of authority delegated to hundreds of officers in the Department of State. Had this delegation not occurred, the day's business could not be done. Out of those 2,100,000 cables, I can recall only 4 or 5 that had to be called back and rewritten because their authors missed the point of policy the president and I expected them to follow, an extraordinary performance by my colleagues.

Administering a department twenty-five thousand strong is not a simple matter. Washington is full of high-powered executives, typically from big business, who proclaim upon their arrival that they are going to cut through red tape, bash some heads, and bring "their people" under control. This approach doesn't work. I found that the best way to deal with the bureaucracy is to capture it and make it work for you. Loyalty is a two-way street; a secretary of state will get loyalty if he gives loyalty in return. And of course, I had no choice. Since I never expected to become secretary of state, I couldn't bring a team of "Rusk men" into the department with me. My constituency was the Foreign Service.

A president soon finds that the Department of State is the department of bad news. It deals with that part of the public business over which the president and the U.S. government have little control. The president, Congress, the Supreme Court, our governors, state legislatures, and local authorities largely determine what we do in domestic affairs. But as soon as we step across our national frontiers, we deal with more than 160 other governments, each living in a different part of the world, each with its own problems, its own aspirations, and its own policies, none of which simply clicks its heels and salutes when we speak. It is a world of negotiation, discussion, compromise, adjustment, conflict, and sometimes violence. Disappointment and frustration are built into the very essence of foreign policy.

In general, the Department of State deals with the most frustrating aspects of our public life. Presidents become impatient with the State Department because events overseas don't always turn out the way they want them to. Occasionally a secretary of state has to say, "Sorry, Mr. President, you can't have it that way because these foreigners just won't do it that way." Thus, it is always difficult for the Foreign Service to earn the confidence of a new president.

Early in his presidency John Kennedy was very suspicious of the Foreign Service and impatient with the deliberate processes of the Department of State. Continuity, tradition, and precedent are built into the bowels of any bureaucracy, and the young John Kennedy, wanting to make a fresh start and "get the country moving again," sometimes became annoyed with these deliberative processes. In foreign affairs the influence of precedent is very important, and sometimes a president does not like to feel bound by what has gone before. But by his second year Kennedy had come to know the Foreign Service well and appreciated that it was a great professional service loaded with talent, dedication, and loyalty.

New presidents sometimes think the Foreign Service's loyalty is suspect simply because it served a preceding president. This contrasts markedly with the attitudes of British politicians about their civil service. On a trip to London I ate lunch with the head of the British civil service and complimented him on the way his people stayed out of party politics. He said, "Oh, no. You've got it wrong. The British civil service supports one political party at a time."

Some of my colleagues were skeptical of the Foreign Service's ability to meet the challenges thrust upon American diplomacy in the sixties. For example, Chester Bowles instinctively looked outside the Foreign Service when we had slots to fill. I felt that career officers had a leg up on another candidates and battled hard for them. Only when needing special talent was I inclined to reach outside the Foreign Service. When staffing, I looked for men and women who were willing to make decisions. The major problem facing bureaucracy is not the struggle for power but the evasion of responsibility; bureaucrats are very reluctant to take action. Never once as secretary did I criticize a colleague for exceeding his authority. My problem was to get my colleagues to fill the horizons of their responsibilities—to stick their necks out and live with the results.

For example, on one occasion Iraq threatened to invade Kuwait, and midway through this crisis our naval commander in chief at Norfolk sent a telegram stating that he had ordered his task force in the Indian Ocean to steam north toward Kuwait. It ended with "Request instructions." I forwarded this message to the Near Eastern Affairs desk and asked for its recommendation. It came back with a convoluted paper outlining all sorts of options. I returned the paper and said, "Now look. All that admiral needs is a compass heading. He can sail north, east, or south. He can't sail west, because he would run into Africa. All I want from you is a compass heading."

I once asked Harlan Cleveland, my undersecretary of state for United Nations affairs and a man to whom I delegated extensively, how he determined when to act and when to ask for direction. "It was very simple," he said. "When I knew what you wanted to do, I would go ahead and act. If I didn't, I'd ask you." The art of the matter was knowing when to act and when to ask.

Whenever traveling, I never tried to run the State Department from a distance. I concentrated solely on the purposes of each trip and left everything else to my undersecretary back in Washington. When Secretary of State George Marshall was in Paris in 1948 for a United Nations meeting, he asked me to cable the department for instructions on some matter. "Instructions for you, sir?" I asked.

"Oh, yes," he replied. "It is the acting secretary of state who has access to the president, congressional leaders, and the talents and resources of the government. Out here on my own, I'm not in a position to make these decisions. I want to know what Washington thinks."

As I said, George Marshall taught me to delegate, and delegate I did. Marshall recruited people in whom he had supreme confidence, delegated massively to then, and gave them as free a hand as possible. I tried to do the same. Sometimes, however, the chain of authority gets broken in interesting ways. We had in John Kennedy a president of insatiable curiosity. He would read something on page twelve of the *Washington Post* and call up State's desk officer in charge of that area, seeking more information. Whenever he did that, two things happened. First, he scared the hell out of the desk officer. Second, whatever that subject was, it had to come to my desk because whatever the president got into, I had to get into. Kennedy's habits and informality sometimes got in the way.

But on other occasions President Kennedy made my job much easier. Soon after taking office, Kennedy sent a very helpful memo to our embassies, placing the ambassador in full charge of all activities and agencies of the U.S. government in that country. As the president's alter ego the ambassador needed access to all communications involving the U.S. government. Kennedy's memo gave every ambassador access to CIA communications. We sought also to eliminate back-channel communications and activities that an ambassador might not be aware of and to make it clear to everyone that the ambassador was the personal representative of the president.

Having long regarded economics as the "dismal science," and lacking personal expertise, I tended to delegate all economic questions to George Ball, Tony Solomon, and other colleagues at State who were more able than I in economic affairs and who covered for me as best they could. This wasn't all that unusual since in my experience, economic policy is the orphan of national decision making. Some revisionist historians argue that economics drives American foreign policy, but that is not so in my experience. On most issues of foreign policy with which I was involved, economic considerations clearly lagged behind political and strategic concerns. For example, economics had nothing to do with the Cuban missile crisis. The Berlin blockade had some economic aspects to it, but the central issues were political and strategic. Similarly, South Vietnam's economic problems demanded our attention but did not explain our commitment. Some claim that we defended South Vietnam because of oil, but I never knew Vietnam had oil until after I left office. Economics rarely entered our discussions on Vietnam. From an economic point of view, it would have been cheaper for us to give every member of the Vietcong a villa on the French Riviera than try to prevent their overrunning South Vietnam.

Fortunately for me, both secretaries of the treasury when I was secretary of state—Douglas Dillon and Henry "Joe" Fowler—understood foreign policy. During my tenure our Treasury Department sought to take international financial power out of the hands of private bankers in Zurich and elsewhere and bring such matters under the responsibility of governments. That fitted the attitudes of the State Department very well. We sometimes disagreed on how to cope, for instance, with unfavorable trade balances, but there were no knockdown, drag-out fights between State and Treasury on international fiscal problems. In general, harmony prevailed. We in the State Department accepted the realities posed by balance of payment problems and trade deficits and did not try to overrule Treasury when it came up with essential actions imposed upon it by these problems. Unfavorable trade balances created genuine problems for the president, and it was up to the Department of State to understand and sympathize with these problems.

On the whole, American businesses do a good job, but in their efforts to encourage favorable conditions for investment, they sometimes become involved in the internal politics of host countries, causing problems for the State Department. And sometimes businesses conclude contracts that can only be described as unfair. To counter these, I established a practice that some businessmen didn't like. In cases where the host country did not perform on a contract with an American company, or a new government took power and denounced an old contract, company executives often asked the State Department for help. Rather than automatically bail them out, I insisted that we review the contract itself. If that contract was corrupt or unfair to the host country, the State Department did not support efforts to require compliance with it. My policy was that we would support diplomatically only contracts that were consistent both with public policy and with what we considered decent business practices here at home. A few of our businessmen got left out on a limb and didn't like it, but I believed that my job demanded focusing on broader American interests first and narrower American business interests second.

At State I was disturbed by the slow reaction time of the political bureaus and the layering of authority between my office and the others—undersecretaries, assistant secretaries, deputy assistant secretaries, and office directors. Many incoming telegrams called for quite obvious answers. I could have easily picked up the phone and said, "Send them a telegram saying yes," or, "Send them a telegram saying no." But I let the machinery work its course. As a result, two weeks after a cable came in, an outgoing and very routine answer would wind its way out of the system. Why so long? An incoming cable had to filter down through all the echelons, and the reply cable to filter back up. Some of the telegrams I saw for approval required twelve, fifteen, even twenty clearances by officers within the department. One cable from the Legal Affairs Office required seven clearances at the bottom—all from the same office! Things were out of hand.

I reduced these many echelons to three and concentrated responsibility in the assistant secretaries. In my scheme the first echelon would be the secretary of state and his undersecretary, the second echelon the assistant secretaries, and the third the country officers. Running the Department of State for eight years provided a fascinating study of the workings of a bureaucracy. Virtually everyone in Washington who thinks he is affected by a decision claims the right to participate in its making. Deputies and assistant directors want to remain part of the decision making, and once they get their feet under the table, it is hard to move them out. This layering created considerable delay and bickering. But my efforts to streamline the bureaucracy did not last, and the causes of the slowdowns often wormed their way back.

At least I kept the beast from growing. When I left office in 1969, there were 350 fewer people in the Department of State than when I arrived in 1961. One doesn't solve problems by adding people. We held the size of the department constant throughout the sixties, even though we established relations with an additional twenty to twenty-five newly independent countries.

In all honesty, I was hardly surprised that my efforts to reform State's bureaucracy had little lasting effect. I had by the early 1960's lived through several reorganizations in government. Each made me more skeptical than the last. More important is to have good people in key positions and allow them freedom to do their jobs. Yet we did make some lasting changes. For example, we established an Operations Center where, in the event of a crisis, we could draw together a task force with full support facilities and have effective communications with our embassies and governments all over the world.

Bureaucratic sprawl was a problem in our embassies overseas as well as in Washington. Our ambassador to Great Britain, David Bruce, reported upon his arrival that forty-four different U.S. agencies operated out of our London embassy. He had more officers attached to his embassy than the British had in their entire Foreign Office! His inventory turned up seven military attachés whose sole responsibility was to give logistical support to a dozen military Rhodes scholars at Oxford. Hell, I had been a Rhodes scholar and nobody gave me any logistical support! A telephone call to Bob McNamara ended that nonsense.

Often I tried to visit those areas of the department that rarely saw a secretary of state, such outposts as the file rooms, code rooms, and shipping department. Sometimes I ate lunch in the general cafeteria instead of the secretary's private dining room because I wanted to see and be seen by those employees. They kept the department going on a day-to-day basis. And they would be eating in State's cafeteria long after I was gone.

I tried to pay special attention to junior Foreign Service officers. When in 1941 as a captain in military intelligence I visited Secretary of State Cordell Hull with one of my superiors, I was deeply impressed that I, a mere captain, had had the opportunity to talk with the secretary of state. Later, when I was secretary, I found ways to meet with junior Foreign Service officers. I often asked assistant secretaries to bring to meetings junior colleagues who were working on the issue at hand. I talked often with younger officers, and I sometimes walked in on lower-level meetings of the department to show junior officers I was interested in their work.

At the policy level, State's Policy Planning Office performed an indispensable function. I met with people in the office frequently, but at the same time I tried to encourage every Foreign Service officer, even every country desk officer, to consider himself a policy planner. I told our people that every officer must think in long-range terms about his job and what the future holds.

One point upon which our Policy Planning Staff and I never agreed was its desire to publish a comprehensive statement of the foreign policy of the United States. The Eisenhower administration started this practice, gathering a rather thick volume called *United States National Security Policy,* a worldwide general catalog of issues and policy responses. During Kennedy's early months the Policy Planning Staff and some White House staffers labored to revise and update this major document on American policy. They wanted a comprehensive statement of Kennedy's foreign policy objectives for the guidance of ambassadors, Foreign Service officers, and other agencies of the government, as well as for the president and secretary of state.

A prodigious volume emerged. But to their dismay, President Kennedy and I did not approve it. There were two reasons. First, how could we know what these generalizations might mean tomorrow morning at nine o'clock, should a particular question arise? And we didn't want anyone else thinking he knew, in advance, what to do about specific problems in the real world. For example, the study spoke of an "Asian policy." My problem with an "Asian policy" was that there was no "Asia." Rather, we had Japan, China, Taiwan, the Philippines, the countries of Southeast Asia, and so on, each distinct in its history, culture, and traditions, highly separate from one another. The same held true for Latin America, Africa, and Europe. Kennedy's sense of pragmatism was offended by this document; he couldn't tell what it meant or what he was being asked to approve. His reaction and mine disappointed George McGhee, Walt Rostow, and others with Policy Planning. But there it was.

Second, although policy planners had undergone a useful exercise in preparing this book, we did not want anyone thinking, "Ah, now we've got the policy," and go to sleep at the switch. Policy planning must be continuous.

In specific situations, policy planning did prove extremely helpful. Take the Berlin crisis of 1961–62. In this case, four-power planning involved Britain, France, West Germany, and NATO. Two decades' worth of contingency planning stood us in good stead when Berlin again became a focal point of crisis. Similarly, when President Johnson evacuated American civilians and landed the Marines in the Dominican Republic in 1965, we used detailed contingency plans prepared at the request of President Kennedy. Actually we tried to have a plan for every reasonable contingency, whether violence, revolution, or natural disaster.

But to try to encompass a complex and contradictory world of more than 160 nations with a generalized study as purposed guidelines for policy is almost fruitless. Dean Acheson once said that the object of American foreign policy is to "try to create a world situation in which this great experiment in liberty that we call America can survive and flourish." As a generalization, that says it all.

Frequently the State Department is pilloried for not coming up with fresh ideas. The criticism is valid, but considering the complexities of foreign policy issues, innovation is difficult. During the Kennedy years I asked some young Foreign Service officers to create a forum for policy analysis, in which they would search for new ideas and challenge basic assumptions about American policy. As I gave them their assignment, I told them, "I think you're going to find this a difficult job." They shot me a rather patronizing look, but a year later they said, "You were right. New ideas are hard to come by." That group evolved into an "open forum" panel where Foreign Service officers met regularly with outside speakers for freewheeling discussions.

Policy planning suffers from the inherent disadvantage of having to deal with the future. We sometimes forget that most foreign policy decisions are about the future, trying to nudge events in one direction rather than another. But Providence has not given us the capacity to pierce the fog of the future with accuracy; a good policy officer knows this and knows that his decisions are made in the conditional mood. "We hope," "possibly," and "if things work out right" are part of his language. Yet a policy officer's decisions are evaluated in the brightness of hindsight.

In today's world the pace and the acceleration of change are continually increasing. The whole scene is in flux. Sometimes, as with bird hunting, a policy planner has to lead with his sights or he will get nothing but tail feathers. Whenever we asked professors and academics to consult with us, we found they had problems with working in the future. Often their reaction was "We need more time to study this." That additional time and factor of delay itself constituted a decision; on that issue at least, at that particular moment, the United States would do nothing. Very often doing nothing was the best policy, but sometimes it was not. Often they would say, "This situation is too complex for the information we now have. We need more information." Unfortunately we often had to make a decision based on whatever information we had, even though we didn't fully understand the complexities involved. By the time professors work out all their footnotes and have taken anywhere from nine months to two years to produce their studies, the issues have often changed and slipped out from under them.

The policy officer facing an important question has a checklist in his mind, somewhat like the checklist that a pilot goes through before taking off his airplane. He thinks about dozens of elements in the problem, constantly haunted by the ghost of the missing factor. Here is a major difference between officials who carry responsibility and citizens who do not. Professors and reporters can isolate several elements in a problem and focus on those, but the policy officer must encompass all. In a world of more than 160 nations, an early question on his checklist is "What are the other governments of the world going to think about this?" Already there are more than 160 concerns on his mind.

Ironically, more often than not, the State Department's office directors and assistant directors play the critical role in policy planning and prophecy. It's at this level that judgments are made about whether a problem needs immediate attention, can be left alone, or will disappear on its own. No administration can take up everything at once. The art of policy is knowing when to act, how to act, through whom to act, with what tools to act, and for what purposes to act.

As an assistant secretary in the Truman administration I frequently reflected upon the extent to which the secretary of state and president were prisoners of judgments made by people at my level and below. The idea that policy is sent down from on high is just plain wrong. The endless stream of business, the pace of events, and the complexity of the modern world require even junior officers in the department to make high-level decisions.

Running the State Department is a hectic job, especially with an action president like John Kennedy. Because of Kennedy's insatiable curiosity and habit of involving himself in many issues, I had to read enormous quantities of memoranda, intelligence papers, studies, and books. But life was almost as busy under Lyndon Johnson. I probably could have conserved my time better than I did. Cutting back on embassy dinners would have helped, but a secretary of state's attendance at those dinners is an issue of protocol. I tried to make myself available to foreign ambassadors, too. By tradition, an ambassador has the right to see the foreign minister and even the head of state of the country to which he is accredited. We frequently sent telegrams to our ambassadors: "Please see the foreign minister" or "Please see the prime minister." Thus, we could not expect our own ambassadors to have access to foreign ministers and prime ministers unless their ambassadors had similar access in Washington. My presidents sometimes became a little impatient when I told them that they had to see somebody as a matter of protocol.

In retrospect, I worked too hard at my job. One reason George Marshall was so effective at State was that he did only those things which only the secretary of state can do. He would leave the rest to his subordinates and go home at four-thirty or five every afternoon. But the world has become increasingly complex since Marshall's day. There were endless White House and embassy dinners that we had to attend. My wife and I had dinner at home with our children perhaps once a month for eight years.

As secretary of state I could never say at the end of the day, "Now I am caught up," because there was always unfinished business and massive amounts of readings. My appointment books show that I talked with individuals or groups over thirty times a day. On each occasion I emptied my mind of one set of data and stocked it up with another set of data relating to the upcoming meeting. This process of changing subjects so frequently in the course of each day, having to unload and reload, exacted its toll in nervous energy.

What surprised me most about the job was the sheer mass of work that needed to be done. I had learned about the department during the Truman years, and much was familiar. But the amount of work was staggering. I am not saying this in terms of self-pity, but it was a tremendous job. My mother could sit in a rocking chair and take a five- or ten-minute catnap at any time of the day. Fortunately I acquired that same ability. As secretary I would frequently take a ten-minute nap in the middle of the day before continuing with the rest of the day's work.

In my final year as secretary, 1968, I was just bone-tired. The job required fourteen- to sixteen-hour days, usually seven days a week, and rarely did I take time off. My longest break was ten days, in 1965, to recover from the flu. Vacations were pointless; the telephone kept ringing whether I was on duty or not. Eight years is just too long for that job. We should treat secretaries of state the way we treat platoon college football: Put in one team, wear it out, and put in another team.

The Soviet Union handles the demands of statecraft far better than we; every year Soviet leaders are required to take a month's vacation. Soviet Foreign Minister Andrei Gromyko once asked me, "By the way, I am planning to take my vacation next month. Will it be all right?" I said, "Sure, go ahead. We're not going to cause you any problems."

The process of decision making is especially strained during times of crisis or ill health. During the Cuban missile crisis John Kennedy and his advisers experienced incredible tension and little sleep for two weeks. I averaged about four hours of sleep per night during the crisis, and John Kennedy could not have slept much either. In his memoirs even Nikita Khrushchev admitted that he slept on his office couch during the crisis. Sleeplessness, suspicion, and ignorance about what the other fellow is going to do all take their toll. In a future crisis how long can human beings hold up? Would there be a point at which exhaustion might affect judgment and some leader might say, "The hell with it," and push the button?

The impact that ill health has on decision making is also an open question. President Kennedy was never affected by his health that I could see, by his back or anything else. Lyndon Johnson was affected by health considerations. He was a man in a great hurry, and I think this related to his massive heart attack when he was a senator. Lyndon Johnson drove himself unmercifully, and his concern about his heart may have contributed to his impatience. It may have influenced his conduct as president, his approach toward administration, toward implementing Great Society legislation, and even his strategy for fighting the Vietnam War.

Whatever the strain of these jobs, though, decisions have to be made and actions taken, by a president elected by the people and those he selects to advise him. None can avoid the awesome responsibility of running the government. My hope is that we can attract the best of our citizens to these positions of great responsibility.

34

Congressional Relations

With the possible exception of Tibet before the Chinese drove out the Dalai Lama, the American constitutional and political system is the most complicated in the world. It was deliberately made complicated by the Founding Fathers to restrain the exercise of power. The late Chief Justice Earl Warren once said, "If any branch of the federal government pursued its own constitutional powers to the end of the trail, our system simply could not function. It would freeze up, like an engine without oil." Impasse is the overhanging threat to our constitutional system.

So complex is it that foreigners cannot understand it. I suspect that many Americans don't understand it either. In the State Department we spent much time educating representatives of other countries about our constitutional system. As I've already related, I personally passed many hours with Soviet Foreign Minister Andrei Gromyko and Soviet Ambassador Anatoly Dobrynin simply explaining how our system works.

Another consequence of complexity is that those who hold positions of responsibility within government, either elective or appointive, devote enormous time just to make the system work. The separation of powers is a vital part of our Constitution, but so is the constitutional necessity for cooperation among and between the branches of government. Our Constitution forces Americans to seek consensus so that government can function.

In foreign policy the most critical avenues of cooperation run between the executive and legislative branches of government. Both presidents whom I served were vitally concerned about their relations with Congress, Lyndon Johnson in particular, dating back to his years as Senate majority leader.

Executive-congressional relations were especially important to the new Kennedy administration. Any new president needs to tap the reservoir of seasoned members of key committees of Congress as well as professional Foreign Service officers. They have been there and seen much. They are the collective memory and provide continuity to American foreign policy.

Congress is important also because almost all foreign policy requires legislation or appropriations. So a secretary of state has to spend a lot of time—and heartburn—with Congress. Henry Kissinger once told me that he compared the amount of time secretaries of state spent in congressional testimony, and I came out on top. That didn't surprise me. Sometimes I thought I spent most of my life there.

A secretary of state is often constrained by congressional legislation. A secretary has a five-foot shelf in his office loaded with statutory law organizing the State Department and setting many lines of policy that he is expected to pursue. As secretary I constantly checked points of law with the department's Legal Affairs Office. I had no other choice if I wanted to stay within the boundaries of congressional statutes.

Full communication between the executive and legislative branches on foreign policy is essential, yet pressures of time make this difficult. Senators and congressmen have little time for in-depth briefings on world events. Often they cannot even attend committee meetings. Senator William Fulbright and I, concerned about absenteeism, figured that one thing would solve it: televised hearings. Sure enough, they all showed up with their pancake on, ready for the show.

I testified before congressional committees and subcommittees dozens of times during my eight years, and every session required two to three days of preparation. There is no rule of relevance in Congress that requires members to ask questions in a particular field; they can throw questions on any subject whatever, and often do. I had to be prepared for anything.

My only real complaint about these hearings was that if my answers consumed more than two or three minutes, the committee chairman usually tapped his gavel and said, "I respectfully ask the witness to keep his answer short so that junior members can ask their questions." I understood the chairman's concerns, but brief answers were the enemy of depth and content.

I devoted about one-third of my time as secretary of state to congressional relations, both testifying and preparing for testimony. It was a major part of the job. Sometimes Congress's demands are excessive. Early in World War II George Marshall as chief of staff of the Army was called to Capitol Hill so often that he finally told Congress, "Now wait a minute, gentlemen. Do you want me to run the war, or do you want me to spend my time here?" They finally let up on him.

But I thought my time on Capitol Hill was well spent. Both John Kennedy and Lyndon Johnson seemed to value the relationship that I nurtured with Capitol Hill. Both administrations did get most of their legislation. I tried to be candid with members of Congress and often told them things which went beyond what they read in the morning newspapers. I remain convinced that the real secret to working successfully with the House and Senate is simply investing enough time.

Sometimes I met with individual members of Congress and sometimes with groups. Committee chairmen and ranking members of the Senate Foreign Relations and House Foreign Affairs committees were especially important, as were chairmen of the various appropriations committees because they controlled my budget. As for groups, members of Congress elected in a particular year formed breakfast clubs, and I often met with them. I had special meetings with congressional leaders during crises when the leaders wanted information and a chance for input. Also, as a matter of courtesy, I tried to give congressional mail top priority. Congressmen are hounded by their constituents, and we at the State Department did everything we could to help members of Congress serve those they represent. Answering congressional mail was one way to help.

On other occasions I joined a senator or representative in a radio or television show that he would sent back to his home district. And sometimes legislators found parked on their doorsteps groups of constituents touring Washington, and they didn't always know what to do with them; once in a while I invited these groups to the State Department to visit with me. I enjoyed the visits. The members of Congress were grateful, and the constituents were happy to meet the secretary of state.

Early in the Johnson years we also began to invite every member of the House of Representatives to weekly Wednesday morning meetings, at which either I or another senior State Department officer answered questions on some aspect of foreign policy. Attendance ranged from 60 to 70 to 350, depending upon the speaker and the subject. Those attending developed a deeper understanding of foreign affairs, certainly more than what British legislators would gain from question time in the House of Commons.

Most foreign policy—the mass of daily business—neither interested Congress nor complicated State's relations with Congress. Much of the day-to-day conduct of foreign policy involves carrying out existing laws or administering treaties already ratified. On every working day throughout the year, roughly three thousand cables go out of the State Department to our embassies and foreign governments all over the world. Conducting this business alone is an enormous undertaking. Of those three thousand daily cables, perhaps only three or four require congressional consultation. If we placed three thousand cables before the Congress on any given day, most legislators would approve all those cables.

At times the executive branch doesn't give enough attention to its relations with Congress, but under Kennedy and Johnson, cabinet officers were expected to push their own legislation through. Getting foreign aid money was like pulling teeth, and neither Kennedy nor Johnson gave me much help. Neither spent political capital on legislation he thought would merely squeak by.

In defending State Department appropriations requests, I often held hearings in my own office three or four weeks prior to testifying. I wanted to know where every dollar in each budget was. When he took my budget to the floor, the Appropriations subcommittee chairman himself had to answer any question about expenditures, and I thought that I ought to know as much about my budget as he did. I became a believer in zero budgeting, in the sense that by following every dollar in department budget proposals, we always found waste, duplication, and inefficiency.

For example, each officer of the department wanted for his own office complete files of everything he dealt with. To cut down on file cabinets and paper, I took steps to centralize these files for every four or five officers. They could step two offices down the hall and get what they wanted. We saved floor space that way and stopped buying file cabinets.

Bureaucrats rarely fight for power; they fight instead for the symbols of power, such as the rug on the floor, a coffee table by the sofa, a flag in the corner, a water bottle on the desk. Grown men would cut each other's throats over vacuum water bottles. I learned in a budget hearing that each water bottle cost the government $82. I could buy one from Sears for $16.50. So I started putting pressure on water bottles.

Congressional relations was not a one-man show. Ours was a team effort, involving not only the secretary of state and our congressional office but undersecretaries and assistant secretaries as well; all testified frequently on Capitol Hill. We were not always successful. On one occasion, when our assistant secretary for congressional relations was holding sway before the House Foreign Affairs Committee, Congressman John Rooney turned to our man and said, "Just what is the function of your office?" The assistant secretary began a monologue about maintaining contact with members of Congress, whereupon Rooney interrupted, turned to the members of his committee, and went right down the line: "Congressman, did this fellow ever come to see you?" In every case the answer was no. Then Rooney turned to our assistant secretary and said, "Now, what do you say to that?" The silence was deafening.

Rooney might have disagreed, but we searched hard for good liaison people with Congress. After Brooks Hays, an effective congressman and a great raconteur, was defeated during his bid for reelection, President Kennedy and I thought he would make a good undersecretary for congressional relations. I asked Speaker Sam Rayburn about him. "Mr. Secretary," he said, "you are still a young man and can still learn. When a congressman is defeated, down here he is dead. Don't ever suppose that an ex-congressman has any influence with Congress."

Fortunately, throughout much of the post-World War II era, congressional support of U.S. foreign policy has been largely bipartisan. In my hundreds of meetings with congressional committees, I rarely saw differences of view turn on party lines with Republicans versus Democrats. One of the most evenhanded in Congress was Senator Arthur Vandenberg. During the Eightieth Congress Vandenberg chaired the Senate Foreign Relations Committee and somehow managed to have every bill and report produced by his committee—with one exception—issued as a unanimous report. Vandenberg somehow made his fellow senators attend meetings, where he hammered out the committee's view.

Vandenberg was a superb chairman, great for the executive branch because we knew where he was, with whom we had to negotiate, and generally how the Senate felt about policy. That greatly facilitated consultation between the two branches. When leadership fragments, presidents and secretaries of state not only have to consult with a lot more senators but also must piece their views together like a jigsaw puzzle to try to figure out where the Senate comes out at the end of the day. Some legislators understand that the powers granted Congress under the Constitution are given to Congress as a corporate body, not to individual members of Congress. Arthur Vandenberg, Richard Russell, and Everett Dirksen—those whom LBJ used to call the "whales of the Congress"—all understood that Congress must act as a corporate body at day's end. With 535 members of Congress, it is impossible to consult with each. Political scientists can make a strong case against leadership in Congress, but trying to deal with 535 minnows swimming around in a bucket is worse.

Presidents and cabinet officers need people in the Congress to talk with, those who could size up Congress for us. In the early sixties we could talk to four senators—Richard Russell of Georgia, Bob Kerr of Oklahoma, Everett Dirksen of Illinois, and Hubert Humphrey of Minnesota—and then go to the House and talk with Speaker Sam Rayburn of Texas, and we knew what Congress would do on a bill or policy issue. Very possibly one reason that they knew was that they often told the Senate and House what to do. But in later years the Young Turks broke up the "whale" system. Now no individuals or small groups can speak for Congress until after a formal vote has been taken. As a result, executive-legislative consultations have been greatly complicated.

One episode from the Truman administration amply illustrates what consultation is and is not. When I was head of United Nations Affairs, Secretary of State George Marshall invited Arthur Vandenberg to spend several hours with us going over the agenda for the forthcoming UN General Assembly. We reviewed forty or fifty items, and when we were done, Vandenberg got up to go. Marshall said, "Thank you very much, Senator. I am delighted to have had this opportunity for consultation." Vandenberg replied, "Not consultation, Mr. Secretary. Conversation." Marshall immediately got the point and said, "Of course. You're right." In those meetings, Vandenberg could not talk with his colleagues.

A similar situation occurred during the Cuban missile crisis. During the first week of the crisis we held close counsel among the ExComm, not wanting anyone to know that a crisis was brewing until we decided what to do. Shortly before Kennedy's speech to the nation, we called in congressional leaders. But we never asked them for advice; we told them what we were going to do. The only real question before them was, Are you prepared to support your country in this moment of danger? This was not consultation. Kennedy did not ask them for advice. But it was the right way to handle this most urgent of crises.

On other occasions we decided not to consult with Congress, usually with good reason. We did not consult with Congress in November 1964 when we cooperated with Belgium to drop a battalion of Belgian paratroopers into Stanleyville to rescue six hundred hostages from the Simbas because we feared that if the slightest word leaked out, those hostages would have been killed. Nor did we consult with Congress in 1967, when we sent three U.S. C-130 transport planes to the Congo to help that government quell a rebellion of white mercenaries. I talked to Senator Russell and Senator Fulbright about this, and they strongly opposed it. I reported their opposition to President Johnson. Nevertheless, he moved these planes to Ascension Island and then into the Congo as the situation worsened. Consequently, even though we did consult with Congress—in a fashion—about the Congo, we didn't agree on what to do. The administration went ahead and took action. Both Fulbright and Russell, in fact, blasted us from the Senate floor for sending planes to the Congo. But the policy decision was correct.

Deciding when to consult is a judgment call, frequently influenced by a need for secrecy and confidentiality. But the issue of confidentiality is complicated by a constitutional provision which grants members of Congress immunity for anything they say on the floor or in committee. The only penalty that can be imposed for breaches of confidentiality is expulsion, and Congress isn't going to do that.

Consultation between the executive and legislative branches usually works. When we negotiated the Limited Test Ban Treaty with the Soviet Union and began to negotiate the Nonproliferation Treaty, we kept in close touch with the Senate Foreign Relations Committee. It always helps to involve Congress in negotiations. At ratification time, senators who were involved can get up on the Senate floor and urge passage.

The initiative for executive-legislative consultation seems to rest with the president and his cabinet. During my tenure as secretary, members of Congress called me only four or five times to say, "Look, the next time you are down here, please drop by my office," or, "Can I come by to see you on the way home?" Rarely do members of Congress take the initiative to consult. Yet often these same people resent not having been consulted. Most preferred to sit like pouting dowagers, waiting to be persuaded. Perhaps they didn't seek me out because of their busy schedules or concern about my own schedule, but they almost always left the initiative for consultation to the executive branch.

Of course, things have changed since my day because of the extraordinary growth of congressional staffs. This had led to an increase in "bureaucratic tendencies" where each staffer must earn brownie points to justify his job. During the Carter years, for example, one report indicated that the White House's congressional relations office received fifteen hundred calls from Congress each day. Most undoubtedly came from staffers who wanted to be able to tell their bosses, "Oh, yes, I talked with the White House about this."

Fortunately Congress itself rarely dreams up foreign policy initiatives, although occasionally we do get a horrible example. During Kennedy's first year I received a congressional proclamation declaring a certain week in July "Captive Nations Week." I called my colleagues and said, "What in the world is this all about?" They brought me this Captive Nations Resolution, which Congress passed unanimously in 1958. It was one of the wildest Cold War documents I ever saw. It called for a dozen or so independent nations to be created from within the Soviet Union, including one, Idel-ural, which cannot be found in the *Encyclopaedia Britannica*. The proclamation implied that separate nationalities in the Soviet Union were entitled to separate countries of their own. The resolution called upon the president to issue an annual proclamation. Each year the Soviet ambassador came in to protest the proclamation, and each year I told him, "Don't get excited. We're not going to war over it." As actors in this play, Soviet Ambassador Dobrynin and I soberly carried out the roles expected of us. For eight years I sent that proclamation to the president, and every year he proclaimed that week in July Captive Nations Week.

There is an interesting sequel. On one occasion William Fulbright tried to weed unnecessary rhetoric out of our legislation, including high-flying preambles and resolutions such as the Captive Nations Resolution. I suggested to Bill Fulbright that his committee tackle that resolution, but he wrote back saying that some of his committee members, up for reelection in districts that had Eastern European immigrant populations, said they could not vote to rescind the resolution. However, they would not object if the president stopped declaring Captive Nations Week!

This and other intrusions of domestic politics into our foreign policy are an inevitable result of democracy. On most foreign policy issues, members of Congress vote for what they perceive the national interest to be. But on some issues, demands of reelection force them to pay close attention to ethnic politics and constituent interests. We always expected a representative from New York City to back Israel, one from Chicago to be conscious of Polish interests, or members from Louisiana westward to be strong supporters of cattle and oil and gas interests. All this is part of the normal play of politics, and at times the trading gets rather tough. I once called upon Senator Bob Kerr of Oklahoma to get his help on foreign aid. He told me, in effect, "Mr. Secretary, if you can do something for me about cattle and oil, perhaps I can do something for you about foreign aid." In dealing with members of Congress, we had to remember that their number one priority was getting reelected.

Another incident is revealing. Early in the Kennedy administration we realized that the United States was violating an agreement with Mexico regarding both the quantity and quality of water moving down the Colorado River to Mexico. After we investigated, we found that irrigation districts outside the Colorado River basin both took water from the river and pumped water into the river. When we tried to do something about this, we ran afoul of Senator Carl Hayden of Arizona, chairman of the Senate Appropriations Committee and president pro tempore of the Senate. He told us to "leave my irrigation districts alone." We had a problem, both with Hayden and with Mexico, and the only way to solve it was to do what Hayden wanted: put desalination plants in Mexico and all sorts of damn things, at great expense. As long as Carl Hayden chaired the Appropriations Committee, we could do little about the Colorado River.

On another occasion I was testifying before a House committee on a foreign aid bill when my good friend Representative Brooks Hays of Arkansas, a marvelous raconteur, got up to leave after the bell rang for a vote. He turned to me and said, "Mr. Secretary, I hope you will excuse me, but I have to go to the floor and vote on an Arkansas River bill. I apologize for leaving, but it won't do me any good to sit here and listen to you talk about the Tigris and Euphrates and the Nile, if I don't vote on this Arkansas River bill."

Clearly, domestic politics plays a big role in foreign policy whenever Congress gets involved, and this was nowhere more true than our many discussions over the Vietnam War. It was also over Vietnam that we had great difficulty with congressional consultation.

Under both Kennedy and Johnson the record shows that we consulted with Congress about Vietnam both freely and frequently. We thoroughly discussed all aspects of policy, although sometimes we took military action without congressional approval. But we didn't discuss troop movements or military actions with Congress during World War

II or Korea either. The full record of our consultation with Congress will be available when the Senate Foreign Relations Committee and the House Foreign Affairs Committee complete the publication of their executive sessions.

For example, during 1966 and 1967, President Johnson invited every senator and representative in groups of about thirty to the White House, where Robert McNamara and I would brief them, answer questions, and listen to comments. Lyndon Johnson covered the entire Congress with those meetings in two successive years.

Of course, the objection could be raised that senators and representatives won't express their real views in such settings. William Fulbright, in particular, complained about this practice of presidents calling senators to the White House for consultation; he said the atmosphere and awe attached to the White House make for an uneven dialogue. He had a point, since the White House is the place where every president beginning with John Adams received members of Congress; Gladstone once said of his relations with Queen Victoria, "It is difficult to argue on your knees." However, members of Congress don't mind speaking up and even defying the president as soon as they leave the White House, so why can't they do so inside? Looking back over the discussions we had with Congress, I firmly believe that Congress supported what we were trying to do in Vietnam.

Other evidence supports my view. At a Senate hearing in 1966, Senator Clifford Case of New Jersey sharply criticized our Vietnam policy, so I told him, "Senator, why don't you put your views in a resolution and have it voted on? What we need to know is what Congress thinks." He didn't respond. And also in 1966, Senator Wayne Morse of Oregon made a motion to rescind the Tonkin Gulf Resolution. There was a countermotion to table his resolution, and only five senators voted not to table.

All in all, despite many congressional voices speaking critically about Vietnam policy, Congress did not change its mind on Vietnam until it rescinded the Gulf of Tonkin Resolution in 1971. The record shows that Congress gave strong and consistent support to our Vietnam policy throughout the 1960's, even though some had strong misgivings. Men like Senator Richard Russell of Georgia did not like our involvement in Southeast Asia but supported the president and our men and women in combat when the national commitment was made. There were probably many in Congress who supported our fighting forces in the field whatever their personal views might have been about our involvement. We deeply appreciated the support we had from Congress, despite the agony which accompanied sending young Americans into battle.

Following my departure from office, Congress in 1973 passed the War Powers Act. Vietnam precipitated this action. In my skepticism I've often wondered if this act was an effort by Congress to find its own alibi for Vietnam. In fairness, other congressional concerns also aided the War Powers Act's passage. Undeclared war has been with us a long time; on over two hundred occasions, dating from the earliest days of the Republic, American presidents have used armed force without any declaration of war or prior authorization by Congress. Sometimes authorizations came after the fact, but there is nothing new about presidential use of military power without specific congressional authorization. It is one of the oldest constitutional problems we have.

Whatever its sources, in my judgment some clauses of the War Powers Act are unconstitutional. An example is the clause which under certain circumstances allows Congress to require the withdrawal of American forces by concurrent resolution. Unlike joint resolutions, concurrent resolutions do not go to the president for signature or possible veto. For Congress to issue concurrent resolutions to bring about a significant policy change weakens the president's legislative role under Article I of the Constitution. And other provisions of the War Powers Act are just silly. One demands that the president report regularly to Congress on the question, How long is this war going to last? What president could ever answer that?

As a private citizen I don't lose sleep over the War Powers Act. If a crisis develops and a president has to go to Congress for something like a Tonkin Gulf Resolution, almost certainly a simple clause will be attached stating, "In carrying out the purposes of this resolution, the War Powers Act shall not apply." In the hoopla of initial action, when everyone is all steamed up and ready to go, Congress will almost certainly adopt language of that nature. No president will commit American troops on a contingency basis.

Despite the conflict that developed between the executive and legislative branches over the Vietnam War, I emerged from my eight years with confidence in our present system. The overwhelming majority of senators and representatives, in that tug of war between the national interest and the local concerns of their constituents, are honest men and women trying to do their best. Lyndon Johnson once said, "I never knew any senator who was trying to do the wrong thing." That may be stretching things a bit, but our system ultimately depends upon the intelligence, integrity, and good faith of people in government.

Yet Congress has not organized itself effectively for reviewing foreign policy. If only the foreign affairs committees and perhaps one or two others were involved in foreign policy, things would be fine, but as it stands, almost every committee of Congress gets in the act. For example, the committess on the District of Columbia are constantly immersed in issues involving the care and handling of foreign embassies and diplomats.

I have long suggested that the Senate and House foreign relations committees be permitted to call before themselves any bill pending before any other committee that affected U.S. foreign policy. Then they could comment on the bill from the perspective of foreign policy as a whole. But committee jealousies are such that this procedure will not likely be adopted. That no one has overall responsibility for foreign policy in Congress—a situation we'll probably have to live with—greatly complicates consultation between the executive and legislative branches.

Members of Congress in general are a fascinating lot, and this goes doubly for senators. One of my favorites was Senator Wayne Morse, despite his being a strong critic of our Vietnam policy. I always respected Morse because he stood up on the Senate floor and stated clearly what he thought. During the debate on the Tonkin Gulf Resolution—he was one of two senators who voted against it—Morse said that South Vietnam was not worth the life of one American soldier. I thought he was wrong, but I respected him. His colleagues called him the tiger of the Senate; in Wayne Morse we had a determined foe. He had a unique facility for forcing his colleagues to look at searching and sometimes embarrassing questions. He pressed the Senate to consider whether the Tonkin Gulf Resolution was an unconstitutional delegation of war power to the president. Although his colleagues thought not, Morse held their feet to the fire on that question.

Despite our strong disagreements, we always remained friends. After I left office and moved to Georgia, Wayne visited me in the midst of his reelection campaign in Oregon, during which his opponents attacked him as a left-winger, soft on communism. I told him, "Wayne, I don't know how it would go over in Oregon, but if you want me to head west and hit the stump on your behalf, I am at your disposal. I'll knock this notion that you are a left-winger clear out of the ball park." The old boy's eyes filled with tears right there in my office.

Another major figure in the Senate with whom I worked closely was Richard Russell of Georgia. For twenty years as chairman of the Senate Armed Services Committee, Dick Russell was the second most powerful man in Washington. He was also de facto chairman of the Appropriations Committee; Carl Hayden was so old he wasn't able to serve actively as chair. Presidents beginning with Harry Truman kept in close touch with Russell. Lyndon Johnson called him at least two or three times a week, and I saw him as well, often in his office; I never called him on the phone. On certain subjects Russell was the czar. If we wanted to sell or lend a destroyer or PT boat to a foreign government, only Richard Russell could make that decision because we needed legislative support. If he said no, the answer was no.

I had a few serious differences with Russell, less on PT boats than civil rights, for example. But Richard Russell was a man of honor. If he pledged his support, he would fight tooth and nail for you. But if he vowed to oppose you, he would do so with every parliamentary trick in the book. At least we knew what our problems were with Russell and what we'd have to do to work with him. In holding the secretary's job, I soon learned who were the men of honor—such as Dick Russell—and who were the other kind. People without honor make conducting public business in Washington very difficult.

Senator Mike Mansfield was another fascinating character who often stated his reasons for opposing the Vietnam War in letters to the president, with copies to me. Ironically, he was a cosigner of the Southeast Asia Treaty in 1955; Mansfield, Senator Alexander Smith of New Jersey, and Secretary of State John Foster Dulles made up the delegation that signed the treaty. When I reminded him of this later, he said that he had signed the treaty "reluctantly." So I went to the *Congressional Record* for the Senate floor discussion on the SEATO Treaty and found that Mansfield at no time told the Senate that he had signed it reluctantly. In fact, he urged his colleagues to vote it through. Mansfield, as most of us, was influenced by the job that he held. When Mansfield was a senator, he introduced resolutions calling for sharp reductions in our NATO forces in Europe. But when he became our ambassador to Japan, he pressed for a buildup of American forces in the Pacific.

As chairman of the Senate Foreign Relations Committee, William Fulbright was an instinctive maverick. He might have learned his iconoclasm in his early days as a Rhodes scholar because at Oxford it is infra dig—Latin meaning "beneath dignity"—to agree with anybody else. There is room in the Senate for mavericks, but when a maverick gets to be chairman of an important committee, that can create some problems.

Senators and representatives also frequently draw criticism for their foreign travel, but I supported these so-called junkets; they help the legislators see and hear and understand the situations they deal with only on paper in Washington. But sometimes members of Congress traveling abroad created extra work for us diplomats. One senator thumbed a ride across the Atlantic on my airplane, had too many drinks, and couldn't keep his hands off the young women on board. I planted him in his chair, put my security man in the seat across the aisle from him, and told him, "Senator, you are going to stay in your seat, and my security man is going to sit here and see that you do." He became very irate and was rough on me during the rest of that plane ride and through that entire congressional term. On another occasion an aged senator on a trip to Greece went up to Queen Frederika at a reception, slapped her on the bottom, and said, "Hello, queenie, how are you this evening?" And a third senator on a trip to Africa told the Africans that they had just climbed down from the trees. On these occasions I practiced damage control as best I could. More frequently, legislators traveling overseas make statements that contradict U.S. policy. Now if the foreigners who hear such statements understand how our system works, no problems arise. But often they don't understand, and we diplomats must exercise damage control.

Whatever the problems of executive-legislative relations in foreign policy—and there are many—ours is a remarkable constitutional system. The awkwardness of checks and balances forces us to seek consensus, even in foreign policy, and I don't believe in tampering with our constitutional arrangements. I oppose most suggestions for constitutional change—for example, selecting the cabinet from members of Congress and a single six-year term for the president. Processes deriving from our present system work better than we realize. There was plenty of consensus in the 2.1 million cables that went out of the State Department with my name signed to them. Ninety-five percent of those would have been approved by Congress in any case. Having lived through many moments of high tension, some involving constitutional issues, I left Washington with a deep sense of awe for our constitutional system. My general approach to the Constitution is "If it ain't broke, don't fix it."

We do need more efficient ways to exchange ideas on foreign policy between the executive branch and Congress. Regular monthly bull sessions between the president and bipartisan congressional leadership would be helpful, not to decide specific points but to develop further consensus about what is going on in the world and what our general responses should be.

Our democracy will always have elements of discord and confusion; they are inherent in our system. A cacophony of voices is a price we pay for democracy. I am glad to pay it even at the expense of some disarray in our relations with other countries. But it is important that the American government speak for the United States in talking with other nations. The quality of that voice is affected by whether we have broad bipartisan support for our foreign policy or confusion and disarray. For example, if we had been confused at home and if the OAS and NATO had not unanimously condemned Soviet actions at the time of the Cuban missile crisis, Nikita Khrushchev might have underestimated American resolve.

Walter Lippmann, George Kennan, occasionally Dean Acheson, and others as well have said that the issues of foreign policy are too complex for Congress and that the elected representatives of the people really shouldn't have a major role in determining foreign policy. I oppose this elitist attitude. I lived and worked with the so-called elite for over forty years, and when it comes to common sense, practical judgment, considerations of right and wrong, and the gap between what is and what ought to be, the "elite" have no advantages over my country cousins in Cherokee County, Georgia, or any other Americans. One flaw of government officials is that they often underestimate the capacity of ordinary citizens to make sensible judgments about public issues.

Political leaders and policy officers must always remember to ask, "What would the American people think about this issue if they knew about it tomorrow morning?" This doesn't mean that the passing whims of the American people are suitable guidelines for policy. Edmund Burke once reminded the electors of Bristol that he was not in Parliament simply to represent their every whim, but to bring to bear his conscience, his abilities, and his judgment on the issues. But respect for the citizenry is fundamental in a democracy, and this must be carried over into the executive branch's attitude toward Congress.

35

Intelligence and Counterintelligence

s secretary of state I was charged with advising my president on foreign policy and carrying out his instructions. But good policies cannot be made without good information. Therefore, as secretary I received a flow of information of all kinds: briefing reports from State's Intelligence and Research office (INR), the Central Intelligence Agency, the Defense Intelligence Agency, and the National Security Agency. Those reports were on my desk every morning when I arrived for work, because some poor devils had shown up at 4:00 or 5:00 A.M. to prepare them. My own staff looked through this material and underlined what it thought important, but it left backup information there if I wanted to read further. Every morning the chief of intelligence and research briefed me, and I often put additional questions to him for further study. Throughout each day INR sent me a constant flow of information, little snippets and short paragraphs calling my attention to developments throughout the world.

With this constant flow of information, it was difficult to determine wheat from chaff. Analysts and policy makers alike tend to interpret information to support their own viewpoints, giving rise to differences.

It is largely to overcome these tendencies that we have competing intelligence services. At the end of World War II Secretary of War Robert Patterson pressed hard for a single, integrated intelligence agency. As his special assistant I supported that view. Later I changed my mind, concluding that it was far more wholesome to have independent and separate intelligence agencies in State, Defense, the National Security Agency, and the CIA, under the coordinating supervision of the CIA director. Multiple agencies can supplement and balance off each other and also highlight disagreements within the intelligence community to policy officers.

Even if intelligence analysts and policy officers were 100 percent objective, on any given day bales of raw data must be digested and distilled to be usable. That process inevitably introduces slippage and distortion.

In addition, policy makers must frequently move on scanty information. They can't pause to commission Ph.D. theses every time a problem occurs. The pace of events won't allow it. Policy makers often realize that they need additional information, but sometimes that information simply doesn't exist or isn't obtainable.

About 90 percent of the intelligence that crossed my desk came from the public domain, even in countries where we had agents in the field. It takes an enormous effort to keep an eye on the blizzard of articles and books published all over the world, to see what significant information can be distilled. Secret intelligence and cloak-and-dagger operations account for less than 10 percent of the CIA's mission.

I thought the "product" of our intelligence community exceptionally good during my tenure, although the occasional oversights were inevitably highlighted. Most shortcomings we experienced were inherent in the intelligence process, rather than the result of poor ability, faulty analysis, or misrepresentation of intelligence at higher levels.

But most breakdowns in intelligence come from the simple fact that future events are difficult to perceive. We expect analysts to predict the future for us, but prophets they cannot be. And intelligence officers need to remind themselves of this. I have told more than one CIA director that strategic estimates ought to begin with the expression "Damned if we know, but if you want our best guess, here it is."

American intelligence has had its share of disastrous lapses; what service has not? Pearl Harbor was the most famous. But the intelligence community should not be graded by its ability to predict the future with certainty. If we demand that intelligence officers be prophets, they will flood policy officers with "cry wolf" predictions, designed to cover all contingencies and around 98 percent inaccurate. Then the policy officer must figure out which contingencies are for real. Policy makers, the press, and, indeed, the American people tend to impose upon analysts the "Pearl Harbor syndrome," forcing them to make sweeping predictions for protection against the unanticipated. I personally would prefer to have the flow of information continue and have too much intelligence rather than not enough. My fear is that if analysts filter too finely, they may filter out essential information.

Many people gather intelligence. It is a primary function of an ambassador to feed his government information. This sometimes leads to sticky situations. In some countries, when our own people make contact with or report the views of opposition political leaders, the host governments are resentful. For example, when Bangladesh was East Pakistan, the West Pakistani government declared our consul general *persona non grata* because he met socially and informally with opposition leaders.

Many countries, including the United States, also use diplomatic cover for intelligence missions. In our case this practice developed because the CIA was always well funded and the State Department was not. The CIA could provide staff in embassies short of State Department personnel. During my years CIA budgets were shown to a few specially cleared officers in the Bureau of the Budget, whisked by the nose of the president, and given to Senator Richard Russell and Congressman Carl Vinson, who proceeded to lose them in the defense budget.

Much secrecy surrounded CIA operations. During my tenure an interdepartmental group called the 303 Committee supervised CIA covert operations, and at various times Llewellyn Thompson, Tom Hughes, head of the State Department's Bureau of Intelligence and Research, and Alexis Johnson served as my representatives on the committee. I also talked frequently with CIA head John McCone.

After the revelations and discoveries of the Church Committee investigation into the CIA in 1975, I look back with chagrin at my performance as a statutory member of the National Security Council charged with overseeing CIA activities, as we were then. We permanent NSC members—not our substitutes—should have focused on the budgets and the personnel manning tables of the intelligence community, at least annually. I never asked to see either. We should also have drawn up our own agendas for meetings and reviewed what was actually being done, rather than just consider items placed on the agenda. The 303 group was not a comprehensive review committee. We learned the hard way that senior officials of the executive branch must review the intelligence agencies; oversight should not be left to our substitutes or congressional committees.

Whatever the error of our oversight procedures, not once did my representatives on the 303 Committee tell me about CIA-hatched assassination plots against Castro and other foreign leaders. I remain convinced that the 303 Committee never discussed them. The closest it came was when Llewellyn Thompson told me about some junior person saying something about the assassination of Fidel Castro. With the exception of that brief reference, I heard nothing more. Thompson and I both laughed about the staffer's remark; we just didn't take it seriously.

The Church Committee revelations of 1975 caught me completely by surprise. Had I known about assassination plots, I would have moved to stop them.

Although these never came to my attention, I vetoed a number of proposed covert actions. Some of these projects evolved from the tendency of intelligence to run away with itself. Analysts tend to look upon intelligence gathering as the end to be achieved, whereas the purpose of intelligence is to inform policy makers about what is going on in the world. Sometimes I vetoed proposals for gathering intelligence, because I would rather not have the information than to use the means proposed to obtain it.

For example, when David Bruce became our ambassador to London, a British official told him, "David, tell your air attachés to stop your planes from flying low over British factories taking pictures. It makes our people nervous. If you want pictures of our factories, just ask and we'll give them to you." Bruce looked into that and found that U.S. military intelligence wanted templates of information on Britain. Included in these templates were categories of bombing targets. American reconnaissance planes therefore flew low over British factories so we would know what to bomb in case the United States and Britain ever went to war. We stopped this absurdity.

When another obnoxious intelligence proposal crossed my desk, I objected to the method that would be used to gain the covert information. "And by the way," I asked, "for whom are you getting this information?" My analysts said, "We're getting it for you, Mr. Secretary." And I said, "Well, I can tell you right now that I don't want this information if that's how you have to get it." The project died.

What made me genuinely angry about the Church Committee revelations was that after President Kennedy was assassinated, we in government searched everywhere to see whether a foreign government might have been implicated; it was potentially a matter of war and peace. I then testified before the Warren Commission that we had found no evidence of foreign involvement. I also said that I did not believe any foreign government had a motive for killing our president.

At that point no one tugged my coattail and said, "Now wait a minute, Mr. Secretary. There is something you should know." Allen Dulles himself sat on the Warren Commission. He said not a word. I felt betrayed that such plans could be made without the knowledge of the secretary of state.

I personally have no idea who authorized the plots to assassinate Castro and other foreign leaders. I find it hard to believe they were discussed in the 303 Committee without my knowledge, because my own representative would not have dared to withhold knowledge of such discussions from me. These plots were likely handled outside the committee. I also doubt that John Kennedy authorized the plots; things like assassinations just were not Kennedy's style.

Other serious problems emerged in the Church Committee hearings. Sometimes the CIA and other intelligence arms bypassed U.S. ambassadors and conducted their own foreign policy. Admittedly, varying degrees of cooperation and tension long marked relations between CIA and State personnel overseas. This was especially so in the fifties, when the CIA head was Allen Dulles, the brother of Secretary of State John Foster Dulles. During the Eisenhower years some bad habits developed. For example, the CIA station chiefs reported to Washington through their own channels their views of the performance of American ambassadors.

This was absolute rubbish. Early in his administration, at my request, President Kennedy issued an order placing the ambassador in charge of all United States government personnel and activities in his country, as well as all communications leaving the embassy. Kennedy's letter cleared up most of this confusion.

Another example of CIA abuse—and this one involved me— emerged from the hearings. Allen Dulles once visited me in New York City in the 1950's, a time when John Foster Dulles chaired the Rockefeller Foundation's board of trustees. Allen had heard, possibly from his brother, that foundation officers traveling abroad had frequent and sometimes intimate discussions with leaders in other countries and often wrote memoranda of conversation about these talks. Allen Dulles asked if the CIA could have access to these memos. I told him no, I couldn't allow that without letting the officers of the foundation know what was being done, in which case they would stop writing memos. Also, if word of that practice leaked, it would spoil the ability of foundation officers to talk with key officials in other countries. Those conversations were necessary to the work of the foundation. In my confrontation with Dulles, my trustees, men like Robert Lovett, John F. McCloy, and Lewis Douglas, backed me up. I was extremely irritated when I learned from the Church Committee that Allen Dulles and his CIA simply went ahead and, enlisting the U.S. Post Office, started reading the mail of the Rockefeller Foundation.

The Church hearings brought to light other intelligence abuses, including illegal wiretapping. Congress investigated these abuses, and I testified on four separate occasions about security and intelligence practices during the Kennedy and Johnson administrations. As secretary of state I don't think I authorized or requested wiretapping or placing under electronic surveillance State Department personnel or journalists. I never had anyone bugged to try to run down leaks, and I never recorded telephone conversations. Some of my visitors may have thought I had recording capabilities, but I never did. On a half dozen occasions I asked the FBI to investigate leaks, but I believe those investigations were conducted by interview rather than electronic surveillance.

I did take precautions to assure the security of my own conversations. I had the ceiling and walls of my office fitted with antibugging devices to prevent anyone from bugging me, and I had that apparatus screened periodically by different agencies. I didn't want a single agency to screen my office in case that agency had fish of its own to fry. I had the pieces of electronics removed—my squawk box for interoffice communications and my scrambler telephone for communicating in code with our embassies. Both are relatively easy to tap.

And I was cautious outside my office as well. My official limousine had a radiotelephone with which I could make calls while driving to and from my office, but there must have been a dozen foreign agents around Washington monitoring radiotelephone chatter. All they ever got was my calling the office and saying, "I'll arrive in about ten minutes. Please have some coffee and a doughnut waiting for me."

Did wiretapping occur during the Kennedy and Johnson administrations? I have no doubt about it. These techniques have been used by many administrations. Wiretapping ebbs and flows with the national mood. During the McCarthy period there was more activity; during the Johnson administration I believe there was less. I did not seek wiretaps in the few instances a leak concerned me, both because I doubted they would succeed and because I was concerned what wiretapping could lead to. Had I been more concerned about the leaks, I might have reconsidered. Wiretapping is tempting because it offers the illusion of a cure, far beyond what is actually gained.

Who authorized wiretapping in the Kennedy and Johnson administrations? J. Edgar Hoover was so extraordinarily independent that in my opinion, no White House staffer or cabinet officer could have told Hoover to wiretap anybody, or not to. The idea that anyone other than the president or attorney general could issue an order to wiretap does not mesh with my experiences with Hoover. Additionally, John Kennedy and Lyndon Johnson were reluctant to issue direct orders to Hoover. They treated him with kid gloves. It is worth remembering that among the first appointments President Kennedy made were Hoover at FBI and Dulles at CIA.

Hoover built a position almost unparalleled in our government, through a combination of professionalism, fear, astute relations with Congress, and good public relations. An experienced bureaucrat, he understood the importance of protecting his flanks. Talking with J. Edgar Hoover was like talking with Charles de Gaulle. He was untouchable. Over the years he had seen many secretaries of state come and go. As far as he was concerned, we were just boys who were in today and gone tomorrow.

Hoover's famous files created a climate of nervousness in Washington, although I was less nervous than some, having learned something about the contents of my own file. Sometimes Hoover passed along gossip to the presidents he served, and that practice could raise questions in a president's mind. What did Hoover know about him? In theoretical terms, that put Hoover in the position of a veiled blackmailer.

During the Truman administration I was thoroughly exposed to national security issues, the workings of the intelligence community, and the investigations of Senator Joe McCarthy. McCarthy's excesses brought many government officials and private citizens under scrutiny. During that time some of my State Department colleagues answered their telephones with a "Hello, you-all," assuming that all lines around the department were wiretapped. Also during the Truman years, an FBI agent came to interview me at Virginia's and my apartment in Parkfairfax, Virginia. He looked through my shelves of books and noted on his pad that I had copies of Karl Marx's *Das Kapital* and Adolf Hitler's *Mein Kampf.* It was ridiculous.

A few years later, when I was president of the Rockefeller Foundation, a young FBI agent came to New York to ask me about someone being considered for a government position. The more he talked, the more it became apparent that he was preoccupied with the fact that this prospective employee was around forty-five years old and a bachelor. This seemed to have raised in the agent's mind the possibility of homosexuality. So I finally said to this agent, "Are you asking me whether this man is a bachelor like J. Edgar Hoover?" He straightened up in his chair and stopped taking notes. I said, "Now look, you asked me the question. You put my answer in your report." Years later I learned that reply was in my FBI file. I had "insulted" the old man.

The FBI stayed after me even after I became secretary of state. That post has several security classifications higher than "top secret," and each requires a full FBI investigation. A neighbor on Quebec Street told me that if the FBI didn't stop coming around asking questions about Dean Rusk, he would think something was wrong with me.

For a while Virginia and I thought the phone in our home on Quebec Street was tapped. Every so often we heard intermittent clicks, so we called in agents to sweep the house, but they couldn't find anything. Finally they discovered that neighborhood squirrels liked the taste of the insulation on the telephone wires and were biting through it. Whenever their teeth hit the wire, we got little clicks. The agents put squirrel-proof insulation on the phone lines.

I viewed domestic surveillance and bugging in particular as a real danger to American society. I felt strongly about this, strongly enough that when I was in a meeting in the cabinet room with President Kennedy, Hoover, and four or five others, I challenged the FBI head. Hoover gave a presentation on a security matter involving electronic surveillance, and when he concluded, I turned to Kennedy in Hoover's presence and said, "If I ever catch anyone in our government bugging me, I will resign and make a public issue of it."

Apart from the constitutional issues bugging raises, using electronic surveillance to run down leaks causes real problems for the State Department. Nothing destroys the Foreign Service's morale as quickly as the belief that its own government doesn't trust it. Also, such surveillance cannot be kept secret, and it certainly won't stop leaks. There are too many ways to pass information.

In fairness to Hoover, he never belabored me with his own judgments about the loyalty or security of anyone in the State Department. He made available summaries of the raw files, but he scrupulously respected cabinet officers' responsibilities to decide loyalty and security cases. He never said, "So-and-so is a security risk; get rid of him." He simply gave me the raw information, and sometimes the information got pretty raw.

In one case a Foreign Service officer in our Warsaw embassy had an affair with a lovely Polish girl who turned out to be a member of the Polish secret police. She blackmailed him for information. Instead of telling the ambassador, "Hey, I'm in a jam. You'd better get me out of the country," he yielded to the blackmail and passed information. He was caught, tried, and given thirty years in prison. A congressman who wasn't very fond of the State Department said, "That's just like the State Department. When they catch one of their people with a woman, they give him thirty years!" Incidents like this led me to give our people two pieces of advice when I sent them overseas: One, pay their U.S. income taxes, and two, keep their zippers zipped up. I accepted resignations from Foreign Service officers who failed to do both.

Despite the diligence of CIA and FBI counterespionage, I took office assuming that our government had been penetrated to its highest levels by foreign operatives. I never looked at McGeorge Bundy or Robert McNamara or others gathered around the cabinet table or at National Security Council meetings and wondered if any of them was a "mole," but I did assume we had been penetrated, so I acted on that assumption. For example, I am certain that at private meetings of NATO foreign ministers where each minister had only one staff person attending, those discussions became known to the Soviet Union. On one occasion I used a private meeting of NATO to send a message to the Soviets, thinking they would pay more attention to it if I sent in that way rather than through official channels.

I am certain that the Soviet Union and other totalitarian countries had more access to the inner circles of American decision making than we had to theirs. We never had enough information or reliable intelligence about what the leadership in Peking or the Kremlin was thinking. We rarely penetrated other governments by old-fashioned espionage, but relied instead on satellite reconnaissance and electronic surveillance. With totalitarian countries we have an intelligence gap because espionage is difficult in closed societies. We had very few agents in China, North Vietnam, and North Korea. I regret our relying so heavily on technical intelligence, which produces limited information, at the expense of the old-fashioned spy on the ground who steals information, infiltrates groups, and eavesdrops on conversations.

Leaks are another matter. Most do not cause national security problems, and as a general rule, secretaries of state are more sanguine about them than presidents. The chemistry of being president and concern for domestic politics causes presidents to try to plug leaks in far livelier fashion than that used by their more relaxed cabinet colleagues. Overreaction can also lead to problems; when presidents or their top advisers become obsessed about leaks, decision making is held in such tight circles that the talents and resources of the government are not brought fully to bear.

Yet leaks are a problem, and anyone who has access to information—junior and senior staffers, members of Congress, private citizens, and special interest groups—can leak it, and even the president and secretary of state themselves can disclose sensitive information.

To illustrate the potential for leaks, I once asked to see the distribution list for a cable sent by an ambassador marked "Eyes only for the Secretary." Forty copies of this cable had been distributed among different agencies of the government. The right to have a copy of a cable marked "Eyes only for the Secretary" becomes a kind of prestige symbol—like a water bottle on the desk or a flag in the corner of the room. But worse, each agency has its own duplicating equipment, and when the Xerox machines get through, several hundred "eyes only" cables could be lying all over town.

To get around this, I invented a special channel called the Cherokee channel, in which I gave a message to a code room officer, who transmitted it to a code room in an overseas embassy. The person who received the message hand-delivered it to the ambassador. I used this Cherokee channel perhaps five or six times in eight years, only for critical messages.

One day I got myself in trouble with one of my secretaries, an extremely able single girl, over top secret information. I wanted to file a highly sensitive document on U.S.-Soviet relations, so I called her in and asked her to take care of it for me. Without thinking I said, "You don't talk in your sleep, do you?" She drew herself up and replied tartly, "If I did, Mr. Secretary, there would be no one to hear!"

Sometimes we Americans get a little paranoid over security. At one point the Soviet Embassy sent staff to the Geodetic Survey Office in Washington to buy detailed maps of the United States. Some of our people wanted to stop this, but that was ridiculous. Anyone can walk into that same office and buy maps across the counter. The incident does illustrate how easily an open society can be "penetrated" by espionage.

State secrets are not as much of a problem as many people think, and the importance of secrecy and the danger of leaks have been greatly exaggerated. At any given time there are only a few truly critical secrets: in the nuclear field, espionage activity, military research, negotiating positions, and maybe a few others. But in truth—and consider that this comes from someone who has held a number of classifications above top secret—I don't know of many subjects on which a private citizen could not make a reasonable judgment by reading information readily available on that subject. I don't believe that secrets impair the judgment of citizens about major policy issues. The argument that "If you only knew what I knew, you would agree with me" is a phony.

I was far less concerned about leaks than about the issue of confidentiality—our ability to talk in confidence with other countries. The preservation of confidentiality in negotiations is a national security consideration. If other governments do not believe they can talk with us in confidence, the process of negotiation is deeply injured. Indeed, some negotiations simply collapsed when it became known that negotiations were being held. Governments must be able to try out ideas on each other and quietly explore the various elements of an agreement before those elements become public. Premature publicity can generate controversy, making agreement impossible. Since leaders of foreign governments have their own domestic political problems in certain negotiations, confidentiality better enables them to work out those problems. Neither we nor our negotiating partners can negotiate agreements or treaties in the atmosphere of a football stadium.

We have even had problems with confidentiality within the U.S. government. During my tenure I had to remove a State Department security officer named Otto Otepka from his role in dealing with personnel matters. The transfer of personnel information seemed to be in conflict with an executive order of President Truman, who wanted to be sure that such information be passed only on proper authorization from senior officers of the department. I decided to be sure that Mr. Otepka was in full compliance with President Truman's executive order and moved in on that situation.

I soon had a telephone call from Senator Eastland, who was chairman of the Senate Judiciary Committee, and he invited me to come to see him. When I visited Senator Eastland, he chided me for moving to interrupt the cooperation between Mr. Otepka and a member of the staff of the Senate Judiciary Committee. From what Senator Eastland told me, it was clear that that cooperation took the form of passing information in apparent violation of President Truman's executive order. I told Senator Eastland that if he wished Mr. Otepka to work for the Senate Judiciary Committee, he should persuade Otepka to resign from the State Department and take a position on the staff of the Senate Judiciary Committee but that if Mr. Otepka was on the payroll of the State Department, it would be necessary for him to comply with President Truman's executive order.

I asked the administrative people in the department to transfer Mr. Otepka away from the personnel section of the department and assign him other duties pending a completion of the investigation. I was told that Mr. Otepka had been offered a position in our consulate in Hamburg, but Mr. Otepka denies ever having heard of this offer.

In any event, Mr. Otepka was given a hearing before an officer of the department who concluded that he had passed personnel information to the staff of the Senate Judiciary Committee without authorization of a senior officer of the department. Mr. Otepka was not continued in his earlier post but was assigned to duties which took him out of the personnel business. With the arrival of the Nixon administration, Mr. Otepka was made a member of the Subversive Activities Control Board and there the matter ended.

To complicate matters, two State Department security officers who investigated Otepka's activities within the department tried to discover if Otepka was, in fact, leaking information to Congress. Having trouble finding firm evidence, they decided to search his trash, looking for carbons of his correspondence, and, worse, tapped his telephone without my permission. One officer was called before a Senate committee to present evidence on Otepka and was less than candid about having bugged Otepka. I couldn't allow that, so I asked for his resignation. Having been raised the son of Robert Rusk, having been an Army officer under the likes of George Marshall, I acquired this funny notion that public servants cannot make false official statements, especially under oath. I expected people to follow that, and 99.9 percent of the time they did. The Otepka affair was not one of State's prouder moments.

Intelligence and counterintelligence raise many constitutional issues, and despite my love of liberty, I am not an extreme purist where public order and the survival of the state may be involved. Both John Locke and Thomas Jefferson recognized that governments must sometimes act beyond the law in order to preserve their constitutional systems. There is a mean, dirty, back-alley game being played around the world in which forty or fifty governments take part. If we simply ignore it or pretend that it doesn't exist, we may learn what Leo Durocher meant when he said, "Nice guys finish last."

Having been raised in the backcountry west and south of the Hudson and Potomac rivers, I find many citizens less concerned about the "people's right to know" than about their need to be governed effectively. If we are not going to allow our intelligence services covert capabilities for gaining intelligence and some secrecy in which to operate, then we had better eliminate the effort. There is no point in operating covertly beneath the public view and then have those activities become known because of press disclosures or congressional inquiry. If we cannot proceed with genuine confidentiality, we should make intelligence gathering an adjunct to the Library of Congress, available to everybody in town, and forget the rest; we can't play it both ways.

There is a place for covert action. But it must be used only rarely and then with complete supervision by the executive branch and Congress. Officers exercising the raw power of the state cannot be left to operate unbridled, and those who occupy such offices must have limited terms. We already limit the terms of the president and the Joint Chiefs of Staff. CIA and FBI directors ought to be limited to six years or less, so that no director can accumulate too much power. Our experiences with J. Edgar Hoover taught us that in spades; he had become so institutionalized that he was virtually untouchable. No one exercising power should be untouchable in our government.

The U.S. intelligence services have made mistakes and occasionally abused their powers. Similarly, those supervising the intelligence services, myself included, have not done the job as well as they should.

But mistakes and abuses should not obscure our need for intelligence and counterintelligence, nor should those mistakes and abuses be universally attributed to the thousands of able, honorable, and dedicated public servants who have served their country well in the intelligence community. If we deny our need for them and for the information they provide, our country's strength will be sorely eroded.

36

Press Relations and the Media

During the 1930's, when Cordell Hull was secretary of state, only a half dozen reporters covered the State Department. He met with them briefly every day at noon, answered many of their questions with a cryptic "Gentlemen, that matter is under the most serious consideration," and moved on to the next question. If I learned one thing during my eight years as secretary of state, it was that the days of Cordell Hull are long gone.

Although I was sometimes called the "Silent American," actually I was one of the more garrulous secretaries of state in terms of congressional testimony, press conferences, and speeches. I prepared thoroughly for press conferences, and only rarely did a questioner catch me unprepared. Once after I delivered a speech in Georgia, a distinguished gentleman in the front row rose and said, "Mr. Rusk, a number of my colleagues and I are convinced that the Second Coming of Christ is imminent and could occur at any moment. What is your view on that?" The audience began to laugh, but not wanting to embarrass him, I said, "Well, I will have to leave that to the good Lord, and He has not taken me into His confidence." That really was a new question.

At first I was rather nervous at press conferences—all those little red television camera eyes staring at me. But it didn't take me long to realize that I knew more about issues than the reporters did. I soon relaxed, but I remain convinced that television appearances require a certain spirit. My wife, Virginia, helped me get over my trepidation about press conferences by suggesting that I take a shot or two of scotch beforehand to help loosen my tongue. That became a regular habit.

Eventually I enjoyed appearing on NBC's "Meet the Press," CBS's "Face the Nation," and ABC's "Issues and Answers." For half an hour, as I interacted with panels of three or four reporters, what I said was not edited in any way. The format made for a more complete program. I had a chance to get across some key points with depth and context. Of course, panelists before broadcasts sometimes said, "For heaven's sake, keep your answers short so we can ask as many questions as possible," but on these three programs in particular, the guest being quizzed had an opportunity to speak his piece.

I did force a minor change in the "Meet the Press" format. Larry Spivak always said, "Our reporters try to get the news, and they are not responsible for their questions." Before I went on "Meet the Press" on one occasion, I said, "Damn it, Larry, these reporters can be as responsible for their questions as I am for my answers. If you say that again, I will say that I'm not responsible for my answers." He said, "You wouldn't do that," and I said, "You try me and see." And by George, he left that out.

Washington's press corps is the best in the world. Its members always drive aggressively for the story. In comparison, the British press is more respectful of public officials, while the French press, especially during de Gaulle's era, was relatively tame. When Charles de Gaulle held a press conference, the press first assembled in a big room in one of the palaces. De Gaulle would enter, simply acknowledge different reporters around the room, and let them ask several questions before he said anything. And then he said whatever he had intended to say even before he entered the room. Then he'd walk out.

The American press shows a vigor not found in many countries. These press veterans have extraordinarily subtle and effective techniques for getting information, particularly from new arrivals untutored in the rules of the game.

James "Scottie" Reston, for example, used the "bedside manner." Scottie would come see me and say, "Gee, Mr. Secretary, I just don't see how you do it! You're working sixteen hours a day, seven days a week, and you've got senators badgering you on one side and these foreigners badgering you on the other. You never have any chance for a private life. . . ." By that time, if I wasn't careful, I had a lump in my throat, and I'd begin to say, "Scottie, you don't know the half of it. Let me give you the rest of the story."

Joe Alsop used the "hand grenade technique." Joe always came through my office door a little breathless and scowling and said something like "Mr. Secretary, how can the government of the United States be so stupid? Any idiot should have known that what you did yesterday made no sense whatsoever!" He'd continue along that trail, and pretty soon the bristles would begin to rise on the back of my neck. Unless I caught myself, I'd begin to say, "Joe, you don't know what you are talking about. Let me set you straight."

Murray Marder of the *Washington Post* I compared favorably to Hercule Poirot, Agatha Christie's famed detective. He got a little piece of a story here and a little piece there and gradually pieced together the puzzle. For example, Murray might be in the State Department garage ready to drive home at the end of the day when he notices the Soviet ambassador coming out of the basement entrance to my private elevator. Murray might say to himself, "Aha! They would not have taken these precautions unless there is a good story." So he goes back to his office and waits for an hour, does some thinking, and figures out that the Soviet ambassador probably brought in a message about Southeast Asia, Berlin, or arms control. He then calls a friend at the Arms Control and Disarmament Agency and says, "I understand the Soviet ambassador has brought you a message about the SALT talks." The ACDA man might say, "Sorry. You've got the wrong scoop; there's nothing in that." So Murray calls a friend in the East Asian Bureau and says, "I understand the Soviet Ambassador came in with a message about Southeast Asia." That office replies, "There's not a thing in it. You're just on the wrong track." Then he calls the Soviet desk about Berlin. Its Berlin specialist has been instructed never to lie to the press, as have all department personnel, and Murray says, "John, I understand that the Soviet ambassador has just come in with a message on Berlin." The man says, "Sorry, I can't say a thing about it. Can't help you at all on that one." Ah! Murray has his confirmation; in the absence of a denial, he knows that he is on the right track. He then figures out what the Berlin problem looks like and calls a friend in the Soviet Embassy. "By the way, what's the attitude of the Soviet Union on this particular point with respect to Berlin?" He listens for a few moments, then publishes his story the next morning on the message that the Soviet ambassador brought in about Berlin. Chances are good that the story is reasonably accurate and that John Kennedy or Lyndon Johnson will call me and ask, "Who in hell has been leaking information at the Department of State?"

Other reporters took advantage of the "big shot syndrome" by talking with officials who simply don't want to plead ignorance and let a reporter know that they are out of the picture. They will pontificate a bit, pretend that they do know, and in the process leak something that should have been kept quiet.

Some reporters used the "cockfight syndrome." Some of the juiciest stories around Washington involve feuds within an administration or between the executive branch and Capitol Hill. A reporter might come in and say, "I talked to Senator So-and-so the other day, and he said that you were off your rocker about so-and-so." Of course, you'd want to respond with "Did that son of a bitch say that? Let me straighten you out about that senator."

Sometimes a reporter wrote his story first, then came in and said, "This is what I am about to publish. Please read it and tell me whether or not it's off base." You'd look it over and comment on whether it was accurate, and your own comments could reveal important information. Sometimes these first-draft stories were simply devices for getting the true story.

I didn't mind inquiring reporters boring in with any techniques short of bribery or theft, but I tried not to fall for these tricks. Fortunately I learned a good deal about press techniques during the Truman administration, and I kept my eyes and ears open. The best way for me to handle the Scottie Restons and Joe Alsops was to sit quietly, smile politely, and let them go on a bit.

Fun and humor sometimes pop up in this give-and-take between government and the press. In 1952, during the United Nations Conference in San Francisco on the Japanese Peace Treaty, we learned that the press in the galleries had telephoto lenses that could pick up notes we passed to each other on the conference floor. I finally wrote a message: "I hope you gentlemen up there are proud of your technical accomplishments and your professional ethics." Later a grinning, although somewhat sheepish, newsman told me that the press had gotten my message.

Although I developed great respect for the Washington press corps, I did have my share of bizarre experiences, especially with some "barons" of the media. One big writer came to see me in the early days of the Kennedy administration and said that if I gave him inside information, he would help me in his writing. As far as I was concerned, that was attempted bribery. With no witness present, I couldn't do anything but throw him out of my office.

In 1961, soon after my taking office, both Walter Lippmann and Arthur Krock sent me messages that if I wanted to call on them, they would be glad to receive me. I am not a stuffed shirt, but I thought that was somewhat unusual even for Washington.

I never gave an answer to one reporter that I wouldn't give to another reporter who asked the same question. The working stiffs in the press corps appreciated that, but some of the big names didn't like it. They wanted privileged information and the machismo that goes with it.

In an effort to help the press, I gave backgrounders for reporters almost every Friday afternoon over drinks on the eighth floor of the State Department, to review past events and look ahead to the coming week. Most of the press and I found these relaxed sessions quite valuable. But the *Washington Post* thought otherwise and once called my eighth-floor weekly backgrounder an "improper instrument of communication" and said that I shouldn't release information in backgrounders that I was not prepared to acknowledge publicly. When the *Post* raised this objection, I said, "It's no skin off my back. If the other reporters want these backgrounders discontinued, I'll stop them." But they wanted them to continue.

In talking with a reporter in my office, I never put something off the record. I would say to the reporter, "Now, I can only answer that off the record. I will leave it to you as to whether you want to accept it on that basis." Then he would decide whether to accept it off the record or take his chances on getting some other colleague in the department to give him that same information without being off the record.

I never lied to the press, but sometimes I had to remain silent or dodge a question. I learned how during the Truman years when a friendly senator advised, "If you get a question that you cannot answer or don't want to answer, answer another question. The questioner will forget that you avoided his first question, because he's eager to get to his second question."

I used this same technique with the media. In one press conference a reporter asked me a question, and I replied in some elliptical fashion. He said, "You didn't answer my question." I said, "I know I didn't. I'm not the village idiot."

By the nature of its job, the press must sometimes press for information, but unfortunately this means that the line between public life and private life disappears for public officials. In an attempt to establish some boundaries, my wife and I had a rule throughout my eight years in office: We never admitted a reporter, photographer, or television cameraman into our home in Washington. We wanted to preserve that small island of privacy. Early one morning a reporter with cameraman in tow turned up on our front doorstep, said that he wanted to interview me for a story, and take some pictures. I explained our policy. As I was closing the door, he protested—and stuck his foot in the way! I came down on his foot with all two hundred pounds and had the satisfaction of watching him hop away on one leg.

One time when Virginia was out of town, my daughter, Peggy, then fifteen years old, and I decided to dress up, go downtown for dinner, and hear Peter, Paul and Mary. She put on a long evening dress and looked like a million dollars, and I wore a black tie. We went downtown, enjoyed the dinner and the floor show, and had a very fine evening. The next day reporters around the department asked, "Who was that chick the secretary was out with last night?" They were clearly disappointed to learn it was my daughter. Had she been anybody else's daughter, they would have had a story.

The fame the media impart is fleeting, thank goodness, and can occasionally lead to some humorous and humbling experiences. Once a little old lady planted herself three feet in front of me at the Atlanta airport and said, "You're on television!" I said, "Oh, you remember Hoss Cartwright of 'Bonanza,' don't you?" She went away very happy. At that same airport a gorgeous young lady came up to me with a wrinkle in her brow and said, "Didn't you come to visit me in Savannah not long ago? I'm sure I've seen you before?" And a few years earlier a gentleman stopped me in an airport and said, "Aren't you John Foster Dulles?" I said, "Well, if I am, there's been a hell of a miracle."

Any secretary of state must be prepared for criticism and adverse comment. I tried to brush aside remarks aimed at me personally, and generally the press avoided that approach. Of course, as secretary of state during the sixties, I became a frequent target of critical press coverage because of the Vietnam War. The hostility of the press didn't bother me as much as its occasional dishonesty. The *New York Post* once ran an editorial calling for my resignation. That wasn't the only newspaper or periodical to call for my resignation, but I remember this one because the *Post* used a picture of me that looked like Al Capone. I never saw such a hideous picture. Shortly afterward I called the publisher and asked to have lunch with her and her editorial board. During my next trip to New York City, over a very pleasant lunch, I referred to this picture and challenged her to go with me to their photographic morgue, get out that picture, and see if the touch-up artist had doctored that photo to make me look as ugly as possible. She declined the challenge.

Reporting from Vietnam varied in quality, but some was false. Reporters and cameramen once went into a deserted village being used as a Marine training base. One reporter gave a Marine a cigarette lighter and asked, "Why don't you light that thatched roof?" He did. That footage went all over the country with the story "Marines torch local village." Another picture went around the country of an old Vietnamese woman with her hands held out, pleading to get on a helicopter. The caption read, "U.S. Forces Refuse to Evacuate Old Woman." We checked into that and found that if that cameraman had turned his camera just ninety degrees, he would have had a picture of a helicopter filled with old women. Had the cameraman gotten his fat tail off that helicopter, that old woman could have gotten on! Both of these stories were fabricated, staged for effect.

But falsified reporting took place outside Vietnam, too. Once on a trip to Montevideo, Uruguay, in November 1965, I went to lay a wreath at the statue of a national hero. I was standing in the main plaza with the VIPs, surrounded by a huge crowd, when suddenly a tiny man ran out of the crowd toward me. He was immediately followed by a six-foot-three two-hundred-pounder. My own security man, a former Pittsburgh Steeler, decided that the big man was the greater threat and tackled him, not knowing that he was a plainclothesman trying to catch the little man. The little man wanted to get close enough to spit at me, but when he got there, he was so scared that he didn't have any spit.

The media's response to this incident was fascinating. For this wreath-laying ceremony, reporters and cameramen surrounded the statue to take their pictures. When this little man ran out of the crowd, did any of them move forward and put himself or herself between that little man and me? Not at all. Everyone backed up three or four paces to focus his camera better. One photographer standing on the statue even started jumping up and down, shouting, "I got it! I got it!" After developing his film and seeing no spit in the picture, the son of a gun dubbed into his negative a blob of spit as big as my fist heading straight for me. That darned picture went all over the United States.

News is falsified in other ways, sometimes unavoidably. The very answer given each day by the news media to the question, What is news?, in choosing what is reported and what is overlooked, creates a distorted picture of the world in which we live. Normality, serenity, agreement are not newsworthy to the media. The controversial, the violent, the extraordinary are. Thus, normality in world affairs is over-looked, and life distorted. Most international frontiers are peaceful, most treaties are complied with, and the overwhelming majority of disputes are settled by peaceful means. Yet that is not the impression of the man in the street. He hears little about normality. Nor does he hear about the many instances of cooperative behavior among governments; they never come to view—not because they're secret but because they're not "newsworthy."

Why do so many newspapers and local programs start by cleaning off the police blotter for that day? What, after all, is newsworthy about a murder? When there were four people in the Garden of Eden, number three killed number four, and this has been going on since the beginning of mankind. Why should murder be the lead story in so many newscasts? Behind the dramatic and violent headlines lies a story of the family of man more encouraging and hopeful than people are permitted to see.

I do not advocate that the media wear rose-colored glasses, but bad news ought to be balanced off with more positive, constructive news. For example, no nation has used a nuclear weapon in anger for over forty years—almost half a century—but with the exception of 1985, on the fortieth anniversary of Hiroshima and Nagasaki, few people in the media mention this fact. It is one hell of a story.

Similarly, despite their many disagreements and differences, the leaders of the world's more than 160 governments over the past four decades put their heads together and worked with the World Health Organization to wipe out smallpox. This great killer of mankind is now eliminated, another dramatic story ignored by the media.

On a daily basis, the contrast between the media's reporting and what is actually happening in international affairs is equally sharp. Every day American delegations attend from twelve to fifteen international conferences somewhere in the world, dealing with everything from the control of nuclear weapons to the control of hog cholera. Only about 20 percent of those meetings ever get mentioned in the press. The rest are lost to public view. When I was secretary of state, I tried for two years to get the *New York Times* to donate four column inches in its Sunday edition—an edition so large you can barely lift it—just to list international meetings for the coming week. I had no luck whatsoever.

I fully understand that selection of the news is forced on editors and producers by the economics of publishing and broadcasting. Readerviewer time and attention span are limited. Editors have only so many column inches for reporting, and producers so few breathless moments of airtime. And on television in particular, there must be a constant flurry of movement; "talking heads" won't do. In press conferences, if I took more than sixty seconds to answer a question, the reporters started shuffling their feet and accused me of filibustering to avoid more questions. A question might require fifteen or twenty minutes to discuss in any degree of depth or context. Yet we in government are only snatching at sixty-second one-line answers. If I discussed one aspect of an issue for sixty seconds one time and picked up another aspect of the same issue for sixty seconds a week later, my change in emphasis was sometimes interpreted as a "change in policy."

The press also has a problem with the future. Since television focuses on today's news, it drives the written press into the future. Reporters at press conferences are not interested in what happened yesterday or last week; they want to find out what will happen tomorrow. About 80 percent of the questions I received were about the future. A secretary of state cannot stand before six hundred journalists and a battery of television cameras and answer 80 percent of his questions with "Damned if I know." If two months later my prediction proved reasonably accurate, the matter lay at rest. But if events took a different course, that became another small contribution to the "credibility gap."

Increasing competition within the media for scoops and lead stories also creates problems. Networks compete for ratings and viewers, and so do radio stations, columnists, and by-line writers; sometimes even reporters on the same newspaper compete with each other for space on the front page. All this competition tends to skew coverage. A columnist hired to write four columns a week must at times sit despairingly before the typewriter: "What in hell am I going to talk about today that will grab some attention?" This pressure for the unusual angle, the offbeat slant produces a tendency toward distortion.

On one occasion Averell Harriman skillfully negotiated some important matters with Indonesian President Sukarno in Tokyo. I mentioned Harriman's effort to a reporter and said, "Here's a good example of real diplomacy of the old style. Why don't you write a story about it?" And he did. About ten days later he showed me the reply from his editor. In big red letters across the page, the editor had written, "Sorry. No blood, no news."

We hear a great deal about the "public's right to know." Our Institution involves balancing many values in which the public has a stake. If the people have a right to know, they also have a right to have their public business conducted in a responsible fashion. It is not an easy line to draw.

Further, the media cannot possibly support the public's right to know when the media do not accept a duty to inform. To the press, the public's right to know extends only to what the press elects to tell. The slogan "All the News That's Fit to Print" ought to have written under it, "At least two percent of it"; the output of information from the wire services is enormous, and someone must select what to print. In a very real sense, those making these selections must "manage" the news; they have to do so.

This leads to another media attitude that I found irritating: the media's view that somehow freedom of the press is their private domain. When I find that the media, organized to sell information for profit, demand rights and privileges which I as a private citizen do not have, I become somewhat skeptical about the media's claimed freedoms. Why can a reporter in a court of law refuse to divulge his sources in the interest of justice if I cannot do the same? The press claims the right to commit trespass, to receive stolen property in the form of information, to suborn the commission of a felony by people in government in terms of leaking classified information to them. If a person goes into the State Department, wiggles out a top secret, takes it down the street, and gives it or sells it to the Soviet Union, he goes to prison. But if he goes into the State Department, gets that secret, and gives it to the rest of the world via the media, he may get a Pulitzer Prize. Something is wrong here, but the media claim such actions are legitimate as "freedom of the press."

And who in the media possesses these freedoms? Is it the reporter or the publisher and editor? There is no question that Katharine Graham and Ben Bradlee had the final word for the *Washington Post.* Did their reporters have any freedom of the press except as Graham and Bradlee permitted them to have? Arthur Hays Sulzberger, a trustee of the Rockefeller Foundation and for many years publisher of the *New York Times,* over a highball told me, "As long as I can keep my wife's vote on the board of directors, the policy of the *New York Times* will be my policy. If anybody wants another policy, they can publish another newspaper."

Despite my irritation over the media's alleged need for confidentiality, I was never too concerned about leaks and unauthorized stories. My two presidents felt differently, of course, perhaps because of the nature of their job and whatever special chemistry goes with being president.

I knew that many stories that appear to be leaked are simply due to intelligent reporters putting bits of news together and figuring things out for themselves. They cover not only the State Department but the Pentagon, Capitol Hill, and Embassy Row. Often leaks attributed to the State Department may have come from an embassy or a senator. Only one leak during my entire eight years as secretary really bothered me: my "eyeball to eyeball" comment during the Cuban missile crisis.

But presidents are different. Once Kennedy called me at seven-thirty one morning while I was still home in my bathrobe. He had read a story on page ten in the morning newspaper, and he blew his top, giving me hell about the "leaky State Department." He told me to find out who leaked that story and fire him. So I went down to the department and, in a most unconstitutional fashion, called in the reporter who wrote the story.

"Now look," I told him. "You have to earn your living around this building. If you think you can do so with any comfort, you've got to tell me who gave you that story." He did, and I called Kennedy back and said, "Mr. President, I found out who leaked that story."

"Did you fire him?" he asked.

"No," I said, "because you gave it to him, yesterday at four o'-clock."

Kennedy laughed. I suspect that when Kennedy gave me hell that morning, he was putting on an act for the benefit of some staff person. I thoroughly enjoyed checking him out on that one.

I learned that reporters in Washington do not protect their sources nearly as much as they claim to. I rarely had a problem getting a reporter to name his source, so if there was a leaker around, we usually learned who it was. Sometimes we figured it out from the internal evidence of the story. Sometimes others were present when the leak occurred. Often our press officers found out from other reporters. Sources for unauthorized stories get back to a president very quickly. Those in the executive branch who leak information to frustrate presidential policy usually don't survive very long.

In a certain sense, as secretary of state I could not leak information because I had the authority to declassify. Once when returning from a press conference, a colleague referred to something I said and remarked, "Mr. Secretary, that is not our policy." I grinned at him and said, "It is now."

One of the biggest leaks from the State Department during my tenure was the release of information that eventually appeared as the *Pentagon Papers,* a multivolume record of U.S. involvement in Vietnam that the *New York Times* got its hands on and published in 1971, nearly three years after I left office. I didn't know that such a study existed. There I was, the American secretary of state, and this forty-four-volume study was prepared under my own nose by, among others, colleagues working twenty yards down the hall from me, and I never knew about that project.

Apparently, in 1967, Bob McNamara asked me if his staff could borrow materials on Vietnam from the Department of State, and since that was a perfectly normal request, I reportedly said yes. The request was so routine I remember neither the question nor my response; we often exchanged papers of various sorts. My executive secretary, Ben Read, remembers that he sent the historical office and others my directive to make available to McNamara's office everything we had. Of course, I did not contemplate anything like the *Pentagon Papers*. Bob told me later that he thought this information was needed to help prepare briefing books for such things as congressional hearings. He claims that the *Pentagon Papers* as they finally appeared were not what he authorized.

There is some mystery in all this. I later discovered a full set of the *Pentagon Papers* was delivered to Undersecretary of State Nick Katzenbach just as we left office in January 1969. But while we were busy turning over power, nobody mentioned their existence to me.

It is important to remember that no one in the Pentagon ever approved or accepted the *Pentagon Papers,* not even by an assistant secretary of defense. They simply exist by dint of analysts who wrote them. I once suggested to the American Historical Association that some enterprising Ph.D. candidate or investigative reporter should do a story about the making of the *Pentagon Papers.* What were they all about? Why were the analysts—about thirty of them, some still not known—not to discuss this project with Walt Rostow, President Johnson, myself, and others? Why was this job not turned over to the historical officers in State and Defense, who are never told how to write their histories and are free to use their own judgment? Why did these analysts not ask for materials in my own office about Vietnam, some of which was not available elsewhere? Why did they not ask for the notes of the Tuesday luncheons, critically important to Vietnam decision making?

I once had lunch with Leslie Gelb, who headed the project, and we discussed the *Pentagon Papers.* I suggested that he had an obligation to tell the full story behind the making of the *Pentagon Papers.* He declined to do so. But some years later, in a BBC interview, he was asked what the *Pentagon Papers* were all about. He replied that some analysts thought they were working on a Vietnam history, and others thought they were working on campaign documents for Bobby Kennedy.

In any event, when the *Pentagon Papers* were published, I never attached importance to the alleged breach of national security. Almost everything in the *Pentagon Papers* was already being discussed publicly. The *Papers* were a public relations problem more than a national security problem. They do reflect the lively discussion within government during the Vietnam decision making. But the *Papers* don't always give accurate impressions of what was in the minds of the president and his cabinet colleagues during crucial moments of decision on the war. No analyst ever asked me what I thought during these critical decisions.

The publication of these *Papers* surely tightened up communication patterns of those in government. By habit, as secretary of state, I never wrote a lot of memoranda. I never felt top officials should author and spread papers all over the landscape. The publication of such documents confirmed this. Unfortunately officials will commit themselves to print even less and find other ways to proceed, and future historians will pay the cost.

Looking back at my experience with the press, as secretary of state I was concerned about the impact that the media, especially television news coverage, had on events. Even during the antiwar demonstrations of the late 1960's, the public usually treated government officials with courtesy and respect. On some occasions I walked down a line of demonstrators and talked with them. I even autographed several posters that proclaimed, "Rusk Go Home!" But when the television cameras arrived, these same young people with whom I had been chatting would ball up their fists and start screaming. Frequently, when I traveled in the late 1960's, the television crews set up their cameras so that when I arrived, antiwar picketers were in the background. Occasionally I infuriated the reporters by walking behind the cameras.

Vietnam was the first armed struggle to be fought on television, in everyone's living room, every day. I shudder to think what could have happened in World War II if Guadalcanal, the Anzio beachhead, the Battle of the Bulge, and the battle for Okinawa had been on television. It could have had a profound effect. War is by nature obscene. Television coverage of any war, no matter how justified, can put great pressure on the patience and understanding of the American people.

Public officials and the news media both work for the public in a sense and wish to keep it informed. No administration can long conduct policy on a major issue without the support of Congress and the understanding of the American people. But for public officials, the press is an uncertain instrument for communication. Its responsibilities and motivations are different. Public officials must deal with the public through the media, yet they have quite limited influence on the style and content of media coverage. There is a built-in tension in the role of the press in a free society, and we must live with it. I tried to do so as secretary of state.

Having exercised my rights of free speech and now free press, with these comments—many critical in nature—I am deeply convinced that the American people are better served by their news media than are the people of any other country.

Everything considered, in thirty years of public life, I had my share of pleasant encounters with the press, as well as the not-so-pleasant. When Virginia and I were about to leave office in January 1969, the press corps covering the State Department gave us a farewell reception. It was a very nice party, and at that reception the press corps presented us with a silver plate with a cartoon from *The New Yorker* engraved on it. The scene was of a stag and a doe in the forest. The stag was saying to the doe, "Remember, dear, if we get through today, we will be out of season."

37

Civil Rights, Human Rights, and U.S. Foreign Policy

Despite what recent U.S. administrations may claim, human rights is not a new concern for U.S. foreign policy. They played a profound role in our policies during World War II and the postwar period and in the drafting of the United Nations Charter. The simple notion that governments derive their just powers from the consent of the governed runs like a scarlet thread through U.S. policy. Thus, our closest friends are the constitutional democracies, and that is why developments in totalitarian countries concern us so deeply.

Even so, we have not always lived up to our ideals. Racism and discrimination are a part of American life. Growing up in Georgia, I was well aware of that from my earliest days. I had attended segregated public schools in Atlanta; Davidson College was segregated as well. It wasn't until I went to Oxford, where I found myself among and made friends with students of all races, nationalities, and religions, that my own racial tolerance took full root. I had found Hitler's Germany, with its wholesale violations of human rights and its notion of a "master race," deeply repulsive. The arrogance of nazism and the horrible crimes committed in its name further consolidated my own views about human rights and civil rights.

But I also found racial prejudice rampant in the United States when I returned from Europe. One incident in particular sticks in my mind. In 1942, while serving in the War Department's military intelligence office, I became friends with a young black Office of Strategic Services (OSS) officer named Ralph Bunche. One day I took him into the officers' dining room for lunch, and apparently that was the first time a black man had eaten there. The timbers began to quiver, but fortunately my commanding officer backed me up. Our innocent stroll into the dining room was quite an incident for its day. The funny thing is, neither Bunche nor I realized it was off limits to blacks. We were just hungry.

Three years later, as a special assistant to Secretary of War Robert Patterson, I worked with him on desegregating the armed forces. Patterson was determined to break down racial discrimination in the military. World War II had enormous impact on racial attitudes; American blacks and whites had fought side by side with each other and with Africans, Asians, and many races all over the world. The U.S. Army was one of the first groups in American society to combat segregation, and as an Army officer I was proud to take part in that effort.

Virginia and I witnessed racial prejudice in our private lives as well. When we lived in Scarsdale, New York, during the fifties, there was a pervasive under-the-rug discrimination against Jewish people. We resisted these attitudes and undoubtedly lost some Anglo-Saxon Protestant friends in the process. Our family did not join the Scarsdale Golf Club, just three blocks away. It would have been a wonderful place for my children, to be able to run down the hill for a swim or tennis match or round of golf. But I could not in good conscience join a club that would not admit blacks or Jews and to which I couldn't invite even trustees of the Rockefeller Foundation.

When we moved to Washington in 1961, Virginia and I continued to try to live our personal lives in a racially tolerant fashion. We sent our children to public schools rather than private, but admittedly part of this had nothing to do with principle. With my annual salary of twenty-five thousand dollars we could ill afford private schools. We also felt, however, that if people like us shunned the public school system, it would slowly divide along racial lines, a process well under way in Washington.

When we bought our home on Quebec Street, just north of American University, we found that the deed stated that the home could not be sold to Africans, Asians, or "denizens of the Ottoman Empire." This deed was obviously written in the nineteenth century. I asked my lawyers how we could knock that stipulation out of the deed, but since the process of changing a deed was complicated and time-consuming, they advised me simply to file a statement with the deed that I considered those clauses unconstitutional and would not comply with them. I also refused to sign a resale contract in which realtors maintained that kind of discrimination.

The world of the 1960's was a different place. I felt this in a very personal way in September 1967, when our daughter, Peggy, eighteen years old, married Guy Smith, a black American. More than twenty years have passed since my daughter's wedding, and I remain reluctant to invade their privacy with the details of their marriage, even in this account. But neither Peggy nor Guy looked upon herself or himself as a newsmaker or promoter of any special clause, and neither did Virginia or I. Peggy and Guy were just two young people in love who wanted to get married, but since I was a cabinet officer, their marriage became a major news story. *Time* ran a cover story on the wedding; it was covered by newspapers all over the world.

They were married in the chapel of Stanford University in Palo Alto, California. We agreed not to announce her wedding in advance because I didn't want antiwar protesters to interfere with the service and light into Peggy when their real object was me.

Prior to the wedding, I told Lyndon Johnson about Peggy and Guy's plans and asked if he thought their wedding would compromise my relations with some members of Congress. I didn't offer to resign, as was reported. Johnson told me later that he spoke to Senator Russell of Georgia about it, and Russell had said, "Forget it. It won't make any difference at all." Russell was right.

On a professional level, racism and discrimination nevertheless had a major impact on my life as secretary of state. During the early 1960's Washington, D.C., was full of racial prejudice, as inhospitable for blacks and other minorities as any other city in the South—or North, for that matter. This sad state of affairs created tremendous problems for our foreign policy. Stories of racial discrimination in the United States and discriminatory treatment accorded diplomats from the many newly independent countries of the old colonial empires began to undermine our relations with these countries.

Black ambassadors in Washington did not know where they could have lunch or dinner except in another embassy. The best restaurants and hotels were closed to them. The Metropolitan Club did not admit black guests, and even the more liberal Cosmos Club had no black members. Black ambassadors had great difficulty finding office space and living accommodations for their families and staffs. They drove their families to public swimming beaches in Maryland and Virginia only to be turned away. The ambassadors' wives frequently asked State Department wives to go to the supermarkets with them to avoid incidents. When black ambassadors wanted to visit other parts of the country, we sometimes sent State Department officers ahead to make travel arrangements and try to avoid embarrassing incidents. We often had difficulty finding suitable buildings or sites for new African and Asian embassies.

Once a newly arrived black ambassador came to my office and asked with some trepidation, "Mr. Rusk, where can I get a haircut?" It pained me to tell him I didn't know. I did say that he could have his hair cut where I had mine cut, a little room next to my office, and that anytime he wanted to come in, a barber would be there within sixty seconds.

When I was secretary of state, scores of racial incidents involving foreign diplomats came to my attention. On one occasion a restaurant refused to serve an ambassador of a West African country about to obtain its independence while he was traveling from Washington to Pittsburgh. This incident was reported throughout Africa, and the State Department worked hard to make amends. Eventually the restaurant changed its policy and began to open its doors to all customers. Local authorities invited the ambassador to pay a return visit. But the damage that such an incident causes is never quite undone. And on another occasion a different African ambassador en route from New York to Washington to present his credentials to the president was ejected from a roadside restaurant.

Early in the Kennedy years a black delegate to the United Nations landed in Miami on his way to New York. When the passengers disembarked for lunch, the white passengers were taken to the airport restaurant; the black delegate received a folding canvas stool in a corner of the hangar and a sandwich wrapped with waxed paper. He then flew on to New York, where our delegation asked for his vote on human rights issues. That same ambassador later became his country's prime minister. We learned later that his chronic bitterness toward the United States stemmed from that incident.

We jumped on that incident right away and told the Miami airport authorities that unless they straightened this out, the American government would move its port of entry to another city. Fortunately they responded.

The State Department's Protocol Office documented many racial incidents. A counselor of an African embassy once wrote about this discriminatory treatment in a letter I entered into the *Congressional Record:*

The result is that a black diplomat is rather cut off. He withdraws to himself and sees only his own people. This creates constant resentment throughout his staff. Some of us are rather bitter. There is so much about America which is good. What America has done for the underdeveloped countries is wonderful. But here, we are dealing on a personal level. When people come to our country, we try to make them feel more at home than they are in their own country. Our general feeling here is that "I am a stranger." There is something about American policy which cannot be explained. It cuts through all your policy—it is the contradiction between what you say and what you do.

My colleagues at State encountered prejudice as well. Carl Rowan, our neighbor in Spring Valley who served as head of the United States Information Agency, was mowing his lawn one day when a Cadillac pulled up to the curb. A lady in the back seat rolled her window down and called out, "Oh, boy? Boy? What are they paying you to mow this grass?" Carl turned to her and said, "Well, as a matter of fact, the lady of the house lets me sleep with her!" Off drove the Cadillac!

Since discriminatory treatment was a severe barrier to cordial relations with many foreign states, the State Department attacked this problem early on. I asked Ambassador of Protocol Angier Biddle Duke and the Protocol Office to tackle problems facing diplomats in Washington. African diplomats were requested to report their difficulties to Duke's office, whether in housing, in schools, opening charge accounts, or hiring baby-sitters. Duke and Assistant Secretary of State for African Affairs G. Mennon Williams personally called upon the African embassies to hear their specific complaints. We also met with Washington realtors, explained the situation, and asked them to make apartments available to African diplomats.

We rapidly discovered that serious headway on the problem—not surprisingly—depended on racial progress throughout Washington and indeed the entire country. We could not expect an African diplomat to gain privileges and services denied black Americans. Nor could we expect him to display his diplomatic passport every time he wanted to eat or get a haircut. Thus, for pragmatic reasons as well as the simple rightness of the cause, the State Department strongly supported efforts to eliminate discrimination. We worked extensively with state and municipal authorities across the nation—real estate boards, hotel owners, police authorities, city councils—and gradually made headway. We worked to strengthen local hospitality committees and volunteer associations of citizens who tried to anticipate problems and insure that visiting diplomats and foreign guests would be treated courteously. We organized the thriving International Club, a place where all diplomats would feel welcome. And the State Department threw its full weight behind the Civil Rights Acts of 1964 and 1965, especially legislation dealing with public accommodations.

The State Department, itself a product of history, was not immune to discrimination and racism. Relatively few blacks held Foreign Service posts in 1961. There were no black ambassadors. Jobs at State for blacks were limited to messengers, custodial positions, and service help. Clearly we had a job to do within our own building. Consequently, I formed a departmental group to focus on racial issues. Carl Rowan and G. Mennon Williams both served on this committee. I also appointed Williams the department's equal opportunity officer. Soapy William worked with characteristic energy to open up the department, and he also did a great job smoothing over the ruffled feelings of diplomats who had encountered incidents. Throughout the Kennedy and Johnson years the department worked to upgrade black employees, recruit qualified blacks for the Foreign Service, and appoint black ambassadors. Progress was not easy, and among our problems was that black Americans qualified to be ambassadors had other jobs waiting for them as the civil rights movement progressed. Many turned us down.

The department's special committee noticed that few graduates of predominantly black institutions passed the Foreign Service exam, unlike blacks from such schools as Berkeley, Chicago, and the Ivy League, so I asked my colleagues to study the exam to see if it was culturally biased. We made some changes, but our group concluded that cultural bias was less of a factor than inadequate practice and test skills.

Admittedly the Foreign Service exam is tough; of sixteen thousand annual applicants, only three thousand pass. One purpose of that exam, of course, was to reduce the pool, so even if we wanted more black Foreign Service officers, if we relaxed admission standards, we might admit some of dubious qualification. We did not relax standards, but the fear of a relaxation led some to resist our efforts at integration.

Without doubt, though, I did place great emphasis on recruiting black FSOs. Black applicants passing the written examination were usually appointed. Very few failed the orals. Even so, they were hard to land. Many blacks expected to encounter discrimination and problems with promotions. They were not convinced that the Foreign Service offered them genuine career opportunities. We lost quite a few good people because of this.

Another problem I tried to alleviate concerned the disproportionately high percentage of blacks working in State's lower echelons. All of the messengers on the seventh floor were black, for example. I appointed a Caucasian as messenger, to make the point that this was not a racist stance. That point was lost: His black colleagues froze him out, and he soon quit.

Carl Rowan went to Finland as one of our first black ambassadors. Shortly after, one African foreign minister advised us to send no black ambassadors to black Africa. We should appoint black ambassadors to other parts of the world and white ambassadors to Africa. Left unsaid was his attitude that since American blacks were still second-class citizens, any black appointment to black Africa would be seen as a second-class appointment.

Given conditions in Washington, D.C., and throughout the country in the 1960's, I was amazed that American racial problems were not brought to the floor of the United Nations, especially since the non-white diplomats at the UN in New York experienced racism and discrimination even as their colleagues in Washington did. New York appointed a hospitality committee to improve conditions for UN delegates, and this helped somewhat, yet many racially inspired incidents still occurred. New York itself was highly segregated, and when the General Assembly was in session, I recall stories that American blacks from Harlem and other areas of the city put on African and Arab robes and went downtown to eat at the best restaurants. It was the only time they were allowed in.

I once asked several black foreign ministers why they never took the United States to task at the United Nations. They told me that we had no monopoly on such problems, that all countries with different races, religions, and cultural groups have similar problems. "We have discrimination in our own countries," they said. Yet it impressed them to see our president, Congress, and the American people moving to improve matters. They also said that events here favorably influenced their attempts to resolve their own racism and discrimination problems.

Another thing that saved us from having our ears boxed at the United Nations was that the United States government as its official policy worked to eliminate discrimination. These efforts deflated the likelihood of UN action. In my talks with diplomats and prime ministers, I found a warm and positive attitude toward the steps we were taking. For example, when the U.S. Army was sent to insure the admission of a black man to a southern university, this had a tremendous impact upon black diplomats in Washington.

Race relations within the United States during the sixties had a profound impact on the world's view of the United States and, therefore, on our foreign relations. While visiting India in 1962, Chester Bowles came across villagers discussing a race riot that had occurred twenty-four hours earlier at a housing project in the United States. Several days later these same villagers of the remote Hindu Kush mountain region were discussing the selection of a black girl as the beauty queen for a state university's homecoming day. We live under the klieg lights of world publicity, partly because of our power and position but also because we have committed ourselves historically to these simple notions of freedom, still the most explosive political ideas in the world.

Because of incidents such as Bowles's experience, I regularly testified before Congress that racial discrimination in the United States had great significance for our foreign policy and that our failure to live up to our proclaimed ideals at home was widely noted abroad. We had to recognize that the breakup of the old colonial empires and the emergence of newly independent nations were one of the epochal developments of our time and that these newly independent peoples, mostly nonwhite, arrived on the scene determined to eradicate every vestige of colonialism and white supremacy. This tremendous transformation has come about partially under the impulse of rights and beliefs set forth in our Declaration of Independence and Constitution. These ideals which we nurtured so much have spread over the earth.

Both policy exigencies and the simple rightness of the cause led us to throw the full weight of the State Department behind the Kennedy and Johnson civil rights programs. President Kennedy asked me as senior cabinet officer to lead off the testimony in support of civil rights legislation. On July 10, 1963, I appeared before the Senate Judiciary Committee in a packed hearing room. These hearings followed several years of intense civil rights activity across the country, the freedom riders, and the historic march of several hundred thousand people on the Lincoln Memorial to hear Martin Luther King, Jr., proclaim, "I have a dream." I was with President Kennedy when he decided, against the advice of some of his aides, not to speak to that rally. He felt that he should not horn in on the show and try to capture or diminish it in any way by his presence. My son David, in the East from California on a research trip, did volunteer work for the march and was so impressed by the event that he quit graduate school and took a job with the Urban League in Washington. There were strong feelings in Congress, in the executive branch, and among the American people that we had to move. Some daring editors in the South—people like Ralph McGill of the *Atlanta Constitution*—helped shape a new public opinion.

Everyone in that packed hearing room on that hot July day knew that historic events were in motion. In my testimony I argued that in civil rights foreign relations were secondary to constitutional and domestic issues and that we should move forward on civil rights to fulfill our own national purposes. Discrimination because of race, religion, and national origin was simply incompatible with American democracy. But I also argued that how we handled civil rights in the United States strongly influenced our relations with the rest of the world. Because the United States is regarded as the home of democracy and the struggle for human rights, we are expected to be the model; no higher compliment could be paid to us. So our failures to live up to our proclaimed ideals are noted—and magnified and distorted. Also, because the white race is a minority in the world, I stressed that we must come to terms with the colored races if we were—or are—to live at peace with other nations.

At one point during my testimony Senator Strom Thurmond of South Carolina asked if I favored recent civil rights demonstrations and marches. "Well, Senator," I replied, "there are various types of demonstrations. I would not wish to make a blanket statement, but if I were denied what our Negro citizens are denied, I would demonstrate." Senator John Pastore of Rhode Island then asked if I believed in the Boston Tea Party. I said that it had had a very wholesome effect on the situation. Thurmond was horrified. He asked if racial turmoil sparked by civil rights demonstrators adversely affected our foreign relations. I told him that it did, but we couldn't avoid the problem. We were facing a crisis that went to the very heart of our society, in which our deeds fell far short of our ideals, and we had to eliminate this inconsistency.

On the way out of the hearing room, Thurmond came up to me and said, "Mr. Secretary, I'm not sure that you understood my questions. I'm from South Carolina."

I said, "Senator, I understood your questions perfectly. I'm from Georgia."

Strom Thurmond and many others, even Alabama Governor George Wallace, eventually changed their minds about race relations. Over time the mood of the country changed dramatically. Martin Luther King, with whom I had sharp differences over Vietnam, rendered a great service by keeping the civil rights movement focused on peaceful change. Had that movement turned violent, there would have been hell to pay.

Yet there were strong opponents of the Civil Rights Act, Senator Richard Russell of Georgia, for one, who believed the federal government should stay out of race relations. In Russell the administration had a formidable barrier to overcome. One of the most skillful parliamentarians the Senate has ever seen, Russell had eighteen or twenty votes in his back pocket, mostly fellow southern senators, that he could deliver on any vote. Thus, despite an apparent national mandate for progress in civil rights, it wasn't easy to get the voting rights bill passed. But we worked hard and received help even from people across the aisle. It was that old conservative Republican Everett Dirksen of Illinois, the minority leader, who could also deliver fifteen to twenty votes in the Senate, who finally unlocked passage of the civil rights bills.

One of the most dramatic evenings I ever spent was the joint session of Congress at which Lyndon Johnson spoke on behalf of the voting rights bill. At joint sessions the Supreme Court justices sit in the front row of one section, and the cabinet sits next to them. Normally whenever the president is speaking, the justices sit quietly and listen. But that evening, with LBJ holding forth on voting rights, out of the corner of my eye I saw these justices actually clapping their hands. In his speech LBJ talked about discrimination he personally had witnessed, beginning in West Texas as a child and continuing into adulthood, even the problems his own chauffeur had in driving between Texas and Washington. He said, "I have known about these problems all my life, but now I can do something about them." And he looked right at Congress and told them, "And you are going to help me."

John Kennedy and Lyndon Johnson, both deeply committed to racial progress, encouraged us to do what we could in our personal and official lives to promote social justice. Little opportunities came up everywhere. In 1961 Smythe Gambrell, then president of the Atlanta Bar Association, asked if I would speak to the bar's annual dinner. The Kennedy cabinet had informally agreed to avoid speaking engagements in segregated gatherings, so I asked Gambrell, "Is the Atlanta bar integrated or segregated?" There was a pause on the end of the line. Back came his reply: "We are not integrated now, but we will be by the time you get here." The evening of my speech was the first time that blacks met with the Atlanta Bar Association and dined in Atlanta's

Biltmore Hotel. In events like these, both small and large, dramatic progress was being made across the country.

One large task remained: an overhaul of American immigration laws to eliminate racial discrimination. I wanted to do away with the national-origin system, under which country quotas were determined, especially the Asia-Pacific triangle provisions which severely limited immigration of Asians. I also wanted to grant immigrants from the newly independent nations, especially those in the Western Hemisphere, the same nonquota status enjoyed by immigrants from other independent nations. We succeeded in all of this. Our immigration reforms received astonishing support in Congress; even conservative senators voted with us. Americans realized that the time had come to move ahead on civil rights, and we at State helped promote it. Passage of immigration reform and the establishment of a racially tolerant immigration policy were major achievements.

South Africa was, of course, a different matter. A solution to the South African problem was—and is—particularly difficult because of the unusual circumstances there. I yield to no one in my abhorrence of apartheid, but sometimes the South African case seems more active at the rhetorical level than at the action level. For example, the overwhelming majority of blacks on the continent of Africa could force change in South Africa if they were prepared to do it. During the early 1960's I had lunch with a dozen black African foreign ministers. All were pressing me for American economic sanctions against South Africa. I said, "Well, let's think about that. Under the UN Charter, if economic sanctions are imposed, steps would have to be taken to alleviate the harshness of these sanctions on any particular country. So let's think of a United Nations sanctions fund. Let's start with one hundred million dollars. Now, the proportionate share for each of you sitting around this table and your respective countries would be the price of a Ford automobile. Would you contribute that much?" They just laughed at me.

In the Kennedy years, at an opening session of the UN General Assembly in New York, in bilateral talks between a group of black Africa's foreign ministers and the South Africans, I tried to negotiate a formula agreeable to both sides. We hoped the South Africans would acknowledge certain principles regarding blacks, and we hoped that both parties would recognize that the implementation of those priciples would take considerable time. We finally arrived at a formula that the black foreign ministers agreed to, but the white South Africans would not even give verbal concessions or words that the black representatives could work with and take home. The South Africans wouldn't play ball, and these exploratory talks went nowhere.

Critics of apartheid have often used the South African Embassy in Washington as a site for demonstrations and sit-ins. I regret protest activity which interferes with foreign embassies, and I offer the back of my hand to those who participate in such protest. The world community has taken many centuries to establish laws and practices for diplomatic exchange, the protection of embassies, and immunity for diplomatic personnel. These are traditions that make international life possible. As the host government we have a duty to protect the South African Embassy in Washington and every other embassy. Fortunately Washington has ordinances that require demonstrators to stay at least five hundred feet from foreign embassies. Sometimes these ordinances are obeyed, sometimes not. Breaking relations with a country is one thing, but abusing its embassy is another. As for sit-ins at the South African Embassy in Washington, only differences in degree separate such action from the Iranian abuse of the American Embassy in Teheran. History reminds us that ancient city-states would sometimes send an emissary to negotiate with the enemy that encircled the fortress, only to have his dead body thrown back over the wall.

Despite the complexity of the South African problem, we almost broke relations with South Africa during the Kennedy administration when Pretoria refused to receive a black Foreign Service officer in our embassy. We did not assign him to South Africa to provoke an incident; his assignment came through regular channels. But we couldn't allow South Africa to remove his name from consideration or accept Pretoria's protest. After a while the South Africans relented.

We also had trouble with South Africa during the Vietnam War when many American ships went around the Cape of Good Hope on the way to Southeast Asia. Frequently they stopped at Cape Town for refueling and shore leave, but when South Africans treated our black sailors and Marines inhospitably, we stopped making port calls there. At considerable inconvenience we thereafter sent our own tankers along to refuel our ships at sea.

But South Africa is only one of many cases of human rights abuses. It is hard to know how to approach these issues. For example, the subject of human rights is difficult to discuss with the Soviet Union. The Helsinki agreements were a step in the right direction, but when we and the Soviets debate human rights, both sides address these issues as each side sees them. The Americans talk about constitutional freedoms, free speech, free press, and universal voting, and the Soviets come right back with economic and social rights, such as public housing, medical care, and education, all provided by their system. Many of their social services reach farther than our own. In such discussions we and the Soviets tend to pass each other in the night; neither of us comes face-to-face with the unfinished business of both societies.

We must also be careful about linkage. It is entirely appropriate for the United States to argue the case for individual liberties and constitutional freedoms. It is also proper for us to use our influence—quietly—to improve human rights in other countries. I have some reservations, however, about linking human rights to the world's business. In the 30 or so constitutional democracies, human rights are in reasonably good order. All of the rest—more than 130 nations—are governed in varying degrees by dictators and authoritarian rule. If we go far down the trail of linking foreign policy to human rights performance abroad, we embark upon a self-chosen path to isolation, one sure to narrow our international participation to the constitutional democracies. I prefer the arts of persuasion and diplomacy to public confrontation on human rights issues.

I have no doubt that in, say, Brazil, South Korea, Argentina, and Taiwan human rights are in better shape because of the steady influence of the United States. President Jimmy Carter can take credit for this, with his administration's focus on human rights. But Carter went further in linking human rights to other issues than I would have advised. Patricia Derian was a very able woman, but when we sent this young assistant secretary of state for human rights to lecture other countries about human rights, she talked to diplomats who remembered racist conditions in Washington. Many went home to leadership positions in their own countries. Indonesian Prime Minister Ali Sastroamidjojo's bitterness toward the United States was partly due to personal snubs and discrimination he encountered while ambassador in Washington during the Truman years.

And with the Soviet Union, we must also remember that pressing human rights issues to the end of the trail may interfere with our need to find ways to share life on this planet. An overemphasis on human rights can complicate already tangled U.S.-Soviet relations. Sometimes a degree of ambiguity on these questions works better. Henry Kissinger worked out an arrangement with the Soviet Union by which the Soviets considerably expanded the numbers of Jews allowed to emigrate. Along came the Jackson-Vanik amendment to a trade bill, an amendment that publicly rubbed Soviet noses into the table on human rights issues, and the Soviets rejected that approach as interference in their internal affairs. The emigration of Jews dropped off sharply after passage of the amendment. American policy should focus on results, not actions that make us feel warmer inside because we have struck a rhetorical blow for freedom.

Human rights have a major role to play in U.S. foreign policy, and we must never lose sight of that. But we must balance our insistence on human rights with awareness of pragmatic policy concerns as well. And we can never afford to be sanctimonious. America has come a long way but still has far to go.

SECTION VII

THE GEORGIA YEARS

Upon leaving the State Department in January 1969, my father lived at home in Washington, wanting to decompress for a year and not rush into another job. He was mercifully out of office but unfortunately also out of money. His Rockefeller Foundation colleagues came to his rescue and named him a "distinguished fellow." He taped oral histories for the Kennedy and Johnson libraries, served on an advisory committee for the Arms Control and Disarmament Agency, and acted as a consultant. He also gave forty-two speeches. It was one of his quietest and least eventful years. I remember it as the worst year of his life.

Once released from the pressure of public life, my dad seemed to come apart at the seams. His eight years of sixteen-hour days and seven-day weeks had caught up with him; now he paid the price in emotional exhaustion and spiritual depression. Suffering as well from a low-grade fever and constant ache in his gut, he visited doctors repeatedly and checked into Walter Reed Hospital and the Mayo Clinic for a battery of tests; the doctors found nothing and suspected stress. My dad vehemently denies this and, in fact, any suggestion that he was suffering during this period, but I remember he thought he was dying. He talked about death as if it were imminent; he had all the appearances of a deeply troubled man.

We Rusks wondered if he would pull through that dismal year, made worse by the fact that the job offers and opportunities normally extended an ex-secretary of state didn't materialize. My dad hoped to return to academic life, but the man was a pariah on many American campuses. Few schools wanted him. The Vietnam War had just gone through its bloodiest phase, and he was reviled by large numbers of Americans. He had time now to see the effects of that war upon American society and time perhaps for reflection. Although he never told us about any second thoughts or soul-searching, his mind was idle, free to wander. Where it went that year we do not know; he would never communicate such thoughts or ask for help. We could only watch from a distance, and worry, and cross our fingers.

"I had trouble trying to wind down from the job," he confessed, but said that lack of money weighed him down more than health concerns.

He had had good job offers while still secretary of state, but he wouldn't discuss them. "I didn't think it was proper," he said. He also turned down book publishers and lecture bureaus. My dad could have made a small fortune in speaking engagements alone, commanding five to ten thousand dollars for his appearances, but "I didn't want to be a pony in their stable." In Georgia I found a file folder of inquiry letters from agents, all refused.

But the University of Georgia was quietly courting Pop. In May 1968, while still in office, Rusk spoke at UGA's law school, despite the presence of a hundred pickets. To some Georgians he was a native son returning home in triumph; to others, a General Sherman who had taken the entire nation on a mission of destruction. But it was a measure of Georgia's civility that Dean Rusk could visit its flagship university in 1968 and not leave the campus in flames. Indeed, the campus newspaper thanked the students "for their commendable conduct" and said "this proved that the University is still a place where free speech is possible."

Pop got the job—the Samuel H. Sibley professorship, a chair created especially for him—but only after an uproar that rocked the state. In what Dean Acheson two decades earlier had called "the attack of the primitives," Rusk was roughed up by Roy Harris, a University of Georgia regent with many hats: former speaker of the Georgia House, member of the White Citizens Council of America, and chairman of George Wallace's campaign in Georgia. "We don't want the university to be a haven for broken down politicians," Harris said. "What galls me most is to have this character sneak in here to my beloved state and get his snout in the public trough. In six years, he'll become eligible for a pension for the rest of his days!

"Why should we manufacture a position . . . just to take care of a man who can't get a job anywhere else?" railed Harris. Insiders felt Harris's real objection to Rusk's being hired was likely his daughter Peggy's marriage to a black man in 1967.

Lester Maddox, having vaulted to the governor's mansion by driving blacks out of his restaurant with an ax handle, also opposed the hire, claiming that Rusk was an "internationalist." So deep was the polarization of American society in the late sixties that my poor father, opposed by Maddox as too liberal, a cog in the "internationalist Communist conspiracy," was rejected up North as too conservative, a phobic crusader against communism.

However, the law faculty voted unanimously to offer him a contract; the regents went along, nine votes to four. "A ringing endorsement of Rusk's coming back home to teach," wrote the *Atlanta Constitution*'s

Reg Murphy. "Cracker politics!" snorted James J. Kilpatrick. "It's a privilege to have him here," editorialized UGA's student newspaper. Even the *Nation* had kind words about his hire. "We never pretended to admire Rusk as secretary of state," it editorialized. "We don't guarantee he'll be a stimulating member of the Georgia faculty. But it may be the best chance Dean Rusk ever had since he left his father's Cherokee County farm."

Much relieved, my folks moved to Athens in the fall of 1970. "After a thirty-year detour, I finally made it," said Pop upon his return to academic life. He settled quietly into university life, a welcome change from the shark-infested waters of Washington.

After eight hectic years as secretary of state Pop had been expected to live the leisurely, academic, semiretired life of an ex-statesman. But he hit the deck running. Trying to satisfy the immediate clamor, he held some classes on closed-circuit television, with hundreds of students tuning in. But he quickly turned to the task at hand, teaching a survey course on international law, a seminar on the Constitution and foreign affairs, and a second seminar on law and diplomacy.

Some students were skeptical. "He was a baby burner, right?" said Charles Hunnicutt, a law student who grew to admire Rusk. "At first I couldn't see how anyone involved in something like Vietnam with its flagrant violations of international law could be teaching international law at Georgia." Most students gave him a fair hearing. Those who remembered only Rusk's blandness and monotonous rhetoric in defending administration policy were surprised by his intellect and speaking ability. With his round, genial face, freckles on his balding head like a shake of nutmeg, eyes that nearly disappeared when he smiled; with his lively sense of humor, surprisingly sociable and witty to those accustomed only to his dour public image, never arrogant or condescending like many ex-statesmen, he soon won over even his critics.

His courses also went well. In short order, Rusk developed a reputation for good teaching, and students flocked to enroll. He prepared hard for each class, graded his blue book exams personally, and never missed a class, except when called for congressional testimony in Washington.

"I had an ironclad rule not to take on outside speaking engagements if it meant missing a class," explained Rusk, calling himself an "old-fashioned professor" who believed that students had "first claim" on his time.

His toughest adjustment to college teaching? "I was taught by George Marshall and Harry Truman to say what I had to say as briefly as possible and then shut up," said Rusk. "But at Georgia whatever I had to say had to last for fifty minutes."

Rusk compensated by encouraging his students to do the talking. Although large classes made this unmanageable, Rusk tried the Socratic method to foster student dialogue. He cut back after his students complained about his wasting time. "We want you to do the talking," they said. He also made the mistakes of rookie professors.

"Rusk had the bad habit of recognizing only two letters in the alphabet," said law Professor Milner Ball, "A and B. He was known as an 'easy mark.' "

"No grading system is worth a damn," my dad replied. "I also had an abhorrence of interfering in other people's lives. . . . I tended to give my students the benefit of the doubt."

As had been true at Mills College, Rusk made little mark as a scholar and failed to publish anything of consequence other than several articles and book reviews. He claimed to be working on a book "in a rather desultory fashion"; his file folder labeled "book" was desultory indeed. A law dean once circulated a study of law faculty publishing, ranking law schools on the total pages published and the number of footnotes crediting articles. Of 109 law schools surveyed, Georgia placed twenty-fourth.

"Dear Dean," Rusk said, firing off a one-page reply. "I can't imagine a more sterile enterprise. . . . Many of these articles did not deserve to see the light of day. I grieve over the number of trees we cut down to make such publications possible."

Where Rusk made his mark was as a teacher. Refusing to teach from textbooks, relating his main points to personal experience, painting large strokes on the canvas, stressing the interrelatedness of law and the world at large, he'd touch upon such issues as human rights, the law of the sea, outer space, environmental law, the population explosion, and methods of settling international disputes, always focusing on the future. He argued passionately that international law is a living force in relations between nations. He tried to do in his classes what he thought university education should do in general: train students to look at life as a whole. His courses weren't technical, detailed, or demanding; they were more a statement of what he personally believed.

Outside class, Rusk was fully involved with his students. There were no office hours; his door was always open. "I had never seen a person of his stature so incredibly accessible," said Pete McCommons, a former Georgia student. "I never saw anyone take that commitment so seriously." He loved to counsel students, talk about their budding careers, point out opportunities and special programs, and occasionally pick up the phone and call Washington on their behalf. He sometimes took them traveling on his speaking engagements for lengthier discussion.

His name created the inevitable confusion. One law student took for granted that Rusk was simply the dean of the law school. "Good morning, Dean," he said each day as they passed. "Good morning, Jimmy," my father replied. A faculty member who witnessed one of these exchanges commented to the student, "I don't know what your relationship is, but do you know that Dean is his first name?" Horrified, anxious to make amends, the student prowled the walkways of the north campus, threading through the magnolias and oaks, until once more he encountered Rusk. "Good morning, Mr. Rusk," he said. "Good morning, Mr. Lunceford," said my father, none the wiser.

As a professor Rusk became so active that he reminded his law colleagues of a junior associate seeking tenure. He guest-lectured all over the campus, in political science, history, journalism classes, even veterinary medicine and programs off the beaten track for a former statesman. "We considered him a campus professor more than just a law professor," said Law Dean Ralph Beaird. He counseled hundreds of students, undergraduates as well as law school students, and became faculty adviser to UGA's black law students. Their association filed a brief with the Civil Rights Commission, charging the law school with discriminatory practices against blacks in recruitment, financial aid, admissions, and grading. Black enrollment increased significantly while Rusk was adviser, as did the retention of black students once enrolled. "Dean helped bring us through some turbulent times," said Beaird.

Rusk served as faculty adviser to Georgia's international law society and its journal, helped screen students for special scholarships, and served on many faculty committees dealing with campus and administrative issues. Off campus, he chaired the advisory committees on the law of the sea and the Georgia Chamber of Commerce, and he was active on countless boards and task forces, working to bolster international trade and commerce and a greater role for international law. He tried to help individual citizens on immigration and visa problems and American businessmen having trouble overseas.

Although never accumulating personal wealth, my father lived his private life consistent with his public philosophy, making numerous contributions to charities of all types, political candidates, the Boy Scouts, Davidson and Mills colleges, memorial funds for his friends. Beyond its use for paying bills, money was of little concern to him. "Filthy lucre," he said. "Why not give it away? I can't take it with me." He trusted the

banks to balance his checking accounts; "they can do that better than I."
Every year he would routinely overpay the Internal Revenue Service at
tax time, not take advantage of all loopholes when filing, and wait
patiently for his refund. "I don't mind paying taxes," he said, "to a
country that allows a barefoot boy from Cherokee County to become its
secretary of state."

Pop's number one charity was the University of Georgia. He had a
habit of signing over honoraria for speaking engagements to the law
school. "Very unusual around this place," observed a colleague. But
during the seventies, according to Dean Beaird, Rusk's honoraria
amounted to thousands of dollars. He often earmarked those funds for
black students or those wanting to study abroad, and he insisted that his
philanthropy not become known.

"Students would thank me, thinking I had given them the money,"
said Dean Beaird. "Actually the whole time I was using Rusk's money."

In between classes, seeking a wider forum for his views, wanting to
popularize international law beyond the legal community, my father
accepted speaking engagements all over the country. At the drop of a hat
he would drive alone to some junior college in a remote corner of the
South, often picking up the tab himself. His audiences ranged from the
Council on Foreign Relations, governors' conferences, and congressional
committees in Washington to grade school assemblies, high school
classes, college commencements, churches, the war colleges, chambers
of commerce, the League of Women Voters, public service and veterans
groups, and trade associations such as plumbers, boilermakers, and
funeral directors. He found time even for such offbeat groups as the
Butler Street Hungry Club, the Optimists Club, and the Fort Gillens Wives
Club.

He was always in demand, and his prestige, availability, and charm on
the lectern made him a popular speaker throughout the South. Speaking
with people at the grass roots seemed to fill a visceral need in him. He
would adapt his speeches to the occasion but, left to his own devices,
would talk about his articles of faith: in American democracy, in the
American people, in the younger generations, and in our ability to cope
with the future. He had a message to deliver, and he worked that
message at every opportunity.

"I would like to share with you a little of the fire that burns within
me," he would begin, staring directly at the young people in his
audiences. He would talk about their formidable agenda—the energy
crisis, population explosion, environmental pollution, depletion of
nonrenewable resources, threat of nuclear war—and remind his young

listeners that his generation had ducked the threat of totalitarian
aggression in the thirties. "We learned some bitter lessons . . . there was
no place to hide, no foxholes into which we could crawl and ignore the
rest of the world."

Rusk would talk about nuclear weapons as well—"these great engines
of destruction"—and how the threat of nuclear holocaust, plus the events
of the last two decades—three political assassinations, Vietnam,
Watergate—have damaged American confidence. "We tend to cut
ourselves to pieces," he'd say. "Prolonged self-flagellation can destroy a
democracy." He believed that hope and confidence were vital to the
functioning of our society and would remind his audiences of the
strengths of American democracy: our "extraordinary constitutional
system," the productivity of a free-market economy, and the American
people themselves. He would talk about his own wellsprings of hope, his
experiences with George Marshall and the presidents he served, those
"simple ideas of human freedom" articulated by the Founding Fathers,
and his conviction that "Mankind was not put on this earth to reach out
and grasp the power of the sun itself to burn ourselves off its face."

Jumping ahead into the future, reaching back into the past, touching
down upon historical events spanning his lifetime and indeed the life of
the American Republic, he would remind his listeners of crises weathered
before: the Civil War; the Great Depression; the resignation of an
American president. He would also remind them of the "grim days of
early 1942," when Hitler's armies were overrunning Europe, North
Africa, and the Soviet Union and the Japanese were overrunning the
Pacific after destroying the American fleet at Pearl Harbor. "In spite of
these dark times when defeat seemed inevitable, Franklin Roosevelt,
Winston Churchill, Joseph Stalin, and millions of us built upon hope and
confidence and necessity and we defeated the Axis powers."

Mildly rebuking recent administrations for ignoring problems and not
calling upon the American people "for the effort we know we ought to
be making," he would say, "There are times when we are not at our
best." He would insist that "the only tolerable way to deal with a
problem or danger is to advance on it," remind his young audience that
hard work, dedication, "even sacrifice" would be required, and quote
John Kennedy: "Problems created by man can be solved by man."

He would talk about the young people he had taught. "I am confident
in you," he would insist, "confident that you will take a piece of the
action and do your job," and he asked his own generation to "go
flat-out" to help them.

Looking directly at his audience, sometimes chopping the air with his hands, Pop would speak with a fire that surprised those who once thought him bland. He took his message all over the South. Talking with a simple, vibrant eloquence, he spoke as if he were making the speech for the first time. Regardless of his audience, whatever its size, however ordinary or distinguished, he made that speech as if he were the American secretary of state addressing the UN General Assembly. And they knew it.

As so often happens with former policy makers, Dean Rusk became increasingly concerned about the threat of nuclear war. Although concern about the nuclear threat had been woven into his speech making since Hiroshima, with increasing frequency as he grew older he talked about the threat of holocaust, about the imperative of arms control, and the necessity for optimism in a nuclear age. During the eighties he worried about President Reagan's apparent indifference to arms control, a quickening arms race, growing acrimony in Soviet-American relations, and the unraveling of past agreements he had helped negotiate. The Strategic Defense Initiative especially concerned him.

"Some years ago," he wrote McGeorge Bundy, "I thought that when I reached my present age I could simply withdraw and let younger people take care of these issues. Unhappily I have become almost passionate about the threat of moving the arms race into outer space."

Getting sassier in his old age, breaking somewhat with his tradition of not criticizing those holding office, and until the INF Treaty genuinely saddened by the Reagan administration's dismal performance on arms control, at every opportunity he blasted Reagan's "Star Wars" program.

"If you want my views on SDI," he would say, and, solicited or otherwise, would volunteer them, "SDI is one of the major blunders of the postwar period." And he would describe the efforts of the Kennedy and Johnson administrations to keep weapons out of space. "We thought that outer space should be a vast arena of peaceful exploration and cooperation between nations," he'd say. "Astronauts and cosmonauts were the envoys of all mankind.

"All this is threatened by SDI. The real question is, Are we going to scrap that approach and make outer space an arena of warfare?

"Star Wars is well named," he said repeatedly, from as many forums as he could address. "In a nutshell, spreading the arms race into outer space is politically inflammatory, militarily futile, economically absurd, and aesthetically repulsive. Otherwise, it is a great idea."

—R. R.

38

Return to Georgia

As the Johnson administration drew to a close, LBJ called me to the White House. He intended to nominate me to the Supreme Court, he said. This was typical of Johnson's generosity toward colleagues; he had already smoothed Robert McNamara's appointment to the World Bank.

Although I wasn't sure what I would do after January 1969, I knew I didn't want to sit on the Supreme Court, nor did I qualify as a justice. "Mr. President," I protested, "World War Two kept me from finishing my degree. I've never practiced law. I've never served on the bench."

"The Constitution doesn't require prior judicial service for the Supreme Court," he said.

"True enough," I said, "but the Senate would never confirm me."

LBJ was ready for that as well: "I've taken care of that. I've already talked to Dick Russell, and he said you'd be confirmed easily."

So I took the only road left. "Mr. President, I appreciate your generosity. But as your adviser I must advise you strongly against it. And as the person under consideration I would not permit my name to go forward." I was one of the few to resist successfully the "LBJ treatment."

LBJ had told us cabinet officers that he wanted a smooth transition with the new Nixon administration, and after the election I met frequently with William Rogers, my successor. "Like any GI in a foxhole," I told Bill, "I welcome my replacement with open arms." My final weeks involved much leave-taking; even the dour Andrei Gromyko drew me aside at a United Nations dinner and spoke in the friendliest terms about our long association and having weathered many crises together. The State Department press corps was among many who threw a reception for Virginia and me. Lyndon Johnson hosted his own, gave me the Medal of Freedom, and established a scholarship in Virginia's and my honor at the University of Texas.

One elderly lady prepared me for the anonymity soon to come. Shuffling through a receiving line at the department, she looked at me and inquired, "What is your name?" I told her, and then she asked, "And what do you do?"

"I work for the State Department," I replied.

"Oh, how nice," she said, moving on.

I left office with few regrets, but one was not writing personal letters to my colleagues, thanking them for their years of service. I don't know why I failed to do that; maybe it was the famous "Rusk reticence."

On January 20, my final day in office, Virginia and I threaded our way through the department's main lobby. A huge crowd had gathered to bid us good-bye. I made no speech on that occasion, other than to say, "Eight years ago Mrs. Rusk and I came quietly. We wish now to leave quietly. Thank you very much."

Virginia and I declined our invitations to the Nixon inaugural, having been through that drill before; we stayed home to watch the proceedings on TV. At the moment President Nixon finished his oath of office, I just floated like a balloon; that job was not my baby anymore. Years later I mentioned this feeling to Lady Bird Johnson, who smiled and said, "That's very interesting because I was sitting next to Lyndon on the platform, and at that same instant Lyndon groaned audibly with relief."

I joined the ranks of the unemployed on Inauguration Day. After eight years in office, I was bone-tired and out of money as well. I needed time to unwind and find work, and fortunately my colleagues at the Rockefeller Foundation awarded me a fellowship. I dictated oral histories for the Kennedy and Johnson libraries, served as an adviser for the Arms Control and Disarmament Agency, and gave a few speeches.

Francis Wilcox, dean of the Johns Hopkins School of Advanced International Studies, offered me a small office in downtown Washington, but some Hopkins students, stirred up over Vietnam, protested. I elected to work out of my home instead. Wilcox and I decided not to tell those students that when I was president the Rockefeller Foundation had put up money to build Johns Hopkins's main building.

But I still had the problem of what I would do after leaving office. Business opportunities were available, but the rat race of business competition and scrambling for money never appealed to me. My secret hope, dating back to studying law at Berkeley in the thirties, was to become a professor of international law. After a thirty-year detour I was drawing closer to a long-held dream.

There was one major stumbling block: no law degree, no Ph.D. The president of a California university once offered me a faculty position, joking that he'd have to bring me on board as a full professor. "Dean," he said, "without a Ph.D., you'll never make it on your own."

Being appointed a full professor on a university faculty, next to being elected president, is probably the most difficult position to achieve in the civilized world. But I was among the lucky few. Late in 1968 Dean Lindsey Cowen of the University of Georgia Law School approached me about joining his faculty as a professor of international law. I would be delighted to come home to Georgia, where thanks to my prolific grandparents, I had hundreds of cousins and many friends. Even though I had not lived in Georgia since 1927, I still considered myself a Georgian.

Virginia and I talked it over, and when the offer came, I accepted it. One small hitch remained: In Georgia's university system, all appointments must be approved by the board of regents. While this is usually a formality, in my case it was not.

When the university and I began talking, someone polled the regents by telephone. They were unanimously in favor of my appointment. Shortly afterward Roy Harris, a regent who also chaired George Wallace's 1968 presidential campaign in Georgia, found an issue. It wasn't over policy like Vietnam or U.S.-Soviet relations or even my lack of a law degree or Ph.D. Apparently he objected to my appointment because my daughter, Peggy, had married a black man. Harris called a special meeting of the regents, who voted to override him and offer me the position.

Shortly thereafter one of Roy Harris's friends introduced a bill in the state legislature to reduce the appropriation to the University of Georgia by the amount of my salary. That was defeated 113 to 12.

Virginia and I moved to Athens in the fall of 1970. Some residents had expected us to buy an old southern plantation home with columns and a wide veranda, fully staffed by servants. We fooled them all by moving into a small town house apartment one mile from the campus. Other than the Harris incident, the reception Virginia and I received was heartwarming. During the height of controversy over my hiring, some Georgia students wrote me and telephoned me, telling me not to pay any attention to the controversy and to come on down. I didn't interpret that as approval by them of my lurid past, but nevertheless, they extended a cordial welcome. Once, as I walked across campus soon after my arrival, a young man approached me, introduced himself as the leader of Georgia's Students for a Democratic Society—an antiwar group of the sixties—and said, "Mr. Rusk, I really didn't care for your war in Vietnam. Nevertheless, welcome to Georgia." And he shook my hand.

My faculty colleagues warmed up, too, despite my lack of formal credentials. When I arrived in Athens, a friend at the Harvard Law School sent me a letter of welcome into the profession. Trying to be helpful, he passed along a story about Harry Truman, lecturing about international law at Harvard after he left office. During the discussion a student asked, "Mr. President, do you know anything about international law?" Truman said, "Hell, yes. I made a lot of it." This may sound a little self-serving, but it would be hard to find anyone in government who had practiced more international law than I had and over a longer period—three administrations.

As a professor I tried to combine the general principles of international law with the kinds of problems practicing lawyers encounter, enlivened with anecdotal experiences from my State Department years. Additionally, I have long felt that international law offered a key to world peace. As Louis Henkin said in *How Nations Behave,* "Most nations, most of the time, comply with international law." Of those three thousand cables that went out of the State Department every day during my tenure, at least 20 percent involved points of international law. The governments of the world already practice international law; it is a living, if unheralded, force in world affairs.

More international law has come into being since 1945 than in the entire history of the human race before them. And yet we must speed the process, as mankind is in a desperate race to find ways of settling its disputes peacefully. I tried to bring as much enthusiasm to teaching international law as was proper and as much as my taciturn Cherokee County style would allow. I asked my students, "Do you believe in international law?," then told them the story of the Baptist who was asked, "Do you believe in baptism by immersion?" "Believe in it?" the Baptist replied. "Hell, I've seen it!"

I felt that teaching and discussing international law with Georgia law students and others I could reach were, in their own small way, a worthwhile contribution to peace. The harvest in teaching is often slow in coming, but hearing from former students about their developing careers is every teacher's delight, as are the continuing contact with young people and their unflagging enthusiasm. Virginia and I came to love Athens, Georgia, and its university; the students I was privileged to teach helped rejuvenate my life and make a new start after those hard years in Washington. Of them I have hundreds of memories; one student wrote indignantly in his exam booklet, after I had asked for the meaning of a Latin phrase, "I'm a Georgian, not a Roman. Would Julius Caesar have known what I meant if I said, 'Go, you hairy dogs'?"

As a professor in a state university I believed that I ought to be totally accessible to the people of Georgia. After all, Georgia citizens are taxpayers, and the university is their university. Instead of spending my time writing academic papers that fifty people might read, I preferred to visit around the state, small communities and large. I also thought that I could show them several things: One, our leaders in Washington, whoever they may be, are human beings like everybody else. Here I was, a boy from Cherokee County, Georgia, also a former secretary of state. They could see for themselves and agree with me that there are no supermen in Washington, only plain, ordinary people. Two, I could try to link their lives in Georgia with the great issues of world affairs which affect us all. For my speech making I declined the services of a lecture bureau and the lure of big honoraria. I also felt that Georgia taxpayers shouldn't have to pay a fee to hear a state university professor speak.

Since returning to Georgia and academic life, like a true academic, I have formed some strong, even opinionated views about American universities. While I don't pretend to be an expert about higher education, there are shortcomings, and some are obvious.

First, I am rather skeptical about the research treadmill in American universities. Fortunately at Georgia I was able to avoid being caught in the "publish or perish" syndrome. If forced to publish, I would have perished in short order. Also, modern universities seem a little suspicious of professors who show too much concern for students. Some professors dream of All Souls College in Oxford, where, with all faculty and no students, they focus entirely on scholarship. I used to read through the annual list of Ph.D. theses in this country, a depressing experience. How much time is spent flogging the obvious. For example, theses on "Why Young Children Fall Off Bicycles" conclude, after two years' study, that the reason children fall is that they lose their balance.

Second, I am concerned about how narrowly focused higher education can be. Universities ought to be more interdisciplinary in structure. Negotiating cooperation between two universities or two departments in the same university is nearly as difficult as negotiating with the Russians. Something about academia seems to get in the way. Each department likes to protect its own turf and attract its own majors. And yet life itself is interdisciplinary; it should be seen and studied as a whole. If we look ahead to the problems of the next three to four decades, problems of overpopulation, environmental pollution, famine, the energy crisis, all merge into an inseparable whole. We're going to need more universal people, men and women like Benjamin Franklin, Eleanor Roosevelt, and Thomas Jefferson. Our leaders also need a universal outlook. We expect our president and secretary of state to look at problems and crises as a whole and examine all elements of a problem. But we don't train our young to look at life as a whole.

At Georgia I once proposed that we offer a Ph.D. in "Nothing at All" and give some talented young people a four-year opportunity to draw the best from the different disciplines and look at life as a whole. Modern problems—the energy crisis, environmental pollution, diminishing resources, the population explosion, and food scarcity—all blend together. My faculty colleagues readily forgave me because they thought I was joking. Had they realized I was serious, they would have driven me off campus.

Third, and closer to my field, lawyers and law schools in general are too possessive of the law. Rather than focus entirely on highly trained specialists, we should take the law to the people and explain our legal system. International law in particular is poorly understood by the American people. There is a strong case to be made for international law and an impressive story to tell, and I think Americans would respond to it. Stronger public awareness of international law would pay dividends for American foreign policy.

During the fifties I spoke to a huge crowd of Harvard Law School alumni in New York City. I liked to think they turned out for me. However, the legendary Judge Learned Hand was also there as guest of honor. He sat on my right at the speakers' table and was obviously the drawing card. I was talking about the need to popularize law and take the law to the people. As I spoke, the old judge, who was quite deaf, thinking he was whispering, urged me on in a loud voice, saying, "That's the stuff! Pour it on! Give it to 'em." These Harvard Law alumni were so fascinated by Hand's enthusiasm that few paid any attention to me.

Believing that universities could improve their teaching of the law, while at the Rockefeller Foundation I once studied the curricula of American liberal arts colleges. Few had courses on the legal system. Yet law is one of the most pervasive aspects of modern life. From our waking until we go to sleep at night, we pass through hundreds of actual or potential legal relationships. Most are not activated unless something happens, like we hit somebody on the snoot on the sidewalk. Nevertheless, those relationships are there. The legal system allows us to predict reliably how the other fellow is going to act. The legal system permits each of us to pursue our eccentric orbits, without colliding with other people's rights. The legal system provides the framework for our own individual rights. Those with the greatest stake in the law are those wishing most to dissent because it is the legal system which prevents the majority from beating them down. I would hope that liberal arts colleges, which should deal with life in the broadest sense, also focus on the nature of the legal system and the majesty of the law.

I was fascinated by the variety of chores that came across my desk as a university professor. Georgia football coach Vince Dooley once brought a well-spoken and heavily muscled young black athlete to my office to discuss criminology and law. We talked for an hour or so, this high schooler and I, and I was very impressed. That young man was Herschel Walker, who soon led Georgia to a national championship. I had inadvertently become a member of the team that successfully recruited perhaps the finest running back in college history!

As an ex-secretary of state I offered sometimes advice but mainly encouragement to my successors at the State Department. I was one of the few who could treat Henry Kissinger like a Dutch uncle, for example. I didn't want anything from him, and he didn't want anything from me, and he seemed to welcome advice without strings attached. He often sent a small jet to Athens to fly me to Washington. I heard from many citizens needing help on such matters as traveling abroad, immigration, and visa problems, American businessmen having trouble overseas, etc. A lawyer once called me from California, waking me up about three o'clock in the morning, to say that one of his clients had lost his passport in Brussels, Belgium, and he had to catch a plane in three hours for an important meeting in Germany. His solution was to call

me in Athens! I said, "Don't you know there's a passport officer on duty
in the State Department twenty-four hours a day to take care of things
like that?" He said no. So I gave him the number for the passport office
and told him to call. One hour later he called back, waking me again
at 4:00 A.M., to say, "Hey, it worked! Thank you very much!"

I was asked to speak by an incredible variety of groups, including
fraternities and sororities, the YMCA, the Athens Newcomers Club,
Young Democrats, trade associations such as boilermakers and funeral
directors, the kinds of groups that had never seen an American secretary of state before and might not ever see one again. I tried to oblige
them all. If one took a map and stuck a pin in every little town I visited,
those pins would cover Georgia. I spoke to many schools and colleges;
kindergarteners and first and second graders were especially tough
audiences. At the blackboard I tried to illustrate my points about
Washington and how the government works with stick figures. Often
the students boned up on questions ahead of time. One little boy asked
me if I had ever disagreed with my president, and I said, "Oh, yes."
Whereupon the next little boy said, "Then why didn't he fire you!" I
usually concluded my remarks by saying, "If a barefoot boy from
Cherokee County can become an American secretary of state, who
knows what might happen to someone sitting in this room?"

I stopped teaching international law full time in 1984, believing that
no one of seventy-five should inflict himself upon students. Because my
salary was funded by private sources, I had already taught ten years
past university retirement age. I had asked several law colleagues to
keep a close eye on me in case I began breaking up. I never did hear
from them, but it eventually became time to step down.

Looking back upon my eighty years, I can truthfully say that I never
had a boring day in my life. Those years were filled with excitement,
accomplishment and failure, and a healthy dose of tragedy. I regret
more than I can possibly say the casualties and suffering of every war
fought in my lifetime. I had devoted my life to the search for peace, and
it was my unique tragedy to participate in three wars and as secretary
of state to preside over one.

I have always regarded my wedding day as the luckiest of my life.
Virginia was diagnosed much later as having multiple sclerosis and is
now confined to a hospital bed and wheelchair, but throughout her
illness we've never heard her utter a word of complaint. Our life together has been my greatest blessing, and the only mystery about her
is how she has tolerated me for more than fifty years. I once asked her
how she managed. "I really don't know," she said.

One final point upon which I've had time to reflect since my liberation from public service: the role of chance and happenstance in life. My journey from Cherokee County to secretary of state to the University of Georgia is a classic example. In tracing it, one should not try to find rare talents and special qualities. Whatever ability I had was shared by millions of others. Rather, one would have to look at accident, chance, happenstance, the roll of the dice, and circumstances themselves which affected what my life would be like. For example, in the spring of 1931, the Rhodes selection committee in North Carolina seemed hesitant to consider my application because I was from Georgia. During the interview I happened to mention that I had paid poll tax in North Carolina. That innocent comment impressed the committee chairman. I probably wouldn't have been awarded a Rhodes had it not been for the happy accident of my paying that tax.

In September 1941 the War Department wanted someone to set up a new section of military intelligence, covering the entire British area in Asia, Afghanistan, the Indian subcontinent, Burma, Malaya, Australia, New Zealand, the British Pacific islands, and Hong Kong. So they dropped hundreds of personnel cards into a sorting machine, and my card dropped out because I had lived in England for three years, not because I was an expert on those areas. I went to Washington, while most of the captains in my division were sent to the Philippines to fight at Bataan and Corregidor. Few survived the infamous death march that followed.

Again, in February 1947, Secretary of War Robert Patterson asked me to join the Regular Army, complete my studies in international law, and become the international lawyer for the Army. That was a very attractive offer. I almost accepted. Three days before I was to take the oath for commissioning, Secretary of State George Marshall invited me to the State Department to run United Nations Affairs. Time after time, the roll of the dice.

There's a lesson in this. The role of accident, chance, happenstance was so pronounced in my life that in counseling young people about their future, I tell them that they cannot plan their lives with certainty. But at least they can prepare themselves to be lucky. They can be ready for whatever opportunities come.

39

Final Thoughts: Developments in Eastern Europe

As this book was going to press in January 1990, dramatic developments in Eastern Europe and the Soviet Union compel comment. The prologue for these events, the forty-year history of the Cold War—the United States' almost complete and almost overnight demobilization after the surrender of Japan; Soviet aggressions in Eastern Europe, Turkey, Greece, Berlin, and Korea; and the Western reaction in the form of NATO, the Marshall Plan, and policies of containment—is told in the foregoing pages. These adventures by Joseph Stalin are the true beginnings of the Cold War, an indefinite period of stalemate between the superpowers or what Arthur Schlesinger once called "the world of coercion" and "the world of consent."

I find myself completely astonished by General Secretary Mikhail Gorbachev's bold initiatives to reform Soviet society and by the revolutionary change in Poland, Hungary, East German, Czechoslovakia, Bulgaria, and Romania toward a measure of incentives and free-market economies. I find it remarkable that the Soviet Union has permitted far-reaching changes among these states of Eastern Europe. Although

I have always thought the Cold War would end only when those who started it decided to call it off, who would have imagined that this would begin to happen now? I never dreamed, for example, that the Berlin Wall, built during my term as secretary of state and the focal point of such dangerous tension, would crumble during my lifetime. I never foresaw the scheduling of free elections in Eastern Europe, free movement of peoples across national borders, or Communist parties voluntarily surrendering political control.

In reviewing these events, this veteran of the Cold War is groping with the question of what to remember and what to forget. I find myself struggling to adjust my thinking to a totally new situation.

Mikhail Gorbachev has shown imagination and courage. Apparently he has abandoned the Brezhnev Doctrine, which claimed the right of the Soviet Union to intervene militarily in any Communist country to ensure that it remain Communist. I never expected a Soviet leader to step out in this way. Who could have imagined that a Gorbachev would emerge from the Soviet political system?

Events are moving so fast and so powerfully it would be foolish to predict how all this will work out. How can I serve as prophet when even the leaders of Eastern Europe do not know what will happen next? But some things seem obvious.

Gorbachev faces enormous problems in trying to reshape Soviet policies and institutions. We should not underestimate the formidable task he has set for himself. Russia's seventy-year history of authoritarian rule and centralized planning, state ownership of all the means of production, and the absence of private capital, a market economy, and democratic expression in their own political and economic traditions almost ensure that *glasnost* and *perestroika* will be rocky roads indeed. The expectations of the Soviet people have outrun the capabilities of their system to deliver. The stirrings of dissent within this huge multiethnic country threaten the unity of the Soviet Union itself. The countries of Eastern Europe, with their smaller, homogeneous populations and cohesive political, social, and cultural traditions, likely have a better chance to succeed. Their reform efforts will not necessarily result in Western-style democratic capitalism but rather in institutions of their own making. But we can anticipate a trend toward market economies, democratic political expression, expanded East-West travel and trade, and greater civility in international affairs.

In my judgment, Gorbachev has already produced changes in Eastern Europe which are irreversible. One cannot unleash forces of this nature and then stuff them back into the bottle. A successor to Gorbachev might try, but repression now would result in bitter resentments and possibly bloodshed. Major elements of the Red Army may not respond to such orders; even in Hungary in 1956 and Czechoslovakia in 1968, Soviet leaders had to replace their occupation forces with East Asian troops.

Even if Gorbachev were ousted tomorrow, he would go down in history as a great leader on the basis of what he has already achieved. He has ushered in prospects of a new world, a sea change in international affairs. I have waited a long time for the Soviet Union to join the human race and work cooperatively to solve common problems. With luck, this seems to be happening.

These events have enormous implications for U.S. policy, although in a time of uncertainty and instability we cannot predict in detail what our lines of policy should be. Radical change ushers in great dangers as well. The Cold War is ending but is not over yet. A half million Soviet troops remain in Poland and East Germany. Soviet involvement in Angola, Nicaragua, Cuba, Cambodia, and other regional conflicts continues. Gorbachev could easily fail. Chaos and anarchy in the Soviet Union would be dangerous for us all. Tens of thousands of nuclear weapons remain in the Soviet arsenal; one can only speculate over who might control them after Gorbachev.

Should the United States actively try to help Gorbachev or sit back and let events take their course? I prefer the former, as long as *glasnost* and *perestroika* move in the direction of liberalized trade, free emigration of peoples and greater respect for human rights, further arms reductions, and reduced defense expenditures. I applaud the results of the Malta meeting between President Gorbachev and President George Bush. The way has opened for a more serious and productive meeting between the two in their planned summit in 1990.

Gorbachev has proven his sincerity by allowing the countries of Eastern Europe to go their own way. We face a historic opportunity to wind down the Cold War, scale back military spending, and reduce superpower involvement in regional conflicts. We should respond positively to Gorbachev whenever his policies and our interests coincide. I prefer that Gorbachev succeed with his reforms and gradually transform his country rather than see it collapse entirely. The Russian bear is dangerous enough without the United States' encouraging the breakup of the Soviet Union.

Yet we must recognize limits in our ability to influence events in Eastern Europe. The magnitude of problems facing the Soviet Union, a country with one of the world's biggest gross national products, is so large that our efforts can help only on the margins. For example, a Marshall Plan for the 1990's, adjusted for inflation, would cost sixty to eighty billion dollars. Even if it were politically possible to float such assistance, because of our massive federal deficit, we simply don't have the dollars. And even this likely would not prove decisive. What the Soviet Union needs to do has to be done at home by the Soviet people themselves.

Surely we must act in concert with our European allies. NATO has done so much to keep the peace during the last four decades. Reductions of NATO forces must correspond with those of the Warsaw Pact. It is to be hoped that reductions will include conventional forces as well as strategic weapons.

On the question of German reunification, we must listen closely and move cautiously. Both East and West Germany have much to do before moving seriously toward reunification. Both Germanys can minimize the importance of their common boundary with all sorts of political, economic, and social linkages, a process well under way.

By treaty, the four occupying powers—Great Britain, France, the United States, and the Soviet Union—hold continuing jurisdiction over the question of German reunification. They are wise to do so. The two Germanys must understand the nervousness with which many countries would view a unified Germany, disconnected from NATO, the Warsaw Pact, and the European Community, rolling like a loose cannon around the deck of world politics.

When viewing recent developments in Eastern Europe, we Americans should not claim victory in the Cold War. These events have their origins in Eastern Europe. Gorbachev is acting in what he perceives to be the best interests of the Soviet Union. He recognized that the Soviet economy has fundamental difficulties, that these satellite countries were an intolerable burden, and that drastic action had to be taken. He saw the evident failings in the Soviet system and is moving courageously to correct them. Communism has not worked in these countries, and to their credit Gorbachev and the peoples of Eastern Europe are recognizing that.

Even so, this is no "victory" for American foreign policy. I have no doubt that the presence of NATO, the patience of the West, and the success of our political and economic systems have contributed to these developments and pointed out alternative models to Marxism-Leninism. We can take a quiet satisfaction in that and in having survived these past forty-five years without general war, no small achievement in this twentieth century. But these changes came about through developments within the Soviet bloc itself. If there is a "victory," it is a victory not for Western democracy but for the entire human race.

It is a time for thankfulness and quiet reflection. I am reminded of the Cuban missile crisis of October 1962. After Nikita Khrushchev announced that the Soviet Union would withdraw its missiles, President Kennedy insisted that there be no gloating by his administration. "If Khrushchev wants to play the role of peacemaker, let him do so," he said. In helping defuse the crisis, Khrushchev had earned the title.

Although events now seem to be moving toward the West, we Americans should remember that the Cold War exacted a terrible price in military spending. For three fiscal years following V-J Day, our defense budget came to approximately eleven billion dollars. If that was our idea of a peacetime military budget, when it is compared with American expenditures over the next four decades in reacting to Soviet policy, the difference is trillions of dollars. It boggles the mind to imagine what could have been done with those resources for peaceful purposes had the Cold War not occurred. Although we didn't start the Cold War, we had to compete with the Soviets in a senseless arms race, a tragic story.

As weaknesses in the Soviet Union and the failings of communism become evident, they should remind us of our own weaknesses and failings. They include the massive budget deficit, the huge deficit in foreign trade, abuses which have beset the savings and loan industry, urgent problems in the environment, our unfinished business in the field of human rights, and a terrible drug problem which is eating the heart out of our society. Our example can be more eloquent than our words.

Entering the 1990's, we Americans face a new situation, no less challenging than that facing American policy after World War II. We must think and act creatively to ensure that the United States does not become a marginal player in the shaping of the post-Cold War period. As East and West enter this period of historical transition, mistakes and misjudgments on both sides will be made. It is impossible now to lay out a precise blueprint for the future, but the general principles which have guided American policy during the past forty years are as valid today as ever. We must act with a balance of restraint and firmness, remain true to our values, yet be tolerant of diversity. We must continually seek those little threads of agreement and compromise which help bind humanity together.

All my adult life I have believed that Thomas Jefferson put his finger on the ultimate political truth when he said, "Governments derive their just powers from the consent of the governed." All other forms of political organization—rule by an aristocracy, the dictatorship of the proletariat, the divine right of kings—must contend with those yearnings for freedom seemingly ingrained in human nature. Those yearnings are now being given powerful expression in Eastern Europe.

AFTERWORD

In July 1984, having moved my family from Alaska to Georgia, I began my journey back into time with my dad. Pop's advancing years led to failing vision. I became his chauffeur and Seeing Eye dog, traveling with him on speaking trips, sharing his Georgia life. In a few short years Pop had gone from "pariah" to "honored native son." My mother told me that their years in Georgia have been the best of their lives.

At home, following my father's career and intellectual journey, I discovered unsuspected passions within myself about issues of public policy but also about Pop's concept of citizenship. Some of his ideas became very dear to me, none more than our shared concern about nuclear war. We teamed up on several teleconferences and educational projects in Georgia, the first time I had collaborated intellectually with my father. And with the urgency of a son whose world is achingly close to destruction and whose own children's lives are at risk, I told my dad that our father-son journey had indeed led to a possible career path for me, that I wanted to focus on Soviet-American relations, arms control, the avoidance of nuclear war—the biggest issue of our times. Sensing my excitement, he understood right away; that is how he lived his life.

I understood my father more clearly now, an old man strapping nitroglycerine patches on his chest and heading out the door on wobbly legs, crisscrossing Georgia and flying the country to spread his gospel of faith and his conviction that somehow "we are going to make it." He worried less about nuclear war from a premeditated strike or accidental launch than that we might lose hope, and although he responded to as many invitations as scheduling and health would allow, any conference, panel show, speech invitation on arms control or superpower relations would grab his attention.

Pop's obsession with nuclear war—primary during the sixties as well—made Vietnam more understandable to me. The American stand in Vietnam, linked in his mind with collective security and the lessons of World War II, had been a means of staving off general war. Shadowing the million lives lost in Southeast Asia was the possibility of further aggression and, in a nuclear age, a billion lives lost. That, for him, was what Vietnam was meant to forestall.

"How will history judge this?" I asked him.

"I am relaxed about it," he said. "As secretary of state I did my duty as I saw it. That's the best one can do. That's all anyone can be expected to do in a job like that."

I wondered how his friends had judged him and whether Vietnam had affected their feelings about him. I asked them point-blank. Some had concurred with his thinking on the war and supported him; others who normally would have opposed the war were unsure what to think, knowing that Dean Rusk was on the other side. "It made me uncomfortable as hell," said a minister friend. A surprising number thought that he was simply being loyal to his presidents and didn't personally believe in the war. Still others had been badly troubled.

"A shattering experience," a foundation colleague had written. "I can't bear to think about it," said a Mills graduate who knew him in the thirties. "I will not allow any critical talk about Dean Rusk in my house!" a family friend had roared at a party in Scarsdale, hosted by him. Most stuck by him; only a few broke off their friendships over the war. However strongly they may have disagreed, most remained unshaken in their convictions about my father and his decency.

After he left office, the Vietnam War dogged Pop. In his classes, speechmaking, press interviews, and correspondence, he was asked repeatedly about it. Still the war's most dogged defender, he answered patiently. Looking back, he openly questioned whether gradualism had been the proper strategy; he wondered whether democracies could truly wage limited war; he admitted mistakes. He worried also about a possible return to isolationism, a withdrawal into Fortress America. But there were no apologies or confessions of wrongdoing. Even in his correspondence, in responding to both friends and perfect strangers, he wrote long letters rebutting criticism and stating his position, point for point, arguing just as hard privately as he ever did publicly.

"I don't know why I take this time," he wrote one colleague, "unless it be to reveal that I am an unreconstructed man from another age."

"I feel like a creature from a distant planet," he wrote another.

In reviewing my dad's record and speeches, I never once found an instance when he tried to duck responsibility for Vietnam or underplay his own role. Nor did he ever—not even once—refer to postwar events in Southeast Asia in an attempt to justify his position. He never referred to Hanoi's violations of the peace negotiated by Kissinger, the North Vietnamese seizure of Laos and Cambodia, their million-man standing army, their allowing Soviet access to naval and air bases in Vietnam, the

boat people, the continuing repression, and genocide in Cambodia.
Developments in Southeast Asia since the American withdrawal have
hardly proved Dean Rusk right, but they do suggest that legitimate issues
were at stake and that the Vietnamese Communists were indeed a
ruthless foe, harshly ideological and inherently expansionistic.

"Why didn't you talk about these events?" I asked him.

"I thought it best just to let things go," he replied. "There's no point
in stirring up old passions and keeping these wounds alive. At least
people can now see what it was we were fighting about."

Gradually, with the passage of time, Pop's views were given a
grudging respect on campus and by a press that earlier had been
stridently critical. Stories about my father now saw such headlines as
DEAN RUSK, WITHOUT APOLOGY and A COLD WARRIER NOW GETS FEW
CAMPUS BOOS. In a column titled "New Respect for the Old Dino,"
written for the July 23, 1971, issue of *Life* magazine after the revelations
of the *Pentagon Papers,* Hugh Sidey said:

> I keep coming out wrong on the *Pentagon Papers.* My regard for
> one of the chief "villains" keeps going up. I think that former
> Secretary of State Dean Rusk emerges from those innumerable
> pages—and from the ongoing tide of electronic comment—as a man
> of singular personal honor and devotion. That may not be what
> Daniel Ellsberg and the *New York Times* had in mind, but more than
> one person in this word-weary city has reached the same conclusion.
> "The Old Dino," said one perennial skeptic (using the private,
> after-hours sobriquet for the Honorable Secretary), "may not have
> been right, but he was a man. He towers over the rest of those
> pigmies."
>
> There is something in that, despite the Vietnam mess in which
> Rusk must share. The papers show that Rusk was warning back in
> 1961 that the United States would start down a long, tough road if
> troops were committed to South Vietnam. Nevertheless, that was the
> road he considered right for the nation when the issue was forced a
> few years later. It was not by any means a lonely position at the time.
> A lot of other important people were marching that way too. But as
> success eluded the American troops, Rusk lost his comrades-in-arms.
> He did not, however, stuff the archives with memos casting doubt on
> others, or air his bitterness, or have the nighttime quivers about the
> policy he had recommended. Some people insist that this was a
> weakness. Maybe it was. But in this age of moral anguish, when
> brilliance is often taken as a license to make up new rules of social
> responsibility, there is something very appealing in Rusk's plain,

old-fashioned sense of decency and loyalty. He still believes he was right, although he readily confesses to making errors along the way. History will be the judge, he says, and we must all wait for that.

"It would have broken the spirit as well as the heart of most men," another columnist wrote, "to have seen the hopes of their professional lives go down the drain of a Vietnam. But Rusk bore the responsibility and did his best."

"How did you rebound so successfully from the war?" I asked him in Georgia, genuinely puzzled. How had he put the carnage of Vietnam behind him and gone ahead with his life when I, who wasn't responsible for any of those decisions, had been ravaged by them at Cornell? Twenty years later I was still groping with that horror.

"What choice did I have?" My father responded sharply to what he considered a silly question. "It was my duty! I had a job to do, and I did it!" he said emphatically. "I cannot redo what has been done. I believed then that I did my duty. I believe it today. Having done my duty as clearly as I could perceive it, I took responsibility for it and tried to get on with my life."

Pop had given me a better answer, perhaps inadvertently, a few years earlier. Sensing my disappointment when a job had ended badly for me in Alaska, he quickly wrote: "What happened is less important than it now seems. Put it behind you and get on with your life. Remember that men are judged not only by their achievements and successes. They are judged by how they handle adversity." In those few words my dad had not only encouraged me but written his own epitaph.

During brief visits home from Alaska, I sensed that life had taken a gentle turn for my folks. But whatever honors came their way were earned. After years of honoraria signed over "anonymously" to the Law School, Dean Ralph Beaird, having decided that enough was enough, told the Georgia Bar Association of Pop's generosity. Later, in 1978, Georgia Governor George Busbee and other civic and business leaders threw a surprise party for my parents, in recognition of these stories emerging from the Georgia Law School and particularly my dad's help in encouraging international trade and investment in Georgia. They gave him a gift as well: keys to a new Cadillac Seville. Pop never directly solicited money, but Law School fund raising increased dramatically during his years. An aggressive dean helped, but so did Rusk's goodwill missions. A South Carolina factory owner, trying to recover his investment when his plant in Bangladesh was nationalized, turned to Rusk for help. He got his money back, and because my dad wouldn't accept a fee, the South

Carolinian willed more than a half million dollars to the Law School. Impressed that Rusk devoted his time after leaving Washington to help young people rather than capitalize upon his government service to make money, an Atlanta-based foundation donated a million dollars to the Law School.

As Pop's travels gradually touched all areas of the state, some people guessed he was gearing up for elective office, perhaps a run at the United States Senate. A grateful public gradually realized that Rusk's mission was as he stated—working with young people, trying to inspire them for public service—and they showered him with further invitations, standing ovations, and awards of all kinds. After Pop retired from the university in 1984, the dean's office stopped counting his outside speaking engagements: more than 700, including 162 visits to other universities and law schools. Despite angina and a weakening heart and the "cardiovascular system of a two-hundred-year-old man," his doctor told me, Pop kept traveling and speaking. "I'll go out with my boots on," he told me.

Politicians and statesmen paying their respects, journalists and TV crews seeking his views beat a steady path to his door. We stopped counting his honorary degrees after thirty-one. Fortunately Harvard had given Pop its degree in the early sixties. "If they had waited a few more years," my father quipped, "the students would have burned the place down." His friends even roasted him in Athens, helping him remember when "this mighty oak was just a little nut." The city of Atlanta named a new elementary school after him—in his old neighborhood in West End. After the ceremony the schoolchildren, most of whom were black, gathered around him. Perhaps tipped off by a teacher who had heard of Rusk's upbringing and the favorite treat his father would occasionally bring from Woodstock, one little boy stepped forward and handed him a can of Vienna sausages. This time the ex-secretary of state was at a loss for words.

In February 1984 Secretary of State George Shultz hosted a party for my father on his seventy-fifth birthday; more than two hundred guests and elder statesmen representing Washington's diplomatic establishment gathered to honor my parents and drink champagne under the crystal chandeliers of state's Benjamin Franklin Room. Lady Bird Johnson, Henry Kissinger, Alexander Haig, William Rogers, Anatoly Dobrynin, George Kennan, Clark Clifford, Alice Acheson—old friends and former colleagues put past differences aside to pay their respects, some even arriving by wheelchair.

"If I had to define the essential quality [about Rusk]," George

McGhee said, "I would use the word 'character.' I don't know what you think the word 'character' means, but I myself would be quite happy to let Dean Rusk's life define it."

They lifted their glasses to him, sang "Happy Birthday", and raised a half million dollars that night and in ensuing weeks for a Dean and Virginia Rusk Scholarship Fund at Georgetown University. It was official Washington's farewell as only Washington can do it, an unprecedented tribute to an ex-secretary of state, and yet my father spoke few words of thanks and farewell. "Hitting on all eight cylinders," as he called it, in his passion stabbing the air with his eyeglasses, he spoke instead about the future and his faith in the younger generations, our constitutional democracy, and the goodness of the American people; of nuclear peace since Hiroshima and the necessity for optimism in a nuclear age. In short, he reiterated in those brief moments the themes of his life. "There have been mistakes, disappointments, frustrations in this postwar period. But when you think of the longer view, the American people have comported themselves with an extraordinary amount of responsibility and restraint and generosity. There is nothing for which to be ashamed, as we look to the future."

Arriving in Georgia in 1984 for our father-son journey, I carried with me some ambivalent feelings. I would have waited longer, but Pop's health was failing. The idea of writing my dad's story excited me; I had dreamed of it for fifteen years. And yet, when I linked it with the Vietnam War, aware of some ambiguity in our relationship, knowing my own capacity for ruthless search, it filled me with dread. I had grown up his son, lived in his house, yet remained a stranger. Are some ghosts better left undisturbed? What was the truth about my father?

What followed was an awkward, sometimes difficult, always fascinating journey researching this story, interviewing family, critics, and friends but mainly my father. Not knowing always how to proceed, trying to shape his story into publishable form, having to make a living out of this venture, after two years I finally realized that I could never write up his story without understanding my own. Reflecting on that complex legacy, having seen the whole man and not just chapters of his life, I found for myself that elusive inner peace. At every stage of Dean Rusk's life—youth, public servant, retired statesman—were signs of mortality. But mainly I found affirmation of the goodness in my dad. Through talking with him as well as with those endless concentric circles of people who had known and genuinely loved my father, I came to know him. Surely they were watching out for me as his son, and perhaps they could guess the somewhat haunted quality of my search. Inevitably one tends to find whatever one is seeking. But to have confirmed with the same, uniform consistency, from Dean Acheson's "a man of shining integrity" to Spec Caldwell's "a man of immaculate character" to similar reminiscences of his childhood friends, to have this affirmed over a life of eighty years was a powerful experience.

Our father-son journey led to two books—his story in these pages and my own book about Pop called *The End of Our Exploring*—and contributed to a third, a biography by Tom Schoenbaum, director of the Dean Rusk Center. It led as well to a Dean Rusk Research Collection at the University of Georgia, for which we retrieved as many of his papers and related materials as we could find. Thanks to the Southern Center for International Studies in Atlanta, we also captured Pop on film—twelve hours of interviews with Edwin Newman as narrator—for eventual rebroadcast on public television and for educational purposes. I even found myself in the family cemetery in Cherokee County, where four generations of Rusks and a few Indians, marked by more than one hundred stones, had been buried. With other Rusks we cut down over sixty loblolly pines that had been killed by Japanese beetles, built a new fence, cleaned the old headstones and rebuilt some broken ones, and planted grass, trees, and flowers. With all this, I couldn't bear to let the official record remain all that was left of my father. I had to push up a few markers of my own.

At this writing Pop has resisted my efforts to bury him eventually in that old family cemetery in Cherokee. Instead, he has picked out a plot next to the University of Georgia's football stadium, "where I can hear the roar of the crowd." Dean Rusk can be a very stubborn man. Yes, there is mystery to my father's life, given his inscrutability and the awesome complexity of human beings. But wherever he is buried, for me at least, there will be no mystery in that coffin, no corroding doubt.

> *No restless ghost*
> *to haunt my footsteps as they pass. . . .*

—R. R.

With a Daughter's Eye: A Memoir of Margaret Mead and Gregory Bateson, by Mary Catherine Bateson (New York: William Morrow, 1984).

Appendices

Dean Rusk's Message to the Young

When it came time for my wife, Virginia, and me to leave Washington, we decided to spend my final years teaching international law and working with young people. Why? Because this generation of young Americans is destined to write a unique chapter in history. For three hundred years commencement speakers have told graduating classes in America just that: You are unique. This time it is true.

There are moments in history when platitudes and clichés suddenly take on new life; when such terms as "harsh necessity," "lethal danger," "issues of survival" ring true. As never before in history, now is such a time. You face problems different in kind and scale from any we have faced before: the energy crisis; population explosion; environmental pollution; the threat of nuclear holocaust. You have a big job ahead. My generation should be going flat-out to find ways to help you get ready.

I would like to share with you a little of the fire that burns within me. My concern these days is with you, our young people. Yes, there is a generation gap. It is obnoxious for young people to hear a person of my age refer to his youth, but youth was a biological necessity for me as well. Along the way the young people of my generation learned some bitter lessons, and one is that there is no place to hide, no foxholes into which we can crawl and ignore the rest of the world. There are no solutions in retreat.

Your generation will discover in the decades ahead whether mankind can organize a durable peace in a world in which thousands of megatons are lying around in the hands of frail human beings. A world in which collective security—what my generation used to try to curb the obscenity of war—is withering away, and we are not even discussing what shall take its place.

As secretary of state I was required to study in great detail the full effects of a nuclear war. Few others have done so. Throughout history it has been possible for us to pick ourselves up out of the death and destruction of war and start over again. We will not have that chance after World War III. In that conflagration—if one occurs—this earth may no longer sustain the human race. And so mankind has reached this point: We must prevent war before it occurs. And that is something different.

In the decades ahead, will the human race so pursue its seemingly insatiable appetites as to destroy this fragile biosphere in which we live? Will we be so wasteful in our consumption of finite sources of energy as to unleash the dogs of war rather than change our indulgent lifestyles? Will we so infest the earth with our own kind as to drive us back to the jungle, tearing and snarling at each other for the sheer necessities of life? At long last we have discovered that our planet's few inches of topsoil and several miles of air and water are a very thin skin, to which man can do irreparable damage. Will we act upon what we have learned?

We Americans, 6 percent of the world's population, consume almost 50 percent of the world's raw materials and energy resources. We take for granted that our gross national product will double every twenty years. A Soviet official once said, "The earth can afford only one United States." He was right. If other nations adopted our standard of living and consumed as we do, our planet would simply collapse. One does not have to be nostalgic about the "good old days" of Cherokee County, Georgia. They weren't good old days at all. But we have to simplify our lives to make lesser demands upon the earth's resources, and that scaling back will be a painful process, given the nature of democracy.

Wouldn't it now make sense to organize a Manhattan Project to develop alternative sources of energy, especially renewable energy—solar, wind, tides, and ocean currents? Dig a hole deep enough and you soon hit temperatures of five hundred degrees. Although I'm no expert, converting that heat into power on the earth's surface shouldn't be as difficult as two astronauts driving a Jeep around the surface of the moon.

Can we live together, different races of people, their different religions and cultures, to share this planet peacefully and overcome that terrible difference between "we" and "they" which has crowded the human story with so much senseless tragedy? Will nations restrain their extravagant notions of sovereignty and join hands to find answers which no one nation can find alone? Will we in our personal lives find more satisfaction in the delights of the mind and spirit and ease our pressure upon material resources? Your generation will discover these things.

Whatever our jobs, training, and backgrounds, can we grasp the essence of arts and letters and science and technology and begin to think of life as a whole, take responsibility for the planet itself, given the global nature of our problems? Will we as a nation recover our will and confidence after twenty difficult years, which began with the assassination of John F. Kennedy?

Kennedy's death was followed by the deaths of Bobby Kennedy and Martin Luther King, Jr., the attempts on the lives of George Wallace and Gerald Ford, the agonies of Vietnam, the corruption of Watergate, the scandal of Iran-contra. For young people today, John Kennedy's murder is the first national event they remember. They have lived their lives when America was in trouble, when our morale sagged, when many believed that somehow the stars had turned against us. They've never seen this great country with a sense of confidence. During these years it became fashionable to cut ourselves to pieces. Are we in danger of repealing the vital elements of hope and confidence, without which democracy and a free-enterprise economy cannot function?

Help me remember back to March 1942, three months after Pearl Harbor. What if Franklin Roosevelt, during a fireside chat, had said the following: "My fellow Americans, I have some serious news. Hitler's armies are smashing at the gates of Leningrad, Moscow, and Stalingrad. Rommel is rushing through North Africa toward Alexandria and Cairo. My intelligence people tell me [as they did at the time] that Russia will be knocked out of the war in six to seven weeks. We cannot mobilize our armed forces except at a snail's pace, because we simply don't have the arms and equipment for them. The Japanese have destroyed the heart of our fleet at Pearl Harbor, and they are rushing through Asia, and we see no way to stop them.

"My fellow Americans, I am sorry, but it is time to withdraw. The jig is up."

Had FDR said that in March 1942, by present-day standards of something called credibility, he would have been telling "the truth." But had he said it, he would also have been telling a profound lie. Because he and Winston Churchill and Joseph Stalin and millions of others acted out of hope and confidence and necessity, and we defeated the Axis powers.

Self-criticism, what the poets call "divine discontent," is the very lifeblood of democracy. But prolonged self-flagellation can be its destruction. Will we continue to cut ourselves to pieces? Or will we rally ourselves and move confidently into the future? Can American democracy mobilize in peacetime the unity and effort this country hasn't seen since World War II? Will we support or even tolerate political leaders who dare look beyond the tips of our noses and demand present sacrifice for a better tomorrow? Will we convince our elected representatives that concern for the future is good politics and that we want them to do now what is vitally important for our grandchildren?

Each of you can add to this list. Yours is a formidable agenda. In my judgment, it is an inescapable agenda. There is no place to hide. But there are many assets on which you can build. For example, in August 1989, we put behind us forty-five years since a nuclear weapon was fired in anger. That's a remarkable fact, considering the dangerous crises of these past four decades. If your generation could add another thirty years to that, by that time the very thought of using these dreadful weapons might become unthinkable.

Other assets? I remind you of a constitutional system of great strength and resiliency and of enormous complexity, made deliberately complex by our Founding Fathers to set limits on the exercise of raw power to foster human freedom. Our constitutional system has been tested grievously by civil war and recently by the resignation of an American president. But we know that a building which rests upon 220,000,000 foundation stones, such as each of you represents, will stand when the storms gather.

A third asset? Our extraordinary free-enterprise economy. It has its imbalances and aches and pains, but it has called upon the energies and dynamism of a free people to produce miracles which have astonished the world. We Americans can generate enormous resources with which to deal with our national and global problems.

And then, the best asset of all, the American people. My mind goes back to the little man from Independence, Missouri. Harry Truman was a great president im part because he had unlimited confidence in Americans at the grass roots. He really believed that the American people at their best are a very good people and will do what has to be done if they understand why.

There are times—one such as now—when we are not at our best. We go through periods when Washington seems afraid to call upon the American people to make the effort we know we ought to be making.

These huge problems, global in scale, threaten to outstrip man's capacity to deal with them. But surely we have learned that the only way to deal with a dangerous crisis is to advance upon it and try to resolve it. That effort will require imagination, hard work to which some are unaccustomed, wisdom of the rarest sort, dedication, restraint, and, yes, even sacrifice. John Kennedy once said, "Problems created by man can be solved by man." If that sounds wildly optimistic these days, I would suggest that we have no choice but to try.

As you leave here today, look around you a little more thoughtfully than usual. Look at your own communities. Your classmates and neighbors are not people who think that we are on this earth to reach out and grasp the power of the sun itself only to burn ourselves into extinction. They aren't people who want to turn this beautiful earth into a moonscape or to fight over diminishing resources and start tearing and snarling at each other for each morsel of food. It means something more than that to be a member of the human race—to be part of the species *Homo sapiens,* or "thinking man."

We need to think about what it means to be a human being.

Or, as some would put it, a child of God.

Forget the doomsayers of my generation! You young people can look to yourselves for hope and confidence and self-reliance. When George Marshall first became secretary of state, somebody remarked at a staff meeting about poor morale in the State Department. The old man straightened up, looked around the table at us, and said, "Gentlemen, it has been my experience that an enlisted man may be entitled to a morale problem, but an officer is not. I expect the officers of this department to take care of their own morale. No one is taking care of my morale." When the word got around the department that there was no shoulder on which to cry in the secretary's office, morale went up to the highest point it has ever been before or since.

In a democracy every citizen is an officer. It's the private citizen who occupies the loftiest position in our constitutional system. It's no accident that we call members of Congress, presidents, and officers of government "public servants." Each of us must accept personal responsibility for the state of our world, maintain our own morale, and get on with life. The very trying is its own reward. We have no choice but to try. Otherwise, we dig a foxhole, lay in a supply of drugs, and crouch there, shivering and hoping for an early death.

Unlike other old men of my generation, I am profoundly optimistic about the future. This is partly a matter of faith. I may also be a Cold War warrior of the old school whose time on history's stage has passed. But I really believe the "family of man" is taking form. This family will not be built upon sentiments of brotherhood or schemes of world government. Rather, it will be bound together by the sheer necessity of resolving life-threatening global problems if mankind is to survive.

I am also optimistic because I believe in American democracy. When we celebrated in 1987 the two hundredth anniversary of the Constitution, we celebrated something very special. More than two hundred years ago, in discussing what the colonists needed to organize their society, Thomas Jefferson, James Madison, and the Founding Fathers articulated some rather simple ideas, not original to them but deeply rooted in the nature of man. The notion that "governments derive their just powers from the consent of the governed" is today the most revolutionary and powerful political idea in the world. Tyrants of the left and right live in terror of this idea, and they go to extraordinary lengths to insulate their people from this virus called freedom. As the future unfolds, this virus will increasingly take hold.

There's another reason for my optimism. It has been my privilege in recent years to visit many campuses throughout the country, to talk with many students. I am deeply impressed by you and your classmates, by this coming generation of young Americans.

I have not tried to tell you what your answers should be; you must find those for yourselves. We shall be fortunate if my generation can help you discover some of the questions. But I am profoundly confident in you. I shall neither patronize nor flatter you by telling you why. But I have no doubt that you are going to make it.

I feel confident that each of you, in your own way, will take a piece of the action and make it yours. In so doing, you will share with each other a great adventure. I am not afraid about how the story comes out. I regret to say that I cannot accompany you on that journey. But I can assure you all, that you carry with you the blessings and best wishes of an old man.

Memorial to President Kennedy at Runnymede

(Note: On May 14, 1965, Secretary of State
Dean Rusk represented the United States at
Runnymede, the Field of the Great Charter, to
receive from Her Majesty Queen Elizabeth II an
acre of Runnymede as a memorial to the late
President John F. Kennedy. The following is
Secretary Rusk's response to the presentation
made by Her Majesty.)

Your presence here, Your Majesty, Your Royal Highness—

This nation, Mr. Prime Minister, which has nurtured freedom for
so many in so many parts of the world—

The British people, Mr. Macmillan, Lord Harlech, who have generously joined their affection and their resources to give life to the
Kennedy Memorial Trust—

This quiet and lovely Runnymede, the Field of the Great Charter,
which began to lay the hand of "the law of the land" upon the exercise
of power—

The extraordinary, incandescent man, Mrs. Kennedy, whom we
honor here today—

All these make this an unforgettable moment for us and for those
we represent.

President Johnson has asked me to exercise personally, on his and
our nation's behalf, my statutory privilege of accepting this acre of land.

I do so with the joy, and the sadness, which shall forever mark those of us who served with John Fitzgerald Kennedy.

When the American people learned about this tribute to our beloved late president, we were deeply moved—not only because you decided to share with us this Runnymede, which is a common and precious symbol, but also because what you have done reflects so sensitive an understanding of John F. Kennedy himself.

No one of us more than he searched out the best of our past as a guide to present commitment and to future action. He would have been the first to recall—

—that his own Massachusetts, in 1641, adopted a "Body of Liberties" in response to a need for what John Winthrop called a fundamental law "in resemblance to a Magna Carta."

—that the lineage of our common liberties runs through the Petition of Right, the Habeas Corpus Act, your Bill of Rights of 1689, and our own Bill of Rights in the Federal Constitution.

—and that there is unfinished business in the endless struggle for human dignity and freedom, at home and abroad.

No one of us more than he was concerned for the future. You have generously provided fellowship opportunities for young men and women to enlarge their capacity to build that decent future which was his passionate concern.

The words you have inscribed on this tablet express not only the deepest resolve of John F. Kennedy but the abiding commitment of the American people: "Let every nation know, whether it wishes us well or ill, that we shall pay any price, bear any burden, meet any hardship, support any friend, oppose any foe to assure the survival and the success of liberty."

We know, because you have proved it on many crucial occasions, that this is also the abiding commitment of the British people.

On behalf of President Johnson and the American people, I thank Your Majesty, your government, and your people. We shall cherish this memorial to a president who shall be forever young. "At the going down of the sun and in the morning" we shall remember him. And we draw strength and confidence from the knowledge that all who pass this way shall be reminded of the common dedication of the British and American peoples to the cause of human liberty—a reminder which has its roots here in seven and a half centuries and its promise through all time to come.

Thank you, Your Majesty, Mrs. Kennedy.

References
and Sources

When Dean Rusk left the State Department in January 1969, taking with him only tax returns and appointment books, he continued a lifelong pattern. Few papers survive from his earlier career.

"Why did you walk away from those?" I asked him.

"Because I never dreamed I would someday become secretary of state," he replied.

Two decades later, with generous assistance from Anne Cox Chambers and the Rockefeller Foundation, the University of Georgia retrieved as many of my dad's papers as it could. These findings—letters, speeches, congressional testimony, press conferences, articles by Rusk, articles, papers, and books about him, research notes for Rusk biographies, photos, film clips, memorabilia of all kinds, family recollections, etc.—are housed in the Dean Rusk Research Collection, at the Richard G. Russell Memorial Library in Athens.

The collection includes Rusk's correspondence and faculty papers generated as a law professor from fall 1970 to the present. It also contains hundreds of hours of taped interviews with Rusk—beginning in 1984 and continuing to the present—from which this book is derived. It contains a wider oral history with friends, family, colleagues, and those who knew him. The Athens collection is the largest single gathering of Rusk material covering all aspects of his life, although the bulk of his papers as secretary of state remains at the Department of State, the John F. Kennedy Library, and the Lyndon B. Johnson Library. Some papers have been copied for the Rusk Collection.

Of special interest are Parks Rusk's lifelong collection of clippings and articles about his younger brother and Rusk's extensive oral history interviews for the Kennedy and Johnson libraries. Taped in 1969, they are now open for review.

For Rusk's career before he became secretary of state, the State Department's Foreign Relations of the United States series is important. The National Archives and the Harry S. Truman Library contain many papers with Rusk's imprint. Oral history collections at Columbia, Princeton, and the Truman Library contain interviews with many of Rusk's colleagues. Oral history projects at the Kennedy and Johnson libraries are useful for his secretary of state years.

The Rockefeller Foundation has a Dean Rusk "diary," his correspondence, and annual reports for the eight years he served as foundation president.

Rusk's assistant secretary of state for Far Eastern Affairs, William P. Bundy, has an excellent unpublished memoir focusing on the Vietnam decision making. The *Pentagon Papers* remain crucially important as well.

Transcripts of Rusk's speeches, press conferences, and television appearances as secretary of state may be found in various issues of the *Department of State Bulletin.* His early speeches during the Kennedy years were reprinted in the book *The Winds of Freedom,* edited by E. K. Lindley (Boston: Beacon Press, 1963). Other articles and speeches by Rusk include:

"Parliamentary Diplomacy—Debate vs. Negotiation." *World Affairs Interpreter,* vol. 26, no. 2 (July 1955), p. 121.

"The President." *Foreign Affairs* (April 1960), pp. 353–69.

"Mr. Secretary on the Eve of Emeritus." Interview. *Life* (January 17, 1969), pp. 56–62B.

"Policy Is About the Future." Address, March 11, 1969, Owens-Corning Lectures 1968–69, Denison University, Granville, Ohio, pp. 3–17.

"The 25th U.N. General Assembly and the Use of Force." *Georgia Journal of International Law* (April 1971), pp. 19–35.

"Dean Rusk's Views of the Washington Press Corps." *Seminar* (December 1973), pp. 4–8.

"Diplomacy and National Power." Lecture at the National War College, Washington, D.C., September 11, 1972. Transcript available at the Dean Rusk Collection, University of Georgia Library.

"Prospective Issues in U.S.-China Relations." Lecture. Reprinted in *China's Open Wall,* edited by Festus Justin Viser (Memphis, TN: Memphis State University Press, 1972).

"The Prospects for Peace in a Strange, New World." Lecture, May 4, 1973, American Experience Program, University of Pittsburgh, 17 pages.

"The American Revolution and the Future." Lecture, June 17, 1974, Institute for Public Policy Research, Washington, D.C.

"Nuclear Advice from One Who Has Been There." *Washington Post,* October 1, 1981.

"A New Secretary of State: At the Pleasure of the President." *Washington Post,* July 18, 1982.

"In Praise of Consensus: Reflections Upon the American Constitution." The Ferdinand Phinizy Lectures (Athens, GA: University of Georgia, 1984), pp. 1–23.

There are now two biographies of Rusk:

Cohen, Warren I. *Dean Rusk.* Totowa, N.J.: Cooper Square Publishers, 1980.

Schoenbaum, Thomas J. *Waging Peace and War.* New York: Simon and Schuster, 1988.

Schoenbaum's book contains the most comprehensive listing to date of reference and source material on Rusk, although Cohen's has an extensive listing as well.

Dissertations and academic papers include:

Gutierrez, G. G. "Dean Rusk and Southeast Asia: An Operational Code Analysis." Paper presented at the 1973 annual meeting of the American Political Science Association, New Orleans, September 1973.

Henry, John Bronaugh. "March 1968: Continuity or Change?" Harvard College, April 1971.

Stueber, Frederick G. "Dean Rusk, East Asia, and the Kennedy Years." Williams College, April 1975.

Hundreds of books have been written about the Truman, Kennedy, and Johnson years. Those especially helpful in prompting my father's memory and preparing this manuscript include:

Abel, Elie. *The Missile Crisis.* Philadelphia: J. B. Lippincott, 1966.

Acheson, Dean G. *Present at the Creation: My Years in the State Department.* New York: W. W. Norton, 1969.

Bowles, Chester. *Promises to Keep: My Years in Public Life, 1961–1969.* New York: Harper & Row, 1971.

Fosdick, Raymond. *The Story of the Rockefeller Foundation.* New York: Harper, 1952.

Goodman, Allen E. *The Lost Peace: America's Search for a Negotiated Settlement of the Vietnam War.* Stanford, Calif.: Hoover Institution Press, 1978.

Halberstam, David. *The Best and the Brightest.* New York: Penguin Books, 1972.

Herring, George, ed. *The Secret Diplomacy of the Vietnam War: The Negotiating Volumes of the Pentagon Papers.* Austin: University of Texas Press, 1983.

Hoopes, Townsend. *The Limits of Intervention: An Inside Account of How the Johnson Policy of Escalation in Vietnam Was Reversed.* New York: David McKay, 1969.

Johnson, Lyndon Baines. *The Vantage Point: Perspectives on the Presidency 1963–1964.* New York: Holt, Rinehart and Winston, 1971.

Karnow, Stanley. *Vietnam.* New York: Viking, 1983.

Kraslow, David, and Stuart H. Loory. *The Secret Search for Peace in Vietnam.* New York: Random House, 1968.

Lowenthal, Abraham F. *The Dominican Intervention.* Cambridge: Harvard, 1972.

O'Neill, Michael J. "The Quiet Diplomat: Dean Rusk," in *The Kennedy Circle,* ed. Lester Tanzer. Washington, D.C.: Robert B. Bruce, 1961.

Schandler, Herbert Y. *The Unmaking of a President.* Princeton, N.J.: Princeton University Press, 1977.

Schick, Jack M. *The Berlin Crisis, 1958–1962.* Philadelphia: University of Pennsylvania Press, 1971.

Schlesinger, Arthur M., Jr. *A Thousand Days.* Cambridge, Mass.: Riverside Press, 1965.

Seaborg, Glenn T. *Kennedy, Khrushchev, and the Test Ban.* Berkeley: University of California Press, 1981.

Seaborg, Glenn T., and Benjamin S. Loeb. *Stemming the Tide: Arms Control in the Johnson Years.* Lexington, Mass.: Lexington Books, 1987.

Sorensen, Theodore C. *Kennedy.* New York: Harper & Row, 1965.

Truman, Harry S. *Memoirs: Years of Trial and Hope, 1946-1952.* New York: Doubleday, 1956.

Tuchman, Barbara. *Stilwell and the American Experience in China.* New York: Macmillan, 1971.

U.S. Department of State. *Foreign Relations of the United States.* Series of volumes that include declassified cables and papers from each year, usually published twenty years later.

The New York Times and the various periodicals indexed in the *Reader's Guide to Periodic Literature* contain many references to Rusk's career and the policies with which he was involved. Articles of special interest:

Alsop, Stewart. "The Trouble with the State Department." *Saturday Evening Post* (March 3, 1962), p. 11.

Clifford, Clark M. "A Vietnam Appraisal." *Foreign Affairs* (July 1969), p. 601.

Gelb, Leslie. "The Pentagon Papers and *The Vantage Point.*" *Foreign Policy* 6 (1972), pp. 25–41.

Henry, John B. "February 1968." *Foreign Policy* (Fall 1971), p. 3.

———, and William Epinosa. "The Tragedy of Dean Rusk." *Foreign Policy* (Fall 1972), p. 166.

Hoopes, Townsend. "LBJ's Account of March 1968." *New Republic* (March 14, 1970), pp. 17–19.

Kraft, Joseph. "Comeback of the State Department." *Harper's* (November 1961), p. 45.

———. "The Dean Rusk Show." *The New York Times Magazine* (March 24, 1968), p. 34.

———. "The Enigma of Dean Rusk." *Harper's* (July 1965), p. 100.

Moskin, J. R. "Dean Rusk: Cool Man in a Hot World." *Look* (September 6, 1966), p. 14.

Nordan, David. "The View from Home." *Atlanta Magazine* (October 1982).

Rovere, Richard. "Notes on the Establishment in America." *American Scholar* 30 (1961), pp. 489–95.

Sidey, Hugh. "New Respect for the Old Dino." *Life* (July 23, 1971), p. 4.

Smith, Loran. "Dean Rusk: A Prophet in His Own Land." *Atlanta Journal and Constitution Magazine* (September 10, 1978), p. 46.

"The Eagle Has Two Claws." *Time* (December 26, 1960).

"The Quiet Man." *Time* (December 6, 1963).

"The String Runs Out." *Time* (February 4, 1966).

Viorst, Martin. "Incidentally, Who Is Dean Rusk?" *Esquire* (April 1968), p. 98.

In spring 1985 Julia Johnson White and the Atlanta-based Southern Center for International Studies produced a series of thirteen one-hour interviews with Rusk.

Narrated by former NBC newsman Edwin Newman, shown on public television, the following films are available through the Southern Center:

The Making of a Public Servant, parts 1,2.
The Making of Foreign Policy, parts 1,2,3.
The War in Vietnam, parts 1,2,3.
U.S.-Soviet Relations, parts 1,2,3.
The Nuclear Age, parts 1,2.

Other films and televised interviews are available at the Rusk Collection.

Index